Shattering the Looking Glass:
Challenge, Risk, and Controversy
in Children's Literature

Shattering the Looking Glass: Challenge, Risk, and Controversy in Children's Literature

Susan Stewart Lehr

Editor

Christopher-Gordon Publishers, Inc.

Norwood, Massachusetts

Copyright Acknowledgments

Every effort has been made to contact copyright holders for permission to reproduce borrowed material where necessary. We apologize for any oversights and would be happy to rectify them in future printings.

All student work used with permission.

Illustration from THE THREE PIGS by David Wiesner. Copyright © 2001 by David Wiesner. Reprinted by permission of Clarion books, an imprint of Houghton Mifflin Company. All rights reserved.

"Giant Story", from THE STINKY SHEESE MAN AND OTHER FAIRLY STUPID TALES written by Jon Scieszka and illustrated by Lane Smith. Text copyright © 1992 by Jon Scieszka. Illustrations copyright © 1992 by Lane Smith. Used by permission of Viking Penguin, A Division of Penguin Young Readers Group, A Member of Penguin Group (USA) Inc., 345 Hudson Street, New York, NY 10014. All rights reserved.

Illustrations from DO NOT OPEN THIS BOOK! By Michaela Muntean, illustrated by Pascal Lemaitre. Illustration copyright © by Pascal Lemaitre. Reprinted by permission of Scholastic Inc.

NCTE Guidelines on Censorship v. Selection (1982) reprinted with permission of the National Council of Teachers of English.

Selected portion of "Censorship of Children's Books" by Amy McClure reprinted with permission from *Battling Dragons*, by Susan Lehr. Copyright © 1995 by Heinemann. Published by Heinemann, a division of Reed Elsevier Inc., Portsmouth, NH. All rights reserved.

Christopher~Gordon Publishers, Inc.
Bridging Theory and Practice

1420 Providence Highway, Suite 120
Norwood, MA 02062

800-934-8322 (In U.S.) • 781-762-5577
www.Christopher-Gordon.com

Printed in Canada
10 9 8 7 6 5 4 3 2 1   11 10 09 08

ISBN-13: 978-1-933760-12-4
Library of Congress Catalogue Number: 2007932390

Contents

Acknowledgments and Dedication

Heartfelt thanks to Susanne Canavan, an extraordinary publisher. Imagine hundreds of emails streaming between Boston and Saratoga Springs.

To Janet Hickman, who helped to make my graduate work at Ohio State a rewarding and intellectual encounter.

Many thanks to Skidmore College, my college home for more than two decades.

To Hans who read many, many rough drafts—36 years!

Dedication

To all of our missing parents who have Alzheimer's

and

To my Mom who read to me when I was little and taught me to love books.

"You look like a picture of someone I know. You remind me of Susan."

I miss you, Mom.

...and to my grandbaby, Evan.

Welcome to the world of books, Evan James.

Foreword

Those of us who care about children's literature in this first decade of the 21st century can find plenty of good news. For one thing, just the quantity of books for children and young adults is stunning—nearly 10,000 published each year, some of which have generated unprecedented sales. Readers with an eye for diversity can now find a range of characters, topics, and issues that would have been almost unthinkable a generation ago. We have many books of outstanding quality and a growing arsenal of awards with which to honor the authors and artists who create them.

Children's literature has found a place in the larger world of literary criticism, thanks to interest in recent decades by English departments and the Modern Language Association. That attention enriches a long-standing tradition of review and critique by librarians and is balanced by new contributions from educators and psychologists who look at literature in terms of its child audience. Furthermore, children's books have proved their worth in the classroom; there are many detailed accounts by teachers and researchers of the positive roles literature can play in children's learning.

Children's literature might seem to be in a very comfortable place, but is it? Unfortunately, every point of celebration listed here has a counterpoint. For instance, high-quantity publishing is no guarantee of high quality or of balance; just note the way picture books have lost ground in the recent burst of enthusiasm for young adult literature or the number of copycat books in general. Titles that become huge commercial successes invite such imitation and contribute to an economic standard that forces other titles out of print before they can find an audience. Although there might be a remarkable range of diversity available, the actual number of books that present characters and viewpoints from underrepresented groups is still disproportionately and disappointingly small.

Even the creation of new awards has been called into question because of the possibility of diluting standards or fragmenting the audience. We have new insights from criticism, but they have a limited impact without lively dialogue; it's regrettable that scholars in education and English still often just ignore one another. Finally, in spite of compelling evidence to the power of literature in literacy and content learning, teachers are forced to negotiate new political, cultural, and economic barriers that restrict access to children's books or to their optimal use.

This last item of bad news would be especially dispiriting if not for the fact that books today have so many impassioned and eloquent advocates.

One of the most notable things in the pages of this volume is the prevalence of high hope for children's literature. We are sure that it will entertain and enrich our children, as always. We have come to depend on it to help them become literate, learn about the world, and think critically. We hope it will sensitize them to differences among people, promote social justice, and bring other benefits not yet defined. Even if we occasionally overreach, it is better to care too much than too little. In the end, these great expectations are crucial. Without them, we might lose our resolve to keep children's literature alive, in school and elsewhere.

Janet Hickman
September 2007

Introduction

~Susan S. Lehr

We are the keepers of the literary tradition. As teachers and parents, we pass these traditions on to our children. We teach children what we know and what we love about literature, expecting them to become competent and astute readers, but more than that, hoping that they will share our passion for good books. Keeping literature alive is part of what we are about.

When I went on sabbatical in 2005 I had no plans to edit a third book. My research agenda lay in an entirely different direction. When I edited my first book in 1995, the title *Battling Dragons: Issues and Controversy in Children's Literature* emerged from what I perceived as a battle between social conservatives, who were attacking specific authors and titles of quality children's literature and challenging the use of this literature in classrooms across the United States, and social progressives, who were committed to effectively using diverse quality children's literature in the classroom. The word *battle* implied that there were two oppositional groups fighting for the right to either implement or exclude the use of certain books in the elementary curriculum. The word *dragon* was open to multiple interpretations, including the idea that dragons were attacking children's literature with the intent of destroying it or making it inaccessible to children. Book burnings desecrating children's books in fundamentalist churches emerged as a metaphorical link to the destructive power of dragon fire.

A critic of *Battling Dragons* suggested that rather than offering solutions, the book described a rather bleak landscape, which perhaps left teachers without strategies to move forward successfully with literature-based programs. Ironically, I view today's landscape with a great deal more cynicism, which is why this book has an entire section devoted to strategic thinking and instructional strategies for the elementary classroom. Reflective teaching based on decades of literacy and literature research is being shattered by frenzied responses to national mandates.

In the 1990s, the status of children's literature in the elementary classroom seemed to be securely established, despite the thousands of challenges to children's books. Why? Two reasons: Research supported literature-based programs, and teachers were using books effectively and innovatively in elementary classrooms across the country. Journals like *Language Arts* and *The Reading Teacher* offered scores of articles detailing success stories. Research had demonstrated that reading aloud daily, using books across the curriculum, allowing independent reading time each day, implementing reader response strategies, and making quality children's literature a central component of the reading program were effective strategies to strengthen and improve literacy instruction. These strategies originated with seminal thinkers like Charlotte Huck, who dedicated her career to establishing a strong presence for children's literature in the elementary classroom back when Dick and Jane were central to reading programs. Researchers and teacher-researchers, like Joy Moss, Laura Robb, Barbara Kiefer, Regie Routman, Shelley Harwayne, Ralph Peterson, and Maryann Eeds, offered scores of practical and effective instructional strategies described in dozens of books for the effective implementation of literature in the classroom

In *Battling Dragons* I was primarily concerned with raising issues and creating controversy for dialogue and intelligent discussion about what I saw as increasing threats to children's literature. Rather than offering practical strategies for implementation, which my colleagues were doing beautifully, I hoped to spark meaningful dialogue in the educational community, particularly among teachers.

As the use of literature in the classroom increased, censorship also increased. Social conservatives increasingly targeted specific authors and book titles, as well as literature-based basal reading programs. Conservative movements against books in the public school curricula became more focused and systematic and began to be quite successful, but in ways that many educators could not have envisioned. Mel and Norma Gabler set off a nationwide censorship frenzy that significantly began to impact the content of textbooks and the position of children's literature in the classroom. Author Penny Colman relates in this volume that her book, *Mary McLeod Bethune and the Power of Education,* was pulled from the publisher's list after Newt Gingrich and his Contract With America gained the majority in 1994. Her publisher admitted that the decision was politically based, because the staff believed that women's history was not going to thrive in that political climate.

Paradoxically, the politics and atmosphere in elementary classrooms across the United States has worsened dramatically in the past decade. How is that possible?

That Was Then, This Is Now: The Altered Reality of Publishing Children's Books

How children's books are marketed and sold has changed significantly in the past decade. Bookseller Frank Hodge says that the number of children's bookstores reached a peak of 400 in the United States, yet they are barely holding steady at about 80 nationwide today. Large book warehouses like Borders and Barnes & Noble, as well as Internet companies like Amazon.com, have overtaken the small independent booksellers by offering a larger selection and cheaper prices while also diminishing diversity in what is available on their shelves for mass market audiences. Even stores like Wal-Mart are becoming competitive booksellers.

Small innovative and independent presses, like Salina Bookshelf, Northland Publishing's Rising Moon, Charlesbridge, and University of New Mexico Press, celebrate and encourage diversity in their publishing lists but are frequently unfamiliar to customers or are unavailable in mainstream bookstores. I often find children's titles from these publishers in museum bookstores, like the Museum of Indian Arts and Culture in Santa Fe, or in regional bookstores, like Page One in Albuquerque. Others, like Lee & Low Books, and Canadian publishers, like Groundwood Press, Kids Can Press, and Tundra Books, continue to offer quality titles and are more widely known and available. It does take work, however, to find these presses and their diverse titles.

Children's literature is increasingly being treated like a commodity. Children's books are becoming much more commercial—tied to movies, toys, and games. Publishing houses that once offered dozens of high-quality titles in spring and fall catalogues have been gradually reducing the number of high-quality children's trade books, replacing them with mass market series books, formula books written by multiple authors, or books connected to mass market commodities. Toys like Barbie and the American Girls Collection have inspired wallpaper, workbooks, and incredibly expensive dolls, along with defecating dogs and a Barbie magnetic pooper scooper. Cute books, silly books, trite books, and poorly written books are suddenly flooding the market.

Record amounts are being paid for books that publishers hope will be blockbusters. It's all about money. Older publishing companies—like Frederick Warne, founded in 1865 and absorbed by Penguin Books in 1983—continue to endlessly "milk" Beatrix Potter's classic characters, like Peter Rabbit, by reformatting and repackaging the books and reselling them to consumers as alphabet books, cookbooks, calendars, diaries, big books, board books, book collections, boxed books, or books with toys. In a new Warne venture, *Miss Potter: The Movie* was linked to *Miss Potter: The Novel* and the official motion picture guide and soundtrack, all of which are available through Amazon.com. *Harry Potter and the Deathly Hallows* (2007) was published concurrently with the fifth movie in J. K. Rowling's series, with U.S. sales for the previous Harry Potter book passing 13 million copies sold.

On the plus side, however, many well-written children's books—both older and more recent titles, many of which have gone out of print—are being republished and reissued in paperback form, giving these books added life and exposure. For example, Catherine Fisher's strongly written fantasy trilogy from 1993 was reprinted and retitled as *Snow-Walker* in one large volume in 2005. This new version should find many new and enthusiastic readers.

Newer and smaller presses, like Roaring Brook Press, founded in 2001, produce small lists of top-quality children's books and have won major awards for their efforts. Now part of the Holtzbrinck Publishing German conglomerate, which also owns Farrar, Straus & Giroux and Henry Holt, Roaring Brook Press is carving out an impressive niche in the children's book publishing world, including an expanded list with graphic novels. Even a successful press must keep reinventing itself.

Many of the large conglomerates, however, are increasingly turning to what I call pulp fiction for the young crowd. Series books proliferate, both old and new. After a century of transforming roadsters, the Nancy Drew books, a favorite series from my childhood, have been updated, rewritten, and repackaged for another generation. Nancy's scheming thieves and thugs now sell drugs, and Nancy has surely dropped several sizes in the past century.

One of the largest growth markets is mass market leveled-series books for the intermediate reader. These books can sell hundreds of thousands of paperback copies, so they are spawning in record numbers. The positive side of this is that intermediate readers suddenly have buckets of books available, whereas once there were too few.

Writers and illustrators are taking innovative risks however, re-creating genres that aren't described in most children's literature texts. Brian Selznick's *The Invention of Hugo Cabret* (2007) combines a fantasy novel with the graphic arts in stunning black-and-white pencil illustrations, taking the illustrated novel and bookmaking to a whole new level through endless illustrations that give the impression of early cinema while innovatively combining history, mystery, and a touch of fantasy.

Crowding out other genres, fantasy series are now increasing, with lots of money as motivation for new authors: $650,000 for fantasy author Matthew Skelton (2006) for *Endymion Spring*, and $500,000 for first-time author David Lee Stone (2004) for *The Illmoor Chronicles*. Vampires have also made a huge comeback in young adult fiction. Despite the proliferation of fantasy series, motivating male readers continues to be a publishing challenge because literacy is increasingly being pegged as a female domain.

The Failure of Boys Threatens the Successes of Girls

New statistics on the failure of boys to engage with literacy continue to distress educators and parents, some of whom connect the successes of females with the failure of boys, which I explored in *Beauty, Brains, and Brawn: The Construction of Gender in Children's Literature* (Lehr, 2001). Girls' successes with higher test scores in math and science as well as record numbers who now attend college have caused some to suggest that we have shortchanged boys, ironically and conveniently ignoring centuries of unequal opportunity for girls. As one college student asked, "Why can't we focus on the success of both boys and girls?"

An equal number of highly qualified females are also entering the field of science, but recent research by Donna Shalala suggests that most university science departments remain male bastions, with most science faculty jobs still given to men. Shrill critics have denounced feminists and feminist agendas and write about the "anti-boy" agenda in classrooms. African-American and Latino males continue to drop out of school in increasing and distressing numbers. Male readers have drifted away from literature and prefer the Internet and video games, whereas literature has been labeled as a feminine pursuit. An article in *Reading Today* suggests that teachers should use any kind of reading material to engage boys with literacy. Alfred Tatum's provocative research, described in this volume, suggests quite the opposite. His case study of a young African-American male headed for jail suggests that high-quality literature showing the gritty side of life enabled an endangered young man to make stronger personal choices. Literature matters.

The Politics of Washington

The cumulative and shattering effects of the No Child Left Behind Act (NCLB) are also becoming apparent. Federal government Reading First funds are dispersed to school districts with high numbers of children living below the poverty line. To receive this high-stakes funding, school districts must prove that they are implementing literacy instruction based on scientific reading research as defined by NCLB. Continued funding is contingent on successful outcomes—that is, improved test scores that align with appropriate instructional programs. Reading First is premised on "scientifically based reading research," which is ultimately defined as systematic and explicit instruction in phonics, phonemic awareness, vocabulary, fluency, and comprehension; this promotes a rather constricting and Machiavellian view of research.

Explicit instruction is premised on teaching new material in small sequential steps, with regular review and reteaching as necessary—sound familiar? Phonemic awareness is taught explicitly with a focus on kindergarten and grade 1, whereas phonics is taught systematically and explicitly through third grade. Readers at risk are given additional explicit instruction. Vocabulary is ironically defined as being of four types: reading, writing, speaking, and listening. Suggestions for teaching vocabulary include providing students with extensive opportunities to read a broad range of texts in and out of school. Because there is supposedly no scientific research to support independent reading, fluency instruction consists of improving decoding and automaticity through monitored oral reading with "aligned student materials."

Comprehension is achieved by teaching students sets of steps to strategically make sense of text. An explicit warning is given in Reading First: "Do not layer scientifically based programs on top of non-research based programs already in use. Supplemental and intervention materials must be scientifically based and coordinated with the core, comprehensive reading program." Teachers are urged to discontinue teaching instruction that is not scientifically based, which indirectly challenges the roles of reading aloud, independent reading, book clubs, and reader response to literature as not having a scientific basis for being implemented in reading programs, although the instructional suggestions for teaching vocabulary suggest otherwise.

In 2006, SAT scores in the written portion of the test dipped significantly, causing some people to suggest that critical thinking is not being taught effectively. This is hardly surprising, with the exclusive focus on skills and drills and the mandated test-taking obsession that now absorbs educators.

An alarming number of superintendents and principals insist that teachers must be on the same basal and workbook pages across grades within school districts, although I could find no support for this curious practice on the No Child Left Behind or Reading First Web sites. Some of the teachers I know who once used children's books as a foundation for teaching literacy have dramatically increased their use of work sheets; many use basal readers exclusively; many teach reading through whole-class direct instruction consisting of extensive phonics drills and grammar lessons. I have recently observed that children's books, now used sparingly, are increasingly being used to teach skills and traditional grammar in elementary classrooms. Other schools are taking precious time once used for reading instruction to take entire grades of children to the cafeteria for weekly test-taking simulations. What sort of madness is this?

I co-taught this year with a veteran fifth-grade teacher who continues to use book clubs and children's literature, but a distressing number of the teachers I observe are abandoning literature at an alarming rate. Veteran teachers tell our student teachers that they are no longer able to find time to use children's literature in their upper elementary classrooms. These veteran teachers are being directed to use the new and expensive basal reading programs exclusively, although they stated a preference for having children read literature.

What kind of message does this send to a preservice teacher? I believe that it sends the powerful message that teachers are disempowered and that they have no legitimate voice in determining how they will teach. This notion of disempowerment is not a new issue in teacher education. Mandated graduate degrees in education are worthless if teachers cannot make basic pedagogical decisions in their own classrooms. Trust remains a core issue between teachers and the public they serve.

I'm not sure that today's children will survive the legacy of No Child Left Behind; politicians are not educators, yet we are currently entrapped with policies based on the opinions of politicians, many of whom are social conservatives with views informed by fundamentalist religious perspectives. I admit that this is a cynical view, but I see power and hope *only* if teachers are willing to stand up for what research-based pedagogy supports. This must include challenging current definitions of scientifically based reading research.

We must make conscious choices to keep literature alive in the classroom. A local principal recently accused a teacher of using literature rather than following the district's curriculum. After returning several times to her classroom to observe and document what she was doing, he told her to shut her door, keep it to herself, and continue using literature. Similarly, Shelley Harwayne (chapter 3) recommends closing the classroom door and teaching what one knows is pedagogically sound. Although I agree, I also think that teachers are once again caught between sound pedagogical research and instruction and the paths of reckless and unknowledgeable politicians.

Teachers: My Hope for the Future

As a result of my cynicism and deep concerns about the far-reaching and negative impacts of the current political mandates, I made the decision to edit a book that would examine these changes in children's literature. This text will offer much wisdom from veterans like Shelley Harwayne and Laura Robb, coupled with strategies from new teachers. New teachers are often the most vulnerable; they have little status and no security and are afraid to rock the boat. They often follow the wisdom of older mentors, who have extensive experience and more power. The young teachers' voices in this volume are at once naive and sophisticated. These teachers believe in the power of literature and literacy in the lives of children, and they are, above all, risk takers. Being a risk taker today might be the one way to effect change.

A few years ago, one of my students went out into the world and implemented a sound reading and writing program using children's literature in her first year of teaching. Hers is a successful folktale. That year, her fourth graders had the highest English Language Arts test scores of any fourth-grade class in the *entire* district. When asked by administrators what her secret was (educators are fond of looking for magic teaching potions), she replied that she was teaching as she had been taught in her college instructional, literacy, and literature courses.

The point is that she was fearless. She taught innovatively, integrated diverse children's literature across the curriculum, and implemented all the rich components mentioned above: daily reading aloud; daily independent reading; providing children with time to discuss and reflect on the books they were reading and time to write about books from multiple perspectives; implementing art, drama, poetry, and music to explore themes and literary elements; using nonfiction and fiction in the content areas. She was a risk taker. She had a set of core beliefs about learning, and her theory was grounded in current research and strong pedagogical practice. She also had an underlying passion for sharing high-quality children's literature with her students. She wanted them to love reading literature as much as she did. She is my iconic hope for the future success of literature and literacy.

How This Book Is Organized

This book is divided into four parts. Part I includes diverse perspectives on the politics of children's literature and the many challenges related to teaching literature and literacy today. National mandates that impact the teaching of literature and literacy have become almost universally conservative, with the result that literature has disappeared in thousands of classrooms.

Belinda Louie examines the multifaceted effects of the current political mandates in education and gives voice to a variety of constituencies—including teachers, parents, children, administrators, publishers, and authors—whom she views as colliding forces engaged in the education of the young.

Patricia Scharer, Evelyn Freeman, and Barbara Lehman continue the discussion by analyzing the status of literature in reading programs across the United States. They consider whether children's literature is essential or marginal in the elementary classroom by examining the literacy research from 2000–2005.

Shelley Harwayne gives teachers encouragement and talks about the perils of abandoning literature in the classroom in an interview with me. As a former administrator at the school and district levels in New York City, she talks about the necessity of putting books into the hands of children.

Amy McClure focuses on current censorship battles over sex, homosexuality, the evils of magic, and diversity, by examining how this obsession with censorship has created a "national curriculum" that is effectively removing literature from thousands of classrooms. I could think of no stronger voice to reflect on the cumulative damaging impacts of censorship than McClure, whose provocative voice laid out both the conservative and liberal positions with such clarity in 1995.

Who supplies all this wonderful literature? Children's bookstores are disappearing, but Hodge Podge Bookstore in Albany, New York, has not closed its doors. Frank Hodge has been getting teachers and librarians excited about children's books for many, many years. He is legendary in the Northeast.

His tiny bookstore caters to thousands of teachers in Vermont, New York, and New Jersey. After more than seven decades, Frank is still teaching, preaching, reading, and selling books. He is a children's book evangelist! For 25 years his conferences have attracted the most dynamic children's authors in the world. He knows this world of literacy and children's books, and he is agonizing over the changes in the classroom and in the publishing industry. I interviewed this provocative educator about his professional life as a professor, bookseller, and conference coordinator.

Marjorie Hancock's reader response research uniquely positions her to categorize and analyze the extensive reader response studies using fiction and nonfiction in the classroom. Because of Hancock's dynamic political implications for and challenges to current literacy instruction, I have placed her chapter in with the politics of children's literature, realizing, however, that her review of the research has powerful implications for strategic instructional strategies for teachers. The research is pragmatic and offers concrete examples for classroom practice. Hancock's call for future studies on reader response with English language learners and a stronger focus on global cultures conflicts with what and how the federal government currently funds research projects.

In Part II, authors and educators consider critical perspectives in children's literature from multiple vantage points in history.

American Indians continue to be marginalized in the social studies curriculum. (Read Deborah Thompson, chapter 23 in this volume, and visit the Oyate Web site, an exceptional Native organization that evaluates texts and resources by and about Native peoples.) Author Joe Bruchac's powerful essay provides insight into the challenges and struggles to write authentically. As an Abenaki Indian, Bruchac, who addresses the importance of names and naming a group, talks about his body of work. Writing from within the American Indian culture entails an enormous amount of responsibility, a commitment of time, and serious research. Even this does not ensure accuracy. His books *Pocahontas* and *Sacagawea* took years of research and provide children with fresh perspectives about American history. In his essay Joe analyzes a book written by a cultural outsider, Ann Rinaldi, and demonstrates how her writing misinforms readers through inaccurate information and a cultural lack of understanding.

The historical record, no matter how distorted, informs what we believe, and because the majority of books about American Indians continue to be written by those outside the culture, many distortions about American Indians remain. Louise Erdrich, who writes about the Ojibwa before European settlers displaced them in the 19th century, provides a rare glimpse into an unfamiliar and intact American Indian culture. In *The Birchbark House* Erdrich imagines what life in a remote Ojibwa village might have been like for her ancestors. Moreover, children rarely get glimpses into the complexity of being an American Indian today. For most educators, Indian studies are relics of the past and end with the last of the Indian Wars in the 19th century. My students are currently reading Bruchac's *The Heart of a Chief*, which explores the complexity of the contemporary landscape through the eyes of a male protagonist. Joe lives 6 miles up the road from me and has worked extensively with my students; they describe him as one of the most powerful educators they have met. Bruchac's voice is an empowered voice.

Because of the work of Barry Thorne, we know about the pollution games that children experience on school playgrounds. Pollution games include taunts and bullying, typically against females and males who are considered effeminate. For girls the taunts can be targeted at physical traits such as weight and the early development of breasts. Those who are disabled can also be challenged or scapegoated for their physical traits. Linda Wedwick and Roberta Seelinger Trites examine how children's perceptions of their own bodies are constructed through the discourse of language and culture, often inauthentically. They focus on how literary depictions of embodiment are shaped by language, how idealized female images related to weight and being physically abled are often considered personal choices, and finally how certain characters are scapegoated for the redemption of other characters. Understanding the role of literature in the shaping of the middle school child's beliefs about her own body illuminates truths about how young readers are socialized "into gendered perceptions of embodiment." Their first heading, "Fat Is a Choice. Really?" captures the absurdity of perfection that is the compulsory diet of young girls who are presented with images of Barbie from their earliest years. A chubby 4-year-old was already being sent to an eating disorder therapist by a working class mother I know, because she feared that her daughter was already destined for obesity. Embodiment is culturally derived and cuts across all levels of socioeconomic status.

Alfred Tatum reframes the literacy dialogue by considering an at-risk population, the African-American male. His theoretical basis challenges current assumptions about males and reading, and his startling research suggests provocative strategies for engaging and enabling African-American males in the classroom. High-quality literature is central to his discussion.

Christopher Paul Curtis's essay reinforces Tatum's research by exploring his own motivation for writing award-winning books like *The Watsons Go to Birmingham* and *Bud, Not Buddy*. Curtis gives voice to the disenfranchised African-American male, but more than that, he gives them relevant and honest books in which they can see reflections of themselves.

Distortions about the historical record exist for most disenfranchised groups, because history is written by the majority shareholder. Who wrote the first realistic fiction novel for children in 1749? (Hint: It was not John Newbery's *The History of Little Goody Two-Shoes*, written in 1765.) Some of the earliest children's writers were considered radical and subversive women who championed lost causes and wrote about the constricted and wasted lives of women. How many of these female children's authors can you name? I explore the history of these radical children's writers from the 1700s, women who challenged their confining roles and wrote children's books that were best sellers. They were eventually censured, labeled didactic, and deleted from many children's literature texts. In a second chapter I draw disturbing parallels between those historical women and contemporary feminist authors who write taboo books that are censored and attacked as being anti-God, anti-family, and anti-boy. Militant women writers are always at risk of being silenced.

Linda Lamme's chapter on gays and lesbians in children's literature provides a frank discussion about one of the most taboo topics remaining in children's literature. Children's books about lesbian, gay, bisexual, or transgender children remain one of the most frequently challenged topics in children's literature. Lamme discusses books written for children rather than for young adults; therefore, she focuses on issues related to children who have gay parents, who have relatives with AIDS, or who are homophobic. *Heather Has Two Mommies* (1990) is one of the most frequently attacked picture books in history, and, ironically, it's not because the illustrations are ineffectively rendered. The most challenged book in 2006, according to the American Library Association, was a true story about two male penguins raising a baby penguin (*And Tango Makes Three*, 2006).

Pam Munoz Ryan shares a harsh letter from a teacher who wrote that her book, *Esperanza Rising*, vilified the early formation of the migrant labor movement. Ryan's response conveys her Mexican-American family's actual role and position in the historic labor movement of migrant workers in the early 20th century. Ryan's response underscores, again, how imperative diverse perspectives are when teaching history. Authors are not bound by politically correct directives or interpretations of history when they write.

Part III reveals the continuing dynamic nature of children's literature, despite the controversies surrounding literature in the classroom and the harsh effects of recent publishing trends. I include this section in a book that is focused on the politics of children's literature so that educators know what's current, what's changing, what's new, and what's available. How does children's literature continue to evolve, even when critics are attacking it? Picture book sales have diminished in recent years, yet some of the most innovative changes in children's literature appear in the art of the picture book. Children's literature is not only alive and well; innovative authors and illustrators continue to create dynamic books for children. Any relevant discussion of the state of children's literature must also consider the vitality and the content of children's literature.

Junko Yokota explores the international explosion of children's books and the issues surrounding this phenomenon. Tom Friedman's book *The World Is Flat* (2005) describes the dissolution of international borders through the instantaneous connections that are possible in this digital age. Books increasingly are accessible across borders, providing children with direct knowledge and access to cultures and politics once contained only in outdated social studies textbooks. Provocative books from the Netherlands (*The Book of Everything* by Guus Kuijer, 2006) and Great Britain (*The Boy in the Striped Pajamas* by John Boyne, 2006) convey troubling yet relevant themes about war, religion, and its aftermath. J. K. Rowling and Cornelia Funke are examples of international book stars who have successfully crossed international borders and sold millions of books. Funke's *Inkheart* (2003) has been translated into English from German. Surprisingly, even Harry Potter's adventures are "translated" for American audiences from British English, causing controversy in Great Britain about the dumbing down of British culture for U.S. readers.

Canadian author Deborah Ellis extends the dialogue on perspective by discussing how she goes about choosing her topics and writing her books. *The Breadwinner* illuminated the plight of women living in Afghanistan under the Taliban's harsh rule. These perspectives would be lost to children if an author like Ellis wrote only from within her own country and culture. Ellis's extensive research and oral histories of women who lived under the Taliban have been published in an adult book, *Women of the Afghan War* (2000), and provide the material for *The Breadwinner*. Most recently, Ellis's *I Am a Taxi* provides a troubling portrait of a contemporary imprisoned Bolivian family in which the children journey to and from prison to school and must earn money to pay the rent for the jail cell in which they live. Ellis's troubling portrait follows the journey of a young boy into the jungle, where opium is processed into a paste that is then smuggled across borders.

Barbara Kiefer, Lawrence Sipe, and Caroline McGuire inform readers about the stunning world of picture books. New technologies, including graphic arts novels and computer-generated illustrations as well as postmodern scenarios, indicate that picture books exhibit vitality and innovation across a range of media. Kiefer also addresses the effects of 9/11 and how illustrators approach complex and troubling images in picture books. Sipe and McGuire explore how authors and illustrators break with convention to produce tableaus in which readers are drawn directly into the confusion and chaos of picture books, as in Jon Scieszka's (1992) *The Stinky Cheeseman* and David Wiesner's (2001) *The Three Pigs*.

Fantasy is being published in blockbuster amounts with many imports from Britain, Australia, Germany, and New Zealand. First-time fantasy authors are receiving $650,000 or more for their books. I explore the many new books cluttering up Harry Potter's world, most of which originate in Britain. Authors writing in this genre have produced and sold more volumes in recent years than in any other. Fantasy series for middle-grade children are enticing and motivating some young male readers while continuing to dominate the best-seller lists. J. K. Rowling is a billionaire and the last installment *Harry Potter and the Deathly Hallows* (2007) will take Harry Potter book sales beyond the current 325,000,000. The fantasy genre cannot be ignored.

Penny Colman provides readers with a provocative insider's account of writing nonfiction. Her perspectives as a writer of biographies about strong women in U.S. history provide balance to social studies curricula that are overburdened and distorted with tales of war, politics, broken treaties, and the efforts of male generals and politicians. Through her books, readers meet Rosie the Riveter, Mother Jones, Frances Perkins, and female spies of the Civil War. They meet an arctic explorer, a botanist, a reporter and a landowner from the 19th century—all females. Colman's personal reflections about the writing process also provide teachers with strategies for thinking about how to teach children to write nonfiction.

This section concludes with an interview I did with Naomi Shihab Nye, poet and author of children's books capturing the voice and spirit of Palestinians today. Naomi's German- and Palestinian-American background, as well as her many visits to her family in the Middle East, merge to form a haunting voice. With her yearnings for peace and understanding between cultures, she has become one of the only voices in the United States writing for children from this perspective. Half of this interview belongs in the previous section, but I wanted to present a coherent voice from this innovative poet who presents readers with thoughts about the Middle East today.

Part IV offers concrete strategies and insights from educators who are working directly with children. Deborah Thompson analyzes social studies textbooks and offers startling insights about their strengths and weaknesses. These collective voices offer insights into the satisfaction and challenge of using literature with children in the 21st century.

Nonfiction has found new health in publishing and in the classroom. Janice Kristo, Penny Colman, and Sandip Wilson examine current research and offer bold instructional strategies for using nonfiction in the classroom. They also dispel lingering myths about the electrifying quality of current nonfiction.

The direct results of censorship are homogenized and noncontroversial textbooks that cater to conservative critics. Deborah Thompson examines the politics of two widely used social studies texts; she analyzes diversity, perspectives of history, and the pitfalls of overreliance on textbooks, which is once again becoming the norm. Multiple perspectives are essential, and Thompson's text sets provide teachers with sterling examples of how to enhance the study of history with relevant and diverse children's literature. The fact that Florida recently passed a law stating that social studies can be taught only through facts underscores the polarizing politics appearing in every part of the curriculum.

Laura Robb's chapter is personal and practical, because the reader is invited into her classroom. A teacher for more than four decades, Robb continues to offer strategies that work. Her description of a thematic unit on social justice links effectively to the text sets that Thompson offers in her chapter on enriching social studies.

Janet Wong, an established poet and picture book author, offers her childhood reflections of an Asian-American child who moved seven times. In this provocative interview by Barbara Chatton, readers understand the evolution of a child who suddenly found herself considered as "other" in a "white-bread" community. This childhood experience helped to shape Wong's "insistence on being seen as culturally American rather than Asian." Wong's powerful recollections of how she struggled with her Asian-American identity and how she read her environment rather than books are compellingly intertwined stories for teachers to know and to understand. How do we successfully invite children into the community of book lovers and readers? How do we teach children to embrace the "other" or to realize the idiosyncratic boundaries that define the concept of "other"?

Finally, what about the school library? Is it now a large closet for unused literature? Linda McDowell was a dynamic classroom teacher for 25 years. Then she decided it was time to fulfill one more career dream: She became a school librarian. McDowell offers a unique and very personal perspective of an educator who has seen it all and knows what works. The school library she runs is a vital place in Lake George Elementary School. Linda works with teachers to implement thematic units, and she talks about how that became a reality. Getting books into the hands of children is her main goal, and she describes how to set up the physical space of the school library and attract readers. She concludes by describing how teachers might reframe their thinking about the current political climate. McDowell's is a very personal voice of experience from the classroom and school library.

For the Love of a Good Book

In the final chapter of this book, I offer the perspectives of eight bright new voices in the field of education, students of mine who have gone out into the elementary classroom. Most of the teachers writing short essays about their classrooms have been teaching for about 5 years—new, but also not new. These bright voices from the trenches present simple but effective encounters with children and good books. Some are eloquent; some are practical; most are passionate. They teach in the country, in the suburbs, and in the city. They teach kids of diverse ethnicities. Their shared belief is that putting good books in the hands of children really matters. Some of their ideas are simple, some are more complex, all are easy to implement. What they share is a vision for literacy that is dynamic, relevant, and child centered. This chapter is the final word on all the essays combined. For those who want a final reflective summation, these essays are my final thoughts on what really matters.

Get books into the hands of children.

Read to children every day.

Don't give up.

Be a risk taker.

Connect children and books.

For the love of a good book!

References

Ellis, D. (2000). *Women of the Afghan war.* New York: Praeger.

Friedman, T. (2005). *The world is flat.* New York: Farrar, Straus & Giroux.

Lehr, S. (1995). *Battling dragons: Issue and controversy in children's literature.* Portsmouth, NH: Heinemann.

Lehr, S. (2001). *Beauty, brains, and brawn: The construction of gender in children's literature.* Portsmouth, NH: Heinemann.

Children's Books

Boyne, J. (2006). *The boy in the striped pajamas.* New York: Fickling Books.

Bruchac, J. (1998). *The heart of a chief.* New York: Dial.

Bruchac, J. (2003). *Pocahontas.* New York: Silver Whistle/Harcourt.

Bruchac, J. (2000). *Sacajawea.* New York: Silver Whistle/Harcourt.

Fisher, C. (2005). *Snow-walker.* New York: Greenwillow Books.

Curtis, C. (1995). *The Watsons go to Birmingham—1963.* New York: Delacorte Press.

Curtis, C. (1999). *Bud, not Buddy.* New York: Delacorte Press.

Ellis, D. (2001). *The breadwinner.* Toronto, Ontario, Canada: Groundwood Press.

Ellis, D. (2006). *I am a taxi.* Toronto, Ontario, Canada: Groundwood Press.

Erdrich, L. (1999). *The birchbark house.* New York: Hyperion Books.

Funke, C. (2003). *Inkheart.* New York: Scholastic.

Kuijer, G. (2006). *The book of everything.* New York: Scholastic.

Newbery, J. (1765). *The history of Little Goody Two-Shoes.* London: Printed for J. Newbery, at the Bible and Sun in St.Paul's-Church-Yard.

Newman, L. (1990). *Heather has two mommies.* (Diana Souza, Illus.) Boston: Alyson Books.

Parnell, P., & Justin, R. (2005). *And Tango Makes Three.* New York: Simon and Schuster.

Rowling, J. K. (2007). *Harry Potter and the deathly hallows.* New York: Scholastic.

Ryan, P. (2000). *Esperanza rising.* New York: Scholastic.

Scieszka, J. (1992). *The Stinky Cheeseman and other fairly stupid tales* (L. Smith Illus.). New York: Viking Press.

Selznick, B. (2007). *The invention of Hugo Cabret.* New York: Scholastic.

Skelton, M. (2006). *Endymion spring.* New York: Delacorte Press.

Stone, D. (2004). *The Illmoor chronicles: The ratastrophe catastrophe.* New York: Hyperion Books.

Wiesner, D. (2001). *The three pigs.* New York: Clarion Books.

At the Crossroads:
Politics in Children's Literature

Chapter

1

Politics in Children's Literature: Colliding Forces to Shape Young Minds

Belinda Louie

"There's no such thing as a politically innocent picture book."

—Fox (1993, p. 656)

Children's literature has powerful influences on young minds because "it reflects the politics and values of our society" (Fox, 1993, p. 656). Politics are concerned with power, control, and regulation. There are those who argue that children's literature has nothing to do with politics: Children's literature appeals to the imaginations and interests of children; how can one use such a venue to manipulate the minds of the young? Irving Kristol (1999) asserts that we cannot deny the influence of literature:

If you believe that no one was ever corrupted by a book, you also have to believe that no one was ever improved by a book (or a play or a movie). You have to believe, in other words, that all art is morally trivial and that, consequently, all education is morally irrelevant. (p. 5)

Although it would be difficult to trace the effects of any single book on an individual reader, social scientists know that books evoke our imagination. Such imagination helps to shape and define the values and beliefs of the readers (Kristol, 1999). For example, imagination developed while reading a biography on Helen Keller will ingrain the value of determination in a reader's mind (Marcus, 1980). Individuals who play a part in young people's lives intentionally or unconsciously use or allow literature to shape those young lives; these are the politics. Authors' worldviews, readers' interests, parents' values, teachers' beliefs, district administrators' goals, the general public's desires, and the publishers' market bring various groups of players into the political arena of children's literature. Embedded perspectives, whether religious, social, or gender based, attempt to control the influences that books have on children. By advocating or rejecting certain books, by highlighting or being silent on certain issues, many stakeholders influence which books make their ways into the hands of young readers. In this chapter, I will discuss the agency of the key players as their choices and values construct the political context of children's literature.

Authors

Authors bring their own worldviews and perspectives to their work. Even when they try to be neutral, their worldviews or underlying assumptions influence what they present in the text (Pinsent, 1997). Hollindale (1988a) notes the influence of authors' passive ideologies, which are unexamined, taken-for-granted assumptions that shape the outlook and values of the author. As authors create literature for children, they draw upon their unique imaginations, which rest "on the private, unrepeatable configurations writers make at a subconscious level from the common stock of their experience" (p. 15). Ernest Gaines (2000), an African-American writer, felt excluded as a reader when authors, writing from their worlds, did not create a textual space in which to invite him:

> Many of these books left me with a feeling of disappointment. Though they spoke of earth, land, water, trees, and the people who lived and worked there, they were not describing *my people*, the people I had left in the South.... They were talking about others, and I did not see me there. (p. 9)

Gaines was not referring to racist literature that attacked his community and identity. He was speaking of the many authors who marginalized his culture and failed to affirm his identity by being silent on his world and his people.

In contrast, some authors are very intentional in sharing their perspectives with the readers. Brent Hartinger, author of *Geography Club* (2003), was a speaker in my graduate seminar that focuses on trends and issues of juvenile literature. He talked about how he wanted to share the worlds of homosexual teenagers with the readers. He said that he aimed at creating characters with whom homosexual teenagers could identify. When he started his writing career, there were so few inspiring "gay" novels. He was confident that he could produce works of better quality. Similarly, in Hazel Rochman's (1990) edited book, *Somehow Tenderness Survives*, she wanted readers to encounter literary characters who were individuals living under the oppression of apartheid. She wanted the book to break down barriers, "with enthralling stories that make us imagine the lives of other" (Rochman, 2003, p. 103). She believes that good stories can break down barriers by enriching people, connecting people, and increasing understanding among people.

In addition to silence and intention, a third key point is that some authors choose to make their worldviews an integral part of their writing. In his *Dark Materials* trilogy (*The Golden Compass*; *The Subtle Knife*; *The Amber Spyglass*), Philip Pullman subverted fundamentalist Christian principles by creating a fantasy world inhabited by "compassionate witches, malevolent theologians and a feeble, disingenuous God" (Wartofsky, 2001, p. C1). Pullman declared his intention "to undermine the basis of Christian belief" during an interview with *The Washington Post*. His final volume in the trilogy, *The Amber Spyglass*, ended with a great war in heaven that resulted in the death of God. Pullman stated that he was not sure about the existence of God. The universe might still have come into being without God as a factor, he said. Pullman observed that many religious zealots demonstrated much cruelty and ignorance as they proclaimed the name of God. "If I were him [sic]," he declared, referring to God, "I'd want nothing to do with them."

Children's literature is therefore political because it reflects the perspectives, worldviews, cultural norms, and biases of its authors (McNair, 2003). Many writers assume that their own ideologies are universal truths. Texts can allure unwary readers into an unconscious acceptance of the writers' values; Nodelman and Reimer (2003) thus encourage readers to "read against" (p. 156) the text so that they can identify the embedded values and arrive at a better understanding of the issues involved. As we continue to examine the influence of the players on the embedded politics in children's literature, we must keep in mind that silence, intention, and worldview are colliding forces that shape children's minds.

Children

Children are the primary consumers of children's literature; their political influence is a little harder to get at than the authors'. Children regulate the publishing industry by choosing books that are pleasant (Squire, 1964). This pleasant orientation occurs among young readers as well as among high school readers. A few years ago, I spent 2 months in a high school classroom studying students' responses to a translated book, *Let One Hundred Flowers Bloom* (Feng, 1995). The students disliked the human suffering, yet they could accept it. However, when the class read to the point where an enemy truck ran over the protagonist's dog, a boy jumped up and threw the book to the floor, yelling, "The book sucks." This class of 17- and 18-year-olds refused to read on because they found the incident very unpleasant. This episode was a critical point in the book. The author used various events to portray the poignant, lasting, and loyal relationship between master and dog. The truck incident was neither sardonic nor melodramatic (Louie, 2005). However, many students refused to read on even though they were analyzing various episodes that built the themes of the book.

As consumers, many school-age readers also reject books with contexts that they do not understand. It takes much motivation to persevere in the beginning pages as readers enter a book with an unfamiliar context. When I was a participant-observer in a sophomore high school class reading Gail Tsukiyama's (1996) *The Samurai's Garden*, many students refused to open the book because they did not understand the term *samurai*. Some students stated that the book must be boring because it was about some "samurai's stuff" that they did not understand. Almost all the students changed their minds after they read the book. In the exit interviews, I asked each student explicitly whether he or she enjoyed the book. The students' answers were affirmative. I asked them why they changed their minds. The students reported that the book was no longer boring after the teacher helped them to understand Japanese society during World War II, the setting of the book.

During the instructional phase of the study, the teacher carefully guided her students to read and to debate two key issues around the text: (a) suicide—shame and honor in Japanese culture, and (b) aggressor and victim—the role of Japan in World War II. Books like *The Samurai's Garden* require much instructional support before students can enjoy them. In settings such as World War II, students need the historical, political, and cultural contexts in order to engage in the text. As they gain knowledge and understanding, their worldviews will be altered, if only subtly, and their outright rejection of strange texts might lessen. Thus, they influence silently by accepting the book and the authors' voice.

It is not unusual that children and adolescents prefer to stay in their comfort zones when they select books to read. They tolerate or even accept stereotypes that affirm their expectations, and they feel uncomfortable when their established notions or values are challenged. In my study of a group of fourth-grade students' responses to a Chinese folktale, *Mulan*, the students identified multiple areas of falsehood in the Disney version of the tale after instruction on authenticity of multicultural texts (Louie, 2006). Some students abhorred Disney's practice of distorting multicultural tales. Many students voiced their insights about Disney's motivation to make money by producing movies that are entertaining to young people in the United States. In its efforts to make movies funny, Disney had little regard for retaining the cultural values of the group being portrayed.

Thus, the children were able to engage in an overtly political discussion of the texts. Still, after a month of instruction, 75% of the class indicated that they preferred the Disney version to other, more authentic versions of *Mulan*. One student succinctly said that "Disney makes movies for American people. I like the funny stuff. I feel more comfortable with the Disney version. It is more like Pocahontas." By demanding books that will conform to American notions, young people constitute a strong political force, regulating the types of books that publishers will bring to the market.

Parents

Regulation and control are elements of politics, and parents, who regulate and control, are always political forces in their children's lives. Most parents want their children to learn from books: reading skills, knowledge, and moral values. The worldview of a piece of literature is often at the heart of parental concerns. A worldview is a framework by which people make sense of their experience. Worldviews are similar to philosophies of life, with an intellectual and emotional coherence (Glanzer, 2004). Parents may object to offensive language or sexual content (Goldwasser, 1997). Some parents want to protect their children from unpleasant realities. Most parents prefer education that favors their particular worldview or that refrains from exposing their children to certain realities of life. Many openly and vocally denounce books that are against their own values and beliefs.

A case in point is some parents' objection to the *Harry Potter* series. Their objection usually centers around the topic of witchcraft. They do not want their children to take the world of Harry Potter as something real. Glanzer (2004) suggests that parental objection goes beyond language, acts, and scenes. When parents want an offensive book removed, they are asking that an overall worldview not be brought into the lives of their children. When parents ask that the *Harry Potter* series be removed, they want their children to have no contact with a world in which a school of witchcraft is a respected place of training for the young. Another example is J. D. Salinger's (1951) *The Catcher in the Rye*. Basically, when parents object to the world of *The Catcher in the Rye*, they are against a world in which vulgar language is accepted. In addition, when some parents oppose Judy Blume's books, they might be expressing their dislike for a world in which casual sexual conduct is permissible. These alternative values are at odds with the foundations of some parents' worldviews. Thus, parents engage in the political acts of control and regulation by limiting their children's exposure to a particular worldview.

In a local school district close to where I live, the president of the PTA told a newspaper reporter that the school district would reduce its problems if minority groups moved out of the district. The parents in that district saw no need to include literature from diverse cultures in the required reading list. A few years ago, they successfully persuaded the district to ban *To Kill a Mockingbird* (Lee, 1960), but the ban was dropped a year later. (The parents were less concerned with the elementary classrooms, where teachers either ignored multicultural texts or used mostly folktales.) What the parents objected to in the book was the issue of racial tension and injustice. Perhaps they believed that if they shielded their children from such volatile issues, then those issues would not exist. Some parents still hold a worldview that racial integration is not a desirable way of life. This worldview affects the literature that they encourage their children to read. Books on racial understanding are unnecessary, in their view, because they expose children to alternative values and alternative ways to interpret life experiences and then provoke them to think about these alternatives.

Thus, parents also choose literature that is comfortable for their children. Some parents might enjoy discussions of values and beliefs with their children, using literature as the basis; others, it would seem, prefer to promote their own worldviews. By encouraging their children to read within a limited selection of books, parents constitute a powerful political force in children's reading choices.

Teachers

Teachers are the fourth group of players in the politics of children's literature. Teachers hold beliefs about the ways in which students learn, how learning should be presented, and what types of teaching texts should be used (Van Dijk, 1998). Teachers do not only engage in teaching; they have personal and social lives, which influence their professional ideologies (Connelly & Elbaz, 1980). Teachers' beliefs, which are the result of their individual past and present experiences, affect their pedagogical and cultural ideologies (Shkedi & Nisan, 2006). For this group, the issues regarding children's literature are paradoxical. On the one hand, most teachers would like to ensure children's access to a variety of books; on the other hand, many teachers resist exposing children to multicultural books that teachers lack either the interest to explore or the contextual knowledge to understand.

Some teachers strongly believe that children's literacy development is directly related to their access to a large number of quality books (Elley, 1992;

McQuillan, 1998). Hence, the classroom library, where books are most easily accessible to all children, plays a vital role in providing children with immediate access to books. Teachers who hold this belief spend their own money to develop their classroom libraries, because many districts do not provide adequate funds for buying books (Lao, 2005). Because many teachers believe that their students' success with literacy is affected by the quantity and quality of their classroom libraries, they refuse to allow a lack of district resources or funding to hinder that successful growth and development.

However, many teachers' desire to increase students' access to books is hampered by their own beliefs, values, and culture. Teachers' cultural beliefs influence the texts they use in the classrooms. For instance, McNair (2003) studied preservice teachers' responses to children's books and discovered their resistance to addressing the sociopolitical dimensions embedded in those books. She reported that many White preservice teachers with whom she worked experienced an enormous amount of discomfort when they were asked to address racial issues within the context of a children's book. Confronting racial issues required the teachers to reflect upon their own beliefs and identities. Such reflection might have triggered defensive responses from the teachers because of the potential threat to some teachers' personal identities. This threat is about self-power, which is inherently political.

Lowery (2002) also found that her preservice teachers felt very uncomfortable when they were guided to challenge gender stereotypes in children's books. The critical examination required teachers to reminisce about their own childhood experiences that had shaped their beliefs in gender roles, another piece of identity. Harris (1999) noted, "Gendered readings of and responses to texts can excite and frighten" (p. 147). Many teachers felt overwhelmed as they pondered their decisions to initiate gender equity conversations in their future classrooms. Racism and sexism are but two politically charged issues in the broader context of cultural identity. Thus, we must wonder how many teacher book choices are driven by maintaining one's own worldview.

Moreover, many teachers do not realize or are not willing to accept that children's books are political (McNillis, 1996). Hollindale (1988b) urged teachers to guide their students to read critically:

> The values at stake are usually those which are taken for granted by the writer, and reflect the writer's integration in a society which unthinkingly accepts them. In turn this means that children, unless they are helped to notice what is here, will take them for granted too. (pp. 12–13)

It is critical that teachers use children's literature to teach students not only to read the word but, more important, to read the world (Freire &

Macedo, 1987). Teachers can guide students to analyze the complexities of the perspectives that the text reflects. Otherwise, common, unexamined ideological assumptions are left alone to do their political work (Nodelman & Reimer, 2003), making young readers believe that those assumptions are universal truths.

District Administrators

In this era of accountability, school district administrators feel the pressure to demonstrate measurable results to show the effectiveness of their literacy programs. Books are selected to enhance the reading skills of the students. Students' reading development is often defined narrowly in terms of decoding and comprehension scores. Last year (2006), I was the northwest regional leader in the Children's Choices Project sponsored by the International Reading Association. Publishers sent us hundreds of books to be placed in K–8 students' hands. Participating classes received numerous new book titles. Students were to read these books and indicate their preferences.

However, when I invited a school librarian to participate in the project, telling her of the deluge of books that her school would receive, her first response was "How many of these books come with an end-of-the-book test?" Many teachers and students choose only books with a prewritten test on which students can demonstrate their reading skills. Although many students in this suburban, middle-class school district read fervently and regularly, they read to earn points from teachers based on the number of pages they finish and the test scores they obtain. Literature reading has become a pursuit of points. Enjoyment, engagement, and transaction with the texts are nonissues in this environment. Because of the district's policy of requiring test scores after book reading, to hold students accountable for the number of books read, the librarian and I both agreed that her school should not receive the books. Thus, the district administrators' policy becomes a political force that shapes the students' motives and purposes in reading children's literature.

Moreover, curriculum committees in some school districts allow teachers to introduce only books that are on an established list. This list is highly influenced by the experiences of the community. Parents feel comfortable when their children read books that the parents read when they were in school. As a result, many district lists essentially consist of award-winning, nonprovocative books from a bygone era. New and exciting titles can hardly find a foothold on district-approved lists. Thus, the district administrators engage in political acts when children's book choices are limited.

The Public

The general public demands a literate workforce. Schools that are supported by local, state, and federal government funds are under tremendous pressure to produce students who can decode. Teachers have to spend a mandated amount of time teaching reading skills in a systematic manner. If students want to read books for pleasure, they can do it outside the classroom. Reading in the classroom means direct reading skill instruction. Armed with free books and ready to go into classrooms, I have encountered many teachers who decline my offer of books because "they are so busy teaching reading that they have no time to read books to students. The students are so busy learning how to read that they have no time for books." A school's reading scores are easily accessible on a district's Web site. Principals and teachers feel the heat of scrutiny when the students' reading scores are low compared to those of other schools. There is a collective effort to raise the scores. The general public's desire for developing literacy skills causes them to regulate the time for literature reading in schools.

Publishers

Publishers are also very concerned about introducing books with unfamiliar contexts because children are very unlikely to purchase the books. Ten years ago, I translated a best-selling Chinese young adult novel, *Jia Li in Junior High* (Qin, 1997). The author, Qin Wenjun, was a finalist in the Hans Christian Andersen Literature Award. *Jia Li in Junior High* was also translated into Japanese and did very well in the Japanese market. However, many American publishers would not publish this book, worrying that American readers would neither understand nor be interested in the lives of their counterparts in contemporary Shanghai.

Johnson-Feelings (1990) considers the publishing of children's literature to be comparable to other business structures in this nation; publishers are very responsive to political sentiments and are deeply committed to profit making. In the last decade, publishers have faced even more competition, so they tend to rely on authors with strongly established sales records. New authors have difficulty getting their manuscripts reviewed. As a result, publishers try to maintain the status quo in the children's literature that they publish by catering to the dominant market.

In recent years, publishing companies have merged or have been purchased by major corporations (Harris, 1994; Nodelman & Reimer, 2003; Taxel, 2003). These economy-driven actions make the industry even more profit conscious. Publishers are less willing to publish new or experimental books. Editors are even hesitant to allow established authors to start a new line of writing on topics or in a genre for which they are not known. In an interview with author Virginia Hamilton, Rochman (2003) reported Hamilton's frustration in not being allowed to write outside the Black experience, for which she was considered a key author. There is little doubt that authors are finding it more difficult to maintain their independence in the face of relentless pressure to keep their book sales strong.

Lee & Low Books, a small independent publisher of multicultural books for children, has set up the exciting New Voices Award, providing cash grants for first-time authors. The publisher sends invitations to authors of color, requesting manuscripts in children's fiction or nonfiction picture books. Independent publishers such as Lee & Low are a rare species, trying to assert their influence in a field dominated by giants. Nodelman and Reimer (2003) observed that these independent publishers "tended to view their work not only as a way of making money, but as a human contribution to the quality of life and literature" (p. 111). Their encouragement of new voices is a political response that goes against the heavyweights of the publishing world.

Conclusion

In this chapter, I have introduced the key players in the political arena of children's literature: authors, whose perspectives prevail in their works; readers, who prefer staying within their comfort zones; parents, who see their role as to protect their children's worldviews; teachers, who like to make choices for their classes; district administrators, who are the guardians of test scores, the public, whose primary concern is a literate work force; and publishers, whose focus is on profit making. Teachers' acknowledgment of these colliding political forces in children's literature is a necessary initial step in cultivating a responsible and intelligent readership among teachers and students.

Children's literature is political. Realizing the political nature of books does not necessarily diminish one's pleasure in reading. Nodelman and Reimer (2003) suggest that reading can be even more pleasurable if readers ask themselves why it is that certain books strike them as so realistic and so enjoyable. Reading a book can be more rewarding if readers remain at some distance from the book and allow themselves to ponder how the views the book presents differ from their own.

References

Connelly, M., & Elbaz, F. (1980). Conceptual bases for curriculum thought: A teacher perspective. In A. W. Foshay (Ed.), *Considered action for curriculum improvement* (pp. 95–119). Alexandria, VA: Association for Supervision and Curriculum Development.

Elley, W. (1992). *How in the world do children read?* Hamburg, Germany: International Association for the Evaluation of Educational Achievement.

Feng, J. (1995). *Let one hundred flowers bloom.* New York: Viking Press.

Fox, M. (1993). Politics and literature: Chasing the "isms" from children's books. *The Reading Teacher, 46,* 654–658.

Freire, P., & Macedo, D. (1987). *Literacy: Reading the word and the world.* South Hadley, MA: Bergin & Garvey.

Gaines, E. J. (2000). A writer's journey. In J. Canfield, M. V. Hansen, & B. Gardner (Eds.), *Chicken soup for the writer's soul: Stories to open the heart and rekindle the spirit of writers* (pp. 6–11). Deerfield Beach, FL: Health Communications.

Glanzer, P. L. (2004). In defense of Harry . . . but not his defenders: Beyond censorship to justice. *English Journal, 93* (4), 58–63.

Goldwasser, M. M. (1997). Censorship: It happened to me in Southwest Virginia—it could happen to you. *English Journal, 86* (2), 34–42.

Harris, V. (1994). Multiculturalism and children's literature: An evaluation of ideology, publishing, curricula, and research. In C. K. Kinzer & D. J. Leu (Eds.), *Multidimensional aspects of literacy research, theory, and practice* (pp. 15–27). Chicago: National Reading Conference.

Harris, V. (1999). Applying critical theories to children's literature. *Theory Into Practice, 38* (3), 147–154.

Hartinger, B. (2003). *Geography club.* New York: Harper Tempest.

Hollindale, P. (1988a). *Ideology and the children's book.* Stroud, UK: Thimble Press.

Hollindale, P. (1988b). Ideology and the children's book. *Signal, 55,* 3–22.

Johnson-Feelings, D. (1990). *Telling tales: The pedagogy and promise of African-American literature for youth.* New York: Greenwood Press.

Kristol, I. (1999). Liberal censorship and the common culture. *Society, 36* (6), 5–10.

Lao, C. (2005). Why teachers buy books for their students. *Reading Horizons, 45* (3), 175–193.

Lee, H. (1960). *To kill a mockingbird.* Philadelphia: Lippincott.

Louie, B. (2005). Development of empathetic responses: New lenses and novel responses. *Journal of Adolescent & Adult Literacy, 48* (7), 566–578.

Louie, B. (2006). Guiding principles for teaching multicultural literature. *The Reading Teacher, 59* (3), 438–448.

Lowery, R. M. (2002). Grappling with issues of gender equity: Preservice teachers' reflections on children's books. *Journal of Children's Literature, 28* (2), 25–31.

Marcus, L. (1980). Life drawings: Some notes on children's picture books. *Lion and the Unicorn, 4* (1), 15–31.

McNair, J. C. (2003). "But *The Five Chinese Brothers* is one of my favorite books!" Conducting sociopolitical critiques of children's literature with preservice teachers. *Journal of Children's Literature, 19* (10), 46–54.

McNillis, R. (1996). *The nimble reader: Literary theory and children's literature*. New York: Twayne.

McQuillan, J. (1998). *The literacy crisis: False claims and real solutions*. Portsmouth, NH: Heinemann.

Nodelman, P., & Reimer, M. (2003). *The pleasures of children's literature*. Boston: Allyn & Bacon.

Pinsent, P. (1997). *Children's literature and the politics of equity*. New York: Teachers College Press.

Pullman, P. (2000). *The amber spyglass*. New York: Knopf.

Qin, W. (1997). *Jia Li in junior high*. Shanghai, China: Juvenile and Children.

Rochman, H. (Ed.). (1990). *Somehow tenderness survives*. New York: Harper & Row.

Rochman, H. (2003). Beyond political correctness. In D. L. Fox & K. G. Short (Eds.), *Stories matter: The complexity of cultural authenticity in children's literature* (pp. 101–115). Urbana, IL: National Council of Teachers of English.

Salinger, J. D. (1951). *The catcher in the rye*. Boston: Little, Brown.

Shkedi, A., & Nisan, M. (2006). Teachers' cultural ideology: Patterns of curriculum and teaching culturally valued texts. *Teachers College Record, 108* (4), 687–725.

Squire, J. (1964). *The responses of adolescents while reading four short stories*. Champaign, IL: National Council of Teachers of English.

Taxel, J. (2003). Multicultural literature and the politics of reaction. In D. L. Fox & K. G. Short (Eds.), *Stories matter: The complexity of cultural authenticity in children's literature* (pp. 143–166). Urbana, IL: National Council of Teachers of English.

Tsukiyama, G. (1996). *The samurai's garden*. New York: St. Martin's Griffin.

Van Dijk, T. A. (1998). *Ideology: A multidisciplinary approach*. London: Sage.

Wartofsky, A. (2001, February 19). The last word: Philip Pullman's trilogy for young adults ends with God's death, and remarkably few critics. *The Washington Post*, p. C1. See also www.philippullman.com/about_the_writing.asp, August 15, 2006.

Chapter 2

Children's Literature in the Classroom: Essential or Marginal?

*Patricia L. Scharer, Evelyn B. Freeman,
and Barbara A. Lehman*

In 1976, Charlotte Huck, professor of children's literature at The Ohio State University, spoke at a general session of the annual convention of the International Reading Association (IRA), advocating for children's literature to be central in the reading program. It is more than 30 years since that important speech, and therefore an appropriate time to consider the current place of children's literature in elementary school classrooms. The 1980s and the 1990s saw an increased emphasis on children's literature, not only to support reading instruction but also to be integrated across the elementary school curriculum. This chapter focuses on the current role of children's literature in the classroom as we progress through the first decade of the 21st century.

The title of this chapter was inspired by an interview with Lea McGee about the *Reading Research Quarterly* article she co-authored in 2000 with Miriam Martinez entitled, "Children's Literature and Reading Instruction: Past, Present, and Future." When asked about the status of children's literature in today's classrooms, only a few years later, McGee worried that quality children's books have been relegated to the margins of classrooms, largely when teachers read aloud to children.

In a separate interview, co-author Miriam Martinez echoed this concern by describing her recent experiences at an IRA convention. First, she noticed the total dominance of the exhibit hall by basal companies. Later, she expressed concern at her presentation that "we have this rich body of knowledge about how to engage children in literature, and I'm afraid it's becoming irrelevant because it's not happening;" the audience responded with a spontaneous and enthusiastic round of applause. Similarly, Martinez explained that her preservice teachers often complain that they cannot read a trade book aloud because it's not written into the district's plan. Hence the question of this chapter: Is children's literature essential or marginal in today's classrooms?

To prepare for writing this chapter, we identified several sources of information to help us study the status of children's literature, including the interviews described above, a questionnaire completed by 13 children's literature professionals across the United States, and a selective review of journal articles published between 2000 and 2005. First we will provide a national context for this discussion, based on the interview and questionnaire data followed by our analysis of recent professional readings. Then we will identify the trends, issues, and gaps that emerged through our analysis before returning to the question posed in our chapter title.

The National Context for Children's Literature (2000–2005)

We asked 13 children's literature enthusiasts to identify the most critical current issues concerning the use of children's literature in elementary and middle school classrooms. The most frequently mentioned issues centered on the detrimental influence of basal or scripted programs, forced curriculum, and testing on the role of children's literature in classrooms. The professionals worried about a "decline in reading done for pleasure" and "the lack of the use of 'real' children's literature," arguing that even though "good literacy teachers know that using high-quality children's literature in literacy instruction has everything to do with helping children become lifelong readers, many doubt themselves and get seduced into using materials that aren't real books."

These initiatives appear to be supported by the recent attention to so-called scientific research-based practices, particularly in terms of federal funding for No Child Left Behind programs. In contrast to the notion that research-based instruction assumes a scripted curriculum or mandated basal, our review of the literature identified an important study comparing phonics-based and literature-based instructional programs. Researchers (Arya et al., 2005) found that the phonics-based program did not result in more accurate reading. In addition, students in phonics-based classrooms had fewer inferences and personal connections in their retellings than did children in literature-based classrooms. These researchers predicted that "the widespread use of commercial phonics-based programs, instead of literature-based programs, will have a debilitating effect on the development of a whole generation of young readers" (p. 71).

A second set of issues identified through the questionnaire focused on helping teachers to handle sensitive issues such as gender, cultural identity, or sexuality in ways that avoid censorship yet broaden students' perspectives during a time of limited resources, both for the purchase of quality books and for professional development. Furthermore, gender issues, literature-based instruction, and multicultural literature were all listed as "What's Not Hot" in the January 2006 issue of *Reading Today*; however, both literature-based instruction and multicultural literature were also listed as "Should Be Hot." In contrast, direct, or explicit, instruction and scientific evidence-based reading research and instruction were both listed as "Hot" but also "Should Not Be Hot." The issues above, raised by the interviews, questionnaires, and some selected reading, begin to describe the challenging context for children's literature in today's elementary and middle schools and form the backdrop for our more comprehensive review of the journal articles published between 2000 and 2005 about the status of children's literature in the classroom.

What's Been Written About Children's Literature (2000–2005)

We decided that one way to view the current state of children's literature use in elementary and middle school classroom instruction was to review journal articles for insights about what was being written and published on the use of children's literature in the 21st century. We selected 10 literacy and children's literature journals to survey: *Language Arts, The Reading Teacher, Reading Research Quarterly, Research in the Teaching of English, Reading Research and Instruction, Journal of Children's Literature, The Dragon Lode, The New Advocate* (now sadly discontinued), *Children's Literature in Education,* and *Children's Literature Association Quarterly.* Because Martinez and McGee's (2000) analysis had extended through the 1990s, we decided to limit our review to articles published from 2000 through 2005. From these journals, we identified 168 articles about children's literature in classroom instruction (Table 2-1).

We included both research and practice-based articles and conceptual pieces with explicit implications for classroom use of children's literature. We did not include editorials or columns with reviews or annotations of children's books. We classified the articles as follows:

- *Data-driven articles.* We divided these into quantitative or qualitative research-based types. Accounts of classroom experiences that were explicitly used within the context of a research investigation were included here.

- *Classroom experiences.* These articles were descriptions of actual class-room teaching events that were not presented as part of a research study.

- *Conceptual articles with classroom implications.* These pieces proposed or advocated specific teaching practices that had not actually oc-curred. They also included articles that presented issues or ideas with implications for teaching with children's literature.

Table 2-1.   Types of Articles

Type of Article (total number)	Data-Driven, Quantitative	Data-Driven, Qualitative	Data-Driven, Both	Classroom Experiences	Conceptual
Literature in the Content Areas (28)	1	4		8	15
Literature Discussion (19)	1	10		7	1
Multicultural Literature (19)		8	1	5	5
Literacy Instruction (18)	3	1		8	6
Response to Literature (16)	3	7		3	3
Nonfiction (15)	1	4		1	9
Critical Issues (12)		1		5	6
Literary Study (13)		4	1	3	5
Bilingual Literacy (11)		3	1	1	6
Read-Aloud (8)	2	5		1	
Technology (5)	1				4
Visual Literacy (4)		2			2
Total (168)	12	49	3	42	62

As we completed our initial review, the following topics emerged accord-ing to each article's primary focus: literature and content areas, nonfiction, literature discussion, multicultural literature, critical issues, reading aloud, bilingual literacy, classroom literacy instruction, visual literacy, response to literature, and literary study. We then read each set of articles looking for descriptions of classroom practices with children's literature; larger themes, trends, or ideas about children's literature and its use in elementary and middle school classrooms; and issues that were raised on the use of children's literature to support literacy instruction, both within each topic and across multiple topics.

The Trends in Children's Literature
(2000–2005)

The first notable trend is the large number of articles related to children's literature supporting content area learning and the use of nonfiction in classroom instruction. The content area category included 28 articles, with nearly half focused on science and math. These articles were diverse in focus and emphasis, advocating the use of many genres of children's literature to enhance the curriculum. The relationship of books to inquiry projects and content standards of math, science, and social studies was explored. Of the 15 articles in the nonfiction category, four dealt with the importance of using nonfiction with primary-age children. Other themes that emerged across multiple articles included effective strategies for sharing nonfiction with children, pairing fiction with informational texts, the importance of illustrations and visuals in informational books, and understanding the nonfiction genre and its text structure. The common belief that children prefer fiction was questioned in many articles.

A second trend relates to talking about books, an explicit focus of articles on literature discussion but also an important trend in the use of multicultural literature. Nearly half of the 19 articles about literature discussions focused on challenges faced by both teachers and students as they work toward the goal of increasing student involvement and engagement during discussions. Learning to participate in high-quality discussions was characterized as requiring considerable time and effort to achieve, but when it was mastered, it led to superior learning opportunities—a trend also seen in half of the 19 articles that focused on multicultural literature. Three articles described the importance of group composition, with specific attention to gender. One important theme raised in the multicultural literature articles was its use to promote awareness, understanding, and empathy for various groups, including people with disabilities, gays and lesbians, and different ethnic groups. (Seven of the literature discussion articles also attended to learning about race, culture, and social justice, and a category of an additional 12 articles focused specifically on critical issues, such as gender, spirituality, homelessness, and bibliotherapy.) In addition to exposure to literature, discussion and other activities were used to help students make meaningful personal connections with their own lives and experiences and develop self-awareness. Having students enjoy literature from their own cultures was also promoted to enhance motivation for reading. The common thread throughout these categories is seeing school as a place for social change and the role that children's literature, discussion, and inquiry in a safe, trusting environment can play in that pursuit.

A third trend highlights the importance of reading children's literature aloud and of oral language, particularly in bilingual classrooms. Oral language—as a way to mediate the story and enhance comprehension in contrast to a more passive, quiet listening experience—was a thread across most of the eight articles in the reading aloud category. Talking before, during, and after the read-aloud helped students to make connections with other texts and each other. The teacher's role to encourage and mediate this talk was central to the argument that having opportunities to respond orally enhanced engagement and understanding and provided a window for the teacher to view students' emerging comprehension. Another 5 of the 11 articles on bilingual literacy each used teacher read-alouds and book discussions, and 3 included drama and oral reading, such as readers' theater. Thus, it appears that oral language is an important medium for sharing children's literature in bilingual settings. Collaborative learning and art and drama in response to literature were identified as important for bilingual learners; so too were repetition (through listening to recordings) and re-reading of literature, teacher modeling through reading aloud, and the use of poetry. The value was noted of affirming bilingual students' self-identity through culturally relevant literature and through including their native languages in class texts. Bilingual literature for all students' language and literacy learning was also emphasized.

A fourth trend related to using children's literature to develop a literate community of readers and writers and the importance of establishing a trusting environment. The most common theme across the set of 18 literacy instruction articles dealt with creating community through reading, writing about, and discussing quality books. Some articles focused on using quality literature to support and motivate struggling readers. Literature, as part of a writer's workshop, helped young writers to notice the craft of their favorite authors of many genres and apply what they found to their own writing. Using picture books with older readers was also supported by recognition of the increasing number of highly complex picture books at a level of sophistication consistent with older children's abilities and interests. Related to this complexity, three of the four articles in the visual literacy category discussed techniques used in postmodern picture books. Overall themes from these articles included the following: the importance of postmodern literature to expand children's understanding of narrative structure and the contemporary world; teacher questioning to support and assist children's understanding; and the need to teach literary language for effective discussions.

A fifth trend—related to previous areas—is the examination of children's response to literature through discussion, as well as the role of drama and role-playing, child participation during teacher read-alouds, readers' theater and other kinds of performance reading, charts, graphs, art, response logs, and music in encouraging response to literature and deepening comprehension and fluency. Of the 16 articles in this category, four specifically focused on motivation to read, recommending the use of independent reading of self-selected materials. They also noted the importance of teacher read-alouds for motivating readers. The following overall themes were suggested: the value of pleasure and engagement with literature; the need for teachers to model responses, pose open-ended questions or problems to solve, and provide specific instruction about the elements of art or historical background for a story; the benefits of exploratory talk for negotiating meanings; the arousal of response and study of issues through intertextual connections; literature as a safe way to explore the complexities of life; and the capability of young children for sophisticated thinking.

The capacity for complex thinking supports the value of studying the literary merits of texts—a final trend. Although many of the 13 articles on literary study focused on genre in some respect, 6 targeted poetry specifically. Overall themes included the importance of literature and literary study for literacy learning (such as how intertextuality strengthens children's sense of story); the importance of learning about genres for literacy development (e.g., learning the different language processes associated with different genres); the need for teacher mediation in literary study through mini-lessons that focus, for example, on the language of literature; and the role of child-centered instruction, such as letting children's interests drive literature discussions and giving children the time and freedom to respond.

Our review clearly identified the relationships among these trends and how one category often overlaps with other topics, which we believe underscores their importance as reflected in the literature. It also points toward issues that were raised in these articles.

The Issues in Children's Literature (2000–2005)

As we looked through all the articles, the issues clustered into six areas. The first area focused on the multiple roles of the teacher and the importance of teacher knowledge and skills. Scripted, teacher-proof programs cannot substitute for a knowledgeable teacher. The role of the teacher was mentioned often in relation to nonfiction books and the need for teachers to have more knowledge about this genre and ways to use nonfiction with children to enhance children's content learning. It is critical for teachers to know how to support book discussions, how to approach controversial issues, and how to select quality books that meet their students' needs and interests. Teachers' limited knowledge in certain areas—such as art and media in picture books, multiple sign systems (e.g., art, music, video) as a means for response, and student reading preferences—was also mentioned.

Although many articles set forth specific implications for teacher education and the kind of information that should be included in preservice courses, it's important to note that a course in children's literature is not frequently required in initial teacher preparation programs, which may account for this knowledge gap.

The second area involved book selection. Teachers need better criteria and assessment tools to review books for classroom use. Specific concern was raised regarding children's books on math and science topics across genres, and how too many books misrepresent concepts and present inaccurate information. Book selection in the area of multicultural literature was also raised as a concern. Teachers need to be knowledgeable about cultural authenticity and have a comfort level with multicultural literature, including books that contain foreign words in context.

The third area revolved around time constraints. Several articles referred to various aspects of time and the need for more time in the school day to devote to literature. The concern was raised about the lack of time for children to read independently and to self-select books. Although articles strongly supported the value and importance of teachers reading books aloud to children daily, time constraints were noted in classrooms with scripted materials, leaving insufficient time for reading aloud and quality interactions.

The fourth area dealt with the access to literature for all children. Educators are losing sight of the importance of grand conversations with students, and students who need quality instruction the most might receive instruction with few opportunities to discuss books that can motivate them to become lifelong readers. The power of quality literature and discussion to support struggling readers, with the goal of having them "fall into a book" (Primeaux, 2001), was argued, as well as the position that "learning does not result from exposure to information, but rather is the result of transactions with that information, with texts, with ideas" (Mills, Stephens, O'Keefe & Waugh, 2004, p. 52). Another aspect of access is the need to implement effective instruction with literature for English language learners' vocabulary, oral language, and comprehension development.

The fifth area involved the way in which teachers' own ideologies and assumptions affect their willingness to expose children to controversial issues. Consequently, teachers might experience discomfort with teaching books that include dialect or violence. Critical issues also included the role of school to promote social justice, to confront concepts of power and subjugation, and to engage children in controversial topics. A question was posed on what literary traditions and perspectives are portrayed in the literature shared with children, especially literature that challenges students' thinking regarding race or sexual orientation, while still connecting to their experiences and interests. The possible consequences to teachers of using literature perceived as controversial were also noted.

The sixth area centered on various aspects of instruction, such as students' motivation to read and the gap between what adults think children should read and what they actually read. The lack of attention to recreational reading in school was pointed out, as well as a lack of books that students prefer. Teachers also need to recognize that not all children engage naturally with written stories. Furthermore, issues about the growing trend of leveling both books and readers (Worthy & Sailors, 2001) were noted, with the concern that the leveling of reading materials according to text difficulty has been overemphasized rather than considered as one particular aspect of matching books with readers. Some authors wrote with concern about whether there is room in the curriculum for literary study in a climate that emphasizes the basics and high-stakes testing. Teachers are challenged to consider what educational practices and classroom environments might restrict, rather than encourage, children's response to literature.

The Gaps in Children's Literature (2000–2005)

Scrutinizing 168 articles provided us with opportunities not only to look for trends and issues but also to wonder about missing pieces as we asked ourselves: What was *not* in the review of the journal articles? Although it was exciting to find so many articles in the 10 selected journals across 5 years, some gaps were clearly identified. As we assembled Table 2-1, for example, we noticed that there were very few quantitative studies—only 12 in the 168 articles. Classroom experiences and conceptual pieces accounted for 104 of the articles, nearly twice the number of data-driven articles. Of the articles based on data, 49 were qualitative; 3 were of mixed methodology; and only 12 were quantitative. This caused us to wonder about the relationship between the status of research on children's literature and the pressures in schools to implement literacy practices that are allegedly research-based but that might not include quality children's literature. In the conclusion of their article, Martinez and McGee (2000) wrote that "what ultimately must be more fully developed is a theoretical rationale for why reading instruction *requires* literature" (p. 166). They argued that the case for children's literature must move beyond emotions into "theory that would suggest that learning to read *is* learning to read literature" (p. 166). Although Martinez and McGee did not specifically discuss the research base for the theory for children's literature, their charge to the field to develop this theoretical rationale supporting children's literature as a requirement for reading appears to need further attention of the kind begun by research we found during this review, particularly on literary study and visual literacy.

　　A second gap arose as we identified and read articles about technology. It was surprising that only 5 of the 168 articles focused on this topic. Four of the five described the advantages of the Internet relative to children's literature such as greater availability of international stories; literature circles via e-mail and chat rooms; or children listening to talking storybooks available for free on the Internet. Web sites were also listed that support teachers looking for author information, storytelling techniques, interdisciplinary resources, lesson plans, or just the right book for their class.

The fifth article (Carter, 2000), however, began by describing the dedication for a new middle school building with a state-of-the-art technology system but no books. To save funds, the school would rely on interlibrary loan until it could add books to its collection gradually over the next 5 years. Carter worried that overemphasizing "Data Land" over "Literature Land" would not help students develop a literature habit necessary for becoming a lifelong reader. This gap may indicate that the relationship between technology and children's literature is not a strong presence in the professional literature, yet in at least one case, technology was financially supported, but it resulted in the exclusion of quality children's books. Likewise, we were surprised at the scarcity of articles about visual literacy, particularly in the context of our highly visual age and the technological advances that make highly complex picture books possible. With the increasing publication of postmodern picture books requiring more visual sophistication, knowledge and techniques for reading and viewing need to be updated.

A third gap centered on the role of children's literature in writing instruction. Although some of the articles mentioned writing in some way (reader response journals or creating charts and diagrams), there was little attention to the influence of quality children's books on children as writers. We would have predicted a greater presence of articles focusing on how children learn about the writer's craft by appreciating and studying the talents of their favorite authors as a way to support their own writing abilities. Literature in the content areas was the largest group of articles, arguing for the importance of children's literature to support content area knowledge, and the number of nonfiction articles was substantial. Yet there was little attention to how children learn to write expository texts through listening to, discussing, and reading quality nonfiction or documenting inquiry projects based on what they learned about nonfiction through quality children's books. Writing nonfiction was not the only genre absent from the articles, however; we found little attention to how mentor texts could help young writers learn about the writer's craft in ways that would help them write first-person narratives, fiction, poetry, or other types of writing. Similarly, writing was identified as "What's Not Hot" by the *Reading Today* survey as well as "What Should Be hot."

Children's Literature: Essential or Marginal?

We now return to the question posed in the title and ask if children's literature is essential or marginal. On the one hand, we found that articles centering on children's literature have clearly been a presence in the professional literature for the past 5 years. Nearly every issue of the 10 selected journals yielded one or more articles for our review and also contained others—such as lists of award-winning books, author profiles, editorials, or book reviews—that we did not include in our analysis. The large number of articles based on classroom experiences is evidence of the strength of children's literature as part of the reading program in those settings.

However, as we read, we also noted that some authors worried about the "subordination of literature" in today's classroom and that children's literature suffers from a "lack of support from a community that sees high-quality children's literature as tangential to literacy instruction, rather than central to it" (Florio-Ruane, Berne, & Raphael, 2001, p. 199). We found words and phrases such as *tangential* or "teaching in the cracks" (Hade, 2002, p. 300) throughout our reading that would support the argument that children's literature today is indeed perceived as marginal, not essential. During our interview with Miriam Martinez, she identified a tension between materials used for learning to read and children's literature as a vehicle for helping children to become strong readers. According to Martinez:

> I don't think we can bury our head in the sand and claim literature for literature's sake. We're going to have to be able to say: Authentic literature is the way to assure that we have strong readers. We need studies that can document and fully describe the kind of really deep understanding and thinking that children do engage in when they are reading authentic literature. I don't think the word is out there.

Struggling readers were a concern during our interview with Lea McGee as she explained, "Lucky strugglers are those who love literature, and they're willing to struggle long enough to get into that world they know is wonderful. That's why we have so many aliterate readers—if they are not caught into the literary world."

The status of children's literature as essential or marginal appears sensitive to local contexts. For the authors of the 168 articles we read and the classrooms they affect, the presence of quality books in the reading program is clearly essential. These contexts were supported by teachers who based their instructional decisions on their theory that children's literature is central to helping their students not only learn to read but also to become deep thinkers, critical learners, strong writers, and, indeed, lifelong readers and writers. Clearly, however, our review identified other contexts in which instructional decisions are based on a contrasting theory of children as learners, resulting in classrooms where quality books are relegated to the cracks, minor moments, and margins of instruction. For these classrooms, the call by Martinez and McGee for a theoretical rationale for why reading instruction *requires* literature is critical. It should shape the research agenda for the future, to ensure that every child has a knowledgeable teacher who makes instructional decisions based on the needs of the individual, with full access to quality children's books—so that *no* child is left behind.

References

Arya, P., Martens, P., Wilson, G. P., Altwerger, B., Jin, L., Laster, B., & Lang, D. (2005). Reclaiming literacy instruction: Evidence in support of literature-based programs. *Language Arts, 83*, 63–72.

Carter, B. (2000). Literature in the information age. *The New Advocate, 12*, 17–23.

Florio-Ruane, S., Berne, J., & Raphael, T. (2001). Teaching literature and literacy in the eye of reform: A dilemma in three acts. *The New Advocate, 14*, 197–210.

Hade, D. (2002). Living well in a time of terror and tests: A meditation on teaching and learning with literature. *The New Advocate, 15*, 293–302.

Martinez, M., & McGee, L. (2000). Children's literature and reading instruction: Past, present, and future. *Reading Research Quarterly, 35*, 154–169.

Mills, H., Stephens, D., O'Keefe, T., & Waugh, J. R. (2004). Theory in practice: The legacy of Louise Rosenblatt. *Language Arts, 82*, 47–55.

Primeaux, J. (2001). "It makes me really want to read": Struggling readers discover literature. *The New Advocate, 14*, 81–85.

Worthy, J., & Sailors, M. (2001). "That book isn't on my level": Moving beyond text difficulty in personalizing reading choices. *The New Advocate, 14*, 229–239.

Literature and Leadership:
An Interview With Shelley Harwayne

Susan S. Lehr

Susan: What are your views on the current state of teaching reading in the classroom?

Shelley: That's such a big question. I visit classrooms and I see wonderful things, but overall, I just worry that the teaching of reading has become so complicated. That's the only way I can describe it. Teachers are second-guessing themselves, and teachers who were good, successful literacy teachers have lost their confidence because of all the mandates that are coming down and all the new fads that are coming in. When I was superintendent, I always worried when a teacher would say, "Am I allowed to…? Am I supposed to…? Is it okay if I…?"

I think teachers have lost their ability to just go with their gut and their instincts. Here I'm talking about very competent, confident teachers who have been using literature in their classrooms for a long time. I think there are also a lot of teachers who are confused by mixed messages in the teaching of literacy. Some districts seem to want everything. I think many teachers are overwhelmed by mandates and have been forced to become mere technicians.

Susan: That's a scary word.

Shelley: Yes. Some teachers have lost their ability to make decisions about what they're going to teach, how they're going to teach it, when, how long, and all those other important choices. And, of course, in some settings teachers are so busy preparing students for tests that they don't have time to prepare for their read-alouds. Some teachers are so busy handing out work sheets that they are not handing out library cards anymore.

I am sorry that not enough time is spent teaching beginning teachers how to read aloud well. We can teach so much through a good read-aloud and its follow-up discussion. We can show students what thoughtful response is all about. We can demonstrate what it means to ask questions of the text, to monitor your own reading, to seek clarification, to have multiple interpretations, to connect to other readings, to be moved emotionally.

Students throughout the grades need ample opportunities to talk richly and deeply about texts filled with big ideas, and then they will know in their hearts and minds what reading is for. They will internalize all those powerful reading behaviors.

Also, of course, I'm still worried about those teachers who are still using basals. I'm especially worried about the ones that are called whole-language basals or literature-based basals. As you know, there's a lot of pressure today to follow prescribed programs. People thought I'd be really happy in New York City when the powers that be decided to adopt one approach and it was balanced literacy. I'd prefer that classroom shelves are filled with real books, but I'm opposed to mandating programs. I'm opposed to the label. I'm opposed to teachers having to ask, "Am I doing balanced literacy correctly?"

Susan: I worry about teachers being overly regulated.

Shelley: We have so many teachers in New York City, and if we asked them all to define balanced literacy, you'd probably come up with 84,000 different definitions. I think one of the problems happening in New York City is that we have a great many literacy coaches—which is a new model and in theory a very fine thing, but teachers complain to me that the coaches are being told to monitor the teaching of literacy in a very dogmatic, absolute way. This is how you should use your time. This is how your room should look. This is what you teach and this is how and when you teach it, and so on. I continue to have many opportunities to visit classrooms across the country. Many are wonderful, but I also visit classrooms in which teachers who don't have adequate or appropriate professional development are attempting to make changes.

For example, I have seen classrooms in which students get to read independent books of their own choosing only when they finish their assignments early. Or I've seen classrooms in which children still have to fill in the blanks with vocabulary words before they're allowed to read their books. Or classrooms in which young students are asked to read very watereddown texts, because first they have to learn how to read, and they don't get to read the good stuff until they are in third grade, when they know how to read. I've seen districts that make the decision that they are going to do this skills stuff in K–2 and then put the real books in third grade to teach comprehension. It's such a strange way of thinking. It's such a bad message for young people. They should always be reading to make meaning.

Of course, there are still classes I visit where I'm appalled at how few books are in their rooms. You know that the money is being spent elsewhere, and the classroom library can hardly be called a library. I'm also surprised when I see, particularly in upper elementary grades, that the teaching of reading has been separated from the teaching of writing. A different person teaches each discipline. They've departmentalized these subjects.

What's interesting to me is that even in the name of literature-based teaching, there's still a lot of literature extension activity that sometimes turns out to be more of an arts and crafts activity. I remember an early childhood teacher had read Jan Brett's *The Mitten*, and as a follow-up, all the kids had to trace these little mittens and decorate them and go home with them. And you know what happens—the families are very happy to hang it on the fridge, and they talk about the mitten, not about the book. So that's troublesome to me.

Please know that I'm not blaming teachers—I think all of these short-comings are a professional development issue. Some teachers are offered in-adequate, dogmatic, or inappropriate professional development. Others are not offered any staff development.

I also think that key components of balanced literacy, such as guided reading, have gotten so complicated. Teachers can feel terrified. There are so many rules to follow, so many ways to seemingly screw up. I think the answer lies in making our teaching public. We need to invite caring colleagues in and be brave enough to teach in front of one another, asking for honest and helpful feedback.

I know when I was principal I tried my hand at guided reading, and I invited Sharon Taberski, a brilliant Manhattan New School teacher, to watch me. Her thoughtful comments were invaluable. Unfortunately, I think many teachers feel uncomfortable allowing a colleague to watch them teach because they think that there is one Good Housekeeping Seal of Approval way of doing things. We must become comfortable saying to one another, "Help me understand why you are doing what you're doing."

There are also upper elementary classrooms where there's a steady diet of whole-class novels, and that, to me, is rather sad, because you can't possibly be meeting the needs of the kids. It's not assessment driven if everyone is reading the same book all the time. Then too, there are some teachers who can't imagine giving up control. They can't imagine letting kids read books of their own choosing. They say, "Well, I haven't read that book. How can I let that child read that book?" I suppose there are also schools and districts that have invested a lot of money in whole-class sets, and they certainly want them to be used.

I think the other worrisome question in the teaching of reading is "What is the rest of the class doing when the teacher pulls a small group together for guided reading?" I don't think any teacher should have to spend his or her Sunday making up center activities. Students are asked to put sentence strips together to re-create poems, play Alphabet Bingo, or illustrate a familiar story. The problem for me is that these activities are usually not assessment-driven. Students rotate from center to center because the teacher has to keep them busy so she can work with one group of four kids. The whole world of classroom management is tied to literacy instruction and the teaching of reading and writing.

Susan: Maybe the problem is the content of the centers. It can become all about making cutesy stuff with no content, like those mittens.

Shelley: At our school, when a teacher worked with a small group, the rest of the class was reading. We didn't do center time. We got them reading. They knew which books they could read and reread, and we had so many books that were appropriate for them, so they weren't doing busywork at all. Maybe there was response attached to the reading, some sort of a drawing or writing, or talking to a friend about the book, or swapping books, but for the most part, they were reading during reading time. With all of the emphasis on creating strategy charts, I've rarely seen students refer to these charts on their own. Some of this thinking comes from my perspective as a superintendent when I visited every classroom every year. And I know that the night before I came, teachers stayed late to freshen up their classroom charts. I think the charts were for me, the visitor, because the kids didn't use them independently. I understand that teachers post them so that they and their students can keep referring back to them, but unless the students are internalizing these strategic behaviors, the charts just remain classroom decorations.

Susan: Where do you think all this preoccupation with that kind of structure for strategies is coming from? What's driving that?

Shelley: I learned from the brilliant Donald Graves to talk to the students, to ask them to explain their classroom lives. "Do you know why the teacher wants you to do that?" I ask that all the time, and most of the kids just shrug their little shoulders. "Do you know why making these connections helps you as a reader?" A lot of kids can't articulate it because their teacher hasn't articulated it, because she's never been involved in studying the topic in depth, because the books are given to teachers and they are told to "do it." You know, we want our school to be P.C.—that is, pedagogically correct. This is the latest stuff—you have to do it. I think that some professional development simply does not go deep enough. So some of these ideas are played out in superficial ways. It takes a lot of time and a lot of hard work to truly understand the research, and overworked teachers feel overwhelmed. They think, "So this is what they want me to do now, and next year they'll ask me to do something else." I think a lot of teachers become cynical.

I think one of the problems is that we don't provoke enough professional conversations publicly. As a profession, it seems to me, we should be having people like Sharon Taberski and Debbie Miller stand side by side at conventions of the IRA [Independent Reading Association] or NCTE [National Council of Teachers of English] and talk about how they teach early childhood literacy—point-counterpoint. "Here's why I do this and don't do that. Here's why I think this is more effective." I'm not talking about personal attacks; I'm talking about intellectual conversations. I'd love to hear these two very accomplished literacy educators chat with one another. We never allow that to happen because we're so polite, but I think it would help teachers to crystallize their thinking about what *they* believe in.

Susan: What big changes have you seen since you were a school principal?

Shelley: Today in New York City there are many citywide mandates, something that never existed when I was principal, nor when I was superintendent. And No Child Left Behind has, of course, left its mark on our city classrooms.

Susan: Can you spell out what some of those mandates are?

Shelley: Well, fortunately for the Manhattan New School, it was on the Excused List because our kids did so well. The top scoring schools didn't have to follow the mandates. You could just keep doing what you were doing. The schools that didn't perform well had to go with the mandated literacy curriculum, which they called balanced literacy. A citywide mandated curriculum in literacy was a first in New York City. We used to have 32 different school districts, each working in its own way; then they were reorganized into 10 regional districts, and I became a regional superintendent. I left very quickly after the restructuring. I was given 170 schools (106,000 students) to take care of, and 70 of them were high schools.

On top of that, there were a lot of "Thou shalts" coming down the pike. This is what we're going to do. This is the reading program we've adopted. This is the math textbook we will be using. That was very different for me. And, of course, the Reading First stuff kicked in, and we were mandated to use the Voyager program, an online skills-based staff development program. I don't know if there are changes now, but certainly if your school was failing and you wanted federal funding, you had to use Voyager. Our principals and teachers were so opposed to it. It was so foreign to them. It's not how we taught. In District 2 we used the balanced literacy approach for years, and we used it for everyone. Our district included Chinatown, Greenwich Village, the Broadway theater district, Hell's Kitchen, the Upper East Side— very diverse areas, some of the wealthiest kids in New York and some of the poorest. We taught all students, asking them to read real books, carefully chosen books; we supported them in myriad ways, and they did well.

Susan: When you were a principal, how did you support literacy, and what were some of the best practices that you saw being implemented?

Shelley: I've written a lot about this. I would have to say that there was no separation between leadership and literacy. What I mean by this is that literacy was woven into everything we did—everything I did. It was just what we believed in. We were passionate. Our top priority at that time was reading and writing. It was a brand new school, and we were just so excited with the possibilities of teaching literacy in very smart ways. We wanted to create a wonderful setting where kids really could learn to read and write—all kids, no matter where they came from, no matter what their schooling had been before. I hired people who knew how to teach reading and writing. It was as simple as that. I brought the best teachers under one roof. So it's always a question of who's doing the teaching, and then devoting big blocks of time to literacy and having lots of appropriate reading material for the students. I think every classroom had a library. To this day, there's no centralized library in that school. The books go right into the classroom.

Susan: So there was healthy funding for it?

Shelley: Not really. We had a very small budget because we opened as a very small school. (We began with 125 kids, and today there are more than 700 students). We never bought any workbooks. All the money went for literature. Any time we had fund-raisers, any time parents wanted to buy gifts, we asked for books—and, of course, I hired people who brought books with them. Then, too, we were always asking for donations of books. You know, I drove out to [fellow teacher] Bee Cullinan's garage in the early years, and she would give me review copies that were stacking up in her garage. We stopped at every flea market. We went to library sales where folks were getting rid of duplicate copies. We went to private schools that were closing and took books off their hands. We did a lot of legwork, and we got the books. To this day, there are just lots of exquisite books in that school, and we didn't settle for mediocre texts. That's another issue—not just any book. We went after good books. It's such a lovely time to be an educator because there is no excuse for mediocre texts.

So in terms of supporting teachers, it was all about making sure that they had the material in their rooms, that they didn't have interruptions all day long, that we pulled together for professional study, that we talked about children who were struggling, that we didn't make any one teacher feel that he or she was alone, that we talked about real kids at our staff meetings, and that we looked at real pieces of literature. We had worthy and energetic staff meetings. I think a teacher would have felt bad if he or she couldn't make it to a staff meeting. We really looked at kids' work, we talked about children; we talked about possibilities. And I taught. I was always in class-rooms; I read aloud a lot; and I knew the kids. When teachers had concerns, I think they felt sure that they had good support. That was my mission, to wrap them in support.

I would also spend time teaching struggling third graders. I would invite staff members to come in and watch me teach. When I did that, the teachers felt supported, the parents appreciated the extra help, and I learned a great deal about teaching and my students. I learned about how annoying interruptions were, about whether our reading materials were adequate, about effective pedagogical techniques. I learned about kids who really couldn't sit still even when there were only eight kids in our tutorial. So you really can say to the teacher, "I get it. What else are we going to do for this child? What can we do differently?" We took each child very seriously.

Susan: That's amazing! How did you bring the parents on board with all the different children's books and all the different things you did with those books?

Shelley: Well, you know, the parents felt very welcome in the school. We always had wish lists of books if parents ever wanted to buy a gift for the class. We ran a lot of workshops for parents. I did a writing workshop for the parents so they would understand how we were teaching. We simulated reading workshops. We invited them in. We had parent reading book clubs. Our fifth-grade parents, in Judy Davis's class, would read the same book as their fifth-grade child and then come and have a pizza party and talk about it. When parents read the same novels as their kids, issues come up that probably would not come up, important issues. If you can read the same book as your child, you talk about things that might never have come up otherwise, or things that are very hard to bring up. We had many rituals that let parents know how important it was to read real books in authentic ways.

We also had all kinds of interesting bulletin board displays that were not your ordinary decorations on the wall. I would send a letter home, for example, that would say, "Can you send in a photograph of your child at home reading and tell us the story of that?" In some families the parents didn't write in English, but the children would do it. We had to give some kids a camera to take the picture, but we got such an interesting array of responses. Everyone was curious, because each day we'd add another photograph with another caption or vignette explaining the scene. "This is me reading a book in Maltese. I brought it with me when we moved to New York City."

Susan: That's powerful.

Shelley: It was very powerful. We also had displays of people's favorite childhood books. We invited the families in, just as we invited the custodian in, and the security guard. Everyone's literacy became gossip [*laughing*]—you know what I mean: interesting, juicy, what's your favorite book kind of talk. We also had a teachers' book club, of course, and it was posted publicly, and then some parents wanted to join, so they formed their own, and they picked books that would be appropriate for them. To this day I hear from families who said it made a difference. It was an all-out effort, and it was natural, it wasn't pretend. We weren't reading because we were teachers. We read because it was one of life's pleasures, and the kids knew it. We were so excited about their reading and our own.

Susan: I like that word *juicy* that you used. Some of those juicy books get people into trouble. One of my questions is related to censorship. The controversy over the picture book *Nappy Hair* was going on at that time in Brooklyn.

Shelley: At our school, we'd have more of an issue if it were a religious book. I came from a district where gender was a big issue and where racism was a big issue. My school board was right up there, the most progressive school board in the world, so issues of censorship were not what I worried about. I'll tell you this interesting story. After Columbine, some of the parents came to me and said they were very concerned about violence and young people, so we invited Dr. Kaiser, our health expert from the district, to meet with the parents. Dr. Kaiser suggested, "Go home and look through the books that are in your kid's bedroom, and if you have books in there where the characters don't show empathy, get rid of them." He told the parents that it's all about being able to show empathy, and that kids who *can't* are the ones we will worry about later on doing these awful things.

Susan: What kinds of things would occur with religious issues, or religious themes in books?

Shelley: We wouldn't share books with religious themes or a lot of religious teaching. When I was superintendent during 9/11, for example, we had to be careful that we didn't give out all the letters that came to us after the World Trade Center disaster. They were very religious. They had Bible passages in them, and our parents might take offense at that. We got a shipment of teddy bears whose belly buttons, when pressed, said The Lord's Prayer. That would be unacceptable to many of our parents.

Susan: In terms of No Child Left Behind and the conflicts with literacy practices that you've been talking about, and then your advice to current administrators who are struggling with all of this, what would you have to say about all those issues?

Shelley: You know, I always say "Close the door and do what's right for kids." In the end, it's the students' only year in the third grade; in the end, it's their only year in fourth grade. So let's keep test prep in perspective. I understand the reality of getting them through the test, and I say to principals that children are more likely to pass a test if they've had good, rich literacy instruction all year long. Two weeks before the test, you say, "Here's what it's going to look like." You show them the protocols and the formats and give them some tips on how to guess. To devote all year to it just gives the students an awful image of what literacy is about. That's not going to help them as readers, you know. It's not going to help them pass the test.

Susan: Teachers are feeling pressure about that, and they don't feel confident that they can close the door.

Shelley: I understand that, but I think that you have to break a few rules if you are going to help students become literate and care about their literacy. You've got to think out of the box, and you've got to act out of the box. It's the only way. If you follow the letter of the law, it's almost impossible. Be careful what you get good at—this is what I tell principals all the time. If you get good at following the letter of the law, they expect you to do it. People used to say to me when I got the job of superintendent, "Aren't you going to get a real haircut and start wearing suits?" I began to think that I had to appear even more nonconforming so that people wouldn't even expect me to listen to all these things. You have to be a little outrageous, you have to be bold, and you have to say, "This doesn't fit with what I know is good for kids." You also have to be incredibly articulate about your beliefs, so your responses won't be immediately dismissed as frivolous. Then you negotiate and you figure it out.

Susan: Think outside the box.

Shelley: Push the envelope. Just keep pushing it. I think it's essential to take principals on field trips, to invite them to see engaging, rigorous, joyful, best practice. I think some folks—including administrators, parents, and government officials—just don't have an image of how exciting and thrilling good elementary classrooms can be. These quiet classrooms with kids filling in the blanks are so deadly. It's a wonder the kids don't walk out the door.

Susan: I've often wondered that myself. You walk down the hallways, and the children look like they are suffering silently.

Shelley: So I want to show nonbelieving educators great schools and say, "Don't your kids deserve these exciting, lively classrooms, with good conversation?" My basic rule, when I would walk into a classroom, was, if I couldn't resist the urge to join the conversation, it probably was not interesting enough for the kids. I don't want to waste kids' time. You have to talk about things that matter. That's why I'm so interested in teachers who actually read the newspaper. When they're reading a novel aloud, or reading a picture book, they can actually say, "You know, this reminds me of..." and let the kids see the relevancy of all this stuff. It's just the most natural thing in the world.

Susan: What were some of your literacy goals when you were a superintendent?

Shelley: When I was a superintendent, there were just a handful of things I was looking for. In terms of best practice, I was hoping to see kids read wonderful books of their own choosing for big blocks of time. I wanted to see teachers pulling alongside them with a notepad in their hands figuring out how to help them grow as readers—noting their strengths, their dysfunctional strategies, and then making smart decisions on how to meet those needs. Is it one-to-one, is it a small group, is it widespread and the whole class needs to hear about it? When they were suggesting certain reading strategies, I wanted to be sure the kids understood why that strategy might help and that they were being asked to practice techniques on appropriate material. I think most kids try to practice on material that's too hard, so they never are able to internalize the strategic reading behaviors. Then, too, I think there is an overemphasis on isolating strategies, teaching one at a time, very slowly. When you or I read, we use many strategies if the text is complicated. We don't rely on one for 2 weeks. We have to be careful that we are not giving young folks a false image of reading.

The other thing that I think is really sad is when good literature is trivialized in order to have a skills or strategy lesson—for example, if a great poem happens to contain a lot of words with suffixes, and a teacher just goes full steam ahead teaching word study, forgetting that the students never had time to talk about the poem. You know, I think one great tip for teachers is to imagine that the poets and the writers are in your classroom watching. Would you be embarrassed by what they saw you do to their text? Cynthia Rylant didn't write her books so that you could have a good reading strategy lesson.

I also expect teachers to be able to help kids select books that will assist them in growing as readers at that point in time. It's almost like *Fiddler on the Roof*, playing matchmaker. Make me the perfect match. That's a major part, but that doesn't mean that everything has to be leveled and labeled in baskets.

Susan: This business of leveling and labeling every book and putting it in a basket worries me.

Shelley: Yes, I worry that some kids will go to the public library one day, and they will think something's missing. They aren't learning how to browse and select appropriate books. It's kind of like when I start feeding my 2-

year-old grandchild, and I realize he should be feeding himself. We want things to be neat and fast, so we do too much for the children. That's not doing them any favors.

I also think that there's a lot of inauthentic stuff done with kids in book clubs. I can understand assigning some roles at the beginning, just to give students a feel for what is possible, but teachers have to remove those scaffolds after a while, otherwise kids never learn to have a really lively and rich talk. Then, of course, the only other thing I want to see every single day is the read-aloud, and that the teachers are reading aloud well. I want them encouraging kids to talk boldly and brilliantly in response to text. I want to see teachers taking notes on the kids' responses, because how else will they know what to teach tomorrow? I am sure you know *Grand Conversations,* the classic Ralph Peterson and Maryann Eeds book. If you want meaningful conversations, you start with the good books. If you want grand conversations, you start with grand books. For teachers, it's all about having content knowledge, content in terms of how to teach reading and content about the world so that you can actually say smart things. That's why I care so much about newspaper reading, helping teachers who don't have that reading habit to acquire it.

Susan: That would be a big one! My college students don't tend to read the newspaper because they say they don't have enough time.

Shelley: How do you make literacy relevant and thrilling for kids? I want teachers to know a lot about literature. Many teachers have not taken a children's lit course since they were undergraduates. I'd be thrilled if teachers had opportunities to take district inservice courses that are devoted to literature. A good children's lit course when you're a teacher—I can't imagine anything better than that.

Susan: I want to close with some personal questions. Who are some of your favorite authors—for adults, for children? What are you reading?

Shelley: Well, I just finished reading *Shadow of the Wind,* a great novel. Oh, I have so many books I've been reading, and most of them are referred by teachers, but *Shadow in the Wind* is a book lover's book. It's a novel; it takes place in Barcelona. The author is Carlos Ruiz Zafon. It's translated from the Spanish. It's an intriguing mystery, and it opens in a book cemetery for all the books that are out of print. I just loved it because it's so different from the novels I usually read. Then for my book club right now I'm reading Marge Piercy's book, *Sex Wars,* which sounds very provocative, but it's a Civil War story. I have a book club meeting every few weeks, and we read a good juicy novel together.

As for children's books, I probably own every Jonathan London book. I also love poets who become picture book writers because I think they care so much about language, and that to me is very significant. I absolutely adore Mem Fox and her books.

Being a new grandma, I have been keeping a record of the books my grandchildren love. and it's actually led me to think a lot about gender issues. My granddaughter was the firstborn—her name is Andie—and now I have lists of her first-year favorites, her second-year favorites, and now the ongoing third-year favorites. I'm starting it now with our three young grandsons, and I will be looking to see the differences for the boys' lists from Andie's lists. Mem Fox books appear on both lists, and they read aloud really well for different-age kids. My grandsons love Bill Martin's books, especially *Brown Bear, Brown Bear: What Do You See?*.

The repetition, the rhythm, the colors—I mean, it's got everything, and you know, they just can't wait to turn the page. They start to shake, they're so excited because they know what is going to happen. All the children love Audrey Wood's *The Napping House* as well.

I just had this wonderful experience. I have a picture book version of C. S. Lewis's *The Lion, the Witch, and the Wardrobe*. It's got a lot of text alongside beautiful illustrations by Pauline Baynes. My granddaughter is three and a half, very articulate, and loves to be read to. I wondered if she was ready for that kind of book. So I started talking about books that are longer and that you don't read all at once. I'll told her, "I'll read you a little bit, and tomorrow I'll read you a little bit more," and so on.

We eventually got to the part where the witch asks the young boy, "What's your favorite candy?" because she wants to entice him. He says, "Turkish Delight." I remembered that my daughter had a colleague at work who just came back from Turkey and brought her a box of Turkish Delight, so I said to Andie, "I think there's a box of Turkish Delight in the house." It was such perfect timing, Andie was so thrilled, and she even liked the taste of the sweet treat. She was so with this character, and it was almost as if she understood why he would come back, because he found it so irresistible, the candy was so good. Would I recommend that everyone read *The Lion, The Witch and the Wardrobe* to 3-year-olds? No! But it's all about knowing your kids and choosing the right time and having fun with the books. We opened the hall closet and said, "What could be behind *our* coats?" You know, it was just so much fun. And she was ready for it because she likes books that scare her. She wants witches and monsters right now. Timing and knowing your kids well is so important.

I was just thinking about my grandkids' favorite books because I'm doing a workshop next week on reading-writing connections, and I was thinking how valuable it would be if we revisited some of the kids' early childhood favorites. You could have fourth graders revisit such books as Bill Martin's *Polar Bear, Polar Bear: What do You Hear?* Listen to those perfect, precise verbs—growling like a polar bear, roaring like a lion, snorting like a hippo, fluting like a flamingo, braying like a zebra. Share Eric Carle's *Slowly,*

Slowly, Slowly, Said the Sloth. I mean, there's just unbelievable language in there when he's talking about not being lazy. He says that he's lackadaisical, unflappable, languid, stoic, sluggish—and the list goes on.

Judith Viorst has always been a favorite of mine. I remember *Alexander and the Terrible, Horrible, No Good, Very Bad Day* being a real hit when I taught second grade many, many, many years ago. I was just reading Viorst's *Earrings!* to my granddaughter, and I realized that I could teach kids in the writing workshop all about repetition by letting them read, and of course reread, that book and figure out all the ways she effectively she uses repetition.

Of course, when kids are surrounded by such literature, their vocabulary grows. They don't need vocabulary workbooks. My granddaughter told me I looked tacky one day and glorious on another, both words she learned from the *Earrings!* picture book.

I like language play books; I like songs that are turned into picture books. I think we don't do enough singing in elementary school, so I have a nice collection of those. The Rosemary Wells one with all the Rodgers and Hammerstein favorites called *Getting to Know You* is such a gorgeous book. I've also had great fun with books like Julie Markes's *Good Thing You're Not an Octopus!* I just love books that lead to rich conversation about content. The bears hibernate in that one, the octopus has tentacles, and the birds eat worms. I also love books for young children that promote wonderful self-esteem. Kathi Appelt, for example, has a book called *Incredible Me*. It's just filled with great language: "I'm the cat's meow"; "I'm the sweet in the pea"; "I'm the dill in the pickle"; "I'm the beat in the jazz"; "I'm the jam in the strudel." I love it. Imagine a classroom ritual: If someone does something kind, we announce it and go around the circle. Everyone invents a compliment. "You're the salt on my pretzel." "You're the rose in my garden." You'd never have to teach kids about simile and metaphor if they lived it. I say to my granddaughter all the time, "You're the dill in my pickle," "You're the sweet in my pea," and now she makes up her own.

There are lots of poets that I love. I love them for myself and for the kids. I love Richard Margulies's *Secrets of a Small Brother*. He also wrote *Only the Moon and Me*, which I think is fabulous. My current favorite new poet would be Kristine O'Connell George. I just love her work. Brilliant, brilliant, brilliant, including *Old Elm Speaks* and *The Great Frog Race*. I could teach students of all ages so many things about reading and writing from these collections. I always count a lot on poetry. When we renovated our house, our contractor built bookcases into one of our bathrooms. I house my entire poetry collection in that one.

Susan (laughing): You're like me. My hallway is a book room.

Shelley: So it's just floor-to-ceiling bookcases built into the bathroom, and I put all my poetry in there. It's in absolutely random order, young adult and children's together. I don't want to sort them. I don't want them to look too neat. So I just browse, and I'm surprised every time.

Susan: Any interesting moments with literature?

Shelley: I had an interesting time once when I was superintendent and I would meet with my staff developers every few weeks on Wednesday afternoons, and we were talking about the read-aloud and how some kids are so passive that you don't know what they're thinking. We lose the quiet kids sometimes because they don't talk, they're well behaved and they never disrupt the class. So I invited some kids who were attending an after-school intervention program at a nearby school to come join us on these Wednesday afternoons. I would read aloud to them, and the staff developers would watch me read aloud to the kids as a group and try to get them all talking, as opposed to just some of them talking.

I remember the first time I did it, I read a book called *Running the Road to ABC* by Denize Lauture, a Caribbean writer. It's about leaving home early in the morning and going to a one-room schoolhouse. It's a very beautiful book. You learn about young children with very unusual names, who walk barefoot early in the morning, carrying herring and yucca in little metal pails. They have backpacks that they wove themselves out of palm tree leaves. So I'm reading the book aloud and I don't ask any questions, I just read it as best I can. I practiced. I tried to be as engaging as I could. It was silent in the room. I closed the book for a minute, and I said to them, "I'm so surprised you guys aren't interrupting me, aren't asking questions. You just heard that when their feet bleed they don't have bandages; that they're walking to school barefoot, their feet start to bleed, and they take crunched-up coffee leaves and put them on their feet, and you have nothing to say?"

They just looked at me and were quiet. I said, "I think the problem is that you think the teacher thinks you're smart when you answer questions. I'm going to tell you a little secret. Teachers think you're smart when you ask good questions." It was so interesting to make it explicit, and to privilege the asking of questions. You should have seen the hands! I mean, it changed the dynamics in the room. It was such a wonderful moment for the kids and for me and for the people watching because—I'll never forget this—one kid said, of course they wanted to know why they don't they have shoes. They were thinking this, but they didn't understand that their role was to ask questions. They're so used to just answering questions. One student asked, "How come in that country if you're poor you can have a house, but you don't have shoes? In our country poor people don't have houses, but they have shoes."

Susan: That's an incredible perspective!

Shelley: We can't underestimate kids just because they're struggling to pass their reading tests. If you put the right material there, and you open up the conversation to get them asking questions, these kids can gossip with the best of us. It *is* gossip. It's good literary gossip. Imagine you're looking out the window and seeing kids with no shoes at 6:00 in the morning, and your grandma is sitting next to you. What would you say to her? "Where do you think those kids are going? What are they saying? Why don't they have shoes on? Look, their feet are bleeding. How did they make those funny backpacks?"

Susan: What advice would you give to new teachers?

Shelley: I do have lots of advice for new teachers. I want them to trust their instincts and never underestimate the power of demonstration. I want them to be fussy about literature. I tell them to treat every child as if he or she is the PTA president's kid. I want them to continually ask themselves "Why?" Build in time for laughter. Create the most beautiful classroom. Be careful of your own language, and imagine that your words are broadcast throughout the building, that everything you say in classrooms can be heard throughout the school. I think that's a good filter. Take notes when students speak. Let students see you read and write frequently and with care. Let students see you treat books passionately and respectfully. Carve out more time for kids to just read. Provide many opportunities for them to read materials that match their writing interests. Always weed your classroom library. Get rid of the stuff that isn't going to delight anyone.

When I think of being fussy about books, I think of one essay in *Remarkable Reads: Thirty-four Writers and Their Adventures in Reading*. It's edited by a man named J. Peder Zane. Writers were asked to submit essays about books that made a difference in their lives. There's one essay in there by Bebe Campbell Moore, and believe it or not, she talks about *The Cat and the Hat*. She writes so eloquently about what that book meant to her. She says that the book has helped her develop her own criteria for having high standards for literature. The questions she asks herself are things like "Does the book delight me? Do the words captivate me? Does the tale horrify me? Make me feel dread? Make me laugh? Does the story resonate? Do I want to share it? Do I walk away with something in my head welded to my heart?"

It's well worth reading. It's an adult anthology. But here she is saying that *The Cat and the Hat* has the most uplifting passages she ever memorized and helped her establish high standards for herself. Of course, when I read it I thought her questions were so brilliant, but I also thought about finding a third-grade classroom with a copy of *The Cat and the Hat*. We'd be hard-pressed to find one in the United States.

That brings me to another point, which is that most of our kids are trying to read too-hard books. If we took the second-grade library and put it in the third-grade room, and the third-grade library into the fourth-grade room, more kids would learn to read. Joanne Hindley, who taught at Manhattan New School, used to occasionally read aloud from easy-to-read series because she wanted to privilege them and elevate them so that the kids who had to read easier books would feel they were okay books.

Susan: What a good basic idea. Thanks, Shelley, for sharing your thoughts and insights. This has been a "juicy" interview!

References

Piercy, M. (2005). *Sex wars*. New York: Morrow.

Peterson, R., & Eeds, M. (2007). *Grand conversations*. New York: Scholastic.

Zane, J. P. (Ed.). (2004). *Remarkable reads: Thirty-four writers and their adventures in reading*. New York: Norton.

Zafon, C. R. (2004). *Shadow of the wind* (L. Graves, Trans.). London: Weidenfeld & Nicolson.

Children's Books

Appelt, K. (2003). *Incredible me* (G. Karas, Illus.). New York: HarperCollins.

Brett, J. (1989). *The mitten*. New York: Putnam.

Carle, E. (2002). *Slowly, slowly, slowly, said the sloth*. New York: Philomel Books.

George, K. O. (1998). *Old elm speaks* (K. Kiesler, Illus.). New York: Clarion Books.

George, K. O. (1997). *The great frog race* (K. Kiesler, Illus.). New York: Clarion Books.

Herron, C. (1997). *Nappy hair* (J. Cepeda, Illus.). New York: Knopf.

Lauture, D. (1996). *Running the road to ABC* (R. Ruffins, Illus.). New York: Simon & Schuster.

Lewis, C. S. (1950). *The lion, the witch and the wardrobe* (P.Baynes, Illus.). New York: Macmillan.

Margulies, R. (1984). *Secrets of a small brother* (D. Carrick, Illus.). New York: Simon & Schuster.

Margulies, R. (1969). *Only the moon and me*. New York: Lippincott.

Markes, J. (2001). *Good thing you're not an octopus!* (M. Smith, Illus.). New York: HarperCollins.

Martin, B. (1983). *Brown bear, brown bear: What do you see?* (E. Carle, Illus.). New York: Holt, Rinehart, & Winston.

Martin, B. (1991). *Polar bear, polar bear: What do you hear?* (E. Carle, Illus.). New York: Holt.

Seuss, Dr. (1957). *The cat in the hat.* New York: Random House.

Viorst, J. (1972). *Alexander and the terrible, horrible, no good, very bad day.* New York: Atheneum.

Viorst, J. (1990). *Earrings!* (N. Langner, Illus.). New York: Atheneum.

Rodgers, R. (2002). *Getting to know you* (R. Wells, Illus.). New York: Harcourt.

Wood, A. (1984). *The napping house* (D. Wood, Illus.). New York: Scholastic.

Chapter 4

Sex, Witchcraft, and Diversity: Censorship of Children's Books

Amy A. McClure

They that can give up essential liberty to obtain a little safety deserve neither liberty nor safety.

—Ben Franklin

Some of my happiest childhood memories are of hours spent curled up in my bed, often with a flashlight under the covers, reading a book: *Nancy Drew*, *Black Beauty*, *Huckleberry Finn*, *Little House on the Prairie*, *Gone With the Wind*, the *Betsy-Tacy* series. I was allowed to read whatever I liked. Reading helped me to learn about the world and where I fit. Today, many of the books I loved as a child have been challenged and sometimes banned in schools and libraries across the country. *Black Beauty* has been removed because it depicts cruelty to animals. *Huckleberry Finn*, *Little House on the Prairie*, and *Gone With the Wind* have been condemned as racist. Maud Lovelace's characters, best friends Betsy and Tacy, have been criticized by feminists. Does this mean that I was reading filth that destroyed my values and mind?

It is true that children's books have changed. Although some still focus on topics like surviving middle school cliques, working through a fight with your best friend, or solving a school mystery, today's books talk about formerly taboo topics like drugs, sex, homosexuality, and witchcraft, and they often use language that some would find offensive. Coincidentally, a segment of our society has become more conservative. These people believe that our country has experienced a collapse of values. Frequently they blame this on what's being taught in school—and can we blame them? Educators have long championed books as influential in shaping children's minds and values. So why should we be surprised that parents, discovering curse words, descriptions of sexual activity, and references to witchcraft, believe that these elements are just as influential on the minds of children as concepts from classics like *Julius Caesar* or *Silas Marner*? They view new ideas and content as capable of corrupting impressionable minds and ultimately destroying the moral fabric of our country. At the other end of the political spectrum, some adults believe that children should be taught tolerance and respect for a multicultural global society and thus should not be exposed to books they consider racist, sexist, or violent. Thus teachers and librarians frequently find themselves in an awkward position as they try to prepare students for the future while addressing community values and concerns.

The debate over what should constitute education is appropriate for a democratic society. It is a debate about how the future of our society—our children—will be shaped. Principals, parents, community groups, and lawmakers all bring their personal concerns to addressing what is taught in classrooms, or what materials students may access in libraries. In a democratic society, opinions on this issue are diverse and wide ranging; ideas for change come from a variety of social, religious, and political perspectives. However, when a few individuals attempt to impose their views on a school or library, not by compromise and open debate but by restriction of materials, based on a single political, religious, or moral perspective, then we have a serious problem; a problem that has the potential to ultimately destroy our democracy (Reichman, 2001, p. 2).

What censors seem to have in common is the desire to protect children from influences they perceive as evil or harmful. This perception arises from their own biases. However, those who cherish the ideals of the First Amendment and intellectual freedom fear that if children don't encounter ideas that are disquieting or different from what they've always believed, they will not grow into thoughtful adults, able to function in a society filled with change and contradiction. Censorship is not a problem of good versus evil but of your perception of good versus my perception of good.

So we must ask: Do children have the right to read anything they want or need in order to attain intellectual maturity? Do adults have the right and responsibility to protect children from what they believe is harmful? Where do we draw the line between "helpful" and "harmful"?

This chapter will address the complex issues related to children's book censorship. I will (a) define the concept of censorship and how it differs from selection, (b) identify general censorship trends, (c) describe some specific works that have been censored, (d) discuss the tensions inherent in balancing the rights of parents, teachers, and educators, and (e) make some final comments about the importance of preserving intellectual freedom.

Censorship or Selection

What is censorship? How does it differ from book selection? Censorship is the suppression of ideas and information that certain individuals, groups, or government officials find objectionable or dangerous. Censors pressure public institutions like schools and libraries to suppress and remove from public access information they judge inappropriate or dangerous, so that no one else has the chance to read or view the materials (American Library Association [ALA], 2006a). A censorship *challenge* is defined as a complaint, filed with a library or school, requesting that materials be removed because of content or appropriateness. A *banning* is the removal of the materials in question. Sometimes banning is done through legitimate means by the decision of a governing body that has considered the complaint. In other instances the offending books are stolen or vandalized (e.g., offensive words marked out, pages torn out), or the offensive book is checked out and never returned. In a worst-case scenario, the book is burned.

In most cases, those who challenge materials are sincerely concerned individuals who believe that censorship can protect children and improve society by restoring moral values (as defined by them). They contend that young people will be influenced by bad ideas and will do bad things as a result. Others believe that there is a clear distinction between ideas that are right and morally uplifting and ideas that are wrong and morally corrupting. Children can be endangered if the wrong ideas are disseminated without restriction. From this perspective, any attempt to keep children from reading certain books could be construed as censorship. Yet is it censorship when librarians cull their collections, removing books that are outdated, worn out, or never checked out? If the book includes references to witchcraft, includes some obscenity, or depicts a sexual activity beyond a chaste kiss, will the librarian be accused of censorship? What about teachers who create summer reading lists or make choices about required readings for literature study? If a teacher chooses to include C. S. Lewis's *The Lion, The Witch and the Wardrobe* rather than J. K. Rowling's *Harry Potter* series for class study, has she or he censored? How do education professionals decide when these choices constitute judicious selection, and when it is censorship?

In 1982, the National Council of Teachers of English (NCTE, 1982) developed a set of criteria (Table 4-1) to distinguish between censorship and selection. They are still relevant today.

For example, consider the topic of sex education. The censor would want this topic ignored because some individuals believe that sex education should be handled only by the family. The selector would defend the rights of children to have access to this information as long as it is accurate and developmentally appropriate.

Table 4-1. NCTE Guidelines on Censorship Versus Selection

Censorship	Professional Guidelines
1. Excludes Specific Materials or Methods *Example:* Eliminate books with unhappy endings.	1. Include Specific Materials or Methods *Example:* Include some books with unhappy endings to give a varied view of life.
2. Is Essentially Negative *Example*: Review your classroom library and eliminate books that include stereotypes.	2. Are Essentially Affirmative *Example*: Review your classroom library. If necessary, add books that portray groups in nonstereotypical ways.
3. Intends to Control *Example*: Do not accept *policeman*. Insist that students say and write *police officer*.	3. Intend to Advise *Example*: Encourage such limiting alternatives for policeman as *police officer, officer of the law*, or *law enforcer*.
4. Seeks to Indoctrinate, to Limit Access to Ideas and Information *Example*: Drug abuse is a menace to students. Eliminate all books that portray drug abuse.	4. Seek to Educate, to Increase Access to Ideas and Information *Example*: Include at appropriate grade levels books that will help students understand the personal and social consequences of drug abuse.
5. Looks at Parts of a Work in Isolation From Each Other and to a Work Example: Remove this book. The language includes profanity.	5. See the Relationship of Parts as a Whole Example: Determine whether profanity is integral to portrayal of character and development of theme in the book.

Essentially, the goal of censorship is to remove or eliminate particular materials, whereas the goal of professional selection guidelines is to provide criteria for selectors, using established standards for literary quality and knowledge of child development.

This perspective does not assume that all books are equally appropriate for children of all ages, nor does it deny that children are influenced by what they read. Rather, it suggests that teachers and librarians must be professional in determining the criteria for book selection and use research to support those choices. This means that we collect reviews from respected sources, guidelines for literary quality, and policy statements to back up our choices. This also means that we must recognize our biases and struggle with them to help ensure that we are providing a balanced program that will enable our students to become not only readers but also lovers of literature. We must be open to a wide definition of quality and accept different points of view about how *quality* is defined. Just because we disagree with a book's perspective (e.g., sexual, racist, satanic), does not mean that we should restrict the reading of it.

General Censorship Trends

Do you use *Bridge to Terabithia* by Katherine Paterson (1976) or *The Giver* by Lois Lowry (1993) in your classroom? Do you encourage children to read the *Harry Potter* series by J. K. Rowling (1998–2007) or Phyllis Reynolds Naylor's *Alice* series (1995–2000)? What about *A Wrinkle in Time* by Madeline L'Engle (1962) or Jean George's *Julie of the Wolves*? All these highly regarded books and more have been challenged in the past two decades by individuals who have requested their removal from classrooms and school libraries. This section will describe some of the general trends in censorship challenges.

It is difficult to discern the pervasiveness of censorship. No one knows for certain how many incidents truly occur, because it is likely that for each reported challenge to a book, as many as four or five go unreported. However, there seems to be agreement that in the 1980s and 1990s the problem was "real, nationwide, and growing" (Reichman, 2001, p. 10). During the mid-1990s, however, censorship incidents began declining. For example, the number of reported censorship incidents in 1999 was 492, in contrast to a high of 762 in 1995. Possibly, the attention of potential censors shifted to other issues, or this trend could be attributed to schools self-censoring by limiting access to potentially controversial materials. Reports of censorship challenges began rising again in the first 5 years of the 21st century, with a high of 646 incidents in 2000 and between 400 and 550 in subsequent years.

It is interesting to note that the total number of challenges in 2005 dropped to 405, the lowest total on record. Speculations about the reasons behind this trend vary, but it could be due to librarians and teachers being better prepared to organize community support for a book, or potential censors focusing more on online content. "There's only so much energy to spend on situations or concerns outside the home," stated Judith Krug, director of ALA's Intellectual Freedom Office (www.mercurynews.com). "Many adults are now so concerned about what's on the Internet that they have refocused."

The most highly challenged books have remained largely unchanged over this time, although the specific targeted works have shifted as new books come on the market. The top 15 books censored (in order of number of incidents associated with each book) from 1990 to 2000 are the following (see www.ala.org for the complete list of 100):

1. *Scary Stories* series by Alvin Schwartz (1981, 1984) (violence, satanism, witchcraft)

2. *Daddy's Roommate* by Michael Willhote (1990) (homosexuality)

3. *I Know Why the Caged Bird Sings* by Maya Angelou (1969) (obscenity, homo-sexuality)

4. *The Chocolate War* by Robert Cormier (1974) (violence, objectionable language, sexual content, religious viewpoint)

5. *The Adventures of Huckleberry Finn* by Mark Twain (1918) (racism)

6. *Of Mice and Men* by John Steinbeck (1937) (offensive language, racism)

7. *Harry Potter* series by J. K. Rowling (1998–2007) (witchcraft, occult)

8. *Forever* by Judy Blume (1975) (graphic sex)

9. *Bridge to Terabithia* by Katherine Paterson (1976) (language, anti-Christian, occult)

10. *Alice* series by Phyllis Reynolds Naylor (1995–2000) (sexual issues)

11. *Heather Has Two Mommies* by Leslea Newman (1989) (homosexuality)

12. *My Brother Sam Is Dead* by James Lincoln Collier (1974) and Christopher Collier (obscene language and violence)

13. *The Catcher in the Rye* by J. D. Salinger (1951) (obscenity)

14. *The Giver* by Lois Lowry (1993)

15. *It's Perfectly Normal* by Robie Harris (1994) (homosexuality, nudity, sexuality)

Compare this list with the one below, which documents the top 10 challenged books from 2000 to 2005. All but two of the books from 2000 to 2005 were in the top 15 on the 1990–2000 list. However, the order has shifted a bit.

1. *Harry Potter* series by J. K. Rowling (1998–2007)

2. *The Chocolate War* by Robert Cormier (1974)

3. *Alice* series by Phyllis Reynolds Naylor (1995–2000)

4. *Of Mice and Men* by John Steinbeck (1937)

5. *I Know Why the Caged Bird Sings* by Maya Angelou (1969)

6. *Fallen Angels* by Walter Dean Myers (1988)

7. *It's Perfectly Normal* by Robie Harris (1994)

8. *Scary Stories* series by Alvin Schwartz (1981, 1984)

9. *Captain Underpants* series by Dav Pilkey (1997–2007)

10. *Forever* by Judy Blume (1975)

Most individuals involved in censorship challenges overwhelmingly seek to limit, rather than expand, student access to the materials in question.

The majority of objections are raised about isolated passages or features of the materials (e.g., explicit illustrations, descriptions of sexual activity, or specific dirty words) rather than the ideas or themes of the work as a whole. In fact, many challengers admitted to not examining the works as a whole. Library materials tend to be challenged more often than classroom materials and were more frequently removed or restricted as a result of the challenge (Reichman, 2001, pp. 12–13).

Those who challenge materials used in classrooms and school libraries are overwhelmingly parents who are typically motivated to protect their children. They believe that they can recognize evil, and that other people, particularly children, should be protected from it. They become concerned when they discover passages in books that contain four-letter words or graphically depict sexual activity. They don't always understand modern teaching methods, and they question why students are reading contemporary fiction and writing in personal journals rather than diagramming sentences and answering lists of comprehension questions. Some are motivated by political convictions, such as when Cuban-American individuals challenged the use of books in Miami, Florida, public schools that they thought praised contemporary Cuban life. Some are motivated by religious convictions, like the parents in Georgia, Michigan, Colorado, and New York who wanted the *Harry Potter* books censored because they believed the books exalted witchcraft and satanism. Others don't want children exposed to racist or sexist stereotyping in the fear that such stereotyping will be perpetuated. Many, however, honestly believe that certain materials will corrupt children or undermine basic values and beliefs, and they want to have some role in what is provided in schools.

Sometimes parental efforts to remove books are guided by political action groups. These arise from diverse political, moral, and religious perspectives and are dedicated to providing information and resources for mounting an informed, organized challenge to a book. For example, the mission of the Parents Rights Coalition is to stop the usurpation of parental authority in relation to the teaching of homosexuality as a valid life choice. Citizens for Literary Standards in Schools is a grassroots organization in Kansas that is concerned about "sexually charged and vulgar" reading assignments required of students in their school district. The group provides critiques of required books so parents can make informed choices about allowing their children to read a particular book. Alternative reading assignments are also suggested. Parents Against Bad Books in Schools provides extensive lists and reviews of "bad" books as well as an "opt-out form" that parents can use to excuse their children from reading a particular book. Typically their concerns focus on passages that are sexually explicit, use obscene language, or advocate homosexuality. Oyate is a Native American group that provides information on books that perpetuate Native American stereotypes. The involvement of these organized, highly sophisticated groups can certainly seem threatening to educators. However, they are within their rights to partici-pate in the debate on what should be taught in America's schools.

Types of Books Censored

Specific reasons for challenging books vary widely and are sometimes diffi-cult to discern. However, the ALA has identified several categories of con-cern that are typically voiced by challengers. From 1990 to 2005, they include (in order of frequency): sexual content; objectionable language; witchcraft and anti-Christian themes; excessive violence; issues of sexism and racism; and anti-American, anti-family, or anti-authority themes. An addi-tional category, "unsuitable to age group," will not be discussed in this chap-ter. This section will describe the various objections to books in more detail. The discussion will focus primarily on books for preadolescents. However, readers should be aware that censorship of literature for young adult read-ers is even more pervasive.

Objections to Sexual Content

Sexual content has continually been the focus of the most numerous com-plaints. Many adults object to children and preteens reading about subjects like masturbation, premarital sex, and homosexuality—all topics addressed in many of today's books. Books that focus on sex education are particularly targeted.

Judy Blume's *Forever* (1975) has been and continues to be a target, land-ing on the top 10 most challenged books year after year. The passage de-scribing sexual intercourse in *Forever* has particularly offended parents, like the father who made the following comments: "It's not just sexually explicit. It's arousing to a teenager. You can't just get them aroused and leave them with no place to go. . . . This is the Bible belt and most people have high moral standards" (Udow, 1992). Judy Blume's *Deenie* (1973) has also long been challenged for references to masturbation.

Phyllis Reynolds Naylor's *Alice* series books are another frequent target. For example, *Alice on the Outside* (1999) was challenged in Shelbyville, Ken-tucky, because Alice asks a family member how intercourse and masturba-tion feel. The adult responds openly, using graphic language (ALA, 2005b). In Webb City, Missouri, a school library removed *Achingly Alice* (1998), *Alice in Lace* (1996), and *The Grooming of Alice* (2000) for references to top-ics like menstruation, puberty, and sex. This particular challenge was backed by Concerned Women of America, a conservative political action group (ALA, 2002). In Mesquite, Texas, the parent of a fifth-grade student re-quested the removal of *Alice the Brave* (1995) from the school library be-cause the title character obsesses over her widowed father's relationships with her teacher and wonders if they are sleeping together (ALA, 2004b). Phyllis Naylor contends that the books deal honestly with issues all girls are curious about as they mature, and her books provide answers to questions they might be too embarrassed to ask. "I believe in honesty and telling kids what they need to know [about] what they ask," she stated. "I am going to keep on doing that" (ALA, 2002). Other examples of books for young readers that have been challenged for sexually explicit content include Sonya Somes's *What My Mother Doesn't Know* (2001) (sexually explicit language, references to masturbation, and a poem about how a girl's breasts react to the cold); Lois Lowry's (1979) *Anastasia Krupnik* series (references to *Playboy* magazine and menstruation); and *My Brother's Hero* (Fogelin, 2002) (reference to a woman "with half her boobs showing"). *When Jeff Comes Home* (Atkins, 1999), about a young boy's recovery after being kidnapped and sexually abused, features flashbacks to the sexual encounters. Parents have asked for its removal from middle school libraries after children as young as 11 checked it out (ALA, 2006b). Typically, challengers requested that these books be removed from the school library or a recommended reading list, or a request was made to move the book to libraries and classrooms for older children.

Nudity seems to be increasingly less of an issue. In the past, Sendak's *In the Night Kitchen* (1970), *A Light in the Attic* (Silverstein, 1981), *National Geographic* magazine, and the *Sports Illustrated* swimsuit issue have been challenged. Concerns about these items have largely subsided, except for the *Sports Illustrated* issue and occasional objections to *In the Night Kitchen*.

Nonfictional sex education books are particular touchstones for censorship challenges. *It's Perfectly Normal* by Robie Harris (written for third to sixth graders) has been a target since it was first published in 1994. The book was written to provide accurate, lucid, unbiased answers to virtually every conceivable question children might have about sexuality, including sexual intercourse, masturbation, menstruation, birth control, sexually transmitted diseases, and the like, all illustrated with humorous yet scientifically correct, graphic illustrations. The book has been widely acclaimed by critics. For example, *School Library Journal* (www.amazon.com) described it as follows:

> Frank, yet playful, they [the illustrations] portray a reassuring array of body types and ethnic groups and illuminate the richly informative, yet compact text, allowing readers to come away with a healthy respect for their bodies and a better understanding of the role that sexuality plays in the human experience.

Some parents are not so positive. They have concerns about the value of text and illustrations that show a naked couple having intercourse, a young boy masturbating, and a young girl leaning over to examine her genitals with a mirror. As one parent stated, "When does good information become too much information? And how much reliable information about sensitive topics should be in elementary school libraries?" (ALA, 2005d). Another parent stated that she became mortified when she reviewed the book and found messages that she believed promoted a licentious attitude toward sex of all kinds, including "have sex with whoever [sic], whenever, whatever," and "don't feel guilty about having sex; if you feel like you are old enough, then you are" (Brown, 2005). The concerns of these parents and others have led to requests for removal of the book from school libraries or at least restrictions put on its circulation. In Ocala, Florida, xeroxed pages of the book were burned after the book was retained in the local library following a censorship challenge. Harris's *It's So Amazing: A Book About Eggs, Sperm, Birth, Babies and Families* (1999), which focuses on teaching second to fifth graders about human reproduction, has also been heavily challenged.

Homosexuality has become an increasingly controversial subject in books for children. The development of the gay rights movement has led many educators and librarians to consider including materials that will educate all students about diverse sexual orientations and gay and lesbian families. The proliferation of gay-theme literature for children has been matched by increased numbers of challenges to these works. In 2004, for example, 3 of the top 10 challenged books were attacked on the basis of homosexual content. This was a higher percentage than at any point in the past two decades. *Daddy's Roommate* (Willhote, 1990) and *Heather Has Two Mommies* (Newman, 1989), which feature gay and lesbian families, were challenged when first published, and they continue to be the targets of many concerned parents. In 1994, *Daddy's Roommate* was the most challenged title in America's schools and libraries. One complaint alleged that "a child below the age of reason having read this book may come to believe that the homosexual lifestyle is common" (ALA, 1995). *Heather Has Two Mommies* has been challenged in libraries across the country because of alleged "obscene and vulgar subject matter and the message is that homosexuality is okay" (Becker & Stan, 2002, p. 37). Opponents of both books in North Carolina accused the library of "taking the lead in promoting homosexuality" and took out newspaper advertisements asking, "Can prostitution, bestiality, and incest be far behind?" (Udow, 1992, p. 4). Similarly, a New York City first-grade multicultural curriculum, "Children of the Rainbow," was rejected by the community school board in Queens because it included these titles and others that celebrated diverse families. Challenges to these books have been largely unsuccessful. In most cases the book was retained or moved to a more restricted section of the school library.

Other books that address this topic have also proved to be controversial. *King and King* (deHaan & Nijland, 2002), a fairy tale about a prince who ultimately chooses to marry another prince instead of a princess, has been challenged across the country. In Lexington, Massachusetts, for example, parents of a second grader protested after the child's teacher read the book as part of a lesson on different kinds of weddings (ALA, 2006c). In other communities parents asked that the book be removed from the school library or put on a restricted shelf because they didn't want their children to accidentally encounter it

Tango Makes Three (Richardson, 2005), based on the true story of two male penguins at the Central Park Zoo who adopted an egg and raised it to a hatchling, has also been challenged due to its "homosexual" theme. Although the book received several national awards, parents from Illinois, Missouri, North Carolina, and Wisconsin asked that the book be removed from their school library or placed in a special restricted section. The parent who initiated the Illinois complaint agreed that pulling the book could constitute censorship but stated, "Of course we know the kids are eventually going to learn about the homosexual lifestyle. . . . Please let us decide when our kids are ready. Please let us parent our kids." In response, the school superintendent defended the inclusion of the book in the library: "My feeling is that a library is to serve an entire population. It means you represent different families in a society—different religions, different beliefs. That's the role of a school library" (Suhr, 2006). Incidentally, the supposed gay partnership was short-lived. As soon as a female penguin from San Diego's Sea World arrived in the enclosure, one of the male penguins mated with her and left his male friend behind.

It's Perfectly Normal by Robie Harris (1994) features a frank discussion of homosexuality as well as other aspects of human sexuality. For example, the section titled "Straight and Gay" features the following text:

The Ancient Greeks thought that love between two men was the highest form of love. . . . Some people disapprove of gay men and lesbian women. . . . usually these people know little or nothing about homosexuals, and their views are often based on fears or misinformation, not facts. (pp.17–18)

Those who challenge books on the basis of sexual content believe that children must be protected from knowledge of these topics, suggesting that early exposure will inevitably lead to experimentation and liberal attitudes toward sex. They contend that the authors of these books are not merely describing but are rather advocating such behavior. Those who oppose this censorship assert that such protection might deny children the very information they need. These issues are significant and of natural interest to young pre-adolescents, and they will certainly learn about sex education. The question is, from whom will they learn it: peers, MTV and movies, or a book in conjunction with frank, honest discussion? Some think that healthy sexual attitudes are better formulated over a book than in the backseat of a car. Furthermore, they contend that children will not pick up a book with content beyond their interest or stage of development, simply because it will be boring to them.

Yet one wonders how much sexual content is acceptable—and where the line should be drawn. Should *Playboy* magazine be part of library offerings? What makes *National Geographic* less objectionable than the *Sports Illustrated* swimsuit issue? Should a book or magazine's literary quality or the nature of the nudity be a determining factor? How is this judged?

Objections to Obscene Language

The second most frequently occurring category of objections is to inappropriate or obscene language. Often these objections are intertwined with objections to sexual content that is described using graphic terms or slang. Judy Blume's books sometimes come under attack for this reason, and so do sex education books. Other books similarly challenged include Peck's *A Day No Pigs Would Die* (1976), for use of swear words and a boy getting hurt in his "privates"; *James and the Giant Peach* (Dahl, 1961), for use of the word *ass*); *Walter the Farting Dog* (Kotzwinkle & Murray, 2001), for use of the word *fart* and *farting* 24 times in the book; and *My Brother Sam Is Dead* (Collier & Collier, 1974), for "vulgar and profane language" (ALA, 2004a). Even dictionaries and thesauruses have been challenged because they include an allegedly obscene definition for words like *bed*, *tail*, *ass*, and *faggot* or provide definitions for common slang related to sexual activity.

In other instances, parents or community members challenge books in which the characters use harsh language or expletives. Many of the challenged books are intended for adolescents but become included in middle school library collections by librarians who seek to meet the interests of their older students. For this reason, individuals have requested the removal of *Bloods: An Oral History of the Vietnam War by Black Veterans* by Wallace Terry (1984) and *Fallen Angels* by Walter Dean Myers (1988) from middle school libraries. In both instances, language used by soldiers in battle was considered inappropriate. *The Chocolate War* by Robert Cormier (1974) has been challenged for inclusion in middle school libraries and eighth-grade language arts classes because of its realistic schoolboy language. For example, in Hartford, Connecticut, one couple requested that no eighth graders be permitted to read the book. When offered a compromise—their child could read an alternative book—the parents continued to protest its use, even sending letters to all eighth-grade parents in the district (ALA, 2006c).

Those who choose to censor on the basis of obscene language and content argue that children should be protected from exposure to these elements. They contend that if teachers and librarians use curse words as they read aloud, and if such books are readily available, children will learn that the use of such words is condoned by the school and community. Their opponents point to the many examples of obscenity that children encounter on playgrounds, bathroom walls, television, and even in their own families. (In one interesting court case, the husband of a woman protesting obscenity found in books testified about the profane language she used at home.)

Katherine Paterson, whose *The Great Gilly Hopkins* (1978) and *Bridge to Terabithia* (1976) have both been challenged for the inclusion of obscenities, has the following response (www.terabithia.com) for those who would censor her books for this quality:

> Gilly is a lost child who lies, steals, bullies, despises those who are different or perceived to be weaker—a child like this does not say "fiddlesticks" when frustrated. I could not duplicate her real speech without drowning out the story in obscenity, but I had to hint at her behavior. She would not be real if her mouth did not match her behavior.

In reference to Jess in *Bridge to Terabithia*, Paterson says the following:

> Jess and his father talk like the people I know in that area. I believe it is my responsibility to create characters who are real, not models of good behavior. If Jess and his dad are to be real, they must speak and act like real people.

An interesting objection related to language has arisen in reference to Barbara Parks's (1992–2007) *Junie B. Jones* series, which follows almost-6-year-old Junie B. through various events in her life. Junie B. talks like a typical 6-year-old, saying things like "I runned straight to the sink"; "They are the gorgeousest pictures I ever saw"; "Mother had a mybrain headache"; and "I got frustration inside me." Critics contend that exposure to such language will lead kids astray and that "they will pick up on the good and bad habits that they see and hear, so why would anyone want his/her child exposed to this constant stream of sloppy language?" (customer review on Amazon. com). However, supporters of these books contend that Junie B. is actually following the rules of English grammar while ignoring exceptions. They suggest that the target audience for these books has typically outgrown these speech patterns and will laugh at Junie B.'s way of talking without taking it on (Ratzan, 2005, p. 36). Readers should also consider that this creative use of language has been used by such well-regarded authors as Lewis Carroll, Dr. Seuss, Peggy Parish, and Beverly Cleary. So when a particular character uses obscene language, nonstandard English, or slang, it does not necessarily mean that the author advocates those words. Rather, the author believed that this language reflected the essence of the character.

So should children be allowed to read obscenity in books? Should these potentially offensive words be blacked out in library books (as is sometimes done) so that children are protected from exposure to them? Should teachers and librarians omit potentially troublesome works when reading aloud to children? What about reading books that feature a character using nonstandard English? Should we eliminate Junie B. Jones, Dr. Seuss, and Lewis Carroll from libraries and classrooms on the chance that children will be enticed to use incorrect grammar after reading them?

Objections to Satanism, Witchcraft, and Anti-Christian Themes

The next most frequently cited rationale for challenges in the last two decades was that the materials were advancing witchcraft and satanism or espousing anti-Christian sentiments. Alvin Schwartz's popular folktale collections, *Scary Stories to Tell in the Dark* (1981) and the other volumes in this series have been and continue to be among the most frequently challenged trade books for these reasons. Objectors stated that the stories "advocate cannibalism, brutality, the religious practice of witchcraft, and violence." The illustrations have been said to "contain a high degree of occult/satanic symbolism" and an emphasis on death over life (McClure, 1995). Challengers often cite as particularly offensive a story in which a child gobbles up her teacher. Other books to which similar objections for references to witches and witchcraft are made include Dahl's *The Witches* (1985); Merriam's *Halloween ABC* (1987), which "heightens awareness of the macabre and piques children's curiosity about the occult"); *The Witch of Blackbird Pond* (Speare, 1958), for references to witches; Rylant's *Missing May* (1992), for references to spirits and ghosts; and Cooper's *The Dark Is Rising* (1973), for teaching satanism and cultism.

Other challenges in this category relate more directly to fundamentalist Christian religious beliefs. For example, Paterson's *Bridge to Terabithia* (1976) was accused of providing students with "contempt for the church through negative religious images and references in the book" and for an allegedly "comic and cruel portrayal" of a preacher. Also cited were 40 instances in which the word *Lord* was used as a curse word and two that used the word *hell*. Objectors further complained that "the book teaches that children are innately good, whereas God's word teaches us that we are all sinners and that the only way to God and heaven is through faith in Jesus Christ" (Becker & Stan, 2002, pp. 38–39). Paterson's *The Great Gilly Hopkins* (1978) faced similar problems for allegedly derogatory remarks about God and religion, in particular Gilly's reference in a letter to her mother that people who pray and read from the Bible are "religious fanatics." The mystical themes of Madeline L'Engle's *A Wrinkle in Time* (1962) raised concerns that children reading the book would "interpret reality mystically and strive to enhance their spirituality through the use of occult practice." Before it was embraced by Christians, C. S. Lewis's *The Lion, The Witch and the Wardrobe* (1950) was challenged for being pagan and anti-Christian. These objections are interesting when one considers that L'Engle and Paterson come from strong Christian backgrounds and that Lewis was a noted British theologian.

It is also interesting that challenges have been made by witches themselves. Wicca, an organization of witches, tried to get "Hansel and Gretel" removed because it allegedly teaches that it is allowable to burn witches and steal their property. The organization also protested the use of another series because it included stories they perceived as portraying witches inaccurately.

However, the most commonly challenged works from 2000 to 2005 in this category were the *Harry Potter* books by J. K. Rowling (1998–2007). "The series makes witchcraft and wizardry alluring to children. It encourages kids to use spells, glorify the occult, and go against Christian teaching," declared one parent in New Haven, Connecticut (ALA, 2003). A parent in Georgia wanted the books banished from school libraries because she believed that they were an evil attempt to indoctrinate children into the Wiccan religion. She further believed that the books fostered the kind of culture that leads to atrocities like the Columbine school shootings. "These [shootings] would not happen if students instead read the Bible," she stated (www.chicagotribune.com/news/opinion/).

Some of the controversy over these books possibly arose when a satirical tabloid *The Onion* ran a story headlined "Harry Potter Books Spark Rise in Satanism Among Children." The story was excerpted in e-mail chain letters, often to people who didn't realize that it was a joke (www.chicago-tribune.com/news/opinion). The controversy was also fueled by Family Friendly Libraries, a group opposing the ALA's intellectual freedom policies, that circulated a warning that the Potter books were not suitable for public school classrooms and should be checked out of school libraries only with parental permission (Reichman, 2001, p. 68). It could also be that its depiction of witchcraft, sorcery, and a sinister evil force naturally caught the attention of individuals who consider those subjects dangerous and against Christian teachings.

In any event, a huge furor arose over the use of the books in school classrooms and libraries, and parents across the country have demanded its removal. Most insidious is the trend toward burning or vandalizing the books. In one incident, two Michigan pastors burned the book outside their Jesus Non-Denominational Church. In Pennsylvania, the Harvest Assembly of God Church held a book, music, and videotape burning in the parking lot of the church. In addition to the *Harry Potter* novels, music from artists like REM and Bruce Springsteen, along with Disney movies, were consigned to the flames. Burnings were planned in Cedar Rapids, Iowa, and Lewiston, Maine, but failed to materialize only because local fire stations denied fire permits. Opponents slashed and destroyed the books instead (Serchuk, 2006).

Nevertheless, most challenges to these books have been unsuccessful, due to the legions of Potter fans. "*Harry Potter* has been a huge gift to child literacy," stated one librarian, who also defended the presence of an evil force in the books as realistic. In the Georgia challenge, the school board's attorney asserted, "There's a mountain of evidence for keeping *Harry Potter*. . . . The books present instead universal themes of friendship and overcoming adversity. . . . Parents, teachers, and scholars have found them a good way to stimulate children's imagination and encourage them to read" (ALA, 2006d). When challenges to these books arose, national publicity frequently resulted in their reinstatement. Even the Vatican went on record as supporting *Harry Potter*: An official stated that the books help children "to see the difference between good and evil. . . . Magicians and witches are not bad or a banner for anti-Christian theology" (ALA, 2003).

The controversy does not seem to have hindered the books' popularity, for the series continues to be the highest-selling children's books of all time. Furthermore, in a contest sponsored by the ALA to celebrate 2006 Banned Books Week, the *Harry Potter* series was overwhelmingly voted the favorite controversial title. J. K. Rowling herself (www.jkrowling.com) considers it an honor that her books are consistently featured on the list of most banned books: "As this puts me in the company of Harper Lee, Mark Twain, J. D. Salinger, William Golding, John Steinbeck, and other writers I revere, I have always taken my annual inclusion on this list as a great honor."

Do the charges that children who read these books will embrace satanism, witchcraft, and the occult have any validity? Some parents are definitely frightened by these issues. Children do question God and the teachings of the Bible. However, other adults are less apt to see a strong connection between reading a book about a witch and becoming one. Even some leading Christian writers have argued for the useful role of *Harry Potter* in children's lives, suggesting that Christians use the books to enlighten their children about the dangers of real occult practices while also teaching them valuable moral lessons (Neal, 2001).

Objections to Violence

Objections to materials considered violent have risen steadily over the past two decades. Most concerns about violence in books focus on allegedly frightening story lines, like those in Schwartz's *Scary Stories to Tell in the Dark* (1981) or Dahl's *The BFG* (1982), or depictions of violent actions in traditional fairy tales like "Snow White" and "The Three Billy Goats Gruff." Violence associated with war is also often a concern. Thus, Collier and Collier's *My Brother Sam Is Dead* (1974) continues to be challenged by parents who object to references to rape, drinking, and graphic violence. Since the book is often required for upper elementary students, in addition to being available in libraries, it is frequently challenged.

The largest number of objections to children's books in this category have been made regarding R. L. Stine's *Goosebumps* series (1992–2007). The *Goosebumps* books were designed to meet 8- to 12-year-old children's interest in things that are creepy and disgusting. Since the books are rarely assigned for classroom reading, the challenge is typically to remove the books from school libraries because they are "frightening," "violent," and "a bad influence." In one incident, a group of well-organized, vocal Canadian parents circulated a form letter that raised concerns about the negative influence of "horror thrillers" on "impressionable young readers." The parents argued that the *Goosebumps* series hooked children on the horror genre and led them to seek ever more violent and evil content as they moved on to similar series for adolescents. The issue became increasingly heated, with some parents supporting the challengers while others raised strong objections to the potential censoring of books. Students also became involved in the issue, writing letters to local newspapers like the following:

Dear Editor:

    I think those three parents who believe we're too young to read those books believe that we think that the books are true and we could not do what the author writes about. We're not dumb. We know that R. L. Stine's are all fiction . . . worse things happen in the real world. Look at O. J. Simpson. (cited in Church, 1997, pp. 528–529)

The issue was eventually resolved with the recommendation that no books be removed from classrooms or school libraries. However, books written specifically for teens (like some of the *Goosebumps* titles) would in the future be purchased only for secondary school libraries.

Those who oppose censorship on the basis of violence contend that children eventually outgrow their interest in books like *Goosebumps* and move on to better fare. Indeed, in the Canadian situation, an articulate group of elementary school students appeared before the district's review committee and explained how reading the *Goosebumps* series had been just a phase and that they had eventually grown tired of reading them, moving on to other books as they became better readers (Church, 1997, p. 529). Many fans of these books say that they enjoy the vicarious thrill of reading about fearful topics and use the books to work through their own anxieties (Reichman 2001, p. 69). Some adults suggest that the subject matter of these books should be readily apparent to anyone picking them up from the shelf (the covers alone clearly depict violent content). Thus, children who are easily frightened will likely turn to less threatening titles.

However, other parents are not so sure. One voiced the opinion of many when she stated, "Childhood is a very special period and should remain free of horrors and unnecessary stress" (cited in McClure, 1995). Although the *Goosebumps* books for younger students contain minimal violence and no sexual content, they do sometimes leave readers with a sense of continually lurking evil. Is this problematic or inappropriate for young readers?

Objections to Racism and Sexism

Increasing awareness of the rights of women and racial minorities has led to more challenges that include alleged incidents of racial and sexual stereotyping or slurs. Considerable progress has been made in creating books and instructional materials that are sensitive to the concerns of these groups. However, occasionally a member of a group that has historically been a target of bigotry and oppression will challenge a book that he or she believes perpetuates that bigotry and oppression (Reichman, 2001, p. 13). The motives are typically the desire to protect children from offending messages or language and to keep such messages from persisting. The problem is not generally an issue with openly derogatory materials. Those are rarely included in school libraries or instructional curricula. It is more common that a work is challenged for the use of offensive or derogatory language without regard for its overall message or context. Sometimes one group might view the work as advancing attitudes of bigotry and thus object to its use, whereas others believe the book does quite the opposite. Those who challenge books on the basis of racist or sexist overtones are typically less likely to call for the removal of an offensive book, although this does occur. Rather, they try to sway the opinions of libraries, teachers, and editors— those who purchase books, use them with children, or determine their contents—to use books that are inoffensive.

The books whose presence in elementary libraries and classrooms have been challenged as prejudiced or stereotypical in depicting a minority group include Wilder's *Little House in the Big Woods* (1953), for references to African Americans as "darkeys" and Native Americans as "savages"; Ringgold's *Tar Beach* (1991), for stereotypical depiction of African-American culture;

and Zemach's *Jake and Honeybunch Go to Heaven* (1982), for misrepresenting and misunderstanding the African-American experience.

Books that use offensive racial slurs like *nigger* or *Jap* are particularly attacked. For example, when *War Comes to Willie Freeman* (Collier & Collier, 1987) was used in Brooklyn and Ithaca, New York, sixth-grade classrooms, the principal pulled it because the word *nigger* is used in a historical context. Christopher Collier defended his use of the epithet as follows (ALA, 1998):

> Our use of "the N-word" is intended to deepen the depiction of the misery of slavery and of the degraded status of free blacks. . . . In all these novels the word *nigger* is unavoidable if anything close to historical verisimilitude is to be drawn. But beyond that, the word is necessary in order to portray, in a way that evokes an emotional response that draws the reader into the story, the horrible condition of enslaved African Americans.

Similar challenges incited by racial slurs occurred with Fox's *The Slave Dancer* (1973) and dictionaries that defined various offensive words. *Baseball Saved Us* (Mochizuki, 1993) was targeted by second-grade parents in Connecticut because the racial slur *Jap* is used to taunt the main character (ALA, 2006c). Twain's *The Adventures of Huckleberry Finn* (1918) is probably the most frequently targeted book for use of the N-word as well as its depiction of the African-American character, Jim, as gullible, simpleminded, and superstitious. Many African-American students have reported feelings of discomfort when the book is read aloud, sometimes to the amusement of White classmates. The book has been reviled as "eroding the dignity, respect and self-esteem of African-American students," "insulting," and "creating, exacerbating, and contributing to a hostile work environment in the school" (McClure, 1995; Zwick, 2006).

Even a book written by an African-American author and intended to build self-esteem in African-American children was perceived as offensive by segments of its intended audience. *Nappy Hair* (Herron, 1997), a story about a Black girl with the "kinkiest, the nappiest, the fuzziest, the most screwed up, squeezed up, knotted up, tangled up, twisted up hair" was challenged after a White Brooklyn, New York, teacher read it to her class of predominantly African-American and Latino students. Protesters swarmed the school, and the teacher was threatened with violence. She soon resigned. "I would hope that other teachers would use books that give children positive images of themselves," stated the superintendent after the incident. "But at the same time we are trying to give children strong messages of themselves, we're also sending a message that you better not do it if you are a white teacher" (Reichman, 2001, p. 75).

Native Americans have also become active in working to educate school personnel on works that are derogatory in their portrayal of the lives and histories of Native peoples. Oyate (www.oyate.org) is an organization that provides critical reviews of such books in the hope that teachers and librarians will select wisely and eliminate books that the organization believes are harmful or derogatory. Some of the books they find objectionable are Banks's *The Indian in the Cupboard* (1980) and its sequel *The Return of the Indian* (1986); Dagliesh's *The Courage of Sarah Noble* (1941); Speare's *The Sign of the Beaver* (1983); Waldman's *Wounded Knee* (2001); and Jeffers's *Brother Eagle, Sister Sky: A Message From Chief Seattle* (1991). Banks's books are criticized for having her Indian character speak in stereotypical short sentences like "I help" and "Want make dance" and for graphic war scenes in which Indians are depicted as bloodthirsty savages. *Brother Eagle, Sister Sky* was criticized for totally misconstruing the intent of Chief Seattle's speech (the focus of the book) and for an inaccurate depiction of Native American culture.

Books that are censored on the basis of sexist stereotyping include *Caddie Woodlawn* (Brink, 1973), because Caddie gives up being a tomboy; *Pippi Longstocking* (Lindgren, 1950), because the strong female character is the fantasy one); *The Giving Tree* (Silverstein, 1964), because the self-sacrificing tree is referred to as a "she"; and my childhood favorite, *Betsy-Tacy* (Lovelace, 1940), because three early 19th-century girls play outside wearing dresses. Various nursery rhymes, which some feminists believe promote negative images of women, have also been challenged.

Thus, if a book includes elements that might be construed as sexist or racist, should it be removed from classrooms and libraries? Will exposure to such materials perpetuate these prejudices? Is this actually censorship or judicious selection?

Others see value in exposing children to such attitudes. Proponents of *Huckleberry Finn* (Twain, 1918), *War Comes to Willy Freeman* (Collier & Collier, 1987), and similar books suggest that such works can develop students' understanding of the historical and cultural roots of racist and sexist attitudes. Regarding supposedly sexist portrayals, one might ask what alternatives in lifestyle were available to young women in rural 1880s Wisconsin (Brink, 1973) or what clothing choices girls had in the early 19th century (Lovelace, 1940). Must all these books be removed because they accurately reflect their times? There can be value in comparing the attitudes, customs, and language in books from historical times to those of today.

Objections to Anti-Family, Anti-Authority, or Anti-American Values

Challenges on the basis of a book's anti-family or anti-authority themes have declined over the past two decades, with two notable exceptions: objections to Pilkey's *Captain Underpants* series (1997–2007) and to Lois Lowry's *The Giver* (1993). The *Captain Underpants* series is a superhero spoof in which two fourth-grade boys hypnotize their principal and turn him into Captain Underpants, a comic book hero who chases bad guys in his underwear. The trio tackles talking toilets, plot against Professor Poopypants, and wrestle the Wedgie Woman, among other adventures. Children, particularly struggling readers, love the bathroom humor and silliness of the stories. Some parents are less enthusiastic, challenging its inclusion in libraries for its alleged modeling of bad behavior and encouraging children to disobey authority. Books in Allard's (1974) *The Stupids* series have been similarly challenged because some adults thought that the books "undermine the authority of parents," "describe families in a derogatory manner," and "reinforce negative behavior" (Becker & Stan, 2002, p. 102). Even parents who normally are against censorship have concerns about these books (http://happyfeminist.typped.com):

> I have to admit that although I would never support [the] banning of any book, when my son was little I struggled with the urge to track down Dav Pilkey and strangle him. My son and his best friend thought the Captain Underpants books were hilarious. . . . Some of their imitative "adventures" almost got my 7-year-old kicked out of school. . . . When I see the books on those banned lists, I tsk-tsk about censorship, but there's a part of me that really, really gets it.

Lowry's *The Giver* (1993) presents a disquieting picture of a utopian community where individuals are spared from making any decisions and feeling any emotions. Complicated issues of infanticide, euthanasia, conformity, and the suppression of personal liberty are explored, with the conclusions deliberately left ambiguous. Parents in Virginia challenged the book because they believe "it will give many children and young adults who read it nightmares for days and weeks. . . . [They] will be ingrained with concepts that will warp their minds possibly for the rest of their lives" (www.trosch.org). Challengers of the book in Illinois thought that the "society of sameness" described in the book is "being held up as an ideal by the schools" (Zammarelli, 2004). Others thought that the book's themes were too mature and unsupportive of family values.

Other works that have long been challenged as "anti-family" or "anti-authority" include such diverse titles as Paterson's *The Great Gilly Hopkins* (1978), which supposedly endorses values like stealing, smoking, drinking, and rebellion against authority; Viorst's *I'll Fix Anthony* (1969), which endorses sibling rivalry; Steig's *Sylvester and the Magic Pebble* (1969), which portrays police as pigs; and "The Three Bears" (because Goldilocks goes unpunished for petty larceny and vandalism).

Proponents of books that explore these issues argue that books should not always present perfect families with no problems or disagreements. They contend that authors must present the world honestly and realistically in order to help children understand that everyone has strengths as well as weaknesses. How much, they ask, are children influenced in their attitudes toward parents and authoritative figures by books? Furthermore, as with other categories of objections, should we let one issue determine the availability of books for children?

A few books for young children are challenged because they allegedly include content that is anti-American, or that differs from some segment of American attitudes and politics. For this reason, Ancona's *Cuban Kids* (2000), a picture book about life in Cuba, was banned by the Miami-Dade County Public Schools. The challenger objected to photos of a child with a rifle and children saluting the Cuban flag with the caption "We will be like Che!" *A Visit to Cuba* (Schreier, 2001) was also challenged by several Cuban-American parents (one who was a former Cuban political prisoner) for painting postrevolutionary Cuba as a veritable paradise. The emotional and political storm surrounding the debate over these books revealed deeply held beliefs about Cuba in the Miami Cuban exile community and their suspicion that other groups remain ignorant of or hostile to their concerns. One Cuban-American school board member voiced the tension surrounding this issue when he sought support for banning the book: "They will have a choice to either define themselves on the side of truth and with the Cuban community or on the side of lies and against the Cuban community" (ALA, 2006d) For similar reasons, Ellis's *Three Wishes: Palestinian and Israeli Children Speak* (2004), a book in which children speak about their lives, was targeted for removal from a fourth- to sixth-grade independent reading program. The challengers were concerned that the book presented inaccurate images of Israel and introduced children to Palestinian youths who aspire to become suicide bombers and kill Israelis.

Balancing the Rights of Parents, Educators, and Children

In the final analysis, is censorship appropriate? Do young children have a fundamental right to intellectual freedom—to read any books that will make them think, question, wonder, dream, laugh, cry, and gain an understanding of the world? Some would argue that they do, that the concept of student rights has been legally affirmed in cases like *Tinker v. Des Moines Independent Community School* (1969) and the case brought by Steven Pico against the Island Trees Union Tree School District (1982). The latter case went to the U.S. Supreme Court, which ruled that "school boards do not have unrestricted authority to select library books. The First Amendment is compromised when books are arbitrarily removed" (Reichman 2001, p. 185). Some interpret this to mean that students, be they 6, 12, or 20, should have access to whatever books they wish to read, in order to develop the understanding and skills to become responsible, thoughtful citizens. Others are not so sure. The justices in the Pico case did identify "pervasive vulgarity" and "educational suitability" as constitutionally valid, acceptable (though vaguely defined) reasons for removing library books. In a minority opinion in the *Tinker* case, one justice voiced what many adults believe: "I cannot support the courts' uncritical assumption that . . . the First Amendment rights of children are co-extensive with those of adults."

Some states have laws and resolutions, often decades old, that condone censorship in some form. For example, Kentucky has a long-standing law that states that "no book or publication of a sectarian, infidel or immoral character, or that reflects on any religious denomination, shall be issued or distributed in any common school." Although some legislators expressed shock when told of the law's existence, few were willing to challenge it for fear of being perceived as "against God and Christianity" (Lockwood, 2006). The Oklahoma legislature passed a resolution that "public libraries should not expose children to material that may be deemed harmful and inappropriate" (ALA, 2005c). It seems safe to suggest that most adults don't believe that a 9-year-old has unlimited First Amendment rights. Yet the extent of these rights has not been precisely determined by law and thus is still open to debate. Since the significant legal cases regarding book censorship have related exclusively to secondary schools, we have yet to precisely define these rights for young children.

We must remember that the trend toward realism is not a recent phenomenon; children's books have always reflected society's evils as well as its ideals. Early children's books were filled with threats of hell and punishment as well as promises of rewards for good behavior. In their own way, these books were just as shocking as the sex and obscenity that disturb parents today. Children know that there is evil as well as good in the world. What we need to do is help them learn to cope with it.

Lois Lowry (2005), in response to those who accused *The Giver* of corrupting young minds, stated the following:

> I feel very strongly that we should question our own be-
> liefs and rethink our values every day with open minds
> and open hearts. . . . I think it is essential that we enter
> the dark places, and face what is too painful, too hard,
> what costs too much. Literature is a way of reminding us,
> perhaps of forcing us, to do that. (pp. 24–25)

Good writers create a story that they passionately believe should be written. Any attempts to limit that passion will most likely result in a book that
is dishonest, superficial, and probably boring.

Children need well-written books that tell them honestly about the
world, giving them a chance to understand it. Even fantasy must be
grounded in reality—with some connection to basic human truths—before
children will accept it. Otherwise literature will seem hypocritical and irrelevant. Books that treat realistic subjects with skill, care, and imagination are
probably preferable to a street-corner encounter. Also, children tend to
read only that which they can relate to or understand. Few children continue to struggle through books that have no meaning for them. Conversely, if they understand the book, they are probably ready to read it. I
remember gulping a bit when my own 13-year-old daughter announced she
was reading *The Lovely Bones* (Sebold, 2002), an adult book with graphic
scenes of rape and murder. However, she ended up loving it and credits it
with instilling in her a strong desire to counsel women and children who
have been abused.

Teachers also believe that they have rights and responsibilities in this
matter. It is true that some educators are not aware of current issues,
trends, authors, and books. However, many do possess knowledge of this
nature, and they feel obligated to provide students with access to a wide variety of high-quality materials that will respect their uniqueness and develop their potential. As one teacher stated when challenged on the use of
stories featuring gay and lesbian characters, "I'm trying to teach tolerance
and respect for all people—and I can't do that and ignore a whole group of
people. Furthermore, I wouldn't present a curriculum that ignored women
or African Americans or Hispanics. How can I possibly teach my students to
embrace diversity if I systematically exclude an entire group from my literature?" (ALA, 2005a).

The National Council of Teachers of English (NCTE, 1981) strongly supports this perspective in its policy statement "The Students' Right to Read":

> English teachers must be free to employ books, classic
> or contemporary, which do not lie to the young about the
> perilous but wondrous times we live in, books which talk

> of the fears, hopes, joys, and frustrations people experi-
> ence, books about people not only as they are but as
> they can be. English teachers forced through the pres-
> sures of censorship to use only safe or antiseptic works
> are placed in the morally or intellectually untenable posi-
> tion of lying to their students about the nature and condi-
> tion of mankind.

This is easier said than done, of course. Making decisions about the content of the literature curriculum is a complex, often political process. Which
authors are included? Which are excluded? On what basis are these decisions
made? One study focusing on the integration of multicultural literature
found that although many teachers advocate the inclusion of diverse works
in their curricula, there is a great deal of confusion and disagreement about
how the teaching of multicultural literature should be implemented
(Stallworth & Fauber, 2006). Teachers must therefore be continually vigilant
in selecting literature for their classrooms that reflect the diversity of perspectives in our society.

Librarians have long been the leaders in opposing censorship, believing
that they are morally obligated to provide a wide range of materials for students. It is in the library that students have the opportunity to choose materials to help them answer questions and address needs that will help them
to grow. The ALA's Bill of Rights (1996) is clear on this issue, stating,
"Books and other library resources should be provided for the interest, information, and enlightenment of all people of the community the library
serves." An additional document, "Access to Resources and Services in the
School Library Media Program" (ALA, 2000), affirms that this policy applies to school libraries at all levels (including elementary):

> The school library media program plays a unique role in
> promoting intellectual freedom. It serves as a point of vol-
> untary access to information and ideas and as a critical
> thinking in problem-solving skills needed in a pluralistic
> society. . . . School media professionals assume a lead-
> ership role in promoting the principles of intellectual free-
> dom within the school by providing resources and service
> that create and sustain an atmosphere of free inquiry.

Yet most schools have limited resources. Librarians can't buy everything
available. Thus, they must balance an obligation to accessibility with an understanding of the school's curriculum and the developmental maturity of
their students. This is a particularly tricky balancing act for middle school
librarians, who often must select books that are appropriate for students as

young as 11 and as old as 15. Librarians have a difficult job balancing the needs of all students while using their funds responsibly and resisting the urge to eliminate a book that could be potentially controversial.

We also cannot deny the very real concerns of parents over the values they wish to transmit to their own children. As one father told a local school board when objecting to the use of Cormier's (1974) *The Chocolate War:* "I have a responsibility to my daughter to protect her from things that I feel are morally not correct for her at this time and age-inappropriate." Many reasonable, intelligent adults believe that their children are not ready for the graphically depicted sex education information in Harris's *It's Perfectly Normal* (1994) or the alternative parental lifestyle portrayal in *Heather Has Two Mommies* (Newman, 1989). It seems healthier for a child and a parent to confront controversial issues in a book together rather than to deny their existence. However, parents who wish to shield their own children from works they consider unsuitable have the right to do so, regardless of professional opinion or the literary merit of the book in questions.

Yet these same parents have no right to make this decision for other children's parents. Censorship should be a private decision. When it becomes a public issue, and one person's (or small group's) will prevails, the rights of all children are trampled. While protecting the minority, we must still allow free choice for the majority.

Conclusion

Censorship does not typically achieve its goal. Often, censored books become best sellers right after a highly publicized incident. A challenged book might be furtively passed from student to student, essentially undermining the censor's intent. In addition, communities can become polarized and teachers demoralized, magnifying the situation beyond its initial importance.

We must continue being vigilant in ensuring that students have access to books that will challenge them to consider new ideas and enlarge their perspectives. Children should have the opportunity to explore far and wide. Each book offers its own gifts to the reader—and the freedom to choose what one reads helps to ensure that those gifts will be understood and appreciated. Reading is one of the greatest freedoms in our society. We must guard this freedom zealously.

Nevertheless, I believe that parents have the right to determine what is appropriate for their own child. We should respect that right. However, teachers and librarians need to communicate why we use a particular book in our classroom or include it in our school library. If we inform parents of a book's value but also truly listen to their concerns, we can often come to an understanding of one another's perspectives, thereby diffusing a potentially explosive censorship situation. The problem is when parents or other community members try to limit what all children read. Such actions are not within their rights.

We cannot afford to stifle the development of critical thinking in our children. Our nation needs thoughtful adults who have the courage to speak their minds, based on an informed perspective. If instead we create people who are suspicious of free speech and incapable of detecting propaganda, illogic, and bias, our democratic nation is doomed.

References

American Library Association (ALA). (1995, March). *Newsletter on Intellectual Freedom.*

American Library Association (ALA). (1996). *Library Bill of Rights.* Chicago: Author.

American Library Association (ALA). (1998, May). *Newsletter on Intellectual Freedom.*

American Library Association (ALA). (2000). *Access to resources and services in the school library media program: An interpretation of the Library Bill of Rights.* Chicago: Author.

American Library Association (ALA). (2002, November). *Newsletter on Intellectual Freedom.*

American Library Association (ALA). (2003, May). *Newsletter on Intellectual Freedom.*

American Library Association (ALA). (2004a, July). *Newsletter on Intellectual Freedom.*

American Library Association (ALA). (2004b, November). *Newsletter on Intellectual Freedom.*

American Library Association (ALA). (2005a, January). *Newsletter on Intellectual Freedom.*

American Library Association (ALA). (2005b, May), *Newsletter on Intellectual Freedom.*

American Library Association (ALA). (2005c, July), *Newsletter on Intellectual Freedom.*

American Library Association (ALA). (2005d, November). *Newsletter on Intellectual Freedom.*

American Library Association (ALA). (2006a). *Intellectual freedom and Q and A.* Available online at www.ala.org/ala/oif/basics/intellectual.htm.

American Library Association (ALA). (2006b, March). *Newsletter on Intellectual Freedom.*

American Library Association (ALA). (2006c, July). *Newsletter on Intellectual Freedom.*

American Library Association (ALA). (2006d, September). *Newsletter on Intellectual Freedom.*

Becker, B, & Stan, S. (2002). *Hit list for children: Frequently challenged books.* Chicago: ALA.

Brown, J. (2005). *Kids' access to explicit library books restricted after Arkansas parent complains.* Available online at www.headlines.agapepress.org/archive/6/12005e.asp.

Church, S. (1997). Values clash: Learning from controversy. *Language Arts, 74,* 525–532.

Lockwood, F. (2006). *"Infidel" book ban unlikely.* Available online at www.kentucky.com/mld/kentucky/living/religion/15248677.htm.

Lowry, L. (2005). *How everything turns away*. Paper presented at the University of Richmond, Richmond, VA.

McClure, A. (1995). Censorship of children's books. In S. Lehr (Ed.), *Battling dragons: Issues and controversy in children's literature*. Portsmouth, NH: Heinemann.

National Council of Teachers of English (NCTE). (1981). *The students' right to read*. Urbana, IL: Author.

National Council of Teachers of English (NCTE). (1982). *Statement on censorship and professional guidelines*. Urbana, IL: Author.

Neal, C. (2001). *What's a Christian to do with Harry Potter?* Colorado Springs, CO: Waterbrook Press.

Ratzan, J. (2005). You are not the boss of my words: Junie B. Jones, language and linguistics. *Children and Libraries, 3*, 31–38.

Reichman, H. (2001). *Censorship and selection: Issues and answers for schools* (3rd ed.). Chicago: ALA.

Serchuk, D. (2006). *Harry Potter and the Ministry of Fire*. Available online at www.forbes.com/technology/2006/11/30/book-burnings-potter-tech-media.

Stallworth, B., & Fauber, L. (2006). It's not on the list: An exploration of teachers' perspectives on using multicultural literature. *Journal of Adolescent and Adult Literacy, 49*, 478–489.

Suhr, J. (2006), *Parents want gay parents book blocked*. Available online at www.boston.com/news/education/k_12/articles/2006/11/16/parents_want_gay_pen_.

Udow, R. (1992). Censorship news. *Newsletter of the National Coalition Against Censorship, 46*.

Zammarelli, C. (2004). *God is not pleased with you*. Available online at www.bookslut.com./banned_bookslut/2004_03_001684.php.

Zwick, J. (2006). *Oklahoma school board votes to keep Huckleberry Finn*. Available online at www.boondocksnet.com/twainwww/essays.

Children's Books

Allard, H. (1974). *The Stupids step out*. New York: Houghton.

Ancona, G. (2000). *Cuban kids*. New York: Marshall Cavendish.

Angelou, M. (1969). *I know why the caged bird sings*. New York: Random House.

Atkins, C. (1999). *When Jeff comes home*. New York: Putnam.

Banks, R. (1980). *The Indian in the cupboard*. New York: Doubleday.

Banks, R, (1986). *The return of the Indian*. New York: Avon Books.

Blume, J. (1973). *Deenie*. New York: Bradbury.

Blume, J. (1975). *Forever*. New York: Bradbury.

Brink, C. (1973). *Caddie Woodlawn* (T. S. Hyman, Illus.). New York: Macmillan.

Collier, J. L., & Collier, C. (1974). *My brother Sam is dead*. New York: Four Winds.

Collier, J. L., & Collier, C. (1987). *War comes to Willie Freeman*. New York: Dell.

Cooper, S. (1973). *The dark is rising.* New York: Macmillan.

Cormier, R. (1974). *The chocolate war.* New York: Pantheon.

Dagliesh, A. (1941). *The courage of Sarah Noble* (L. Weisgard, Illus.). New York: Scribner.

Dahl, R. (1961). *James and the giant peach.* New York: Farrar, Straus & Giroux.

Dahl, R. (1982). *The BFG* (Q. Blake, Illus.). New York: Farrar, Straus & Giroux.

Dahl, R. (1985). *The witches.* New York: Farrar, Straus & Giroux.

deHaan, L., & Nijland, S. (2002). *King and king.* Berkeley, CA: Tricycle.

Ellis, D. (2004). *Three wishes: Palestinian and Israeli children speak.* Berkeley, CA: Groundwood.

Fogelin, A. (2002). *My brother's hero.* Atlanta, GA: Peachtree.

Fox, P. (1973). *The slave dancer* (E. Keith, Illus.). New York: Bradbury.

George, J. (1972). *Julie of the wolves* (J. Schoenhert, Illus.). New York: Harper Collins.

Harris, R. (1994). *It's perfectly normal* (M. Emberley, Illus.). Cambridge, MA: Candlewick Press.

Harris, R. (1999). *It's so amazing: A book about eggs, sperm, birth, babies and families* (M. Emberley, Illus.). Cambridge, MA: Candlewick Press.

Herron, C. (1997). *Nappy hair.* New York: Knopf.

Jeffers, S. (1991). *Brother eagle, Sister sky: A message from Chief Seattle.* New York: Dial.

Kotzwinkle, W., & Murray, G. (2001) *Walter the farting dog.* Berkeley, CA: Frog.

L'Engle, M. (1962). *A wrinkle in time.* New York: Farrar, Straus & Giroux.

Lewis, C. S. (1950). *The lion, the witch and the wardrobe.* New York: Macmillan.

Lindgren, A. (1950). *Pippi Longstocking.* New York: Viking Press.

Lovelace, M. (1940). *Betsy-Tacy,* New York: Harper & Row.

Lowry, L. (1979). *Anastasia Krupnik.* Boston: Houghton Mifflin.

Lowry, L. (1993). *The Giver.* Boston: Houghton Mifflin.

Merriam, E. (1987). *Halloween ABC* (L. Smith, Illus.). New York: Macmillan.

Mochizuki, K. (1993). *Baseball saved us.* New York: Lee & Low.

Myers, W. D. (1988). *Fallen angels.* New York: Scholastic.

Naylor, P. R. (1995). *Alice the brave.* New York: Atheneum.

Naylor, P. R. (1996). *Alice in lace.* New York: Atheneum.

Naylor, P. R. (1998). *Achingly Alice.* New York: Atheneum.

Naylor, P. R. (1999). *Alice on the outside.* New York: Atheneum.

Naylor, P. R. (2000). *The grooming of Alice.* New York: Atheneum.

Newman, L. (1989). *Heather has two mommies.* Boston: Alyson.

Parks, B. (1992–2007). *Junie B. Jones* series (D. Brunkus, Illus.). New York: Random House.

Paterson, K. (1976). *Bridge to Terabithia* (D. Diamond, Illus.). New York: Crowell.

Paterson, K. (1978). *The great Gilly Hopkins.* New York: Crowell.

Peck, R. (1976). *A day no pigs would die.* New York: Knopf.

Pilkey, D. (1997–2007). *Captain Underpants* series. New York: Scholastic.

Richardson, J. (2005). *Tango makes three.* New York: Simon & Schuster.

Ringgold, F. (1991). *Tar beach.* New York: Crown.

Rowling, J. K. (1998–2007). *Harry Potter* series. New York: Scholastic.

Rylant, C. (1992). *Missing May.* New York: Orchard.

Salinger, J. D. (1951). *The catcher in the rye.* Boston: Little, Brown.

Schreier, A. (2001). *A visit to Cuba.* Chicago: Heinemann.

Schwartz, A. (1981). *Scary stories to tell in the dark* (S. Gammell, Illus.). New York: Lippincott.

Schwartz, A. (1984). *More scary stories to tell in the dark.* New York: Lippincott.

Sebold, A. (2002). *The lovely bones.* Boston: Little, Brown.

Sendak, M. (1970). *In the night kitchen.* New York: Harper & Row.

Silverstein, S. (1964). *The giving tree.* New York: Harper & Row.

Silverstein, S. (1981). *A light in the attic.* New York: Harper & Row.

Somes, S. (2001). *What my mother doesn't know.* New York: Simon & Schuster.

Speare, E. (1958) *The witch of Blackbird Pond.* Boston: Houghton Mifflin.

Speare, E. (1983). *The sign of the Beaver.* Boston: Houghton Mifflin.

Steig, W. (1969). *Sylvester and the magic pebble.* New York: Windmill Books.

Steinbeck, J. (1937). *Of mice and men.* New York: Covici Friede.

Stine, R. L. (1992–2007). *Goosebumps* series. New York: Scholastic.

Terry, W. (1984). *Bloods: An oral history of the Vietnam War by Black veterans.* New York: Random House.

Twain, M. (1918). *The adventures of Huckleberry Finn.* New York: Grosset & Dunlap.

Viorst. J. (1969). *I'll fix Anthony.* New York: Harper & Row.

Waldman, N. (2001). *Wounded Knee.* New York: Atheneum.

Wilder, L. I. (1953). *Little house in the big woods* (G. Williams, Illus.). New York: Harper.

Willhote, M. (1990). *Daddy's roommate.* Boston: Alyson.

Zemach, M. (1982). *Jake and Honeybunch go to heaven.* New York: Farrar, Straus & Giroux.

Bookseller Extraordinaire:
An Interview With Frank Hodge

Susan S. Lehr

Susan: Tell me about yourself and Hodge Podge, and then we'll jump into the books.

Frank: I think the easiest way to describe myself is to say that I got bored easily, and after I spent 6 years doing something, I found I had the itch. My feet were itching. I needed to get out, see some people, and try something different. So I taught school for 6 years, then I went for my doctorate for 6 years, and then I came to the university to teach for 6 years. I spent time visiting in schools and talking to kids. I would do the third grade at 9:00 in the morning in an auditorium or gymnasium. The first question I would ask them is "What class during the day do you hate the most?" and without hesitation, they would all scream, "Reading!" It really knocked me back, you know. I just couldn't imagine that this would be the worst.

So I kept asking that question, and no matter where I went—suburban school, rural school— it was the same response. And there was no hesitation; they yelled, "Reading!" I was so appalled, so I talked to them about the various kinds of reading we have to do in school. Then I'd say, "Well, there's another kind of reading, and that's the reading we do for fun. We have a good time with it." Then I would introduce the books to them.

It really got sort of frightening, so I went to the university and talked to my department, where I was still teaching part-time. They had a reading conference every year, and every year they had sessions on vocabulary skills, critical thinking skills—all of these technical kinds of things. The attendance was consistent, maybe 100–120 people. So the chairman of the department said to me, "Why don't you plan a conference, Frank, and we'll do it. You can do the reading conference this year. You plan it."

I said, "Well, before we do it, I'll plan it and then bring it to the department to see if they'd approve." So I planned a conference revolving around writers and poets. I had things with which to stimulate kids to read. I took it to the department, and their faces fell down to their kneecaps. One of them said, "Well, we couldn't possibly support something like this, because all our teachers are more interested in vocabulary development and critical thinking skills. Besides, if a teacher needs to have a kid read a book, she can send the kid to the library to get a book." Now *my* face fell down to my kneecaps. They voted it down, but the chairman supported it. We started Let the Reading Begin in 1983.

The bookstore came about as a result of my meeting all these kids who hated reading. I thought there had to be something else I could do about that. However, I knew I couldn't get to all the kids, but through their teachers I certainly could get to a number of them. On October 28, 1982, we opened a bookstore and the rest is history. We had a wonderful time. The the name of the store came from junior high school kids who were sitting in the park one day. I was talking with them, and I said, " We're opening a bookstore for children. What should we call it?" I had all these names— Magic Moment, and all this other crap—and one of the little boys looked up and said, "Well, if you've got anything to do with it, Frank, it'll be a hodge-podge." So I said, "Well, you just named the store." He's a very good friend to this day. I see him frequently. He's married now with several children. His kids are great readers.

Susan: I would expect that. We've been the winners in the Albany region as a result because of all the readers you've helped to create and nurture!

Frank: I've never had the itch to leave. When the sixth year at the store came, I thought, "Am I going to get the itch?" and, you know, I've never had the itch.

Susan: From your position as a bookseller and as an expert in the field, what changes have you seen in the past decade or so in children's literature?

Frank: The changes have been monumental. I think we've gone from a focus on providing children with literary experiences to almost entertaining children. When you look through the catalogs today for quality literature that will be around, there are fewer and fewer choices. I mean, look at the company with the Barbie Doll books. Now, those are probably written by hacks, paid a flat fee of several hundred dollars. The company is making money on those hand over fist. They sell like crazy—they're all over the popular press. The parents who come in to buy books for kids say, "Oh, a Barbie book." So they'll buy the Barbie book. Or now a book has to have a television connection or a movie connection. It's got to have a plush toy. What happened to the old concept of a book you snuck into the bed, read with your flashlight under the covers at night so your mother didn't see that you were reading? What about the books that you treasured? There still are books like that, and there are still a lot of kids who are into that kind of thing. But unless the book has a big hype publicity machine working, publishers don't feel it's going to succeed. Look at the hype over *Harry Potter*. Those books are abominably poorly written.

Susan: I guess I'd like to hear what some of the "flashlight books" are that you've been finding lately. I'm using your term, which I really like—the book you're going to crawl into bed with.

Frank: Oh heavens, yes. Look at *Stone Fox* by John Gardiner. Published, what, in 1984? Now, it's way over 3–5 million copies that have been sold. He just died, about 3 weeks ago. But he would go out to visit schools and to talk to kids about this book. He was selling thousands of paperbacks a month. Now, he could write. He's written three books all together, but he went back to the company where *Stone Fox* was originally published, and the people there told him, "Don't bother sending us any more manuscripts, because we don't want books like that any more." They said the same thing to [author] Gloria Houston.

Susan: How long ago would you say that that message started coming from publishers?

Frank: About 8 or 9 years ago. John became so discouraged. "Don't bother sending us any more. We don't want that kind of book." As for Gloria Houston, when you look at *My Great Aunt Arizona* or *Year of the Perfect Christmas Tree*, alone, just those two books, they have sold thousands of copies and still sell hundreds of copies every year.

Susan: Well, I was just looking for some of the stats on *Harry Potter*, and I saw that in 2005 alone, just in our country, *Goblet of Fire* sold 13.5 million. So everybody's looking for the next megahit.

Frank: One publisher purportedly said in a meeting with his editors, "When you get a manuscript, look at it and say to yourself, 'Will this sell 150,000 units in 6 months?' If the answer is 'no,' don't publish it." Now that's a frightening, frightening situation.

Susan: Where do you see independent booksellers ending up?

Frank: Oh well, look at how they have diminished over the last 5, 6, 7 years. Look at the number of children's bookstores. At one point, there were more than 400 in America, and now they're down to about 80.

Susan: Do you carry mass-market books in your bookstore? I would guess that people ask for them.

Frank: They do ask, and I just say, "No, I'm sorry, we just don't carry it. I don't believe in carrying everything they carry at the chain stores. Just go to the grocery store or chain stores and buy it, or go someplace else, because my space is limited." My store is 240 square feet. I have to fill it wisely and carefully. Now recently I had 25 copies of a book called *The Little Boy Star*, which is a fable of the Holocaust, and I'm down to three. We had a book, *Mother's Wish*, and I had, I think, 55 of those and I'm down to 2. I had 75 of *Lily's Big Day*, the new Kevin Henkes book, and I think I'm down to 10 of those.

Susan: What other kinds of changes have you seen?

Frank: Well, I think the major change is the fact that if a book is intellectual, or if publishers think a book is going to be hard for kids, 9 times out of 10 they won't publish it. There are companies that used to be what I call a literary press, like Harper, now HarperCollins. They did a lot of wonderful, wonderful books. Now they have series after series. And when you read them and you compare them, they're just all basically the same kind of thing.

Susan: Formulaic.

Frank: Yes. Very formulaic. Very formulaic. A lot of young authors are getting started, and that's great. I love to see new people coming into the field. After the first successes they do not seem to become consistently good writers publishing interesting stuff. Too many publishers are trying to be Scholastic.

Susan: What do you mean by that?

Frank: Well, Scholastic has geared itself toward the school market for years and years, and they've published a lot of books designed for second graders, third graders, fourth graders, specifically written for that particular level. A lot of companies couldn't possibly do that because they were catering to the lowest common denominator. Now they're all doing it. They're getting a lot of that schlock in their programs, with the exception of places like FSG [Farrar, Straus & Giroux], which has published consistently high-level, very good books, marvelous writers. Look at the editor, Frances Foster. My heavens. What a goddess she is in the world of children's literature. Oh, she is fantastic.

Susan: A goddess. I like that. What makes you say that? What is it, the fact that she's been able to hang onto a high-quality list?

Frank: Yes, because she recognizes the talent. She recognizes good writing, and she encourages her people to continue with this good writing. Beverly

Horowitz, one of the other editors there, does the same thing. They bring people along. They recognize that here is a person of considerable talent, now let's work with this person and bring him or her along. Peter Sis is a good case, an example here, a marvelous illustrator and author. And you watch him grow as he works with Frances Foster at FSG. Cynthia de Felice is a master storyteller in all the books that she has done. Last night I just finished a galley of the sequel to *Weasel*, written 15 years ago. And finally she has been able to do what she wanted to do with *Weasel*, to make sure that Ezra [the main character] has a place. It was a wonderful book, a wonderful sequel.

Susan: What's the title of that?

Frank: *Bringing Ezra Back*. The other set of books that I think hasn't lowered its standards is Walker Books. Walker has always been strong in nonfiction. Their children's editor, Emily Easton, I think, is perceptive and has recognized some very special, fresh talent when she did the *Miss Malarkey* books by Judy Finchler. Judy was a librarian, and she wrote a book about kids. It was illustrated by a very clever man, Kevin O'Malley, and was a big success. Emily was able to see that talent in Judy and to develop that talent through a whole series of books about this teacher, which speaks to kids and teachers. Then she also has another librarian, Beth Evangelista, who has written a book called *Gifted*. It's a fantastic piece of writing. She's done an amazing, amazing job. And Emily sees this potential in people, encourages it, builds on it, and makes that person a writer.

Walker was purchased by Bloomsbury, which is British. There is something about British writing that I think is very special. I have a lot of friends over there who are writing.

Susan: I have to agree. They can tell a story exquisitely.

Frank: David Almond. Tim Bowler. Melvin Burgess. The three hottest young writers in England. Tim Bowler, who is the leader of that trio called The Three Musketeers, said to me, "Frank, we will come to America for you, do anything you want us to do. All three of us will come to be at a conference."

Susan: That'd be a powerhouse conference. The British are just hot right now anyway, especially in fantasy. What changes have you observed in schools in the use of literature? I don't want to sound a death knell to our conversation but—

Frank: I think you just did, dear.

Susan: I think I did.

Frank: I had a fourth-grade boy in the store here the other day, and I've known him since he was in first grade. He's been coming to the store. I smiled at him and said, "And what are you reading?"
  "Nothing. I mean nothing!" he said.
  "Don't you get time to read in school? What's your teacher reading to you?" I asked.
  "She doesn't read to us.
  "Well, what do you do in reading class?"
  "We do pages—workbook pages."
  "Don't you have free time to read?"
  "If we have free time, we do test prep."
  I said, "You do *what*?"
  "We do test prep, Frank. Those g.d. sheets of paper."
  And that's what they're doing.

Susan: Well, that's what I'm observing a lot of, but I wanted to hear it from your lips.

Frank: Susan, it is frightening. There was a big article in the paper not too long ago about the fact that humanities, art, and music are less and less known in schools. There's going to be less of history, and less science, less language arts, because kids are doing test prep. What do they really think is being accomplished by No Child Left Behind?

Susan: I'm finding that some of the teachers who used to use literature have abandoned it—completely. Or they've basalized it totally— and it's skills and drills and quotation marks.

Frank: One local teacher has been a literature buff for years and years and years. She's been teaching probably 26 years and has a room filled with books. The principal called her in one day and said, "You'll have to get rid of all of the books in your room."
  She said, "What do you mean, get rid of all the books?"
  "A complaint has come from a mother that the books that you have in your room are distracting her son."

Susan: That doesn't even sound legal.

Frank: After school that night, the principal showed up with boxes, and they loaded up all the books and took them out.

Susan: So that's where we are. But what are teachers saying to you—the good, the bad, and the ugly?

Frank: The teachers whom I would classify as really good teachers—who can take a book and make it into magic for kids—are still using literature in subtle ways, but they're hiding it. They're disguising it as a lesson. They take a thing from their workbook or their basal, a skill, and they say they're reinforcing this particular skill when they're caught reading the book.

Susan: "Caught."

Frank: Yes, it's a sneaking kind of thing that they have to do. Other teachers who find time every day to read to the kids justify it in a variety of ways. They take time off their lunch recess time, and they're able to read, and of course the kids love it. The kids can hardly wait for it. A special ed teacher started reading *The Miraculous Journey of Edward Tulane* to them. The kids are tough little nuts; they begged to not go out for lunch. They would stay in the room if she would read to them. When they finished the book, the teacher told me there were actually tears in the eyes of the kids. She said, "Are you sad?"

And they all said, "No, we're happy. We're so happy. He's home. He found the love."

Now these are slow kids. And she said, "Frank, when I say 'slow,' I mean slow."

Some schools are still doing a fantastic job. When the authors go there, they're treated like princesses and princes because the kids have read the books. The kids are surrounded by literature all the time. One school has had a visit from Elizabeth Winthrop, who wrote *Castle in the Attic* and *Battle for the Castle* . They recently were visited by Trinka Hayes Noble, who wrote *The Day Jimmy's Boa Ate the Wash*. They've had Mem Fox, Bruce Coville, Gloria Houston, and Cheryl Harness. They have two or three authors a year.

Susan: I bet this school is testing well, too.

Frank: When the newspaper publishes the report card on test results, the school is in the top 10 every year.

Susan: Why is no one making this connection?

Frank: I say that to principals. Look at the schools that are in the top 10 and go find out what those schools are doing. When you do, you go to the schools that are literature based. The kids are reading all the time. They don't have test prep booklets. They have books. They read.

For the last 3 years in one school in Vermont, the new principal, for Teacher Appreciation Week, has brought me and a load of books over to the school. We get the teachers all together and she says to every teacher, "Each of you can buy $125 worth of books at Frank's store."

Susan: You must still have schools that send teachers your way with vouchers to buy books.

Frank: Not like they used to. But, see, these teachers will spend the day. I'll go over and I'll sit with teachers in the third grade, and they'll say they really are looking for this kind of thing in nonfiction, this kind of thing they want to do as a theme for literature. So I'll rush around, and I'll bring the books over to them. They'll look at the books. They'll read the books and talk about the books and then they might put in an order for eight copies of a title, five copies of another to go along with things that they've already got. At the end of the day we come home with very few books and a big order.

This year she [the Vermont principal] is principal of two buildings literally across the street from each other, so we're going to do the two buildings this year. I think one easy way for you to see what the condition of American literature is for kids is by looking at *Publishers Weekly*. It publishes a list of the children's best sellers. Years ago, *The New York Times* started to do a weekly children's best-seller list. One of the editors called me and asked if I would be willing to be one of the stores submitting titles. I said, "Oh, I'd love to!" So I submitted.

And then the issue comes out, and of course none of my books is mentioned. So I submitted again, and I went through this for months, and then the editor called me one day, and I said, "This is really sort of silly, isn't it? Every book that is a big seller for me goes nowhere on the list. It's never on the list. I have never had a book on the list. I'm not going to do it any more."

She said, "Oh, Frank, please. Please keep it up."

And I said, "Well, what good is it?"

She said, "I'll tell you what happens. Your list comes; the staff duplicates it; they take it to the bookstores, and they buy the books for their families."

I said, "You're kidding."

She said, "No. That's how we get books for our kids that we know are worthy of reading." And I thought, well, that's really, really something.

I was at NEBA, Northeastern Booksellers Association—a big meeting in Providence, Rhode Island, with thousands of people, hundreds of exhibitors—and we're having dinner. I started quizzing the women at the table from three different bookstores. I started asking them questions about authors. They'd never heard of them. I asked them who their favorite authors were and who the big-selling authors were at their stores. They named the Berenstain Bears. I said, "The Berenstain Bears? My God, you get those at the chain store for half price."

"Well, they love the Berenstain Bears. Oh, my God, they've got a whole section of the Berenstain Bears," they said.

Susan: When you go to present in schools, what kinds of questions do the teachers ask you?

Frank: Usually the questions they'll ask me are curriculum related, like "I want to refresh my Holocaust unit." They want to refresh something—you know, some kind of character development or something like that. "Do you have anything that you can think of that would go with the War of 1812?" they'll ask.

I'm working right now on how I'm going to introduce books down in New Jersey. I'm going to begin by doing *Lily's Big Day*, Kevin Henkes's book. And this is going to be my big day because we're talking to all those people. I'm going to use *Little Boy Star*, and I'm going to use the new *Boy in the Striped Pajamas*. I think I'm probably going to end the evening by reading *Mother's Wish*, which is a beautiful, lovely, wonderful story.

And then I'll be using early readers, middle grades, junior high school, senior high school. You have to cover all the ranges. I just get excited about the books. There's a book called *The Book of Everything* that I'm going to insist everybody go out and buy a copy of immediately because it's so fantastic. A little boy talks to God, talks to Jesus, and it is wonderful. It's not religious at all. It takes place in Amsterdam. It won the equivalent of the Newbery Award in the Netherlands. The father is a religious bigot; he insists that the only book worthy of reading is the Bible; the boy helps the old lady next door, who's called a witch by all the kids. He carries her groceries in one night, and she asks him to come in and sit. They become friends. She introduces him to literature, and she gives him *Emil and the Detectives* by Erich Kastner.

And, of course, he's amazed that they're writing books about kids. He's never read a book about kids. He falls in love with this neighborhood woman, who has lost her leg. She has a prosthesis that's leather, and it squeaks. Plus, she's only got one finger on one hand. Well, he's never seen anyone like that. He goes up to her and he asks her if she'll marry him. He's 8. And, of course, she says yes, she'll wait for him. Well, he's just got the world by the tail. He's got this new book, a book about kids, and the old lady convinces him that they should start a read-aloud club. So they have a read-aloud club over at her house, and she introduces him to reading poetry. It's all done so simply and so beautifully.

Then she says one day, "Shouldn't we have the meeting at your house?" She knows that the father is an abusive father. Well, he couldn't possibly have the meeting there. But then his father's going away, so they can have the meeting at the house; he invites his mother and his sister and the woman he loves. This older lady brings three of her aged cronies to this read-aloud club because they all like to listen and enjoy being read to. They're right in the middle of this when the father comes home, and—wowee, what a book!

Susan: I guess I have to read that one. I haven't read that one.

Frank: Oh! It is wonderful. *The Book of Everything* is a Scholastic publication, and it's a novel by Guus Kuijer. It comes to us in translation. When you get finished with the book, you are drained, but you are so excited because it's so wonderful. You're going to just love it all the way through, because he doesn't understand. He simply doesn't understand.

You've also got to read *The Boy in the Striped Pajamas*. It's written as a fable from the perspective of a little boy in Berlin; he's 8 years old, and he is so mad because he has to leave his friends. That damned Fury was over at the house the other night, and every time he walks in you have to stick your hand up in the air. His father is being sent away and the little boy goes to this place and there's nobody to play with, but he looks out the window from the top floor of the house and he sees all these buildings back there and this barbed wire. His father is now the new commandant at Auschwitz.

So one day the boy looks around in desperation, and he finds another little boy on the other side of the barbed wire. This little boy is wearing striped pajamas. And he says to him, "I'd love some of those striped pajamas. I've never had striped pajamas. And you have a little cap that goes with it. Oh! I'd love a pair of those striped pajamas." The boy in the striped pajamas tells about the soldiers coming one night. His father was a tailor. They lived over the shop. And they came one night and killed his mother and took him away. He doesn't know why. He doesn't know what he's there for. And there are lots of kids there.

"Do they play?" the little boy asks the boy in the striped pajamas . . . Well, no, they don't. They can't play. The boy in the striped pajamas is hungry.

So our little boy begins to steal food for him; however, it's quite a distance to walk from the house up to the camp. If he starts with a piece of chocolate, by the time he gets there, there's no chocolate left because he has eaten it. Sometimes he takes a cookie, but there are only pieces left, so he gives them to the little boy in the striped pajamas. They gradually work the wire loose away from the post so they can hold it up, and the little boy sneaks under the wire. But that's the day the Russians are coming, and the commandant orders that everyone in the camp be killed. And then the commandant and his wife spend the rest of their lives wondering what happened to their boy. He disappeared and they can't find him. It's a fable written by a man from Ireland, John Boyne.

Susan: That's haunting. It reminds me of *Rose Blanche* by Roberto Innocenti.

Frank: You've got to read it. Sue, you'll just sit there and say to yourself, "Oh my Lord, and we're allowing Darfur; we're allowing this to happen. What is the matter with us? Haven't we learned anything?"

Susan: Apparently not. Do you want to get political, talk a little bit about that?

Frank: It's a bit frustrating, so frustrating. It's so frightening what the current administration is doing, but also what teachers are doing. Two years ago, at my conference called "Got Books? Let's Read," my luncheon speaker was Brent Runyon. He wrote *The Burn Journals*, his first and only book at that time. And the teachers said to me, "Why is he coming to be our speaker?"

"Because he is a kid," I replied. He was a child, and he's very young. He was in trouble at school and acted out, begging for help. He didn't get any help. So he went home one night, put his bathrobe on, soaked himself with gasoline and set himself on fire. He burned himself over 85% of his body. And he lived! The only reason he lived is that he was in the shower when he did it, and his brother was able to turn the shower on. And when he was in therapy, the therapist said to him, "Brent, why don't you tell your story? Why don't you write your story?" So he did. It was published as *The Burn Journals*.

You know, kids are crying out all the time for help—We can listen and direct them someplace. I don't care what level you teach; kids are in trouble all the time. The advice that I used to give kids wasn't any good. I used to say, "Oh, Honey, you'll grow out of it." Kids don't grow out of it if they've got serious problems.

Brent began his speech by saying that he spent all his teenage years trying to kill himself. Yet no one recognized the fact that he wanted help—none of his teachers nor his parents. Well, he's up there talking, and one of the other speakers is right across from where I'm sitting. I look over at him, and the tears are literally flowing out of his eyes. As soon as Brent finished, I ran over and asked the man, "What is the matter? Are you all right?"

And he said, "Frank, years ago I was so discouraged, and one day I turned on NPR, and I heard this man talk. It was Brent Runyon. I said to myself, if he can do it, I can do it. So I went back to the dining room table and I finished my book. I sent it in, and it got accepted for publication. I always wanted to thank the man whose voice I heard on the radio. Now here I am in Albany, New York, at a children's literature conference, and there's the man who inspired me."

He couldn't get over it. So he went right over to Brent, and the two of them were hugging and holding on to each other as he told his story.

Susan: You've got so many stories like that.

Frank: Oh. Just so beautiful. When John Gardiner died, *The Los Angeles Times* called his wife, and she talked about John, his life as an engineer. She said to the obituary writer, "If you want to know about his literary world, call Frank Hodge in Albany, New York." So the reporter asked me how did I first get in touch with him. I told her about having a conference and all this stuff. She said, "Are you a bookstore? Are you a publisher?"

I said, "I'm just a bookstore."

"A bookstore that has a conference bringing authors together? I never heard of anything like that," she said.

The obituary was syndicated; it went all over the country, and I got calls from as far away as Bangor, Maine, saying, "I read about you in the obituary of John Gardiner, and I'd like to talk with you." The fallout from that has been really interesting. I'm doing more things with people through e-mail. That seems to be the vehicle of choice at this point. People are telling me that they've written a book, and I give them, you know, lecture number 416: Don't Give Up on Yourself. Somebody would say he's discouraged, and I would just say, "Believe in yourself. That's what John Gardiner would tell you, and it took him 7 years to get his book published."

It took Madeleine L'Engle 23 rejections to get her book published. She had written it for adults, and finally the editor at Farrar Straus said to her, "Madeleine, you should take this book across the hall to the children's division." She was insulted. She hadn't written it for kids, but she took it across to the children's division, and that was the magic moment. She tells that story, and she tells it with great gusto. What a fool she was all those years, thinking she'd written for adults.

Jerry Spinelli—all the writing he did at first was for adults, too.

Susan: And then they got on the right side of the hallway.

Frank: Then Jerry went to work one day, opened up his Tupperware dish expecting a piece of chicken, and it wasn't there. One of the kids had eaten it and put the dish back in the refrigerator. So he sat down and he started writing *Space Station, Seventh Grade*, took it home, and said to Eileen, his wife, "Read this." She read it; she looked at him and said, "You've made it. You've hit it. This is it. This is it." He's a fabulous, fantastic person. I sent him a Christmas card, and on the Christmas card I just typed all this stuff. I was talking to the two of them, good friends of mine. Then the day before Christmas I got a long, long handwritten letter from Jerry saying how wonderful it was to get a letter. He hates cards with just signatures because they're so cold. Two days later I got a long handwritten letter from Eileen saying how much they enjoyed my note. So I'm not going to send Christmas cards anymore. I'm going to send letters—because we don't do that anymore. We just don't write letters, and they're so special.

Susan: *Loser*, I just love that book.

Frank: My favorite is *Wringer*. But my real favorite would be *Space Station, Seventh Grade*. I called the publisher after he wrote that book, and I said, "I'd like to get hold of Jerry Spinelli and have him come to a conference."

"Oh, Jerry Spinelli doesn't do visits," the publisher told me.

"Oh really? That's too bad," I replied.

Then his second book comes out, *Who Put That Hair in My Toothbrush?* I call the publisher again and I say, "I *really* want to get hold of Jerry Spinelli."

"He doesn't do conferences."

"Well, would you let *him* tell me? Give me his phone number?"

"I'll call him one more time."

So five minutes later, my phone rings. "Hello. This is Jerry Spinelli. Somebody wants to get hold of me up there?" He had been trying for years to get out to schools, and he never got any calls. Mine was the first call he ever got.

I said, "That's absolute insanity. I've been trying for years to get you."

So he came. The first time he came was right here in Albany. He walked into that room and everybody applauded as he walked down the aisle, before he said a word. He stood up in front of the group and he was overwhelmed. We went out for dinner that night, and I remember sitting across from him at the restaurant, and he said to me, "Frank, should I give up my day job? Or should I give up my writing?"

I said, "Never give up your writing, young man. You're going to make it." So then he won the Newbery!

We're doing conferences now called "Got Books? Let's Read." I had to give up "Let the Reading Begin." I said in my newsletter that I was going to give up the conference. Well, the phone started ringing, letters started coming in, and people volunteered to come back—the Spinellis and Karen Hesse and all these wonderful people who had been here for years before. So we had a list of speakers that was unbelievable. We had, actually, three Newbery authors, and the next year's Newbery winner, Kate DiCamillo. I have a picture of the four of them together: Linda Sue Park, Karen Hesse, Jerry Spinelli, and Kate DiCamillo. It's been amazing. We bring in authors, and the authors talk about themselves and their books.

Susan: So you just keep on going. You're better than the Energizer bunny.

Frank: You've heard about the Frank Hodge Reading Association? A bunch of people got together and they formed the Frank Hodge Reading Association. They collected money and they're giving teachers a chance to write a proposal to get $350 worth of free books for their classrooms. There are eight of them this year.

Susan: That's marvelous, Frank! If you had a message, something that you wanted to say to lovers of children's literature, what would you say to them?

Frank: What I keep saying to people all the time is, "Don't give up. You've got to sweat your way through. There are real gems lurking on these lists and in these companies. You've just got to push a lot of that schlock aside, and don't cater to the lowest common denominator. Just because a kid or the parents happen to say that they only like these kinds of stories, that's not true. You've got to introduce them to the other kinds of stories, too. If we fed a baby a steady diet of pablum, we would have the largest, fattest, happiest little baby in the world, but we wouldn't have any development of bones or muscle or sinew or anything. We need to vary the diet. It's the same way with kids in school.

When I taught school once, I had a girl who read Marguerite Henry—in fourth grade, in fifth grade, and in sixth grade. According to the reading record that they used to pass along in the school, every year she read the same books over and over again. So it was my job as the seventh-grade teacher to find a book that had a horse in it, but a horse and a boy. Now at the end of the book, she could kiss the boy and kiss the horse and ride off on the horse. That would be perfectly all right. But I would be introducing her to a new concept, and that would be the boy. I worked like hell until I found a book where she kissed the boy and the horse at the end of the book but didn't ride off on the horse. All of a sudden this student started looking at other books, and she expanded her horizons—something as simple as that. She's now an English teacher, and I've heard she tells the kids her story.

Teachers are notorious nonreaders. Booksellers are notorious nonreaders. Librarians are notorious nonreaders. I said to them, when I went to the first library group that I did down on the Hudson, "I really should be sitting down, and you should be talking to me about the books."

And they all said, "Oh God, no, Frank. You read the books. We shelve the books."

I thought, "Oh my heaven." The chairman of the conference said that he would let me do a small group, but he didn't think that I would get many people in my group because I was not a librarian. So he gave me a group, and you couldn't get in the room. I said, "I'm the speaker. Can I come in? Can I come in?" So they finally moved us to another, big room, and by the time we got started we had four times as many people as we should have. The next year, I was the keynote speaker at the convention.

Susan: That says it all, Frank.

Children's Books

Boyne, J. (2006). *Boy in the striped pajamas.* New York: Fickling Books.

de Felice, C. (1990). *Weasel.* New York: Atheneum.

de Felice, C. (2006). *Bringing Ezra back.* New York: Farrar, Straus & Giroux.

DiCamillo, K. (2006). *The miraculous journey of Edward Tulane.* Cambridge, MA: Candlewick Press.

Evangelista, B. (2005). *Gifted.* New York: Walker Books.

Finchler, J. (1995). *Miss Malarkey doesn't live in Room 10* (K. O'Malley, Illus.). New York: Walker Books.

Gallaz, C., & Innocenti, R. (1985). *Rose Blanche.* (R. Innocenti, Illus.). Mankato, MN: Creative Education.

Gardiner, J. (1980). *Stone fox.* New York: HarperCollins.

Hausfater, R. (2006). *The little boy star.* New York: Milk and Cookies Press.

Henkes, K. (2006). *Lily's big day.* New York: Greenwillow.

Houston, G. (1992). *My great Aunt Arizona.* (S. C. Lamb, Illus.). New York: HarperCollins.

Houston, G. (1998). *Year of the perfect Christmas Tree* (B. Cooney, Illus.). New York: Dial.

Kastner, E. (2001). *Emil and the detectives.* New York: Penguin. (Original work published 1929).

Kuijer, G. (2006). *The Book of everything.* New York: Scholastic.

Noble, T. (1980). *The day Jimmy's boa ate the wash* (S. Kellogg, Illus.). New York: Dial.

Rowling, J. K. (2000). *Goblet of fire.* New York: Scholastic.

Runyon, B. (2004). *The burn journals.* New York: Knopf.

Spinelli, J. (1982). *Space station, seventh grade.* Boston: Little, Brown.

Spinelli, J. (1984). *Who put that hair in my toothbrush?* Boston: Little, Brown.

Spinelli, J. (1997). *Wringer.* New York: HarperCollings.

Spinelli, J. (2002). *Loser.* New York: HarperCollins.

Wargin, K. (2006). *Mother's wish.* (I. Roman, Illus.). New York: HarperCollins.

Winthrop, E. (1985). *Castle in the attic.* New York: Holiday House.

Winthrop, E. (1993). *Battle for the castle.* New York: Holiday House.

Chapter 6

The Status of Reader Response Research: Sustaining the Reader's Voice in Challenging Times

Marjorie R. Hancock

Louise Rosenblatt's (1938, 1978) transactional theory of reader response provided the theoretical foundation of a plethora of meaningful research studies conducted during the past 40 years. The transactional view of reading implies an active, constructive experience that blends the voices of the reader and the author, with personal meaning becoming the collaborative product of reader and text during the act of reading (Galda & Liang, 2003). Time-honored quantitative and qualitative research studies revealed the thoughtful, unique responses to literature that take place in the mind and heart of the reader. Beyond the content of reader response, however, has been the effort to provide insights into the varied dimensions of the response process itself. Respected studies have affirmed the developmental nature of response (Applebee, 1978; Cullinan, Harwood, & Galda, 1983) and the importance of reader stance (Many, 1991), whereas case studies have showcased the idiosyncratic nature of the reader-responder (Galda, 1982; Hancock, 1993). Research conducted in authentic classroom settings has described patterns of response (Hickman, 1981; Kiefer, 1983), and teacher action research of the previous decade has reflected the strength of blending reader response research and literature-based classroom practice (Roller & Beed, 1994; Wollman-Bonilla & Werchaldo, 1995).

During the height of reader response research— the 1990s—trends in the research became apparent as journal articles and professional books continually applauded individuality and celebrated higher level thinking surrounding reader response to literature (Hancock, 2000). Response to multicultural literature (Altieri, 1995), oral response through literature circles (Short, Kauffman, Kaser, Kahn, & Crawford, 1999), the artistic response to literature (Whitin, 1996), and responses of young children to literature (Shine & Roser, 1999) provided research studies that energetically filtered into classroom practice. Many teachers remain committed to reader response and transactional theory as the basis of effective instructional decisions.

Although this introductory, retrospective view of reader response research rekindles fulfillment in those who fully participated in the aura of the reader response era, researchers are currently challenged to make the transition from the worthy studies of the past to the dynamic studies of the present and the future. Building on an honored reader response research tradition, researchers on the horizon of change are utilizing the respected theoretical foundation of reader response theory, adjusting their research focus to ongoing educational changes while reaching beyond the traditional studies in reader response to challenging areas of current and future response-based research. Devoted teachers, on the other hand, anticipate the transition from the latest research findings to classroom practice even in an educational climate that supports the commonality rather than the individuality of the reader.

The Impact of Multidimensional Change on Response Research

Ongoing changes in society and in the nation's schools—philosophical, cultural, political, technological—have altered the face of reader response research in the new millennium. The gradual decline of the literature-based instructional era, which appears to be a shadow of its former self, still exhibits its powerful presence in the continued role of authentic literature in the classroom. Believers in whole language, a philosophy challenged as nonscientific, stood tall, both retaining and maintaining the literature base that had inspired meaningful teaching during the 1990s. Many classrooms remain filled with shelves of the highest quality books across genres, heartfelt writings in response journals, and energetic talk of book clubs.

The changing face of students in American schools through increased diversity has also resulted in a challenge to reader response research. The increased use of multicultural literature, the desire to extend response to second-language learners, and the increased focus on differentiated instruction to reach all readers have opened researchers' eyes to fresh possibilities in investigation.

The No Child Left Behind legislation initially presented another hurdle to reader response as one-size-fits-all programs and single answers to national and state test questions moved the comprehension spotlight from individual response to cloned reading focused on the sole "right" answer. Yet many classrooms retain the best of the response base by focusing on national and state standards that lean toward the use of authentic literature to model reading strategies, multigenre instruction, and oral and written interactions in response to literature.

The new technologies in our society have actually resulted in dynamic changes in reader response research. The inclusion of viewing and visual representation in the *Standards for the English Language Arts* (IRA & NCTE, 1996) opened the door to exploring and broadening the definition of response to literature. Visual literacy provides an inspired challenge to those who desire to blend the worlds of literacy and technology in their research. As a result of innovations such as the production of postmodern picture books and graphic novels and the use of technology for delivering literature-based instruction, the new generation of reader response research lies on a threshold of change that will continue to impact the new century and the changing era of American education.

Although the passing of the passionate voice of Louise Rosenblatt left a personal void in the heart of researchers and practitioners alike, the spirit and drive of the transactional theory of reader response will forge ahead. Reader response readily adjusts to the changing times, climate, and opportunities that await its continued contribution to various research efforts.

Trends in Reader Response Research

In order to discuss the current status of reader response research, I have reviewed studies from the past years (2000–2006). Eight trends in reader response research emerged:

- Cultural diversity and response
- Response modes in young children
- Response to nonfiction or informational books
- Literature discussion as response
- Critical literacy as response
- Multiple sign systems as response
- Response to postmodern picture books
- Technology connections to response

A selective discussion of published research and unpublished dissertation studies in each of these eight trend areas provides a fresh look at the movement of reader response research in the new decade. More studies than can be covered in a book chapter are available, but the most influential and promising studies that have expanded reader response research are featured.

Research findings and implications for classroom practice provide the nudge needed by classroom teachers to continue to apply response-based findings in their classrooms. Building on the past can bring light and life into future instructional dimensions providing optimal conditions for continuing to create lifelong readers and heartfelt responders in a literate society.

The Multicultural Dimension of Reader Response

The role of multicultural literature in soliciting reader response provides a major focus of this expanding area of research. Lehr & Thompson (2000) set the stage for a "dynamic response" to multicultural literature by sharing Jerry Spinelli's (1990) *Maniac Magee* and Mildred Taylor's (1987a) *The Friendship* with urban and rural fifth graders. The methods of response included paired and silent reading, drama and art, journal writing, and small- and large-group discussions. The resulting framework for analysis showcased the potential of response through literal thinking, inferring, moral response, personal connections, interactive meaning-building, background knowledge, and dialogic response. The depth and breadth of response provided incentives to delve further into response to multicultural literature with multicultural audiences of readers.

The report of aesthetic and efferent responses of 11th and 12th graders to the evocative narrative paintings portrayed in Tom Feelings's (1995) wordless *The Middle Passage: White Ships/Black Cargo* further supported African-American literature and reader response (Connor, 2003). Twenty-five high school students of different races enrolled in a Minority Authors elective course focused on a semester of African-American literature titles. Oral discussion and written response to prompts focused on Feelings's paintings as an expression of history and the author's personal feelings toward slavery. After their initial response, the students were invited to use a variety of formats—poems, art, letters, essays—as a means of personal response. An analysis of these response modes showcased the power of the book to enhance ethnically and culturally diverse students' critical understandings of the Middle Passage through the use of multiple reader response formats. The study supported the personal connections of African-American literature through the picture book format in secondary English language arts classrooms.

A dissertation study conducted by Miller (2003) utilized literature discussion groups to respond to culturally relevant children's literature in a kindergarten classroom. The specific African-American literature selected for this inquiry invited low socioeconomic African-Americans students to critically analyze culturally relevant texts in a platform that honored their discourse and urban background. In related dissertation research, Connor (2004) explored female biracial adolescents' transaction as they read and responded to biracial literature in an out-of-school book club. The study concluded that teachers need to seek out literature as a means to develop critical consciousness about racial, cultural, and ethnic diversity in today's classrooms.

Dressel (2005) implemented a multicultural, middle school literature unit to explore the link between personal response and social responsibility in response to literature across cultures. Surveys, dialogue journals, and a book club organizer provided response data from Suzanne Fisher Staples's (1989) *Shabanu: Daughter of the Wind*, Walter Dean Myers's (1993) *Scorpions*, Sherry Garland's (1993) *Shadow of the Dragon,* and four other novels. Analysis of 123 eighth-grade responses revealed momentum from neutral feelings about reading novels to positive feelings about the self-selected multicultural literature. Students' cultural knowledge influenced their interpretation of the novels, but they held firmly to attitudes reflective of their own cultural groups. The study indicated the need for teachers of dominant-culture students to include much more multicultural literature in the curriculum so their students gain experience with different worldviews within our increasingly global society. The role of the teacher remains crucial in providing students with a response opportunity to examine their otherwise unchallenged cultural assumptions. Moving beyond multitcultural units toward a critical literacy curriculum is essential if teachers intend for students to read beyond *who they are* toward changing cultural attitudes and behaviors from *what they read.*

Belinda Louie's (2005) observational case study of empathetic response to Feng Jicai's (1995) Chinese novella, *Let One Hundred Flowers Bloom,* embedded reader response in an intense cultural, political, and historical context. With a focus on the development of reader empathy outside one's own culture and time, the study identified five types of empathy: cognitive, historical, parallel emotional, reactive emotional, and cross-cultural. Drawing on prereading knowledge, students discussed, composed response journal entries, and constructed an emotional timeline of the main character. The study concluded that rich contextual information, multicultural literature, and response opportunities developed empathy for characters who live in a different world. The implication of this study is a first step toward a broader curriculum addressing a global perspective and encouraging empathy for cultural differences.

The changing face of America has also created a response focus for second-language learners as research delves into literature as a mirror of a culture for children of that culture. Ruth Elizabeth Quiroa (2005) investigated the oral, written, and artistic responses of young Mexican-origin children to Mexican-theme picture storybooks. This qualitative, descriptive inquiry explored how culturally specific children's literature can intersect with the cultural backgrounds of students. In this study, children's responses included high levels of aesthetic and critical thought when a familiar cultural aspect of the book related to their lives.

The trend in multicultural response to literature has grown from multiethnic literature to both a homegrown focus (e.g., Hispanic or Latino literature) and a more global perspective for response. Future studies invite the response to both translated literature from world cultures and literature from around the world in a setting surrounded by a rich historical and cultural context to deepen the level of discussion, cultural understanding, and reader empathy.

Reader Response With Young Children

Although most reader response research in the 1990s focused on intermediate, middle school, and high school students, the new century has shifted the spotlight to responses of young children emerging into literacy in kindergarten, first grade, and second grade. A key researcher, Lawrence Sipe (2000), is noteworthy; he focused his research on the literary responses of K–2 students to picture storybooks. His research developed a grounded theory of literary understanding specifically concerned with young children. The theory suggests that young children follow three impulses and five types of responses when they experience literature.

The *hermeneutic impulse* is driven by a desire to know, as the children understand and interpret stories. This impulse incites *analytic responses* in which the child tries to understand the internal workings of plot, character, setting, and even the language of story. In addition, children create *intertextual responses* as they link previous texts, videos, television shows, and artwork to the current picture storybook.

The *personalizing impulse* connects the world of story to children's own lives; the resulting *personal response* is that the children connect the current story to their experiences.

Children enact the *aesthetic impulse* as they enter the "lived through" (Rosenblatt, 1978) literary experience and share the uniqueness of their personal interpretation. *Transparent responses*, or faint suggestions of deep engagement, occur as the world of story and the children's world become transparent to each other. Children also engage in *performance responses* as the story serves as a foundation for their own creative expression.

A university researcher and teacher-researcher study (Sipe & Bauer, 2001) placed reader response in an urban kindergarten setting of primarily minority students from low socioeconomic backgrounds. A focus on the picture storybook genre of fantasy resulted in these emergent literacy participants making meaning with both words and illustrations through the impulses and responses characterized by Sipe's (2000) study. Titles included *Swimmy* by Leo Lionni (1987), *The Mitten* by Jan Brett (1989), *The Gingerbread Boy* by Paul Galdone (1979) and a newer version of the same title by Richard Egielski (1997), and several other fantasy and/or traditional tales. The number of and cumulative percentage of intertextual connections throughout the study increased as more and more titles were introduced.

The read-aloud storybook resulted in literary talk, empowered children who bring their own culture and backgrounds to the discussion, and provided the opportunity to bring school-based literacy to these children.

Sipe (2002) also focused on the early literacy response of expressive engagement gained from his numerous studies of young children's literary understanding developed during storybook read-alouds. He constructed a set of five conceptual categories to describe conversational turns that reflect expressive engagement. These meaningful response categories for young children are the following: spontaneous dramatization of the story; talking back to the story or the characters; critiquing by suggesting alternative plots, characters, or settings; inserting oneself into a story; or taking over the text and using the story as a launch for one's own creativity. Sipe supports each of the five categories with authentic sample responses that inform primary teachers of the power and possibilities of reader response at this early literacy level. Teacher reactions to these responses encouraged active participation, pleasure, and engagement in literature.

Undoubtedly, continuing studies with young, emergent readers will build on the theory established by these groundbreaking studies of Sipe. Recognition of the capabilities of reader response in emergent readers is the key to ongoing research.

Response to Nonfiction

The explosion of the nonfiction or informational genre of literature has extended and enhanced interest in reader response to the expository domain of children's books. Although professional books have dominated the readings in the expository text genre, nonfiction stands at the threshold of continuing response-based research.

A parent-researcher case study (Maduram, 2000) examined the responses of Amy, from age 4 to age 6, to informational books beyond the parental read-aloud. Amy's spontaneous, unstructured response episodes included mention of facts in casual conversation, reevaluation of facts, reflections of complex thinking, life and literature connections, and portraits of personal inquiry. Amy's responses to informational books in the home setting represented the richness of the meaning-making process between life and nonfiction text at an emergent literacy stage.

A case study of preschool children's responses to read-aloud informational books by Cathy Tower (2002) involved a group "pretend" reading of the book as nondirected response. Pretend readings were analyzed to reveal children's knowledge of informational book language as well as ways that the text and illustrations helped them to make sense of the text. Nonfiction texts included Allan Fowler's photographed *Please Don't Feed the Bears* (1991), Linda Glaser's illustrated *Wonderful Worms* (1992), and Mary Ebeltoft Reid's photographed *Let's Find Out About Ice Cream* (1996). Children used informational language during their retelling responses, mixing science language features with specific descriptions of illustrations. The results indicate that young children are attuned to text characteristics, including illustrations, and these have a great impact on early response to nonfiction text. Tower's study contradicted earlier studies that indicated that young children favored narrative text for response (Shine & Roser, 1999).

An observational, descriptive study of interdisciplinary response research (Porter, 2006) celebrated the enhancement of science and social studies curricular units through integrated Orbis Pictus Award–winning nonfiction. Although the findings analyzed both oral and written responses, the transcripts of students in response to interactive read-alouds of the informational titles showed the power of integrating quality nonfiction into a standards-based content curriculum.

Christine Pappas (2006), whose research has focused on the interdisciplinary use of literature, targeted the information book genre and its integration into science literacy. Through identifying seven atypical, hybrid types of informational text in children's illustrated nonfiction trade books, she has opened the door to response research with this subgenre of literature by seeking out children's responses to simultaneous narrative and expository text on a selected science topic. Her analytic scheme for types of hybrid texts has the potential to serve as a tool for investigating the responses of young children to the publishing frenzy of atypical narrative-expository informational books.

Literature Discussion

Professional educators who are dedicated readers of books and journals would not be surprised by the amount of research and teacher-action research focus on literature circles, literature book clubs, and oral discussion as response. Based on a sound foundation from the 1990s and plentiful professional books (Hill, Johnson, & Schlick Noe, 1995; Daniels, 2002; Raphael, Florio-Ruane, George, Hasty, & Highfield, 2004), recent researchers have found that talking about books is a fruitful arena for expanded research. Classroom practice has revealed that teacher intervention guides and gradual transitions from teacher-led to student-led discussions actually raise the level of reader response within a literature discussion. Studies of the new decade have focused on improvement of oral response, while avoiding the manipulation of response, through selective transitional and engagement strategies.

Beth Malloch (2002, 2004) focused on the transition period that now appears necessary as literature discussion moves from teacher-led to student-led conversations. Building on the teacher-as-facilitator research of Short and colleagues (1999), Malloch spent more than 5 months in a third-grade classroom to document the transition process to student-led literature circles. Her research found that literature circles require a complex transition into classroom practice. If educators want children to have opportunities to share personal response through substantive, meaningful conversations, students need procedural knowledge of how to initiate, enter, and maintain a response-based literature circle.

Two university researchers (Long & Gove, 2003) focused on the use of literature circles as a means to higher level thinking, or critical response, in a fourth-grade urban classroom by utilizing titles by Mildred Taylor focused on social justice: *Song of the Trees* (1975), *The Friendship* (1987a), and *The Gold Cadillac* (1987b). Valuing Rosenblatt's (1978) view of reader response of independent readers, this study used teacher read-alouds, inviting students to connect, reflect on, and question the text as a means of critical response. Engagement strategies were implemented alongside encouraging personal response: ask, listen, honor, respond, and encourage; investigate and find out; and pose and solve problems. The mix of literature circles and engagement strategies as a form of scaffolding caused students to read, discuss, question, experience the text firsthand, and act on textual possibilities with others. The authentic situations created by the teacher allowed readers to publicly share affective responses to literature in a context of emotional response, resulting in investment in and enthusiasm about reading.

Unquestionably, talk about literature remains an open avenue to continuing research. The more one reads, the more one desires to share personal connections, innermost thoughts, and controversial reactions to literature.

Critical Literacy Response as Comprehension

McLaughlin and DeVoogd (2004) proposed expanding reader response beyond the aesthetic and efferent stances familiarized by Rosenblatt (1978). Through thinking actively, extending reasoning, and seeking out multiple perspectives, they suggest a third stance—the critical stance—which resides and fluctuates along the aesthetic-efferent continuum. When reading from a critical stance, readers use prior knowledge to link their own experiences to the ideas of the author. Readers have the power to envision multiple ways of viewing the topic when they read a text from a critical stance. Beyond understanding the words, they interpret purpose in their own analytic and evaluative minds.

McLaughlin and DeVoogd (2004) provide a substantive list of literature titles that represent critical literacy and invite response in this suggested stance. Lois Lowry's (1989) *Number the Stars*, Eve Bunting's *Fly Away Home* (1991) and *Smoky Night* (1994), and Jane Yolen's (1996) *Encounter* provide initial critical-stance selections. Chapter books at the intermediate level include Paul Fleischman's (1993) *Bull Run*, Avi's (2002) *Crispin: The Cross of Lead*, and Michael Dorris's (1999) *Morning Girl*. Middle and high school readers may select a critical stance to Karen Hesse's (2001) *Witness* or

Beverly Naidoo's (2000) *The Other Side of Truth*. The attempt to locate the critical stance on Rosenblatt's aesthetic-efferent continuum invites further research across genres and age levels.

A higher level form for critical thought is problem solving. A dissertation study by Shari Griffin (2006) explored common traits of effective problem solving and how these traits are portrayed in literature for intermediate grades. Twenty school stories were analyzed, using the processes of reader response and structural analysis to identify the portrayal of problem-solving traits. National standards focus on problem solving, and children's responses to vicarious experiences through response can provide character support for their own attempts at problem solving.

Reminding educators of the role of readers as text critics in daily life, these researchers advocate the comprehension of information from a critical stance as naturally as response from an efferent and aesthetic stance. The findings of these studies remind educators of the ultimate goal of literacy instruction: the empowerment of readers through independent, critical thinking by accessing all modes of communication.

Multiple Sign Systems as Response

As educator knowledge of learning styles expanded in the last decade, so too did research in expressive modes beyond oral and written response. Fresh areas for reader response have extended the possibilities to all readers and, for some, instilled vitality and motivation into the response process.

Short, Kauffman, and Kahn (2000) gave impetus to the concept of multiple sign systems of response from classroom-based research. Whereas most classrooms had been incorporating written response through literature logs and oral response through literature circles, many children in this study thrived on the invitation to incorporate diagrams, sketches, webs, storyboards, and charts as a means to response. The combination of words and images encouraged further reflection and analysis of those responses through transmediation (across sign systems), intertextuality (across books), and presentations (synthesis of response). Using sign systems (art, music, movement, drama, mathematics, and language) as tools for thinking about, responding to, and extending understanding through transmediation makes response available to all learners as meaning makers and inquirers.

Building on her own previous research in multiple ways of knowing (Whitin, 1996) and the sketch-to-stretch activity, Phyllis Whitin (2005) provided a longitudinal teacher-research study from fourth-grade children's sketched interpretations about literature supplemented by their written commentaries as well as conversations before, during, and after sketching and writing. Titles incorporated in her research included Robert Coles's (1995) *The Story of Ruby Bridges*, Patricia MacLachlan's (1985) *Sarah, Plain and Tall*, and Julius Lester's (1994) *John Henry*. The blending of visual symbols and exploratory talk to mediate thinking about reading was the key to the uniqueness of the findings of this study. Making sketches to represent literary ideas involves higher level thought and generated multilayered interpretations of literature, thus implying pedagogical practice for an extended view of reader response.

Response to Postmodern Picture Books

The advent of new technologies in the creation of digital artwork as illustration paved the way for the creation of postmodern picture books. The emphasis shift from an even blend of text and illustration moved toward a greater focus on the illustrations themselves as a meaning-making and critical response to literature. Sylvia Pantaleo (2004) fully described the radical change of the metafictive devices of postmodern books to include graphics in new forms and formats, sophisticated relationships between text and illustration, nonlinear and nonsequential organization, multiple layers of meaning, interactive formats, and multiple levels of visual and verbal perspectives.

Two studies of postmodern picture books conducted by Pantaleo (2002, 2003) with first-grade children included responses to David Wiesner's (2001) *The Three Pigs* and other postmodern picture books. Pantaleo (2002) revealed, through an analysis of written and visual art responses, that changes demanded that readers must assume an active role in constructing meaning through interpretations, hypotheses, inferences, and connections. An expanded study (Pantaleo, 2003) included small-group conversational responses to related, illustrated texts focused on response to peritext—that is, anything in a book beyond the printed text. Titles included Anthony Browne's (1997) *Willy the Dreamer*, David Macauley's (1995) *Shortcut*, and David Wiesner's (1991) *Tuesday*.

Barbara Chatton (2004) invited fourth and fifth graders to "think like critics" and write book reviews in response to several postmodern picture books, including Chris Raschka's (1998) *Arlene Sardine*. Often critiqued quite harshly by reviewers, this title was reviewed most positively by the intermediate readers. Related response discussion exposed the students' willingness to share their opinions in contrast to published reviews. Additional studies by Serafini (2005), Styles and Arizpe (2001), Goldstone (2002), and Lohfink (2006) showcase the changing role of reader response as it transcends visual literacy. Postmodern picture book characteristics influence oral and written response and meaning-making in children for this new subgenre of books.

Although picture books have always required readers to fill in gaps and generate predictions, postmodern texts escalate readers to a higher level, demanding interaction, engagement, and response to nonlinear, multilayered, and nonsequential text and illustrations. Tolerating and dealing with these challenging characteristics in postmodern picture books is fundamental to children's growth in response to increasingly complex texts.

Technology Connections to Response

Technology has provided a new vision and dimension for reader response research. Carico & Logan (2004) addressed the promise of online literature discussion. Real-time, online chats provided an alternative space for engaging eighth-grade readers and preservice teachers in meaning-making through literature in a WebPal project. Three tools linked cyberspace to reader response: (a) e-mail, for discussing literature with WebPals; (b) bulletins boards, where groups enter responses to posted topics and to the response of others; and (c) real-time, online chats in which pairs discuss a book read in common. The analysis of transcribed student conversations revealed broadened perspectives, increased knowledge, enhanced communication skills, and more satisfying and effective reading processes through the use of technology for initiating and recording reader response.

Further research in the area of technology promises to open time and space from the walls of our classrooms to the world community. The exchange of reader response to literature between related groups of readers is no longer prevented by distance or context. The aesthetic and cognitive domains of reader-responders to commonly read literature promises interactions and experiences through a technological means of communication that shares and expands personal perspectives on response to books.

A Vision of the Future

Looking toward the future of reader response research, we can envision the types of research that might dominate the next decade and continue into the evolving century. These are based on personal visions of the direction that reader response research must assume to continue its role in creating greater understanding of the unique reader's transaction with individual text. Undaunted by current educational trends toward sameness and mandated national reports, research must maintain an open view of the reader and the importance of the individual response in creating lifelong readers.

English language learner response. Undoubtedly, the need for more research with multicultural literature reigns supreme. In a country with an increasing English-as-a-second-language population, more research is necessary to access the identities and language of the real reader in authentic literature. Discovering the impact of culturally relevant literature on the responses of readers across various cultures requires more studies across grade levels and ethnic backgrounds. Blending culture and reading through response can actually provide evidence of motivation for reading and succeeding in one's second language.

Global cultural response. In an increasingly global society, the need exists to explore the possibilities of responding to translated text from children's and young adult literature originally written in foreign countries. International award-winning books, such as the Mildred Batchelder Award books, provide rich literary experiences for gifted readers or international traveling students. Integrating background knowledge of world historical events in preparation for global reader response provides an even broader area for study.

Response to the nonfiction genre. The dramatic interest in expository text generated by national and state standards as well as the increase in publication of informational texts for children and young adults make this genre an outstanding area for response research. The variety of formats, respected authors, award-winning titles, and text structures invite reader response research. Organizing studies of response to text structure and to type of visual transmission of information seems inevitable. The infusion of nonfiction to enhance existing curricular units and the response of all readers to the genre itself identifies nonfiction as an ideal genre for response generation and exploration.

Response and visual literacy. Continued research on response to postmodern picture books and graphic novels seems inevitable as the increased publication of these subgenres encourages further investigation. Even chapter books that blend illustration and text provide new reading opportunities for response. The role of illustrations in generating response and making meaning requires further research as digital technology impacts children's book illustration.

Technology's role in reader response. Research in the electronic mode of reader response has only begun. Exploring how a reader responds to text delivered as electronic books or on CD-ROMs, how blogs influence the quality and quantity of written response, and the potential of online conversations that share response are only a few of the technological research possibilities for the future. Even as the context of Rosenblatt's transactional theory is preserved, technology itself can provide insights into the responses that result through technological reading, writing, and conversations about literature.

Response as assessment. One way to preserve the richness of response is to document response as a way to enhance comprehension and reading accountability. Researchers need to capture and link the connections between personal response to literature and comprehension. With the spotlight on comprehension, more research should explore the levels of comprehension that occur in reader response through several modes of response.

The response domain of intertextuality. As reader response supports text-to-text connections, so too does it invite text-to-video, text-to-music, text-to-videogame, and text-to-television responses. The impact of popular culture and media on reader response truly requires more specific study. Readers in today's world are surrounded by visual literacy, and the possible response connections from this visual background have yet to be documented and investigated in depth.

Although research in each of these suggested areas may be initiated by university researchers, the importance of the authentic classroom setting for reader response must not be forgotten. The role of collaborative teacher-action and university-researcher research looms as a continuing means to enact and analyze authentic responses. Qualitative research still holds promise for descriptive studies, but response lends itself to categorization and quantification, too. Mixed qualitative and quantitative methods provide sound scientifically based research studies that blend the best of both experimental and descriptive worlds of research.

To summarize and conceptualize the vision for a response-based research agenda, Mills, Stephens, O'Keefe, and Waugh (2004) remind both researchers and teachers that Rosenblatt's theory and vision for a democratic society come alive when students and teachers engage in authentic response surrounding literature. They describe Rosenblatt's image of the teacher as both noble and democratic. When teachers are guided by Rosenblatt's theory and related response-based research, instructional decisions lead to the democratic thinking to which she aspired. The current vision for 21st-century education, however, appears less noble and democratic than the educational freedom of the past. The pressure and scrutiny of test-score performance, mandated curriculum and programs, and teaching to the test are striving to force researchers and teachers to lose sight of Rosenblatt's vision for the potential of reader response in a democratic world. To keep Rosenblatt's legacy and theoretical premises alive, continuing research must forge ahead if we are to create the independent, critical thinkers needed for tomorrow's world. Research that blends the trends of a changing society with the strengths that reader response research has established across almost five decades will create the vision for the future that Rosenblatt spent a lifetime professing, endearing, and articulating to the educational community.

References

Alteri, J. (1995). Multicultural literature and multiethnic readers: Examining aesthetic involvement and preferences for text. *Reading Psychology, 16*, 43–70.

Applebee, A. (1978). *The child's concept of story: Ages two to seventeen.* Chicago: University of Chicago Press.

Carico, K. M., & Logan, D. (2004). A generation in cyberspace: Engaging readers through online discussions. *Language Arts, 81* (4), 293–302.

Chatton, B. (2004). Critiquing the critics: Adult values, children's responses, postmodern picture books, and *Arlene Sardine. Journal of Children's Literature, 30* (1), 31–37.

Connor, J. J. (2003). "The textbooks never said anything about . . .": Adolescents respond to *The Middle Passage: White ships/black cargo. Journal of Adolescent and Adult Literacy, 47* (3), 240–246.

Connor, J. J. (2004, October). *Seeking "free spaces unbound": Six "mixed" female adolescents transact with literature depicting biracial characters*. Unpublished doctoral dissertation, University of Illinois, Urbana-Champaign.

Cullinan, B. E., Harwood, K. T., & Galda, L. (1983). The reader and the story: Comprehension and response. *Journal of Research and Development in Education, 16,* 29–37.

Daniels, H. (2002). *Literature circles: Voice and choice in book clubs and reading groups* (2nd ed.). Portland, ME: Stenhouse.

Dressel, J. H. (2005). Personal response and social responsibility: Responses of middle school students to multicultural literature. *The Reading Teacher, 58,* 750–764.

Galda, L. (1982). Assuming the spectator stance: An examination of the response of three young readers. *Research in the Teaching of English, 16,* 1–20.

Galda, L., & Liang, L. A. (2003). Literature as experience or looking for facts: Stance in the classroom. *Reading Research Quarterly, 38* (2), 268–275.

Goldstone, B. P. (2002). Whaz up with our book? Changing picture book codes and teaching implications. *The Reading Teacher, 55* (4), 362–370.

Griffin, S. L. (2006, March). *It's the thought that counts: The portrayal of problem solving in children's literature*. Unpublished doctoral dissertation, University of Wyoming, Laramie.

Hancock, M. R. (1993). Exploring the meaning-making process through the content of literature response journals. *Research in the Teaching of English, 27,* 335–368.

Hancock, M. R. (2000, July 11). *Reader response to literature: Retrospective reflection and the promise of future inquiry*. Paper presented at the International Reading Association's 18th World Congress of Reading, Auckland, New Zealand.

Hickman, J. (1981). A new perspective on response to literature: Research in an elementary school setting. *Research in the Teaching of English, 15,* 343–354.

Hill, B. C., Johnson, N. J., & Schlick Noe (Eds.). (1995). *Literature circles and response*. Norwood, MA: Christopher-Gordon.

International Reading Association (IRA) & National Council of Teachers of English (NCTE). (1996). *Standards for the English language arts*. Newark, DE: Authors.

Kiefer, B. Z. (1983). The responses of children in a combination first/second grade classroom to picture books in a variety of artistic styles. *Journal of Research and Development in Education, 16,* 14–20.

Lehr, S., & Thompson, D. L. (2000). The dynamic nature of response: Children reading and responding to *Maniac Magee* and *The friendship*. *The Reading Teacher, 53,* 480–493.

Lohfink, G. (2006, April). *Responses to postmodern picture books: A case study of a fourth-grade book club*. Unpublished doctoral dissertation, Kansas State University, Manhattan.

Long, T. W., & Gove, M. K. (2003). How engagement strategies and literature circles promote critical response in a fourth-grade urban classroom. *The Reading Teacher, 57,* 350–361.

Louie, B. Y. (2005). Development of empathetic responses with multicultural literature. *Journal of Adolescent & Adult Literacy, 48,* 566–578.

Maduram, I. (2000). "Playing possum": A young child's responses to information books. *Language Arts, 60,* 202–209.

Malloch, B. (2002). Scaffolding student talk: One teacher's role in literature discussion groups. *Reading Research Quarterly, 37,* 94–112.

Malloch, B. (2004). One teacher's journey: Transitioning into literature discussion groups. *Language Arts, 81* (4), 312–322.

Many, J. E. (1991). The effects of stance and age level on children's literary responses. *Journal of Reading Behavior, 23,* 61–85.

McLaughlin, M., & DeVoogd, G. (2004). Critical literacy as comprehension: Expanding reader response. *Journal of Adolescent & Adult Literacy, 48* (1), 52–62.

Miller, T. D. (2003, September). *Literature discussion groups respond to culturally relevant children's literature in a kindergarten classroom.* Unpublished doctoral dissertation, University of Pennsylvania, Philadelphia.

Mills, H., Stephens, D., O'Keefe, T., & Waugh, J. R. (2004). Theory in practice: The legacy of Louise Rosenblatt. *Language Arts, 82* (1), 47–55.

Pantaleo, S. (2002). Grade 1 students meet David Wiesner's *Three pigs. Journal of Children's Literature, 28* (2), 72–84.

Pantaleo, S. (2003). "Godzilla lives in New York": Grade 1 students and the peritextual features of picture books. *Journal of Children's Literature, 29* (2), 66-77.

Pantaleo, S. (2004). Young children and radical change characteristics in picture books. *The Reading Teacher, 58* (2), 178–187.

Pappas, C. C. (2006). The information book genre: Its role in integrated science literacy research and practice. *Reading Research Quarterly, 41* (2), 226–250.

Porter, D. (2006, July). *Oral and written responses of sixth graders to interactive read-alouds of Orbis Pictus Award nonfiction in a curricular setting.* Unpublished doctoral dissertation, Kansas State University, Manhattan.

Quiroa, R. E. (2005, May). *Literature as mirror: Analyzing the oral, written, and artistic responses of young Mexican-origin children to Mexican-American-themed picture storybooks.* Unpublished doctoral dissertation, University of Illinois, Urbana-Champaign.

Raphael, T. E., Florio-Ruane, S., George, M., Hasty, N. L., & Highfield, K. (2004). *Book club plus! A literacy framework for the primary grades.* Lawrence, MA: Small Planet Communications.

Roller, C. M., & Beed, P. L. (1994). Sometimes the conversations were grand, and sometimes . . . *Language Arts, 71,* 509–517.

Rosenblatt, L. M. (1938). *Literature as exploration.* New York: Appleton-Century-Crofts.

Rosenblatt, L. M. (1978). *The reader, the text, the poem: The transactional theory of the literary work.* Carbondale, IL: Southern Illinois University Press.

Serafini, F. (2005). Voices in the park, voices in the classroom: Readers responding to postmodern picture books. *Reading Research and Instruction, 44* (3), 47–64.

Shine, S., & Roser, N. L. (1999). The role of genre in preschoolers' response to picture books. *Research in the Teaching of English, 34,* 197–251.

Short, K., Kauffman, G., & Kahn, L. (2000). "I just need to draw": Responding to literature across multiple sign systems. *The Reading Teacher, 54* (2), 160–171.

Short, K., Kauffman, G., Kaser, S., Kahn, L, & Crawford, K. (1999). Teacher watching: Examining teacher talk in literature circles. *Language Arts, 76,* 377–385.

Sipe, L. R. (2000). The construction of literary understanding by first and second graders in oral response to picture storybook read-alouds. *Reading Research Quarterly, 35,* 252–275.

Sipe, L. R. (2002). Talking back and taking over: Young children's expressive engagement during storybook read-alouds. *The Reading Teacher, 55* (5), 476–483.

Sipe, L. R., & Bauer, J. (2001). Urban kindergarteners' literary understanding of picture storybooks. *The New Advocate, 14* (4), 329–342.

Styles, M., & Arizpe, E. (2001). A gorilla with "grandpa's eyes": How children interpret visual texts—A case study of Anthony Browne's *Zoo. Children's Literature in Education, 30* (4), 261–281.

Tower, C. (2002). "It's a snake, you guys!": The power of text characteristics on children's responses to information books. *Research in the Teaching of English, 37,* 55–88.

Whitin, P. (1996). Exploring visual response to literature. *Research in the Teaching of English, 30,* 114–140.

Whitin, P. (2005). The interplay of text, talk, and visual representation in expanding literary interpretation. *Research in the Teaching of English, 39,* 365–397.

Wollman-Bonilla, J. E., & Werchaldo, B. (1995). Literature response journals in a first-grade classroom. *Language Arts, 72,* 562–570.

Children's Books

Avi. (2002). *Crispin: The cross of lead.* New York: Hyperion Books.

Brett, J. (1989). *The mitten: A Ukrainian folktale.* New York: Putnam.

Browne, A. (1997). *Willy the dreamer.* Cambridge, MA: Candlewick Press.

Bunting, E. (1991). *Fly away home* (M. Wimmer, Illus.). New York: Clarion Books.

Bunting, E. (1994). *Smoky night* (D. Diaz, Illus.). San Diego: Harcourt.

Coles, R. (1995). *The story of Ruby Bridges.* New York: Scholastic.

Dorris, M. (1999). *Morning girl.* New York: Hyperion Books.

Egielski, R. (1997). *The gingerbread boy.* New York: HarperCollins.

Feelings, T. (1995). *The Middle Passage: White ships/black cargo.* New York: Dial.

Feng, J. (1995). *Let one hundred flowers bloom.* New York: Viking Press.

Fleischman, P. (1993). *Bull Run.* New York: HarperCollins.

Fowler, A. (1991). *Please don't feed the bears.* Chicago: Children's Press.

Galdone, P. (1979). *The gingerbread boy.* Boston: Houghton Mifflin.

Garland, S. (1993). *Shadow of the dragon.* San Diego: Harcourt.

Glaser, L. (1992). *Wonderful worms* (L. Kurpinski, Illus.). Brookfield, CT: Millbrook Press.

Hesse, K. (2001). *Witness.* New York: Scholastic.

Lester, J. (1994). *John Henry* (J. Pinkney, Illus.). New York: Dial.

Lionni, L. (1987). *Swimmy.* New York: Knopf.

Lowry, L. (1989). *Number the stars.* Boston: Houghton Mifflin.

Macauley, D. (1995). *Shortcut.* Boston: Houghton Mifflin.

MacLachlan, P. (1985). *Sarah, plain and tall.* New York: HarperCollins.

Myers, W. D. (1993). *Scorpions.* San Diego: Harcourt.

Naidoo, B. (2000). *The other side of truth.* New York: HarperCollins.

Raschka, C. (1998). *Arlene sardine.* New York: Scholastic.

Reid, M. E. (1996). *Let's find out about ice cream.* New York: Scholastic.

Spinelli, J. (1990). *Maniac Magee.* New York: HarperCollins.

Staples, S. F. (1989). *Shabanu: Daughter of the wind.* New York: Knopf.

Taylor, M. (1975). *Song of the trees.* New York: Dell.

Taylor, M. (1987a). *The friendship.* New York: Dial.

Taylor, M. (1987b). *The gold Cadillac.* New York: Dial.

Wiesner, D. (1991). *Tuesday.* New York: Clarion Books.

Wiesner, D. (2001). *The three pigs.* New York: Clarion Books.

Yolen, J. (1996). *Encounter.* San Diego: Harcourt.

Part
II

Issues of Diversity and Authentic Voice

Some Thoughts on Writing About Native Americans for Young Readers

Joseph Bruchac

First, a word on terms: I'll be using *American Indian* and *Native American* interchangeably throughout this essay. There are several reasons for this. One is that both terms are English and are equally representative—or unrepresentative—of the ways in which the original tribal nations of what is now the United States view themselves. It is true that the word *Indian* comes from the misunderstanding that the Americas were part of South Asia, and with the increasing number of South Asian citizens, we now have both Indian Americans and American Indians; it can be confusing. However, a *native American* (usually spelled with a small *n*) refers to any person born in North America—or South America—regardless of their racial background. In fact, there was a native American anti-immigration movement a century ago that defined native Americans as northern and western European White people born in this country.

More than 300 languages were spoken by the various tribal nations within the United States. Every Native people has its own word for itself, usually a word meaning "human beings." Among my own Abenaki people, that word is *alnobak*. However, after centuries of use, the terms *Indian* and *American Indian* have become both familiar and widely accepted by Indians, especially in the pan-tribal context. *Indian* also can be found in the U.S. Constitution and in the many treaties that have been the law of the land. Although most indigenous Americans refer to themselves first by their tribal background—such as Lakota or Dine' or Haudenosaunee—they also call themselves Indians, and they do so much more than they refer to themselves as Native Americans. Consider the fact that the two most popular pan-Indian newspapers are called *News From Indian Country* and *Indian Country News* and that with the blessing of this country's many tribal nations, the new museum in Washington that is devoted to representing the indigenous nations of the Western Hemisphere as they wish to be represented is named the National Museum of the American Indian.

Also, consider the fact that most non-Indians who have written books about Indians are unaware of what I've just passed on to you in these first paragraphs.

Few subjects have captured the imagination of those who write for young readers as much as the American Indian. As a result, there have been countless books written about Native Americans for young readers. The vast majority of those titles are still by non-Native authors. Most of them, to a greater or lesser degree, are flawed. Some are even worse than that; they are filled with inaccuracies and racist depictions. I am not, I must add, talking about the past. More than a few books published within the last two decades are among the worst offenders.

Why have Indians so captured the imagination of children's writers? Indian stories have been popular for centuries in the United States. Some of the best-selling books of the 18th and 19th centuries were the "captivity narratives," first-person stories of White men and women who were taken prisoner by Native Americans (first in the northeast and then in the west), living among these strange people for a time before being "redeemed" and returned to "civilized society." Indians were the subjects of the first motion pictures, and it is impossible to have any knowledge of American television or cinema without encountering thousands of depictions of Indian life, often from the point of view of a White person among the tribes—the *Dances With Wolves* paradigm. Imagined Indians have now become so much a part of the mythology of this continent that many people think they can understand Native Americans simply by being Americans. Furthermore, if they are writers who are sympathetic to the Indians' plight and they read a few books, they can not only write about Native Americans, they can more or less "be" Indian. Thus we end up with not captivity narratives but captured narratives, White writers literally "playing Indian."

Ironically, that so-called sympathy often gets in the way of seeing Native Americans as real human beings and not as figures from the collective unconscious. These writers imagine the poker-faced noble Indian, the ecological Indian who instinctively knows how to live in balance with nature, the vanishing Red man riding over the hill with head bowed. However, they've never met a modern Native American, they do not know any of our languages, and, in fact, when they picture an Indian in their mind, their vision is almost always that of a 19th-century Lakota warrior on horseback with a tipi and a herd of buffalo in the background.

Some writers think that they know Indians so well that they don't even have to do research. They write about a "generic" or "homogenized" Indian.

It's easy to spot this kind of writing—books in which the descriptions and the illustrations depict Plains Indians in birch-bark canoes or northeastern Native peoples with Plains headdresses and buffalo-skin tipis. For images of this sort, turn to the popular but very inaccurate picture book *Brother Eagle, Sister Sky* (Jeffers, 1991). Even the title betrays the author's lack of understanding of our cultures. The sky is invariably associated with the masculine force, and earth with the feminine. The text is based on a famous speech given by Chief Seattle, but even the text that was chosen is questionable—especially when one considers the images with which it is paired. The book also begins and ends with Indians pictured as ghostly figures—implying that they are all long departed and the day of the Red man is gone. Such books always seem to keep Indians in the past, like insects caught in amber, relegating the Native American experience to a status of picturesque extinction like the vanished herds of buffalo and the great flocks of passenger pigeons. For every book that gives any clear picture of American Indians surviving the 19th century, there are dozens that make it seem as if American Indian existence ended after Geronimo's final surrender in 1886.

In fact, placing the Native American in a time capsule is the usual approach in works "about Indians" by writers who have apparently done most of their research in their local library or, these days, online. These writers either immerse themselves so deeply in the past that they fail to register the existence of living American Indians, or they seem to think that those who know the most about "real" Native Americans are not the direct descendants of those famous figures they've written about. The results are that the same misinformation keeps getting recycled.

Since this is a brief essay, I'm not going to spend my time critiquing a long list of books that are prime examples of bad (in the sense of being misleading, stereotyped, or inaccurate) writing about Native Americans for younger readers. Anyone who wishes to know more can go to either of two excellent texts that deal with these issues: *Through Indian Eyes* (1998) and *A Broken Flute* (2005), both edited by Doris Seale and Beverly Slapin.

I would, however, like to bring in a book that disturbed me greatly when it was published and that is the subject of several incisive essays in *A Broken Flute*. That book, *My Heart Is on the Ground* by Ann Rinaldi (1999), is extremely useful as an example of what a writer should *not* do when writing about other cultures. Although it was conceived as the fictional journal of a late 19th-century Lakota child at the famous U.S. Indian Industrial School in Carlisle, Pennsylvania, it contains numerous errors about not only Lakota history and culture but also everyday life and events at the Carlisle Indian School itself. The author clearly did some research and even visited the school, but she did not take advantage of any number of scholars—Native and non-Native alike—who could have read her manuscript and helped to correct her errors. For one thing, they could have told her that naming her characters for real students who died and were buried in the Carlisle graveyard was incredibly insensitive, to the point of being sacrilegious. Then, perhaps, she might not have excused herself in her afterword by saying that she was certain that "in whatever happy Hunting Ground they were," those deceased students approved of her theft of their names.

Perhaps I am being naive in assuming that she would have listened to such criticism. A few years ago I was asked to read the manuscript of a novel by another author with a long history of imagining Indians—Lynn Reid Banks. Supposedly, the author wanted to avoid some of the errors she'd been criticized for in her earlier books, including *The Indian in the Cupboard* (1980). I declined, but my sister, Margaret Bruchac, whose specialty is that period of New England history, took on the task. She read *The Key to the Indian* (Banks, 1998) and wrote a long, detailed, and helpful response to the manuscript, pointing out dozens of errors—not only in the history and portrayal of the Native American characters, but also in the British author's depictions of White colonial life. Marge even offered suggestions on how some changes could easily be made. Instead of being grateful, Banks was outraged. She wrote back an angry letter accusing my sister of "failing to respect an elder." She refused to change a word. Her vision of her book was more important to her than mere facts.

There are, fortunately, a number of excellent writers who are succeeding in presenting authentic stories of our past and a present that contains hope for the future. Although all of them are American Indians, I do not believe that only Native Americans can write good books about Indians. However, most non-Natives do not seem to have either the patience or the interest in investing the kind of time—and I am speaking of decades, not months—necessary to gain the deep understanding that is needed.

Several of those are authors who first gained attention as writers of adult fiction. The first—now, sadly, deceased—was Michael Dorris (Modoc). His several young adult novels portrayed history through the first-person narratives of Native children whose voices were intelligent and whose experiences were accurately rendered. His books were also not lacking in that one element that so many books about Indians by non-Native writers lack: a sense of humor.

Louise Erdrich (Turtle Mountain Chippewa) has written and illustrated novels and picture books, such as *The Birchbark House* (1999), that have gained critical acclaim and delighted young readers. One of the best of the younger generation of American Indian authors, Sherman Alexie, is also now writing for kids. I believe that an understanding of the need for good books about our people and their own experiences as parents led those authors to their new roles.

Two other Native authors whose work excites me are Cynthia Leitich Smith (Creek) and Tim Tingle (Choctaw). Tingle is a professional storyteller and thus really understands the narrative voice. His *Crossing Bok Chitto* (2006) is a moving tale about the Trail of Tears. Cynthia Leitich

Smith is primarily a children's writer. Her books include *Rain Is Not My Indian Name* (2001) and *The Jingle Dancer* (2000). Both titles are that rarest of commodities in Native American literature for children: stories about present-day Native American kids. Tingle and Smith are examples of the new wave of Native Americans writing for children, authors who are sharing what they know and doing so with accurate and excellent writing.

What I would like to do now—and I hope that the reader will not think me vain in doing so—is to talk a little bit about one of my own experiences as a Native author writing for young people. I want to do so in particular because it shows that just "being Indian" is not enough when one wishes to write with integrity and honesty about our many and diverse cultures and histories.

I recently completed a novel entitled *Geronimo* (2006a). It tells the story of the Chiricahua Apache Geronimo (or Goyathlay), who still is one of the most famous of all Native Americans. I decided to tell his story from the viewpoint of an Apache boy who views Geronimo as his grandfather. Because I am not Apache, but a person of northeastern Native descent, I knew I had to do a lot of work if I hoped to get it right. That meant research—but not just by going to the library. The deepest research that I did for the story began not with my signing of the book contract with Scholastic Publishing 2 years before its publication, but more than 30 years ago. That was when I first heard stories about Geronimo and that period of southwestern American Indian history from such Apache and Pueblo elders as my friend Swift Eagle. Over the course of many years I traveled to the parts of the country where Geronimo's story took place—not just the mountains and deserts of the southwest, but also those places in Oklahoma, Florida, and Alabama where the old man was held captive by the U.S. Army.

Because I was trying to write from a Chiricahua viewpoint, I studied the Chiricahua language. I corresponded with contemporary Chiricahua Apache historians and sent them drafts of my manuscript. Whenever someone offered a suggestion, I took it. For example, Michael Darrow, tribal historian of the Fort Sill Apaches, pointed out to me that there is no word for *warrior* in Chiricahua. He explained that certain words, frequently used by most authors when referring to Geronimo and other Chiricahuas of the period, were culturally inaccurate and insulting to Chiricahuas. *Raider* and *renegade* are two examples. As a result, those words did not appear in my novel.

However, I did go into detail about the fact that even in the 1880s Chiricahuas were being taken as slaves by both the Mexicans and the New Mexicans, who hunted Apaches as if they were wild animals. It was common for peaceful Apaches to be attacked by Mexicans who first pretended to be their friends. Geronimo's mother, his first wife, and all their children were killed in such a massacre. Those bitter experiences of tragedy and betrayal make it understandable that he and other Chiricahua men fought with such determination for so long.

The result of all this is that my portrayal of Geronimo ended up being at odds with almost every other book ever written about him for young readers. Rather than seeing Geronimo as a ruthless killer or a noble savage, I had learned to see him as a complex man who loved his family, tried to protect his people, and yet was also a truly clever survivor who always was quick to find a way to turn any situation to his advantage—even when he was being held as a prisoner of war for the last 23 years of his life.

I haven't done my work alone. Any success I've enjoyed with the various novels I've written about events and people out of Native history is due in large part to the help I've been given by individuals from the tribal nations on which I've focused. When I wrote my novel *Sacajawea* (2000) about the Lewis and Clark expedition, I turned to Wayland Large, the tribal historian of the Wind River Shoshone. In writing *Code Talker* (2004), a novel about the Dine' (or Navajo) marines who created an unbreakable code using their own language during World War II, my manuscript was read not only by such Dine' elders as Keith Little, himself a code talker, but also by my friend Harry Walters, the director of the Dine College Museum. Although he himself is Navajo, Harry also had the manuscript read by another elder to make sure that the many words in Dine' in the book were properly spelled and correctly used.

There is an old tribal tradition of not just asking for help from an expert but also getting that help from more than one individual. Other authors have observed this. When John Neihardt was writing down the story of the Lakota medicine man Black Elk, Black Elk told his story in the presence of other elders who had been there during the events of his life and could step in to either add details or correct what he said. I've tried to follow this tradition whenever I can. I did so in my recent writing of a novel (2006b) in the first-person voice about Jim Thorpe, the American Indian who won the Olympics and was named the greatest athlete of the 20th century. I listened to the stories that many people had to tell about Jim.

I'm doing even more of this right now because I'm working with a documentary filmmaker on a public television show about Jim Thorpe's life. Over the past few months I've interviewed his children, his grandchildren, and many others—both Native and non-Native—who have been deeply connected with Jim Thorpe. Often they have told the same stories, but from different points of view, so that makes it easier to see the whole. Through listening to many voices so intimately connected to him, as well as reading the written record, which included much that Jim Thorpe had to say about himself over the course of his life, I believe that I was able to come close to finding a narrative voice that was close to Jim's own.

I am amazed that more authors have not taken this approach: simply asking living people for help when you are writing about their ancestors, their relatives, their tribal members. The worst that can happen is that they will say no when you ask for that help. (Well, let me take that back. The *worst* that can happen is that people do offer you that help and then you don't listen to them, à la Lynn Reid Banks.) I am not talking just about Indians. It is not only American Indians who follow the tradition of looking at their history through more than one person's point of view. In 1992, when my son Jim and I were in Mali, West Africa, collecting traditional stories from the Dogon people in the village of Tirali, not one but two village elders sat with us to relate certain important and sacred histories. Whenever Meninyu paused, Asama would either agree or add something, or vice versa. That kind of sharing of history and seeking of consensus is one reason I believe that oral history can be just as accurate as written history—and sometimes more so. It is also why it has always been so important for me to listen, listen, and then listen some more, and to advise others to do the same.

What I hope I achieved in *Jim Thorpe*, in *Code Talker*, and in *Geronimo* is what I aim for as an author and what always attracts me to all good writing—an authentic and interesting voice, the feeling of being taken into the confidence of a living person. What I strive for in my own work and hope for in the writing of others who tell stories of our Native cultures is the patience and the ability to listen and learn, which will make it possible to do the following necessary things: avoid the traps of an imagined past, unbind our captured histories, and see the present through free eyes.

Children's Books

Banks, L. R. (1980). *The Indian in the cupboard.* New York: Avon Books.

Banks, L. R. (1998). *The key to the Indian.* New York: Avon Books.

Bruchac, J. (2000). *Sacajawea.* New York: Harcourt.

Bruchac, J. (2004). *Code talker.* New York: Dial.

Bruchac, J. (2006a). *Geronimo.* New York: Scholastic.

Bruchac, J. (2006b). *Jim Thorpe: Original All-American.* New York: Dial.

Erdrich, L. (1999). *The birchbark house.* New York: Hyperion Books.

Jeffers, S. (1991). *Brother eagle, sister sky.* New York: Dial.

Rinaldi, A. (1999). *My heart is on the ground: The diary of Nannie Little Rose, a Sioux girl.* New York: Scholastic.

Seale, D., & Slapin, B. (Eds.). (1998). *Through Indian eyes: The native experience in books for children.* Los Angeles: American Indian Studies Center.

Seale, D., & Slapin, B. (Eds.). (2005). *A broken flute: The native experience in books for children.* Walnut Creek, CA: AltaMira Press.

Smith, C. L. (2000). *Jingle dancer.* New York: Morrow.

Smith, C. L. (2001). *Rain is not my Indian name.* New York: HarperCollins.

Tingle, T. (2006). *Crossing Bok Chitto.* El Paso, TX: Cinco Puntos.

Chapter 8

Embodiment and Discourse
in Fiction for Girls

Linda Wedwick and
Roberta Seelinger Trites

Some poststructural theorists, such as Judith Butler (1990), have written about the human body—especially gender—as a discursive construct; that is, as something that is defined more by a culture and its language than by biological considerations. Although many academics might well be prepared to understand how powerfully language affects our perceptions of our bodies, most children and adolescents are unlikely to think of their bodies in those terms. No amount of theorizing is ever going to make a schoolchild believe that the physical signs of maturation—acne, growing breasts (or not), increased hairiness (or not), voice changes, growth, menstruation, or sexuality—are defined by language rather than by biology. Schoolchildren in the middle grades understand that teenagers undergo puberty, regardless of the culture—and even regardless of the presence of language. How children learn to view their bodies is entirely influenced by discourse, but their bodies are not, in and of themselves, constructed by language. As the French philosopher Maurice Merleau-Ponty (1945/1962) observes, the Cartesian tendency in Western culture to split mind from body as if they were separate entities is a spurious distinction. Embodiment, those aspects of humanity that are physical, cannot exist separately from the mind, just as all languages require bodies to comprehend and communicate them.

On the other hand, the depiction of human bodies in literature is entirely a matter of language—since *everything* in literature is, obviously, constructed from language. There is no human body in literature that exists without words defining it. Thus, to study embodiment in literature creates an odd conjunction of language and body, culture and biology, all of which are terms that have concerned feminist for years. If embodiment is defined as those aspects of our selfhood that we understand to be rooted in the physical biology of the body, it follows that in literary studies, embodiment involves discursive depictions of human bodies as constructs of language and culture. Such discussions of literary depictions of embodiment in youth literature are usually part of the ongoing feminist dialogue about the relationship between adolescents' perceptions of their physical bodies and their socially constructed self-images.

For example, studies of adolescents and preadolescents demonstrate clearly that embodiment is influenced by social bias. Rice (2000) investigated the gendered frame of reference of sixth-grade boys and girls "by examining the bias in their memories of a 'feminist' folktale that included male and female characters with both traditional and nontraditional traits" (p. 211). After 1 month, girls included more of the nontraditional traits in their recall of the folktale than boys did; however, both boys and girls transformed the physical description of the main character. In the original story, Maru-me is described as round and fat. In their recall, however, the students either deleted these descriptions of Maru-me or they changed them to "fit with their cultural values, such as 'beautiful'" (p. 226). Rice's study reveals two things: how individuals' perceptions of embodiment are linked to their culture's values and how young readers can be vulnerable to misinterpreting or reorganizing their memory of literary discourses about embodiment.

Another study investigates how children's exposure to issues of embodiment can negatively affect their own self-image. Kuther and McDonald (2004) show that both boys and girls identify Barbie dolls—those ultimate icons of American femininity—as damaging to girls' sense of their own embodiment. As one male respondent wrote, "Barbie is not the best toy for girls because . . . Barbie has . . . the perfect style and body, so that other girls would feel they want that, too. . . . girls would just try to lose weight and everything and forget about the importance of life" (p. 48). Female respondents wrote similar statements: "Barbie has this perfect body and now every girl is trying to have her body because they are so unhappy with themselves" and "I think she is too thin and does not show the best example for young kids" (p. 48). Other girls responded, "They should make a fat one" or "They are all so skinny and that's mean to fat people" (p. 43). The middle school students in this study understand that there is cause and effect between what children are exposed to and what they internalize in terms of gender and body image. Like these children, we share a concern with the effect of discourses about the "perfect" female body, especially on girls. *Perfect*, after all, implies that one is both thin and physically abled.

Because girl readers are taught to identify with female characters and boys are taught to identify with male characters, female readers are particularly at risk of internalizing negative messages about body image and the importance of some impossible standard called perfection. As Perry Nodelman (1977) observed 30 years ago in an article that still rings true today, nothing in our current cultural practice is motivating children to ignore gender identification in their reading. Susan Lehr (2001) also discusses children's literacies as a function of their gender socialization, noting that "society ensures its own continuance within existing social structures that separate and stratify groups based on gender, ethnicity, and economic position" (p. 2). She argues cogently that girls are shortchanged in their educations by cultural expectations, by teachers who reinforce gendered behaviors, by the language choices that children and educators use, and by the ways that children are socialized to think of their literacies as circumscribed by a matrix of gender and genre.

Girls who have been taught from very early ages to identify with female characters in books—a process that is reinforced when they are overwhelmingly exposed to toys that are gendered female, such as Barbie, Bratz, and Polly Pocket—are not suddenly, in middle school, going to start identifying with male characters in novels or disidentifying with the bodies of the female characters about whom they read. Girls have been taught to read books as they read their toys and other cultural artifacts: to find images that they can identify with and emulate. Thus, physical embodiment is depicted in the literature that children in the middle grades read in ways that are highly gendered, especially within those books in which physical imperfection plays a major role.

Since girls are particularly vulnerable to perfectionism regarding their bodies, the focus of this essay involves two aspects of embodiment that manipulate notions of what is perfect and what is not: weight and physical ability. We focus herein on books that are marketed to female readers in the hope of raising awareness about the issues that surround literary depictions of embodiment.

Thus, we will explore three related concepts to demonstrate the relationship between female embodiment and gender in novels written for an audience of middle-grade readers: (a) embodiment as it is constructed by language; (b) weight and ability as aspects of embodiment that are often tied to personal choice; and (c) embodiment as an aspect of abjection—that is, as a form of social ostracism in which a character's scapegoating allows for other people's redemption.

Understanding these three concepts depends on reading strategies that focus on analyzing such discursive constructs as ideologies, metaphors, and characterizations. We have included here six novels that we think usefully demonstrate embodiment in terms of discursive language, choice, and abjection. All the novels have female protagonists and are targeted to the middle grades: readers who are 9 to 14 years old. We have chosen three novels that focus on weight as a factor of embodiment and three that focus on physical ability. Although many novels participate in negative discourses about ideals of physical perfection, these six novels are particularly useful in demonstrating how all these manifestations of embodiment work together to socialize readers into gendered perceptions of embodiment. First we will discuss novels about weight; then we will discuss novels about physical ability. Finally, we will synthesize the discursive similarities between novels about weight and ability. A glossary of terms appears at the end of the chapter.

Fat Is a Choice. Really?

In Cherie Bennett's *Life in the Fat Lane* (1998), Joan Bauer's *Squashed* (2001), and Judy Blume's *Blubber* (1974), the language that constructs the overweight female character relies on character self-descriptions, narrator descriptions, and descriptions from other characters, who might taunt or victimize the fat person. Alternatively, she might be self-deprecating because she believes she is imperfect. Each novel presents the reasons for fatness differently: In one, fatness is caused by a fictitious metabolic disease; in another, by emotional distress; and in the third, by overeating. However, the discourse that valorizes thinness as a cultural value persists.

Even though there are numerous etiological factors that contribute to fatness, most authors for youth share a perception that body size is merely a choice. For example, a recent sampling of novels for youth with fat characters estimates that 83 percent of those texts depict fat as something that characters choose—as something that they can change if they are only strong-willed enough or self-actualized enough or motivated enough to do so (Wedwick 2005). What word could possibly be more evocative of the feminist movement than *choice*, since that has been our rallying cry for so long? As feminists, we equate choice with power. Even though human beings do not often have power over their own embodiment, fat female characters are regularly depicted as having a power over their bodies that they are simply unaware of, and they only need to be reminded to enact this power. Thus, studying weight issues in novels for the middle grades is a particularly apt place to demonstrate how the discourse of human embodiment is often both gendered and stereotyped, even by authors with the best of intentions.

Although the physical process of maturation, genetics, overeating, and emotional distress are proven etiological factors for body size, novels for middle-grade readers take a complicated set of factors and reduce them to a simple binary that fat is a choice or not. Adolescent novels with overweight characters tend to validate the belief that the reasons for fatness are irrelevant because fat people are imperfect, no matter what (Wedwick, 2005). Even in novels that attempt to explain how fatness can be beyond the control of the individual, the author's underlying assumptions still participate in the dominant cultural values placed on thinness.

Bennett's (1998) *Life in the Fat Lane* attempts to explain how fatness can be beyond the control of the individual. Unfortunately, the novel's mixed ideological messages about fatness will leave middle school readers believing that fatness is more about choice than etiology. The novel sets up embodiment as a binary opposition that most of us know to be false: Bennett implies that people are either thin or fat.

Lara Ardeche is the protagonist, who takes the reader into the worlds of thin and fat people—and their worlds in this novel are very segregated. Lara is perfect—a popular, former beauty pageant winner—until she develops a fictional metabolic disorder called Axell-Crowne Syndrome. This disease causes Lara to gain a large amount of weight in a short amount of time. Axell-Crowne is in direct opposition to what we typically believe about food consumption: For people with Axell-Crowne, "the less they eat, the more efficient their bodies are, so they actually gain more weight by ingesting less food" (p. 110). Lara begins the novel at 5 feet 7 inches tall and weighing 118 pounds (which is underweight according to the Body Mass Index chart), and she gains 100 pounds in about 7 months. The fact that Axell-Crowne is a fictional disease is significant because all the other fat characters in *Life in the Fat Lane* are fat only because they overeat—and there are many more of them: Molly, Molly's mom, Patty Asher, Perry, Suzanne, and Cleo. In an interview with Smith (n.d.), Bennett explains that she wanted to focus more on the *what* of fatness rather than the *why* because people make assumptions about a fat person when all they know is that the person looks fat.

Although Bennett might believe that she is sending a message to girls not to obsess about their bodies, all she really succeeds in doing is preying on their fear of being fat. As a fat person, Lara feels isolated and ridiculed in every public setting she experiences, and she discovers that "fat is fat," regardless of what causes it (p. 205). People just don't care about the reason she is overweight. Although Lara's ultimate lesson is to conclude that being thin "wasn't *everything* anymore" (p. 260), this epiphany immediately follows the declaration that Lara "long[s] to be thin . . . So much" (p. 259). With Lara's final thoughts, the reader knows that Lara's disease is in remission, and she could very likely return to her starting weight of 118 pounds. So if thin isn't everything, why is Lara being rewarded with it in the novel's denouement? The ideology deconstructs itself.

In *Squashed* (Bauer, 2001), Ellie Morgan is a 16-year-old girl in a small Iowa town who grows giant pumpkins in her backyard. Ellie is 5 feet 7 inches tall, and her weight fluctuates between 140 and 147 pounds throughout the novel. According to the Body Mass Index charts, both 140 and 147 fall within the normal weight range. Nevertheless, Ellie describes herself as "pudgy" (pp. 5, 9), "round" (p. 8), and 20 pounds overweight (p. 5). Ellie's dad believes that "being overweight keeps [Ellie] from discovering [her] true potential" (p. 3). He is anxious for Ellie to lose weight and offers to help her with dieting because he has had his own "battle with weight" (p. 10).

As a motivational speaker, Ellie's dad "specializes in difficult cases, which is why he holds out hope for [Ellie]" (p. 4). Ellie's father, then, sets the expectation for ideal body weight, and Ellie finds herself unable to meet this standard.

Ellie is in a perpetual state of body dissatisfaction, setting unrealistic goals for her own body weight and conveying a distorted body image to the reader. When Ellie does not state her actual weight, the reader can infer Ellie's weight based on what she wears. Ellie describes a pair of khaki pants that do not fit if she is above 140 pounds (p. 36). Ellie feels "thin and stunning" (p. 40) in these pants and mentions having them on at the beginning, middle, and end of the novel (pp. 45, 108, 161). However, Ellie never experiences body satisfaction, believing that she is overweight and that it is necessary to diet throughout the novel. For Ellie, even at 140 pounds she is still not perfect and has 20 pounds to lose. But if Ellie weighed 120, she would fall on the border of being underweight on the Body Mass Index chart.

The underlying ideology, then, suggests that normal body weight might not be thin enough for a female. If it weren't for Ellie's continual food indulgences, dieting, and narrative reminders that she needs to lose pounds, the reader might believe that Ellie is experiencing normal development. Perhaps the only real purpose for developing Ellie as a fat character is to compare her to the giant pumpkin, Max. While caring for Max, Ellie beams "healthy, fat thoughts through his vine" (p. 33). Later, Ellie draws her own comparison: "I weighed 144 pounds and was dreaming about chocolate chip cheesecake. Max weighed 430 pounds and was dreaming about victory" (p. 40). For Ellie, both her weight and Max's weight are entirely within her control.

It follows logically that if fat people can choose not to be fat, then they have the power to change the victimization that follows from being fat in these novels—and being fat is surely a matter of victimization in novels for the young. The ideology of victimization presents itself discursively in a variety of ways: through character isolation, name-calling, ridicule, self-deprecation (as with Ellie in *Squashed*), or antipathy. Fat characters in children's novels are called an extraordinary number of names—like Blubber, for example—and they are often compared (unfavorably, of course) to animals, such as the whale metaphor inherent in the insulting nickname Blubber, or to food, such as when Ellie compares herself to the giant pumpkins she grows: "They were round, I was round" (Bauer, 2001, p. 8).

In *Blubber* by Judy Blume (1974), Linda Fischer is characterized repeatedly as being victimized by her fifth-grade classmates simply because she is overweight. Nicknamed Blubber because she gives a report about whales, Linda endures both verbal and physical abuse at the hands of her peers. Even Linda's teachers don't believe her when she tries to get help. On board the school bus, a student shouts, "Here comes Blubber!" (p. 8). Then a few boys on the bus make spitballs and "sho[o]t them at Linda" (8). Some of the girls in Linda's class instigate a series of assaults on her: They try to strip her to see the blubber under her cape (p. 33); compel her to say, "I am Blubber, the smelly whale of class 206" (p. 89) before she can use the bathroom, get a drink, eat her lunch, and get on the bus to go home; cause her to vomit by making her eat a chocolate-covered ant; and put her on trial for being a tattletale (p. 129).

All the students get "weighed every fall and again every spring" (p. 77), and Blubber's weigh-in becomes a must-see spectacle for Jill. When Blubber tries to go on a diet, her classmates tell her that her name will always be Blubber. Wendy says that "even if you weigh fifty pounds, you'll still be a smelly whale" (p. 61). Later, Linda's classmates find Linda's weight a source of entertainment as they jump rope to the following rhyme, "Oh, what a riot / Blubber's on a diet / I wonder what's the matter / I think she's getting fatter" (pp. 79–80). Blume's novel is about the evils of bullying—but Linda never has an identity independent from her weight. Her characterization is entirely passive.

Perhaps the most pervasive and insidious experience of the discursively fat character in children's literature is the way that fat characters often serve as a source of amusement or as a catalyst for someone else's growth. Think of Chet in *The Hardy Boys* or Bess in *Nancy Drew*: Both provide comic relief and are more likely to be conduits through which Frank and Joe Hardy or Nancy Drew find information than they are to be crime solvers themselves. When such characters serve as sources of entertainment for the "normal" people in the novel (i.e., the thin people), they are serving in the capacity of a busker, or street entertainer. Blubber's discursive construction as a spectacle in her class demonstrates how fat characters are typecast as buskers in children's literature. These buskeresque characters sometimes serve as performers, sometimes as sources of humor, and sometimes as circus freaks, but in all cases, the authors rely on discourses that validate the practice of objectifying the human body.

Most fat characters hope to avoid becoming the object in the gaze of their peers, but one of two things typically happens: Fat characters see their peers seeing them and experience disgust in the gaze of others, or the fat character becomes symbolically invisible and thus resides in the gaze of no one. Furthermore, the gaze affects fat characters because they are often ridiculed on sight, before they even have an opportunity to use language to engage their own subjectivity, affecting the gaze of the Other to regard them as being more than simply an object. In other words, fat characters in novels for youth might be depicted as being fat by choice, but ideologies, metaphors, and characterizations often create a discourse in which fat characters are depicted as being deprived of the choices required to define their own subjectivity.

Disability Is Disturbing. Really?

With her early work on disability studies, Thomson (1997) defines physical ability as residing more in the domain of minority discourse than in the domain of medical discourse. She makes the point that disabled characters more often serve as foils for White male protagonists in American literature than they do as protagonists themselves (p. 9), a point that Heim made in 1994. Coats (2001) extends Thomson's work, arguing, "Whether disabled characters are seen as shoring up an individual identity or deconstructing the terms of that identity, they remain in the service of something" (p. 16). Disability has a utilitarian function in children's literature—just as obesity does—that almost always resides in an objectification of the human body and that almost always serves a didactic function. Coats (2001) even refers to obesity as "a form of culturally constructed disability" (p. 12), and Gilman (2005) describes the Equal Employment Opportunity Commission, Americans with Disabilities Act, and World Health Organization policies that equate obesity with "impairment" and therefore "disability" (pp. 514–515). Disability's utilitarian function becomes gendered when we recall what Shakespeare and Watson (2001) observe: that disability "sits at the intersection of biology and society . . . agency and structure" (p. 19). Those are certainly some of the terms of feminist engagement with literature: *biology*, *society*, *agency*, and *structure*. Moreover, the ideologies, metaphors, and characterizations of disabled characters frequently construct discourses that depict disability as disturbing, especially in terms of gender.

Cynthia Voigt's (1986) *Izzy Willy Nilly* self-consciously draws the reader's attention to embodiment as something that is defined by objectification and the gaze. The protagonist, nicknamed Izzy, has had one leg amputated after a boy she is dating crashes their car in a drunk-driving incident. Izzy thinks her missing leg makes her look "grotesque," a concept that reinforces her concern about being the object of other people's gaze. She reiterates the phrase three times on one page alone (p. 211). She defines herself as a "cripple" (pp. 54, 98, 270) and as an "amputee" (p. 138), and she observes that "crippled people do make other people nervous" (p. 137). She also draws repeated parallels between herself and her physical therapist, who is African American:

> I saw, out of the corner of my eye, Adelia's bright white uniform and her dark skin. I thought again that she and I had the same kind of problem: Everybody who saw us knew right away what label to use. When Adelia said there wasn't anything to do about it, she knew what she was talking about. (p. 212)

Izzy has adopted this ideological attitude from her best friend, who says, "You know—there are things about the way you look . . . that would be the thing about being black—people see it right away, black skin. . . . If you're black, well, the first thing people see is your skin color. You can't hide it" (p. 138). The same friend tells her:

> The trouble is, you're used to people looking at you and envying you, wishing they were you. You're not used to people looking at you and pitying you and being glad they aren't you. But if you look at it from another angle, they're both the same mistake, because people aren't ever seeing *you*. (p. 241)

In other words, Izzy has been used to thinking of herself as perfect, before her accident. Of course, the envious "people" Izzy's friend is describing are implied as physically abled, White, and—very likely—thin.

In Voigt's (1986) discourse, race and disability are both an "external mark" (p. 182). Izzy understands—rightly or wrongly—that being the object of someone else's gaze is a major factor in how we as a culture define embodiment. She reinforces that by forcing her girlfriend to have a makeover. Girls know that people look at them. Girls know that people pass judgment on them based on how they look. Consciously or not, girls experience this process of being looked at as objectification—that is, as the result of being the object of someone else's regard. That panoptic sense of always being observed—regardless of ability or race or weight—is an almost unavoidable motif in children's literature that deals with embodiment.

The discourse of embodiment in children's literature also relies heavily on animal or plant metaphors that objectify the human body, just as in fictional discourses about weight. Sometimes the use of metaphor is poetic, as when an author such as Virginia Hamilton (1999) writes about embodiment, and sometimes it is forced, as when Bauer (2001) can't quit comparing a young girl's growth to a pumpkin—but such metaphors are as common in the discourse of embodiment as objectification is.

Bluish is Hamilton's (1999) novel about a fifth-grade girl who is recovering from leukemia and whose body has been devastated by chemotherapy. She is wheelchair bound and cannot control her bodily functions: Sometimes she vomits, and at other times she loses bladder control, much to her classmates' horror. Because her skin has turned an odd, blue color, her classmates call her Bluish. Her mother objects to that term because, as she explains, "Blewish" is derogatory New York lingo for people who are Black and Jewish, as Bluish herself is. Bluish's classmates, however, are much more preoccupied by her disability than they are by her ethnicity and religion. Although sometimes they are horrified by Bluish, sometimes they envy her.

For example, she is allowed to hold a puppy during class because it calms her. The puppy is nicknamed Lucky, and he eventually becomes something of a mascot for the whole class, just as Bluish does.

The more important animal metaphor in the novel, however, revolves around the narrator's perception of Bluish as a moth, someone who is fluttery and fragile and associated with moonlight. Dreenie, the narrator, mentions moonlight in connection with Bluish 8 times. Bluish's hands "look like moonlight fishes about to dive and flop off the arms of her wheelchair" (Hamilton, 1999, p. 8); she is "pale, glowing fluttery" (p. 11). Initially, Dreenie fears Bluish's fragility, and she describes her fear through the metaphor of moonlight. She thinks, "Pale moonlight. Scary Bluish" (p. 18) and "Scary sickness, and I was afraid it'd rub off on me. . . . All the moonglow" (p. 38). Dreenie articulates her fear that Bluish's disability is contagious. (Dreenie isn't alone in thinking of disability this way. Izzy, too, has thought of disability "as if her troubles were contagious. As if something would show up on my skin if I said hello" [p. 69].) Dreenie says to her mother, "Moonglow is what . . . what she reminds me of. And . . . and . . . scary-looking? . . . And she is so pale!" (p. 39). The discourse is poetic and beautiful, but it nonetheless communicates Dreenie's fear of Bluish's imperfection.

Eventually, however, Dreenie reconciles herself to her friend's difference as she gets to know Bluish better. The last discursive instance of Hamilton (1999) relying on the light or moonlight metaphor to describe Bluish occurs in the girl's self-description of her chemotherapy: "It hurts so bad. It sucks, man! Like sucking on a straw. It sucks your insides out. It sucks out your light" (p. 93). Once Bluish acknowledges that she is now only a pale reflection of her former self, her class goes on a field trip to see the butterfly conservatory in the Museum of Natural History. The class learns about butterflies—including the fact that many of them are poisonous. Bluish compares herself to a Blue Morpho butterfly: "Me, Bluish, toxic me" (p. 105). Dreenie rejects the comparison, insisting that Bluish wasn't "born that way" (p. 105); hers is an acquired disability, and not even necessarily a permanent one. The discourse, however, still subtly insists that Bluish is defined by her fragility and by her color, whether she was born that way or not.

The text resolves itself as virtually all middle-grade novels about disability do: The characters in the story accept disability, and the character with the disability is welcomed back into the community. Echoing the Kwanzaa proverb "I am because we are; because we are, I am," Dreenie tells their group of friends, including Bluish, "Bluish is, because we are; we are, because Bluish—is—us" (p. 122). Bluish has found a community, regardless of physical ability. Nonetheless, her identity throughout the text has been defined by her disability. Her skin color is a constant marker of her identity, and she is frequently objectified. She is moth; she is moonlight; she is butterfly; she is scary. The language is poetic, but it is still discourse that emphasizes difference as negative.

In *Gathering Blue*, Lois Lowry (2000) is less poetic, but the discourse about disability is also less dominant. Kira is an orphan in a post-apocalyptic world that might well be related somehow to the world in which Jonas lives in *The Giver* (Lowry, 1993). Kira's community, however, is more barbaric: agrarian, tribal, and patriarchal. Kira was born with a twisted leg but is spared from death because her mother protected her while she was an infant. Kira proves to have a talent as a weaver and needleworker, which gives her value in a community that posits all of its historical memory in the work of a singer, who annually sings the epic tale of their culture, wearing a robe that Kira is expected to mend. She does so, beautifully. Their community, however, has lost the ability to dye threads blue. The title of the book (Lowry, 2000) refers to Kira's efforts to find blue dye.

She cannot go on a quest for the dye, however, for two reasons: her disabled leg, which causes her frequent pain, and her fear of the beasts that roam about the woods of their community. Pain and fear commingle in this book as discursive constructions of disability. Kira's physical pain is reported at least 8 times in terms of her disability, and fear defines both her life and the life of all the villagers. They fear each other, they fear their elders, and most of all they fear the beasts, who are relatively obvious metaphors for the unknown.

Kira's confrontation with the *unheimlich*—in German, literally, "the unhomelike," the unknown, which unsettles us or causes us to face or displace our fears—occurs when she finds an elderly woman who mentors her in the art of dy(e)ing. The elderly woman teaches Kira everything she knows about dyes, and she also teaches her that there are no beasts—that beasts are just a discursive construct that the Elders have invented to control and repress the villagers. Kira tells one of the Elders that the old woman has told her that there are no beasts; the next day, the woman is found dead. Thus, Kira learns to fear the Elders and what they represent. She also learns that there are worse things than the imperfection of disability. She understands death as inevitable better than she ever has before. Eventually, a friend helps her to find a plant that can be used to make blue dye, and she is reunited with her father.

Like Bluish (Hamilton, 1999)—another character for whom blue represents uniqueness—Kira finds a community, even saying to her friends, "I need all of you. We need each other" (Lowry, 2000, p. 177). The beasts are the metaphor for her own fear and her own difference. Once she defines these beasts as gone, they, like her disability, cease to trouble her. Her fears and her disability recede in importance when she confronts the *unheimlich* and refuses to let it conquer her. Like Bluish, she is discursively compared to an animal, albeit an unknown one, and like her, she finds community. But *Gathering Blue* is particularly useful for demonstrating the *unheimlich* at work. Disability is strange, disturbing, fear inspiring, and painful.

Kira (Lowry, 2000), Bluish (Hamilton, 1999), and Izzy (Voigt, 1986) all must acknowledge their disability as being part of the unfamiliar, and they all must do so while people stare at them and in the context of metaphors of difference.

Embodiment and Abjection

Whether these female characters are fat or differently abled, they have a utilitarian function that can be tied to Kristeva's (1982) concept of abjection. Abjection represents the rejection of the unclean in psychological theory. For example, we rid ourselves of bodily fluids because they are abject: unclean, unacceptable, impure. According to Coats (2004), abject characters, who represent this rejection of the impure or the unacceptable, come in two forms in literature for youth: the socially abject character, who is effectively scapegoated by other people; and the psychologically abject character, who embraces his (gender specificity intended) own abjection as a way to escape from social pressures.

Psychologically abject characters are "ordinary people who refuse to reintegrate into society under its terms but instead haunt and disrupt its borders" (Kristeva, 1982, p. 149). Socially abject characters experience some sort of separation from others, followed by "a liminal experience of individuation" and a reintegration into society (p. 150). All the characters we've investigated in this chapter—Blubber, Ellie, Lara, Izzy, Bluish, and Kira— are more socially abject than they are psychologically abject. They do not choose to haunt the borders of their cultures; they are all forced to do so because of some aspect of their embodiment. In other words, they are made abject against their will and without a choice in the matter, but they are responsible for choosing to reintegrate themselves back into the appropriate social sphere by adjustments to their bodies or their attitudes. Indeed, they all overcome their abjection by asserting their own agency, advancing the ideology that we all have "choices" about our social positions and how we are viewed by others.

It is significant that all the female characters we describe are socially abject, and all the psychologically abject characters that Coats (2004) describes are male. Discursively constructed female characters rarely choose their own abjection in children's literature—but the discourse surrounding the female body in children's literature almost always defines the physical as being a matter of choice. Over and over, characters whose embodiment marks them as different, as imperfect, and as Other are presented as having either physical choices or psychological choices that allow them to reintegrate themselves into society as nonabject characters. They employ their agency to redefine their biology and change the structures of society. They are portrayed as being fortunate to have choices.

This emphasis on choice surrounding embodiment is startling. Whether the role of choice in defining discursive embodiment is a misapplication of feminist principles or whether it has surrounded the discourse of female embodiment in children's literature all along is an investigation for another paper. For now, we can't help wondering: Is all this discourse about embodiment and choice honest? Is it accurate? Is it a message that benefits either female readers or male readers to experience with such repetition?

Bérubé (2005) observes how figural our interpretations of bodily discourse often are within the field of disability studies. He notes that the goal of much of the literal criticism that treats characters with disabilities as if they were real people is to ask readers to consider what constitutes the human body and what defines difference.

Our goal with this essay is exactly that. We want others to interrogate not the literal definition of the human body but its discursive representations that somehow circumscribe perceptions with this constant, hounding implication that the physical is always already a matter of choice. Even if the only choice that discursive characters have is to psychologically redefine themselves, young readers are still left with the impression that we have more choices about our physical bodies than we actually do. Grownups know that not everything physical is a matter of choice. Certainly, some people can choose to go on diets and lose weight, redefining themselves and their self-image, but not everyone can do that. Not everyone can change her embodiment. Just ask anyone with cancer or incipient Alzheimer's what choices they think they have. For that matter, ask someone who's experiencing puberty. So why do writers for the young keep writing the discourse of embodiment in such choice-laden terms?

Embodiment and the Discourse of Stereotypes

Authors use language to perpetuate stereotypes, even when they are trying to reject cultural stereotypes about gender and race, as Louis Sachar (1998) tries and fails to do in *Holes*. In that novel, the fat boy ends up skinny, of course, whereas the righteously indignant White woman turns into a raging, homicidal ballbuster; moreover, that newly thin White male is the strong guy who has to carry the victimized male of color up a mountain in order for both of them to achieve a putative victory.

If we think about embodiment as the physical manifestation of the individual, we can think about embodiment in ways that seem, in childhood, to have little to do with choice, like race, gender, or physical disability. Certain transgender and intersex children are given choices about gender; certain racially mixed children are given choices about how they self-identify with race (especially if they live outside the United States). Physical ability, however, is not a matter of choice, nor are any of the neurological disorders that leave children appearing physically normal but that wreak havoc on their behavior because of physical causes. (We're thinking here about attention deficit disorder, cognitive development disorders, or autism spectrum disorders, for example.)

The truth is this: Physical disability is often depicted in children's literature in the same way that fatness is, just without the element of choice as a causative factor. As Heim (1994) points out, disabled characters are far more likely to serve as catalysts for other character's changes than they are to be agents of change themselves or characters whose dynamic emotional development drives the plot structure. Think of Charlie in *The Summer of the Swans* (Byars, 1970), Kevin in *Freak the Mighty* (Philbrick, 1993), or Mary in *Little Town on the Prairie* (Wilder, 1941). All these disabled characters are defined by language that focuses on their embodiment.

Even when authors have the power to create something new, something that defies cultural expectations and subverts stereotypes—as Sachar (1998) attempts in *Holes* or as Philbrick (1993) attempts in *Freak the Mighty*—they still can't help themselves. They still fall victim to the stereotypes that few young readers notice, like "fat people are stupid"—since Freak is so much smarter than Mighty—or "the physically disabled don't mature like 'normal' people do." After all, Freak doesn't grow up; he dies. For all we know, Mary in *Little Town on the Prairie* (Wilder, 1941) never marries, in the heteronormative way that Laura does.

Do we really want to teach our children that weight is entirely a matter of lifestyle, when medical research indicates otherwise (Gibbs, 1996; Homeier, 2005; Whigham, Israel, & Atkinson, 2006) and when children often have far less choice in their lifestyles than adults do, anyway? Do we really want to imply that disabled characters don't mature on the same emotional trajectory that other characters do? Do we really want issues of embodiment to saturate the literature of maturation? It follows all too frighteningly that if you can choose a "perfect" body, you will, and if you can't, you'll never be as mature as "normal" people.

Glossary

Abjection: Moving to the edge or the periphery of a group that is unacceptable because it is socially suspect or unclean. The abjected is purged from the social body to make it more clean. In literature for youth, abject characters are often scapegoats.

Agency: An individual's ability to take action or assume the subject position in a given situation.

Characterization: The formal literary term used to describe the depiction of people or personified beings within a narrative. Because characters are always constructed from language, they are always discursive.

Discourse: The language system, both written and verbal, within which an individual or society functions. Discourse is necessarily composed of language. That which is **discursive** is constructed from language.

Embodiment: Aspects of the physical body, including gender, physical ability, and appearance.

Etiology: Pertaining to causes; the study of causes or causation.

Ideology: A sociopolitical belief. Whether directly stated or only implied, the sociopolitical statements that inform children's literature often result in the text manipulating the child reader's understanding of the world. Because ideology is always constructed from language, it is always discursive.

Metaphor: A comparison between two unlike concepts or objects. Frequently in literature for youth, the comparison is made for thematic purposes. Because metaphors are always constructed from language, they are always discursive.

Subject position: Having the ability to act, as opposed to being acted upon. The term has specific implications in terms of language study: the subject of a verb takes action, whereas the object of the verb receives it. In the sentence "Lee kisses Terry on the cheek," Lee is in the subject position and is assuming agency as the one who kisses; Terry is in the object position, as the one who is being kissed.

Unheimlich: Literally, the "un-home-like"; the uncanny; that which is so unfamiliar to us that it is startling or disturbing in ways that force us to renegotiate our feelings about what we are confronting.

References

Baynton, D. (2005). Slaves, immigrants, and suffragists: The uses of disability in citizenship debates. *PMLA, 120*, 562–567.

Bérubé, M. (2005). Disability and narrative. *PMLA, 120*, 568–576.

Breen, M., & Blumenfield, W. (Eds.). (2005). *Butler matters: Judith Butler's impact on feminist and queer studies*. Burlington, VT: Ashgate.

Butler, J. (1990). *Gender trouble: Feminism and the subversion of identity*. New York: Routledge.

Coats, K. (2001). The reason for disability. *Bookbird: A Journal of International Children's Literature*, 39 (1), 11–16.

Coats, K. (2004). *Looking glasses and neverlands: Lacan, desire, and subjectivity in children's literature*. Iowa City, IA: University of Iowa Press.

Gibbs, W. (1996). Interview with Rudolph L. Leibel. *Scientific America*. Available online at www.sciam.com/article.cfm?articleID=00087E84-E0CB-1CD9-B4A8809EC588EEDF&pageNumber=1&catID=4

Gilman, S. (2005). Defining disability: The case of obesity. *PMLA, 120*, 514–517.

Halperin, D. (1997). Forgetting Foucault: Acts, identities, and *The history of sexuality*. *Representations, 63*, 93–120.

Heim, A. (1994). Beyond the stereotypes. *School Library Journal, 40*, 139–142.

Homeier, B. (2005). Obesity. *TeensHealth*, Available online athttp://kidshealth.org/teen/food_fitness/dieting/obesity.html

Kristeva, J. (1982). *Powers of horror* (L. Roudiez, Trans.). New York: Columbia University Press.

Kuther, T., & McDonald, E. (2004). Early adolescents' experiences with, and views of, Barbie. *Adolescence, 39*, 39–51.

Lehr, S. (2001). The hidden curriculum: Are we teaching young girls to wait for the prince? In S. Lehr (Ed.), *Beauty, brains, and brawn: The construction of gender in children's literature.* Portsmouth, NH: Heinemann.

Merleau-Ponty, M. (1962). *Phenomenology of perception* (C. Smith, Trans.). New York: Humanities Press. (Original work published 1945)

Nodelman, P. (1977). How typical children read typical books. *Children's Literature in Education, 12*, 177–185.

Nussbaum, M. (1999, February 22). The professor of parody. *The New Republic,* pp. 37–45.

Paley, V. G. (1998). *The girl with the brown crayon: How children use stories to shape their lives.* Cambridge, MA: Harvard University Press.

Pinsent, P. (1997). *Children's literature and the politics of equality.* London: Fulton.

Rice, P. (2000). Gendered readings of a traditional "feminist" folktale by sixth-grade boys and girls. *Journal of Literacy Research, 32*, 211–236.

Saunders, K. (2004). What disability studies can do for children's literature. *Disability Studies Quarterly.* Available online at www.dsq-sds.org/_articles_html/2004/winter/dsq_w04_saunders.html

Shakespeare, T., & Watson, N. (2001). The social model of disability: An outdated ideology. *Research in Social Science and Disability, 2*, 9–28.

Smith, D. (n.d.). *Life in the fat lane:* Author Cherie Bennett tackles the tough subject of kids and weight. Available online at http://teenagerstoday.com/resources/articles/weight.htm

Thomson, R. G. (1997). *Extraordinary bodies: Figuring physical disability in American culture and literature.* New York: Columbia University Press.

Wedwick, L. (2005). *Socialization of a reader: The representation of fatness in adolescent literature.* Unpublished doctoral dissertation, Illinois State University, Normal, IL.

Whigham, L., Israel, B., & Atkinson, R. (2006). Adipogenic potential of multiple human adenoviruses in vivo and in vitro in animals. *American Journal of Physiology, 290*, 190–194.

Children's Books

Bauer, J. (2001). *Squashed.* New York: Putnam.

Bennett, C. (1998). *Life in the fat lane.* New York: Bantam Doubleday Dell.

Blume, J. (1974). *Blubber.* New York: Bradbury Press.

Byars, B. (1970). *The summer of the swans.* New York: Viking Press.

Cormier, R. (1974). *The chocolate war.* New York: Dell.

Crew, G. (1993). *Strange objects*. New York: Simon & Schuster.

Crutcher, C. (1993). *Staying fat for Sarah Byrnes*. New York: Greenwillow.

Fine, A. (1997). *The tulip touch*. Boston: Little, Brown.

Glenn, M. (1996). *Who killed Mr. Chippendale?* New York: Lodestar.

Glenn, M. (1997). *The taking of room 114*. New York: Lodestar.

Hamilton, V. (1999). *Bluish*. New York: Blue Sky Press.

Hinton, S. E. (1967). *The outsiders*. New York: Dell.

Lowry, L. (1993). *The giver*. Boston: Houghton Mifflin.

Lowry, L. (2000). *Gathering blue*. New York: Laurel Leaf.

Myers, W. D. (2000). *Monster*. New York: HarperCollins.

Philbrick, R. (1993). *Freak the mighty*. New York: Blue Sky Press.

Sachar, L. (1998). *Holes*. New York: Dell Yearling.

Voigt, C. (1986). *Izzy willy nilly*. New York: Atheneum.

Walter, V. (1998). *Making up megaboy*. New York: Dell.

Wilder, L. I. (1941). *Little town on the prairie*. New York: HarperCollins.

Chapter 9

African-American Males at Risk: A Researcher's Study of Endangered Males and Literature That Works

Alfred W. Tatum

Almost 20 years ago, Jewelle Gibbs (1988) used the descriptor *endangered* to explain the status of young Black males miseducated by the educational system, mishandled by the criminal justice system, mislabeled by the mental health system, and mistreated by the social welfare system. She explained "that all of the major institutions of American society have failed to respond appropriately and effectively to their multiple needs and problems" (p. 2). She was describing African-American males in the 15- to 24-year-old age group who live predominantly in inner-city neighborhoods but who can also be found in rural areas, working-class suburbs, and small towns all over America. Gibbs noted:

> They are the teenagers and young adults from families of the lower end of the socioeconomic spectrum, many of whom are welfare-dependent and live below the poverty line. They are the black youth who are seen when one drives through inner-city ghetto neighborhoods, hanging out on dimly lit street corners, playing basketball on littered school lots, [or] selling dope in a darkened alley. (p. 2)

Now, 7 years into the 21st century, the plight of African-American males in the communities described above is worsening. The incarceration rates for these young men are increasing while college enrollment rates are decreasing.

Jobless rates among African-American male teenagers in underprivileged areas are experiencing a precipitous incline while graduation rates are experiencing a decline from the past two decades. The volume of despair for young African-American males from impoverished communities in the United States becomes louder as they enter adolescence. They need successful school experiences that will help them to become resilient in communities characterized by social and economic suffering. Gradually, more and more African-American males living in these communities are opting for maladaptive solutions that lead to negative life outcomes.

Beyond engaging in personally defeating behaviors, many of these young men also engage in morally reprehensible behaviors with perceived short-term rewards that often lead to long-term repercussions. Recently, a young teenage male who will be discussed later in this chapter was arrested for allegedly possessing a small amount of cocaine. This arrest followed several months of our working together to improve his reading and reshape his identity. His attempt, like the attempt of so many other young men living in similar conditions, to remove the immediate stings of poverty often manifest as a dual victimization. The young men become victimized by their actions as they begin to victimize others. As a result, communities and community structures (e.g., schools, businesses) become paralyzed by fear, cynicism, hopelessness, and a depleted sense of self-efficacy. Analysis of quality-of-life indicators such as life expectancy rates, homicide rates, incarceration rates, college enrollment and graduation rates, and jobless rates suggests that the *endangered* label has legitimate applicability to young African-American males.

Being endangered, or placed at risk for failure, by variables such as poverty, violence, drug-infested communities, and substandard educational practices contributes to a diminished sense of selfhood that is psychologically corrosive to many young people. The outgrowth of this psychological impact is a literacy gap on a smaller scale and a life outcome gap on a grander scale. Too often, however, the literacy achievement gap and the focus on closing it suffer from oversimplification and underestimation. This is reflected in proposed solutions to close the literacy achievement gap by focusing solely on reading skill-and-strategy development for adolescents.

A skill-and-strategy approach, in its deliberate attempt to help adolescents become better readers and writers, fails to acknowledge the significance of *what* they read. We must critically question *what* we want adolescents to read and *why* we want them to read, particularly in a society where many of them function along clearly demarcated race-influenced and class-influenced lines. Answering *what* and defining *why* will move educators closer to closing not only the reading achievement gap but also the life outcome gap.

Following a logical argument, high-quality skill-and-strategy instruction is absolutely essential to move students toward reading text independently.

It is not logical, however, to assume that a sole focus on skills and strategies is sufficient to address the myriad needs of adolescents who live in communities in which their literacy development is shaped and often adversely influenced by environmental and cultural variables. Environmental and cultural variables influence identity development and how the role of schooling is perceived. The community forces influence students' adaptation to school, their perceptions of and responses to school, and their beliefs about schooling (Ogbu, 1998). Ogbu (1987) explains:

> School performance is not due only to what is done to or for minority students; it is also due to the fact that the nature of minorities' interpretations and responses make them more or less accomplices to their own school success or failure. (p. 317)

Unfortunately, a simplistic approach that ignores environmental and cultural variables is often taken in an approach to revive struggling adolescent readers. Such an approach does not acknowledge the influence of text on the human development of individuals and groups in society.

One only has to look at the role of biblical text and its influences on groups and individuals. In addition, an examination of democratic principles—such as equality, fairness, and human rights, found in American documents such as the U.S. Constitution and the Declaration of Independence—and how these principles helped to shape the conscience of American society, in times of both turbulent revolt and national calm, forcefully demonstrates the importance of text in the lives of individuals and society. However, the focus on skills and strategies devoid of meaningful texts dismantles opportunities to shape the conscience or nurture resilience among African-American adolescent males. This is problematic because meaningful texts can be used to help these young men move beyond community forces such as observed joblessness or perceived barriers in the adult opportunity structure. Although community forces may remain stagnant, response to community forces is continually negotiated (Lareau & Horvat, 1999). They suggest that although an individual's class and race affect social reproduction, the response of individuals to their community forces is shaped moment by moment within their social environments.

Children's and young adult literature can be used with African-American adolescent males to help them critique and understand their experiences outside school. Literature can also be used to support their academic, cultural, emotional, and social literacy development. These young men can make more productive choices aimed at overcoming societal barriers if they have an increased understanding of their experiences. Rich and meaningful experiences with literature can also support these young men to better navigate their experiences in schools where they are often alienated and rejected because of behavior problems that are associated with academic underperformance on reading-related tasks.

It has been argued that there is a need for literature that offers discussions of race, gender, and class—literature that illuminates the problems caused by racism, sexism, and classism (Harris, 1997). Sims (1997) has noted the following:

> It is possible for literature to contribute to children's understandings of how they are viewed and valued by the school and society of which schools are reflections. Ultimately, to the extent that school achievement is tied to a sense of self-worth, multicultural literature can have a beneficial effect on the school achievement of children who have historically been denied realistic images of themselves and their families, community and culture. (p. 4)

There is sufficient guidance for selecting and engaging African-American students with literature. Some identified strategies are leading daily readalouds, creating art centers with books illustrated by major artists, having oratorical contests, and posing essential questions related to the text (e.g., What does it mean to be responsible?).

Harris (1997) identified several characteristics of exemplary literature for African-American children. The exemplary texts have high literary quality, appeal to children and adolescents, address sociocultural concerns, and potentially serve multiple functions. She also identified authors who capture the multifaceted complexity of African-American children and adolescents and the African-American experience. Among them are Christopher Paul Curtis, Sharon Flake, Virginia Hamilton, Angela Johnson, Sharon Bell Mathis, Walter Dean Myers, and Jacqueline Woodson. These authors, who generally write for adolescents, embrace traditional controversial themes and characters. They willingly depict characters in all their "beautiful-ugly selves" as they wrestle with topics such as gangs, drugs, and other societal problems. In line with the changing conceptualization of adolescent literacy (Alvermann, Hinchman, Moore, Phelps, & Waff, 2006), many of these writers focus on the multiple identities of adolescents—race, gender, and class—and how young people are shaped by these identities across different contexts.

In spite of our knowing more about using literature with African-American children, of the proliferation of children and young adult literature over the past 40 years, of the emergence of new writers who write for adolescents, and of the research that supports using a wide range of text with adolescents, there is still relatively little guidance for using young adult literature with African-American adolescent males. Several solutions that have been proposed in the last 10 years specifically address the literacy needs of African-American adolescent males. They include providing culturally responsive literacy instruction that links classroom content to student experiences, developing character development programs, and initiating rite-of-passage programs.

However, there is a glaring omission: the role of literature in their literacy development. Although curriculum is often a significant consideration for improving the education outcomes for African-American males, specific texts and text characteristics that should inform curriculum selection is strikingly absent (Tatum, 2006b). I have suggested the following:

> By selecting appropriate reading materials, teachers can engage African American adolescent males with text . . . that will lead to positive life outcomes. . . . Modifying curriculum on the basis of such texts . . . can foster meaningful discussion among students against a backdrop of standards and accountability. A meaningful program should include texts that shape a positive life trajectory and provide a road map that can help students resist nonproductive behaviors. (p. 45)

I was describing "enabling" texts that move beyond a sole cognitive focus such as skill-and-strategy development to include a social and cultural focus. These types of text move these young men to be, do, or think differently as a result of their reading. I often share personal accounts of how I began to pray differently after reading Judy Blume's (1970) *Are You There God? It's Me, Margaret.* I also share how Dick Gregory's (1964) autobiographical novel, *Nigger,* functioned as an enabling text in my life. His words released me from the stigmatic trapping of poverty. My childhood dreams were no longer polluted by environmental conditions as I began to absorb his messages. I learned to be resilient like the author.

By definition, enabling texts do the following:

1. Provide a road map for action
2. Connect to personal and community experiences
3. Nurture identity development
4. Stimulate inner reflection

Unfortunately, African-American adolescent males suffer from an underexposure to high-quality literature in an era of accountability. Also, the types of texts that African-American adolescent males as a group encounter in schools are characteristically disabling. These texts either reinforce their perceptions as struggling readers or ignore their local contexts and their desire as adolescents for self-definition. In this chapter, I discuss how a young adult novel was used along with another nonfiction text with a young African-

American adolescent male who fits the *endangered* descriptor. The literature was selected to help him become academically and emotionally resilient among some of the personal turmoil he was experiencing inside and outside school.

Introducing Quincy

Quincy, a 15-year-old African-American male, was retained in eighth grade 3 times because he failed to meet the minimum reading standard on his district's reading assessment. He is the oldest child of three siblings. His family lives in a relatively high-crime area in one of Chicago's West Side communities, where very few jobs opportunities exist for the residents. At the time of the study, Quincy lived with his mother and his stepfather and had an antagonistic relationship with the latter. His biological father was incarcerated.

I began working with Quincy a month after he appeared in court for driving without a license. When I asked him about the experience, he stated, "I stole the car, I didn't plan on driving everywhere, but I got carried away and drove off. I am going to court now, and I have to learn from my mistakes." He was forced out of his aunt's house, where he was living at the time of the joyride, because he refused to attend counseling for his increasingly negative behaviors. He did not believe that counseling was necessary.

Quincy's father's incarceration had had a profound effect on him. He shared, "My dad going back to jail really hurt me because he told me if I don't get bad grades he would stay out of jail. He went back. I got mad and I just started failing school." Other issues affected Quincy's views of himself. He shared, "[My family] all think I am dumb." He also shared, "The majority of the world don't think [African Americans] are worthy enough to take control and handle what we need to do....They think we are worthless." Quincy suggested that cultural and environment barriers impacted his views on schooling. He stated the following:

> Wherever you go, you see the average Black male right [on] the corner. Wherever you go in the prison, you'll see the average Black male in prison. Or, you'll see an average Black male in a fight, or killing somebody, or they [are] kidnapping for instance, basically doing wrong. We don't have education on our side.

Quincy was experiencing an emotional overload outside school, and negative behaviors were beginning to manifest more frequently in school and outside school. I decided to help Quincy become a better reader in the hope of reshaping his identity so that he would not continue to engage in negative activities. Therefore, I designed a study to identify and describe the aspects of texts that he found most useful for improving his reading and shaping his identity. The primary goal of the study was to gather his views on how reading materials affected the way he viewed himself. Quincy agreed to participate in the study by agreeing to do the following:

1. Read books, articles, newspaper clippings, and speeches I recommended. He was given the final decision about the materials he chose to read.

2. Participate in 20 hour-long audiotaped discussions about the reading materials; these took place every other Saturday morning for 40 weeks at a bookstore or library near his home.

3. Write reflections in a journal during the last 10 minutes of each discussion.

4. Participate in four 30-minute interviews to reflect on the discussions. The interviews were scheduled at 10-week intervals.

Quincy and Reading

I asked Quincy to describe himself as a reader the first time we met. He stated, "I can read, but I really do not comprehend what I am reading. I read and pay attention to some things, but I imagine things I know I miss. . . . I just think I read to get through the books, basically." The following excerpt is from the first interview:

Tatum: Have you read anything that really affected you?

Quincy: Nope.

Tatum: Is there any book that just stands out that you remember?

Quincy: To say the truth, I ain't read a book. And the book I just started on [*he did not remember the title*], that's the only book that I took the time to read at home. And it really ain't got nothing to do with my life.

Tatum: Have you ever read a book from the front cover to the back cover?

Quincy: Nope.

Tatum: Do teachers assign novels at school?

Quincy: No.

Tatum: Do you only read [text] in the textbook?

Quincy: No. The last book I read from cover to cover was *Harry Potter.* This is what they had in school. Anything else, I used to think like, man, after 5 hours there ain't no way I'm coming outside and turn around to go home and read a book on my own. I gotta have my childhood. Basically I just either do the homework or wait until the morning at school to do my homework for that day's assignment.

Tatum: That is interesting, because I am asking you to participate in a study that is going to focus on books. How do you feel participating in a study that will require you to read books?

Quincy: I mean, I know I gotta start getting straight, trying to get back on track. . . . Basically what you are doing is giving me a challenge because I don't [read] normally.

Tatum: If I had to recommend certain types of books to you, what would you want me to recommend?

Quincy: I don't know, because I really don't know about books out there now. I really don't know what's good for me that I will pay attention to, that will help me.

Several issues emerged from our first meeting. First, Quincy had little to no experience with reading materials that he found meaningful. Second, his exposure to books and his expectations of reading them were limited in the schools he attended. Third, he viewed reading as a barrier to enjoying his life outside school. Finally, he could not provide insight into the types of reading materials he liked because he had limited knowledge of the wide range of reading materials that exist.

It was clear by the end of the first interview that Quincy was experiencing an imbalance between an out-of-school literacy overload and an in-school literacy underload (Tatum, 2006b). This imbalance often shapes a trajectory of negative life outcomes, particularly for African-American adolescent males, when in-school literacy instruction fails to help them figure out what they want to do with the rest of their lives. Therefore, I decided to initially select literature that would help Quincy critique and understand his experiences outside school. The major criterion was to identify texts that would provide Quincy with capital to become resilient amid some of his negative environmental conditions. I wanted the literature to function as enabling— texts that moved Quincy to be, do, or think differently. *Yo', Little Brother* (Davis & Jackson, 1998) and *Handbook for Boys: A Novel* (Myers, 2002) were among the first books that I recommended and that Quincy selected. In the remainder of this chapter I will explain how these books affected Quincy. This is followed by the implications for selecting literature that works for African-American males who fit the *endangered* descriptor.

I Wish I Had Had This Book Earlier

During the second week of the study, Quincy discussed his reading of *Yo', Little Brother* (Davis & Jackson, 1998). He was asked to discuss the following:

- Why he selected the book
- How he was affected by the book
- Which parts of the book stood out to him
- How this book compared to what he was required to read in school
- If he would recommend this book to other African-American adolescent males

I initiated the conversation by asking Quincy to discuss how he was affected by the book. He responded, "I just know it helped me out with a lot of problems I had. I wish I [had] had this book earlier so I [could] know more things about life." Curious as to why he read this book after having never read a book from cover to cover in 15 years, I asked Quincy to explain why he read the book. He shared the following:

> How it started off. I don't really know what made me read, but I was totally involved with what [the authors] were saying. To tell you the truth, I read this book in 1 day. I ain't started until Monday . . . cause I wasn't going to read it at first. . . . So as I flip the pages and start reading I'm like I like this book for some reason, so I'm going to try to read. Then, I seen "Street smarts" [a chapter subtitle] right at the top. I know I know a lot about the street, so I just read to see what [the authors] were talking about. Then some of the things they were saying were true.

Quincy's admission that he was not going to read the book was not surprising. This can be expected from a teenager who never completed a book. However, the structure of the book and the subtitles (Table 9-1) led Quincy to give the text a chance.

Table 9-1. Partial List of Subtitles From *Yo', Little Brother*

Table of Contents

Homies
- Don't let peer pressure get to you 38
- Avoid known troublemakers 38
- Play organized sports 40
- Support your brothers 41A

Time to Learn
- Learn from the mistakes of other brothers 51
- Study hard 52
- Become computer literate 53
- Listen to old folks' stories 62

Cross Cultural
- Don't blame your problems on the white man 85
- Speak without slang 86
- Speak standard English 90

It's Your Money
- Stop worrying about designer labels 103
- Forget about the Joneses 105
- Know the difference between wants and needs 107

Quincy cited 21 subtitles without looking at the table of contents when I asked him to describe and explain the parts of the text that stood out to him. I asked him how he remembered so much. He shared the following:

> I mean, cause, I have been through a lot of stuff during the 16 years of my life. It ain't been no bad stuff, but it is some stuff that is good enough to make me remember these titles in these book.

He was surprised that he could remember so much, and equally surprised that he completed a book. Here is his reaction to reading his first book:

> As I was going along, I wanted to stop but I couldn't. I was like, I started it and I ain't go to sleep until 6:00 a.m. That's how into it I was. I didn't really know I could get into a book like that. To tell the truth, I forgot I was reading. I was just totally imagining at the same time. So

> that's how I knew I was really understanding what [the authors] were saying. I don't know how I know all these titles by heart, but this is a good book; it helps you out a lot. . . . I mean, I thought I [was] just going to give up.

Ironically, Quincy did not believe that this book would have had the same effect on him if it had been assigned in school. He shared the following:

> It is something that we should be reading, but the teachers would read it and use it like a story. They ain't going to explain what it means. They [are] going to give us things to write about it and all, but they ain't going to really explain it. . . . If they are going to start a book like this, they got to let [the students] know what the [authors] mean. Especially what they mean.

He was suggesting that literature is more effective when it is discussed in ways that give students access to the meaning and when it is connected to students' lived experiences, not reduced to school stuff (Tatum, 2004). I asked Quincy to describe the impact, if any, that the book had on him. The end of our conversation was as follows:

Tatum: What do you think you will do differently after reading this book?

Quincy: I think I should go and take care of myself.

Tatum: Is that what you really think you will do after reading this book?

Quincy: Yeah, I think I would.

Tatum: But these are just words on the page.

Quincy: But I understand what [the authors] are saying, where [they are] coming from.

Trying Not to Make Mistakes

From the next recommended texts I provided, Quincy selected *Handbook for Boys: A Novel* (Myers, 2002). This novel was selected to serve as a road map text for Quincy. The young protagonist is given the choice by a judge to go to a youth facility or to a community mentoring program for 6 months. Duke, an African-American barber and mentor in the story, believes the male protagonist is worth the effort. There were many parallels between Quincy's life and the life of the young man in the novel. This novel also had chapter subtitles, which I hoped would attract Quincy's attention. Some of the subtitles are "Victims," "The Blind Monkey Strut," "Does Life Work?", "Reading," "Take Care of the Ball," "S-E-X," and "Change." I was hoping that the adult male characters in the novel would become Quincy's mentors. When asked to describe what he liked about the text, Quincy stated the following:

> What I like about this book is a young boy, and he had people that stayed on him about his problems. They talked to him. Like in the beginning, he went to court for beating up a boy, and the judge had him go to a place where a person keeps him out of trouble or something. As the story goes on, Duke [teaches] him. You know what I am saying? There [are] a lot of people coming in there that are messing up, and he [is] telling them that he should learn from the mistakes that people make.

Quincy began to reflect on his personal experience with the criminal justice system. He shared the following:

> I just got to learn from the mistakes that [the characters] in the story make, that they [are] telling about in the book. And if I do that, maybe it will make me better before I go out and make the mistakes that they made. I already made a mistake, and I am trying to learn from it. I just hope that I don't make any more mistakes. I try to keep my life going and keep my life better.

As with his reading of the first book described in this chapter, Quincy did not intend to read this novel in its entirety. However, the literature and its ability to draw Quincy into the story led him to give the text a chance. He stated the following:

> I felt a whole different change when I read the first book. It's like when I started reading, I thought I was just going to go through it and see what the chapters [were] about and then go to the next chapter to, like, glance at it a little bit, but I kept going because it was like I was in the story myself. I was understanding what [the characters] were talking about. It was like I was reading and visualiz-

ing what was happening and putting my feet in his shoes. That's how I kept with the book. I mean, I kept reading and reading and reading. The book started getting good because I gave it a chance . . . I just gave it a chance and kept reading.

Quincy gave the text a chance because it connected to his personal backdrop, his community backdrop, his gender backdrop, and his social backdrop. He used the text to critique his own life. The chapter "Does Life Work?" appealed to Quincy. He stated, "When I read that title, I thought about it for a minute. So I just got to reading." When I asked him if life works, he responded, "I mean, life works, but it ain't going to work if you ain't doing right to make your life better." Following is an excerpt from our conversation that illustrates how Quincy began to engage in self-reflective behaviors stimulated by reading the literature.

Tatum: How do you think this text will help you think about your life?

Quincy: Think about the mistakes I made. Maybe I need to just take my time, calm down, and think about things, think about stuff that I do before I do it and learn from the mistakes. Because you might do a mistake that might mess up your life for real. You might do something to get put in jail, and it's going to mess up your life when you come out of jail....This book tell you the truth from the cover....Until I started reading it, what made me really start reading it is [that] he caught a case and I had a case. I wanted to see what was going to happen in the story. I wanted to see what was going to happen to him. Then maybe I could learn from his mistake.

Tatum: Is that how you are going through life—trying not to make mistakes? Or are you trying to find something? I do not go through life trying not to make mistakes. I have goals that I strive toward. What is your position?

Quincy: The reason I say that is [that] since I've been in sixth grade, I've been making mistakes. I've been making bad mistakes that [are] messing me up right now today. From my mistakes right now I am not in school. I'm supposed to be a junior, but I'm not there yet. I'm letting all my family

> pass me up, besides my brother, and that's hurt-
> ing me because now some people look at me as
> a dummy....The reason I'm trying not to make
> mistakes is [that] every chance I get I make a
> mistake.
>
> *Tatum*: Have you ever shared that with anyone?
>
> *Quincy*: To tell you the truth, I wouldn't express myself to
> nobody—even my grandmother, and I love talk-
> ing to her.

Quincy became extremely reflective because of the literature that provided him with insight into his own existence. The novel prompted him to
ask real questions and seek real answers. The literature moved him toward
self-correcting tendencies. After reading this novel he kept saying, "I got to
get it right, I got to get it right."

Self-Correcting Tendencies

Ten weeks into the study, and after reading two novels and other nonfictional reading materials (e.g., poems, essays) not described in this chapter,
Quincy began to engage in self-correcting tendencies. He was becoming accountable for his out-of-school behaviors that were influenced by social and
academic variables that contributed to his personal turmoil. For example,
this young man successfully enrolled himself in an alternative high school
after being out of school for several months. This was a major step because
he made the decision to approach the school after his mother failed to enroll him. I wanted to know if he attributed changes in his behaviors to the
reading materials. Here is part of our discussion:

> *Tatum*: Do you feel different as a result of the literature
> you have been reading?
>
> *Quincy*: I'm starting to think. Before I started reading, I
> didn't think, period. So what I am saying now is
> I'm starting to think about things. Before I started
> reading I didn't really care. I just did what I do.
>
> *Tatum*: Do you really feel yourself changing, or are you
> coming up with the right things to say?
>
> *Quincy*: I am thinking positive instead of negative. I used
> to stay in trouble every day. Now you can't pay
> me to get in trouble.

> *Tatum*: Do you think it is because of reading?
>
> *Quincy*: I don't know what it is, to tell the truth, but it's got to be reading or something. Because before I started reading I stayed in trouble. Normally, I don't help my mama clean up; [now] I be cleaning up myself for her. The books ain't told me nothing about cleaning up and learning how your parents are stressing out. But, like I said, I am starting to see stress in them. I don't know what it is, but I'm changing a little bit.

The following paragraph written by Myers (2002) captured Quincy's attention:

> "You mean to tell me," Duke said, speaking slowly, "that you can see half the young men on this street without jobs, more people than you want to know from this block ending up in jail, and you still need a bomb and a sign to tell you want to do?" (pp. 85–86)

Quincy's actions began to indicate that he did not need a bomb to go off to tell him what he needed to do. This literature was providing the direction and the road map. He was learning to become resilient outside school and hoping to practice that same resilience once he returned to school.

From Endangered to Engaged: Literature That Makes a Difference

Like Quincy, many African-American adolescent males fit the *endangered* descriptor. Many of these young men also experience an underexposure to high-quality literature in school that helps them to shape their lives outside school. They might be exposed to literature that reinforces their perception as struggling readers, neglects their desire to define themselves, or denies them the opportunity to engage in self-reflective behaviors. Young adult literature is robbed of its potential to mitigate some of the problems experienced by African-American adolescent males. Quincy's case illustrates that literature can lead young men to engage in self-correcting tendencies that they might not imagine for themselves if they are not exposed to literature that connects to their multiple backdrops—personal, community, economic, gender, and cultural—through which they filter their lived experiences.

Literature must be selected with a clearer understanding of African-American adolescent males and of how cultural and environmental variables potentially shape their reading of literature. The impact of literature on the lives of African-American adolescent males cannot be overestimated. Quincy also informs us that educators should not rob young adult literature of its significance in order to be "schoolish." All too often, we wait for the endangered African-American adolescent male to heal himself. This is reflected in statements such as "if only he were motivated," "if only he wanted to be smart," and "if only he would read more." I offer a counter statement: If only we can place the right literature in his hands, we can motivate him, make him smart, and make him want to read more. Quincy teaches us that we must pay attention to the structure of the literature, the content, and the discussions of the literature.

With the knowledge acquired over the past 40 years for using literature with African-American children, with the reconceptualization of adolescent literacy, and with the emerging body of young adult literature that captures the complexity of the African-American experience, we now have a great starting point for identifying literature for endangered African-American adolescent males.

Years ago, Martin Luther King Jr. wrote about an African-American boy put to death in a gas chamber. As the gas pellets were released in the chamber, the young boy screamed out, "Save me, Joe Louis, save me!" He believed that the boxer Joe Louis would understand him and fight for his right to live. Joe Louis became the young man's appointed advocate. I suggest that literature can be used in the same way to advocate for the lives of African-American adolescent males. However, we must understand each young man and be willing to identify the literature that speaks to his multiple needs, inside school and out, particularly if we believe he is endangered.

References

Alverman, D., Hinchman, K., Moore, D., Phelps, S., & Waff, D. (Eds.). (2006). *Reconceptualizing the literacies in adolescents' lives* (2nd ed.). Mahwah, NJ: Erlbaum.

Gibbs, J. (1988). *Young, Black, and male in America: An endangered species*. Westport, CT: Auburn House.

Harris, V. (Ed.). (1997). *Using multiethnic literature in the K–8 classroom*. Norwood, MA: Christopher-Gordon.

Lareau, A., & Horvat, E. (1999). Moment of social inclusion and exclusion: Race, class and cultural capital in family-school relationships. *Sociology of Education, 72*, 37–53.

Ogbu, J. (1987). Variability in minority school performance: A problem in search of an explanation. *Anthropology & Education Quarterly, 18*, 312–334.

Ogbu, J. (1998). Voluntary and involuntary minorities: A cultural-ecological theory of school performance with some implications for education. *Anthropology & Education Quarterly, 29*, 155–188.

Sims, R. (1997). Selecting literature for a multicultural curriculum. In V. Harris (Ed.), *Using multiethnic literature in the K–8 classroom* (pp. 1–19). Norwood, MA: Christopher-Gordon.

Tatum, A. W. (2004). Moving beyond school stuff: Literacy instruction that honors students' realities. *Illinois Reading Council Journal, 32* (1), 22–29.

Tatum, A. W. (2006a). Adolescent multiple identities and teacher professional development. In D. Alvermann, K. Hinchman, D. Moore, S. Phelps, & D. Waff (Eds.), *Reconceptualizing the literacies in adolescents' lives* (2nd ed., pp. 65–79). Mahwah, NJ: Erlbaum.

Tatum, A. W. (2006b). Engaging African-American males in reading. *Educational Leadership, 63* (5), 44–49.

Children's Books

Blume, J. (1970). *Are you there God? It's me, Margaret.* New York: Bantam DoubleDay Dell.

Davis, A., & Jackson, J. (1998). *Yo', little brother.* Chicago: African-American Images.

Gregory, D. (1964). *Nigger.* New York: Pocket Books.

Myers, W. D. (2002). *Handbook for boys: A novel.* New York: Harper Trophy.

The Literary Worlds of Bud, Kenny, Luther, and Christopher: Finding Books for Me!

Christopher Paul Curtis

If, as a writer, you visit as many classrooms as I do, it doesn't take long before a couple of things dawn on you. The first is that during the inevitable ask-the-author sessions you will face a very limited number of questions. City to city, state to state, students all want to know the same few things. I'm not sure why, and I'm not sure it's really important, but what *is* important is that this constant repetition of the same queries will eventually lull the visiting author into a form of cruise control. Without much thought, the same answers are given to the same questions, again and again and . . . (multiply these *agains* by the number of visits you do a year).

This sense of complacency can cut both ways. It can be positive because the students' questions are met with well-rehearsed answers. Jokes, witticisms, and learned authorial insights can be inserted in the proper places, "uh" and "um" and "you know" can be culled, and, once you've done it many times, even a sense of spontaneity can be perpetrated on the unsuspecting kids. However, this system of rote answers can also be a source of danger, particularly to an author's ego. Precisely because you've had plenty of opportunities to think out and practice and fine-tune the answers you'll give, you are eventually bound to sound a whole lot smarter than you really are. Worse, you're bound to start *believing* you're a whole lot smarter than you really are, and therein lies the peril. Keep that in mind. The second thing that will dawn on you after a number of these visits is that a love of reading is something that absolutely burns in some young people, and it's not something they can easily hide. They might as well have a scarlet *B* (for *bookworm*) emblazoned on their foreheads. Experience has taught me that these scarlet *B*s are to be avoided at all costs. Not only do the questions of these kids show uncanny insight and intelligence, they are also the ones fraught with the risk of being most embarrassing.

I learned the hard way. The 541st question-and-answer session of the year was winding down, and I called on the 10- or 11-year-old girl at the back of the room. Something about her was different, which I thought at the time was nice. Wrong.

She prefaced her question with a sigh, then said, "Mr. Curtis, what books really, *really* touched you when you were a kid?" She sighed again, then eagerly looked at me, waiting, no doubt, to be regaled with a lengthy and detailed discussion of Christopher Curtis's favorite formative classic literature.

However, I was thinking, "Hey, wait a minute, that's nowhere on the List of Standard Questions! What kind of nonsense is this little nerd trying to pull?"

I quickly analyzed her question and realized just how loaded it was. First, she'd assumed that books had been a very important part of my childhood, so much so that particular ones were touchstones that I could easily and fondly recall. Second, she had said *books* as opposed to *book*, as if there were going to be dozens or hundreds from which to choose— which was undoubtedly the case with her.

I looked over at one of the teachers; I know they spend a good deal of time before these visits explaining to their charges what constitutes an appropriate question (nothing involving age, money, favorite colors, shoe size or pet's names). There was no help there, however; the teacher was also eagerly watching. She'd obviously missed my e-mail entitled, "RE: Inappropriate questions—none that require too much thought on the visiting author's part."

I hate to admit it, but I fell back on one of my baser instincts: politics. I remembered a lesson from my year of working for the campaign of one of Michigan's U.S. senators. I learned that if you're asked something you either don't know the answer to or you don't want to answer, all you have to do is say, "Hmm," to give the impression that you're deep in thought, then repeat the question and answer a completely different one! By the time the questioner catches on to what you've done, you have moved on to the next person.

I said to the little bookworm, "Hmm." I even stroked my chin twice, always a nice effect. I repeated, "What book really touched me as a child?"

What came next I've conveniently forgotten. I can't say with any certainty how I answered, but my response was full of *um*s, *uh*s, *you know*s and even included two references to my cat Suki's name. One thing I *can* say with certainty is that all the capital I'd gained from my previous witty, charming answers was shot. The teachers exchanged confused looks, the little bookworm's nose wrinkled, and I pointed at the other side of the auditorium and said, "Next question, please."

It was true: I couldn't think of one book that would actually apply. Unfortunately, I didn't gain the scarlet *B* on my own forehead until my late teens, when I began to gobble up books while working at a factory in Flint.

Not being one who savors the taste of humiliation, especially my own, I realized I had to give this question some serious thought. If, heaven forbid, this came up again, I had to be prepared and rehearse a brilliant, thought-provoking reply as to why no titles leaped to mind when I was asked what book had touched me as a child.

I ran through a list of three usual suspects that are probably familiar to most educators. First, perhaps I hadn't been exposed to books and encouraged to read as a child. This was certainly not true. Both of my parents had the scarlet *B* emblazoned on their foreheads; they were *always* reading. Any enduring mental pictures of Mom and Dad include a book in their hands.

I also remember coming home from school one day and noticing a strange smell in the house. My father lined up the four older Curtis siblings and marched us into the hallway. Huddled against the wall was a new bookcase and the most beautiful, coruscating, awe-inspiring set of books we'd ever seen. The top two rows of books were green and white and gold and had WORLD BOOK on their spines, and the bottom two rows were red and white and gold and read CHILDCRAFT.

Dad told us, "These books cost over $300." He looked over the top of his glasses, always a bad sign, then said, "If I see a crayon, a pencil, an ink pen, or bubblegum, chewed or not, within a mile of any of them, heads will roll."

My older sister, Lindsey, and I would spend hours sitting cross-legged in that hallway while she read to me and taught me everything from *Dogs of the World* to *The Great Artists*. One of my earliest and greatest senses of accomplishment came from these books and lessons.

Lindsey pointed at a painting and said, "What do you think this one is called?"

I studied the picture and said, "*Starry Night*."

She looked shocked and said, "Wow!"

My heart soared; I was so proud of myself. Years later I realized that the painting was actually the *Mona Lisa*, but that did nothing to diminish my sense of accomplishment. I've learned that when it comes to feeling accomplished, you'd better accept it when it comes along.

Thus it was clear that I'd been exposed to books and encouraged to read from a young age. So maybe I'd never been touched by a book because I was one of those boys who just didn't like reading. No, that wasn't it, either. The introduction to Jon Scieszka's *Guys Who Read Guys* could have been written about me. I truly enjoyed reading—just not books, particularly not fiction. I did, however, read comics, *National Geographic*, *Time*, and *Newsweek* from cover to cover. I even had a subscription to *Mad* magazine! I also remember praying that I'd live at least until 1985, when everybody would have one of those cool flying cars from the cover of *Popular Science*. (What happened?)

I loved reading and I loved the library; I just had never gotten into fiction. So might the final suspect, Mr. Not-a-Good-Reader, be the culprit for my dodging the young woman's question? Wrong again—I was an absolutely excellent reader.

I'm sure many of you remember the old S.R.A. boxes that used to be in the back of English classes. They contained folders in which the reading became progressively more involved and difficult. Each folder had its own color, and the beginning ones were the primary colors. The colors became more and more complex as the readings did.

By the time I left sixth grade, I was reading from "plaid," with mauve undertones.

I also breezed through books that were assigned at school. *Johnny Tremaine*, *Great Expectations*, *1984*, and *Brave New World* were to different degrees enjoyable, but none rose to the level of being "touching." Thus, being a poor reader wasn't the reason I couldn't find a book that touched me, so what's left?

After much thought, I think I've hit on at least one very important reason. I believe that there were no books that *really* touched me as a child because there were no books that were written for, by, or about me. There were no books from an African-American perspective.

I must quickly add that I'm not professing that young people should read only books specific to themselves. I shudder to think what a horrible, bland, confused world that would make. (I shudder even more when I think what that would do to the sales of my books!) I'm suggesting that if a book is to attain the lofty level of being "touching," as a bookworm would define the word, there has to be something in it to which he or she can relate on more than just a superficial level.

Not only must the book be beautifully written and compelling, there also to be something of the *me* in the book. Reading it must produce a series of nods followed by an instant, shared assumption of "I know where you're coming from," an assumption I never knew as a reading child. It was completely missing, and on some, probably subconscious, level the absence became acute.

This absence is compounded when there is nothing that comes remotely close to having some of the *me* in it. This was true in my youth. I'm reminded of the early 1960s, when one of my siblings would be watching one of the two channels the TV could pick up and he or she would shout something that would start a stampede of Curtii (the correct plural of Curtis) to the living room. All we'd need hear was "Quick! There's a Negro on the television!"

That absence, I think, is why I fumbled so badly at the young woman's question. That absence is also why I feel so fortunate today. It is incomprehensibly gratifying to know that my books, along with those of Jacqueline

Woodson and Walter Dean Myers, among others, are offered to young people. It is such a wonderful feeling to know that *Monster* or *The Watsons* or *I Hadn't Meant to Tell You This* or *Bud* or *Elijah* just might supply the missing *me* to some nascent bookworm. I can't help but glow when I think that some child might not have to sacrifice the years that I did before I learned the wonder of reading—or, as the little bookworm might put it, before I learned what it was like to "*really* be touched by a book."

Who knows, maybe 15 or 20 years from now, some African-American author will have had options, and a title will readily come to mind when he or she is asked that question. Maybe he or she won't have to resort to "Hmm, what book really touched me as a child? . . . Next question, please."

Feminist Women Writers of the 18th Century: Those Barbarous and Didactic Women

Susan S. Lehr

> *Damn them! I mean the cursed Barbauld Crew, those Blights and Blasts of all that is human in man and child.*
>
> —Charles Lamb, writing to
> Samuel Coleridge, 1802

Like Charles Lamb, many of today's social conservatives passionately insist that books undermine social values, religious beliefs, and the cultural fabric of Western society. Such conservatives abhor many of the topics addressed in children's books; they believe that it will harm their children to read about empowered female and male characters who face the complexity of struggles, abuses, and diversity found within contemporary family structures.

I use the term *social conservative* broadly, to describe people who share morals and mores in any given society, who are resistant to changing or challenging those values, and who often base their values on religious precepts, all of which can vary across time and place. The Latin root of the word *conservative* (i.e., *conserve*) has to do with guarding and keeping, a role that many social conservatives take quite seriously. Their detractors may share many of the same core values, but they see nothing sacred about challenging, destroying, or replacing certain ethics or customs. These social tensions are not new, and although the parameters change across time and place, the basic conflict is often between maintaining versus challenging society's traditions. Central to these traditions is the positioning of males and females within the family and society's larger network.

Charles Lamb's quote about the children's author Anna Barbauld and her "cursed crew" in 1802 could have been published today about Lois Lowry, Katherine Paterson, Judy Blume, Phyllis Reynolds Naylor, Jacqueline Woodson, or Madeleine L'Engle, whose works have been attacked by social conservatives for destroying or undermining the family and traditional values. Anna Barbauld, an enlightened and intelligent woman, was described by Lamb as "a witch bent not on nurture but destruction," an absurdly defamatory accusation that denigrated the significant body of literature that she generated for adults and children (Clarke, 1997). Barbauld was a teacher who wrote innovative age-leveled literacy textbooks in the *Lessons for Children* series in 1778; she was also a prolific poet with a substantial body of work, including her well-known *Hymns in Prose for Children*. In the capacity of editor she also produced *The British Novelists* in 50 volumes and the letters of Samuel Richardson in 6 volumes. Finally, Barbauld was an activist who wrote against slavery and war (Clarke, 1997) and who started a successful boarding school with her husband (Meigs, Eaton, Nesbitt, & Viguers, 1953). The personal assaults that Lamb made on her character attempted to publicly degrade the significant body of work she produced in which she urged child readers toward rational and humane behavior.

Women writing for English-speaking children have broken with tradition for more than two centuries by portraying strong female protagonists, since the publication of *The Governess or Little Female Academy* by Sarah Fielding (1749/1968). By breaking the silence about taboo topics hidden within families and offering strong protagonists, particularly females who seek their own agency, women writers have been vehemently criticized and have faced censure. Trites's (1997) definition of a protagonist's agency includes both the concept of a growing self-awareness and the ability to assert personality and enact personal decisions. Many children's novels are predicated on feminism's core notion of the equality of males and females, manifesting itself through the choices and options that their protagonists enact. Although the parameters of feminist topics have expanded in the modern era, some of the earliest books written for children contained "flickers of feminism" that the prevailing critics were determined to extinguish (Langford, 1989, p. 565), to the extent that 19th-century male literary critics felt compelled to protect impressionable young female readers by assuming the role of "strict literary police," as Stephen and Gifford referred to them in 1809 (Ferris, 1991).

While attending the Children's Literature New England workshop at Newnham College in Cambridge, England, in 1999, I purchased and read *Opening the Nursery Door: Reading, Writing and Childhood, 1600–1900*

(Hilton, Styles, & Watson, 1997), a book that is now out of print; it was the catalyst that led me to the primary works of the feminist women writers. I was simultaneously thrilled and agitated to learn about the significant roles that British women had played in education and in writing many of the earliest children's books at the end of the 18th century, and how they eventually were censured and silenced by socially conservative critics. These essays led me to the field of scholarship about 18th-century feminists and ultimately back to the primary sources at the British Library, where I examined the original works of these women and their critics. I looked at dozens of primary sources and secondary sources now out of print. I also used many excellent sources that provided biographies of the individual women writers and an extended discussion of the historical context of feminism in the late 1700s (Bree, 1996; Ferris, 1991; Fielding, 1749/1968; Myers, 1986; Rowe, 2005; Taylor, 2003; Todd, 2000).

Many male critics essentially considered female novelists, including the famous female novelists of books for adults, an inferior breed of writer—both dangerous and contemptible—so it is rather remarkable that women wrote prolifically for child audiences in the last decades of the 18th century. By the beginning of the 19th century and throughout the 20th century, however, these best-selling female children's authors were often caricatured by male critics as didactic women who were "destructive, dreary and inhuman" (Hilton, 1997), and who "utterly overlooked" the real child "except as a *tabula rasa* for a heavy pen" (Darton, 1932/1999, p. 174). (The word *didactic* includes both the concept of teaching and the concept of excess moralizing; the term is certainly justified when referring to this body of work.) Although the female novelists were initially praised by many socially conservative critics in the late 18th century, the success of the novelists and the sheer amount of books published by them caused a backlash among male critics, who began censuring women writers who were seen as being intellectually pretentious and moving beyond their accepted stations (Ferris, 1991). The critics eventually silenced the female children's authors, and their works were largely forgotten and dismissed as didactic novels written for children.

In the late 20th century, historians, feminists, and literary critics began a lively reexamination of the historical context of these British female writers, reconsidering their importance in feminist and literary history and historical children's literature. Mitzi Myers (1986) contends that the late 18th-century women writers constitute an "undervalued and almost unrecognized female literary tradition the more revelatory precisely because it *is* didactic, because it accepts and emphasizes the instructive and intellectual potential of narrative" (p. 33). Myers's groundbreaking analysis of what she called the "impeccable governesses, rational dames, and moral mothers" initiated a serious reevaluation of the roles of these women in the development of children's literature. Authors of children's fiction, including Anna Barbauld, Hannah More, Mary Wollstonecraft, Sarah Trimmer, Eleanor Fenn, and Maria Edgeworth, sought social justice through "their self-conscious didacticism," which presented readers with "a female mode of cultural reform directed toward improvement of both self and community" (p. 55). The "manipulation of gender" was always central to the critical examination of the novel because it was largely considered a female field (Ferris, 1991). Target the books. Attack the authors. Protect the readers. For more than 200 years there has been a conscious movement by social conservatives to shield children from dangerous books, including classics like *Little Women* by Louisa May Alcott (1868/2004) and *Bridge to Terabithia* by Katherine Paterson (1976).

Women in the 18th century were considered "children of a larger growth—passive, weak in mind and body, charming, frivolous, [and] fixated on beauty"; this description is found in a letter from Lord Chesterfield, a British statesman and author, to his son in 1748 (Root, 1929). Myers suggests that authors like Mary Wollstonecraft were offering women new visions of what motherhood entailed, including depictions of a rational and morally autonomous female—a new vision of the female heroine, a new vision of being a mother, a new vision of being a daughter, a new vision of the female activist who could effect social change and move more freely in society. Social historians have reenvisioned that era both in England and in the United States as a time in which the role of the mother was being redefined (Bloch, 1978) meaning that the adult female was being entrusted with the "social and moral development of young children and fledgling adolescent girls" (Rowe, 2005, p. 43). As a friend reminded me, this does not sound very radical, but the impact of this meant that women had an increasing presence as early childhood educators, wrote texts about education, novels for women and children, and began literacy outreach programs for the lower social classes—all of which was within the domain of the middle- and upper-class woman's domestic position in society and gave women more freedom of movement.

I will briefly examine the historical context and children's works of 18th-century female writers in Britain who "went against the grain" by empowering young female readers. Sarah Fielding has been examined in depth by scholars from other fields but has received scant attention in the field of education. Knowledge of her contributions and the powerful themes she explored are relevant to today's educators because she wrote the first children's book describing females who experienced freedom of physical movement, and her adult books challenged the restrictions of a woman's intellectual world. Fielding's single children's book influenced the popular female children's authors who wrote prolifically decades later, including Mary Wollstonecraft, who was the most strident proponent of female rationality.

Despite the extensive works of female authors at the beginning of the 19th century, children's literature moved away from a view of the rational female toward a romantic view of the male's journey. The didactic female writers were attacked, dismissed, and largely forgotten, whereas the didactic male writers like John Newbery and John Bunyan became icons of success, pillars in literary history. Parallels to the censure of modern female children's authors and their controversial works will be explored in chapter 12. The connections are powerful and startling. Then, as now, freedom of movement and freedom over one's own body are central to the discussion.

Sexual Repression Then and Now

Juxtaposed with the emerging model of the female activist in late 18th-century Britain was the prevalent model of the subordinate Christian woman, considered by Lord Chesterfield to be the large child in the nursery whose company would make 18th-century men despicably effeminate. A publication for women entitled *The Lady's Magazine* told women how to dress, how to control the tongue, how to be an obedient wife, how to read, and what to read. Physicians warned that reading novels could lead to female diseases, breakdowns, and other physical or psychological illnesses (Ferris, 1991).

This attempt to control what women could read was challenged by Sarah Fielding in her book *The Adventures of David Simple* by a Lady (Fielding, 1744), through the character of Cynthia, whose parents forcibly take books from her, except for silly stories and romances, because the knowledge in intellectual books will ruin her ability to attract a husband and "Miss must not enquire too far into things, it would turn her brain" (p. 188). Cynthia laments:

> Thus was I condemned to spend my youth, the time our imagination is at the highest, and we are capable of most pleasure, without being indulged in any one thing I liked, and obliged to employ myself in what was fancied by my mistaken parents to be for my improvement when in reality it was nothing more than what any person, a degree above a natural fool, might learn as well in a very small time, as in a thousand ages. (pp. 188–189)

At age 16 Cynthia meets a well-read woman and enjoys talking to her, but her mother is "frightened out of [her] wits to think what would become of them if they were together too much" (p. 199). "I verily believe she thought we should draw circles—and turn Conjurers" (pp. 199–200). How painfully constricting life must have been for an intelligent woman!

Sermons for young women addressed the seductive and corrupting powers of men, the afflictions of beauty, the safe confinement of the female in the home, the pitfalls of being a "Learned" Lady, and lists of acceptable female hobbies and appropriate reading materials (Fordyce, 1768). Fordyce actually *preached* that women should engage in needlework and that shading with color in needlework was a delicate and lost art that should not be abandoned by women, thereby showing how men attempted to regulate *every* aspect of a woman's life—no detail was too small.

First acknowledging the distinguished learning and success of skilled female authors, an essayist identified only as "N." then told readers of *The Lady's Magazine* (1789) the real message: The writing of novels was "well adapted to female ingenuity," and writing poetry was a "pleasing employment for their vacant hours," but classical knowledge was forbidden for women to study—because this pursuit was "repugnant to female delicacy" (p. 297). Female pedantry was the object of this author's ridicule. "I know no way of rendering classical knowledge so ridiculous, as by clothing it in petticoats" (p. 298). With ultimate contempt and ridicule, N. conjectures that ladies might ultimately usurp the male academy with their "rapid advance towards manhood" and go on to battle in war with superior skill (p. 300).

Alexander (1779), a misogynist, suggested that husbands have limited contact with their wives and that boys be taken away from their mothers, to whom he referred as that "dangerous female parent," as soon as they were weaned. Mary Hilton (1997) suggests that this kind of tract was commonplace at the end of the 18th century and that women fought the patriarchy even as they were entombed in their domestic roles. Alexander's rhetoric was meant to present an ideal family in the 1700s, as advocated by the Church and supported by a political structure in which women were captive, analogous to today's global religious and political institutions that continue to deny women basic rights and freedoms, such as freedom of movement, freedom over one's body, freedom to publicly express one's views, freedom to attend school (Ramdas, 2006).

Because death was common, the concepts of original sin and a burning afterlife converged as tangible threats that intimidated many people, as they still do today; excellence in every detail of personal behavior mattered. Christianity embraced a fear and respect of patriarchal values premised on obedience to a distinct male hierarchy. Two centuries later, little has changed. Most Christian denominations today do not allow women to become ministers or priests (e.g., the Lutheran Church Missouri Synod, the Roman Catholic Church) or hold certain positions of authority over men (e.g., church elder), and until recently they did not allow women to vote in church meetings (e.g., women's suffrage is still *optional* for congregations in the Lutheran Church Missouri Synod, an archaic position that was difficult to find on the Synod's Web site). Rather, women spoke through their husbands or other male members, a practice that some churches continue to this day. The Southern Baptist Church in the United States has reinserted the word *obey* in marriage vows for women—men do not have to obey.

Kavita Ramdas (2006), president of the Global Fund for Women, reminds us "that there is no culture…that intrinsically values women's rights" (p. 103), yet she has witnessed women who are locked in oppressive societies take enormous risks for the sake of personal and public freedom. Women in 18th-century Britain were no less wedged within their social, cultural, and political hegemonies and, not surprisingly, wrote within those strictures. That they spoke at all is remarkable.

Mary Wollstonecraft, writing in 1788, described the ideal woman of her era as idle, vain, and empty-headed, a profile that she considered decadent and worthy of her contempt; she focused much of the blame on parents who were not fulfilling their obligations to their children. Today's similarities are compelling. Women have obvious freedoms and choices that were not available to women in the 18th century, yet females tottering on high heels that permanently injure their backs are still fixated on cultural ideals of beauty that result in anorexia, bulimia, Botox injections, breast implants, liposuction, and plastic surgery. Females also continue to be vulnerable to violence within the family. Assault and rape of females continue to be rampant within the family, wrapped in terms like *sexual abuse* and *domestic violence*—isolating that violence from mainstream violence by locating it specifically within the family. Until recent decades, these topics have remained taboo in children's literature.

Some components of feminist theory address how the patriarchal structure negatively impacts males and females, and how eliminating inequality would benefit both males and females (Dresang, 2002). Sexuality, however, is one of the primary means of enforcing and maintaining inequality. "Foucault's *The History of Sexuality* demonstrates that regulating sexuality is central to the ways that Western cultures define themselves" and that "sexuality depends on a power/repression dynamic: sex is so powerful that it must be but cannot be controlled" (Trites, 2000, pp. 86–87). Given the beauty myths and mystiques that parallel sexual and predatory violence against females in Western society, it is hardly surprising that repression and silence continue to dominate the discourse in children's literature.

Understanding the historical context in which 18th-century women lived, and acknowledging that these writers were didactic, perhaps to their credit, I propose that we need to move beyond restricting labels and toward understanding what precipitated the didactic genre, as Mitzi Myers (1986) has called it. Reenvisioning history and the works of these 18th-century women writers will enable educators to understand how and why these authors were marginalized and to proactively consider the future role of children's literature, which has been under attack for several decades. Understanding the purposes and positioning of 18th-century didactic authors may illuminate how and why the works of contemporary feminist authors are slowly being removed from the elementary curriculum.

Positioning Female Writers in the 18th Century

A group of radical English women dominated writing in the late 1700s and challenged the tightly constricted lives of females in public and private spheres by writing intelligently and passionately for children. These female writers "sought to oppose the whole basis of the masculine ideology that was simultaneously working in society to enclose women's competence in the private and domestic sphere" (Hilton, 1997, p. 6); at the same time, they offered alternative views of the female heroine and of female potential in ordinary female life (Myers, 1986). Many of these women wrote books for both adults and children, with the specific intent of improving the lives of children, promoting female rationality, and providing mothers with models of teaching their daughters and sons. Some would be considered extreme feminists by today's labels and standards, and in their day many of their ideas were considered quite radical, a word I like to use because it encapsulates the concepts of fundamental, uncompromising, and far-reaching change. Many were active in a range of social issues of the time, such as improving the living conditions of the lower classes, establishing schools and teaching literacy to the poor, working against slavery, writing against the physical abuse of women and children, protesting cruelty to animals, and developing literacy texts and story anthologies (Clarke, 1997; Meigs et al., 1953; Myers, 1986).

In 1693, John Locke, in *Some Thoughts Concerning Education*, embraced popular notions not entirely original to him that male children needed explicit guidance in terms of moral principles that were considered to be the essence of an educated person (Bree, 1996). Influenced by Roger Ascham and Richard Mulcaster, who wrote 100 years earlier, Locke wrote that children should be treated as rational creatures, experience a childhood, not be burdened with excessive rules, and have books that brought them pleasure (Hunt, 1995; Meigs et al., 1953). Locke's view of childhood impacted Sarah Fielding and the single book that she wrote for children in 1749 (Fielding, 1749/1968; Meigs et al., 1953). Locke's views that children should laugh, play, and have physical exercise essentially focused on the education of males, but Fielding took his philosophies to heart and applied them to a school filled with girls (Hunt, 1995).

Sarah Fielding: Opposing Masculine Ideology in *The Governess*

Sarah Fielding (1749/1968) is considered the author of the first English full-length contemporary realistic fiction novel with real characters for real children (Myers, 1986; Rowe, 2005; Watson, 1997). Fielding wrote about ordinary people, as did her brother Henry Fielding; she used conversations and everyday dialogue to reveal character, a practice still used in contemporary fiction today. Fielding's female characters in *The Governess or Little Female Academy* were essentially middle-class boarding school students—as was Sarah Fielding—unbound by the restrictions of the home (Bree, 1996), which makes this the earliest prototype of the boarding school genre, a British literary tradition that includes thousands of titles and on which J. K. Rowling's *Harry Potter* books are premised (Whited, 2002). Sarah Fielding's major contribution to "feminist" children's literature, however, might be the fact that she challenged the physical confinement and structured time of 18th-century women.

Sarah Fielding challenged prevalent assumptions about women's roles, abilities, and movements by providing fictionalized spaces where young girls could become self-aware, although that's not a term that she would have used. When I write that the movements of girls were tightly controlled, modern readers don't fully appreciate how literally that statement can be taken. For example, at the beginning of the 19th century, didacticism reached its peak in the writings of Mary Butt Sherwood, who actually re-wrote *The Governess* because she considered Fielding's version too liberal for including two fairy tales. Meigs and colleagues (1953) relate how young Mary Sherwood was forced to wear an iron collar with a backboard all day as she studied, and like other females of the era, she was also made to stand in wooden stocks as she studied banal lessons on posture, manners, and dressing properly. Sarah Fielding believed that girls should exercise the body as well as the mind to achieve peace and harmony.

The governess in the story was Mrs. Teachum, an independent widow who earned her livelihood by operating a boarding school for girls. At Mrs. Teachum's female academy, girls had leisure time and exercise before and after meals, including 4–6 miles of walking each day. Make no mistake, Fielding was a product of her time, and happiness for women was achieved through obedience and submission to men and governing the passions rather than being ruled by them. Rowe (2005) writes that Fielding's "whole intent" was the "proper socialization" of young women into the sisterhood, albeit focused obediently on community rather than on "individual ambitions." Fielding was vehemently opposed to cruelty and violence of any kind, particularly birching children and torturing animals, and she wove these lessons into her stories through the voice of Mrs. Teachum so that her readers and their parents might desist using these common but violent practices.

Mrs. Teachum was a self-sufficient woman whose "chief delight" as a married woman of 9 years had been receiving her clergyman husband's instruction concerning the education of children. Within a year of his death, she lost both of her daughters to a violent fever. Mrs. Teachum was an enlightened and mature woman who allowed the girls independent time and interfered as little as possible, using persuasion rather than force and encouraging the nine girls to run in the fields and gardens, pick flowers, laugh, talk, and sing as they lived in harmony with each other. This was revolutionary in a time when the movements of women were tightly controlled.

The Governess begins with an epic fight over the largest apple in a basket of apples while Mrs. Teachum was away. This is an impressively vicious fight by any standards. The central character of the book is 14-year-old Jenny Peace, a knowledgeable young adolescent who has already achieved inner tranquility, is an active problem solver, and has much wisdom to dispense— a character in control, not unlike J. K. Rowling's Hermione Granger. As the other eight girls whine and explain why each deserves the best apple, Jenny tosses the beautiful apple over the hedge, at which point the girls explode into pulling off one another's caps, tearing hair, dragging off clothes, scratching, pinching, and screaming. Miss Dolly Friendly attacks a pincher like an enraged lion on its prey, and not content only to return the Harm her Friend had received, she struck with such Force, as felled her Enemy to the Ground. [The girls] fought, scratch'd, and tore, like so many cats, when they extend their Claws to fix them in their Rivals Hearts. (Fielding, 1749/ 1968, p. 7)

This female fight is a first in children's literature—these girls are pent-up wildcats. This is a bar brawl. The girls have fists filled with hair, pieces of ripped caps and aprons, and the ground is spread with the tatters of their clothing. Mrs. Teachum returns, restores order, and spends the remainder of the book teaching her young fictitious females how to control their feral passions. The fight scene must have been enormously popular with young female readers, who were being scripted into physical and emotional control and confinement. Sarah Fielding's fight was possible only because of the boarding school setting that gave the young women a context in which social conventions could be broken (Bree, 1996). Fielding begins the book with the fight to show why control and subordination of one's passionate emotions are essential, and then she presents her individual characters, each having a different story, each having different character flaws.

She begins with the oldest, 11-year-old Sukey, who does not easily relent. "For if I could but hurt my Enemies, without being hurt myself, it would be the greatest Pleasure I could have in the world" (p. 14). Her personal narrative reveals that she has no memory of her dead mother, and that after her father remarried she was left to the care of an old servant who always let her have her own way, a theme that becomes the main premise of Wollstonecraft's *Original Stories* (1788). From the age of 4, Sukey has beaten her little companion servant. Sukey thinks that the distance between them is so great that she has never considered that the girl could feel pain or grief.

Sukey further reveals that she cannot sleep in peace because she has not taken revenge on the girls who offended her during the apple fight. Through Socratic dialogue, Jenny challenges Sukey's obstreperous behavior, and while alone that night, Sukey ponders her behavior and intrinsic unhappiness and grieves all night over her quarrelsome nature. The next morning, Sukey mumbles a reluctant confession of her faults, which reveals Fielding's didactic agenda of achieving self-discipline and subordination of emotion for each individual girl (Bree, 1996), highlighting themes of rationality that would later be echoed in the work of Mary Wollstonecraft. Fielding might have had self-discipline as her ultimate goal, but what a vicious romp the girls have had achieving it, and what nasty faults they have all revealed—jealousy, tantrums, revenge. Imagine how a young female reader might have reveled in this kind of naughty physical and emotional freedom. Labeling it naughty gave it a legitimate right to be described in detail.

Juxtaposed with Fielding's vision of female physicality was John Newbery's bleak depiction found in *A Little Pretty Pocket-Book* (1744/1760), an alphabet book of uppercase and lowercase movements published 5 years before *The Governess*. Small woodcuts show boys actively playing or moving in *all* the pictures—hopping, stepping, jumping, kiteflying, playing shuttlecock, hoop and hide, chuck farthing, blind man's bluff, maypole, base-ball, cricket, pitch and hussel, fives, tip cat, hop-hat, hopscotch, and leapfrog. The boys are also depicted swimming without clothes, riding, and fishing—all of which indicate the male's extensive freedom of movement, lack of restrictions, access to games, and ability to roam without supervision.

Conversely, girls appear in only 5 of the 38 miniature alphabet woodcuts. Two woodcuts show women standing: One shows three polite women standing in front of a bowing man, and the other shows a vexed woman holding a hankie to her cheek as she converses with a male. Only three woodcuts show women actively moving: Two depict males and females dancing, and one shows males and females playing blind man's bluff; in the latter, however, the text indicates that one of the "overly proud" women has lost the treasure of her heart.

Although Fielding's book is a novel and Newbery's is an alphabet book. the oppositional views of female physicality are evident. Newbery's woodcuts show females as essentially invisible bystanders rather than active participants. "Half empty or half full" is the notation I made in my journal at the British Library in 2000, which indicates my own conditioning and my low expectations for successful and active females.

The fact that Fielding purposely empowered the female characters within the constraints of the social milieu in which she lived makes this the earliest feminist book for children. Mrs. Teachum influenced children's authors for decades, including John Newbery, who turned *Little Goody Two-Shoes* (1765) into Margery, the "Trotting Tutoress", and whose Mr. Loveworth was a male version of Mrs. Teachum, according to Grey (Fielding, 1749/1968). Sarah Fielding's provocative works influenced Mary Wollstonecraft 39 years later. Fielding's name, however, never appeared on *The Governess* during her lifetime, even though the book remained in print until 1903; it has recently been republished for purposes of scholarship.

Mary Wollstonecraft's Planet:
Rejecting a Decadent Model of Womanhood

No one has been more vilified or ignored in historical children's literature than Mary Wollstonecraft, the most militant of the women writers, who was also strongly influenced by Sarah Fielding's writings. Wollstonecraft advocated the intellectual rights and independence of women. Her lifestyle was considered so scandalous that even after her death, *A Defence of the Character and Conduct of the Late Mary Wollstonecraft Godwin* was published by James Wallis in 1803. The author was obviously a great admirer of Wollstonecraft and suggests how vicious the personal attacks were. "Geniuses are not to be estimated by common rules—they are planets, and must be reviewed upon their own principles" (p. 10). The attacks continued as late as 1995, when John Rowe Townsend referred to her *Original Stories* (Wollstonecraft, 1788) as "perhaps the most repellent piece of English Rousseauism" and to Wollstonecraft herself as being "better known as an early propagandist for the rights of women" (Townsend, 1995, p. 26). Indeed.

Wollstonecraft was a steadfast advocate of the rights of women, although Townsend's use of the words *repellent* and *propagandist* suggests that she was fiercely misguided. Her vision of daughters and mothers was based on her passionate beliefs about the rational female and her rejection of the vain and frivolous idleness of women and the silly romances they read. Wollstonecraft's caustic writings about the idealized roles of women made her an icon for feminism in the late 20th century. Taylor (2003) writes that Wollstonecraft sought no less than "universal equality" and "moral perfection" for women, premised on the utopianism of Britain's radical Enlightenment.

Wollstonecraft (1788) viewed reading as the "highest branch of solitary amusement," wherein "the heart is touched, till its feelings are examined by the understanding" (p. 116). She believed that "reason regulates the imagination" and wrote that it took years to acquire, but knowledge becomes a mine to which one can return. Hers was a transformational view of writing and reading that she used to challenge the establishment by tackling what she called the miseducation of daughters. She used story to transform—a brilliant application of the didactic genre.

Original Stories from Real Life with Conversations, calculated to regulate the affections and form the mind to truth and Goodness (1788) is a family story in which two wealthy parents have left the management of their two daughters to servants. Because their father finds them troublesome, a surrogate mother in the form of a governess takes over after the death of his wife and becomes the first real mother that the children had ever known. Wollstonecraft indicates that the girls were morally deficient because they "had caught every prejudice that the vulgar can instill" (p. XII), reflecting the social divide in Wollstonecraft's world. A modern-day character like

Katherine Paterson's (1978) Gilly Hopkins exhibits deviant behaviors, as do the abandoned Mary and Carolyn, suggesting the universality of Wollstonecraft's characters.

The dual premises of *Original Stories* are that of the mother-teacher governess, Mrs. Mason, who had the knowledge to transform two misguided daughters and who would serve as a role model for mothers who read the book. Wollstonecraft was later ridiculed for believing that women are capable of such rational behavior. Like Mrs. Teachum, Mrs. Mason believes in exercise and being outdoors, providing freedom for the confined female. Throughout the book Mrs. Mason teaches the girls by taking them on walks in the fields and in the woods, which was typical of early childhood models of active learning promoted by educators like Eleanor Fenn. Both daughters are considered guilty and innocent within the microcosm of their interior worlds—guilty because they have to take control and overcome their vulgar and violent tendencies; innocent because they have never been given proper nurture and instruction but have been allowed to grow up untutored. Wollstonecraft believes that it is not too late for Mrs. Mason's surrogate daughters to become self-aware. The important lessons are taught, digested, and learned, and the reader knows that the girls will be rehabilitated successfully into society, but into a society that Wollstonecraft envisioned rather than society as it actually existed.

The Difference Between Male and Female Didacticism

How did the odious word *didactic* become a permanent slur to describe the children's books of Sarah Fielding, Anna Barbauld, Maria Edgeworth, Sarah Trimmer, Hannah More, Mary Wollstonecraft, and Lady Eleanor Fenn? Why were these and other authors attacked, marginalized, and then excluded from the literary canon? What relevance could it possibly have today? I will answer that question by briefly reenvisioning the work of two widely read didactic authors who are held in high esteem by the literary community and included in the literary canon. The negative connotation that has evolved with the word *didactic* includes the idea of dreary excessive moralizing that was common in early books of instruction for children. Those books, written by both men and women, included rules for living a moral life within meticulously delineated gender roles. Children's writers spelled out the reward system for adhering to these didactic rules; they encompassed heavy-handed warnings about heaven and hell and all the severe punishments in between. John Bunyan, writing *A Book for Boys and Girls or Country Rhymes for Children*, in 1686, employed the voice of an "awakened" child to lament his original sin:

and as I was born naked
I was with filth bespaked . . .
My filth grew strong and boyled
and me throughout defiled
It's pleasures me beguiled
My Soul! how art thou spoyled!" (p. 2)

Bunyan went on to didactically lament this state-of-sin muck for 29 verses and concluded, "But God has condescended, and pardon has extended, to such as have offended, Before their lives were ended" (p. 6). Bad behavior was punished most vehemently, even violently. Bunyan wrote this about the disobedient child: "Their sinful Nature prompts them to rebel, And to delight in Paths that lead to Hell." (p. 71) The disobedient child despised the type of love given by his indulgent parents and brought birds to pick out their eyes. Bunyan well understood the didactic genre and thought it appropriate for children, but he was neither chastised nor personally attacked for his writings. How ironic that Townsend (1995) referred to this work as having a "rugged sternness," whereas he considered the works of the didactic women as being "unspeakably cruel" with their threats of damnation for common faults (p. 29).

John Newbery's hearty use of didacticism is rarely mentioned in historical children's literature. Rather, Newbery is extolled for his publishing contributions in the history of children's literature. *The Norton Anthology of Children's Literature* (Zipes, Paul, Vallone, Hunt, & Avery, 2005) reduces Newbery's original 156-page *The History of Little Goody Two-Shoes* (1765), to a mere 7 pages, calling the original version "diffuse and digressive" (p. 50). This shortened version creates the impression that Newbery wrote a compelling and compact story, unique in its times and didactic-free. In *Goody Two-Shoes*, Margery Meanwell, the orphaned female protagonist, becomes a "trotting Tutoress" who uses didacticism explicitly to teach literacy to her students. As in *The Governess* (Fielding, 1749/1968) and *Original Stories* (Wollstonecraft, 1788), plot and pleasure are to be found in this book; however, didacticism plays a central role in this children's literature icon of 156 pages, which Darton (1932/1999) describes as being "utterly dead" and "not even a good readable story" (p. 131).

Using explicit scripted instruction on how to learn to read, the author of *Little Goody Two-Shoes* inserts prayers exhorting children to moral behavior:

The Lord have Mercy upon me, and grant that I may be always good, and say my Prayers, and love the Lord my God with all my Heart, with all my Soul, and with all my Strength; and honour the King, and all good Men in Authority under him. (Newbery, 1765, pp. 37–38)

In the last prayer, the children are exhorted to pray for their enemies, to which Polly Sullen objects.

"Not pray for your Enemies," says Little Margery; "yes, you must, you are no Christian, if you don't forgive your Enemies, and do Good for Evil." Polly still pouted; upon which Little Margery said, though she was poor, and obliged to lie in a Barn, she would not keep Company with such a naughty, proud, perverse Girl as Polly. (p. 38)

Why is it that Bunyan and Newbery are praised and extolled for their contributions to historical children's literature, whereas the significant contributions of female authors who advocated social justice and a repositioning of the female's role in society have traditionally been denigrated and denied their rightful status? The difference between Bunyan's and Newbery's use of didacticism and the censured women writers' use of didacticism is that women used it to circumvent the male agenda. The books that I have briefly examined by Fielding (1749/1968) and Wollstonecraft (1788) indicate how women became direct proponents of a female agenda, with their own purposes, seeking to shape the content and reality of their own lives, but within the context of the subordinate Christian female. This was not a full-scale rebellion. Women were seeking more latitude in their lives, more autonomy, more wiggle room.

A fierce conflict ensued between the rational didactic books and the rise of what Rowe (2005) calls "a culture of radical romanticism." At the beginning of the 19th century, Tucker (1997) suggests that the battle over children's literature became more pronounced because social conservatives longed for a bygone feudal era in which everyone had a specific social slot, even as some women fought for the acceptance of the intelligent and rational female activist. Similar to today's battles, the controversy then was political and included personal attacks.

Closing Thoughts:
Why Should This Matter to Educators Today?

I see troubling parallels between the politically charged scene today and the atmosphere in which the radical women writers and educators of the 18th century lost their autonomy, which no one would have thought possible in 1788. Will the voices of today's innovative children's authors be silenced and ultimately disappear? In the next chapter I will examine the books of the modern women writers who have broken with tradition to write stories with empowered female and male characters living within diverse families. In the past four decades, a group of female children's authors have been harshly challenged by social conservatives and caricatured as anti-family and anti-God. Yet divorce, abortion, homosexuality, abandonment, sexual predators, violence, and death have all existed in families throughout history. Contemporary authors have not restructured families, nor have they invented current domestic tableaus. They have, however, written truthfully about diverse family structures and the complexities that swirl within and around them. They have written sensitively and with insight about the difficult lives that some children live and the difficult choices that some children make.

Many of these controversial works have been excluded from or rewritten for anthologies because their themes are considered too raw and too revealing of the darker side of family life. Certain books have been censored outright and removed from libraries, have been put on booklists that are unavailable for classroom use, or require parental permission to check them out from libraries. Books that contain characters with a strong sense of self-determination who challenge traditional gender roles, who ask the wrong questions, or who are victims surviving within destructive families have been frequent targets of censors. What parallels can be drawn between these women writers separated by more than 200 years?

References

Primary Sources

Alexander, W. (1779). *Female government or letters from a gentleman to his friend on the education of the fair sex.* London: Fielding & Walker.

Anonymous. (1789, February). Hints on reading. *The Lady's Magazine, 20,* 80.

Anonymous. (1812). On novel reading and the mischief which arises from its indiscriminate practice. *The Lady's Magazine, 43,* 222–224.

Bunyan, J. (1686). *A book for boys and girls on country rhimes for children.* London: Printed for N. P. and Sold by the Booksellers in London.

Darton, J. (1932/1999). *Children's books in England: Five centuries of social life* (Brian Alderson, Ed.). London: British Library and Oak Knoll Press.

Fielding, S. (1744). *The adventures of David Simple.* London: A Millar.

Fordyce, J. (1768). *Sermons to young women* (7th ed.). London: Printed for J. Williams in Skinner Row.

N. (1789, June). On female authorship from the Trifler. *The Lady's Magazine, 20,* 297–300.

Newbery, J. (1760). *A little pretty pocket-book* (10th ed.). London: Printed for J. Newbery, at the Bible and Sun in St. Paul's-Church-Yard. (Original work published 1744)

Newbery, J. (1765). *The history of Little Goody Two-Shoes.* London: Printed for J. Newbery, at the Bible and Sun in St. Paul's-Church-Yard.

Wallis, J. (1803). *A defence of the character and conduct of the late Mary Wollstonecraft Godwin founded on principles of nature and reason as applied to the peculiar circumstances of her case in a series of letters to a lady.* London: James Wallis.

Wollstonecraft, M. (1788). *Original stories from real life with conversations, calculated to regulate the affections and form the mind to truth and goodness.* London: J. Johnson.

Secondary Sources and Children's Books

Alcott, L. M. (2004). *Little women.* New York: Signet Classics. (Original work published 1868)

Bloch, R. (1978). American feminine ideals in transition: The rise of the moral mother, 1785–1815. *Feminist Studies, 4* (2), 101–126.

Bree, L. (1996). *Sarah Fielding.* New York: Twayne.

Clarke, N. (1997). The cursed Barbauld crew: Women writers and writing for children in the late eighteenth century. In M. Hilton, M. Styles, & V. Watson (Eds.), *Opening the nursery door: Reading, writing and childhood, 1600–1900.* London: Routledge.

Dresang, E. (2002). Gender issues and Harry Potter. In L. Whited (Ed.), *The ivory tower and Harry Potter.* Columbia, MO: University of Missouri Press.

Ferris, I. (1991). *The achievement of literary authority: Gender, history and the Waverley novels.* Ithaca, NY: Cornell University Press.

Fielding, S. (1968). *The governess or little female academy* (J. Grey, Ed.). Oxford, UK: Oxford University Press. (Original work published 1749)

Fitzgerald, P. (1876). *The works of Charles Lamb.* London: Moxon.

Hilton, M. (1997). Introduction. In M. Hilton, M. Styles, & V. Watson (Eds.), *Opening the nursery door: Reading, writing and childhood, 1600–1900.* London: Routledge.

Hilton, M., Styles, M., & Watson, V. (Eds.). *Opening the nursery door: Reading, writing and childhood, 1600–1900.* London: Routledge.

Hunt, P. (Ed.). (1995). *Children's literature: An illustrated history.* Oxford, UK: Oxford University Press.

Langford, P. (1989). *A polite and commercial people: England, 1727–1783.* Oxford, UK: Clarendon Press.

Marrs, E. (Ed.). (1976). Letter 136. *The letters of Charles and Mary Anne Lamb* (Vol. 2, pp. 81–82). Ithaca, NY: Cornell University Press.

Meigs, C, Eaton, A., Nesbitt, E., & Viguers, R. (1953). *A critical history of children's literature.* New York: Macmillan.

Myers, M. (1986). Impeccable governesses, rational dames, and moral mothers: Mary Wollstonecraft and the female tradition in Georgian children's books. *Children's Literature, 14,* 31–59.

Paterson, K. (1976). *Bridge to Terabithia* (D. Diamond, Illus.). New York: Crowell.

Paterson, K. (1978). *The great Gilly Hopkins.* New York: HarperCollins.

Ramdas, K. (2006). Feminists and fundamentalists. *Current History, 105* (689), 99–104.

Root, R. K. (1929). *Lord Chesterfield's letters to his son and others.* London: Dent.

Rowe, K. (2005). Virtue in the guise of vice: The making and unmaking of morality from fairy tale fantasy. In D. Ruwe (Ed.), *Culturing the child, 1690–1914: Essays in memory of Mitzi Myers.* Lanham, MD: Children's Literature Association and Scarecrow Press.

Taylor, B. (2003). *Mary Wollstonecraft and the feminist imagination.* Cambridge, UK: Cambridge University Press.

Todd, J. (2000). *Mary Wollstonecraft: A revolutionary life.* New York: Columbia University Press.

Townsend, J. (1995). *Written for children.* London: Bodley Head.

Trites, R. (1997). *Waking sleeping beauty: Feminist voices in children's novels.* Iowa City, IA: University of Iowa Press.

Trites, R. (2000). *Disturbing the universe: Power and repression in adolescent literature.* Iowa City: IA: University of Iowa Press.

Tucker, N. (1997). Fairy tales and their early opponents: In defence of Mrs. Trimmer. In M. Hilton, M. Styles, & V. Watson (Eds.), *Opening the nursery door: Reading, writing and childhood, 1600–1900.* London: Routledge.

Watson, A. (1997). Jane Johnson: A very pretty story to tell children. In M. Hilton, M. Styles, & V. Watson (Eds.), *Opening the nursery door: Reading, writing and childhood, 1600–1900.* London: Routledge.

Whited, L. (2002). *The ivory tower and Harry Potter.* Columbia, MO: University of Missouri Press.

Zipes, J., Paul, L., Vallone, L., Hunt, P., & Avery, G. (Eds.). (2005). *The Norton anthology of children's literature.* New York: Norton.

Chapter

12

Contemporary Women Writers: "Undercutting the Patriarchy"

Susan S. Lehr

> *It is a platitude in the criticism of children's literature that social agendas in children's fiction tend to fall twenty years behind the social movements of a given culture. This is especially true in such cultures as ours that hold an inherently conservative and Romantic view of childhood, believing that childhood is a time of innocence and that children should be protected from politics. As a result, the ideologies in children's fiction tend toward upholding the status quo, traditionally affirming the patriarchy and capitalist culture. Feminist children's fiction is nowhere near as radical as is feminist fiction written for adults, but in its own quiet way, the genre is very neatly undercutting the patriarchy in a variety of innovative ways.*
>
> —Trites (1997a, pp. 3–4)

The Destruction of the Family by Women Writers of the Modern Era

Women writers who "undercut the patriarchy" with feminist children's fiction have been accused of destroying the family and of being anti-God, a phenomenon that parallels the vituperative attacks against women writers and educators that began at the end of the 18th century, when critics like Charles Lamb derided female children's authors as "blights and blasts of all that is human." The attacks against these established 18th-century female writers of children's books continued throughout the 20th century. Percy Muir (1954) referred to these magnificent female writers as a "monstrous regiment of women," whereas most textbook authors simply dismissed their works as being didactic and therefore not worthy of merit or even mention in historical children's literature, a practice that continues today. The term used by Percy was originally penned by John Knox in a 1558 tract, "First Blast of the Trumpet Against the Monstrous Regiment of Women," in which Knox attacked what he considered to be the "unnatural rule" of the Catholic Queen Mary. Ironically, Percy Muir's sexist comments in 1954 preceded by less than a decade the earliest modern feminist books for children—books like *A Wrinkle in Time* (L'Engle, 1962) and *Harriet the Spy* (Fitzhugh, 1964), both of which are radical books that challenge traditional gender roles and whose authors could therefore also be considered part of the "monstrous regiment."

Susina (1997) writes that "the great works of children's literature have always been subversive, if not revolutionary" (p. 2); this was true in the 18th century and is still true today. Social conservatives attack "subversive" children's authors and educators today, using the term *feminist* as the ultimate slur for writers who explore the tapestry of family life. The term is also used for the educators who use these books in the elementary curriculum. *Didactic* has been replaced with *anti-god* and *anti-family* and, most recently, *anti-boy*. O'Beirne (2006) rails against the gender warriors who emasculate young boys, beginning in elementary school, which she calls feminist reeducation camps. Trites (1997a) suggests that before the women's movement in the 1960s, "most children's books subjected the child reader to some fairly heavy-handed indoctrination into gender roles" (p. 1). This practice, bizarrely, is supported today by online booksellers who specialize in 18th- and early 19th-century children's books that depict historical gender roles and that are targeted for homeschooled children.

Rosemary Tong (1998) writes that postmodern feminism embraces diversity within the female experience and, I would argue, within the male experience.

> As bad as it is for a woman to be bullied into submission by a patriarch's unitary truth, it is even worse for her to be judged not a real feminist by a matriarch's unitary truth. . . . As I see it, attention to difference is precisely what will help women achieve unity. (p. 279)

I would add that postmodern feminism embraces diversity within the male experience as well; bullying males into a patriarchal or matriarchal unitary truth is equally disempowering, because successful feminist writers give agency or self-determination to both genders (Dresang, 2002; Gilligan, 1982; Trites, 1997b; Vandergrift, 1996). Feminist literature has become the means of expression for the disempowered, including both males and females, which I will address in my analysis of feminist books. Dresang (1999) describes contemporary books as having three broad types of male and female characters: those who survive and thrive; those who survive with some thread of hope; and those who have doubtful futures.

Using Dresang's three broad types of male and female characters as a framework, I will examine how males and females "find strength and agency despite their marginalization," which encapsulates the definition of the feminist children's novel (Dresang, 2002, p. 218). Much has already been written about the "darker topics" found in books for young adults, but little has been written about how authors address feminist topics for younger children in elementary school. The focus of this essay, therefore, will be on feminist books written specifically for children at the edge of becoming young adults (Dresang, 1999). Vandergrift's (1996) model of "female voices in youth literature" considers the feminist stance of both the writer and the reader, but not all the women writers that I will consider in this chapter consciously produced feminist texts advocating female equality; therefore, like Dresang (2002), I will examine the books based on what the authors have done, not on what could have been done.

In this chapter I will focus on selected works of female writers, although the time is ripe for an examination of the feminist works of male authors. Guus Kuijer, for example, has written the miraculous *The Book of Everything* (2006), in which a young boy endures his father's formidable and twisted religious wrath and beatings. Thomas says that when he grows up, he will be happy. Translated from Dutch, this book is set in a culturally turbulent post-World War II Holland.

I believe that many contemporary high-quality children's books written by feminist authors are in danger of being erased from the curriculum. An entire class of college students in children's literature was unfamiliar with Katherine Paterson's name, although I discovered later that many had been assigned *Bridge to Terabithia* (1976) in elementary school. Paterson, winner of National Book Awards, the Newbery Awards, and the Hans Christian

Andersen Award for lifetime achievement, had just won the 2006 Astrid Lindgren Memorial Award for her body of work, yet these well-read students did not know who she was, nor were they familiar with her other books. In my concluding remarks I speculate how this could be possible.

This essay will provide an overview of the significant feminist works of contemporary female authors, underscoring their importance and vitality in the field of children's literature. At the end of this chapter I will draw explicit parallels to the women writers of the late 18th century and suggest that we consider their eventual demise as a cautionary tale for today's writers and educators, echoing warnings given by Judy Blume and others during the past decade. Before analyzing feminist children's books of the modern era, I will define the parameters of the contemporary context in which these women wrote and continue to write, which will provide a sociocultural framework in which to consider their works.

Defining and Extinguishing "Flickers of Feminism" Today

> *If we think to regulate printing, thereby to rectify manners, we must regulate all recreations and pastimes, all that is delightful to man.*
>
> —John Milton, 1644

A range of social conservatives seeks to ban specific feminist books in schools, to control public school curricula, to censor content in textbooks, and to restrict library holdings and access to books. This manipulation manifests itself at times through publishing conglomerates that cater to conservative constituents and conservative education agendas.

In 2006 Patricia Polacco cancelled an appearance to speak at the International Reading Association because there was an attempt on the part of the client sponsoring the event, SRA McGraw-Hill, to preview the content of her remarks and limit those remarks to noncontroversial, nonpolitical topics. Polacco has responded in an open letter on her Web site, www.patriciapolacco.com, as follows:

> My speeches certainly do inspire teachers. . . . I truly believe they are among the last heroes we have in our country . . . but I always mention the destructive path

> that is laying waste to our schools, and that is the No
> Child Left Behind mandate! I did mention to them [SRA
> McGraw-Hill] that I considered that this request ap-
> proached "censorship" and a violation of my freedom of
> speech.

Polacco countered their request to be "upbeat" by stating that

> the plight of American teachers is far from "upbeat" and
> that they are caught in the vice grip of the most controver-
> sial and political LIE that has ever been perpetrated on
> the American teacher. . . . Profits and money seem to
> matter much more than truly making changes to our edu-
> cational systems that would truly help our children.

Religious and political conservatives have united in their efforts to restore traditional values through a "moral crusade" that is now firmly situated within the Republican Party (D'Emilio & Freedman, 1997) and often plays out in the elementary classroom or the public library, although some Republican politicians are beginning to reassess and distance themselves from the extremity of their party's moral positioning.

Kavita Ramdas (2006), president of the Global Fund for Women, writes that "the one thread [that fundamentalists] share is the attempt to control women's bodies, the ability of women to move freely, and their ability to speak with any kind of free voice within their societies" (p. 102). Ramdas maintains that the irony is that fundamentalists, from Kabul to Cambridge, seek an idealized past in which women are restored to their rightful collective places despite the fact that the international community agrees that women's rights are a "global good." No global developmental goals can be achieved without a major investment in the education of girls and the full participation of women in all aspects of international institutions. In Afghanistan under the Taliban the physical movement of women was controlled, education for women was repealed, and yet women passed books illegally to one another and met secretly to discuss them and educate their daughters.

In the United States, social conservatives have been successful in their attempts to control the national curriculum by targeting reading instruction and methodologies. Rather than encouraging free access to children's literature in the classroom, there has been a systematic attack on literature-based programs, much of it motivated by fundamentalist religious conservatives. In thousands of elementary classrooms, a return to direct instruction, emphasizing skills and drills is replacing much of the rich children's literature that was found in classrooms across the United States in the 1980s and 1990s. William Bennett's *The Book of Virtues* (1993) has become symbolic of how contemporary children's literature is being usurped by traditional stories with moral absolutes, what Henry Carrigan, writing for the *School Library Journal* (1993) has called a "McGuffey's Reader for the Nineties." I would add that the virtuous in Bennett's stories are primarily White Western males, which reinforces the marginalization of females and minorities and continues the miseducation of both males and females in the classroom.

Feminist discourse continues to divide and alienate women. Kate O'Beirne, author of *Women Who Make the World Worse* (2006), blasts feminists and feminist research, specifically targeting Hillary Clinton, Gloria Steinem, Maureen Dowd, Eleanor Smeal, Peggy Orenstein, Mary Pipher, and the American Association of University Women (AAUW, 1995) report, *How Schools Shortchange Girls*, by accusing these women of poisoning public discourse through their claims that a hostile patriarchy makes women its helpless victims. Ignoring the status of women in history, O'Beirne declares that the silencing of adolescent females by the Western patriarchal culture is a myth, and she contends that the discourse of feminists is devastating American society and fracturing families. It is indicative of a shift in the focus of social conservatives in recent years. There is little that is specific against feminist literature for children in her writing. Rather, she talks in generalities about the devastation of the family and of children in the classroom by feminist principles, feminist teachers, and feminist agendas.

In *The War Against Boys*, Sommers (2000) shreds feminist educational researchers and their research by attacking the methodology, the interpretation of results, and the motivation of the researchers, like Carol Gilligan, whom she demonizes. Sommers makes the case that because boys are now at risk educationally, feminist agendas are somehow to blame. Must the female's success be sacrificed so that boys might succeed?

Cheaney (2005) makes a general case against authors who "teach" children through gloom and "edgy" subjects. She suggests that the zeal with which some authors, teachers, and librarians "push" problem novels at middle school children borders on the sadistic. Cheaney also resurrects the didactic label and says that children's authors accept this preachy role with gusto for their captive, impressionable, and pliant child audiences, suggesting that "the existential dilemma that infected literature in the early 20th century has worked its way down to 10-year-olds," offering them bleak world views and abandoned protagonists. This vision of childhood seems to be premised on safe clean children who live in safe clean homes with safe and nurturing adults. When has that ever been the reality for the majority of children in the world? This worldview is not even a realistic picture of the local neighborhood. Children cannot safely avoid the human condition, and I don't believe that attempts to shelter them from seeing the world is ultimately a wise choice. Understanding and compassion are not the exclusive domains of the adult world.

An oppositional and radical feminist stance recognizes that institutions are being shattered out of necessity so that females can finally become empowered rather than be helpless. Drawing on the older work of Helene Cixous (cited in Trites, 1997a), one finds a powerful statement of why she believes this devastation is necessary:

> A feminine text cannot fail to be more than subversive. It is volcanic; as it is written it brings about an upheaval of the old property crust, carrier of masculine investments; there's no other way…it's in order to smash everything, to shatter the framework of institutions, to blow up the law, to break up the "truth" with laughter. (p. 7)

Building on Cixous's statement, Trites writes:

> Any time a character in children's literature triumphs over the social institutions that have tried to hold her down, she helps to destroy the traditions that have so long forced females to occupy the position of Other. . . . Laughter emblemizes the girl's transcendence, and her transcendence is the key to her feminism and is the greatest factor that separates her from prefeminist protagonists. She does not simply grow, she grows in power. (p. 7)

Who are today's "destructive" women writers who seek social justice by presenting child readers with "female mode[s] of cultural reform directed toward improvement of both self and community" (Myers, 1986, p. 55)? What makes their works of the past four decades so dangerous? Feminist children's writers either destroy the family and emasculate males, as O'Beirne (2006), Sommers (2000), and Cheaney (2005) imply, or they reenvision a world in which patriarchal traditions are destroyed and females transcend with laughter, as Cixous and Trites imagine.

Probing Madeleine L'Engle's Universe: Religion, Science, and Gender Implode

Prior to the late 20th century, many family topics were taboo in books for children, and if they were written they were not published. Contemporary issues that have been forbidden, marginalized, or considered subversive include children who live in gay and lesbian families, who are raped by family members, who are assaulted by violent parents or siblings, who live in homes where the adults are unmarried, who experience the suicide of a loved one, who are exposed to the concept of abortion or to characters who believe that it is an option for women, who talk about human sexuality, or who question religion.

Consider the difficulty that Madeleine L'Engle had publishing her groundbreaking book *A Wrinkle in Time* (1962), in which she portrayed a strongly defined, intelligent, atypical female character with a scientist mother as her role model, all within an unorthodox religious framework. L'Engle's universe was boldly rational and scientific, as were her female characters, which might explain why 26 publishers rejected this book. L'Engle embraced the principles of Albert Einstein and questioned the place of humans in the universe. Her view of evil included a bleak suburban neighborhood in which all children bounced their balls at the same time and in the same manner. Was she anti-family, or simply reflecting a caricature of the middle-class family? Zipes (2002) writes that evil can be characterized by a "lack of imagination and compassion" (p. 182).

Long before Lois Lowry's *The Giver* (1993) explored a dysfunctional family in a dystopian future world, L'Engle explored the powerful themes and hazards related to total conformity and authoritarian governments, and she did this through the lens of rationality situated within the strong bonds of family. Some religious conservatives still reject L'Engle's bold scientific questioning and see the book as anti-God. In contrast, some feminists continue to be uncomfortable with her fantasy framework and have questioned the muddled and occasionally whiny nature of the female protagonist, Meg Murray, who they believe became disempowered when she got married and became pregnant in the third book of the trilogy.

Madeleine L'Engle imagined a world in which females and males were empowered with self-determination and transcended stereotypes, and, as such, I believe she was *the* groundbreaking female children's author in the modern era. I believe that her work was as significant for depicting empowered females in 1962 as Sarah Fielding was in 1749 (see chapter 11). L'Engle opened the door for future feminist writers, but she has not often received credit for this impact because her protagonist was less than the ideal image for many feminists and existed in the science fiction fantasy genre.

In contrast, Louise Fitzhugh's *Harriet the Spy* (1964) has long been considered significant because Harriet was a feisty female protagonist situated within a contemporary setting, and as a result the book has been given prominence by feminists (Trites, 1997b). We have long passed the era in which a book like *A Wrinkle in Time* (L'Engle, 1962) should be considered subversive, with 6 million copies sold; even so, this book remains one of the most challenged books for children, with criticisms ranging from supporting witchcraft, demons, and un-Christian thought; lacking a feminist protagonist;

and promoting New Ageism (American Library Association, 2006; Blume, 1999).

L'Engle's fictional mother, Dr. Murray, was a brilliant scientist who heated up food on a Bunsen burner and was not singularly focused on cleaning her house; in fact, she was a bit of a slob, an antithetical mother to television's June Cleaver of *Leave It to Beaver* and Mrs. Anderson of *Father Knows Best*. L'Engle wrote this book in the 1950s, and through it she offered daughters new thoughts about self-determination and mothers alternatives to being relegated to the nursery as permanent caregivers—reminiscent of Wollstonecraft's agenda in 1788.

Betty Friedan's *The Feminine Mystique* was published in 1963, a year after L'Engle's (1962) *A Wrinkle in Time*. "The problem that has no name" was Friedan's term to describe women's feelings of worthlessness and dependency on their husbands—emotionally, intellectually, and financially—a mental condition that also came with the expectation that women would define their worth through their husbands and their children.

In contrast to the world envisioned by L'Engle (1962) in *A Wrinkle in Time*, Karen Cushman (2006) captures Betty Friedan's world in *The Loud Silence of Francine Green* through the voice of a female protagonist who is a poster child for the compliant female of the 1950s. Francine's world is simple. Obedience, submission, and silence are the parameters of her young female universe. Using the era of McCarthy blacklisting and the building of atomic bomb shelters as a backdrop, Cushman shows how Francine's friend Sophie, a Jewish girl in a Catholic school, exercises her freedom to think out loud, to question God, the president, communism, the pope, and even the repressed and self-righteous teacher Sister Basel, a cruel woman who bullies her students into submission. In contrast, Francine wears her silence like a shield. Cushman states that one of her explicit purposes in writing this book was to address the necessity that each individual has to defend the First Amendment.

The silencing of women has been pernicious throughout history, and Cushman tackles this theme with passion. In a scene reminiscent of one in Sarah Fielding's *The Adventures of David Simple* (1744), Francine's mother worries that being friends with Sophie will contaminate her daughter. Throughout history, compliant daughters have frequently had compliant mothers who seek social safety for their young. Francine says of herself: "I myself was so patient, moderate, and self-controlled that sometimes I felt invisible and I liked it that way. Let others get noticed and into trouble. Let Sophie get into trouble. It seemed a sure bet that she would" (Cushman, 2006, p. 2).

Sophie, who was kicked out of a public school, found herself battling a contentious nun who abhorred disbelief and tried to crush Sophie's self-assured quest for knowledge. She's too bright, too angry, too impatient, too smart, too irreverent, too inquisitive. In contrast, Francine is Betty Friedan's emerging woman from the 1950s:

> I tried so hard to be invisible, sometimes I felt like I wasn't here at all, like if I looked in the mirror, I would see no one there. What if someday there really was no Francine there, her having been smashed to bits by a super bomb?" (Cushman, 2006, p. 98)

Cushman's didacticism is subtle but clear. Women should not remain silent, nor should they be content with invisibility.

Jennifer Holm (2006) effectively uses the frame of the 1950s as a backdrop for *Pennies From Heaven*, but she does so using Cixous's (cited in Trites, 1997a) notion of laughter to examine stifling traditions. Ironically, but effectively, Gennifer Choldenko (2001) time-warps a 1950s mother into a 21st-century plot in *Notes From a Liar and Her Dog*, suggesting that "the problem that has no name" has not disappeared. By the end of this book the mother in the story has begun to become empowered, but she remains an anachronism.

A Wrinkle in Time (L'Engle, 1962) had to be a fantasy because girls were not allowed to have bold adventures in the 1950s. Meg Murray is a resilient and forceful character whose stubbornness and anger were used didactically by L'Engle to save the world, flaws that real girls were encouraged to extinguish, just like the character of Francine. L'Engle upheld the status quo even as she wriggled within its constraints, and that is why she has not been given a greater presence in feminist children's literature. Dr. Murray's laboratory was attached to the house, making her an unconventional but, nonetheless, stay-at-home mom; she was a responsible and productive mother of four, and it was, of course, a male in the family, Charles Wallace (the youngest son), who was the genius of the bunch. It was her adventuring husband, using their combined research, of course, who went tesseracting across the universe—but he was saved by his daughter. In fact, Meg's father and brother were both duped by the evil persona of Camazotz because of their arrogance. L'Engle broke significant conventions while reinforcing others, which will always be the tension of those who defy social traditions juxtaposed with ritualized institutions.

Surviving and Thriving:
Strong Female Protagonists Emerge

Landmark feminist books that followed *A Wrinkle in Time* (L'Engle, 1962) over the next two decades included the development of bolder female characters who did forbidden things, thought unconventional thoughts, questioned accepted beliefs, chose complex paths, and struggled with alienation and Carol Gilligan's knotted dilemma about difficult choices that women make for themselves and others, although most were situated within stable heterosexual two-parent families—typifying characters who survived and thrived. Examples are *Harriet the Spy* (Fitzhugh, 1964), *From the Mixed-Up Files of Mrs. Basil E. Frankweiler* (Konigsberg, 1967), *Are You There, God? It's Me, Margaret* (Blume, 1970), *Summer of the Swans* (Byars, 1970), *Julie of the Wolves* (George, 1972), *Roll of Thunder, Hear My Cry* (Taylor, 1976), *Bridge to Terabithia* (Paterson, 1976), *Anastasia Krupnik* (Lowry, 1979), and *Homecoming* (Voigt, 1981).

Women writers of the late 20th century were every bit as brilliant and gutsy as the forgotten women from the 18th century as they invented females who would survive and thrive (Dresang, 1999). As a result, censorship became common and many of these books were attacked. In the beginning, individual titles and authors were targeted. Characters like Anastasia Krupnik (Lowry, 1979) and Margaret Simon (Blume, 1970) were considered dangerous. Complex themes related to death, attempted rape, human sexuality, and mental illness were viewed with suspicion, derision, and outright censure, and consequently were labeled inappropriate for all children.

Conversely, the books were widely read by children, extolled by adults, and received numerous awards for excellence. A dynamic emerged in which excellent children's authors were simultaneously praised and condemned for exposing children to complex themes about family life. Most of these children's writers were women, and their books were set squarely within domestic tableaus where their empowered female protagonists survived and thrived.

Only eight years after L'Engle (1962), Judy Blume's *Are You There, God? It's Me, Margaret* (1970) was applauded for daring to explore the uncharted territory of early adolescence and emerging sexuality, territory that Phyllis Reynolds Naylor eventually charted quite explicitly in her *Alice* novels, which began in 1986 and are still being written 20 years later. Blume's concept of family was brilliant and fraught with difficulty. Margaret fretted about religion, menstruation, and the size of her breasts. Meg Murray, who came before (L'Engle, 1962), was less interested in increasing the size of her breasts than in saving the world, and Alice, who came after (Naylor, 1986–2007), worried about letting a boy touch those breasts.

Are You There, God? It's Me, Margaret (Blume, 1970) continues to be challenged 37 years after its publication, but the *Alice* series by Naylor now dominates many of the challenges that Blume once garnered. Early on, Judy Blume was troubled by the censorship of her books and became an active member of the National Coalition Against Censorship. In her anthology of short stories, *Places I Never Meant to Be: Original Stories by Censored Writers*, Blume (1999) wrote the following:

What I worry about most is the loss to young people. If
no one speaks out for them, if they don't speak out for
themselves, all they'll get for required reading will be the
most bland books available. And instead of finding the
information they need at the library, instead of finding the
novels that illuminate life, they will find only those materials to which nobody could possibly object.

In this age of censorship I mourn the loss of books that
will never be written, I mourn the voices that will be silenced—writers' voices, teachers' voices, students'
voices—and all because of fear. How many have resorted
to self-censorship? How many are saying to themselves,
"Nope...can't write about that. Can't teach that book.
Can't have that book in our collection. Can't let my student write that editorial in the school paper. (pp. 8, 9, 10)

Quirky and spunky females in literature became prominent in children's
books. Anastasia Krupnik (Lowry, 1979) was another version of Meg and
Margaret, a successful little kid with a big brain, big questions, a big heart,
and an intelligent and supportive nuclear family. She became an immediate
target of censors because she asked the wrong questions, and, worse, her parents
answered them honestly. Characters like Anastasia were oppositional females because they were not passive, docile, or obedient. They expected to be heard.
They were freethinking girls on the edge of adolescence who got into little
troubles, like their younger counterparts Ramona Quimby (Cleary, 1955) and
today's Junie B (Park, 1992). Profanity, questioning God, asking about love
affairs, taking a sip of alcohol, exploring sexuality, lying, and spying made
the books controversial, but the nuclear family was still firmly in control,
and a mother and father were still lovingly somewhere on the sidelines, although Harriet the Spy's parents were rather distant and somewhat neglectful.
Feminist books presented a new generation of empowered young females.

Reenvisioning the Historical Record

The combined impact of the civil rights movement and the women's movement gave birth to rich and complex female characters situated across genre,
within diverse families and outside diverse families, within conventions and
at the edge of conventions. Mildred Taylor's powerful stories about the Logan family, which began with the classic *Roll of Thunder, Hear My Cry*
(1976) cast Cassie Logan as an African-American girl growing up under oppression, a child who was supported and shielded by her parents from the
institutionalized racism of the 1930s. Cassie's first exposure to violent racism is a chilling portrait of how racism becomes embedded within families.

Taylor's portrayal of the Logan family, based on stories passed down orally in her own family, was a first, and it offered all children images of a resilient African-American family decades before the civil rights laws were passed in the 1960s. It broke many White myths about oppression and showed how African-American families lived richly textured lives within their own communities. Taylor examined the tensions of a loving and resilient family living within and apart from the White community and the complexity of survival in a racist society. Her historical portrait of three generations of strong women continues to be a significant contribution to children's literature and is widely used in elementary and college classrooms in the United States, with more than 2.6 million copies sold.

Rural and urban fifth graders reading about the Logan family in *The Friendship* (Taylor, 1987) were unfamiliar with Cassie's world in different ways, indicating the continued importance and relevance of Taylor's books about segregation in the 1930s. Rural children did not understand certain concepts related to segregation and civil rights, whereas many urban children understood racism all too well. Both groups were confused about the chronology of events in history and where specific people were located historically (Lehr & Thompson, 2000).

Western World history has been dominated by the political, cultural, and scientific exploits and accomplishments of men. Yet scholarship (Davis, 1995) has uncovered rare written records showing empowered females who lived within the parameters of the 17th century autonomously and on the margins (i.e., a merchant, a researcher, an immigrant, the founder of a school). In the 1990s Karen Cushman offered children invigorating new portraits of the roles of women in history. Cushman explored the medieval roles of midwives (*The Midwife's Apprentice*, 1995) and young girls who were forced into marriages (*Catherine Called Birdy*, 1994), effectively questioning the myth that all women were submissive historical commodities.

Controversies swirling around Cushman's depictions of independent and empowered females suggested that she was misrepresenting history by presenting 20th-century characters in medieval plots. In *The Ballad of Lucy Whipple* (Cushman, 1996), she showed the spirited Lucy Whipple being transported across a continent and then starting a library in California territory. From the authentic journals and diaries of pioneer women, we know that women like Lucy Whipple and her mother existed in U.S. history but aren't typically described in books for children, and they certainly aren't presented as protagonists in their own stories.

Katherine Paterson's *Bread and Roses* (2006) tells the story of the mill-worker strikes of 1912 from the perspective of an Italian immigrant family led by a single mother. This slice of history reveals the determination and courage of these militant and desperate women marching for wages to feed their families. Because the historical written record of the acts of females is rare, it is difficult to locate the actions of females in history. As Janet

Hickman (2001) points out, it is even more difficult to find the female child in history, and yet authors like Cushman and Paterson provide readers with stories of heroic women in history.

Surviving With a Thread of Hope

During the first half of the 20th century, the children featured in stories were part of a family, but they were absorbed in play and the challenge of growing up and isolated from adult concerns (MacLeod, 1994). MacLeod suggests that children's literature was dominated by stories in which adults were in control and could solve most conceivable problems that a child protagonist might face by offering guidance and direction. During the mid-1960s there was a shift in the relationships between children and parents in children's literature. The focus turned toward the inadequacies of adults and parents rather than their capabilities. It became more common for an adult to be portrayed as inept, abusive, neglectful, or substance-abusing.

Dresang's (1999) second category of male and female characters are those who face difficulty but survive with hope. These books are particularly appropriate for elementary-age readers because they reveal truths about life but do so without leaving the reader desolate and hopeless. When Beverley Naidoo's (1985) *Journey to Jo'burg*, a book banned in South Africa, was published in the United States, young readers were confronted with the indignity, injustice, and violence of apartheid in South Africa through the eyes of two young children, Naledi and Dineo, who left their small village to find their mother and bring her home because their little sister was sick. Naidoo skillfully left readers with a greater understanding of how children could live and survive under such a harsh system of institutionalized racism, yet she also left readers with a small amount of hope for the future of these two young children. That thin thread of hope is what makes these books relevant for young readers who are beginning to learn about injustice in their studies of history and who, in their own personal observations and experiences, also see how children experience injustice in their own neighborhoods.

Abandoned Children and the Surrogate Parent

Urban survival fiction gained momentum in the 1970s, particularly in young adult fiction. Harris (2002) suggests that these stories, rather than condemning adults, simply removed them. Children were placed in more independent adult roles, while social changes in family life accounted for the "prevalence of abandonment as a theme in children's literature" (74). Authors like Katherine Paterson began to explore alternate concepts of extended family, suggesting that children might find refuge outside conventional family structures.

Stories about contemporary children who are unwanted or abandoned personalize the reality of many children and show young readers how characters can transcend oppressive circumstances, although honestly written stories also show how some children will never be safe. Once the domain of young adult literature, absent, abusive, and neglectful fathers and mothers are now common motifs in children's literature. Fathers are frequently absent in books, thereby reflecting the reality of children who are raised in single-parent homes by their mothers. Social class is often a key factor in defining the child's status in society, which reflects statistics on low incomes in many single-parent homes. Many children struggle with emotional abandonment in foster situations. Cultural identity has also become a new area of exploration for feminist authors, illuminating the alienation and isolation of some children who belong to two cultures and feel part of none. Violent events in Paris recently echoed this theme for young French Arabs who feel estranged and disempowered in French society.

One of the first authors to portray an abandoned and unwanted child was Katherine Paterson, who sends out themes of comfort and hope to abandoned and neglected children—whom she calls the "throwaway kids"— in many of her books. *The Great Gilly Hopkins* (1978) is a groundbreaking feminist children's book, because Gilly shared many of her peers' alienation and irreverence, but without family she lacked their security nets and stability. This disposable kid was tossed aside as a love child of the sixties, and through Gilly's voice the idea of the nuclear family begins to shift. Gilly was situated outside the parameters of family, so her alienation and lack of cultural norms were too outlandish and raw for some. Gilly was tough, devious, foul-mouthed, racist, and so vulnerable that her foster mother, Trotter, showed what the power of love might accomplish.

One of the strengths of Paterson's writing is that her characters suffer the consequences of their actions. Early in the book, when Gilly wrote a belligerent letter to her mother stating that Trotter was unfit to be a foster parent, Gilly established a sequence of events that was irreversible. Paterson indicates that Gilly might survive, but she needed the love and guidance of a surrogate mother. Ironically, she lost that surrogate mother before she was able to stand on her own two feet, illustrating another of Paterson's strengths: The future is uncertain. Life does not offer guarantees. One cannot always choose one's circumstances.

Paterson's surrogate parents are often at the fringes of family and include grandparents, foster parents, uncles, or teachers who offer adult support and guidance, a long tradition in children's literature. *The Same Stuff as Stars* (Paterson, 2002) offers a similar tale of abandonment, rejection, and suffering by a strong female protagonist and her brother. Angel experiences the ultimate rejection from her mother when the mother comes to reclaim her cute and cuddly male child and leaves Angel behind. The truth as Paterson sees it is devastating, but it must be confronted and then endured.

These characters face multiple obstacles, including poverty, absent parents, and abusive parents, but Paterson's characters are resilient and move toward empowerment. Other exceptional authors who first wrote about abandoned and alienated children include Jean Craighead George (*Julie of the Wolves*, 1972), Cynthia Voigt (*Homecoming*, 1981), and Betsy Byars (*The Pinballs*, 1977). The reader knows that the women in these books should not be raising children, because they are not competent mothers who nurture their young—and the fathers never show up. Therefore these books expose the awful truth that some children are victimized by their parents.

Establishing Cultural Identity

Recent books like Ryan's *Becoming Naomi Leon* (2004) show how some children exist in two cultures, lack personal definition in both, but ultimately gain personal agency. These protagonists deal with the complexity of cultural differences and with isolation. Naomi Leon lives on the edge of poverty in a trailer, with her younger brother, Owen, and her quirky great-grandmother. This surrogate parent gives her great-grandchildren tremendous emotional stability and buckets of love, which is why Naomi's empowered character is believable. When the abusive mother reappears, she tries to force Naomi to go with her new family as a live-in babysitter, but the mother is not interested in taking Owen. The mother is depicted as callous, harsh, and threatening, and her boyfriend is even scarier. When Naomi learns that her biological father is a well-known Oaxacan artist, she talks her great-grandmother into taking a road trip to Mexico in a desperate effort to find him and seek his help. The eventual meeting with Naomi's father is touching and realistic, as Naomi discovers the other half of who she is. The legal system makes the final decision about where and with whom the children will live, and in this fiction, at least, the decision is right for Naomi and Owen. Both children will not only survive, one suspects that they are already beginning to thrive. Readers understand that characters suffer and are scarred, but they also see that life can hold promise.

Poverty and social class have been common motifs in exploring the complex lives of abandoned or single-parented children, but life can also be complex and painful for children who do not live in poverty; one can feel estranged or isolated at any stratum in society. In *Naming Maya*, Krishnaswami (2004) uses the common device of the camera to distance her protagonist from her life as an Indian and an American; through that third eye the character is able to detach and see more clearly. The camera's view becomes a metaphor for examining Maya's reality. When her grandfather dies, Maya is forced to spend a summer with her high-powered mother in Chennai, India; she feels estranged there, as she does in her all-girls' school in the United States; she also lacks a father in her life, which is all too common for many children. Maya feels that she belongs nowhere.

As her family connections in India strengthen, Maya begins to accept and understand both parts of herself, similar to Naomi's odyssey. The plot also centers on the family's housekeeper, who shows the early stages of dementia. Maya knows that something is wrong, but she does not have the knowledge to bridge that gap. Because her mother is engrossed in the details of burying her own father, Maya is left to fend for herself. A plot like this can easily become overloaded and superficial, but Krishnaswami skillfully brings all the thematic threads together. Such authors offer children complex stories about the diverse cultures found within the United States and provide insights about the struggle to belong and the struggle to find one's personal voice.

Other authors convey the emotional and economic complexity and isolation of living as ethnic minorities in the United States. In the Newbery book *Kira Kira*, Cynthia Kadohata (2004) provides a historical perspective of the Takeshimas, a Japanese-American family uprooted from Iowa to Georgia because of economic hardship in the 1950s. The experiences of this family are conveyed through the tensions that the parents face from working long hours under harsh conditions in a poultry plant, while the children bond to each other. That the family manages to find stability and warmth in this small town, despite the racial prejudice they experience and despite the eldest daughter's lymphoma, is a tribute to the resilience of children and the strong bonds of family.

Lensey Namioka (1992) and Lenore Look (2006) are two other authors who successfully bridge the gaps cross-culturally in their series about the Yang family and Ruby Lu, respectively. Namioka and Look use humor rather than tragedy to bring insight to the Chinese-American experience, but they wedge much laughter between realistic slices of contemporary life in the United States.

The Stigma of Mental Illness and Suicide

Cynthia Voigt was one of the first authors to raise issues related to mental health by telling the story of the Tillerman children, which began with *Dicey's Song* (1983), and continued with the prequel, *Homecoming* (1981). Dicey Tillerman's spirit of survival is legendary. Dicey's song of survival is living off the land and hiding from the authorities so that she and her abandoned siblings might remain together. When she finally reaches her grandmother's home and the temporary lukewarm safety it offers, Dicey is able to return to being a child only with great difficulty because of her role as a surrogate parent. The Tillerman saga shows how three disempowered children and one abandoned and emotionally empty grandmother survive and thrive.

Similarly, Janet Taylor Lisle's excellent *The Afternoon of the Elves* (1989) shows how one young girl copes with her mother's mental illness by creating a safe backyard fantasy world that she controls. In both of these books, the parents are essentially absent and are unavailable to parent their young.

In several newer books, the authors have approached the topic of mental illness and suicide from the perspective of young protagonists who experience the loss of a family member. Refreshingly, fathers are present in the lives of these children, and extended family support is central to the story.

In *Keeper of the Night*, Kimberly Holt (2003) has written about the shock waves resulting from a mother's ongoing mental illness, depression, and suicide. The year after her suicide is one of isolation for each member of the family; there is no talk about what has happened within the family or within this small community on the island of Guam. The father withdraws from the family through silence, long absences at work, and beer, while Isabel, the protagonist, is left to comfort her younger sister, who has nightmares, and her younger brother, who retreats into silence and self-mutilation. The emotional tableau of how the characters react and cope with their mother's, wife's, and sister's suicide is realistically depicted, along with the meetings with a psychiatrist, which positively demystify the experience. However, Isabel must find her own voice and personal agency as she takes on a role similar to that of Dicey's in *Dicey's Song* (Voigt, 1983).

Ann Martin's *A Corner of the Universe* (2002) deals with the undefined mental illness of a young man who has spent many years at a special school, and it reveals old attitudes of shame and embarrassment toward mentally ill family members, as told from the perspective of his cousin. In *Walk Softly, Rachel* (Banks, 2003), a young girl strains to be seen by her parents, who mourn their son's suicide by keeping his room as a shrine. Rachel's emotional scars are hidden, and she does not understand what happened to her brother and how it has impacted her family until she begins to read his journal years later.

These three books show the numbness that families face when a family member is mentally ill and commits suicide. They also show how family members emotionally retreat and isolate themselves to heal or decay. All three authors present a singular moment when the truth is finally spoken. The authors deal honestly with the topics of suicide and its destructive impact on families, but they also envision characters who survive these traumas and begin to heal.

Violence at Home

Violence has become more central and graphic in young adult literature in the past decade (Dresang, 1999). Carl Tomlinson (1995) writes that violence in literature should be justified rather than gratuitous and that it should provide a "deeper understanding . . . of past events and present conditions" and be integral to the story. "Violence, like a thin but noticeable thread, runs through every inch of the fabric of children's literature. . . . Violence cannot be avoided in literature, even literature for children, for literature serves to explain the human condition" (pp. 39–40). To calls for sheltering children from difficult information, McDaniel (2001) counters that "instead of focusing on superficial, meaningless topics because we want to preserve children's innocence as long as possible, we should provide literature that deals with the significant issues and questions children must face in real life" (p. 221). Authors give voice to the topic of family violence for younger children. Carolyn Coman (1995) wrote the first significant and accessible feminist children's book, *What Jamie Saw*, about living in a family where a man assaults his wife and stepchildren, by showing how a powerless female and male find their own personal agency and worth. Writing through the eyes of the main character, a young boy who is in a position of weakness, Coman shows how Jamie survives an abusive stepfather. "WHEN JAMIE SAW HIM THROW THE baby, saw Van throw the little baby, saw Van throw his little sister Nin, when Jamie saw Van throw his baby sister Nin, then they moved" (Coman, 1995, p. 7). This one scene from Jamie's memory haunts the entire book.

Jamie never stops worrying that Van will return and hurt his family, nor does the reader. Coman reveals what can happen within families, but she does not overwhelm young readers with repeated scenes of violence. Coman shows how a disempowered mother finally chooses safety for her family, and how that family begins to reconstruct its life; however, the threat does not disappear, nor does the intense fear. Whereas many women feel trapped and intimidated and unable to leave abusers and abusive homes, Jamie's mother, heroically, chooses to leave. Jamie's fear is palpable, and the reader shares his shaky existence and rebuilding. He is a boy who is sensitive, scared, and scarred, but he has survival strategies that his mother has taught him. Jamie begins to recognize his own agency and overcomes his obsessive fear that his abusive stepfather will return and hurt Jamie and his family. Jamie begins to believe in himself, and in the end the reader is left believing that he will triumph, even though he is only a 9-year-old boy.

The final confrontation between Jamie's mother and stepfather instills hope and confidence in Jamie. Power cannot always come from within young characters. Sometimes adults must act courageously and responsibly to ensure the safety of their children. Child readers will know that there is hope and that one can survive. *What Jamie Saw* opens the door to a home where a man beats his family. When is it ever easy to see and know this kind of truth? Coman knows that what is hidden can remain hidden—and thus unchallenged and unchanged. By bringing light to the darkest corners of family life through the direct experiences of her protagonist, she offers young readers knowledge, choices, and perhaps hope.

Leading young readers into the topic of domestic violence through fantasy seems like a risky strategy, but Lois Lowry's *Gossamer* (2006) does exactly that. I wonder about the readers who will be drawn, unaware and unprepared, into the gentle story of the invisible dream-givers and the lonely old woman. When 8-year-old John appears later in the book, one is not ready for his memories of being forced to eat dog food on the floor after having his face smashed into it. His father is a cruel tyrant who beats his wife and child. No longer present, he remains a menace only in John's violent nightmares, brought by the evil Sinisteeds. These nightmares are challenged by the dream-giver with the gossamer touch, who weakens them by sending John healthy hopeful dreams, including a song, a seashell, and a dog named Toby. Like Carolyn Coman's (1995) Jamie, John ends up with hope, a lot of hope. His mother slowly seams her life together, while the old retired teacher who fosters John is a bastion of love and acceptance.

Although Lowry (2006) acknowledges that there is evil in the world, the book's strength is its focus on the dream-givers who come in the night, gently touch objects that reveal memories, and weave dreams of hope, delight, and comfort. Once again, Lowry works with the powerful images of memory, as she did in *The Giver* (1993), and empowers her characters realistically through fantasy.

The topics of assault, rape, and violence in the home have been thoughtfully explored by contemporary writers like Hahn, Voigt, Coman, Byars, Woodson, Fine, and now Lowry. A book can be "realistic without being overly graphic," and "very few subjects are inappropriate in themselves; it is all in how the author treats them" (Kiefer, 2007, p. 474).

The Ultimate Taboo in Children's Literature: A Lesbian Mother

Along with abortion, lesbian and gay issues are among the most frequently mentioned targets of fundamental religious conservatives; however, I could not find a balanced discussion about children with lesbian or gay parents. Books like *Heather Has Two Mommies* (Newman, 1990) and *Daddy's Roommate* (Willhoite, 1990) are condemned for their content and for allegedly promoting homosexuality, but there is no discussion about the child's positioning within those families. Certain groups like Concerned Women of America (CWA) believe that the best place for children is in a family with a mother and a father, but that is not the reality for all children. Beverly LaHaye, founder of CWA, warned her members that homosexuals "want their depraved 'values' to become our children's values. Homosexuals expect society to embrace their immoral way of life. Worse yet, they are looking for new recruits!" (CWA, 2006).

What does a 13-year-old boy do with his love of his mother when that mother does something that he finds inexplicable and unlovable? Jacqueline Woodson (1995) won the Newbery and Coretta Scott King Awards when she explored a young African-American boy's relationship with his mother in *From the Notebooks of Melanin Sun*. When Melanin Sun's mother reveals that she is a lesbian, he rejects her and stops talking to her for weeks. He is terrified about what that says about his own sexuality, and he is afraid that his family life will be destroyed. He is also afraid of what his friends will say and how they will treat him. For a time he hates his mother—passionately. Woodson poignantly explores his thinking and his agonizing through his own voice.

Whether one supports the personal choices of Melanin's mother, one cannot fail to be conscious of Melanin's struggle and heartache. Melanin ultimately decides that his mother is his family. Without her he is alone in the world. He makes the conscious decision to hold on fiercely to that love. In the end, what else is there? Woodson's message is powerful for child readers. Melanin's struggle is not resolved by the end of the book, but he is aware of his own agency and begins to give voice to his own feelings; the reader hopes that he will prevail.

Doubtful and Hopeless Futures: Darker Visions of Family

A strand of books written in the 1990s began to move into darker visions of the family, revealing some of the rank and violent secrets that are hidden but, unlike *What Jamie Saw* (Coman, 1995), described children who had doubtful futures. Marsden (1994) says the following:

> If we accept that children are not automatically innocent and angelic, that they are complex, subtle humans, who are trying to overcome their ignorance, trying to acquire knowledge so that they can move to the positions of strength that the knowing adults seemingly occupy, then we can get a clearer idea of the role of fiction in their lives. (p. 103)

In contemporary books, violence is likely to be found in realistic fiction with a focus on the experience of a child who is living in a violent setting (Dresang, 1999), but not all books offer hope for the protagonists. Hopeless protagonists have been present in adolescent literature for many years, but books for children have typically offered readers hope. In fact, that has been one of my ongoing definitions of the children's book and what distinguishes it from books for older readers.

Woodson's *I Hadn't Meant to Tell You This* (1994) is a dismal anomaly in which a sexually abused poor White child has no safety net, no understanding adult, and no hope except for escaping with her young sister. Woodson provides an ending that is ambivalent and distressing, especially for the middle-class Black female protagonist, who knows the secret but has kept it to herself. We know she'll survive, but she was not being abused. Although Woodson tackles other complex themes in this short book, the ending is bleak and leaves the reader with no grasp of what will happen or what might have been done differently, representing Dresang's (1999) notion of the character who has a doubtful future reflected by bleak circumstances. The difference between an adult book and a children's book is often that the child would probably not survive in the adult book or in the adult world. Dresang's theory of Radical Change challenges the notion of children's literature as nurturing good, hopeful child readers by bringing pleasure exclusively; she queries whether good literature experiences that are embedded with lessons are of equal value.

Alfred Tatum (see chapter 9) uses the term *enabling texts* to describe books by African-American authors who willingly depict characters in all their "beautiful-ugly selves" wrestling with society's harsh and complex problems. His list of such authors includes Sharon Flake, Virginia Hamilton, Angela Johnson, Sharon Bell Mathis, and Jacqueline Woodson—female authors who focus on the multiple identities of adolescents and show how race, gender, and class shape their young protagonists. Tatum describes how disabling texts ignore local contexts and the adolescent's desire for self-definition, whereas enabling literature can help students to achieve the emotional and academic resiliency to face personal instability and chaos at home and at school. Tatum is discussing young adult books, and his premises are illuminating; the ultimate choices that the fifteen-year-old African-American male in his study makes suggest a strong role for enabling texts that show the "beautiful-ugly" side of characters and the complexities that they face.

Woodson's (1994) two girls, arriving on urban streets, would not last much longer than 48 hours before being exploited by predators. I wonder what the purpose of Woodson's bleak and hopeless tale was. Is her ultimate message that there is no escape from being raped by your father unless you run away? Is she trying to say that some secrets should never be kept and that children should tell a responsible adult if they know someone is being abused? Or, as Dresang (1999) suggests, was Woodson showing the power and impact of a fleeting friendship in the lives of two girls, both of whom had lost their mothers and were living with their fathers, with no promise of a happy resolution? Dresang writes that young protagonists are not always able to overcome their situations triumphantly but that they might be better able to cope. Somehow, one does not feel that Woodson's abused female character will be able to cope at all, but Tatum's research makes me marvel that reading about the turmoil and devastation in the lives of fictional characters can help real children achieve resiliency and make stronger personal choices.

Lena (Woodson, 1999) is the sequel to *I Hadn't Meant to Tell You This* (1994) in which Woodson continues the story of Lena's and her sister's escape from their sexually abusive father. Lena and Dion make a harrowing journey to reach their mother's hometown. The hopelessness of their earlier suffering and trauma haunts them throughout the second book. How does a child like Lena find help and healing after years of sexual abuse? Lena's harsh story is told in her own strong voice, with which she honestly echoes the confusion that children feel toward their abusive parents. This book ends with hope but no justice. Parents who rape their children seldom receive the prison sentences that other rapists are given, thus underscoring society's ambivalence toward rape in the home.

Woodson's narrative of family rape and violence parallels Anne Fine's *The Tulip Touch* (1997), in which two female protagonists wreak chaos and eventually experience the long-term effects of either positive or destructive parenting. What is seen as mischievous in elementary school turns to destructive behavior during the teen years. The character with caring parents survives; the abused child ends up in detention. Although Fine implies that it's about personal choices, it's just as easily about nurturing and supportive parents contrasted to systematically violent and destructive parents. As in Woodson's books, the effect of having violent or nonviolent parents determines the child's destiny. Are these books appropriately labeled as children's literature, or are they more appropriate for older readers? Are the parameters of what constitutes a children's book perhaps changing as authors begin to explore complex topics for younger readers?

Parallels in Two Centuries of Feminist Writing

Women have been writing "against the grain" since a literature for children was firmly established in the 18th century. The parallels between contemporary feminist writers and the earliest children's authors are salient. Women writers, then and now, have explored the complexity of the domestic domain within the constraints of the Western patriarchy, although those parameters and constraints have changed over time. One wonders how the oppositional female characters, within those parameters and throughout two centuries, have impacted the thinking of female and male readers. Strong female and male characters have been given options and choices in dozens of books written for children, offering complex models of what it means to be a female or male who achieves personal agency.

For the past 250 years, many oppositional female characters have been highly regarded by much of the public even as they have been simultaneously dismissed or challenged by other segments of the public, thus indicating the tensions that remain within Western society. Feminist writers have faced severe public criticism and challenges to their works by social conservatives who have written forcefully against the themes and issues raised in their works, both then and now. These children's authors have been maligned, and many have been labeled as enemies of the family and as anti-God. In the modern era, many social conservatives have organized nationally and have systematically moved against the inclusion of targeted topics, authors, and books in the school curriculum. Historically, many women writers were excluded from the literary canon, and their works, when mentioned, were referred to as malignant. The reexamination of their works in recent years has reaffirmed the relevance and importance of their voices in literary history.

Over time, the range of these women writers has been diverse; they have never been a homogeneous set of women with a homogeneous set of beliefs. Many would not have considered themselves radical or feminist. Some would have considered themselves religious, with moral obligations to write truthfully and to direct the course of the education of children through didactic stories. Some have been activists who advocated equality for many disenfranchised groups in society. Many aligned themselves with and found inspiration from parallel social movements that occurred at the time in which they were writing, such as abolition and the civil rights movement.

What these women share over time is the belief that their writing mattered, that they could effect social change through their writing. They believed in female potential—that women should be given the opportunity to live unrestricted lives. The earliest writers believed that the physical movements of women should be unrestricted and that women should be free to choose the books they wanted to read. Sensitive authors today have also begun to consider the potential of the disenfranchised male, as described in the works of Jacqueline Woodson and Carolyn Coman, which I view as necessary if feminist children's literature is to be relevant to all its readers.

Conclusion: The Power of Words and the Role of Those Barbarous Feminist Writers

Who kills a man, kills a reasonable creature, God's image; but he who destroys a good book, kills reason itself, kills the image of God, as it were in the eye. . . . If we think to regulate printing, thereby to rectify manners, we must regulate all recreations and pastimes, all that is delightful to man.

—John Milton, *The Areopagitica*, 1644

If we lie to children, if we are silent, if we protect them from the truth, we leave them in ignorance. Books have been considered dangerous enemies from the beginning, because the written word is powerful, and those who fear it do so with good reason. Throughout history people have tried to control or eradicate dangerous ideas, as far back as the time of John Milton (1644), when the British government wanted to precensor books before they were even published. People have tried to protect children, to keep them safe from unsanctioned ideas, as if children really could be locked up safely and shielded from ideas until they are older.

This battle over the books is a true divide between two broadly defined groups who stand in opposition to each other. Their beliefs are different, and their goals are different. Their means of obtaining knowledge and education are different. One group is intent on limiting the content to which children can be exposed—all children, not just their own children. Many use fundamentalist religious ideas and morality as their motivation. The other group supports children's authors who tackle complex and difficult topics in a sensitive and relevant manner, and they want their children to have access to these books at home, at school, and in the public library. Their beliefs are often premised on civil liberties rather than religious ideas. I see no bridging of the chasm between them.

In classrooms across the United States, there is a battle going on over what and how children can be taught, what they can read, and what teachers can use as materials in the classroom. Textbooks in the past decade have become more sanitized, carefully scripted, and politically nonoffensive. It's all about safety and safe content, sinful and not-sinful content. The values, topics, and themes in many realistic fiction books are labeled by some as inappropriate for inclusion in textbooks, and the restriction of those books in school libraries continues. Publishers are replacing quality children's books with formulaic series books often written by multiple authors or based on television characters or cartoons. Educators are losing the battle to engage children with quality literature if children don't see the relevance of becoming lifelong readers who talk about the books they are reading.

Literature is being marginalized in the elementary curriculum. Time to read aloud, to read independently, and to talk about literature is being replaced with explicit skills instruction and test preparation. What began as censorship of individual titles in the 1980s has morphed into an agenda of skills and drills, test preparation, and sanitized texts that leaves little time for reading literature. Publishers often won't do anything because they can't get quality literature past the censors, and as Frank Hodge says in his interview (see chapter 5), publishing is about profits.

Passionate teachers still teach literature to their elementary students, but for too many, literature is being eliminated or is becoming a subversive activity. Scholastic's publisher, Horton, fears that the burdens of the *No Child Left Behind Act* have caused teachers to have less time to learn about books and less time for individual reading in the classroom, and that children are being taught to read for instruction rather than pleasure. Skills and drills are not about reading and writing.

What's the real agenda? Many social conservatives do not want their children to become critical readers and writers and thinkers. Victory means maintaining the status quo. Ironically, the critical reading and writing portions of the Scholastic Aptitude Test have declined for the past two years.

Modern feminist women writers are central to these controversies because they will not be silenced. Like their predecessors in the 18th century, they will not stop writing, nor will they be manipulated by those who find their books offensive. Will these women be remembered for their important works 200 years from now, or will they ultimately be silenced through the erosion of the literature that is available in classrooms and libraries? Will children's literature continue to explore the tapestry and diversity of the family?

Just as the radical women of the 18th century were eventually dismissed as being destructive, barbarous, and didactic, will the labels of anti-God, anti-family, and anti-boy be invoked to marginalize the voices of Madeleine L'Engle, Katherine Paterson, Lois Lowry, Cynthia Voigt, Jacqueline Woodson, Judy Blume, Janet Taylor Lisle, Karen Cushman, Kate Banks, Phyllis Reynolds Naylor, Sharon Creech, Naomi Shihab Nye, Audrey Couloumbis, Carolyn Coman, Mildred Taylor, Deborah Ellis, Anne Fine, Virginia Hamilton, Pam Munoz Ryan, Patricia McKissack, Penny Colman, Kimberly Holt, and all the other female voices who question our place in the universe?

References

American Association of University Women (AAUW). (1995). *How schools shortchange girls: A study of major findings on girls and education.* New York: Author.

American Library Association. (2006). *Intellectual freedom.* Available online at www.ala.org/ala/oif/bannedbooksweek/bannedbooksweek.htm

Blume, J. (Ed.). (1999). *Places I never meant to be: Original stories by censored writers.* New York: Simon & Schuster.

Carrigan, H. (1993). Review of *The Book of Virtues.* School Library Journal. Available online at Amazon.com

Chase, C. (1998). *Suncatcher: A study of Madeleine L'Engle.* Philadelphia: Innisfree Press.

Cheaney, B. (2005). All alone in the world? *World Magazine, 20,* 26. Available online at www.worldmag.com/articles/10811

Colman, P. (2005, April). *Birth of a book.* Paper presented at the University of Maine, Orono, ME.

Concerned Women for America. (2006). Available online atwww.cwalac.org/

Davis, N. (1995). Women on the margins: Three seventeenth-century lives. Boston: Harvard University Press.

D'Emilio, J., & Freedman, E. (1988). *Intimate matters: A history of sexuality in America*. New York: Harper & Row.

Dresang, E. (1999). *Radical change: Books for youth in a digital age*. New York: Wilson.

Dresang, E. (2002). Gender issues and Harry Potter. In L. Whited (Ed.), *The ivory tower and Harry Potter*. Columbia, MO: University of Missouri Press.

Fielding, S. (1968). *The governess or little female academy* (J. Grey, Ed.). Oxford, UK: Oxford University Press. (Original work published 1749)

Friedan, B. (1963). *The feminine mystique*. New York: Norton.

Gilligan, C. (1982). *In a different voice: Psychological theory and women's development*. Cambridge, MA: Harvard University Press.

Harris, M. (2002). Bleak houses and secret cities: Alternative communities in young adult fiction. *Children's Literature in Education, 33*, 63–76.

Hickman, J. (2001). Truth as patchwork: Developing female characters in historical fiction. In S. Lehr (ed.) *Beauty, brains, and brawn: The construction of gender in children's literature*. Portsmouth, NH: Heinemann.

Janeway, J., & Mather, C. (1771). *A token for children*. Boston: Printed and sold by Z. Fowle, in Back-Street, near the Mill-Bridge. (Original work published 1672)

Kiefer, B. (2007). *Charlotte Huck's* Children's literature in the elementary school (9th ed.). New York: McGraw-Hill.

Lehr, S., & Thompson, D. (2000). The dynamic nature of response: Children reading and responding to *Maniac Magee* and *The friendship*. *The Reading Teacher, 53* (6), 480–93.

MacLeod, A. S. (1994). *American childhood: Essays on children's literature of the nineteenth and twentieth centuries*. Athens, GA: University of Georgia Press.

Marrs, E. (Ed.). (1976). Letter 136. *The letters of Charles and Mary Anne Lamb* (Vol. 2, pp. 81–82). Ithaca, NY: Cornell University Press.

Marsden, J. (1994). More power to them! In A. Nieuwenhuizen (Ed.), *The written world: Youth and literature* (pp. 100–115). Port Melbourne, Australia: Thorpe.

McDaniel, C. (2001). Children's literature as prevention of child sexual abuse. *Children's Literature in Education, 32*, 203–224.

Milton, J. (1644). *Areopagitica*. Available online at http://darkwing.uoregon.edu/~rbear/areopagitica.html

Muir, P. (1954). *English children's books, 1600–1900*. London: Batsford.

Myers, M. (1986). Impeccable governesses, rational dames, and moral mothers: Mary Wollstonecraft and the female tradition in Georgian children's books. *Children's Literature, 14*, 31–59.

O'Beirne, K. (2006). *Women who make the world worse: And how their radical feminist assault is ruining our schools, families, military, and sports*. New York: Sentinel.

Ramdas, K. (2006). Feminists and fundamentalists. *Current History, 105* (689), 99–104.

Salvner, G. (1998). A war of words: Lessons from a censorship case. *The ALAN Review*, 25 (2), 45–49. Available online at http://scholar.lib.vt.edu/ejournals/ALAN/winter98/salvner.html

Sommers, C. (2000). *The war against boys*. New York: Simon and Schuster.

Susina, J. (1997). Subversive children's literature. *American Book Review*, 19, 2.

Tomlinson, C. (1995). Justifying the violence in children's literature. In S. Lehr (Ed.), *Battling dragons: Issues and controversy in children's literature* (pp. 39–50). Portsmouth, NH: Heinemann.

Tong, R. (1998). *Feminist thought: A more comprehensive introduction*. New York: Westview Press.

Trites, R. (1997a). Feminist subversions in children's fictions. *American Book Review*, 19, 2, 8.

Trites, R. (1997b). *Waking Sleeping Beauty: Feminist voices in children's novels*. Iowa City, IA: University of Iowa Press.

Trites, R. (2000). *Disturbing the universe: Power and repression in adolescent literature*. Iowa City: IA: University of Iowa Press.

Vandergrift, K. (1996). *Mosaics of meaning: Enhancing the intellectual life of young adults through story*. Lanham, MD: Scarecrow Press.

Young, K. (1930). *Social psychology: An analysis of social behavior*. New York: Knopf.

Zipes, J. (2002). *Sticks and stones: The troublesome success of children's literature from Slovenly Peter to Harry Potter*. New York: Routledge.

Children's Books

Banks, K. (2002). *Dillon, Dillon*. New York: Farrar, Straus & Giroux.

Banks, K. (2003). *Walk softly, Rachel*. New York: Farrar, Straus & Giroux.

Bennett, W. (1993). *The book of virtues*. New York: Simon & Schuster.

Blume, J. (1970). *Are you there, God? It's me, Margaret*. New York: Bradbury.

Brooks, W. (1927–1958). *Freddy* series. New York: Knopf.

Burnett, F. H. (1905). *The little princess*. New York: Grossett.

Burnett, F. H. (1910). *The secret garden*. New York: Grossett.

Byars, B. (1970). *Summer of the swans*. New York: Viking Press.

Byars, B. (1977). *The pinballs*. New York: Harper & Row.

Choldenko, G. (2001). *Notes from a liar and her dog*. New York: Putnam.

Cleary, B. (1955). *Beezus and Ramona*. New York: HarperCollins.

Coman, C. (1995). *What Jamie saw*. Arden, NC: Front Street.

Coolidge, S. (1994). *What Katy did*. London: Puffins. (Original work published 1872)

Couloumbis, A. (1999). *Getting near to baby*. New York: Putnam.

Couloumbis, A. (2002). *Say yes*. New York: Putnam.

Cushman, K. (1994). *Catherine called birdy*. New York: Clarion Books.

Cushman, K. (1995). *The midwife's apprentice*. New York: Clarion Books.

Cushman, K. (1996). *The ballad of Lucy Whipple*. New York: Clarion Books.

Cushman, K. (2006). *The loud silence of Francine Green*. New York: Clarion Books.

Dickens, C. (1843). *A Christmas carol*. London: Elliot Stock.

Fielding, S. (1744). *The adventures of David Simple*. London: Millar.

Fine, A. (1997). *The tulip touch*. Boston: Little, Brown.

Fitzhugh, L. (1964). *Harriet the spy*. New York: Harper & Row.

George, J. C. (1972). *Julie of the wolves*. New York: Harper & Row.

Holm, J. (2006). *Pennies from heaven*. New York: Random House.

Holt, K. (2003). *Keeper of the night*. New York: Holt.

Janeway, J., & Mather, C. (1728). *A token for children*. Boston: Printed for T. Hancock at the Bible and Three Crowns near the Town-Dock.

Kadohata, C. (2004). *Kira Kira*. New York: Atheneum.

Konigsberg, E. L. (1967). *From the mixed-up files of Mrs. Basil E. Frankweiler*. New York: Atheneum.

Krishnaswami. (2004). *Naming Maya*. New York: Farrar, Straus & Giroux.

Kuijer, G. (2006). *The book of everything*. New York: Scholastic.

L'Engle, M. (1962). *A wrinkle in time*. New York: Farrar, Straus & Giroux.

Lisle, J. T. (1989). *The afternoon of the elves*. New York: Orchard.

Look, L. (2006). *Ruby Lu. Empress of everything*. New York: Atheneum.

Lovelace, M. (1940). *Betsy-Tacy*. New York: Harper & Row.

Lowry, L. (1979). *Anastasia Krupnik*. Boston: Houghton Mifflin.

Lowry, L. (1993). *The giver*. Boston: Houghton Mifflin.

Lowry, L. (2006). *Gossamer*. Boston: Houghton Mifflin.

MacDonald, G. (1872). *The princess and the goblin*. London: Strahan.

Martin, A. (2002). *A corner of the universe*. New York: Dial.

McKay, H. (2002). *Saffey's angel*. New York: Simon/McElderry.

Naidoo, B. (1986). *Journey to Jo'burg*. New York: Lippincott.

Namioka, L. (1992). *Yang the Youngest and His Terrible Ear*. Boston: Little, Brown.

Naylor, P. R. (1986–2007). *Alice series*. New York: Atheneum.

Newman, L. (1990). *Heather has two mommies* (Diana Souza, Illus.). Boston: Alyson.

Park, B. (1992). *Junie B. and the stupid smelly bus*. New York: Random House.

Paterson, K. (1977). *Bridge to Terabithia*. New York: Crowell.

Paterson, K. (1978). *The great Gilly Hopkins*. New York: Crowell.

Paterson, K. (2002). *The same stuff as stars*. New York: Clarion Books.

Paterson, K. (2006). *Bread and roses*. New York: Clarion Books.

Ryan, P. M. (2000). *Esperanza rising*. New York: Scholastic.

Ryan, P. M. (2004). *Becoming Naomi Leon*. New York: Scholastic.

Taylor, M. (1976). *Roll of thunder, hear my cry*. New York: Putnam.

Taylor, M. (1987). *The friendship*. New York: Dial.

Turner, A. (2002). *A corner of the universe*. New York: Scholastic.

Voigt, C. (1981). *Homecoming*. New York: Atheneum.

Voigt, C. (1983). *Dicey's song*. New York: Atheneum.

Voigt, C. (1994). *When she hollers*. New York: Scholastic.

Wilder, L. I. (1932–1971). *Little House* series. New York: Harper & Brothers.

Willhoite, M. (1990). *Daddy's roommate*. Boston: Alyson.

Woodson, J. (1994). *I hadn't meant to tell you this*. New York: Delacorte Press.

Woodson, J. (1995). *From the notebooks of Melanin Sun*. New York: Scholastic.

Woodson, J. (1999). *Lena*. New York: Scholastic.

Chapter 13

Literature About Lesbian, Gay, Bisexual, and Transgender People and Their Families

Linda Leonard Lamme

Lesbian, gay, bisexual, and transgender (LGBT) children's literature has gradually expanded since the 1980s and now includes books about children with LGBT parents, children who are themselves LGBT or questioning, homophobia in schools, gay relatives with AIDS, and books about diversity that include LGBT families. In terms of picture books with gay or lesbian story characters, there has been a steady flow of one or two books published each year since 1989. The first books were about AIDS and homophobia, whereas more recently, families and school issues have been addressed. Picture books about LGBT families tend to be superficial and perpetuate stereotypes. Several have been widely banned even though most merely describe lesbian or gay families. There are a few about commitment ceremonies and several about homophobia in schools. The publishers of these books are small book presses, including some that specialize in LGBT books. Many of the picture books appear to be written to inform heterosexual audiences that lesbian and gay families exist. *Kirkus Reviews* notes that "Gay picture books are unfortunately still rare enough that they all matter regardless of literary and artistic quality" ("Mom and Mum . . ., 2005). Therefore all the books are listed in this chapter, but not all are discussed.

Today's novels for young people are replete with gays and lesbians in the background, in stereotypical minor roles such as the lesbian gym teacher, a gay uncle, lesbian neighbors, or the young girl with a lesbian crush on a heterosexual story character. These books have been omitted from this analysis because they are token encounters and not relevant to the plot. Most of the novels about young people with LGBT families and about LGBT youth are well written, tell intriguing stories, and are published by mainstream presses. Practically all the books about lesbian or gay parents are written by lesbian or gay authors and are therefore authentic stories about the culture. Books about LGBT youth that might be of interest to older elementary students feature story characters who are questioning their sexual orientation or gender identity.

This chapter analyzes the nature of literature about LGBT families and youth and explains why this marginalized population is somewhat marginalized in children's literature as well. The books that are analyzed contain almost the same number of lesbian or gay story characters. These books vary widely in quality according to the Horn Book Scale, which rates books from 1 (excellent) to 6 (not worthy). The reasons that some books are not rated (NR) at all are that they are published outside the United States, they are recently published, or they are produced by small presses that are not reviewed by Horn Book. There are many other prestigious awards given to LGBT books, including the Lambda Literary Award for outstanding LGBT books for children and young people; these are shared in a separate section of this chapter.

Lesbian and Gay Parents in Picture Books

According to the 2000 U.S. census, same-sex couples lived in 99.3% of the counties in America. Many of these households include children. In 1990 there were an estimated 6–14 million children in the United States living with a lesbian, gay, bisexual, or transgender parent (COLAGE, 2006). With advancing reproductive technologies and more liberal adoption laws, more lesbian, gay, and transgender couples are deciding to have children than at any time in our history, causing a sharp rise in the number of LGBT families. Researchers find that children who are raised by one or two lesbian or gay parents fare as well as children of heterosexual parents in emotional, cognitive, and social functioning (Perrin, 2002).

Children enter gay and lesbian families in many different ways, which the collection of picture books shown in Table 13-1 accurately depicts. Some are born to straight parents who divorce because one parent discovers that he or she is gay, as in *Daddy's Roommate* by Michael Willhoite (1990), *Jennifer Has Two Daddies* by Priscilla Galloway (1985), and *Zack's Story* by Keith Greenberg (1996). These children, like any children of divorce, have to deal with divorce issues; in addition, they must deal with belonging to an LGBT family. Most divide their time between two homes. Some of the children are parented through planned conception by artificial insemination, as in *Heather Has Two Mommies* by Leslea Newman (1989); others are adopted, as in *Felicia's Favorite Story* by Leslea Newman (2002) and *How My Family Came to Be: Daddy, Papa and Me* by Andrew Aldrich (2003).

Table 13-1. Children's Picture Books About Children with Gay and Lesbian Parents

Title	Author	Horn Book Scale
Jennifer Has Two Daddies	Priscilla Galloway	NR
Heather Has Two Mommies	Leslea Newman	NR
Daddy's Roommate	Michael Willhoite	5
Gloria Goes to Gay Pride	Leslea Newman	NR
How Would You Feel If Your Dad Was Gay?	Ann Heron & Meredith Maran	4
Zack's Story: Growing Up With Same-Sex Parents (nonfiction)	Keith Elliot Greenberg	3
Felicia's Favorite Story	Leslea Newman	NR
How My Family Came to Be: Daddy, Papa and Me	Andrew Aldrich	NR
The Daddy Machine	Johnny Valentine	5
King & King & Family	Linda deHaan & Stern Nijland	4
And Tango Makes Three	Justin Richardson & Peter Parnell	4

Because they are born into a homophobic society, children with lesbian and gay parents face discrimination to the same degree as LGBT students (Ray & Gregory, 2001), but few of these books present those experiences. Only in *How Would You Feel If Your Dad Was Gay?* by Ann Heron and Meredith Maran (1994) is prejudice and children's responses to it incorporated into the story. A small girl believes that she has the right to talk about her two dads, but her older brother is aghast that she has made that information public because it sets the kids up for harassment.

Zack's Story by Keith Greenberg (1996) is a nonfiction introduction to Zack's family, written for children who have little exposure to LGBT families. Zack's lesbian mother's partner has a baby, so he now has two half siblings, because his father also has a child with his second wife. There are color photographs of Zack and his family throughout the book. Like Zack, Jennifer spends time with both parents and meets her father's new partner in *Jennifer Has Two Daddies* by Priscilla Galloway (1985). As with any family, there are adjustments when a family member departs through divorce or separation or becomes married or partnered.

Heather Has Two Mommies by Leslea Newman (1989), illustrated with black-and-white sketches by Diana Souza, explains how Heather was conceived and raised. Newman wrote this book because her friends could not find any picture books about LGBT parents. She and illustrator Souza unsuccessfully tried to sell the book to many publishers and ended up self-publishing it. A year later, in 1990, when Alyson Wonderland Press opened, *Heather Has Two Mommies* became the first book it published. In Heather's school, the children come from diverse cultures and family structures; one child has two fathers. The original edition of the book explains in detail how Heather was conceived, but when the book was republished in 2000 the artificial insemination information was edited out.

Daddy's Roommate, written by Michael Willhoite (1990) and dedicated to his father, is a concept book rather than a fictional story. The child narrator explains that his Mommy and Daddy divorced, and now Daddy and his roommate, Frank, live together. Then he lists all the things they do together: "eat together, sleep together, shave together," and so forth. On weekends the boy has fun with his dad and Frank. His mother explains to him that they are gay.

And Tango Makes Three, by Justin Richardson and Peter Parnell (2005) and illustrated by Henry Cole, is based on the true story of two penguins in the Central Park Zoo in New York. Roy and Silo build a nest together, even though they are two males. The keeper then takes an extra egg from another nest and places it in Roy and Silo's nest. When the egg hatches, the penguin fathers raise their baby together just like the other penguin couples in the zoo. The penguins make playful subjects for artist Henry Cole's watercolor illustrations of the somewhat anthropomorphized parents and child. This appealing story is a gentle introduction to the literature of gay families.

King & King & Family by Linda deHaan and Stern Nijland (2004) and *The Daddy Machine* by Johnny Valentine (2004) are off-the-wall fantasy picture books. King and King find a girl in the jungle and bring her home to start their family. In *The Daddy Machine,* two girls with lesbian mothers create a daddy machine because they wonder what it would be like to have a daddy, only the machine produces many daddies. These two books reflect the kind of exaggerated and offbeat humor that oppressed groups sometimes use when there is a need for laughter and absurdity about matters that otherwise might be serious.

The LGBT family stories in picture books are not highly rated on the Horn Book Scale and rarely win many awards. One reason might be that quality fiction has to be well written and subtle in theme. Many of these books have very obvious topics that overwhelm the plot and are written like informational books. A second reason could be the illustrations, which in most cases are not realistic. Furthermore, the content is controversial to some reviewers. Two of the books about gay parents are high on the American Library Association's list of most frequently banned books. Between

1990 and 2000, *Daddy's Roommate* (Willhoite, 1990) was the 2nd most frequently banned book, and *Heather Has Two Mommies* (Newman, 1989) scored 11th. This fits public attitudes that look more kindly on women rather than men raising children. Finally, large publishers view LGBT literature as a niche market that will not be highly profitable, so most of these books are from small presses, such as Alyson Wonderland, Tricycle, Women's Press, Two Lives, New Family, and Children's Book Press, which do not have huge resources to devote to the creation of really excellent children's books.

Gay Marriage, Commitment Ceremonies, and/or Separation in Picture Books

In 1989 Denmark became the first country to grant registered same-sex partners the same rights as married couples. Since then, 14 more countries around the world have instituted some type of marriage rights for LGBT couples, including the Netherlands, Belgium, South Africa, Spain, and Canada. In the United States, as of this writing, the state of Massachusetts recognizes same-sex marriage, and five other states have enacted legislation to provide some benefits for same-sex couples, but many of these laws are being contested. These laws impact the ability to adopt, obtain insurance and retirement benefits, and inherit joint property, and they affect many other rights taken for granted by heterosexual spouses. In places where domestic partnerships are available, couples go before a judge or to a courthouse to receive the legal paperwork. Clergy often preside at commitment ceremonies held in churches or synagogues or in public or private places.

The children of LGBT parents know how important these issues and the ceremonies surrounding them are, so it is not surprising that they become excited when their parents decide to hold a commitment ceremony, whether it involves legal rights or not. Table 13-2 lists the picture books for children on this subject.

Table 13-2. Children's Picture Books on Same-Sex Marriage

Title	Author	Horn Book Scale
Saturday Is Pattyday	Leslea Newman	5
Daddy's Wedding	Michael Willhoite	NR
King and King	Linda deHaan & Stern Nijland	2
Mom and Mum Are Getting Married	Ken Setterington	4

In *King and King,* Linda deHaan and Stern Nijland (2000), who live in the Netherlands, where gay marriage is possible, create a twist to a normal marriage fairy tale. When the queen decides she wants to retire, her son must get married. In colorful, fanciful illustrations, the prince meets a series of princesses and rejects them all, until the last princess arrives with her brother, a prince, and it is love at first sight—with him. The princes get married by a minister in a small church. The three-tier wedding cake has a figurine of two men on the top. The book is funny and the art creative. It is enjoyable to be able to laugh about a serious topic like gay marriage. This book has been contested for library and classroom display because of its frivolous treatment of marriage and because of the gay characters. *King and King* would fit well into a unit on fairy tales.

Mom and Mum Are Getting Married by Ken Setterington (2004) and *Daddy's Wedding* by Michael Willhoite (1996) describe commitment ceremonies. In Setterington's book, the mothers decide on a party at their cottage for family only. Mom's father bakes a cake, and rings are exchanged, but there is no ritual. In Willhoite's book, Daddy and Frank dress formally and hold their ceremony at Frank's house, which is festooned with rainbow flags and balloons. Nick, the narrator, is the best man, and most of his family attend the celebration; there is a short ritual conducted by Reverend Powell. Frank and Daddy read the vows they have written, and Nick is the ring bearer. The ending, when their dog Clancy takes a big bite out of the three-tier wedding cake, leaves readers chuckling.

Saturday Is Pattyday by Leslea Newman (1993) is the only picture book about separation or divorce between gay parents. Frankie is upset after his mothers, Allie and Patty, "divorce," but Patty assures Frankie that he will spend Saturdays with her. When Allie comes to pick him up, Frankie sees how sad Patty is, so he leaves his beloved stuffed dinosaur for her to take care of until next week. Any child of divorce will relate to this touching story.

All together, these books present a fairly complete picture of the creation and division of families, from a child's perspective. None of them mentions ostracism of gay people within families; this is a huge omission, because some of the most hurtful kinds of prejudice come from the relatives of people in LGBT families. Sometimes lesbian and gay couples choose not to have commitment ceremonies because they know that their family members would not attend. These books, like the books about same-sex parents, have little plot. They show present commitment ceremonies as being smaller than traditional weddings, but the details, such as the ring exchange and wedding cake, show them to be very similar otherwise.

Novels About Children With Lesbian or Gay Parents

Four excellent novels for the upper elementary grades address almost all the issues that children with lesbian or gay parents will encounter (Table 13-3). Two concern families in which children have grown up with two lesbian mothers. Nancy Garden's (2000) *Holly's Secret* is about 11-year-old Holly, her brother, Will, and her mothers, who move from New York City to western Massachusetts. In New York, Holly's family had been out (i.e., they did not hide their lesbian identity), but in summer camp Holly experiences teasing and wants to avoid that situation in the future. In order to be popular, she tries to hide her family's identity. Her efforts backfire, but her mothers stand beside her throughout the ordeal.

Table 13-3. Older Children's Novels on Gay and Lesbian Parenting

Title	Author	Horn Book Scale
From the Notebooks of Melanin Sun	Jacqueline Woodson	2
Holly's Secret	Nancy Garden	2
Box Girl	Sarah Winthrow	1
Between Mom and Jo	Julie Anne Peters	NR

In *Between Mom and Jo* by Julie Anne Peters (2006), 14-year-old Nick tells about his life growing up with two mothers. His birth mother, whom he calls Mom, is a busy lawyer. Jo, her partner since before Nick's birth, conquers alcoholism and can't keep a job, but she provides Nick with an entertaining, love-filled childhood. His mothers intercede when he faces name-calling in kindergarten and a homophobic third-grade teacher who won't post his drawing of his family or give him fair grades. The family lives through his birth mother's discovery that she has cancer, her hospitalization, and her recovery. When his parents separate, Nick, at age 13, is devastated because Jo does not have custody. Mom refuses to let Nick see Jo as she prepares to sell their house and buy another one with her new partner. The story has a happy ending, but only because moral rights overcome legal ones.

Between Mom and Jo (Peters, 2006) also deals with legal issues and parental rights. When Mom and Jo wanted to have a baby and decided that Mom would be the birth mother, they idealistically thought that there was no need for Jo to adopt the baby. Even today, that kind of adoption would be illegal in many places. The legal issue of hospital visitation rights also arises in this story, when Jo realizes that she has no right to be there with the woman she loves. Many of these issues concern children of lesbian and gay parents.

These two stories accurately portray the need for a support system at home for children who face discrimination or teasing at school. The stories also show the wonderful relationships between the mothers and their children, with the humor, drama, and everyday occurrences that make life interesting in all families.

In another two novels, the children are older when they discover that one of their parents is gay. Melanin Sun is 13 when his mother reveals that she is in love with a woman in *From the Notebooks of Melanin Sun* by Jacqueline Woodson (1995). Melanin reacts with disbelief and shuts his mother out of his life until gradually their close relationship is rebuilt. Melanin has to deal with issues involving both race and sexual orientation, because his mother is African American and her lesbian partner is White.

Box Girl by Sarah Winthrow (2001) received the highest Horn Book Scale rating. Gwen loses her best friend at the end of seventh grade when she reveals that her father is gay. Thus, when Clara moves to town, and she and Gwen work together on school assignments and develop a close friendship, Gwen does not divulge her family structure. Also, Gwen's mother, who disappeared 5 years earlier when she learned that her husband was gay, has begun sending Gwen postcards from France with no return address, and her father's partner moves in with her and her father. When Clara begs Gwen to invite her overnight, everything is revealed, and Clara remains her friend. Although there is some stereotyping—such as her father's partner being a flamboyant gay artist—Gwen's struggles are genuine and the story is entertaining.

The difference between these two stories is that the parents, for a while at least, become the source of the conflict rather than the support system for the child.

The ultimate goal for any marginalized group is to fit into the mainstream. In two short novels for children 8 to 12 years old (Table 13-4), there are children with lesbian or gay parents, but that is just one of the characteristics of the parents and has nothing to do with the plot. Nancy Garden is writing a series of books for this age group called the *Candlestone Inn Mysteries*. These chapter books are not about lesbian issues; they are mysteries. The main characters, Nikki and Travis, have lesbian mothers who run the Candlestone Inn, but the stories feature the two children solving mysteries. In *The Case of the Broken Scarab* (2004a), Nikki and Travis have just moved into their new Vermont home and helped their mothers to set up the bed-and-breakfast. They discover that one of their first patrons has stolen a scarab from a museum in New York City and brought it with her to Vermont.

Gay parents are even more invisible in *The Trouble With Babies* by Martha Freeman (2002). Holly has just moved into a new home and befriended a boy who lives next door. When she knocks on his front door, his dad answers the door, and when she asks if he is Xavier's dad, he responds, "One of them; my name is Jim," which goes right over her head. Later Xavier tells Holly that his grandmother says he favors Alan, and when

Holly asks who Alan is, Xavier explains that it is his other dad. At first Holly thinks that, like her, Xavier has a stepdad, but he goes on to explain that he has two dads and no moms. "Alan and Jim are partners." Holly says, "Oh, now I get it, you mean they are gay." When he asks her if she thinks that is weird, she says that it is unusual but not weird.

Table 13-4. Younger Children's Novels on Gay and Lesbian Parenting

Title	Author	Horn Book Scale
The Trouble With Babies	Martha Freeman	3
The Case of the Broken Scarab	Nancy Garden	NR

Both of these stories set the stage for a time when lesbian and gay parents are no long invisible in children's books.

Homophobia in School and the Outside World in Picture Books

Children from LGBT families often fear being teased by homophobic (or ignorant) classmates. Many face homophobic comments and actions repeatedly, and schools are the primary location for this type of harassment (Bott, 2000). Their parents are often invisible in schools where personnel do not know how to approach them, according to Ryan and Martin (2000). There are five picture books that realistically present school experiences of children with lesbian or gay parents and therefore could fit into an antiprejudice, tolerance, diversity, or family theme curriculum (Table 13-5).

Table 13-5. Children's Picture Books on Homophobia

Title	Author	Horn Book Scale
Asha's Mums	Rosamund Elwin & Michele Paulse	NR
Molly's Family	Nancy Garden	4
Antonio's Card/ La Tarjeta de Antonio	Rigoberto Gonzalez	4
My Two Uncles	Judith Vigna	3
Uncle What-Is-It Is Coming to Visit	Michael Willhoite	5

In *Asha's Mums* by Rosamund Elwin and Michele Paulse (1990), Asha, an African-Canadian girl, returns her permission slip for a field trip to her teacher, who tells her to take it home and get it signed correctly because she can't have two mothers. Clearly this teacher is ignorant or homophobic or both. Asha's mothers come to school and take care of the situation, but not before the other students overhear the discussion, and one child makes it clear that her family thinks that having two mothers is bad.

Molly's Family by Nancy Garden (2004b) is set in a kindergarten classroom where Timmy, one of the students, challenges Molly by telling her (and the other classmates) that she cannot have two mommies. Molly is upset and takes her drawing of her two moms home. The teacher, once she figures out that Molly does have two moms, explains to Timmy and the class that there are all kinds of families. At home Molly talks with her mothers about her feelings, and they explain that one of them birthed her and the other adopted her. The watercolor illustrations by Sharon Wooding portray an idyllic family in soft tones. Most kindergarten children, however, would already know their family origins, and most kindergarten teachers would have previously met their students' parents or at least know about them prior to the start of the school year.

In the bilingual book *Antonio's Card* by Rigoberto Gonzalez (2005), Antonio is teased after his classmates see his mother, whom he calls Leslie, in overalls splattered with paint when she meets him after school. Antonio urges Leslie to join him across the street as they wait for Mami, his other mother, to pick them up. In school Antonio makes a Mother's Day card, and when his teacher asks him whom his card is for, he says without thinking, "Mami and Leslie." Like Molly, he has drawn a picture of himself and his two mothers. He finally confides to Mami that kids are teasing him about Leslie's appearance and that the teacher is posting artwork on the wall the next day. Mami leaves it up to him to decide what to do about his picture. He loves both his moms, but he does not like to be taunted by other children. When Leslie brings him to her art studio and unveils a picture she is painting of Mami, he has a change of heart and realizes that he wants to share his picture at school, even if Leslie is taller than the other parents and a lesbian. Many children feel embarrassed about their parents for one reason or another. They could relate to this story as a realistic portrayal of a child who overcomes embarrassment about his or her family. Children's Book Press provides a teachers' guide on its Web site (www.childrensbookpress.org/teachersguide.html) to support the use of this book in the classroom.

Sometimes homophobia can be blatant, as in Antonio's case, and at other times it is subtle. Judith Vigna (1995), who is known for writing children's books on sensitive topics, presents *My Two Uncles*, a realistic story about homophobia within a family. Elly has worked hard constructing a diorama for her grandparents' 50th-anniversary party with her uncle and his partner, who is never invited to family functions even though they have been together for 5 years. On this occasion her uncle decides that he will not attend if his partner is not invited. Elly is distraught but takes the diorama to the party. Afterward her grandmother comes to the uncles' house to thank them. Grandpa can be seen in the illustrations, waiting for his wife outside his car and waving to the rest of the family. These kinds of family tensions are common in LGBT families, so many children, even those from heterosexual families, will be able to relate to this story, where for one reason or another a family member is rejected.

Uncle What-Is-It Is Coming to Visit by Michael Willhoite (1993) depicts two children's ignorance and fear when their mother tells them that their gay uncle is coming to visit. In their imaginations they conjure up stereotypes, so they are surprised when he walks in the door looking normal and enjoys playing baseball with them. Without discussion this book could reinforce stereotypes, but used in an instructional manner it can be informative. This is shown by one primary-grade teacher who developed a lesson in moral education from the book, believing that if children are old enough to hurt one another, they are old enough to learn about homophobia (Powell, 2003).

Picture Books About AIDS in LGBT Families

Four picture books about uncles with AIDS have received several awards (Table 13-6). Three are in the Adventuring With Books Collections from the National Council for Teachers of English (NCTE), and one, Leslea Newman's (1995) *Too Far Away to Touch*, received a star by *Publisher's Weekly* and is on the Children's Literature Choice List. One reason for the more highly rated LGBT books on the topic of AIDS might be because the books focus on a real problem and develop a story line, unlike some of the stories about LGBT families that are just informational.

Table 13-6. Children's Picture Books on AIDS

Title	Author	Horn Book Scale
Losing Uncle Tim	Mary Kate Jordan	2
Tiger Flowers	Patricia Quinlan	3
Too Far Away to Touch	Leslea Newman	2
A Name on the Quilt: A Story of Remembrance	Jeannine Atkins	5

The AIDS stories are all very similar. A female child has a close relationship with an uncle who has AIDS and copes with the uncle's death. "Since 1981, AIDS has killed over 25 million people worldwide. Today over 40 million live with HIV," according to *Newsweek* (Gerlach, 2006), so it is appropriate that there should exist some children's books on this topic. Nevertheless, these books were all written in the 1980s and 1990s, and nowhere, even in an endnote, does the reader learn about the magnitude of the disease outside the family in the book. There are mothers, fathers, sisters, brothers, and aunts who also live with HIV and die from AIDS. Most AIDS victims are not white or gay. So the children's literature on this topic stereotypes in its narrow range of story characters.

Two of the books deal with preparing a child for the death of her uncle, and two celebrate and remember the loss of an uncle due to AIDS. *Too Far Away to Touch* by Leslea Newman (1995) actually describes the uncle whose hair is falling out, who is taking pills, and who is tiring quickly. *Losing Uncle Tim* by Mary Kate Jordan (1989) is a sad story about Uncle Tim's death. In *Tiger Flowers* by Patricia Quinlan (1994), Joel dreams of his Uncle Michael and his uncle's "friend," Peter, who also died of AIDS. In *A Name on the Quilt* by Jeannine Atkins (1999), a family gathers to make a panel for the AIDS Memorial Quilt, which is explained in an endnote. Since AIDS is not emphasized in these books, they make good choices for a child to read when any family member is approaching death or has recently died. They might also be a useful addition to a science curriculum on diseases.

Nonfiction Family Books

Another kind of literature is informational books on families (Table 13-7). Several are alphabet or counting books that display only lesbian and gay families in the pictures. These are most useful for children from lesbian and gay families, so they can see many other families similar to their own. Bobbie Combs (2000a, 2000b) created two of these multicultural books.

Other books present lesbian and gay families alongside families with straight parents. *All Families Are Special* by Norma Simon (2003) and illustrated by Teresa Flavin presents a classroom of diverse children, with a Black teacher who asks her students to talk about their families. Twelve children discuss their families, and the discussion ends with "No families are the same. All families are special." One of the children is Hanna, who tells about her two mommies.

Some books feature gay and lesbian families alongside other families in photographic essays. Robert Skutch (1995), in *Who's in a Family?*, includes a lesbian couple with two children as well as a girl who has two fathers. There are 14 other kinds of families, including some animal families, with the theme being "who[m] you love forms your family." *Families: A Celebration of Diversity, Commitment and Love* by Aylette Jenness (1989), highlights 17 diverse families. *Families* by Ann Morris (2000) contains one illustration of two lesbians with their daughter. The best book in this genre is *Families* by

Table 13-7. Children's Books About Lesbian or Gay Families

Title	Author	Horn Book Scale
ABC: A Family Alphabet Book	Bobbie Combs & Desiree Keene	NR
1, 2, 3: A Family Counting Book	Bobbie Combs	NR
The Family Book	Todd Parr	4
It's OK to Be Different	Todd Parr	4
Families: A Celebration of Diversity, Commitment, and Love	Aylette Jenness	3
Who's in a Family?	Robert Skutch	5
Families	Ann Morris	3
All Families Are Special	Norma Simon	4
Families	Susan Kuklin	NR

Susan Kuklin (2006), because the author interviewed children and they selected the photographs that represent their families. Through children's interviews, readers are introduced to Ella, an African-American girl with gay dads and Lily and Jacob and their lesbian moms. Todd Parr includes lesbian and gay families in both *The Family Book* (2003), and *It's OK to Be Different* (2001). With cartoonish illustrations in bold primary colors, it features many different kinds of families, including some families that have two moms and some families that have two dads.

Children from gay and lesbian families will leaf through each book searching for "their" family to be represented, and when it is, they will be delighted. Children from straight families can broaden their concept of family from reading these books. A book like Kuklin's (2006) in a classroom library is one of the best ways that a teacher can validate the multiple cultures and diverse families of students in his or her classroom.

LGBT Young People

In the contemporary media, issues of sexual orientation and, to a lesser extent, gender identity are prevalent, and many young people begin questioning their identity while they are in the upper elementary grades. Because the media representations and cultural stereotypes are often negative, most young people are nervous about their feelings. Some deny them, at least initially. Others quickly learn to embrace their identity and find allies for support. Several novels share the school experiences of LGBT students (Table 13-8). According to the Gay, Lesbian, and Straight Education Network (GLSEN,

2005), 74.9% of lesbian, gay, bisexual, and transgender students frequently hear derogatory terms like *faggot* at school, and 89.2% often hear "that's so gay," meaning stupid or worthless. More than 33% have been physically assaulted at school.

Table 13-8. Children's Novels on Sexual Orientation and Gender Identity

Title	Author	Horn Book Scale
The House That You Pass on the Way	Jacqueline Woodson	1
The Misfits	James Howe	2
Stitches	Glen Huser	NR
Luna: A Novel	Julie Anne Peters	NR
So Hard to Say	Alex Sanchez	4
Absolutely, Positively, NOT	David Larochelle	3
Totally Joe	James Howe	4
The Manny Files	Christian Burch	NR

Three novels directly address gay-bashing in schools. In *Stitches* by Glen Huser (2003), a seventh grader narrates his middle school experiences. He lives in a trailer with his aunt, nieces, and nephews, whom he entertains with handmade puppets. His mother shows up from time to time. Glen makes friends with bright but disabled Chantelle. In school, they join two other students to produce elegant puppet performances for the entire school, which are wildly popular. Glen tries to ignore bullies who call him names, and he appreciates the teachers who allow him to explore his talents. When he is the first and only boy to take a class called fashion studies, he is harassed, attacked, and ends up in the hospital while his tormenters are jailed. Finally, Glen gets a scholarship to a fine arts high school in the city, and his mother finds him an apartment so that he can attend. This great story of a close friendship and sensitive teachers portrays a realistic homophobic school environment.

In a story laced with humor, James Howe (2001) addresses the school climate in *The Misfits*. Four "different" seventh graders—unkempt Skeezie; tall, activist Addie; gay Joe; and overweight Bobby—meet weekly in an ice cream shop for discussions. Bobby is the narrator. Addie decides that the seventh grade needs a third political party for school elections so that the popular kids won't win all the time. She organizes a Freedom Party for oppressed minorities (who don't feel so oppressed), and when that fails, the group sets up a No Name Party, lists all the names each of them has been called, and creates large print versions of each word in a large orange circle with a line through it. They post the signs around the school, and even though they don't win the election, the school administration decides to have a No Name Week and eventually a No Name school policy. The nice thing about this book is that Joe is part of a larger group that addresses prejudice broadly.

Another boy, Keats, is harassed by Craig throughout fourth and fifth grade. Ostensibly it is because he is the smallest student in the class, but in reality it is because Keats is different in many ways that would associate him with being gay. At home he has a new male nanny, whom they call the "manny" and who reminds him of Mary Poppins, doing outlandish things with him and his brother and sisters. The manny understands Keats and is able to make him laugh and feel good about himself. Students who babysit or have had a nanny will laugh uproariously while reading this book, and students who are different, for whatever reason, will relate to the bullying and the strategies for dealing with it. In the end, at Thanksgiving dinner, when each family member tells what he or she is grateful for during the past year, Uncle Max (another gay uncle) says that he is most happy that Matthew (the manny) has come into his life, and he kisses him. This tender moment adds a sweet realism to the family ritual of sharing gratitude at Thanksgiving. Several award-winning LGBT novels that might be of interest to upper elementary school students are about young people who are questioning or just discovering their sexual orientation or gender identity. *Totally Joe,* also by James Howe (2005), is written in the form of an "alphabiography" that Joe writes as an assignment for his seventh-grade English teacher. His frank, humorous, and poignant writings about accepting his sexual orientation, as well as the responses of his family members and friends, provide highly entertaining reading. Joe's best allies are his aunt and a straight friend who urges him to help her start a gay-straight alliance in his school.

Although Steven in *Absolutely, Positively, NOT* by David Larochelle (2005) is 16, and the book opens with him practicing his driving with his mother, his behaviors are typical for younger people, even those much younger, who are trying to determine their sexual orientation. Steven lives in rural Minnesota, where there is not a lot of information about or exposure to LGBT culture. He uses the public library and the Internet as sources of information. In one book for parents, he finds "warning signs" that a child might be gay. For example, "Does your son prefer the company of girls to boys?" Steven's best friend is Rachel. The book also asks if your son participates in activities such as playing with dolls. Steven has two plastic bins of collectable Superman action figures and wonders if they are considered dolls. Steven goes square dancing with his mother. One of his male teachers is also a member of the square dancing group, and Steven later realizes that he is gay. Rachel notices an advertisement for a gay support group, and Steven begs his mother to let him take his driver's license test so that he can drive to a neighboring town to attend the meeting. Because Steven is just figuring out his sexual orientation, this story would be appropriate for students much younger that Steven.

In a similar story, *So Hard to Say* by Alex Sanchez (2004), Frederick, an eighth grader who has just moved to California, becomes close friends with Xio, who begins to think of him as a boyfriend. Frederick, on the other hand, looks at Xio as a best friend and begins to have romantic feelings for Victor, the leader of the soccer boys. He begins to think that he might feel about boys the way most boys feel about girls.

Sugarlee, in *The House That You Pass on the Way* by Jacqueline Woodson (1997), briefly kissed a girl in sixth grade, so like Steven she is questioning her identity. Her father is from a famous Black family and her mother is the only White woman in the town, so Sugarlee, being biracial, has already faced identity issues. When her cousin, whom she has never met, visits for the summer, the girls discuss what it might be like to fall in love with a girl, and Sugarlee is attracted to Trout in an innocent way. The end is surprising and reflects the complexity of sexual orientation issues.

Luna: A Novel by Julie Anne Peters (2005), on the transgender experience, is appropriate for middle school students. Using flashbacks, the female character Regan tells how her brother Liam has lived a life of a girl in a boy's body. From an early age Liam has secretly cross-dressed and pretended to be a girl, which would have infuriated his father had he known what was going on. His mother did know, but she chose to ignore it. Only Regan watches her brother dress up in girls' clothing in the middle of the night, and she agrees to call him Luna. She accompanies Luna to shopping malls, where he tests whether he can pass as a girl. The book covers the span of Liam's life from ages 3 to 18. When he decides to have sex-change surgery, Liam flies to Seattle in order to work to earn money for the operation. His sister is distraught and emotional at the airport, but she can see that his choice to eventually get surgery is the right one for him. Any young person who has held family secrets or who has been harassed will enjoy this story.

These novels are well written, have complex characters, and provide wonderful insights into LGBT life. Because they are multifaceted, many older elementary or middle school students can relate to the stories and gain insight about living as a lesbian, a gay man, a bisexual, or a transgender person in today's world.

Lambda Literary Awards for Children's Books in this Chapter

Since 1988 the Lambda Literary Foundation has given awards to outstanding books on LGBT topics. One section of those awards is for books for children and young people. Eight of the books in this chapter have won this prestigious award (Table 13-9). In 2005 more children's books won this award than in any previous year. In past years most of the awards went to young adult literature and were about students who were seniors in high school. It appears that books for elementary and middle school readers are now breaking into award-winning status in children's literature.

Table 13-9. Lambda Literary Foundation Awards

Year of Award	Title	Author
1989	*Losing Uncle Tim*	Mary Kate Jordan
1995	*From the Notebooks of Melanin Sun*	Jacqueline Woodson
1997	*The House That You Pass on the Way*	Jacqueline Woodson
2002	*Felicia's Favorite Story*	Leslea Newman
2000	*King and King*	Linda deHaan and Stern Nijland
2004	*So Hard to Say*	Alex Sanchez
2005	*Antonio's Card*	Rigoberto Gonzalez
2005	*Totally Joe*	James Howe
2005	*And Tango Makes Three*	Justin Richardson and Peter Parnell

Publishers of LGBT Fiction for Children

An examination of publishers who produce fiction books about lesbian and gay families and young people is revealing (Table 13-10). Mainstream publishers such as Clarion and Dial produced books about gay men dying of AIDS, but no books about LGBT families in general. In 1995, mainstream publisher Scholastic produced one novel about a child's mother coming out to him as a lesbian, written by a well-established, award-winning African-American author. Not until 2005 did Scholastic publish another, under the Arthur Levine imprint. Four large companies published more than one book in this genre: Atheneum, with four, published books by James Howe and Christian Burch; Little, Brown published Julie Anne Peters. Farrar,

Table 13-10. Publishers of Children's LGBT Fiction

Publisher	Dates of Books	Focus
Albert Whitman	1989, 1995	Cultural diversity
Alyson Wonderland	1989, 1990, 1991, 1993, 1994, 1996, 2004	LGBT
Atheneum	1999, 2001, 2005, 2006	Major publisher
Children's Book Press	2005	Bilingual/multicultural
Clarion	1995	Major publisher
Delacorte	1997	Major publisher
Dial	1994	Major publisher
Farrar, Straus & Giroux	2000, 2004	Major publisher
Groundwood (Canada)	2001, 2003	Major publisher
Holiday House	2002	Major publisher
Little, Brown	2005, 2006	Major publisher
New Family Press	2003	No information
New Victoria	1993	Lesbian-feminist
Scholastic Arthur Levine/Scholastic	1995, 2005	Major publisher
Second Story (Canada)	2004	Diversity
Simon & Schuster	2004, 2005	Major publisher
Tricycle (Ten Speed)	1995, 2000, 2004	Progressive
Two Lives	2000, 2000, 2002, 2004	Alternative families
Women's Press	1985, 1990	Feminist

Straus & Giroux produced two by Nancy Garden, and Groundwood and Simon & Schuster produced two each.

Both Nancy Garden and Julie Anne Peters credit their editors for encouraging them to write books about LGBT people and their families (see sidebars). The majority of large book publishers have never published a book about LGBT young people or children with gay or lesbian families. Given the number of books produced by mainstream publishers each year, which runs in the

Julie Anne Peters

Meet Julie Anne Peters, a woman who avoided English classes, majored in science and math, held numerous jobs, quit her job as a systems engineer, and announced to her partner that she was going to be a children's book author because she never wanted to work again in her life. Little did she know that writing would be the hardest work she's ever done. Julie visited her local public library and read many young adult novels. In 1989, she started writing for publication. Memorable early titles include *The Stinky Sneakers Contest* (1992), *How Do You Spell Geek?* (1996), and the *A Snitch in the Snob Squad* (2001) series.

It was her editor, Megan Tingley of Little, Brown, who suggested that Julie write a lesbian love story. Her next two books were ground-breaking novels. *Luna* (2005), about a young male-to-female transsexual, won a National Book Award nomination and many other awards. *Between Mom and Jo* (2006) is about a lesbian couple with a son who separate. Her topics are contemporary and her writing style mesmerizing, using contemporary language that kids will recognize as their own.

Julie typically creates a book by writing the ending first so that she has a goal and will not veer too far off the track as she creates her story. She then writes scenes that aren't chronological and builds the story around those scenes. That process becomes evident to the reader; each scene is crafted with details and suspense that makes it difficult to stop reading. The scenes fit together as a logical whole. Perhaps her systems engineering background supports her writing.

For *Luna* (2005), Julie visited a transsexual support group and asked if she could interview the members. They all offered enthusiastic support; they were eager to help her write a book about them because there were no books written about their experiences

hundreds for the larger presses, it becomes obvious that LGBT families are marginalized by most major children's book publishers.

Several small book publishers specialize in literature about LGBT people and their families. Alyson Wonderland produced 10 books; Two Lives, 4 books; and New Victoria, 1. Other small presses fit LGBT families into their collections. For example, Children's Book Press, a multicultural imprint, published one about Latina lesbian mothers and their son. Tricycle, a subdivision of Ten Speed Press, has three books. Women's Press, which is feminist, has two books, and diversity presses Albert Whitman and Second Story have two and one, respectively.

Taken all together, small presses are the major supplies of picture books about LGBT families. Major publishers produce excellent novels about children with LGBT families and young people who are questioning their identity, as well as nonfiction works on families in general. It would appear that publishing LGBT books targeted at young children is more risky than producing LGBT books for older readers. Elementary schoolchildren from LGBT families are being deprived of wonderful books that reflect their culture. The list of major publishing houses that publish no books about the LGBT culture is long.

Conclusion

One of the best ways to counter homophobia, and the teasing that accompanies it in elementary schools, is to surround children with books that include children with lesbian and gay parents. What at first might seem strange or unusual can then be seen as normal for some children. Widening the picture of family to include many different types will benefit all children who do not live in a one-father, one-mother household. Today, in the United States, this includes more children than ever. Teachers who share these books with their classes take an important step in welcoming children from LGBT families into their classrooms (Lamme & Lamme, 2003). There are few well-written and illustrated books about LGBT families, although increasingly these families are included with other types of families in picture storybooks on other topics. The novels for middle school children are excellent and cover a variety of issues and topics. However, a single lesbian or gay parent doesn't exist in children's books but is frequent in real life.

There are few young adult novels with LGBT story characters, but several are excellent, award-winning books. In the United States, conditions have changed in the past few years for lesbian and gay families. Children in middle school are discovering their identities and coming out at earlier ages than ever before. Young lesbian and gay adults who are partnered are choosing to have families at earlier ages. These family situations make some of the books about gay and lesbian parents seem outdated. Many of today's families teach gay pride to their children from day one.

These new conditions do not appear in the books. Not mentioned in any of the gay and lesbian family picture books are the LGBT activities that provide social opportunities. There is only one book about gay pride parades or celebrations, *Gloria Goes to Gay Pride* by Leslea Newman (1991). There are no family picnics during LGBT Pride Week or travels to Family Week at Provincetown or mentions of Children of Lesbians and Gays Everywhere (COLAGE) or the Family Pride Coalition events. There are no playgroups or experiences at open

for young readers. To make her story more authentic, she created a younger sister for Luna to tell the story. The result helps readers to relate to the ally voice rather than to Luna's.

Julie's parents divorced when she was a teenager, so writing about Nick's lesbian mothers splitting up in *Between Mom and Jo* (2006) might have had some grounding in personal experience. Her own partner relationship has lasted more than 30 years, however. Her research on the legal issues and how they impact lesbian couples as well as same-sex couples with children makes that story realistic and relevant. Julie's characters are real and consistent in their behavior. Readers will feel as if they know them as people and will almost be able to predict how they will act.

Julie has great support for her writing. She values Megan Tingley's long-term mentoring. Julie is a member of a critique group and credits her "generous, brilliant, astute, caring, rigorous, invested readers." She receives literally thousands of letters and e-mail messages from her readers. Julie views young adult literature as being in its infancy and evolving at a fast pace.

As with any LGBT literature, adults sometimes ban or limit access to Julie's books. When a librarian said that she had tossed one of Julie's books into her wastebasket, Julie's brother, a children's librarian in the New York Public Library, told her that "throwing a book in the trash is a surefire way to get kids to read it." He is probably right.

In an interview with professional writer and editor, Peggy Tibbets (2000), Julie says that she balances humor in her stories the same way she does in life:

> A measure of laughter, a measure of tears, always tipping the scale on the side of laughter. Humor is, I think, our saving grace when it comes to coping with the hardships and tragedies of life. It can be helpful. It can be healing. For young people, especially, humor is a positive response to dealing with life's larger dilemmas, such as loss, death, disease, unwelcome change. It's certainly healthier than anger and violence. Reluctant readers—the audience I most hope to capture—seem to gravitate toward humorous books. Maybe because they make reading fun, not such a chore. But all kids love to laugh. And I love to hear them laughing. If my humor has a subtext, it's "Don't take yourself so seriously. Lighten up."

and affirming churches. There are no positive or negative neighborhood experiences. Nor is there any mention of laws that target LBGT families and the fact that so many believe they must be closeted or lose jobs or housing.

The books in print come largely from people who live in Massachusetts, New York City, or California, the more progressive areas in this country. The books are so focused on the sole topic of family composition that they fail to depict an accurate or complete view of the life experiences of a variety of lesbian and gay families. Most of the families in these books appear to be middle class, with the exception of Jo in *Between Mom and Jo* (Peters, 2006).

The only LGBT people in all these books are parents, uncles, or LGBT children. There are no lesbian aunts or LGBT grandparents. For *Winter Poems,* a collection of poems by famous poets compiled by Barbara Rogasky (1994), Trina Schart Hyman paints illustrations of her family in their New Hampshire home. The grandparents (Rogasky and Hyman) are a lesbian couple, and their grandson is a biracial child. However, this information comes only from an author's note and the illustrations. Clearly a broader definition of family would make the books about LGBT families relate more closely to reality.

Race is an issue in both of Jacqueline Woodson's books, *From the Notebooks of Melanin Sun* (1995) and *The House That You Pass on the Way* (1997). Racial-minority families are represented only in illustrations in the picture books. Adriana Romo paints Felicia's mothers as two different ethnicities in *Felicia's Favorite Story* (Newman, 2002). Danamarie Hosler creates multicultural families in *1, 2, 3: A Family Counting Book* (Combs, 2002b). Cecilia Concepción Alvarez portrays a Latina family in *Antonio's Card* (Gonzalez, 2005). Asha and her mothers, in *Asha's Mums* (Elwin & Paulse, 1990), are represented as Black. Daddy and Papa are White, but they adopt an African-American son in *How My Family Came to Be* (Aldrich, 2003). The family ABC book (Combs, 2000a) contains families of many different ethnicities and races.

On the positive side, it is wonderful that several publishing companies—like Little, Brown and Farrar, Straus & Giroux—are now urging authors like Julie Anne Peters and Nancy Garden to specialize in LGBT literature. It is encouraging that books are appearing like the Candlestone Inn mysteries by Nancy Garden (2004a) and *Box Girl* by Sarah Winthrow (2001), in which being lesbian or gay is not the issue, yet there are LGBT characters. It is satisfying to have these books out at all, when two decades ago there were none. There are great opportunities for new authors and new books to fill in the gaps in this lexicon.

References

Bott, C. J. (2000). Fighting the silence: How to support gay and straight students. *Voice of Youth Advocate, 23*, 22, 24, 26.

Children of Lesbians and Gays Everywhere. (COLAGE). (2006). http://www.colage.org/resources/facts.htm

Gay, Lesbian, and Straight Education Network (GLSEN). (2005). *National school climate survey on experiences of lesbian, gay, bisexual, and transgender (LGBT) students.* Available online at www.GLSEN.org

Gerlach, D. (2006, March 15). A global menace. *Newsweek, 123* (20), p. 52.

Lamme, L. L, & Lamme, L. A. (2003). *Welcoming children from sexual-minority families into our schools.* Bloomington, IN: Phi Delta Kappa.

Mom and Mum are getting married! (2005, January 1), *Kirkus Reviews, 73* (1).

Perrin, E. C. (2002). Technical report: Coparent or second-parent adoption by same-sex parents. *Pediatrics, 109*, 341–344.

Powell, M. (2003). Homophobia—hate's last refuge. *Montessori Life, 15*, 14–16.

Nancy Garden

Nancy Garden is a prolific and well-known author of children's and young adult books about lesbians and about children growing up in two-mom families. She began writing lesbian fiction for young adults ages 10–24 because none was available when she was growing up as a young lesbian in the 1950s, and because most of the adult lesbian fiction she found was very negative. She published her landmark novel, *Annie on My Mind*, about two high school girls who fall in love, in 1982.

From her start in the early 1970s, Nancy wrote about kids who crossed traditional boundaries, such as the cross-racial friendship in *What Happened in Marston* (1971) and a boy who falls in love with a girl on drugs in *The Loners* (1972). Nancy also wrote non-fiction informational books on such topics as vampires, werewolves, witches, devils, and demons, as well as a history of Berlin during and immediately after World War II. Among her other books are a historical novel about Joan of Arc called *Dove & Sword* (1995), a fantasy sequence called *Endgame* (2006), which is about bullying, and a serial novel that is still running in a number of newspapers. Her lesbian novels continued with *Lark in the* Morning (1991), *Good Moon Rising* (1996), and *The Year They Banned the Books* (1999). During this era there was considerable backlash against LGBT people, for they had become more open about their sexuality. LGBT kids, who have always been subject to bullying, were teased and beaten in greater numbers than before, and Nancy felt it important to reflect that in fiction.

The 1990s also brought the "gayby" boom, in which large numbers of gay and lesbian couples, including several of Nancy's friends, began adopting or having children more openly and in greater numbers than ever before. Nancy was concerned that some of those children might be teased or ostracized because of their families. An editor asked if she would be willing to write about a child with two moms. She had been thinking of doing that, anyway, so she jumped at the chance, and the result was *Holly's Secret* (2000).

However, the children her friends were adopting were infants, so Nancy wanted to write a picture storybook, something she had never done before. She had a lot to learn. Nancy explains that books for very young children look simple, but that is not the case, especially if one is a novelist. Every word in a picture book, like every word in a poem, has to be exactly right. It took years, a lot of guidance from her editor and from Nancy's good friend Barbara Seuling, who has written for that level, and many versions of roughly the same story before *Molly's Family* (2004b) was completed.

Today, Nancy is establishing another trend with the Candlestone Inn mystery series (2004a) published by Two Lives Publishing, for middle school students. In writing these books, Nancy is responding to a child from a lesbian family who, at a gay

Ray, V., & Gregory, R. (2001). School experiences of the children of lesbian and gay parents. *Family Matters, 59*, 28–41.

Ryan, D., & Martin, A. (2000). Lesbian, gay, bisexual, and transgender parents in the school system. *School Psychology Review, 29*, 207–216.

Tibbets, P. (2000). *Her Humor Hits Home: An Interview with Julie Anne Peters.* Available online at www.writing-world.com/children/peters.shtml

Children's Books

Aldrich, A. P. (2003). *How my family came to be: Daddy, Papa and me* (M. Motz, Illus.). Oakland, CA: New Family Press.

Atkins, J. (1999). *A name on the quilt: A story of remembrance* (T. Hills, Illus.). New York: Atheneum.

Burch, C. (2006). *The manny files.* New York: Atheneum.

Combs, B. (2000a). *ABC: A family alphabet book* (D. Keene & B. Rappa, Illus.). Ridley Park, PA: Two Lives.

Combs, B. (2000b). *1, 2, 3: A family counting book* (D. Hosler, Illus.). Ridley Park, PA: Two Lives.

deHaan, L., & Nijland, S. (2000). *King and king.* Berkeley, CA: Tricycle.

deHaan, L., & Nijland, S. (2004). *King & king & family.* Berkeley, CA: Tricycle.

Elwin, R., & Paulse, M. (1990). *Asha's mums* (D. Lee, Illus.). Toronto: Women's Press.

Freeman, M. (2002). *The trouble with babies* (C. B. Smith, Illus.). New York: Holiday House.

Galloway, P. (1985). *Jennifer has two daddies* (A. Anul, Illus.). Toronto: Women's Press.

Garden, N. (1971). *What happened in Marston.* (R. Cuffari, Illus.) New York: Four Winds Press.

Garden, N. (1972). *The Loners.* New York: Viking Press.

Garden, N. (1982). *Annie on my mind.* New York: Farrar, Straus & Giroux.

Garden, N. (1991). *Lark in the morning.* New York: Farrar Straus & Giroux.

Garden, N. (1995). *Dove and sword.* New York: Farrar, Straus & Giroux.

Garden, N. (1996) *Good moon rising.* New York: Farrar, Straus & Giroux.

Garden, N. (1999). *The year they banned the books.* New York: Farrar, Straus & Giroux.

Garden, N. (2000). *Holly's secret.* New York: Farrar, Straus & Giroux.

Garden, N. (2004a). *The case of the broken scarab.* Ridely Park, PA: Two Lives.

Garden, N. (2004b). *Molly's family* (S. Wooding, Illus.). New York: Farrar, Straus & Giroux.

Garden, N. (2006) *Endgame.* Orlando, FL: Harcourt.

Gonzalez, R. (2005). *Antonio's card / La tarjeta de Antonio* (C. Conception, Illus.). San Francisco: Children's Book Press.

Greenberg, K. E. (1996). *Zack's story: Growing up with same-sex parents.* Chicago: Lerner.

Heron, A., & Maran, M. (1994). *How would you feel if your dad was gay?* (K. Kovick, Illus.). Los Angeles: Alyson Wonderland.

Howe, J. (2001). *The misfits.* New York: Atheneum.

Howe, J. (2005). *Totally Joe.* New York: Atheneum.

Huser, G. (2003). *Stitches.* Toronto: Groundwood.

Jenness, A. (1989). *Families: A celebration of diversity, commitment, and love.* Boston: Houghton Mifflin.

Jordan, M. K. (1989). *Losing Uncle Tim* (J. Friedman, Illus.). Morton Grove, IL: Whitman.

Kuklin, S. (2006). *Families.* New York: Hyperion Books.

Larochelle, D. (2005). *Absolutely, positively, NOT.* New York: Levine.

Morris, A. (2000). *Families.* New York: HarperCollins.

writers' conference, said that she would like good stories for kids with gay parents in which the family structure is not the focus of the story. The mysteries take place in an old inn run by a lesbian couple and their children, 12-year-old Nikki and 11-year-old Travis. The kids solve the mysteries; the moms are present but in the background.

Nancy credits her editor, Margaret Ferguson of Farrar, Straus & Giroux, for helping her to create good books. They have worked together on 16 books. Nancy sees LGBT literature as being in a transition, from portraying LGBT as being a problem to portraying all aspects of it, the good and the bad. "Thank goodness," she says, "we're moving away from the idea that gay literature needs to concentrate on the bad!"

Nancy also thinks that we need more books about bisexual and transgender teens, and more books about younger gays and lesbians. Kids are now coming out at younger ages than ever before, and books for middle school students should reflect that. She points out that we're seeing more positive and neutral LGBT minor characters in books that aren't focused on homosexuality, and that's a good sign, too. Again, Nancy says, it reflects life.

Newman, L. (1989). *Heather has two mommies* (D. Souza, Illus.). Los Angeles: Alyson Wonderland.

Newman, L. (1991). *Gloria goes to gay pride* (R. Crocker, Illus.). Boston: Alyson Wonderland.

Newman, L. (1993). *Saturday is Pattyday* (A. Hegel, Illus.). Norwich, VT: New Victoria.

Newman, L. (1995). *Too far away to touch* (C. Stock, Illus.). New York: Clarion Books.

Newman, L. (2002). *Felicia's favorite story* (A. Romo, Illus.). Ridley Park, PA: Two Lives.

Parr, Y. (2001). *It's OK to be different.* Boston: Little, Brown.

Parr, T. (2003). *The family book.* Boston: Little, Brown.

Peters, J. (1992). *The stinky sneakers contest.* (C. Smith, Illus.). Boston: Little Brown.

Peters, J. (1996), *How do you spell geek?* Boston: Little, Brown.

Peters, J. (2001). *A snitch in the snob squad.* Boston, Little, Brown.

Peters, J. (2005). *Luna: A novel.* Boston: Little, Brown.

Peters, J. (2006). *Between Mom and Jo.* Boston: Little, Brown.

Quinlan, P. (1994). *Tiger flowers* (J. Wilson, Illus.). New York: Dial.

Richardson, J., & Parnell, P. (2005). *And Tango makes three* (H. Cole, Illus.). New York: Simon & Schuster.

Rogasky, B. (1994). *Winter poems* (T. S. Hyman, Illus.). New York: Scholastic.

Sanchez, A. (2004). *So hard to say.* New York: Simon & Schuster.

Setterington, K. (2004), *Mom and Mum are getting married* (A. Priestley, Illus.). Toronto, Ontario, Canada: Second Story Press.

Simon, N. (2003). *All families are special* (T. Flavin, Illus.). Morton Grove, IL: Whitman.

Skutch, R. (1995). *Who's in a family?* (L. Nienhaus, Illus.). Berkeley, CA: Tricycle.

Valentine, J. (2004). *The daddy machine* (L. Schmidt, Illus.). Los Angeles: Alyson Wonderland.

Vigna, J. (1995). *My two uncles.* Morton Grove, IL: Whitman.

Wickens, E. (1994). *Anna Day and the O-ring.* Boston: Alyson Wonderland.

Willhoite, M. (1990). *Daddy's roommate.* Boston: Alyson Wonderland.

Willhoite, M. (1993). *Uncle what-is-it is coming to visit.* Boston: Alyson Wonderland.

Willhoite, M. (1996). *Daddy's wedding.* Los Angeles: Alyson Wonderland.

Winthrow, S. (2001). *Box girl.* Toronto, Ontario, Canada: Groundwood.

Woodson, J. (1995). *From the notebooks of Melanin Sun.* New York: Scholastic.

Woodson, J. (1997). *The house that you pass on the way.* New York: Delacorte.

Living in Esperanza's World: Writing About the Mexican-American Experience

Pam Munoz Ryan

I am often asked, "What's the best thing about being an author and what's the worst?" The answer is usually the same: the letters I receive. I have been moved to tears from the touching responses from children. Their letters are gratuitous in the most honest and charming ways. I adore the students who continue to encourage me, who tell me, "Keep up the good work!" or who sign their letters "Your Reader." I'm pleased to hear from teachers who write and share the innovative ways they use my work in the classroom. I am grateful and amazed at how they enrich my stories, especially those who use my books as read-alouds. They are my heroes.

Occasionally, I receive accusatory, negative letters. I've had teachers write that they will never use a particular book with their students because the story brought up their own long-repressed childhood memories, and "nobody should have to revisit those types of situations ever again!" Once I received a letter from a woman who was upset that *Becoming Naomi León* (2004) depicted a character with alcohol-related problems. She was instrumental in subsequently having the book banned from her school district. I have been admonished because someone dies in a story and it is too sad. I have been criticized for ending a story with "too much hope and not enough reality." One teacher fiercely reprimanded me because she didn't appreciate that my characters figured out their problems on their own. Her allegation was that my characters should have prayed for answers.

I respect the reader's right to express his or her feelings about a book. Sometimes I feel the need to respond to a letter. Recently I received an intelligent and thought-provoking letter about *Esperanza Rising* (2000). The teacher took issue with my presentation of a strike in the book. She thought that my story relayed an anti-strike message that was damaging to children. Her interpretation was that I normalized the plight of the strikebreakers and "demonized" the picketers. She pleaded with me to think about the messages I put in my books. She suggested that since I have many readers, I also have the responsibility to give insight to the side of an issue that is not prevalent in our society.

I must be honest and say that when I sit down to write a story, I don't think about whether the slant of my story will be the road less traveled or the more accepted view; I think about the story I *need* to tell. My allegiance is to the truth in my character's reality, the verity of the situation in which I place him or her. There are many truths from many different perspectives for every story. Certainly, my character's truth should not be the only epiphany a reader experiences. A reader should have many singular revelations.

Children often approach a book with an open heart. Adult readers often come to a book with an agenda. Sometimes I am compelled to distinguish my own. Following is my response to the teacher:

Dear Teacher,

I received your letter and am confused and disheartened by your interpretation of *Esperanza Rising*. Although the book has been examined, studied, reviewed, and analyzed in great depth by any number of professors of children's literature and committees, I have never once had anyone write or ask me about the issues you suggest are in the book.

I did not write to "demonize the side of organized labor." I wrote to depict what happened to one family during that time period at DiGiorgio Farms, the actual camp where my mother was born. This story is a family story, and although it is fiction, it closely parallels my grandmother's immigration experience. Many people during that time period chose not to strike. Right or wrong, it is the truth.

The strike and social organizing issue was only one of many circumstances that affected my characters' lives. The characters do not know the language, they are desperate to have work, and their main concern is to put food on the table and exist at a basic level. When Esperanza and her family come to the United States, like so many others they live in "survival mode," not in a self-actualized mode like the character Marta. I purposefully and deliberately brought the strong and determined Marta into the story so I *could* tell the other side of the story. My intent was that in the end, the reader would recognize the compassion that Esperanza felt toward Marta. I hoped that the reader would be able to see Esperanza's growth. I also wanted to show the compromises that many Mexicans had to make. I wanted the reader to be appalled and indignant at their treatment and at repatriation. Many readers make these connections.

I agree that educators have a social responsibility to be mindful of the stories they tell or read to their students. I feel even more strongly that educators should expose *all sides* of a story, not just one. I often hear from teachers and professors of children's literature who teach the book. Many use it in ninth-grade English along with with *The Grapes of Wrath* (Steinbeck 1939/2002) and biographies of Cesar Chavez. With younger students, it's often used along with biographies of Dolores Huerta and/or Cesar Chavez. It's often read to inspire discussions about these very subjects. Many teachers have written to tell me that they divide their classroom down the middle and have one-half take the strikers' side and the other half take the nonstrikers' side. This exercise has been the impetus for extensive discussions. Aren't inquiry and deliberation important aspects of education?

I love my profession and take it seriously. Please know that I was not cavalier in my approach to this book. My research was extensive and arduous. I interviewed many people who lived in the camps at the same time as my grandmother. I researched in depth at the local history room in Bakersfield, California. I read about many strikes in the San Joaquin Valley in the 1930s. Believe me when I tell you that any negative incidents I mentioned in *Esperanza Rising* were tame in comparison to what the strikers actually did to nonstrikers, which included killing them. An academic researcher on the Great Depression reviewed the book for authenticity before publication. His only suggestion was that I was not graphic enough in that regard.

One of my greatest joys has been receiving letters, almost daily, from Latino children who tell me how very much the story has meant to their lives and, *just as important*, from non-Latino children who tell me that they have been enlightened by a story that is different from their own. For those letters, I am always grateful.

I'm sorry that as a writer, I failed you as a reader. I have learned after years of writing and speaking and answering letters that there is one thing I cannot control when a reader picks up a book. It is that every reader brings his or her own experiences to the story: family circumstances, travels, politics, likes and dislikes, emotional history, bravado, insecurities, and expectations. All affect the reading of any book. I respect that.

I don't write today to change your decision about using *Esperanza Rising* with students. I write to simply let you know that I read your letter carefully. What is ultimately important in the classroom is that students have a dedicated teacher who feels passionate and enthusiastic, rather than one who simply does not care at all. Your students are very fortunate.

Sincerely,

Pam Muñoz Ryan

Children's Books

Ryan, P. M. (2000). *Esperanza rising.* New York: Scholastic.

Ryan, P. M. (2004) *Becoming Naomi Leon.* New York: Scholastic.

Steinbeck, J. (2002). *The Grapes of Wrath.* New York: Penguin. (Original work published 1939)

Currents of Change

International Literature: Inviting Students Into the Global Community

Junko Yokota

More than ever before, it is important for today's students to grow up with a sense of who they are as members of a global community. It is essential that we, as teachers, purposefully introduce students to the cultures and lives of the wider world beyond their own communities so that they can begin to situate the context for their own lives within the world community. A powerful means for helping to develop this world context is through children's literature. What impact does literature have on children's understanding of the world and their perceptions of what they don't yet know? How does the literature affect teachers and librarians and other adults who work directly with children? What do adults need to know and do in order to maximize children's experiences with international literature? What challenges do we face as we bring international literature into the classroom? This chapter explores these questions and offers some suggestions.

Defining International Literature

The most widely accepted definition of international literature in the United States is books originally published outside the country and subsequently published here. Furthermore, if the book was originally written in a language other than English, it was translated to English for publication in the United States (Tomlinson, 1998). Books from other English-speaking nations like Canada, Britain, and Australia therefore count as "international" because of their country of origin.

International literature is not the same as multicultural literature. Multicultural literature typically refers to books that reflect cultural diversity within the United States. Multicultural literature includes stories and information on ethnic groups within the United States, but it also includes the stories and information on the root countries of the various U.S. heritages. As a result, it includes the folklore as well as the historical and contemporary stories of life outside the United States. What distinguishes multicultural books from international books is that multicultural books are published in the United States for a U.S. audience, whereas international books are published outside the United States for an audience in the country of their publication.

This very important distinction is reflected in the ways that authors and illustrators create their works and in how editors and publishers shape the creation—their perceptions of the intended audience. Each country prepares its books for its own children. However, due to the circumstances of economics, different goals in publishing, and differences in what constitutes quality literature, there is occasionally more in print in the United States about some cultures than in the country in which the story is set. Another reason that we should find value in multicultural books set in countries outside the United States is that sometimes the "outside" perspective of an author who is not from the targeted culture is able to notice what is of interest to the readers who are also outside that culture.

Muddying the definitional waters, however, are the different ways in which we have become increasingly inclusive since the 1990s in discussing international literature. For example, some people also designate as *international* books that are published in the United States but written by authors who have immigrated from another country—for example, Peter Sís or Yumi Heo. Sís was born in what was Czechoslovakia, and Heo was born in Korea; both grew up in their homelands, but both now reside in the United States.

Others (Freeman & Lehman, 2001) include books written and published in the United States but set entirely in a foreign country (e.g., *Shabanu: Daughter of the Wind* [Staples, 1989]). Staples is an American citizen who writes about a country she lived in but published her book in the United States; therefore, this makes *Shabanu* less clear as an international book by traditional definition. Yet a Canadian counterpart, such as Deborah Ellis's (2001) *The Breadwinner*, is clearly seen as an international book, despite the fact that like Staples, Ellis is also a North American writing about a story set in a country based on her years of living there.

For the purpose of this chapter, I use the traditional definition of international literature: books originally written in a country outside the United States, published for an audience of readers in its country of publication, and subsequently made available in the United States through translation (if necessary), publication, and distribution. I have chosen to retain this somewhat narrow but focused definition because I want to explore books that children around the world are reading in their own countries. What happens when these books cross national borders and are shared with a global community?

I examine how international literature is distinct from multicultural literature, and because of the limited space of this chapter, I leave the discussions of multicultural literature to the volumes that have already been published on the topic (e.g., Cai, 1998; Yokota, 1993). My objective is to get beyond the question of definition, because the real question, as Mingshui Cai pointed out in his article, is: "Is the debate really just ivory tower bickering?"

Why International Literature Matters

Why should we care about international books for our children? Garrett (2006) cited the work of three people who were historically influential in establishing the purpose of international books for all children. The first was French educator Paul Hazard (1932/1960), who, in his book *Books, Children, and Men,* described children's books as "diplomats," because diplomats travel easily across borders. Hazard viewed children's books as "ambassadors of peace."

The second was Jella Lepman, a Jew who fled Germany in the 1930s and returned after the war to eventually establish the International Youth Library, to date the only library to systematically collect as many books as are donated in original publication format from around the world. Lepman proposed that books were "emissaries of international diplomacy." Her autobiography, *A Bridge of Children's Books* (1969/2002), chronicles how she worked tirelessly to help realize her belief that children growing up with international books would come to view other nations with an understanding that would make it unimaginable to enter wars.

The third person cited by Garrett (2006) was Sheila Egoff, the Canadian author of *The Republic of Childhood: A Critical Guide to Canadian Children's Literature in English* (1966), who contended that children essentially belong to a singular republic—that of childhood. Garrett expands the views of these scholars, contending that there are many republics of childhood rather than one. By this he means that childhood can be characterized as a republic, but there is more than one republic of childhood.

International literature lets us see the lives of people as they represent themselves in their own countries. There could be no more honest a depiction than one created by local people for their own audiences. We can learn how people live their daily lives, what activities they engage in, and what decisions guide their lives. Meanwhile, our students have the opportunity to read—in their own language—the highest quality of books that have been published and read all over the world.

Issues Concerning International
Books for Children

The issues concerning international books for children are numerous. Following are a few:

- The lack of international books published in the United States, especially from non-European countries

- Translations as lenses through which we read books that were originally published in a foreign language

- The availability of and preference for books that have been published in the United States, and the question of authenticity

Most countries in the world import a substantial proportion of their children's books from outside their own land. The most notable exception to this trend is the United States. Whereas many countries import 28% to 67% of their published books annually, the United States imports only 1% of its books annually. What does this imply? The Batchelder Award (see awards sidebar), given for the highest quality translated book in the previous publication year, seldom has more than a handful of books to consider. Another issue is that most available international books are European. How do we find books from cultures that do not have their books available to us? The reasons for this lack of access range from the economics of the publishing industry to a widely varying definition on what constitutes a "book."

Awards Related to International Literature

- Hans Christian Andersen Award for Writing and Illustration, awarded every two years by the International Board on Books for Young People (IBBY)

- IBBY Honor List, awarded for writing, illustration, and translation to books nominated by national sections of IBBY

- U.S. Board on Books for Young People (USBBY) Outstanding International Books, an annual list of international books published the previous year in the United States. USBBY also sponsors the Bridges to

This condition is exacerbated for children. Children's books are translated only half as often as adult books. Stephen Roxburgh (2006), who has a reputation for publishing more international books than most publishers, describes a hesitation about expenses, prospective sales, and the ability of editors to read in multiple languages and make decisions about the quality of foreign-language books firsthand, among other reasons. Then the inevitable language barrier must be dealt with in terms of how the translation is done and with what lens.

Even when books are translated, the U.S. market does not purchase many international books. The books are often perceived as quirky or out of the mainstream. They address subject matter that is often elusive in U.S. books. Librarians eventually end up weeding books from collections when they lack circulation. Ultimately, it is this inability to cross boundaries that limits the potential for international books to succeed in the United States. Readers look for what is comfortable and familiar, not understanding the importance of making the effort to cross boundaries.

Roxburgh (2006) cites this discomfort with the unfamiliar, along with an aversion to seeing "translated by [difficult-to-pronounce names]" as off-putting to readers in the United States. Yet he publishes international books because he finds them exciting. He describes how exhilarating it is to be in a heightened state of awareness when he finds himself in unfamiliar territory, and how when his vision adjusts he sees even familiar things in a new light. How can we, as educators who work with children, also help our students to become interested in engaging with the unfamiliar, find it exhilarating, and come to new understandings? This is a challenge we must undertake.

Understanding Award, which rewards projects and programs that offer connections between countries through literature. Criteria and application forms can be found at www.usbby.org/bridge.html.

· Mildred Batchelder Award, American Library Association and Association of Library Services to Children (ALA & ALSC), for the best book in translation published in the previous year.

The issue of translations is particularly important because the translator plays the most significant role in making the book accessible to the English-language audience. The translator does much more than a mechanical job in bringing a book to life in a new language. In fact, the translator creates a version of the story by interpreting the meaning and various nuances in ways that he or she believes are more authentically communicative than a literal word-by-word translation would be. Such authentic communication might mean the following (Temple, Martinez, & Yokota, 2006):

- Creating a flow in the translated language, despite differences in the sentence structures of the two languages

- Balancing the amount of foreign information to maintain readability and reader attention while retaining the unique details that make the work authentic

- Explaining foreign situations that are unknown to readers while maintaining the pace of the original text

In essence, translators are offering the lens through which we view the book, and they serve as storytellers.

Rather than using imported international books to depict people in their own countries around the world, the United States more often creates American-produced images of other countries, cultures, and people. This sometimes sacrifices authenticity, because the author or illustrator might have limited firsthand experience in the country. Sometimes the book is created by people who have only visited a country, or who have done some research on it without living there or even visiting. One factor that has improved this situation significantly in the last decade is that more people who are first-generation immigrants from other countries have begun to tell their own stories and create their own images. It is legitimate to explore questions of how authentic a depiction of a country is when it is created by people outside that country.

Here are some more examples that raise questions of authenticity: Does a fantasy book set in Italy but written in German and translated into English count as an international book? How about a book written by an author, Susie Morgenstern, who was born and raised in the United States but who now lives in France, and whose books are translated to English from the original French edition and published in the United States? What about a book from France, written and illustrated by a French author and illustrator, that is set in Japan?

Trends in International Books for Children

Despite the issues discussed above, there are signs that international children's literature is coming into its own. An increasing recognition of the importance of international books for children can be noted in the establishment of regional international literature conferences, the number of international authors being published and invited to speak in the United States, and the number of books and articles being published in this area compared to a decade ago.

In addition, international books are being promoted through such awards (see awards sidebar) as the U.S. Board on Books for Young People (USBBY) Outstanding International Books list on an annual basis. The American Library Association/Association of Library Services to Children's (ALA /ALSC) International Relations Committee has published its first list, entitled "Growing Up Around the World," and plans to update the list every few years. These books are published in the United States but offer authentic images of people outside the United States.

There are increasing opportunities for networking and learning about international books through organizations and conferences. Every other year the International Board on Books for Young People (IBBY) holds a conference that is committed to promoting books for young people from around the world. Going to IBBY means meeting people from many different countries who are authors, illustrators, publishers, translators, educators, and librarians—all interested in children's literature from a global perspective. You listen to speakers, you engage in discussion groups, and you informally chat with people from all around the world.

Within the United States, there are IBBY regional conferences every other year, sponsored by the USBBY. These conferences are intended to bring together people who are committed to international literature for children.

Book discussion groups, issues discussion groups, keynote speakers, session speakers, and exhibits of books from many countries offer participants an opportunity to learn about international literature. In addition, the Dorothy Briley Lectureship invites one international keynote speaker. The speaker in 2007 is Meshack Asare of Ghana; previous speakers have included British author Nina Bawden and Norwegian author Mette Newth.

Digitized formats of international books are helping to overcome the barriers of economics and access. The International Children's Digital Library (ICDL) acquired 1,562 books in 37 languages in the first 3 years after its inception in November 2002. Its Web site makes available the full text and complete illustrations of books that have been identified by national libraries as available for digitizing and posting for free access. The Web site has been visited more than a million times, by people in at least 158 countries. Each book is presented in its original language, with a summary in English when the language is other than English. The goal of ICDL is to expand its collection to 10,000 books by 2008.

Implications

Authors such as Margaret Mahy, Philip Pullman, and Beverly Naidoo have offered us rich reading materials written in English but published originally outside the United States. Authors whose works in translations have also richly increased our international literature include Uri Orlev, Astrid Lindgren, and Cornelia Funke. Illustrators such as Mitsumasa Anno, Lisbeth Zwerger, and Tomi Ungerer have added to the richness of illustrated books. Children can share the best books worldwide and create a world community of readers. This kinship is an important part of having some shared experiences that connect us.

International literature for children is important to all of us, and as teachers we must not only believe in it but also make a commitment to it. This means that with limited time, limited funds, and limited support we must be creative in how to make space for it in our priorities when teaching. We all know that we do what must be done—that which sustains our lives. In the physical sense, that means we eat, we drink, we take care of health issues. Likewise, we must feed our minds and souls with what matters. Because international literature has yet to enjoy widespread exposure, those of us who believe in it must promote it and "talk up" individual books, purchasing them as gifts for our libraries and classrooms as well. They should be part of classroom and school libraries, placed in proximity with other books that are meaningfully related.

First and foremost, we must all read, read, and continue to read. There's nothing that substitutes for our firsthand knowledge of international books. We have to personally experience the power of international literature before we can truly share what it offers to others. We have to read at the adult level in addition to reading the books that are appropriate for our students. Books at the adult level expand our own understanding in a way that goes beyond what the books for children alone can offer. Then, with our adult-level awareness, we can more deeply scaffold children's experiences with their books. The further away a book's experiences are from the students' own life experiences, the more important it is for teachers to scaffold the book experience so that students don't become frustrated or uninterested. Reading aloud such books gives us the opportunity to do think-alouds and ask questions in ways that monitor comprehension of experiences that may differ from students' prior knowledge.

Collaborating with other teachers and with librarians is one way to share the effort. Assess student needs and interest in people from other countries, determine what curricular goals can be met through international literature, and teach in ways that foster meaningful connections between the literature and learning. Such meaningful connections should be grounded in basic similarities across cultures while recognizing the differences. For instance, intergenerational relationships can play out very differently in each culture, but the basic idea of having meaningful relationships across age groups is essentially the same.

What are the "right" international books for our students? Certainly, they should be books that are *not* selected on the basis of their ability to "educate" our students about another culture in a didactic way. Rather, they should be books that are engaging, reflect the personal interests of readers, and stretch and teach children in a natural way. They should reflect diversity of all kinds, particularly showing diversity within a culture. Another benefit of international literature is that students are introduced to books that are visually interesting in ways unlike books originally published in the United States, because artistic sensibility around the world varies.

What is really important, however, is not just selecting the "right" books; it is how we facilitate students' understanding through international literature. What matters most is the way in which we ask questions and promote discussion, facilitating it so that stereotypes are dispelled and meaningful connections are made. How do we think about people in other countries in relation to ourselves?

It is also important to balance reading materials so that students are reading a range of genres. Often, what gets published in international literature is folklore and historical fiction. The danger in

---

Teaching Tip: Pair an International Book With a Book From the United States

Pairing a book that is unfamiliar with a book that is more familiar allows readers a chance to make comparisons and contrasts between the two books. The similarity can be in theme, illustration style, tale type, or any other factor. For example: *Chibi* by Julia Takaya (1996) and *Make Way for Ducklings* by Robert McCloskey (1941).

reading those materials prominently is that it gives international books a sense of representing the long ago and far away. Having a supply of informational texts is important, and it is engaging to see the information presented in ways that are authentic. However, the power of contemporary, realistic fiction cannot be overlooked (Yokota, 1999). Children then have an opportunity to "peek" into the lives of their contemporary peers around the world, making comparisons between their lives and with their own.

Author-illustrator Mitsumasa Anno (1996) conceptualized and created the book *All in a Day*, inviting eight illustrators around the world to depict children in various countries. On each double spread, there are images of children eating, sleeping, playing, celebrating, and going through their day. However, the time zones and the hemisphere they live in determine what they are doing at that moment. Each time you turn the page, 3 hours have passed. Throughout the 24-hour day, each of the children is engaged in daily activities that are essentially the same but that vary in detail by country. In the preface to the book, Anno notes that despite our differences, "the expressions on our faces and the sounds of our voices when we laugh or cry are very much the same, no matter where we live." It is this understanding that realistic fiction set in countries around the world allows our students to see.

How can we make a commitment to international literature a reality in our practice? First, join a network of professionals who are similarly committed; this can provide timely information, organized meetings, and a support group for promoting the cause. The IBBY is *the* organization, and many countries around the world have national sections, such as the USBBY in the United States. Subscribing to journals such as IBBY's *Bookbird* will keep readers informed of international issues, books, and other information that will deepen readers' understanding of international literature.

There are places around the world with collections of international books available for study. The oldest and largest collection is at the International Youth Library in Munich, Germany. In Japan, there is the Osaka Institute for Research in Children's Literature. In the United States, there is the Center for Teaching Through Children's Books in Chicago; it has rotating exhibits from the International Youth Library of Munich, the Hans Christian Andersen nomination dossiers and books from around the world, the USBBY Outstanding International Books, the ALA/ALSC Growing Up Around the World, and the IBBY Honor List Books. It allows visitors to examine firsthand international books that are considered exemplary.

Northwestern University hosts a virtual exhibit (www.library. northwestern.edu/exhibits/hca/index.html) that followed the actual exhibit in the summer of 2004, as well as an extensive collection of international books and Andersen dossiers that they own. Other university libraries and some public libraries around the country are also collecting international books. IBBY's Web site (www.ibby.org/index.php?id=598) hosts the virtual

---

Teaching Tip: What Country Do These Book Friends Come From?

Generate a list of book characters that children are familiar with, and find their homelands on a map or globe. Familiar characters might include Heidi, Pinocchio, Peter Rabbit, Winnie the Pooh, Babar, Pippi Longstocking, and Anne of Green Gables. Talk with students about how these characters were all born in the imaginations of authors who live in countries outside the United States, and that children in those homelands, as well as in many other countries around the world, are enjoying their stories as they are translated into many languages. Some students might wish to do research on the Internet to see how many different languages the books have been translated into.

---

exhibition called "Books for Africa, Books from Africa."

In the foreword to *Crossing Boundaries With Children's Books*, Hans Christian Andersen Award winner Katherine Paterson (2006) encourages everyone to make friends across boundaries through books. Going to war against a friend is unthinkable; she believes that when we have friends in another country, we will make every effort to understand them better. Thus, establishing such friendships through reading is taking a giant step toward peace.

Her Majesty, Empress Michiko of Japan (1998), reminds us that "no one book or number of books can be the key that will open wide the doors of peace." Rather, those books leave "buds" that later grow into "ways of thinking and of feeling." She believes that reading helped her to come to understand the depth of other people's emotions and hurts and that learning of such pain and sorrow can add depth to our own lives and deepen our ways of thinking about others. Likewise, we, as adults who influence children's reading materials and scaffold their thinking about these life issues, can bridge the way for all our students to begin to contextualize themselves in the global world; we can nurture the "buds" so that as children grow throughout their lives, they will come to understand those who are very different from themselves. In this way, we can take on the challenge of re-focusing the images we see of the world through the "looking glass."

References

Anno, M. (1986). *All in a day.* New York: Philomel.

Book Bird: A Journal of International Children's Literature, published quarterly.

Cai, M. (1998). Multiple definitions of multicultural literacy: Is the debate really just "ivory tower" bickering? *The New Advocate, 11* (4), 311–324.

Egoff, S. (1966). *The republic of childhood: A critical guide to Canadian children's literature in English.* Toronto: Oxford University Press.

Ellis, D. (2001). *The breadwinner.* Toronto, Ontario, Canada: Groundwood.

Freeman, E., & Lehman, B. (2001). *Global perspectives in children's literature.* Boston: Allyn & Bacon.

Garrett, J. (2006, September). *The many republics of childhood: Children's books as international ambassadors.* Paper presented at the grand opening of the National-Louis University Center for Teaching Through Children's Books, Chicago.

Hazard, P. (1960). *Books, children, and men* (4th ed). Boston: Hornbook. (Original work published 1932)

Lepman, J. (2002). *A bridge of children's books.* Dublin, Ireland: O'Brien Press. (Original work published 1969)

McCloskey, R. (1941). *Make way for ducklings.* New York: Viking Press.

Michiko, Empress of Japan. (1998). *Building bridges: Reminiscences of childhood readings.* Tokyo: Suemori Books.

Nye, N. S. (1998). *The space between our footsteps: Poems and paintings from the Middle East and North Africa.* New York: Simon & Schuster.

Paterson, K. (2006). Foreword. In D. Gebel (Ed.). *Crossing boundaries with children's books.* Lanham, MD: Scarecrow Press.

Roxburgh, S. (2006). Si sie müssen den Amerikanischen sector verlassen: Crossing boundaries. In D. Gebel (Ed.), *Crossing boundaries with children's books.* Lanham, MD: Scarecrow Press.

Shima, T. (2006, September). *Listening, looking and reading: Three aspects of children's literature.* Paper presented at the International Board on Books for Young People (IBBY) Congress, Macau, China.

Stan, S. (Ed.). (2002). *The world through children's books.* Lanham, MD: Scarecrow Press.

Staples, S. F. (1989). *Shabanu: Daughter of the wind.* New York: Knopf.

Takaya, J. (1996). *Chibi.* New York: Clarion Books.

Temple, C., Martinez, M., & Yokota, J. (2006). *Children's books in children's hands: An introduction to their literature* (3rd ed.). Boston: Allyn & Bacon.

Tomlinson, C. M. (Ed.). (1998). *Children's books from other countries.* Lanham, MD: Scarecrow Press.

Whalen, G. (2000). *Homeless bird.* New York: HarperCollins.

Yokota, J. (1993). Issues in selecting multicultural children's literature. *Language Arts, 70,* 156–167.

Yokota, J. (1999). Ten international books for children. *Journal of Children's Literature, 25* (1), 48–54.

Worlds Apart: Writing About the Taliban and the Repression of Woman

Deborah Ellis

I came of age at a time when Ronald Reagan and Leonid Brezhnev were engaged in a very dangerous snarling contest. Reagan was planning to bury giant MX missiles on rolling tracks under the earth, and Brezhnev sent his tanks rolling into a small Asian country called Afghanistan. Annihilation was in the air, the streets of Europe were filling up in opposition to the Cruise missile, and there was talk of a nuclear winter that would encompass all the Earth after the bombs went off.

I grew up in a small town in Ontario and was very eager to leave, so the initial attraction of political action was the escape route it gave me from my own constricted life. Borders began to fall away, and although a sense of independent power was still far off for me, the seeds of it were sown with my first political involvement.

I wrote constantly as I was growing up, bad novels and indulgent poetry. Because I was straining at the bit to leave home, my favorite books took place in New York City: *A Tree Grows in Brooklyn* by Betty Smith (1943), *Harriet the Spy* by Louise Fitzhugh (1964), and the marvelous *The Teddy Bear Habit* by James Lincoln Collier (1967). So much of childhood is about constraints—wanting to see places you can't get to, waiting around for adults to get it together, being stuck someplace and unable to leave, having the power to dream but not to act. I felt those constraints keenly as a kid, and even now I hate going anywhere unless I know I can get up and leave whenever I want.

In *Looking for X* (1999), my first published novel for young readers, 11-year-old Khyber is constrained by her circumstances of poverty, the autism of her brothers, and the judgments of others. Part of the beauty of writing is that you can create characters who are braver, smarter, and kinder than you are, and Khyber is all those things. She doesn't see the obstacles. She inhabits a parallel world, one in which she renames herself after the famous Afghani mountain pass; she uses her thrift-store atlas to pack her mother off to Siberia after an argument and to bring her back again, the imaginary journey being sufficient outlet for her anger.

She is aided in this separate world by her mom—who she knows will not hit her, no matter how much she messes up—by a grouchy waitress at the local greasy spoon, and by a troupe of female Elvis impersonators. The adults who are on Khyber's side are the ones who haven't left their own childhoods behind, but who still inhabit them even as they execute their very grown-up responsibilities.

Constraint was very much part of life in Taliban-controlled Afghanistan (and still is, in spite of all the Afghanis we've killed in the so-called War on Terror). After the Soviet withdrawal in 1989, Afghanistan dropped from the headlines until the Taliban took over Kabul in September 1996; then their crimes against women hit the newspapers. In Canada, as in many places, women came together to oppose the regime and to support our sisters living under that particular brand of tyranny.

A fan of Studs Terkel, I thought that one way I could be useful would be to go over there and gather the stories of the survivors, to put names and faces to the news clips. While there, I heard about a girl who was masquerading as a boy in order to be able to work and feed her family. I knew in that instant that I'd write *The Breadwinner* (2000). This was followed by two sequels—*Parvana's Journey* (2002b) and *Mud City* (2003).

Months spent on the Afghani-Pakistani border introduced me to new and harsher forms of constraints on women, ones blessed by the society at large and sanctified in law. The Taliban's rules are now familiar to most of us: Women could not show their faces, make noise when they walked, leave the house without a male relative escorting them, go to school, or work outside the home. Add to that no music, no freedom of the press, and a nation whose communications and infrastructure have been bombed by the superpowers back to the Stone Age, and we can get a glimpse into the grimness of their situation.

The refugee camps were cities made out of mud and whatever scraps people were able to bring with them out of Afghanistan. In the heavy winter rains of northwest Pakistan, the streets became rivers of sticky mud and overflowing sewers. Boredom, hunger, trauma old and new, children growing old with one day much like the last—these were the stories I heard. Women welcomed me into their tents and hovels and shared their stories and their tea with a hospitality that was no less genuine for its formality. All the things that any society has to deal with—such as rape, mental illness, male violence, child abuse, and unemployment—happened within the added impossibility of being far from home in a hostile environment with very few tools of liberation available.

One of the more horrifying aspects of long-term life in a refugee camp or similar situation of limbo is that people stop having a sense of the future. We all have hopes and make plans, and we have a reasonable expectation that we can make those plans and maybe even those dreams come true. For many of the people I met in the camps, all belief in their power to influence the future, and therefore change their present, was gone. Too many years had been spent in dirt-scratching survival; there had been too many false starts when relief was promised but never delivered. Their eyes had a deadness that was truly frightening. We place too much faith in the resilience of people. Sometimes people just get lost.

Even so, and in the squalor of the camps, people constantly search for ways to express their humanity—by holding secret schools for girls, sweeping the dirt in front of their hovels, and trying to re-create a sense of normality and decency.

It is this decency, and the struggle for it, that keeps coming up in my novels.

In my travels, I have been repeatedly amazed by people's capacity for kindness even in the midst of utter destruction. The children in my books survive by the kindness of themselves and of strangers, coming up against too many examples of adults' meanness, indifference, and falling down on the job of being human.

The question of courage comes up a lot in my books: How and when do we decide to be courageous, and how and when do we decide to be cowards? In *A Company of Fools* (Ellis, 2002a), medieval choirboys see many examples of both choices as they entertain people in 1348 Paris who are suffering from the Black Plague. Whether the enemy is disease, ignorance, foreign terrorists, or warmongering governments, some of us allow ourselves to be ruled by fear, and some of us act with integrity in spite of our own fear. Most of us go back and forth, in moments great and small. Children as well as adults travel that road, and that journey is often reflected in their literature.

After writing about the Plague, it was natural to move on to AIDS. I've done two books about this modern challenge, which being faced with more courage by those who are surrounded by it than by those who are removed from it. Travelling to Malawi and Zambia, I was honoured to be able to learn from kids who are affected by this. The first book, *The Heaven Shop* (2004), is a novel about 13-year-old Binti, whose world falls apart when she becomes an AIDS orphan, and she has to find a way to rebuild it. The second book, *Our Stories, Our Songs* (2005), is a nonfiction book, containing the interviews I did with the kids I met. They were such wonderful children, and the fact that they have to struggle the way they do is nothing short of a crime by all of us who allow it to continue.

I am struck by how cheap the lives of children are, especially the lives of poor children. Warlords, narcotics producers, and multinational corporations all have cold disregard for children at the core of their policies and practices. I believe that one of the roles of children's literature in such a world is to reflect the realities of the most forgotten, and to give permission to young minds to think beyond the world with which they are presented to a greater one, a golden one, which they have the power to create.

Children's Books

Collier, J. L. (1967). *The teddy bear habit*. New York: Norton.

Ellis, D. (1999). *Looking for X*. Toronto, Ontario, Canada: Groundwood Books.

Ellis, D. (2000). *Breadwinner*. Toronto, Ontario, Canada: Groundwood Books.

Ellis, D. (2002a). *A Company of Fools*. Toronto, Ontario, Canada: Fitzhenry and Whiteside.

Ellis, D. (2002b). *Parvana's Journey*. Toronto, Ontario, Canada: Groundwood Books.

Ellis, D. (2003). *Mud City*. Toronto, Ontario, Canada: Groundwood Books.

Ellis, D. (2004). *Heaven Shop*. Toronto, Ontario, Canada: Fitzhenry and Whiteside.

Ellis, D. (2005). *Our Stories, Our Songs*. Toronto, Ontario, Canada: Fitzhenry and Whiteside.

Fitzhugh, L. (1964). *Harriet the spy*. New York: Harper Trophy.

Smith, B. (1943). *A tree grows in Brooklyn*. New York: Harper.

Chapter 17

Visual Images in Children's Picture Books

Barbara Z. Kiefer

What is a picture book? For most of the 20th century, a picture book was defined as any book in which pictures carried a heavy responsibility for conveying meaning and eliciting an aesthetic response from the reader, usually within a 32-page format. Wikipedia defines a picture book as "a popular form of illustrated literature—more precisely, a book with pictures in it—popularized in the 20th century. Picture books are normally aimed at young children." Barbara Bader's (1976) definition, in her introduction to *American Picturebooks: From Noah's Ark to the Beast Within*, is widely quoted by scholars of children's literature:

> A picture book is text, illustrations, total design; an item of manufacture and a commercial product; a social, cultural, historical document; and foremost an experience for a child. As an art form it hinges on the interdependence of pictures and words, on the simultaneous display of two facing pages, and on the drama of the turning page. (p. 1)

By these definitions, wordless books, ABC and counting books, concept books, nonfiction books, and picture storybooks can be included under the umbrella term of *picture book*. Illustrated books, in which a picture is included only occasionally to decorate or elaborate on the words, are not considered to be true picture books.

Although these definitions have been used to describe 20th-century picture books, it is not a stretch to say that whenever sequences of images and ideas work together to create an aesthetic experience for a reader, it is a picture book. Such a description could apply to an Egyptian scroll from 1295 B.C.E., an illuminated manuscript from the Middle ages, an *Aesop's Fables* printed in 1484, or a "toy book" printed by Edmund Evans in the late 1800s. These works join with 20th-century forms to compose the art objects we refer to as picture books. What has changed over the centuries is not the basic definition but the form and format of the picture book, its media, its topics, and the technology that produces it—and therefore its audience. What has remained fundamental is how the artist and the author contribute meaning to our experience with the book.

The Meaning-Making Power of Art

Picture books are singular art forms in which images and ideas interact to create an experience that is more than the sum of its individual parts. Any art form can be seen as a form of communication (Kaelin, 1989; Langer, 1942), yet each one has a unique way in which meaning is symbolized. For example, although both language and visual art have a meaning-expressing potential, the two are not identical and cannot be matched at a word or sentence level. Gombrich (1982) argues that although both language and visual images have the capacity to express, arouse, and describe, the visual image is more effective in evoking emotions but unable to match "the statement function of language" (p. 138).

This lack of specificity in pictorial images, however, could be what lends them their emotional punch. Whereas an author can be more unequivocal about meanings through word choice and composition, an artist can enhance our affective response to a book through the choice of elements of art, knowing that there are emotional associations that we bring to certain configurations of line, shape, color, texture, and value. We might, for example, interpret wavy lines as serene, or angular, jagged lines as tense and exciting. In addition, the artist chooses principles of composition and layout that are highly effective in expressing meaning and evoking emotion. In a picture book, even technical choices relating to book production—such as the original medium, the design of the end papers, or the typeface—can enhance the impact of the book.

When the illustrator's choices in the elements of art, the principles of composition, and the technical elements of book production work with the author's words to extend and enhance the meaning of the work, it produces an art object that can evoke complex emotional and intellectual responses (Kiefer, 1995b). Such an art object can provide the reader with an important aesthetic experience that will be qualitatively different from viewing a television news report or seeing a photograph.

Various authors have explored the changes that are taking place in litera-ture for children. Dresang (1999) refers to new developments in books for children as part of a trend toward "radical change" and categorizes these changes as follows:

1. Changing forms and formats: nonlinear, nonsequential, multilayered, interactive graphic words and pictures

2. Changing perspectives: multiple perspectives, previously unheard voices, speaking for oneself

3. Changing boundaries: new subjects, new settings, new characteriza-tions, new communities, new endings.

Sipe and McGuire (chapter 18) explore the movement toward the postmodern in picture books. Based on the kinds of changes identified by these authors, I would predict that the picture book we hold in our hand today will be vastly different 100 years from now. However the picture book evolves, we will still judge its quality by the type of response it evokes in its reader. In our current era, the artists of picture books are experimenting with a variety of forms and media. They are exploring new topics and en-gaging new audiences. In this chapter I take a look at books that seem to ex-emplify these trends in the first decade of the 21st century.

Forms and Formats

Bader (1976) refers to the picture book as an "art form that hinges on the interdependence of pictures and words, on the simultaneous display of two facing pages, and on the drama of the turning page" (p. 1). It is part of a category of artworks (which includes drama, film, and comic strips) in which time is as much a factor as visual space. The first comic strips were developed in America in the late 19th century, and comic books followed in the 1930s. These books, containing brief text and pictures in panels, were generally printed on inexpensive paper under poor production values.

However, illustrators of children's books have made use of the sequential form in well-made picture books. Raymond Briggs, a noted British artist, first used the panel format in 1973 in *Father Christmas*, a book that won the prestigious Kate Greenaway medal for illustration. Briggs has continued to use this form in more recent books such as *Ug, Boy Genius of the Stone Age* (2001). The strip art format suits the ironic tone of many of Briggs's works. His delicate line drawings and softened color tones, arranged in the small panel drawings, lead the reader to expect comical or outlandish adventures such as those found in *Archie* or *Superman*. Instead, we enter the world of an "everyman" or "everywoman" who is caught up in the drudgery of day-to-day living, as in *Fungus the Bogeyman* (1977), or experiencing the horrors of a nuclear holocaust, as in *When the Wind Blows* (1982).

The comic strip format has continued to inspire today's authors and illustrators, who use the format for more lighthearted purposes. Kevin O'Malley's (2005) *Captain Raptor and the Moon Mystery,* illustrated by Patrick O'Brien, is a wonderful tribute to superhero comic books like *Captain Marvel* and *Superman.* Captain Raptor, however, doesn't have quite the same attributes; instead, he bears an uncanny resemblance to *Tyrannosaurus rex.* Captain Raptor and his assorted saurian crew climb aboard the USD *Megatooth,* to aid aliens on a distant planet (a certain blue-green planet, third from the sun). Their adventures pit them against sea monsters and air monsters until they achieve their aim and send the stranded aliens back to their Earthly home. In *Captain Raptor,* the panel art format and vivid paintings of Patrick O'Brien heighten our enjoyment of their grand adventure. The pacing of smaller panels set against several double-page spreads underlines and reinforces the most exciting moments of the drama.

In the late 20th century, the comic book format that had been exported from the United States to the rest of the world was embraced by the Japanese, and *manga* (graphic novels) blossomed and caught fire with adolescent audiences in Japan and then in the West. Authors and illustrators such as Neil Gaiman (1993) and Art Spiegelman (1986) began exploring the graphic novel format for adult audiences. In 1993 author Avi and artist Brian Flocca produced one of the first graphic novels for children, *City of Light, City of Dark.* Since then the appetite for graphic novels has soared even higher, and children's book publishers have devoted more and more attention to the phenomenon.

Among the many graphic novels published recently, there is something for every age. Andy Runton's *Owly* (Figure 17-1) is a totally appealing character who, so far, has appeared in three graphic novels for younger children. In books such as *Owly: Just a Little Bit Blue* (2005), the sequential panels contain almost no words. Instead we follow the adventures of Owly and his unlikely friend, Wormy, through the bold contrasts of black and white. The meaning of the stories relies heavily on Runyon's expressive drawings, thought bubbles, and punctuation marks, as well as on the pacing and shape of the panels. The few written words are unessential to the basic meaning and so invite even the youngest reader to enjoy the visual stories.

Jennifer L. Holm and Matthew Holm (2005) have collaborated on amusing graphic novels about a character named Babymouse and her classmates, Wilson the Weasel and Felicia Furrypaws. These characters inhabit a whimsical yet realistic adolescent world fraught with bullies and bad hair days. The illustrations are presented in black line panels with alternating black and white spaces. These drawings vary in size and are sometimes contained in boxed frames. Other images are freed from the tight borders. This visual design, along with rounded speech bubbles or rectangles of narrative text, sets up a lively pacing to the story. The addition of bright pink to contrast with the more fanciful imaginings of Babymouse with her day-to-day realities is a delightful touch.

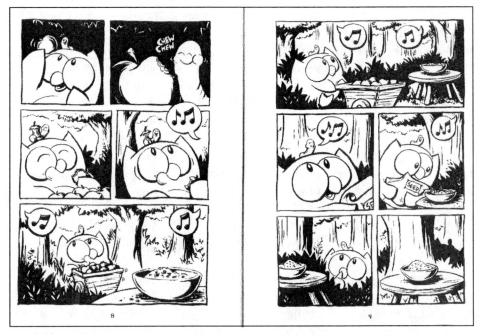

Figure 17-1. Owly

Although many of the early graphic novels were produced in black-and-white by small-press publishers, the field is rapidly changing. Many of the major publishing houses are adding imprints devoted to graphic forms and are providing budgets that cover higher production values. Titles such as *American Born Chinese* by Gene Luen Yang (2006) and *Sardine in Outer Space* by Emmanuel Guibert and Joan Sear (2006) are printed in full color by First Second Books, an imprint of Roaring Brook Press. Although they are different in form from traditional picture books, graphic novels are appropriately categorized as picture books, and they can be evaluated through criteria that consider the contributions of words and images to our response to the book.

Another book format that began to take hold in the late 20th century was the nonsequential book. Dresang (1999) explains that these books are inspired by hypertext associated with computers. Such texts allow readers to enter the book and move around in it at any point in any direction, rather than the "begin at the beginning and move to the end" approach of most books. DK (Dorling Kinderley) Publishing was one of the first publishers for children to apply this format.

The nonsequential form has been increasingly popular for both nonfiction and fiction and has extended the traditional picture-book format as well as the age of its audience. Among the most successful of the fictional nonsequential books are Candlewick Press's "ology" series, which began with

Dragonology by Duggald Steer (2003). These books add an element of play-fulness (or postmodernism) to fiction as they purport to be factual and based on primary sources. Everything you'd want to know about dragons, wizards, and pirates is divulged in visually rich compilations whose visual success relies on the design and layout of each double-page spread and the tactile objects and artifacts that are embedded or attached to each page. *Pirateology*, also by Steer (2006), includes letters, maps, drawings, diagrams, charts, and a bag of pirate gold. These elements break away from the traditional limits of texture and movement that normally applied in a flat, 32-page picture book. The books are clear reflections of our increasingly multimodal world. Like graphic novels, nonsequential picture books ask us to redefine our understanding of *picture book*.

New Technologies

Throughout the picture book's history, its form has been shaped by the media available to its artists and the technologies available for its creation. A *biblia pauperum*, a type of illuminated manuscript produced in the Middle Ages, could be created in full color, embellished in gold leaf, and handwritten in elegant script. However, such books were created one at a time for rich patrons. With the invention of movable type, more books could be created for more readers, but printing in color was seldom an option. Instead, illustrations were executed with woodcuts, and books were printed in black-and-white with a few exceptions. Woodcut illustrations were soon supplemented by copper engraving, wood engraving, etching processes, and then lithography (in 1788), all of which allowed for a wider range of detail and tone in pictures.

All these techniques were used in book illustration by the 1800s, but color printing was still an expensive luxury, not considered profitable in books for children. Then in the 1860s, engraver and printer Edmund Evans perfected a multiblock wood engraving technique that allowed high-quality, inexpensive color reproductions. This technology and the huge interest in providing children with entertaining and attractive picture books ushered in the modern picture book for children.

By the 20th century, photomechanical reproduction made color reproduction much more efficient. The process of preparing original art for reproduction was still somewhat tedious, and a book printed in full color was costly to produce. The original art had to be preseparated into four colors of yellow, red (magenta), blue (cyan), and black in order to be photographed and transferred to printing plates. This lengthy process meant that the original art was limited to media that was suited to a flat surface, such as printmaking, drawing, or painting. However, technology continued to improve, and by midcentury it allowed for finer color fidelity and the use of original media such as collage.

Another huge step in technology occurred in the 1980s with the advent of computers and laser scanners into the printing process. The scanner and computer took over the mechanics of color separation and did a better job of it. The artist, in turn, was freed up to imagine and create and to do so in almost any medium imaginable. By the end of the 20th century, talented artists began to experiment with original media. New audiences were ready to respond.

New Media

One of the outcomes of such improvements in color reproduction seemed to be a burst of fully saturated color picture books. Black-and-white or two-color books almost disappeared from the scene (with the notable exception of such artists as Chris Van Allsburg and Peter McCarty). The wonderfully subtle work of artists of the 1940s and 1950s, such as Robert McCloskey and Clement Hurd, was replaced by picture books that seemed to come directly out of a trend toward dazzle and pizzazz rather than thoughtful choice on the part of the illustrator. This trend might have been aided and abetted by the common belief that children prefer color in picture books.

However, black-and-white or limited-color picture books seem to be making a comeback in the early 21st century. Ian Falconer's (2000) *Olivia* is a prime example of the effectiveness of a limited palette. Olivia, a highly original iconoclastic pig, is rendered in black-and-white, and the addition of subtle shades and tints of red in the world surrounding her reinforce her individuality and liven the story.

Kevin Henkes took a whole new direction in style in his Caldecott Medal–winning *Kitten's First Full Moon* (2004). To tell a simple story of a little cat who confuses the moon with a bowl of milk, Henkes switched from his usual thin-line ink drawings and full color washes for books such as *Chrysanthemum* (1991) to black gouache (tempra) paintings done with a thick brush. He then created softer textures with a gray colored pencil. The original art was separated into four colors using computer scanning methods. This technique produced a final product that is subtly richer in tone and depth, with a hint of red, than traditional black-and-white illustrations. Of course, there is more to *Kitten's First Full Moon* than just Henkes's choice of original media and modern bookmaking technology, but these two elements do seem notable as we look at trends in picture books.

Other recent picture books that make effective use of black-and-white or a limited-color palette include Chris Van Allsburg's (2006) *Probuditi!* and Amy Schwartz's (2006) *Bea & Mr. Jones*. Both books ask the reader to enter a fantasy world, and the impossible seems far more likely in a world almost devoid of color. Black-and-white is highly effective in Bill Thomson's illustrations for Carol Nevius's (2004) *Karate Hour*, a book that celebrates children's physical energy and self-esteem (Figure 17-2). In this book, black-

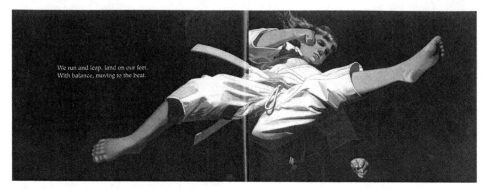

Figure 17-2. Karate Hour

and-white—with touches of color for the children's belts—shines a spotlight on the children's joyous movements. In addition, Thomson's exaggerated points of view make the characters seem to fly around, if not off, the page.

Randolph Caldecott and Walter Crane would likely have been astonished to see how the reproduction of original art in picture books had changed by the end of the 20th century. Not only had tone and gradation of line, texture, and color become much more subtle; original media had also expanded to three dimensions to include stitchery and fabric (Ringgold, 1991), found objects (Bang, 1994), natural objects (Ehlert, 1991), plasticine (Reid, 1999), and paper sculpture (Wisniewski, 1996).

A notable outcome of the computer age was computer-generated art. Many of these illustrations, such as those found in David Kirk's *Miss Spider's Wedding* (1995) or his *Nova's Ark* (1999), resemble computer-animated films such as Walt Disney's *Toy Story*. Such art is immediately recognizable as computer created. More recent developments in software have expanded artistic possibilities. Salisbury (1994) suggests that the most common approach in computer-generated art includes the use of original drawings that are scanned into the computer and then further developed using software such as Adobe Photoshop to add color and texture.

Frank Asch and Devin Asch (2004) used Corel Painter and Adobe Photoshop to create the illustrations for the macabre *Mr. Maxwell's Mouse*. In this story, a debonair cat named Mr. Howard Maxwell goes to his favorite bistro to celebrate his promotion. Changing his regular routine, he orders fresh, rather than baked, mouse as his entree. When it is served, the wily mouse plays on Mr. Maxwell's sense of ego and importance to make his getaway, in the long tradition of cat-and-mouse stories. The color scheme of the book is dark and muted, very much in keeping with the dark comedy. The pictures resemble heavy gouache paintings and contain a great deal of dark space; the words are printed in white type on a solid black background. The decorative details of the setting recall the art nouveau movement of 1920s Paris. All these features deepen the drama and the mood of mystery. The printed words are placed in columns on the left or right of each double-page spread, and the pictures take up three-quarters of each space until the story's climax. Then the type disappears; the full impact of the visual art, and the mouse's successful escape, is apparent.

Mr. Maxwell's Mouse (Asch & Asch, 2004) seems to indicate that the use of computer techniques does not necessarily make it easier to create the art for picture books, but it does allow the artist new ways to experiment, and even play, with visual meaning-making. As with other recent trends and innovations in the art of the picture book, we will want to learn more about how the illustrators who use computer art make artistic choices and how children and other audiences respond.

New Topics

Ever since Edmund Evans began publishing his toy books for children, the topics of picture books have implied an idealized childhood. The stories have been whimsical, and the nursery rhymes and poetry have been light-hearted. Even the folktales were cleansed of violence for many years. Humor in picture books was, for the most part, directed at the developmental level of the young child, with silliness rather than satire as its aim.

Although childhood has never been ideal, and children have always been aware of the unpleasantness and tragedies of life, the advent of television and the challenges of the Vietnam War exposed children to the realities of life as never before. One of the outcomes of these events was the rise of dark comedy in picture books for children. The picture book is particularly suited to the elements of irony or fatalism that are found in dark comedy, because the artist can fill the gap between what the words mean on the surface and what the author really implies. Raymond Briggs's *Father Christmas Goes on Holiday* (1973) and John Burningham's *Come Away from the Water, Shirley* (1977) are examples of dark comedies that resulted from the influences of the 1960s. After these came two British works, Anthony Browne's (1983) *Gorilla* and Babette Cole's (1986) *Princess Smarty Pants*, both of which focused on the surrealistic twisting of expectations, visual as well as verbal. David MacCaulay's (1985) *Baaa* and Lane Smith and John Scieszka's (1989) *The True Story of the Three Little Pigs* were American dark comedies. Picture books entered the postmodern era.

Emily Gravett's (2006) *Wolves* is a wonderful example of how dark comedy has evolved over the last decades, and it illustrates many of the trends we have discussed. The cover is largely devoid of color—a matte white—with the exception of the title, the author's name, and a shiny pinkish-beige rabbit in the lower left-hand corner. The title is placed squarely in the upper middle in bold, black, sans-serif type. The author's name appears underneath, almost in opposition, printed in a red serif type. Even before we open the book we have a sense of irony or opposing forces. The white front-cover flap, set against brownish textured end papers, declares that contrary to book lore, wolves don't like to eat little girls in red hoods; instead, "this book has the facts." A note in parentheses asserts that the book follows the National Carroticulum. The puns, word play, and wry visual humor continue throughout the book. The text never strays from the nonfiction expository style. If we didn't have the pictures, we would come away with a few simple (and not very interesting) facts about wolves.

In the best tradition of other authors of ironic picture books, Gravett (2006) uses the pictures to tell an entirely different story: a rabbit who has gone to the library and checked out a book on wolves (the very one we are holding in our hands). As the rabbit reads, pictures show the wolves emerging from the pages and growing larger and larger until the rabbit becomes wolf dinner. In addition to playing with words throughout (including listing herself as Emily Grrrabbit on the title page), Gravett limits her use of color and makes optimum use of pictorial space. She mixes media to include paint, pencil, and collage and mixes referents to include many intertextual messages (e.g., overdue letters from the library, a postcard with rabbit and wolf stamps, a catalog from Angora Organics). She shifts her point of view to enhance the drama, and she kills off her protagonist; at the same time, she provides an alternate "happy" ending for "sensitive readers." Whether we label *Wolves* as a postmodern picture book or as an example of radical change, *Wolves* is a pure picture-book delight, well deserving of the 2006 Kate Greenaway Medal.

The 1960s, the decade that gave rise to dark comedy, also gave birth to stories and picture books about divorce, death, war, and discrimination. British illustrator Charles Keeping (1970) was a groundbreaker in dealing with serious emotional subjects in picture books such as *Though the Window*. By the 1980s these realities began to be dealt with more broadly in picture books. Among Raymond Briggs's sequential picture books was *When the Wind Blows* (1982), a highly ironic and ultimately terrifying story about a nuclear holocaust. In 1980 Toshi Maruki published *Hiroshima No Pika*, a survivor's account of the bombing of Hiroshma, and in 1985 Christopher Gallaz and Roberto Innocenti created *Rose Blanche*, about the Holocaust. Picture books would soon deal with almost every sad aspect of the human condition: slavery (Feelings, 1995), the Japanese-American interment (Hamanaka, 1995), the Vietnam War (Myers, 1992), homelessness (Bunting, 1991), and refugees (Williams, 2006).

Many of the picture books that deal with serious topics have come from outside the United States (the reasons for this are not within the scope of this chapter). Roberto Innocenti is Italian; Raymond Briggs and Charles Keeping are both British.

Australian authors and illustrators have contributed some ground-breaking picture books that deal with difficult topics. In 1991, Margaret

Wild wrote and Julie Vivas illustrated *Let the Celebrations Begin*, a picture storybook set in a Nazi concentration camp.

Australian illustrator Shaun Tan has broken tradition in both his subject matter and his artistic style. In *The Rabbits* (Marsden, 1998), Tan's unique visual imagination is perfect for conveying an allegory of the British invasion and destruction of the indigenous peoples of Australia. Children will not need to know Australian history to apply the message of the book to other tragic cultural encounters, past and present.

In *The Red Tree* (Figure 17-3), Tan (2000) anticipates the despair that followed 9/11 and seems to signify a world that is spiraling out of control. His written text taps into our deepest human fears and anxieties when, "without sense or reason," all our troubles seem to come at once. The book begins with a small illustration placed on the right-hand side of the double-page spread. A tiny figure, head bent, is sitting up in bed. She seems lost in a pale, reddish-gray room, which has been rendered in thick paint that seems to weigh her down even more. A few brown leaves seem to float down from the ceiling. This image is encased on all four sides by a large, almost colorless border and set against a blank opposite page. This layout enhances a feeling of entrapment and is repeated on the next double-page spread as the figure leaves her room, now almost filled with dead leaves.

Figure 17-3. The Red Tree

On the next two pages the image expands to fill the space. Now the colors and the light have darkened. The figure is almost lost on the lower part of the right-hand page, shadowed under a huge fish that floats over her head. These nightmare images, the layout, and color scheme are repeated on the next two pages. Then suddenly a full double-page illustration is rendered in a bright red and yellow collage. The sharp-edged shapes and objects in the scene seem to overwhelm the tiny girl, and the reds and yellows imply danger rather than warmth.

On subsequent pages the child remains tiny, overwhelmed by the images around her and separated from any human contact. At the end she struggles back to her room. On the last double-page spread, the layout reflects that of the book's first pages, except that the huge border surrounding the image is a deep, dull gray. However, the leaves that had seemed to smother the room are gone, and one red leaf is illuminated by the light spilling in through the open door. When we turn to the final page, the image is placed on the left. The picture is still encased in a gray border, but now the opposite page is a warm golden color. In the middle of the girl's room a huge tree has suddenly grown, its leaves a brilliant and heartwarming red.

Conclusion: What Works

To get a sense of how picture books have changed over the last century, look back at Beatrix Potter's (1902) *The Tale of Peter Rabbit*. This tale is about a rabbit who gets lost in a garden, is almost captured (and eaten) by a relentless farmer, and returns home, safe but contrite. Then look at *Rosie's Walk* by Pat Hutchins (1968), where another hapless animal leaves home, is menaced by a dangerous fox, and arrives home safely, but without a clue as to her escape. Compare these two books to Gravett's (2006) *Wolves,* where a rabbit sets off to the library, is threatened by dangerous predators—and *doesn't* arrive home safely.

Then compare *The Red Tree* (Tan, 2000) to another groundbreaking story written in the mid-20th century. Maurice Sendak's *Where the Wild Things Are,* first published in 1963, broke new ground in children's picture books for its distinct illustrations and also for its treatment of its subject matter. Max, the main character, has been called the first antihero in children's literature, and his arrival heralded a growing willingness to show children the world as it is, not the world as their parents wish it were. If Sendak was one of the first to suggest that children were not perfect beings, *The Red Tree* acknowledges that the world is an imperfect place.

Examining these titles and other books discussed here, we can see how the format, the artistic media, the technology of book production, and the subject matter has changed over the years, as well as how these changes imply new audiences rather than the demise of the picture book. What makes any picture book work is the how the author and illustrator make use of their imaginations to choose verbal and visual choices that provide readers with aesthetic experience. Such imaginative choices will create an experience that is more than the sum of the pages of the book, one that engages intellect and emotion at the deepest level and that changes and intensifies over time.

References

Bader, B. (1976). *American picturebooks: From Noah's ark to the beast within*. New York: Macmillan.

Dresang, E. T. (1999). *Radical change: Books for youth in the digital age*. New York: Wilson.

Gombrich, E. H. (1982). *The image and the eye: Further studies in the psychology of pictorial representation*. Ithaca, NY: Cornell University Press.

Kaelin, E. F. (1989). *An aesthetics for art educators*. New York: Teachers College Press.

Kiefer, B. (1995a). The disturbing image in picture books: Fearful or fulfilling. In S. Lehr (Ed.), *Battling dragons: Issues and controversy in children's literature*. Portsmouth, NH: Heinemann.

Kiefer, B. (1995b). *The potential of picture books: From visual literacy to aesthetic understanding*. Columbus, OH: Merrill.

Langer, S. K. (1942). *Philosophy in a new key*. Cambridge MA: Harvard University Press.

Salisbury, M. (1994). *Illustrating children's books: Creating pictures for publication*. London: Barron's.

Sipe, L., & McGuire, C. (2007). *The Stinky Cheese Man* and other fairly postmodern picturebooks for children. In S. Lehr (Ed.), *Shattering the looking glass: Challenge, risk, and controversy*. Norwood, MA: Christopher-Gordon.

Children's Books

Asch, F., & Asch, D. (2004). *Mr. Maxwell's mouse*. Toronto, Ontario, Canada: Kids Can Press.

Avi. (1993). *City of light, city of dark* (B. Flocca, Illus.). New York: Orchard.

Bang, M. (1994). *One fall day*. New York: Greenwillow.

Briggs, R. (1973). *Father Christmas goes on holiday*. London: Hamish Hamilton.

Briggs, R. (1977). *Fungus the bogeyman*. London: Hamish Hamilton.

Briggs, R.. (1982). *When the wind blows*. London: Hamish Hamilton.

Briggs, R. (2001). *Ug, boy genius of the Stone Age, and his search for soft trousers*. London: Cape.

Browne, A. (1983). *Gorilla*. London: McRea.

Bunting, E. (1991). *Fly away home* (R. Himler, Illus.). New York: Clarion Books.

Burningham, J. (1977). *Come away from the water, Shirley*. New York: HarperCollins.

Cole, B. (1986). *Princess Smarty Pants*. London: Hamish Hamilton.

Ehlert, L. (1991). *Red leaf, yellow leaf*. San Diego: Harcourt.

Falconer, I. (2000). *Olivia*. New York: Atheneum.

Feelings, T. (1995). *The Middle Passage: White ships, Black cargo*. New York: Dial.

Gaiman N. (1993). *The sandman*. New York: Vertigo.

Gallaz, C., & Innocenti, R. (1985). *Rose Blanche* (R. Innocenti, Illus.). Mankato, MN: Creative Education.

Gravett, E. (2006). *Wolves*. New York: Simon & Schuster.

Guibert, E., & Sear, J. (2006). *Sardine in outer space*. New York: First Second Books.

Hamanaka, S. (1995). *The journey*. New York: Scholastic.

Henkes. K. (1991). *Chrysanthemum*. New York: Greenwillow.

Henkes. K. (2004). *Kitten's first full moon*. New York: Greenwillow.

Holm, J. L., & Holm, M. (2005). *Babymouse: Our hero*. New York: Random House.

Hutchins, P. (1968). *Rosie's walk*. London: Bodley Head.

Keeping, C. (1970). *Through the window*. London: Oxford University Press.

Kirk, D. (1995). *Miss Spider's wedding*. New York: Scholastic.

Kirk, D. (1999). *Nova's ark*. New York: Scholastic.

MacCaulay, D. (1985). *Baaa*. Boston: Houghton Mifflin.

Marsden, G. (1998). *The rabbits* (S. Tan, Illus.). Melbourne, Australia: Lothian.

Maruki, T. (1980). *Hiroshima no pika*. New York: Lothrop.

Myers, W. D. (1992). *Patrol* (A. Grifalconi, Illus.). New York: HarperCollins.

Nevius, C. (2004). *Karate hour* (B. Thomson, Illus.). New York: Marshall Cavendish.

O'Malley, K. (2005). *Captain Raptor and the moon mystery* (P. O'Brien, Illus.). New York: Walker.

Potter, B. (1902). *The tale of Peter Rabbit*. London: Warne.

Reid, B. (1999). *The party*. New York: Scholastic.

Ringgold, F. (1991). *Tar beach*. New York: Crown.

Runton, A. (2005). *Owly: Just a little blue*. Marietta, GA: Top Shelf.

Schwartz, A. (2006). *Bea & Mr. Jones*. San Diego: Harcourt.

Sendak, M. (1963). *Where the wild things are*. New York: HarperCollins.

Smith, L., & Scieszka, J. (1989). *The true story of the three little pigs*. New York: Viking Press.

Spiegelman, A. (1986). Maus: *A survivor's tale*. New York: Pantheon.

Steer, D. (2003). *Dragonology*. Cambridge, MA: Candlewick Press.

Steer, D. (2006). *Pirateology*. Cambridge, MA: Candlewick Press.

Tan, S. (2000). *The red tree*. Melbourne, Australia: Lothian.

Van Allsburg, C. (2006). *Probuditi!* Boston: Houghton Mifflin.

Vander Zee, R. (2003). *Erika's story* (R. Innocenti, Illus.). Mankato, MN: Creative Education.

Wild, M. (1991). *Let the celebrations begin!* (J. Vivas, Illus.). New York: Orchard.

Williams, M. (2006). *Brothers in hope: The story of the lost boys of Sudan* (G. Christie, Illus.). New York: Lee & Low.

Wisniewski, D. (1996). *The golem.* New York: Clarion Books.

Yang, G. L. (2006). *American born Chinese.* New York: First Second Books.

The Stinky Cheese Man and Other Fairly Postmodern Picture Books for Children

Lawrence R. Sipe and Caroline E. McGuire

In the world of picture books, there has been a pronounced trend in the last 15 years toward a particular type of book that many would label *post-modern*. Although this term is used by theorists, researchers, and practitioners in widely different ways and is notoriously difficult to define, there has been a growing body of literature that seems fascinated with picture books, such as *The Stinky Cheese Man and Other Fairly Stupid Tales* (Scieszka, 1992), *Black and White* (Macaulay, 1990), and David Wiesner's (2001) version of *The Three Pigs*. These books do seem to have stretched our conventional notion of what constitutes a picture book, as well as what it means to be an engaged reader of these texts. As more of these types of books are published, it seems important to examine them closely and to attempt to reflect on their unique contributions to both the field of children's literature and the development of new literacies (Anstey, 2002) for child, adolescent, and adult readers.

In this chapter, we describe a number of attributes that seem to distinguish these types of books and that have the potential for eliciting intriguing and novel responses on the part of children. In our review of theory about postmodern picture books, we have identified six characteristics: blurring, subversion, intertextuality, multiplicity of meanings, playfulness, and self-referentiality. We view these characteristics not as totally discrete, but rather as interconnected nodes, with different books displaying different constellations of these characteristics. Thus, although we do not think it is useful to conceive of these types of books as an entirely separate category of the range of contemporary picture books, we do believe that as more of these characteristics are displayed in any one book, that book is more likely to be identified as postmodern.

As we discuss these six characteristics, we describe them theoretically and then give examples from picture books. We also include examples from young children's talk about these books that illustrate the children's playful and insightful grasp of the quirky and transgressive nature of the books. We end the chapter with a discussion of the affordances—the intrinsic potentials—of postmodern picture books for extending, refining, and developing children's literary understanding in new ways.

Blurring

One general characteristic of postmodern picture books is that they seem to blur a number of commonly assumed distinctions: the bifurcation of high and low culture, the categories of traditional literary genres, and the boundary between author and reader. Contemporary culture flattens the traditional hierarchy of fine art and popular culture (e.g., through the use of masterpieces of past centuries in media advertisements for products for our consumer society). In the same manner, many postmodern picture books present unlikely juxtapositions, such as the appearance of the classic paintings of Da Vinci's *Mona Lisa* and Frans Hals's *The Laughing Cavalier* on a bleak urban sidewalk on the fifth opening (the fifth set of facing pages since the text of the story began) of Anthony Browne's (1998) *Voices in the Park*. In contrast to the original paintings, both figures have tears running down their faces. Two openings later, the Cavalier and Mona Lisa have emerged from their paintings to dance joyfully on the sidewalk, now in the company of Santa Claus and King Kong. One third grader offered this explanation of the change across the two illustrations:

I know why they were sad in the picture right there: because they got split up. And then they finally met at a dance or something like that, and ran into each other, and they just started dancing and trying to get their old moves back.

The children had previously recognized the paintings as works of art that they had seen elsewhere, but now these classic figures were recast in a story of thwarted love and long-forgotten dance moves—a blurring Browne might not have anticipated!

Another type of blurring present in postmodern picturebooks is the juxtaposition of literary genres and their corresponding linguistic registers. For example, in "The Princess and the Bowling Ball," the second story in *The*

Stinky Cheese Man (Scieszka, 1992), the title alone juxtaposes the word *princess*, commonly found in fairy tales, with *bowling ball*, an object seldom associated with the genre of traditional stories. The story begins with traditional fairy tale language: "Once upon a time there was a prince." As the story continues, however, our expectation of fairy tale language is punctured by references to the prince's "dad and mom" and their invitation to princesses "to sleep over." Of course, none of the princesses feels the tiny pea underneath 100 mattresses, so in desperation, the prince replaces the pea with a bowling ball and deceives his parents into believing that the princess has sufficient sensitivity to be genuine royalty. Thus, the elevated style of most fairy tales and the style of everyday colloquial speech blur into each other, and one of the pleasures of reading this story is for children to notice the breaks with traditional terminology. As one first grader remarked, "You're not supposed to have a bowling ball in a fairy tale, and you're not supposed to call the King and Queen the dad and mom!"

A third boundary that postmodern picture books tend to blur is the traditional separation between the author, who communicates the message, and the reader, who receives it. Postmodern texts invite greater participation or performance on the part of readers. The literary critic Roland Barthes (1974) has forwarded a useful distinction between "readerly" texts, which involve a relatively passive consumption by readers, and "writerly" texts, in which readers play a more active, equal role and are seen as co-authors and producers of text rather than mere consumers. For example, *Do Not Open This Book!* (Muntean, 2006) addresses the reader directly, beginning with the title on the front cover, and continues, "Excuse me, but who do you think you are, opening this book when the cover clearly says do not open this book!?... The reason you are not supposed to open this book is because it is not yet written." This implies that the reader will have an important role to play as the book proceeds, in conjunction with the hard-working pig (the "author") who continues to address the reader and admonish him or her not to turn the page. The pig even goes so far as to promise the reader, "I will make this story about you... I will leave a blank like this: _____ so whenever you see a _____ like this, say your name." At the end of the book, the pig acknowledges the reader's writerly involvement: "Thank you for helping me write this book. I couldn't have done it without *you*."

Additional Theoretical and Empirical Work on Postmodern Picturebooks

Arizpe, E., & Styles, M. (2003). *Children reading pictures: Interpreting visual texts.* New York: RoutledgeFalmer.

Goldstone, B. (1998). Ordering the chaos: Teaching metafictive characteristics of children's books. *Journal of Children's Literature, 24,* 48-55.

Goldstone, B. (2004). The postmodern picturebook: A new subgenre. *Language Arts, 81,* 196-204.

Kümmerling-Meibauer, B. (1999). Metalinguistic awareness and the child's developing concept of irony: The relationship between pictures and text in ironic picturebooks. *The Lion and the Unicorn, 23,* 157-183.

Lewis, D. (1990). The constructedness of picturebooks: Picturebooks and the metafictive. *Signal, 62,* 131-46.

Lewis, D. (1996). Going along with Mr. Grumpy: Polysystemy and play in the modern picturebook. *Signal, 80,* 105-119.

Lewis, D. (2001). *Reading contemporary picturebooks: Picturing text.* London: RoutledgeFalmer.

Nikolajeva, M., & Scott, C. (2001). *How picturebooks work.* New York: Garland.

Nikola-Lisa, W. (1994). Play, panache, pastiche: Postmodern impulses in contemporary picture books. *Children's Literature Association Quarterly, 19*(1), 35-40.

Paley, N. (1992). Postmodernist impulses and the contemporary picture book: Are there stories to these meanings? *Journal of Youth Services in Libraries, 5,* 151-162.

Pantaleo, S. (2004). The long, long way: Young children explore the fibula and syuzhet of *Shortcut. Children's Literature in Education, 35*(1), 1-20.

Serafini, F. (2005). Voices in the park, voices in the classroom: Readers responding to postmodern picture books. *Reading Research and Instruction, 44(3)*, 47-65.

Stevenson, D. (1991). "If you read the last sentence, it won't tell you anything": Postmodernism, self-referentiality, and *The Stinky Cheese Man. Children's Literature Association Quarterly, 19(1)*, 32-34.

Trites, R. (1994). Manifold narratives: Metafiction and ideology in picture books. *Children's Literature in Education, 25*, 225-242.

Subversion

The sense that postmodern picture books differ from the norm stems in part from the way in which these books gesture toward convention just as they proceed to disrupt it. By mocking traditions and destabilizing or questioning certainties, these texts acknowledge their understanding of the norm while announcing their intention to march to the beat of a different drummer. For instance, the tale of "The Really Ugly Duckling" in *The Stinky Cheese Man* (Scieszka, 1992) harks back to the traditional story of the ugly duckling who grows into a beautiful swan. However, Scieszka's parody explicitly undermines the normative discourse of beauty's triumph:

> He knew that one day he would probably grow up to be a swan and be bigger and look better than anything in the pond. Well, as it turned out, he was just a really ugly duckling. And he grew up to be just a really ugly duck. The End.

Both the reader's and the duckling's expectations are confounded, for "as it turned out" in this case, tradition had been shunted aside. In fact, in the illustrations, the six "normal" duck siblings, rendered in traditional-looking woodcuts, are pushed to the margins in favor of a focus on the zany, ugly duckling. Convention is decentered (literally!) and replaced with a more sarcastic, cynical view.

Beyond its individual stories, *The Stinky Cheese Man* (Scieszka, 1992), taken as a whole, operates as a parody of picture books by playing with their conventions. At one point, Jack the narrator alters the book's construction to aid his escape from the Giant, making the reader complicit in his plan: "Shhhh. Be very quiet. I moved the endpaper up here so the Giant would think the book is over. The big lug is finally asleep. Now I can sneak out of here. Just turn the page very quietly and that will be The. . . ." Before Jack's explanation was even read, a first grader remarked, "That's funny—the endpaper isn't supposed to be there." Indeed, the book is funny because it does what it's not supposed to do: it disobeys the accepted norms of bookmaking and the telling of traditional tales.

The boundary between the story and the outside world might also be subverted, making "diegetic border crossing" (Mackey, 2003), or movement in and out of the narrated world, a pronounced part of the act of reading. In Wiesner's (2001) *The Three Pigs*, for example, the narrated world actually consists of several different stories, and the three pigs move among the story worlds, changing appearance as they break in and out of different frames. On the second opening of the book, the first story border is crossed: the text reads, "So the wolf huffed and he puffed, and he blew the house in . . .," while the illustration shows an explosion of straw, and the pig seems to be falling off the page by breaking the frame of the illustration. His speech balloon reads, "Hey! He blew me right out of the story!" First-grade children's comments suggest their wonderment at this odd event:

Steven: It looks like he's falling out of the story.

Anthony: I don't think he's in the story.

The children proceed to figure out the book's internal logic of boundary crossing and to chart the landscape of the narrated world: "It's like a bunch of picture frames all over the place." They are able to navigate several sets of boundaries between the story and the world and to make meaning from violations of those boundaries. Postmodern picturebooks "break frame" both literally and figuratively; on the fourteenth opening of *The Book That Jack Wrote* (Scieszka, 1994), we see the picture frame bordering the illustration being shattered by a falling book—none other than *The Book That Jack Wrote*. The book we are reading appears, paradoxically, as a character within its own pages, crossing the border between the narrated world and the reader's world, and thus breaking the hermetic seal that conventionally surrounds a story.

Intertextuality

According to Roland Barthes (1977), every text is made up of many others; no text is new or *sui generis*. Rather, each text is constructed from bits and pieces of other previous texts. In the case of postmodern picturebooks, this reference to other texts is explicit and manifold. Unlike images are juxtaposed and related to one another, often constituting a pastiche, a frequently amusing blend of texts from many recognizable sources. For example, in *The Stinky Cheese Man* (Scieszka, 1992), the "Giant's Story" is a pastiche of phrases from a number of different fairy tales, arranged higgledy-piggledy:

"The End / of the evil stepmother / said 'I'll huff and snuff and / give you three wishes.'/ The beast changed into / seven dwarves / happily ever after / for a spell had been cast by a Wicked Witch / Once upon a time." Each phrase is set in a different typeface, indicating the multiplicity of sources of this "Unbelievably Stupid Tale." First-grade children's responses were predictably incredulous: "That *is* a stupid story—it's lots of stories, and it doesn't make any sense."

Another way that intertextuality occurs in postmodern picturebooks is through a confluence of fairytale characters within a new story. In *Beware of the Storybook Wolves* (Child, 2001), for example, Herb, the main character, meets the wolf from "Little Red Riding Hood," the evil fairy from "Sleeping Beauty," and the fairy godmother from "Cinderella" as they emerge from his cherished storybooks. Other books in which a "Who's Who" of fairy tale protagonists makes an appearance are Janet and Allan Ahlberg's (1986) *The Jolly Postman*; Lauren Child's (2003) *Who's Afraid of the Big Bad Book?*; Anthony Browne's (2004) *Into the Forest*; and Colin and Jacqui Hawkins's (2004) *Fairytale News*.

Thus, as Gerard Genette (1997) claims, postmodern texts are heavily "layered," with the layers of previous texts made visible, as in a palimpsest—a medieval vellum manuscript that contains multiple texts, each erased in order to write a new text on top of the old one, but in which the old texts are still partly visible. Many postmodern picture books contain this type of visible multiplicity of texts in the form of multiple stories. For example, in *Black and White* (Macaulay, 1990), each page is divided into four quadrants, and each quadrant is illustrated in a distinctly different style and tells a different story; the four stories might be related to each other, or they might not, as the title page states: "Warning. This book appears to contain a number of stories that do not necessarily occur at the same time. Then again, it may contain only one story. In any event, careful inspection of both words and pictures is recommended."

Moreover, these multiple texts might contradict or contest each other, competing for our attention. Which of the four quadrants in *Black and White* (Macaulay, 1990) should we read first? Should we assume that the traditional left-to-right, top-to-bottom order is the way in which we should consider them, or should we choose at random? Should we read the upper left-hand quadrant from start to finish through the whole book, and then read the upper right-hand quadrant in the same fashion? Or should we read the four quadrants on each page before proceeding to the next page? It's up to us, as the children and teachers in McClay's (2000) study decided, because we as readers are in control.

Another example of a different employment of a multiplicity of texts is found in Wiesner's (2001) *The Three Pigs*, where, as mentioned above, the pigs literally get blown out of their own story. They make a paper airplane from a page of their own story and then sail into several other stories, meeting various characters on the way (a cat and a dragon from other stories), bringing these characters back to their own story, where the dragon confronts the terrified wolf and drives him away. Children understood this movement from one text to another and were particularly fascinated by one double-page spread (in which one illustration runs across two facing pages), in which the pigs seem to be in a "space between" stories, which are arrayed in rows of storyboards. Also, the fish from one story (whose setting is clearly the ocean) are drifting into the other stories. Here are the children's reactions:

> *Mandy*: This is weird because this story's [*points to the picture*] going into this story. And this is another one. The fish are like floating in nowhere.
>
> *Dominique*: It's like a bunch of pictures.
>
> *Mandy*: This story is going into every story. The fish are going crazy and going everywhere!

Thus, the children were cognizant of the presence of multiple stories, as well as the potential for these stories to blend and remix with each other.

Multiplicity of Meanings

Another common characteristic of postmodern picture books is that plots are not linear or univocal. In other words, there can be multiple stories within a story with multiple narrators, as well as multiple pathways through the text-world. This results in strong ambiguity, a high degree of what Wolfgang Iser (1978) calls *indeterminacy*. According to Iser, indeterminacy is an integral part of all literary texts; but in postmodern texts it runs rampant. Most traditional narratives have an easily traceable plot, with a beginning, a problem or difficulty, and an ending that resolves the problem or difficulty. Postmodern narratives often favor nonresolution and open-ended "endings" instead.

   In *Voices in the Park* (Browne, 1998), we hear the same story, told from four entirely different (and frequently contradictory) perspectives: a well-to-do, strict mother; her timid, compliant son; an unemployed lower-class father; and his friendly, outgoing daughter. The story involves a walk in the park and the meeting of the two children; but what a difference there is among the four "voices"! The narration of each voice is printed in a different typeface, and these fonts correspond in subtle ways to the personalities of the characters. For example, the timid boy's narration is in a thin, delicate typeface, whereas the outgoing girl's narration appears in an informal, casual, bold font. Thus, even the typefaces utilized in this book add to readers' perceptions of multiple voices, a type of polyphonic narration (Bakhtin, 1981).

The Stinky Cheese Man (Scieszka, 1992) provides a good example of a different type of polyphonic narration. The book is narrated by Jack, who might be the Jack in the rhyme "Jack and Jill," because he signs himself "Jack Up the Hill." However, he might also be the Jack in "Jack and the Beanstalk," because his own story, "Jack's Bean Problem," clearly refers to elements in that traditional tale. Thus, there is an ambiguity and indeterminacy about Jack's identity. Moreover, the book begins with an exchange between Jack, who says, "I'm the narrator," and the Little Red Hen, who intrudes, providing her own querulous narration and reappearing several times in the course of the book.

Adding to the complexity and multiplicity of the narration, the main part of the book consists of nine parodies of other traditional tales—such as "The Really Ugly Duckling" (already described) and "Little Red Running Shorts"—which are told by a variety of narrators, some of whom interact with Jack. In "Little Red Running Shorts," for example, Jack introduces the story by commenting, "This next story is even better than the last three.... So anyway, this girl is running to her granny's house when she meets a wolf." Jack proceeds to tell the whole story, irritating Red Running Shorts and the wolf so much that they say, "You just told the whole story...we're not going to tell it again," leaving Jack complaining that he now will have a blank page because "Your story is supposed to be three pages long."

Thus, there is a bewildering assortment of narrators, as well as a resulting ambiguity and indeterminacy about who is really telling these stories. Also puzzling is the question of how each story relates to the others: some seem to stand alone, whereas others are porous to each other, with characters (and narrators) intruding into other characters' stories.

Postmodern picture books might not resolve or end in traditional ways. Readers are left not with a sense of completion but rather with an "ending" that invites multiple interpretations and might leave us hanging. For example, in "Jack's Story" in *The Stinky Cheese Man* (Scieszka, 1992), Jack is being squeezed by the Giant, who is about to eat him. So, Scheherazade-like, he tells a story that has literally no ending but that circles perpetually around to the beginning. The typeface of the story gradually becomes smaller and smaller, until it disappears off the bottom of the page. First graders who listened to this story understood this lack of resolution: "It's going to go on forever—it won't ever end! Maybe we'll never know what happens to Jack."

Playfulness

Postmodern picturebooks are texts that do not take themselves seriously. There is a certain playfulness about these texts that invites readers to explore them as linguistic and visual playgrounds. Reading them is, therefore, a type of intellectual game, meant to evoke pleasure in the sense that Roland Barthes (1976) describes as *jouissance*. Barthes distinguishes between two types of texts: texts of *plaisir* (translated as "pleasure") and texts of *jouissance* (rendered as "bliss"). We feel pleasure when we can easily master a text; Barthes writes that pleasure is linked to a "comfortable practice of reading" (p. 14). This type of text reinforces our cultural and social expectations. Texts of bliss, on the other hand, unsettle our comfortable assumptions and jar us, opening up new vistas of experience.

Postmodern picture books are frequently texts of *jouissance* for readers, primarily because of their playful, mischievous nature. *The Stinky Cheese Man* (Scieszka, 1992) is a book in which even the Table of Contents acts as a character: it falls on everyone and knocks one story out of the book entirely. Even the fine-print copyright information is playful; instead of the usual serious information about the artistic media used in the illustrations, there is this humorous note, "The illustrations are rendered in oil and vinegar," insouciantly inserted within the obligatory (and boring) publishing information. Moreover, these texts seem to evoke playful and mischievous responses from young children. In one of the Little Red Hen's tirades in *The Stinky Cheese Man*, she demands, "Where is that lazy narrator? Where is that lazy illustrator? Where is that lazy author?" Upon hearing this, a first grader sardonically replied, "The illustrator and the author are probably making another stupid book!" This child jokingly pretends that the Little Red Hen is directly addressing her, and she replies in kind.

Children seem inspired to make puns on these texts—a linguistic playfulness that purposefully misreads someone's meaning, just as the books themselves engage in intentional transgressions of conventional meaning. The dust jacket of *Black and White* (Macaulay, 1990), for example, contains a gold medallion, indicating that the book has won the Caldecott Medal. If we remove the dust jacket on the trade edition of the book, we see a gray board cover with a stamped image of a cow. A first grader's response to this was to say, "Look, Miss Bigler—it won the *Cow*-decott Medal!" Another example of playful punning occurred during the reading of the front flap of *The Stinky Cheese Man* (Scieszka, 1992):

> 100 *Teacher* (*reading flap*): Only $16.99! 56 action-packed pages. 75% more than those old 32-page "Brand-X" books. 10 complete stories! 25 lavish paintings! New! Improved! Funny! Good! Buy! Now!

101 *Terry*:	Why?
102 *Julie*:	It got a medal, too!
103 *Gordon*:	"Why," just say, "why," just say "why," just say it.
104 *Teacher*:	What? OK, "why"?
105 *Gordon*:	How come? Because. Where? When? Who? [*Dissolves into giggles*]
106 *Teacher* (*laughing*):	OK. New! Improved! Funny! Good! Buy! Now!
107 *Terry*:	I don't wanna go "bye" now. I don't wanna go bye-bye now!
108 *Gordon*:	Me neither!
109 *All*:	Bye-bye! Bye-bye!
110 *Terry*:	I don't want to go to the bathroom and be the stinky cheese man!

At 101, Terry interrogated the text: Why should we buy the book, just because it tells us to do so? Julie tried to keep the group on track with her comment at 102, but the other children were having none of it. At 103 and 105, Gordon set up a playful imitative display of the language of the book, which the teacher fed into by rereading part of the text (106). At 107 and 110, Terry made moves that deconstructivist critics would be proud of, punning and using the text as a springboard for his own transgressive text-to-life connection. This whole sequence exemplifies what we call—adapting Mikhail Bakhtin's (1968) terminology—a "carnivalesque romp." The children took over the story, playing with its language and rejecting its authority, just as the text of the book rejects literary and authorial conventions. They became caught up in the excesses of their own hilarious responses.

Self-Referentiality

Most books are written in a manner that assumes the reader's desire to "enter" the world of the story in some way, and many theories of literary understanding assume that this is the case. Rosenblatt (1978), for example, writes of the "aesthetic stance" as one in which the reader has a "lived-through" experience of the text. Michael Benton (1992) writes of the "secondary world" that the reader enters as the primary world of immediate experience is forgotten or drops away, leaving the reader free to experience, vicariously, what the characters in the story are experiencing. Thus, most books (as well as many theories of reader response) assume that the readers will immerse themselves in stories, becoming "lost in [the] book" (Nell, 1988).

In postmodern texts, all these assumptions are turned upside-down. Rather, the postmodern text constantly interrupts or punctures the illusion of the secondary world of the story by drawing attention to itself *as* a story, as if to say, "What you're reading here is an artifice—don't attempt to immerse yourself in it or 'enter' it—it's only a literary construction." Texts that are unconventional in this way are often referred to as "metafiction" (Waugh, 1984), or fiction that is *about* writing fiction itself. Postmodern picture books exhibit self-referentiality as well. In a way, this is the most sophisticated of their qualities; however, even young children can understand that their expectations of being *in* the story are shattered.

Postmodern picture books also frequently puncture the story world by emphasizing the sheer physicality of the book. We have already mentioned Jack's strategic moving of the back endpaper in *The Stinky Cheese Man* (Scieszka, 1992); in addition, the title page in this book draws attention to itself by being called "Title Page"! Lauren Child's (2003) *Who's Afraid of the Big Bad Book?* refers to Herb's habit of reading his books while eating, and several of the illustrations show evidence of this carelessness, as well as his "scribbling phase," and his tendency to cut out parts of the illustrations. Herb's penchant for snipping holes serves him well, for he is able to escape a dangerous situation by cutting a hole in the floor. The page itself, at this point, contains an actual ragged hole. Thus, the physical page becomes an integral part of the story, and the story becomes tangible for the reader.

Similarly, when Herb attempts to open "an enormous door" to a palace, he has difficulty "because the illustrator had drawn the handle much too high up." This draws attention to the artifice of the illustration, because we do not usually consider an illustration as the product of human effort if we are immersed in a story-world. The reader is enabled to assist Herb by opening a double French fold that mimics the palace doors, thus reinforcing the physical correlates of the narrated events. In all these examples, readers are not allowed to forget the physical book they hold in their hands, and they are thus prevented from immersing themselves in the secondary world of the story.

Conclusion

With these six characteristics, we have attempted to describe some ways in which postmodern picture books differ from conventional picture books. Eliza Dresang (1999) argues that this special subset of picture books results from a more far-reaching change in children's literature since about 1990; she uses the term "Radical Change" to describe the following trends: changing forms and formats; changing perspectives; and changing boundaries. In any case, because the nature of texts influences child response, we would expect that these books would have unique potentials for engendering new ways of responding. Research has borne this out and has proven that postmodern picturebooks, complex as they may be, are well within the intellectual grasp of young children (McClay, 2000; Pantaleo, 2002, 2004).

One caveat for using these books is that children should probably already be conversant with traditional picture book aesthetics (Sipe, 1998), as well as with traditional narrative structure, in order to perceive the ways in which postmodern picture books play with, subvert, and reverse those traditions. To put it in simplest terms: If children don't know the usual placement and uses of endpapers, they are not going to fully grasp the humor in Jack's desperate attempt to move the endpapers in *The Stinky Cheese Man* (Scieszka, 1992). Thus, we recommend that children have some broad acquaintance with conventional picture books before tackling postmodern ones. One way to do this is to read a series of picture book variants of the same traditional story, ending with a postmodern version. In one first-grade classroom (Sipe & Brightman, 2005), children heard a sequence of four variants of "The Three Pigs." The first three versions were traditional narratives; the fourth was the postmodern Wiesner (2001) version, discussed above. With the background of the first three variants, the children were prepared for the intricacies and surprises of the Wiesner tale. One important outcome of this exposure to multiple variants is that children automatically compare and contrast the texts, thereby increasing their higher level thinking skills.

In general, we believe that children can more easily see themselves as controlling and being active engagers in postmodern picture books, rather than being passive recipients; we have already argued that these texts tend to be "writerly" rather than "readerly," inviting (even demanding) a high degree of involvement from children. Thus, exposure to these books prepares children in a unique way for the active role they must learn to play in reading *all* texts on their own. The high degree of indeterminacy in postmodern texts increases children's opportunities (and abilities) to make inferences that fill in multiple gaps.

Moreover, we believe that self-referential, metafictive elements are precisely the right stimulus for encouraging children to become more aware of their own thinking: engagement with metafiction encourages metacognition. In other words, it is the startling and unexpected qualities of postmodern picture books—and their drawing attention to the behind-the-scenes work of writing, designing, and producing a book—that jar children out of the "comfortable practice of reading" (Barthes, 1976, p. 14) and make them aware of their own behind-the-scenes reasoning processes as they engage in the hard intellectual work of making meaning from these texts.

Another potential of postmodern picture books for children's literary understanding and literacy development is that children come to see that texts have no absolute, authoritative, unshakable meaning. Respect for a multiplicity of other readers' interpretations follows. The development of this stance is also important if children are to develop into critical readers.

We have found that children truly enjoy postmodern picture books; they present challenging and intriguing literary puzzles to solve. Also, because of the texts' subversive and transgressive nature, children are likely to relish the knowledge that the literary world (and perhaps the real world) is not quite as seamlessly ordered and predictable as it might appear. When children encounter postmodern parodies of traditional texts, they have the pleasure of understanding the elements that make the text recognizable, as well as the pleasure of the novel, unexpected elements that make postmodern texts unique.

Because of this high degree of enjoyment and engagement, teachers should be prepared for (and encourage) the types of carnivalesque responses we have described above, and they should feel free to treat postmodern texts as playgrounds, alongside the children. Carnivalesque responses may be understood not as off-task but as expressively aesthetic acts on a high level. They represent a type of literary understanding that sees the text as "a vessel of associations helplessly open to the mastery of [our] response" (Grudin, 1992, p. 105).

References

Anstey, M. (2002). "It's not all black and white": Postmodern picture books and new literacies. *Journal of Adolescent and Adult Literacy, 45*(6), 444–457.

Bakhtin, M. (1968). *Rabelais and his world* (H. Iswolsky, Trans.). Cambridge, MA: MIT Press.

Barthes, R. (1974). *S/Z: An essay* (R. Miller, Trans.). New York: Hill and Wang.

Barthes, R. (1976). *The pleasure of the text* (R. Miller, Trans.). New York: Hill and Wang.

Barthes, R. (1977). The death of the author. In S. Heath (Trans.), *Image/Music/Text* (pp. 142–148). New York: Hill and Wang.

Benton, M. (1992). *Secondary worlds: Literature teaching and the visual arts.* Buckingham, UK: Open University Press.

Dresang, E. (1999). *Radical Change: Books for youth in a digital age.* New York: Wilson.

Genette, G. (1997). *Palimpsests: Literature in the second degree* (C. Newman & C. Doubinsky, Trans.). Omaha, NE: University of Nebraska Press.

Grudin, R. (1992). *Book: A novel.* New York: Penguin Books.

Iser, W. (1978). The act of reading: A theory of aesthetic response. Baltimore: Johns Hopkins University Press.

Mackey, M. (2003). At play on the borders of the diegetic: Story boundaries and narrative interpretation. *Journal of Literacy Research, 35*(1), 591–632.

McClay, J. (2000). "Wait a second...": Negotiating complex narratives in Black and White. *Children's Literature in Education, 31*(2), 91–106.

Nell, V. (1988). *Lost in a book: The psychology of reading for pleasure.* New Haven, CT: Yale University Press.

Pantaleo, S. (2002). Grade 1 students meet David Wiesner's three pigs. *Journal of Children's Literature, 28*(2), 72–84.

Pantaleo, S. (2004). Young children interpret the metafictive in Anthony Browne's *Voices in the Park. Journal of Early Childhood Literacy, 4*(2), 211–233.

Rosenblatt, L. (1978). *The reader, the text, the poem: The transactional theory of the literary work.* Carbondale, IL: Southern Illinois University Press.

Sipe, L. R. (1998). Learning the language of picturebooks. *Journal of Children's Literature, 24*(2), 66–75.

Sipe, L. R., & Brightman, A. E. (2005). Young children's visual meaning-making during readalouds of picture storybooks. *Yearbook of the National Reading Conference, 54,* 349–361. Oak Creek, WI: National Reading Conference.

Waugh, P. (1984). *Metafiction: The theory and practice of self-conscious fiction.* New York: Methuen.

Twenty Notable Postmodern Picturebooks

Ahlberg, J., & Ahlberg, A. (1986). *The jolly postman or other people's letters.* Boston: Little Brown.

Browne, A. (1998). *Voices in the park.* New York: DK Ink.

Browne, A. (2004). *Into the forest.* Cambridge, MA: Candlewick.

Child, L. (2000). *Beware of the storybook wolves.* New York: Scholastic.

Child, L. (2002). *Who's afraid of the big bad book?* New York: Hyperion.

Feiffer, J. (1997). *Meanwhile.* New York: HarperCollins.

Felix, M. (1988). *The story of a little mouse trapped in a book.* La Jolla, CA: Green Tiger.

Hawkins, C., & Hawkins, J. (2004). *Fairytale News.* Cambridge, MA: Candlewick.

Lehman, B. (2004). *The red book.* Boston: Houghton Mifflin.

Macaulay, D. (1990). *Black and white.* Boston: Houghton Mifflin.

Macaulay, D. (1995). *Shortcut.* Boston: Houghton Mifflin.

Muntean, M. (2006). *Do not open this book!* New York: Scholastic.

Scieszka, J. (1994). *The book that Jack wrote.* New York: Viking.

Scieszka, J. (1992). *The Stinky Cheese Man and other fairly stupid tales.* New York: Viking.

Vail, R. (1998). *Over the moon.* New York: Orchard Books.

Van Allsburg, C. (1995). *Bad day at Riverbend.* Boston: Houghton Mifflin.

Wattenberg, J. (2000). *Henny Penny.* New York: Scholastic.

Whatley, B. (2001). *Wait! No paint!* New York: HarperCollins.

Wiesner, D. (2001). *The three pigs.* New York: Clarion.

Wilson, A. (1999). *Magpie magic.* New York: Dial.

Heroes in Children's Fantasy: Secondary Worlds Worth Visiting

Susan S. Lehr

> If it be true to its roots, a fantasy tale must always have a moral—yet in the telling, should entertain primarily and never preach. At its worst, when it is created to manipulate the masses, it is merely propaganda; at its most sublime, it is as enlightening as an ethical or metaphysical tract, and as uplifting as any great poem.
>
> —Grace Chetwin (1995, p. 177)

Fantasy in children's literature has a richly textured history, going back to the classics of the late 19th century—*The Princess and Curdy* (MacDonald, 1872/1986), *At the Back of the North Wind* (MacDonald, 1871/2001), *Alice's Adventures in Wonderland* (Carroll, 1865), *Water Babies* (Kingsley, 1863)—but the genre found new authority and direction with the emergence of *The Hobbit* by J.R.R. Tolkien (1937/2001). Leonard Marcus (1863/2006) writes the following:

> Fantasy is storytelling with the beguiling power to trans-
> form the impossible into the imaginable, and to reveal our
> own "real" world in a fresh and truth-bearing light. It has
> the surprising power to make everything it touches upon
> seem new, unpredictable, and—in Tolkien's fine phrase—
> "arrestingly strange." (p. 2)

Although J.R.R.Tolkien's (1954) *The Lord of the Rings* books are not considered children's books, the influence that Tolkien has had on generations of
fantasy authors of both adult and children's books is significant. The success
of Peter Jackson's *Lord of the Rings* movies, the *Harry Potter* books and movies, and the reappearance of C. S. Lewis's Narnian tales in film, combined,
have fueled a fantasy rage in the publishing world. The success of the *Harry
Potter* series forced *The New York Times* to create a separate best-seller list
for children so that books in this series could be removed from long-term
positions on the adult list. Despite its popularity, J. K. Rowling's magic and
wizardry have caused considerable controversy, provoking book burnings
in Pennsylvania. Even the Vatican has taken conflicting stances for and
against the magic and morality of Harry Potter's world.

> "Of course it's tempting to say that Harry Potter raised the
> awareness of children's fantasy to a new level and I think
> that is true. I do believe that publishers were encouraged to
> try publishing fantasy who had not done so before. And I do
> think that more British authors are trying their hands at writ-
> ing fantasy. I think this is attributable to Harry Potter, but also
> to Philip Pullman's *His Dark Materials* trilogy and Brian
> Jacques's *Redwall* series and other successful fantasies of
> recent years. Fantasy is a well-established genre in
> children's literature and always has been... Editors are look-
> ing for books that they are passionate about, books that are
> good literature." Lodge, 2003, unpaged

In this chapter I will consider the categories and characteristics of contemporary fantasy. Focusing on new fantasy with human characters, three broad
strands emerge in contemporary fantasy: (a) the fantastic adventures of preadolescents originating in the known familiar world, (b) the adventures of preadolescents residing in secondary worlds, and (c) the epic quests of adolescents
residing in secondary worlds. What is the nature of these types of fantasy? What
are the characteristics of these types of fantasy? How do authors successfully
transport readers into these secondary worlds? Because of J. K. Rowling's incredible success, I will first consider the *Harry Potter* series as a separate phenomenon,
situating the Rowling books within the wider context of children's fantasy.

Harry Potter: Arrestingly Strange

Jack Zipes (2002) attempts to pierce the cultural obsessions that have created this megamonster by stripping away the institutions and conglomerates that control mass media and the publishing market. His view of this megamonster is one of obsession, fetishism, and consumption, what he terms "an induced experience calculated to conform to a cultural convention of amusement and distraction" (p. 172). Young readers might be having the times of their lives, but he cautions that this has all been carefully manipulated and marketed by corporate conglomerates that own publishing companies, toy companies, movie companies, and news media.

Zipes also raises the issue about the mythos surrounding Harry Potter's creator, J. K. Rowling, a welfare mother who wrote in a coffee shop and was rejected by publishers (Zipes, 2002). Zipes maintains that Rowling's rags-to-riches transformation occurs through a rather ordinary and predictable work that follows the structure of the basic fairy tale: A modest protagonist departs, enters a perilous realm, finds gifts and helpers along the way, realizes he has powers, encounters an evil entity, defeats his antagonist, and returns home. Zipes is right, but fairy tales have endured precisely because of their predictable and reassuring structure; audiences rely upon structure across all modes of storytelling. Because of fairy tales' endurance across centuries, one suspects that humans psychologically need the predictability and reassurance that this genre offers, grappling with reality from safely structured stances. The predictability of the Rowling books is not necessarily damning, as Zipes would have us believe.

Conformity is another issue explored by academics. Rowling's depiction of a British White world is real enough and reveals a classist society. The British Harry Potter has been described by scholars as an all-American boy (Thompson, 2001), a fairy tale prince and an archetypal hero (Grimes, 2002), living in the White patriarchal world found in fairy tales (Zipes, 2002), in a "likable but critically insignificant series" (Sutton, 1999, p. 1). Westman (2002) suggests that the series is appealing precisely because it is conservative in its "rendering of [the] British childhood experience" (p. 305). Mendlesohn (2002) suggests that each character has a rightful place in the story: the poor but noble Weasley family; the house elves, who are content with their birthright of service; the aristocratic but evil Malfoy, who is in a dark competition with Harry; and the nouveau riche and vulgar Dursley family, with whom Harry lives in the detested suburbs. Harry, however, is the heir apparent based on birthright.

Some critics are appalled by Rowling's sexist worldview. Rowling has managed to keep her female characters confined to stereotypical female roles, with the exception of the emerging Hermione Granger, whom Thompson (2001) rates as the brilliant but overachieving and overextended know-it-all girl. In the media Rowling has clearly claimed Hermione as a caricature of herself. Hermione begins to loosen up after book 3 of the series, when she flaunts her looks, champions the oppressed house elves, gobbles her food, and taunts Harry and Ron because she has no homework (Dresang, 2002). Dresang proposes that no apology be given for Hermione's overbearing and somewhat obnoxious personality—men act this way "without castigation." Surely girls will gain greater independence and visibility in future Rowling books that don't exclusively involve giggles, whines, and hiding in the background. In *Harry Potter and the Deathly Hallows* (2007) Hermione still squeals and hides behind Ron and Harry, but she is also valiant and proactively ready to battle Voldemort.

Finally, the real world in which Harry lives is considered by some to be a strength of Rowling's *Harry Potter* series. His home life is troubled, but at Hogwarts his wizardry helps him to define and develop his own powers (Natov, 2002):

> The interpenetration of the two worlds suggests the way in which we live—not only in childhood, though especially so then—on more than one plane, with the life of the imagination and daily life moving in and out of our consciousness. The two realms, characterized in literature as the genres of romance and realism, are located in the imagination, which is, always, created by and rooted in the details of everyday life. (p. 129)

What propels a person to overcome obstacles when family, school, church—every level of society—has positioned one in an inferior slot? Trites's (2000) notion of interior self-determination is, I believe, what propels Harry, Hermione, and Ron onward and is a core strength of the books. All three characters are successfully growing up, despite being orphaned, poor, or born of the wrong parents, although they have the insider societal advantage of being born White and, in the case of Ron and Harry, male. The adventures and battles with evil that they have along the way mirror contemporary society. Crago (1999) believes that fantasy's power lies in its ability to help readers grow up. As a metaphor, Crago insists that the *Harry Potter* books are not simply escapism; rather, readers identify with problems at a deeper and more symbolic level.

Children at the Edges of Adolescence Residing in the Real World

The success of the *Harry Potter* series has injected the publishing world with a frenzy of fantasy books in all sorts of shapes, colors, and sizes. One of the significant trends has been the revival of fantasy with contemporary settings and heroes at the edge of adolescence who experience adventures against evil forces—not cosmic, as in epic fantasy, but nonetheless dangerous and important to the local neighborhood. The fantasy books are often written for middle- to upper-elementary audiences and occur in a bundled series of adventures, not unlike the seven books about Narnia by C. S. Lewis. Many seem to be targeted at male readers. Most begin with the unlikeliest hero, often a boy, who is awkward or bullied, new at school, unpopular, not very athletic, shy or introverted, frequently nerdy, with equally nerdy male or female companions. This young boy is typically very intelligent but unwilling to reveal this to his peers, because he knows that he will be persecuted. Many of the heroes are initially reluctant, not in a cowardly way, but, like their parents, they do not want to get involved, and they hope that it will all just go away. It never does, however, or there would be no adventure.

Fantasy that is written within the realistic framework of the known world mirrors the type of child who might actually read fantasy and, as such, typifies Crago's (1999) notion of fantasy as a metaphor for the real world of young males. Art imitates life. I maintain that young males desperately need these fantastic heroes to survive. Fantasy provides safety from a distance—the safety to explore one's fears, which are often rooted in everyday interactions, and the vicarious experience of meeting and defeating monsters and bullies that are everywhere in real life.

Fantasy typically works by convention, with certain characteristics that bridge the real world of fiction and the world of make-believe. Applying certain elements from the fairy tale cycle to the fantasy structure, I will consider several new series for young readers through the lens of two vital conventions that authors use to transport readers into secondary worlds. If this bridge is successful, in the words of Tolkien, one suspends disbelief. If this bridge is not successful, the reader is constantly adrift, unable to connect with the imaginary world.

The Familiar Settings of Home and School

The first characteristic of bridging the real world to the world of make-believe involves creating a realistic modern world that is familiar to readers. Natov (2002) describes this as being rooted in the details of everyday life—as the leap readers take into imagination. Many of the new series, such as Garth Nix's (2003) *Keys to the Kingdom* series, use a public school framework to structure the child's world, with teachers depicted as unapproachable, pre-occupied, or ancient, except for those who aid or impede the hero's actions. In some cases, a Dumbledore from Hogwarts will offer support and guidance and then mysteriously disappear when danger threatens. As in realistic fiction, adventures occur more readily when parents are not hovering or coddling their children protectively, although innovative authors can frame stories within supportive families as a refreshing respite from the stream of absent, dead, or abusive families. School-age children enjoy a certain amount of freedom, which is known quite well by most boys and girls in the Western world (from which these fantasy authors originate). If this real world is set up realistically, and if enough clues are embedded to indicate that the familiar is fading, the child can successfully shift to the imagined reality.

The school setting is a long and familiar tradition in British literature; since 1749, thousands of books have been written using the setting of the boarding school (Bree, 1996; Steege, 2002). *Harry Potter* is considered by some British critics to be primarily a boarding school story with the fantasy frame as a secondary device (Steege, 2002). Many writers have used the school framework to launch their fantasy adventures. One of the best known is a tale from Narnia, *The Silver Chair* (Lewis, 1953), which begins and ends briefly at school—behind the gym, where poor Jill is hiding from bullies. Upon her return from Narnia at the end of her fantasy adventure, Jill faces the real world of school bullies and has some lessons to teach them. This story is very satisfying and safe for young readers, who face all sorts of bullies at school.

Some contemporary heroes attend schools for the magically gifted, like Harry Potter's Hogwarts. One example is Charlie Bone, a British boy who attends the Bloor Academy for the endowed (Nimmo, 2003). Each day Charlie returns to his modest London home, where he lives with his mother and two grandmothers, and dodges his Yewbeam aunts, all of whom seem to be conniving relatives with separate agendas. Charlie Bone's magical ability is that he can hear what is being said in photographs and even knows what the people were thinking. At age 11 he has come into this new ability and is identified by his aunts as being a descendant of the Red King, which means he must attend the Bloor Academy to develop his powers. Charlie Bone, quite simply, is nice and has nice friends and nice adventures. He reminds me of Charlie in *Charlie and the Chocolate Factory* (Dahl, 1964), because he is inherently nice. Predictability aside, and in spite of the criticism of Nimmo's lack of understanding about the conventions of magic, the *Charlie Bone* series is solid for middle-grade children because his familiar world and his scheming aunts make his adventures entertaining—not outstanding, but nonetheless satisfying.

In contrast, Anne Ursa's (2006) *The Shadow Thieves* introduces a slightly older protagonist who is surly; *nice* would not describe Charlotte Mielswetzski. Ursa builds the story slowly as she invites the reader to become acquainted with the protagonist and her everyday world. She hints at the gray creatures who loom and lurk in tuxedos, not even noticed by Charlotte at first, because she is preoccupied with the stray cat that decides to follow her home. Diligent readers will notice and will be chewing on their fingernails with wonder and anticipation. The setting is a public school in Minnesota, where two cousins are ultimately the last children standing against the forces of Philonecron, a Greek immortal who hopes to overcome Hades' dominion of the underworld by stealing the shadows of children and creating an army.

Ursa understands the world of the eighth-grade child and has created two distinctly different children, one of whom is a loner, Charlotte, and one of whom is unaware of his own popularity and innate appeal, Charlotte's biracial cousin, Zee, from London. Ursa realistically weaves the complexities of school life while hinting at dark doings and evil occurrences; the tension heightens as more children become sick and do not return to school. Zee finally tells his cousin why he thinks he has caused all this misery. In the second part, Ursa takes the reader back to England to discover why Zee was sent to Minnesota in the first place.

Ursa skillfully retells the ancient Greek myths, weaving them artfully throughout the story. At school the children study the Greek myths with Mr. Metos, a mysterious teacher who comes to their aid. Charlotte's mother and father hover lovingly and protectively in the background; however, it is Zee and Charlotte who must enter the underworld and recover the stolen shadows of their schoolmates. Ursa's humor is clever, at times subtle. Her caricature of the modern corporate structure of Hades, with its complex but efficient bureaucracy, is hilarious. Hades is too busy to control his kingdom directly because he is preoccupied with finding his wife, Persephone, who hides in a cave and undermines him. She has never forgiven him for tricking her into becoming his immortal wife. With the aid of Persephone, Zee's grandmother, from Malawi, returns from Hades to help her grandson in his time of need. A clever twist. Exquisite writing, an entirely original plot, humor, believable characters, and a real sense of danger make this a compelling new fantasy series for grades 5–9.

Using the familiar everyday world of London, in which magicians reside openly and actually govern the country, Jonathon Stroud (2003) offers a quirky novel, *The Bartimaeus Trilogy: The Amulet of Samarkand*, with extensive footnotes, as told by a magic djinni. This blend of the familiar, with the secondary world residing openly within the primary world, is quite effective. Some gifted children are apprenticed to tutors who are eccentric but wise magicians; however, the tutor in this story is a petty, jealous, inept, and aging magician who is unwilling to teach his pupil anything important. Because Nathaniel has been humiliated by the evil magician Simon Lovelace, he takes charge of his own education, secretly reading his master's books to concoct dangerous spells. Nathaniel is a twisted and naive hero—his motivation is revenge; without guidance he unleashes great forces. The story is told tongue in cheek by Bartimaeus, a 5,000-year-old djinni, who is summoned by Nathaniel to steal an amulet of power from a powerful magician, the same Simon Lovelace who so humiliated him. Nathaniel is a younger version of the older and reckless Ged in *A Wizard of Earthsea* (Le Guin, 1968), who also unleashes great misery because of his petty jealousies and arrogance, but this is a gentler journey, told with more humor and in a familiar urban setting. One learns again that tutors who don't fulfill their obligations come to bad ends.

Sometimes magic resides at home, especially when characters move into a new unfamiliar setting. These new homes are often large mansions ripe for exploration, like the one in which C. S. Lewis placed his Narnian children during the bombing of London in World War II.

The action in *Ulysses Moore: The Door to Time* (Baccalario, 2006) takes place in one day in a mysterious mansion, in the form of a treasure hunt to find the key to a mysterious door. This door leads to an abandoned ship in a cave that transports three children to ancient Egypt, paralleling the concept of Sciezka's Time Warp Trio for younger readers. Of the three characters, the two boys take most of the risks and make most of the decisions, whereas obnoxious Julia constantly attempts to subvert the adventure through endless whining and complaining. This adventure could have been strengthened if Julia had been simply dropped off at the mall, which is where she longs to be. She doesn't deserve this adventure, and children don't deserve to listen to her complain through an entire series. Her cardboard character is a tall distraction that weakens the plot and reinforces tiresome gender stereotypes.

Shifts of Time and Place

The second and more difficult characteristic of bridging the real world to the world of make-believe is the means by which the children shift time or place through portals to other worlds, and what they see or experience when they first enter. Kiefer (2007) describes time-shift fantasy as a literary device for communicating with those of the past without losing one's current reality. Maiya Williams (2004) cleverly transports children from modern-day Maine back in time on "Alleviators" to the French Revolution in *The Golden Hour*. In most of these series history is a backdrop, but the fantasy takes precedence. The same is theoretically true for time shifts into the future. Shifting place, however, involves entering imaginary new realms that are not connected to the familiar world even historically. A time or place shift is actually the most perilous device that fantasy authors face, because the evocation of the secondary world is successfully made or shattered with the first step into it. The first impression must be formidable. Authors use familiar places, words, and animals to transport readers through portals into imaginative realms.

Making the shift from one world to the next, from one time to another, is complex and can leave the reader in disbelief, wondering why this shift to an imaginary land lacks authenticity. Time- and place-shift fantasies occur through portals that can be ships or books, mysterious doors, or even a grate in a laundry room. C. S. Lewis imagined an ice world of witches and stone animals that could be reached through the back of an ordinary wardrobe. In *The Shadow Thieves,* Ursa (2006) cleverly transformed the mundane and familiar—a shopping mall, a long empty hallway painted in a dreary color, and a locked door—into a portal to Hades. The dismal hallway is barely worth notice, but if one noticed it, one would immediately be desperate for a large pretzel from the mall's food court. Ursa's magic portal was dramatic in its utter drabness. We've all ignored doors like that.

Many secondary worlds are located right beneath our feet. Authors use unlikely and unexpected portals to reach these underground worlds, like the hole that Alice fell into to enter Wonderland. Alice was a worthy character who met each challenge with bravado and escaped unscathed; however, Lewis Carroll (1865/2005) brought her back to the real world by waking her up from a dream—clever, because it left the reader wondering if her adventures really happened.

These between worlds are quite effective and believable. One enters, at times, unwillingly. In *Gregor the Overlander* (Collins, 2003), 11-year-old Gregor journeys underground to retrieve his baby sister, who has disappeared through a grate in the laundry room in the basement of an apartment in New York City. Adventure is waiting right next to the coin-operated washer and dryer in a dreary but seemingly safe basement. This is an urban retelling of *Alice's Adventures in Wonderland* (Carroll, 1865/2005), with a well-developed but reluctant protagonist who only wants to get back safely with his baby sister before his mother comes home from work. By taking the urban setting underground, Collins (2003) builds a believable parallel world where Gregor meets the enemy rats and simple-minded cockroaches, all of which are gigantic and able to speak. Gregor is believable as a reluctant participant in an underground war because he wants to protect his sister. The humans, who have built a walled city and travel by underground river, slowly pull Gregor into their war against the rats—a believable underground city and a realistic urban foe.

Underground inhabitants are occasionally summoned above ground. In *Artemis Fowl* (Colfer, 2001), Artemis schemes to summon a fairy from underground, and what he gets is the spunky and determined Captain Holly Short, member of LEPrecon Unit. Colfer deftly shifts between the fairy perspective and that of the young Artemis Fowl, a 12-year-old genius who has stolen fairy secrets and is intent on extorting an elf ransom. Holly is summoned to the top to take out a troll who is rampaging through an Italian village, because the Mud People (humans) might be hurt. These events have been diabolically manipulated by Artemis Fowl. Colfer makes the world of fairies believable through large and small details, from Nettle Smoothies to explanations of chutes and elevators that connect deep underground.

Cornelia Funke would have us believe that words are so powerful and so magical that when read aloud they can change the molecular structure of people and characters. Her character Silvertongue is such a powerful reader that he breathes characters into life, and people into characters, when he reads *Inkheart* aloud. Unfortunately, the escaped breathing characters are villains of the worst sort, and his wife disappears into the very same book, which he now treasures as his only link to her. Mo, whose secret name is Silvertongue, has never read aloud to his daughter, Meggie, for fear that she will disappear, and Meggie knows nothing of his silver tongue. This adventure takes place across the dark and remote areas of the Italian hills. The imagined world is brilliantly intertwined with the real world because the storybook villain, Capricorn, is intent on destroying the last existing copy of *Inkheart*. Funke is in love with books, and she skillfully weaves them throughout every imaginable nook of *Inkheart* (2003).

Her second book in the series, *Inkspell* (Funke, 2005), takes place inside the first book. Meggie is now an apprentice to Dustfinger, the fire-eater. Anthea Bell has beautifully translated both stories from German to English, which adds another layer of mystery to the books. A book within a book is a clever device for a secondary world and reminds one of David Wiesner's (2001) brilliant rendering of the three pigs escaping from their own picturebook onto blank white pages, as the wolf, trapped in his illustration, stands with his mouth agape. In the current era of skills and drills, one longs for silver-tongued teachers who breath magic into words. Words can be dangerous, but they are so magical.

Not all historical settings are serious. Dave Barry and Ridley Pearson (2004) have teamed to create the slapstick and swashbuckling *Peter and the Starcatchers,* set on the *Never Land,* a ship belonging to a pirate named Black Strache. Readers find out how Black Strache got his hook to become the Captain Hook found in J. M. Barrie's (1904) *Peter Pan.* The second book of this series, *Peter and the Shadow Thieves* (Barry & Pearson, 2006), is set in a familiar but magical London.

In less successful hands, however, word bridges can become trivial if the imagined kingdoms are too silly or too irrelevant. Two authors begin with innovative ideas and strong writing but present convoluted or trivialized plots. Matthew Skelton's (2006) bold concept for *Endymion Spring* becomes contrived as he flips back and forth between the historical Germany of Gutenberg and contemporary Oxford, England. He dwells largely in the present, but his premise, plot development, and characters remain superficial. Kristin Kladstrup's (2006) *The Book of Story Beginnings* uses the effective device of a book of story beginnings as a bridge to a secondary world. She creates a trivial plot, however, that might work well in a picture book, but is silly as a premise for a chapter book. If the reader is unable to successfully suspend disbelief, the secondary world is not worth the visit.

At times characters meet magical animals in the real world that lead them into the fantasy world. These animals guard the hero against intruders and often lead them to portals. In secondary worlds for older readers, these guides are often wild animals, like Philip Pullman's (1996) northern white bears, or Michelle Paver's wolf brother (2004), who guides his ancient young human in a battle against an avenging bear. In real world tales, the guides are often reassuring dogs or cats, with cats being the most prevalent. Younger children find comfort in these familiar guides and hope that their pets will be as valiant, whereas older children enjoy the danger of having a wolf brother or of riding on the back of a polar bear. At times these guides have even been known to hurl themselves at dangerous predators or pounce on the hero in the middle of the night to warn of immediate danger. Cats are often chosen as a guardian because of their feline characteristics—they pounce, they mince, they sneak, at times they talk, and when all else fails they scratch; but most important, they choose their caretakers and give them guidance. The perception is that cats are smarter than dogs, and even if they are not perceived as being as loyal as dogs, they do seem to exhibit their own distinct brand of allegiance to their chosen hero.

In Jane Johnson's (2006) *Eidolon Chronicles: The Secret Country*, a cat named Iggy chooses Ben when the boy goes into Mr. Dodd's Pet Emporium to buy two Mongolian Fighting Fish. Iggy has been kidnapped from the Secret Country and is becoming quite sick in the real world. He ultimately leads Ben to a stone portal in the park and then disappears for many chapters, but Ben now knows two important things: how to enter the Secret Country, and that he has an ally there. Animal links to secondary worlds can be effective because they are reassuring and familiar companions who lead readers into believable plots.

Young Victimized Preadolescents Save Imaginary Worlds

Few books set in imaginary worlds are written for the young child, but those that are often revisit themes from classic fantasy tales. *Lowthar's Blade*, a series by R. L. LaFevers (2004), shares similar images and themes with Tolkien's books. *Lowthar's Blade* is a good series for the middle-grade child as an introduction to fantasy with Robin Hood themes and settings. Predictability, believable and familiar characters, linear plots, and solid writing make these books effective for younger readers. The *Rowan of Rin* series by Emily Rodda (2001) and Nancy Springer's (2001) *Rowan Hood* series are also strong books for young readers. Similarly, Paul Stewart and Chris

Riddell's *Edge Chronicles* (2004) are episodic adventures about a boy search-ing for his father. The imagined world is both humorous and dangerous, filled with an assortment of bizarre creatures living above and below ground. Riddell's small drawings enhance Quint's journeys.

Sage's (2005) *Septimus Heap: Magyk* —about two babies, one royal and one with "magyk," abducted at birth—is not a new motif in fantasy. How-ever, the unique setting—consisting of a jumble of magicians' homes run-ning beneath the castle walls, a Dickensian family, some enslaved orphans who are given numbers in place of names, an escape to the marshes, and a relentless character named Hunter—all combine to give this fantasy innovative magyk.

Sage undermines her rich characters and strong plot, however, by at times resorting to a sort of mindless stereotyping with both class and gen-der. A powerful magician, Marcia, is trivialized by her irritating preoccupa-tion with the latest fashions and her abhorrence of mud. There is also an abundance of women who are ridiculed for being fat. The men go to work and the women gossip; even a female rat is compelled to gossip, whereas her mate has a real job, although it's considered menial. When Jenna and Boy 412 run for their lives while being chased by the Hunter, who is a wonder-fully wicked tracker, Boy 412 holds, pulls, and drags Jenna, who tires imme-diately. This stereotypical female helplessness and the constant stream of female preoccupation with fashion, gossip, and comfort food detract from a rather compelling plot. Educators should be aware of and discuss the limi-tations that continue to be placed unwittingly and unceasingly on females in literature. I would not necessarily avoid a well-written book like this, but one should be aware of the negative stereotyping and use it as a tool for dis-cussion, perhaps asking, "Why do you think the author chose to make her such a whiny, helpless, and weak female?" "What could Jenna have done dif-ferently?" Gender stereotyping like this is common in children's literature and continues to trivialize and minimize female roles.

A strong new series for upper elementary age children, *Ranger's Appren-tice: The Ruins of Gorlan* by Australian John Flanagan (2005), includes famil-iar images, characters, and intrigues from the perspective of the Rangers, those loners who guard and protect the borders of the realm. Young Will longs to be apprenticed to the Battleschool, but because he is too small to train as a warrior, he reluctantly accepts a Ranger's invitation to become an apprentice. The world of apprentices has the same bullies of the real world, and some of the most powerful scenes in this book occur between bullies. The close relationship that develops between the main characters is well de-veloped, and when danger is met in the guise of two giant bearlike crea-tures, the Ranger and his apprentice work together to defeat this threat, but not without cost. This new series for middle and upper elementary age chil-dren offers compelling new experiences with fantasy that have previously been limited for this age group.

Imagined worlds also reside in familiar epochs or explore ancient cultures, as in Ursa's (2006) depictions of the Greek gods and their underworld.

Adolescents Battle the Age of Darkness

Authors writing for adolescents explore acts of evil, treachery, and deceit in opposition to acts of courage and integrity. In these provocative books, dark forces coalesce against all living creatures, and the actions of individuals matter; without heroic acts of selfless courage, much would be lost. In these books for older readers, authors explore contemporary issues related to gender, diversity, oppression, personal freedom, war, and the ravages of abusing the planet Earth, while other authors present innovative settings and diverse cultures. Strong new roles for females have emerged that Tolkien (1954) never envisioned in his Middle Earth.

Adolescent Females in Fantasy

When I first wrote about females in fantasy (Lehr, 1995), there were essentially two roles for women, with a third emerging in newer works: the traditional subservient woman, the woman as warrior, and the wise woman who rejected the magic of men. I explored the first role by reconsidering the classics and the depictions of women in fantasy and found that authors essentially presented women in traditional and subservient roles, although some of the women had spunk and some took a lot of initiative within the confines of their limiting cultures: princesses, mothers, companions to male protagonists, worriers, captives waiting to be rescued. I rejected the term *heroine* because of its historical baggage and used the term *hero* instead. Tamora Pierce's (1983) Alanna encapsulated the woman-as-warrior role, what Dresang (2002) refers to as role reversal. The third role emerged in the works of Monica Furlong (1990) and Ursula Le Guin (1990), who created wise women who did not accept or conform to men's magic and who took on apprentices so that their knowledge would not disappear. These wise women were typically healers who were also ostracized targets who could be burned as witches, thereby echoing themes from history.

A provocative new strand of fantasy presents young women who have been born under humble circumstances—no weepy princesses need apply, although there are still plenty of current books fitting this description—and must make their own way in a difficult and often harsh world. Some have fallen from high places. These females share a deep sense of justice, have been greatly wronged, are barely aware of their own emerging powers, live on the edge of nowhere, are immersed in a sense of innocence, and challenge evil. They transcend their origins with tears, laughter, and a great deal of courage (Cixous, cited in Trites, 1997).

Like many heroes, this female adolescent protagonist is often unaware of her magical aptitudes, but her transcendent role has been prophesied. Dark forces, once defeated, are now escaping and gathering strength, and in some small cot the hero is being raised unaware. This female hero is often a victim of abuse, slavery, political intrigue, or exile, and she is sometimes mentored by an older and wiser guide who will instruct and lead her to the edge of danger. The edge includes battles against minions, flights and fights against evil hordes, and an eventual confrontation with the dark leader. This resilient adolescent is a doubtful hero and is unaware of her own powers, but she perceives that she is different, an outsider, a loner—all of which is reinforced by the locals. This strand of fantasy often operates in books of three. Several of the more innovative series work outside old feudal structures and envision worlds in which men and women are not preoccupied with tightly defined gender roles. One's worth is not immediately decided based on one's genitalia, unless one is born into slavery, and then gender becomes an issue of safety.

This bold strand of literature shows the potential of women and men in societies where gender need not be an impediment. The females in these series are not merely positioning themselves against men; rather, they have definition and purpose and are not merely vassals or appendages. At times they begin within patriarchal boundaries but then move to differently structured societies. Alison Croggon (2005), from Australia, leads the pack with her *Pellinor* series about a young girl, Maerad, who loses her home, most of her family, and is sold into slavery with her mother. She grows up in Gilman's Cot at the edge of nowhere, tucked into a fortress.

Croggon (2005) describes Maerad's existence as "an endless cycle of drudgery, and exhaustion, and dull fear" (p. 1). The Thane's men are rough and crude sexual predators, who drink and grope. Maerad has learned to take care of herself and trusts no one after her mother dies. Because of her dark hair and blue eyes, the men consider her a witch, and she uses their superstitions against them. Life is dismal for everyone in this cot, and at the age of 16, Maerad is without hope and without a future, except for the lyre that has been given to her by her mother and that a minstrel has taught her to play. As in many fantasy series, music is significant to Maerad's eventual success. Her dreams of escape are now seen as childish dreams:

> Freedom was a fantasy she gnawed obsessively in her few moments of leisure, like an old bone with just a trace of meat, and like all illusions, it left her hungrier than before, only more keenly aware of how her soul starved within her, its wings wasting with the despair of disuse. (Croggon, 2005, p. 2)

Croggon (2005) offers a powerful vision of freedom that fades but does not disappear. She breathes life and a tingle of hope into this depressed young woman. Maerad is wary and does not trust easily; however, she begins to accept the kindness of the Bards she meets. Maerad's eventual quest with the Bard Cadvan, her mentor, is long, dangerous, and difficult, but whenever a tub is available, Maerad is in it soaking off the miles, pure delight for a former slave. Like Tolkien (1954) and his ever-hungry hobbits, the details make the secondary world poignant.

Maerad is a worthy hero and yet like any hero, she has a tangle of inner distortions that she must sort through and understand. Like Le Guin's (1968) archetype, Ged from Earthsea, Maerad has a dark side that she must integrate and accept. Her coming of age is remarkable, and the journeys that Croggon (2005) imagines are at times breathtaking. This coming of age and coming into powers is a common motif in fantasy. The third book in the series about her brother's journey is equally compelling. Both brother and older sister must eventually reunite in order to restore balance to the world.

David Randall's (2004) *Clovermead: In the Shadow of the Bear* and Betsy James's (1989/2005) *Long Night Dance* both have strong female protagonists who feel an awakening to power as they reach adolescence. Unfortunately, Randall's sequel falls into the trite traps of courtly behavior, which many fantasy authors cannot resist but should. Watching the young spirited hero suddenly struggle with dance steps, pimples, and bad hair days derails the freshness and strength of the first volume and renders the second volume clichéd. I find this preoccupation with courtly dancing and gendered manners a pedestrian preoccupation in many series while an author struggles to maintain the momentum of a first book. The superficial effects of courtly life and its rigid roles are often a retreat from a compelling narrative. Tolkien (1954) resisted that temptation by transforming clichéd situations and by challenging the banality of courtly virtues, which is what ultimately separates the mundane from the mystical.

In an unusual recasting of elves and goblin tales, a young girl awakens to her elfin powers in *The Hollow Kingdom* (Dunkle, 2003). Clare Dunkle has given fresh energy to the superstitions about the frightful folk who live under the hill. The king of the goblins attempts to capture a wife and to bring her underground for the rest of her life, where she will be honored and protected and give birth to the heir to the kingdom. In Dunkle's reshaping of old motifs, the young woman resists heroically and resourcefully, honors a promise to save her sister, and is eventually called upon to save the goblin kingdom. The underground goblin kingdom is exquisitely described, as is Kate's tension in being locked beneath the earth. In the second book, her sister's story is told, and in the third book the ancient battle between the elves and the goblins is revived.

Kate Constable (2002) and Lene Kaaberbol (2004) have also developed extraordinary protagonists who battle dark forces and help to restore balance to the world as their powers become realized. Constable, from Australia, achieves balance through song, whereas Kaaberbol, who also translates her books from Danish to English, uses the unusual gift of shaming, making one face the truth. Exposing truth is the shamer's gift and mission, passed from mother to child.

Australian Isobelle Carmody's (2005) *The Gateway Trilogy* begins effectively in the real world, when a young girl's mother lies comatose in the hospital. Rage Winnoway, the girl, is not allowed to see her mother, nor is she given any options about her own future. About to lose her four dogs and to be sent into foster care, Rage flees from her farm, becomes lost in the barren hills, and is lured through a magic gate with the hope of finding a cure for her mother. Carmody parodies destructive gender roles by creating a sexist and hierarchical valley of dying magic in which Rage's questions are heretical. The old magic is dying but is propped up by blackshirts and other guards who are certainly distant relatives of the Taliban. As Grace Chetwin (1995) says good fantasy exposes the depth of truths about heart and soul, by reflecting the past, scrutinizing the present, and helping to shape the future (p. 177).

Catherine Fisher's two provocative trilogies are distinct from each other. *The Oracle Prophecies* (2004a) is set in an ancient desert world with priestesses who are responsible for the sacred selection of the ruler; *Snow-Walker* (2004b) is set in a medieval world of ice and snow. *Snow-Walker* first appeared as three separate books in Great Britain and was republished as a single volume in 2004. Hopefully the revival of fantasy will help this excellent trilogy to find a strong audience.

In *Snow-Walker,* Fisher tells the tale of Kari, who was imprisoned from birth as a result of his mother's malicious acts. His exile to the desolate north, is haunting. Years later, when his cousin, Jessa, is exiled to Thrasirshall, she is terrified because of rumors about a beast, which has lived in isolation for many years. The two exiled cousins find each other, and they form a remarkably strong bond. That they will combine their gifts and overcome the evil enchanter is assured. Fisher's (2004) two protagonists are like Ursa's (2006): Both are empowered and need each other to succeed. Each has gifts distinct from the other. Although Fisher's world has a traditional gender imbalance, her two protagonists and their interactions suggest possibility. Her female embodiment of evil controlling and manipulating the duped Jarl, her husband, also exposes evil as being gender-free.

Innovative Settings and Diverse Cultures

Most fantasy books originate in imagined realms, within medieval patriarchal structures, but a few fantasy authors have begun to create innovative settings and to explore diverse cultures. In doing so, they reveal the contemporary world "in a fresh and truth-bearing light" (Marcus, 2006, p. 2), often setting their stories in the distant future or a reimagined past. Although most fantasy books are set in preindustrial worlds, English author Philip Reeve (2001), like Philip Pullman, has reenvisioned a machinated but geographically familiar world. In *Mortal Engines* and in all his books that follow, Reeve's giant cities roll on gigantic treads searching for resources. Stationary towns and cities have been gobbled up by cities like London and no longer exist, whereas small towns moving on treads cower in the shadows of hidden valleys or swamps.

Set thousands of years in the future, after the world's resources have been devoured, cities swallow cities just to survive. New mountain ranges have emerged and old mountain ranges have diminished. A remote kingdom safely tucked behind the now-diminishing Himalayas is in danger of being invaded, and other human clusters hide on the northern fringes of a devastated North American plain. Scenes from a fabled north Alaskan village evoke a mystery about a world that is reshaped and unfamiliar. If this is hard to follow, it is because Reeves has imagined a future in which humanity has self-annihilated and begun again. Tragically, history's lessons have not been learned.

Authors explore the clash of science and theology, beginning with the Age of Enlightenment. In *The Golden Compass*, Phillip Pullman (1996) reimagines the development of science and theology and its consequences on history. Garth Nix divides the familiar world into two separate realms, magic and modern, machine and machine-free, in *Sabriel* (1996), *Lireal* (2001), and *Abhorsen* (2003a). Reimaging the familiar world by separating science from magic with concrete boundaries is innovative.

Jeanne Du Prau (2003) creates an underworld city in *The City of Ember* as a haven for humanity when the known world is at the edge of destruction. Centuries later, however, the inhabitants are no longer aware of any boundaries beyond their own underground kingdom, but the light bulbs are dimming, and resources are no longer available for long-term survival. In the sequel, she explores a world devastated by disaster and left with few humans and limited resources. Authors like Du Prau effectively explore contemporary themes related to global warming and diminishing resources by envisioning future scenarios in which disaster has already struck. Adolescent protagonists show tremendous courage as they work together to defeat evil and achieve balance in the world.

Diverse cultures can provide unique perspectives in modern fantasy. Nancy Farmer's (2004) *The Sea of Trolls* incorporates Saxon England, berserker Vikings, and ancient trolls from Nordic myths in an enthralling and expansive epic. Her story of two kidnapped children is compelling and historically feasible even when the remote and dangerous kingdom of the trolls is breached. Her sequel, *The Land of Silver Apples* (2007), is equally exciting!

Louise Siegler's (2005) *The Amethyst Road* is set in a region similar to the northwestern United States and is told through the eyes of a young biracial girl, Serena, who lives on the edges of two races, the Yulang and the Gorgio, neither of which accepts her, her sister, or her sister's child. They are *ma'hane*, untouchable. Their mother has disappeared, and they live as outcasts. When the social services—the Cruelty—come to take her niece, Serena pushes the callous official down the stairs and then flees for freedom. Serena's quest to find her mother takes the reader deep into the northwest setting and into a Roma ("Gypsy") culture that is fierce and rugged. Serena aches with her loneliness:

> I could escape my loneliness only when I was alone, roaming in the mountains, searching for shiny objects like the solitary, sharp-eye Magpie I had become. And maybe it wasn't so bad, this scavenging in the wild, since it released me from the sentence of solitude. Only when I was alone was I not an outcast, not shunned as if the very air I breathed were infected. (Spiegler, 2005, p. 99)

Powerful themes of racial hatred and prejudice make Serena's journey potent.

Rarely does the tapestry of non-Western countries and customs become the setting in which fantasy is set. In *The Conch Bearer* by Chitra Banerjee Divakaruni (2003), 12-year-old Anand befriends a beggar and ends up on a dangerous journey to return the magical conch shell to the Brotherhood of the Healers in a magical valley in the Himalayas. This journey is reminiscent of Farmer's (1994) folktale fantasy through Zimbabwean culture in *The Eye, the Ear, and the Arm*, because Divakaruni takes the protagonist through a richly textured journey into contemporary India. In the sequel, *The Mirror of Fire and Dreaming* (Divakaruni, 2005), Anand has found his vocation as the keeper of the conch, but because of his recklessness he is thrust into an ancient Indian kingdom. There is no precedent for remaining locked into medieval worlds with horse and foot as the chief means of travel and medieval gender customs and hierarchy as the cultural norm and rule of government. Authors who envision scenarios like these bring unique perspectives and worlds of possibility to fantasy.

Final Thoughts About the Rejection of Gom Gobblechuck and the Child's Need for Heroes

Grace Chetwin (1995) once wrote that the ethical hero "is one who dares fly in the face of some outworn, cultural shibboleth according to some inner and overriding sense of right" (p. 184). She writes that her greatest hero, Gom Gobblechuck (Chetwin, 1986), encounters "harsh judgment, intolerance, and unkindness from those who do not recognize his singular gifts" but that Gom "is born with qualities that will one day render him a savior of his world—if he can learn how to use them effectively" (Chetwin, 1995, p. 184). Chetwin characterizes the hero's charge: Challenge cultural conformity, learn to use one's gifts effectively and ethically, and overcome the adversities of youth, which are often harsh and unfair.

Like Joseph Campbell, Chetwin has characterized the hero's quest as an inner quest to conquer the self, maintaining that we are all heroes. Her questing heroes are on allegorical journeys and, like Crago (1999), she views them as metaphors of inner struggles. Living, breathing, making it through the day, the week, the month, the year, we carry on heroically. Small acts of bravery. Large acts of courage. Noble deeds. Ethical decisions. Some applauded. Most are not seen. Children need to think of themselves as independent agents and to consider how they can choose to live heroically. Children cannot survive without heroes. Perhaps that is why Harry Potter and the hobbits continue to disarm us with their courageous chutzpah.

References

Bree, L. (1996). *Sarah Fielding*. New York: Twayne.

Campbell, J. (1949). *The hero with a thousand faces*. Princeton, NJ: Princeton University Press.

Chetwin, G. (1995). Creating ethical heroes who know how to win: Or muddling through. In S. Lehr (Ed.), *Battling dragons: Issues and controversy in children's literature*. Portsmouth, NH: Heinemann.

Crago, H. (1999). Can stories heal? In P. Hunt (Ed.), *Understanding children's literature*. London: Routledge, 163–173.

Dresang, E. (2002). Gender issues and Harry Potter. In L. Whited (Ed.), *The ivory tower and Harry Potter*. Columbia, MO: University of Missouri Press.

Grimes, K. (2002). Harry Potter: Fairy tale prince, real boy, and archetypal hero. In L. Whited (Ed.), *The ivory tower and Harry Potter*. Columbia, MO: University of Missouri Press.

Hunt, P. (1995). *Children's literature: An illustrated history*. Oxford, UK: Oxford University Press.

Kiefer, B. (2007). *Charlotte Huck's* Children's literature in the elementary school (9th ed.). New York: McGraw-Hill.

Lehr, S. (1995). Wise women and warriors. In S. Lehr (Ed.), *Battling dragons: Issues and controversy in children's literature*, (pp. 194–211). Portsmouth, NH: Heinemann.

Lodge, S. (2003, June 30). Beyond the wizard's wand: A look at the growing field of fantasy books for children. *Publisher's Weekly*. Available online at www.publishersweekly.com/

article/CA308239.html?text= children%27s+fantasy

Marcus, L. (Ed.). (2006). *The wand in the word: Conversations with writers of fantasy.* Cambridge, MA: Candlewick Press.

Mendelsohn, F. (2002). Crowning the king: Harry Potter and the construction of authority. In L. Whited (Ed.), *The ivory tower and Harry Potter* (pp. 159–181). Columbia, MO: University of Missouri Press.

Natov, R. (2002). Harry Potter and the extraordinariness of the ordinary. In L. Whited (Ed.), *The ivory tower and Harry Potter* (pp. 125–139). Columbia, MO: University of Missouri Press.

Steege, D. (2002). Harry Potter, Tom Brown, and the British school story: Lost in transit? In L. Whited (Ed.), *The ivory tower and Harry Potter* (pp. 140–156). Columbia, MO: University of Missouri Press.

Sutton, R. (1999). Potter's field. *The Horn Book, 75,* 500–501.

Thompson, D. (2001). Deconstructing Harry: Casting a critical eye on the witches and wizards of Hogwarts. In S. Lehr (Ed.), *Beauty, brains, and brawn: The construction of gender in children's literature* (pp. 42–50). Portsmouth, NH: Heinemann.

Trites, R. (1997a). Feminist subversions in children's fictions. *American Book Review, 19,* 2, 8.

Trites, R. (2000). *Disturbing the universe: Power and repression in adolescent literature.* Iowa City: IA: University of Iowa Press.

Westman, K. (2002). Specters of Thatcherism: Contemporary British culture in J. K. Rowling's Harry Potter series. In L. Whited (Ed.), *The ivory tower and Harry Potter* (pp. 305–328). Columbia, MO: University of Missouri Press.

Zipes, J. (2002). *Sticks and stones: The troublesome success of children's literature from Slovenly Peter to Harry Potter.* New York: Routledge.

Children's Books

Baccalario, P. (2006). *Ulysses Moore: The door to time.* New York: Scholastic.

Barrie, J. M. (2003). *Peter Pan.* New York: Holt. (Original work published 1904)

Barry, D., & Pearson, R. (2004). *Peter and the starcatchers.* New York: Hyperion Books.

Barry, D., & Pearson, R. (2006). *Peter and the shadow thieves.* New York: Hyperion Books.

Carroll, L. (2005). *Alice's adventures in Wonderland* (H. Oxenbury, Illus.). New York: Candlewick Press. (Original work published 1865)

Chetwin, G. (1986). *Gom on windy mountain.* New York: Morrow.

Chetwin, G. (1987). *The riddle and the rune.* New York: Simon & Schuster.

Colfer, E. (2001). *Artemis Fowl.* New York: Hyperion Books.

Collins, S. (2003). *Gregor the overlander.* New York: Scholastic.

Constable, K. (2002). *The chanters of Tremaris trilogy: The singer of all songs.* New York: Scholastic.

Croggon, A. (2005). *The first book of Pellinor: The naming.* Cambridge, MA: Candlewick Press.

Dahl, R. (1964). *Charlie and the chocolate factory.* New York: Knopf.

Divakaruni, C. (2003). *The conch bearer.* New York: Roaring Brook Press.

Divakaruni, C. (2005). *The mirror of fire and dreaming: Book 2 of the brotherhood of the conch.* New York: Roaring Brook Press.

Dunkle, C. (2003). *The hollow kingdom.* New York: Holt.

Du Prau, J. (2003). *The city of ember.* New York: Random House.

Farmer, N. (1994). *The eye, the ear, and the arm.* New York: Scholastic.

Farmer, N. (2004). *The sea of trolls.* New York: Atheneum.

Farmer, N. (2007). *The land of silver applies.* New York: Atheneum.

Fisher, C. (2004a). *The oracle prophecies: The oracle betrayed.* New York: Greenwillow Books.

Fisher, C. (2004b). *Snow-walker.* New York: Greenwillow Books.

Flanagan, J. (2005). *Ranger's apprentice: The ruins of Gorlan.* New York: Philomel.

Funke, C. (2003). *Inkheart* (A. Bell, Trans.). New York: Scholastic.

Funke, C. (2005). *Inkspell* (A. Bell, Trans.). New York: Scholastic.

Furlong, M. (1990). *Juniper.* New York: Knopf.

James, B. (2005). *Long night dance.* New York: Simon Pulse. (Original work published 1989)

Johnson, J. (2006). *The Eidolon chronicles: The secret country.* New York: Simon & Schuster.

Kaaberbol, L. (2004). *The shamer chronicles: The shamer's daughter.* New York: Holt.

Kingsley, C. (2006). *The water babies: A fairy tale for a land baby.* London: Dover. (Original work published 1863)

Kladstrup, K. (2006). *The book of story beginnings.* Cambridge, MA: Candlewick Press.

LaFevers, R. L. (2004). *Lowthar's blade: The forging of the blade.* New York: Dutton.

Le Guin, U. (1968). *A wizard of Earthsea.* New York: Atheneum.

Le Guin, U. (1990). *Tehanu.* New York: Atheneum.

Lewis, C. S. (1953). *The silver chair.* New York: Collier Books.

MacDonald, G. (2001). *At the back of the north wind.* New York: Everyman's Library. (Original work published 1871)

MacDonald, G. (1986). *The princess and Curdy.* New York: Dell Yearling. (Original work published 1872)

Nimmo, J. (2003). *Midnight for Charlie Bone.* New York: Orchard.

Nix, G. (1996). *Sabriel.* New York: HarperCollins.

Nix, G. (2001). *Lirael.* New York: HarperCollins.

Nix, G. (2003a). *Abhorsen.* New York: HarperCollins.

Nix, G. (2003b). *The keys to the kingdom: Mister Monday.* New York: Scholastic.

Paver, M. (2004). *Chronicles of ancient darkness: Wolf brother*. New York: HarperCollins.

Pierce, T. (1983). *Song of the lionness: Alanna—the first adventure*. New York: Atheneum.

Pullman, P. (1996). *The golden compass.* New York: Knopf.

Randall, D. (2004). *Clovermead: In the shadow of the bear.* New York: Simon & Schuster.

Reeve, P. (2001). *Mortal engines.* London: Scholastic.

Rodda, E. (2001). *Rowan of Rin.* New York: Greenwillow Books.

Rowling, J. K. (2005). *Harry Potter and the half-blood prince.* New York: Scholastic.

Sage, A. (2005). *Septimus Heap: Magyk.* New York: HarperCollins.

Siegler, L. (2005). *The amethyst road.* New York: Clarion.

Skelton, M. (2006). Endymion spring. New York: Delacorte.

Springer, N. (2001). *Rowan Hood: Outlaw girl of Sherwood Forest.* New York: Philomel.

Stewart, P., & Riddell, C. (2004). *The edge chronicles: Beyond the deepwoods.* New York: Random House.

Stroud, J. (2003). *The Bartimaeus trilogy: The amulet of Samarkand.* New York: Hyperion Books.

Tolkien, J.R.R. (1954). *The lord of the rings: The fellowship of the rings.* London: Allen & Unwin.

Tolkien, J.R.R. (2001). *The hobbit.* New York: HarperCollins. (Original work published 1937)

Ursa, A. (2006). *The shadow thieves.* New York: Atheneum.

Wiesner, D. (2001). *The three pigs.* New York: Clarion Books.

Williams, M. (2004). *The golden hour.* New York: Abrams.

Chapter 20

On Writing:
One Writer's Perspective

Penny Colman

I wrote for years before I was brave enough to think about how I did what I did—how I got my ideas; how I did my research; how I wrote articles, essays, stories, and books.

Brave, you may wonder? Yes, brave, I reply, because I was afraid that by analyzing and articulating my process I would lose it. Poof!—there goes the magic spell that makes me a writer.

So what made me take the risk and begin to examine my process? There are three reasons: First, I discovered that many authors wrote and talked about their writing and I love to read their books. Second, I discovered that people were curious about my process; they—including children—asked questions, and I could never *not* answer a child's question (Where do you get your ideas? How long does it take to write a book? How do you do research? How do you do interviews?). Third, several years after I started writing full-time, a friend made a helpful comment. This occurred while I was writing *Rosie the Riveter: Women Working on the Home Front in World War II* (1995a). My friend's comment had to do with my beginning the book with the recollections of Dot Chastney, who was a child during World War II. Although I knew that Dot was a key ingredient in how I structured the book, I could not articulate why. That is when my friend observed, "Dot takes the reader by the hand and draws the reader into the story," and I realized, in a flash of insight, "Yes, of course!"

That exchange prompted me to reflect more on how I used Dot, and it resulted in my article for *Social Science Record* (Colman, 1998b), in which I wrote that Dot

would be my hand to the reader, a commentator of sorts
who moved the chronology and commented on daily life.
For example, I included Dot's memories of Pearl Harbor,
the Battle of the Bulge, the atomic bomb, as well as how
she had to wait for four years to get a two-wheel bicycle,
the effect of synthetic rubber in her favorite bubble gum,
and how she and her classmates knitted squares to make
afghans for the Red Cross to distribute. (p. 19)

As I continued to analyze my process, I was relieved that there was no
"poof." Happily, I discovered that I could examine my process and still be a
writer. I became aware that my writing has less to do with magic and more
to do with growing up with adults who wrote, including my maternal
grandfather; my father and mother; my mother's college roommate Eda
LeShan, a widely published writer; and my mother's friend Marian Potter
(1953), who wrote the children's book *The Little Red Caboose* (although I
did not remember this influence until recently when I read the book to my
granddaughter). My writing has to do with having an English teacher,
Meredith Coe, who loved grammar and delighted in good writing. It has to
do with taking two adult education courses in writing from top-notch
teachers: Laurie Peters and Roberta Roesch. It has to do with reading good
writing and practicing the skill and art of producing writing that is clear,
coherent, and compelling (the 3Cs).

Whenever I talk or write about my writing process, I hasten to point out
the following: (a) What works for me will not necessarily work for someone
else, and (b) my process is contrary to much of the conventional advice put
forth for writers. For example, I do not write every day. I do not keep a
journal. I like to write about what I do *not* know. When I am confronted
with a writing prompt, I freeze. I do massive amounts of conceptualizing,
structuring, and writing in my head. I do not write rough drafts. I write
and revise as I go forward. I have to have just the right title and the right
first sentence before I can start writing.

As a writer, I am always thinking about how to keep readers turning the
page. One of my strategies is to use a variety of literary elements. I focus on
diction, or the choice of words, and on transitions. I listen carefully to the
music—the tone, rhythm, melody, harmony, and timbre—of my writing.
The opening sentence of *Rosie the Riveter* (1995a) is an example of all
three—diction, musicality, and transitions: "The summer between second
and third grade Dot Chastney had her first inkling that things weren't quite
right in the world" (p. 1). My focus on diction resulted in my selection of the
key word in that sentence—*inkling*—the brain-tickling, attention-catching
word; the word that adds the music, specifically the rhythm, to the sentence.
The rest of the sentence "that things weren't quite right in the world" is a

foreshadowing transition to my writing about the outbreak of World War II in Europe.

Here are some examples of three other literary elements or devices: telling details, providing a sense of place, and using action to convey information. The following examples are from my (2006) essay about Louise Boyd, an Arctic explorer. A telling detail is Boyd's comment that she always "powders her nose before going on deck, no matter how rough the seas" (p. 17). A sense of place is provided by the following description of the ice (itself a main character in the essay) that Boyd saw when she traveled to

> Spitsbergen, an Arctic island northwest of Greenland, and to the edge of the pack ice, a jumble of massive hunks, and blocks, and piles of ice. Ice that forms in the polar basin and gets carried southward by the ocean currents. Ice that for much of the year forms barriers around the thousands of islands in the Arctic region. Ice that can crush a ship that stays too long as winter is settling in." (pp. 9–10)

Action is used to convey information about one of Boyd's expeditions in the following example:

> They met the ice—dense, heavy ice and floes, some of which had fifteen-foot-high hummocks—on July 12. It took them fourteen days to bump, push, pull, wiggle, and dynamite a way through it. At times, they could see the coast of Greenland, but their progress was "a tantalizing game of ice-pack tag, a sort of hide-and-seek with the coast." (p. 22)

I have been a full-time writer since October 1, 1987, one month after my 43rd birthday. That was also the year my eldest son graduated from high school and his twin brothers entered their senior year. I started as a journalist and wrote research-based nonfiction articles and essays for magazines and newspapers for adults. I also wrote nonfiction articles and fiction stories for children's magazines. As a journalist, I learned that every word counts. For example, if a magazine editor wanted a piece that was 1,000 words long, it had to be 1,000. Once I had an assignment to write a piece with 450 words and I sent it to the editor with 451. "Penny," she said when she called, "You've got to get rid of that extra word." And I did, although it wasn't easy, since I had already gotten rid of all the adjectives and adverbs, but it was excellent discipline. Making every word count taught me to think like a poet, a great skill for a prose writer. A more detailed account of my background and writing process can be found in my "Autobiography Feature" (2005a).

In 1992, my first two nonfiction books for young readers were published: *Breaking the Chains: The Crusade of Dorothea Lynde Dix* and *Spies!: Women in the Civil War*. In 2006, my 15th book for young readers was published: *Adventurous Women: Eight True Stories About Women Who Made a Difference*. In between, I have written books about the history of bathrooms, burials, strikes, and women in the United States. I have also written more biographies: Mary Harris "Mother" Jones, a legendary labor leader (1994b); Frances Perkins, the pioneering secretary of labor of the United States (1993d); Fannie Lou Hamer, a bold civil rights activist (1993a); and Madam C. J. Walker, a businesswoman and philanthropist (1994a). Currently I am working on three books: one about the true history of Thanksgiving; a second about the friendship between two champions of women's rights, Elizabeth Cady Stanton and Susan B. Anthony; and a third about women's fierce fight for the right to vote.

Where do I get my ideas? My one-word answer is *everywhere*. Those of you who have read my preface in *Toilets, Bathtubs, Sinks, and Sewers: A History of the Bathroom* (1994c) know that I got the idea for that book during a white-water raft trip down the Colorado River through the Grand Canyon. Those of you who have read my preface in *Corpses, Coffins, and Crypts: A History of Burial* (1997b) know that an editor wrote me a letter asking me to write a book on that subject. As for *Adventurous Women* (2006) it came out of a luncheon meeting with an editor who wanted me to write a book about women's history, and I proposed writing about adventurers. A discussion with inservice teachers who were taking a class I was teaching at Queens College inspired my forthcoming book *Thanksgiving: The True Story* (in press).

There are three aspects of my writing process: mechanical, cognitive-emotional, and interactive. They dance from start to finish—sometimes alone, sometimes in tandem, sometimes all together. Here are the highlights of each aspect.

The mechanical aspect includes a supply of mechanical pencils, paper, note cards, and file folders; my computer and Internet connection; my home office, with its many books and other source material; a puzzle and a mystery (I can take breaks without losing my focus by putting a piece or two in a puzzle or reading a page or two of a mystery); and music (I write each book to music). Every book gets its own plastic box, with a rim for holding file folders, and a three-ring binder. The box is for storing research material. The three-ring binder is for storing the pages of the manuscript as I finish each one. This chapter does not require a box, but it does have a three-ring binder—a red one—that at this point holds six manuscript pages.

The cognitive-emotional aspect of my writing process is about feeling safe enough to do deep thinking. This means that I know I will not be interrupted unless I choose to be. I spend huge amounts of time thinking. I think about "What's my point? Is my point clear? Do I care enough about the project to carry me through the hard work of writing?" I think about structure. I think about what I need to know and how I am going to find out about it. I think about diction, or my choice of words. I think about transitions. I think about how to keep the reader turning the page. (Students who are being taught to write typically do not get much, if any, practice with thinking, an essential part of worthwhile writing.)

The interactive aspect involves two activities, research and writing; the research is much more interactive than the writing. Actually, I rarely interact with anyone about my writing until I have produced the best writing I can. Then I seek constructive feedback. I give my manuscript to a friend, colleague, or family member for feedback. Then I send it to the editor and enter the interactive process of line editing and copyediting.

When I do research, I interact with anyone and everyone who is or might be a source of expertise, material, information, or insights. For my Thanksgiving book, I gathered information through a survey that I sent to former students, old friends, and new friends. I also contacted two groups of people I did not know: graduates of a college I attended and members of a professional nonfiction writers' association. The response rate was an amazing 53%.

In addition to doing text research, I do my own picture research, a time-consuming but essential endeavor that involves locating vivid, unusual, and interesting images, ordering prints, getting permissions, writing captions, and cuing the images into the text. I have also taken photographs for my books, including the cover photograph and most of the 131 photographs in *Corpses, Coffins, and Crypts* (1997b) and a number of the photographs in *Adventurous Women* (2006).

At what point do I do the picture research, I have been asked—before or after I write the text? Simultaneously, I answer. That is because I am a very visual writer, and I immerse myself in relevant images while I write. For example, while writing about Louise Boyd, an Arctic explorer, I surrounded myself with images of Arctic ice. I tracked down a picture of the flower that Mary Gibson "fell in love with" before I wrote that she was "in love with a flower, *Linnaea borealis,* a tiny, usually pink, bell-shaped flower borne in pairs (hence its common name, Twinflower) atop delicate stems that rise above a cluster of evergreen leaves" (p. 27). I drove to Los Angeles to visit and photograph the Biddy Mason Memorial before I wrote that "I stepped into an exquisite, narrow, vest-pocket park. . . . To my right, I saw a long, black wall with ten gray granite panels" (p. 133).

To select visual images for the text, I consider three elements: the visual narrative; the relationship of each image to the text; and the overall aesthetic of the text, the images, and the book design. Each image I select serves a particular purpose: it augments or clarifies the text, adds emotion, elicits curiosity, adds complexity or nuance, provides evidence, or creates a particular aesthetic. Visually, I think about each book thematically or from a particular point of view.

For example, for *A Woman Unafraid: The Achievements of Frances Perkins* (1993d), I went to great lengths to find pictures that showed an energetic, self-assured Frances Perkins who cared about workers, because early in my writing research I was struck by the mismatch between the Perkins whom I was discovering and the frequently reproduced photographs of her in which she seems passive and disconnected. I was thrilled to discover the picture of Perkins visiting shipyard workers in California that shows her standing shoe-deep in mud, her body stretched over a puddle, her hand holding the worker's muddy glove, and with a smile on her face (p. 78).

For my book *Where the Action Was: Women War Correspondents in War World II* (2002), I included photographs taken by war correspondents: Margaret Bourke-White, Toni Frissel, Lee Miller, and Dickey Chapelle. I also included images of their newspaper and magazine articles. These, of course, are all primary source documents, as are the illustrations in all my books, including *Rosie the Riveter* (1995a), which features posters, cartoons, a page from a ration book, an advertisement, a letter, and pictures of children and of women war workers.

Since 1990, I have focused on writing nonfiction. Before that I wrote both fiction and nonfiction. In fact, my first two children's books were fiction—*I Never Do Anything Bad* (1988) and *Dark Closets and Noises in the Night* (1999a)—and I wrote a number of fiction stories, including my favorites, *Storm* (1990b) and *Really Red Hair* (1991c) for children's magazines. Writing fiction, especially fiction with a sense of humor, was great fun. I loved making up stories and characters.

Why, then, do I write so much nonfiction for young readers? In my article "Nonfiction Is Literature, Too" (1999), I recounted how I, a nonfiction lover and writer, moved from innocence to disbelief to indignation as I realized that fiction dominates K–12 classrooms and curricula. In a speech I gave (2004) entitled "Hooked on Nonfiction: How About You?" I coined the word *anti-nonfictionism* to describe the all-too-common state of affairs in schools across America. I described how anti-nonfictionism manifests itself and discussed how fiction came to dominate classrooms and curricula. I asserted the following: Nonfiction literacy matters!

Nonfiction material is the crucible within which readers can gain the skills that enable them to identify and assess made-up and factual material; these are skills that are vital to making sound decisions in all arenas of life—skills that are antidotes to gullibility and essential for informed and active citizenship. Nonfiction is the language of ordinary things—laws, tests, reports, letters, documents—and of extraordinary things, such as the Declaration of Independence and the Constitution, of Abraham Lincoln's Gettysburg Address and Elizabeth Cady Stanton's Declaration of Sentiments. Nonfiction is the currency with which public policies are enacted, societal needs are discussed, cultural aesthetics are defined, life lessons are conveyed, and historical narratives are transmitted. It is the currency with which matters of war and peace are decided. It is the stuff of everyday life. Nonfiction is here, there, and everywhere.

I think it is important that women write nonfiction because the majority of visible nonfiction writers are men. If you doubt that, quickly list the nonfiction authors for young readers who first come to your mind. When I ask people to do that, a typical list includes Seymour Simon, Jim Arnosky, Russell Freedman, James Cross Giblin, Jim Murphy, Steve Jenkins, and Gail Gibbons. As for writers of national general interest magazines for adults, Ruth Davis Konigsberg (Seligson, 2005) reported that the ratio of male to female writers is 525 to 170. I checked Konigsberg's Web site (www.WomenTK.com) on July 9, 2006, and discovered that the male-to-female ratio was 1,157 to 391. Another study (Seligson, 2005) found that during one week, only 12% of the front-page articles in *The New York Times* were written by women. What explains the dominance of male nonfiction writers? Perhaps it is because nonfiction is rooted in authority and expertise and universality, all of which are culturally ascribed to men. If you already read nonfiction by women, read even more. If you do not read it, get started!

Since 2001, I have been teaching college and graduate courses in nonfiction literature to preservice and inservice teachers. When I ask for definitions of nonfiction, I get a range of answers. Fiction is fake, and nonfiction is not, say some teachers. Other teachers say that fiction is not real and nonfiction is real. There are teachers who define fiction as based on imagination and nonfiction as based on facts. I also hear that nonfiction requires research and fiction does not. Frequently teachers assert that fiction is read for pleasure and nonfiction is read for information.

All these definitions are misleading. For example, thinking that fiction is fake or not real undermines the verisimilitude that many fiction authors strive to achieve. It is also misleading to pair imagination with fiction because that dismisses the role of imagination in nonfiction. "I began to write from the imagination, but I did not write fiction," Le Anne Schreiber (1996) said about writing her memoir *Light Years*. "It took all the imagination I had to try to find words that were faithful to the complexities, contradictions, and subtleties of being alive, sentient, irreducibly particular" (p. 7). Biographer Leon Edel (1984) noted, "I'm using one kind of imagination and a novelist uses a different kind. . . . My imagination is used in finding a structure and form" (p. 10).

As for the issue of research it depends on the project. Some nonfiction requires very little research (e.g., I am doing very little research for this chapter), and some fiction requires a great deal.

Marguerite Henry (1947) did considerable research for her realistic fiction *Misty of Chincoteague*. "She talked with everyone that had a pony all over the island," recalled Jeanette Beebe, the owner of Misty. Henry (1965) used Beebe as the model for a character in *Stormy—Misty's Foal* (Mooar, 1997, pp. 1–6).

The novelist John Jakes (McKinney, 1998) spends half his time on research: "Even when the writing starts, I'm always looking back and referring to my research notes. Looking up things goes hand in hand with the writing process. The research never really stops" (p. 29).

Designating fiction as reading for pleasure and nonfiction as reading for information miseducates students about what to expect from fiction and nonfiction. Many students derive pleasure from reading nonfiction materials, including video game instructions and books about dinosaurs. Many fiction books convey information. Through *Julie of the Wolves* and her many other fiction books, Jean Craighead George (1972) conveys information about nature and ecosystems along with information about a wolf pack, falcons, owls, weasels, foxes, prairie dogs, alpine tundra, and tropical rain forests.

When thinking about definitions, I kept asking myself what is the essence of the difference between fiction and nonfiction. Both can have facts and information. Both can employ imagination. Both can provide pleasure. As a writer, I asked myself, what is the difference in terms of what I can or cannot do? The answer is that in fiction, I can make up material, but in nonfiction, I cannot. That insight led me to these definitions: Nonfiction is writing about reality (real people, places, events, ideas, feeling, things) in which nothing is made up. Fiction is writing in which anything can be made up (Colman, 2005c).

I categorize books that are labeled nonfiction (or "juvenile literature" in the Library of Congress schema) but that nevertheless contain made-up material (e.g., *The Magic School Bus Explores the Senses* by Joanna Cole, 1999) as hybrid books. Carol Avery (1998a), an elementary school teacher, and her students use the word *faction* for such books. Other teachers call them blended books.

In my books for young readers I specialize in what I call *historical nonfiction*, a genre that I think should be as familiar and popular as historical fiction. And why not? Readers are always asking, "Is this true?" "Did this really happen?" Think of their reaction when you respond, "Yes!" Think of the conversation you can have about people who really lived, events that really happened, objects that really existed, ideas that really mattered.

Adventurous Women (2006) is the 11th book featuring historical women that I have written in 14 years. I have also written articles and essays and a curriculum featuring women. I written so much about women because there are so many fabulous women to write about, women whose commitment and courage and contributions are integral to the history of every person, family, community, and country, and, indeed, of the whole world!

I also write about women because they are all too often marginalized or trivialized or ignored. For example, in movies made for children, a recent study (Kelly & Smith, 2006) of 101 widely viewed G-rated films released between 1990 and 2004 found the following:

> There are three male characters for every one female character; fewer than one out of three (28 percent) of the speaking characters (both real and animated) are female; fewer than one in five (17 percent) of the characters in crowd scenes are female; more than four out of five (83 percent) of the films' narrators are male. (p. 3?)

In a study I did (2005b) I found that female characters constitute only 15 percent of the main characters in Newbery, Orbis Pictus, and Sibert award-winning nonfiction books. The imbalance is apparent regardless of whether the author is female or male. Although it is impossible to attribute this discrepancy to a single reason or cause, consideration should be given to the possible roles played by publishers and editors, reviewers, award committees, writers, librarians, and teachers. For example, publishers typically publish books that feature women during National Women's History Month in March, thus possibly contributing to the belief that books about women have limited appeal or use. In addition, a March publication is not optimal for the award-decision process.

As for award committee members, they might favor books that feature male characters over those that feature females for any number of reasons, including the perception that men's stories are inherently more important, more interesting, more exciting, or more worthy than women's stories. Librarians may skew their purchases toward award winners and unwittingly reinforce the publishers' decisions to continue prioritizing those types of books.

Because women's speech was restricted throughout much of American history, I make sure that women's voices are an integral part of all my books. I described what I look for in my article *On Writing Labor History* (1997a):

> In selecting voices, I look for quotations that make something happen—move the narrative, spark insight, evoke feelings, amplify ideas, inspire action, illuminate personalities, flesh out facts, and/or provide life lessons or good role models. A good example of the life lesson/role model function of quotes are the words of Dolores Huerta in *Strike! The Bitter Struggle of American Workers from Colonial Times to the Present* (1995): "One thing I've learned as an organizer and activist is that having tremendous fears and anxieties is normal. It doesn't mean you should not do whatever is causing the anxiety; you should do it." (p. 70)

At this point, it is time for me to stop writing about writing and to turn my attention to the three books that I am currently committed to creating. These are books that I am eager to write because I am curious; because I feel a sense of responsibility to tell the whole story, the real story; and because I hope that my passion for nonfiction and for history, especially social history and women's history, is contagious.

References

Avery, C. (1998a). Nonfiction books: Naturals for the primary levels. In R. Bamford & J. Kristo (Eds.), *Making facts come alive: Choosing quality nonfiction literature, K–8.* Norwood, MA: Christopher-Gordon.

Colman, P. (1997a, Winter). On writing labor history. *Organization of American Historians' Magazine of History,* pp. 17–19.

Colman, P. (1998, Summer). On writing *Rosie the riveter: Women working on* the home front in World War II. *Social Science Record, 35,* 15–19.

Colman, P. (1999, Summer). Nonfiction is literature, too. *The New Advocate, 12* (3), 215–223.

Colman, P. (2004, January). *Hooked on nonfiction: How about you?.* Paper presented at the Children's Literature Conference, Ohio State University, Columbus.

Colman, P. (2005a). Autobiography feature. *Something About the Author, 160,* 49–68.

Colman, P. (2005b, June). *Where are the women? Gender in award-winning books for young readers.* Paper presented at the Berkshire Conference on the History of Women, Scripps College, Claremont, CA.

Colman, P. (2005c). *Writing, selecting and teaching children's literature: A dynamic model.* Paper presented at the Presidential Roundtable, Queens College, City University of New York, Flushing.

Edel, L. (1984). *Writing lives: Principia biographica.* New York: Norton.

Kelly, J., & Smith, S. L. (2006, February). *Where the girls aren't: Gender disparity saturates G-rated films.* A Research Brief Commissioned by the Jane Program at, Dads & Daughters Conference, Duluth, MN.

McKinney, D. L. (1998, February). John Jakes: "I'll never stop." *Writer's Digest,* pp. 26–30.

Mooar, B. (1997, November). Marguerite Henry wrote "Misty of Chincoteague." *The Record,* p. L-6.

Schreiber, L. A. (1996). *Light years.* New York: Lyons & Buford.

Seligson, H. (2005, December). One by one, women count bylines. *Women's eNews.* Available online at www.womensenews.org

Children's Books and Short Stories

Cole, J. (1999). *The magic school bus explores the senses* (B. Degan, Illus.). New York: Scholastic.

Colman, P. (1988). *I never do anything bad.* Mahwah, NJ: Paulist Press.

Colman, P. (1990b, September). Storm. *Cricket,* pp. 62–67.

Colman, P. (1991b). *Dark closets and noises in the night.* Mahwah, NJ: Paulist Press.

Colman, P. (1991c, July). Really red hair. *U*S*Kids: A Weekly Reader Magazine,* pp. 14–16.

Colman, P. (1992a, 2007). *Breaking the chains: The crusade of Dorothea Lynde Dix.* Cincinnati, OH: Betterway Books.

Colman, P. (1992b). *Spies!: Women in the Civil War.* Cincinnati, OH: Betterway Books.

Colman, P. (1993a). *Fannie Lou Hamer and the fight for the vote.* Brookfield, CT: Millbrook Press.

Colman, P. (1993b, September). Girls and sports. *Sports Illustrated for Kids,* pp. 50–59.

Colman, P. (1993c). *101 ways to do better in school.* Mahwah, NJ: Troll.

Colman, P. (1993d). *A woman unafraid: The achievements of Frances Perkins.* New York: Atheneum.

Colman, P. (1994a). *Madam C. J. Walker: Building a business empire.* Brookfield, CT: Millbrook Press.

Colman, P. (1994b). *Mother Jones and the march of the mill children.* Brookfield, CT: Millbrook Press.

Colman, P. (1994c). *Toilets, bathtubs, sinks, and sewers: A history of the bathroom.* New York: Atheneum.

Colman, P. (1994d). *Women in society: United States of America.* New York: Marshall Cavendish.

Colman, P. (1995a). *Rosie the riveter: Women working on the home front in World War II.* New York: Crown.

Colman, P. (1995b). *Strike!: The bitter struggle of American workers from colonial times to the present.* Brookfield, CT: Millbrook Press.

Colman, P. (1997b). *Corpses, coffins, and crypts: A history of burial.* New York: Holt.

Colman, P. (2000). *Girls: A history of growing up female in America.* New York: Scholastic.

Colman, P. (2002). *Where the action was: Women war correspondents in World War II.* New York: Crown.

Colman, P. (2006). *Adventurous women: Eight true stories about women who made a difference.* New York: Holt.

Colman, P. (in press). *Thanksgiving: The True Story.* New York: Holt.

George, J. (1972). *Julie of the wolves.* New York: Harper & Row.

Henry, M. (1947). *Misty of Chincoteague.* New York: Macmillan.

Henry, M. (1965). *Stormy—Misty's foal*. New York: Macmillan.

Potter, M. (1953). *The little red caboose*. New York: Little Golden Books.

On Poetry and the Middle Eastern Experience: An Interview with Naomi Shihab Nye

Susan S. Lehr

Susan: I thought we could start by talking about your childhood, and what stories you heard about your family and your father's homeland.

Naomi: Childhood was a very precious time for me. I felt extremely attached to it even as it was happening. That is something I have contemplated as I get older, because many people I know say their childhoods were occasionally pleasurable, but they couldn't wait to grow up. In my case, though there were rugged aspects—my mother suffered from chronic depression, there was never any extra money, things that make a child a little nervous along the edges—it was just so precious to have the continual acute awareness, wonder, and giant curiosity of spirit, that I felt stricken that I would have to depart those early days. I did not want to grow up, become a teenager, or even worse, an adult. Adulthood had little to recommend it. So I've thought about all that for years now. Was the part of my brain that would make me a poet so engaged in reverie that the prospect of becoming a literal, schedule-oriented adult was just disgusting to me? What was it, exactly?

I was fascinated by mixtures of cultures—not only in my house, but in the world. My best friends on my street were French Canadian and Italian American. I knew no other Arab-American kids as a child. My father certainly knew many Arabs, but we didn't seek out families who were just like ours. My parents were ecumenical in all their tastes. My German-American grandparents (my mother's family) lived near us when I was growing up. Her relationship with them was loving, but they didn't bless her marriage

and were a little stand-offish from her artistic temperament and her willingness to cross borders. They were very straitlaced Missouri-Synod Lutherans.

Susan: That's my background—long ago. It's not what I am currently.

Naomi: Oh my! How fascinating! So you know about that strain. Well, my
mother rejected it at the time of going to art school. She had a full scholarship to Washington University in the great heyday of that university's art
school, when people like Philip Guston and Max Beckmann were teaching
there. She was a very gifted artist. Luckily for her children, she was always
open-minded—toward people of different backgrounds, various spiritual
strands. I guess she would have been considered way ahead of her time, a
New Age mom, interested in principles of natural health and organic foods
back in the 1950s, when those things weren't so popular. No matter how
little money we had, we were going to attend the live production of *Raisin
in the Sun*, we were going to the symphony, we went to art museums every
Sunday afternoon, we were going to the lectures on King Tut.

Susan: What an amazing childhood!

Naomi: It *was* very amazing. So it wasn't just that my father was an Arab. A
mother's willingness to expose her kids to so many intriguing cultural things
gave me more than I can say. Because she had been kept in a narrow little
crevasse as a child, she wanted us to have another kind of childhood. I always felt a sense of wide horizons, but I didn't see the Middle East for my
first 14 years. Our home had a strong emphasis on literacy, reading, writing. Both my parents cared very much about language. I still can't beat
them at Scrabble. They were sticklers for the proper use of language. If our
mom heard someone use bad grammar on a television show, she would
write the show a letter and correct them and urge them to be grammatical
in the future. She wouldn't let me watch *Mighty Mouse* because it was too
violent. Can you imagine? It was a conscious household. The older I get, the
more I'm grateful for that. Going to the library, reading so many books,
having so many books, newspapers, and good magazines in the house all the
time was critical. My sense of wealth connected to how much we had to
read. Writing was naturally connected.

Susan: What about your father?

Naomi: My father's Arabness was woven into our lives—in the delicious
food we ate, his little sayings and philosophies, the stories that he told us so
exquisitely. To this day he remains one of the greatest storytellers I'll ever
know. He has a memoir coming out from Syracuse University Press, *Does
The Land Remember Me?*, and is writing another book of stories in Arabic
right now.

Susan: What kinds of stories did he tell you?

Naomi: Well, the famous Joha stories—the wise fool, the iconic figure who appears in folktales all over the Arab world. In some countries he's known as Nasser Eddin.

Susan: Yes, I've heard of that—the "noodlehead" strand of stories.

Naomi: He's very beloved, he's kooky, he's nonviolent. He's the comic who's in the margins, an eyewitness to daily life who is always making wisecracks, or little odd wise remarks, that suddenly spin everything into a different light. I don't know, I wonder sometimes what could this have done for our government if it had taken a weeklong course in the wisdom and mysticism of Joha before it invaded Iraq, what would this have done to its sense of who these people are, what their humor is? I'm so haunted by the loss of the consciousness of Middle Eastern humor, which is so profound, versus the tragedies in the headlines these days. I tell kids that the Middle East is generous, it's hospitable, and it's very, very funny. None of this is being transmitted. Can you just bulldoze over a whole reality?

In my book called *You and Yours*, which came out in 2006 from BOA, I have a poem called "Johnny Carson in Baghdad." I was thinking how, when the Persian Gulf War happened, Johnny Carson was still alive. What would it have done if we could have sent one of our icons of humor to a region that really responds to humor? With all the troubles and all the fundamentalists, humor is still something that binds people. If we had been able to communicate through humor, what would that have done?

When we were growing up, we knew our father was a refugee. We knew his family had lost its home during the Arab-Israeli war of 1948. They lost their money in the bank, they lost their Jerusalem lives, they were booted out. They went to a village where they had relatives and where they happened to own an ancient house, thank God, so they never went to a refugee camp. This was the only house I ever knew as my grandmother's home. We were always quizzing our father to tell us more about what happened, please—he dropped wisps and tidbits. It pained him to speak of it all. We would ask questions like "How did your father feel when he lost everything he worked for?" I remember my mom not wanting us to press too deeply. Here he was, trying to make a new life in the United States, to be positive, not to be bitter. So there was something mysterious about the injustices when I was very little.

As we got older, our father was often invited to speak at churches because he was a very good speaker. Especially around Christmas, this native of Jerusalem would speak about the Holy Land; he gave a beautiful talk, about the mixed city of Jerusalem that he had known early in his life, when his neighbors were Jewish, Greek, Armenian, Palestinian Muslims, Palestinian Christians, priests from Europe—all living together in the Old City of

Jerusalem. My dad's own decision at a young age was that, even though his family was Muslim, he did not want to be a practicing Muslim, which fascinated me as a child. I'd heard my mother's stories about how she was dragged to Sunday school and felt proud of my dad for being able to stand up for his own secular leanings. Even when he was very little, he told his parents, "I respect Islam. I'm glad you're Muslim. I like the traditions and the practices, but I don't want to fast; I don't want to pray five times a day; I don't ever want to go on a pilgrimage." And they said, "Okay, that's fine. Just love God and love other people and respect everyone." So when my father spoke in churches, it was interesting when Christians held themselves up as the only open-minded religion. My father would say, "Well, I don't think so—it all depends on who's practicing it." I was interested in how delicate he was about never wanting to offend anyone. As a child, he used to march with the pilgrims to Bethlehem at Christmastime. He liked their hymn-singing.

He made a distinction between Jews and Zionists. He was also clear about Jews and Arabs being cousins, being from the same Semitic roots. My Jewish friends have always loved my dad.

Susan: You've written something about how love means you breathe in two countries?

Naomi: Maybe more than two countries—many countries. We're all going to need to connect with the other, whoever that other might be. I was also fascinated as a child by segregation—when I was growing up, we didn't have Black kids in our school, but we had all these other kids from mixed cultures. I knew where the Black school was, and I didn't understand why we didn't get to know those kids. So I took a job when I was 11 on a farm that exists to this day, picking berries. All the other berry pickers were Black boys who went to the other school. My father didn't understand why I wanted such a job. My mother understood perfectly. "She wants to know those kids," she said. Now when I go back to the neighborhood, it's completely integrated. That's the big difference. The school became the school I dreamed of. It's ironic to me, retrospectively—all my schools have become what I wanted them to be after I left them. The high school I graduated from here in Texas, which at the time was a big football school, became one of the great oases of art education in our city. I always wondered—where did "other" begin? My German grandfather was nervous about the Black population of St. Louis. His street was becoming a completely Black street at the time I was growing up. He would go to the public laundry at 3:00 in the morning so he could be the only person there. I knew this and thought, "So weird!" Consequently, I was obsessed by people like Langston Hughes, who was one of my favorite poets when I was 7 years old. I wanted to read Black writers. My mother loved Black music. We listened to spirituals in our house all the time at top volume.

Susan: It seems unusual that a child of 7 would love Langston Hughes. You must have been very well-read or been read aloud to as a child.

Naomi: Well, luckily, I also read other people at age 7, like William Blake and Emily Dickinson, thanks to a great second-grade teacher who is a legend to this day. Her name was Harriett Barron Lane. She was an elderly teacher when I had her, described in those days as "the teacher who won't retire." She marked us in great ways. She was a stern disciplinarian but an incredibly devoted lover of poetry. She really believed that poetry was at the center of the universe—through poetry, we could find out so many things we needed to know. Her curriculum was completely poetry-based.

I had already fallen in love with poetry. In my preschool days and in the first grade, when I started writing poems myself, I had already recognized that poetry had something strong for me. In the first poems my mother read to us when we were little, before I could read, I could identify a poem by the fact that it sat in the center of the page and there was space around it. I can remember telling her, "Read that again," and she would, because it was a poem, it was short; she could read it more than once before bed. I loved the resonance of the language in poems. I loved the way that a poem left you floating or drifting somewhere. Years later I would read that Carl Sandburg says that a good poem leaves something happening in the air after it's over.

By the time I entered Mrs. Lane's class, I was a minor devotee. Here was a teacher surrounded by poetry books, who had us writing a poem on the blackboard every Monday. It could be by a famous beloved poet, or we could write one ourselves. She'd have us come up to the front of the class, recite the poem, and tell something about why we selected or wrote it. So this turned us all into detectives for poetry. She said she would teach us not to mumble—that was one of the goals of her class. She just loved words. When we would come to a hard word in a poem, a word like *radiate* or *splendor*, she would have us say it over and over again. If the poem was about butterflies, we'd start looking up interesting details about butterflies. There was a sense that the poem became ours the better we got to know it. By Friday, after each person had had a chance to go up and recite a poem, Mrs. Lane would ask us to copy (in our best printing, because we didn't know cursive yet) the poem we liked best that someone else had put on the board, not the one that we had put up. Then she taught us to make big books, sewing them together with giant needles and yarn, illustrating them—so we made four anthologies that year of our favorite poems.

I've said to other teachers: Notice how one teacher, with no extra expense, turned such young and passionate students into writers, editors, public speakers, bookmakers, and poets ourselves. By the end of the year, most of us were writing our own original poems and realizing how much fun that was. It was really a miraculous and simple curriculum that she developed.

She never suggested that anything was above our heads. She never said, "Well you know, William Blake's a little hard for you. Why don't you go find another poet?" She would say, "Oh! William Blake! What a magnificent mind! Do you know that he was also an artist?" And she would look in her files and come in the next day with something by William Blake on a scrap of paper that she had saved from when she was in school 70 years ago. There was always a sense of richness and supplementary information; we were on the brink of discovering all these voices.

Years later, when I was in college, I took a William Blake course and an Emily Dickinson course, and I remember saying to the teachers, "You know, here we are analyzing these poems and doing all this research and writing fancy papers, but somehow I feel I was closer to Dickinson and Blake when I was 7 than I am now."

I never had another teacher at any level who loved poetry as much as Mrs. Lane did. Thank God, when she was 98 years old, I was able to thank her publicly in St. Louis at one of my first readings. I asked someone from the old neighborhood to find her, if she was still living. Somehow I knew she would be. My knees were knocking together, and I didn't want to mumble!

Susan: I'd like to talk a bit about *Sitti's Secrets* (1994). In other places you've talked about how important your grandmother is to you. And then you wrote this picture book about a grandmother, Sitti, in Arabic.

Naomi: I wrote that book during the Gulf War, when I was stricken by the thought of all the humble people of Iraq who might die in this military action of our country in Kuwait—all the innocent people who always die every time there's a military action somewhere. I wanted to write a book that was not primarily political at all but that does include a letter to the president by the little girl in the book. It's a testimonial to connections, how we're all connected in the world, at some recent point or in our long-ago histories—people on all sides of the earth. If we knew each other, we'd like each other. That girl in the book is not really me; I'm just imagining a young Arab American going to visit her grandmother for the first time and discovering that even though they don't speak the same language, there are little details of life they can share with gusto. I wanted it to be a two-way dynamic.

When the little girl feels the source of her life and her connection to her grandma, it's difficult for her to leave. Later she keeps looking up into the night sky and feeling how connected they still are—our family histories are their own constellations. I often ask in classes, "How many of you feel connected to people, maybe even people you've never met in another country, because of your own cultural heritage?" So many hands go up. Of course, in Texas, so many kids feel connected to Mexico. With all the immigration controversies going on now, it's haunting to think how our lives are nothing without connections. So when I wrote *Sitti's Secrets*, it was out of a sense of despair for all the innocents who would die. Certainly that has only been underscored endlessly during this current catastrophe in Iraq.

Susan: Please tell us about your grandmother.

Naomi: Well, my grandmother was a lover of peace, without any question. She wanted peace in the world. Shortly before her death at 106, someone was asking her how she felt about some round of peace talks and she said, adamantly, in Arabic, punching her own chest with her fist, "I never lost my peace inside." That idea—that peace is not some abstract concept we grant or take away from others, it's something we hold close to *ourselves*— has to guide the ways we live and everything we do. In the same way, democracy is not something we pour down from the sky; as Dr. Shireen Ebadi, the Nobel Prize winner from Iran, said recently when she spoke in San Antonio, "You don't give other people democracy by dropping cluster bombs on them." My grandmother used to say, "Good luck to all these men trying to make peace, but many of us have always had peace." Even though she had lost her own home, she believed that we must live in a spirit that is willing to be peaceful. That's not always easy to do.

My grandmother never committed an act of violence, and she would have been horrified by the fact that the perpetrators of the 9/11 crimes were Muslim. Her Islam was a peace-loving religion. I think the whole idea that politicians are the ones who make peace needs to be questioned— continually. I stand with whoever it was—some group of Middle Eastern women, I think— who said, "Peace is far too important to be left to politicians." Politicians aren't going to be able to *give* it to us, we have to declare it, seize it, live it, be it, make it, all the time—we citizens. With that in mind, how could we not be political? Politics is daily life.

Susan: In a letter you wrote to the [9/11] terrorists you said, "Poetry humanizes us in a way that news or even religion has a harder time doing. A great Arab scholar, Dr. Salma Jayyusi said, If we read one another, we won't kill one another." You really spoke from the heart in that letter.

Naomi: Well, that was written a week after September 11. I was in such a state of despair and shock, thinking about what a terrible injustice had been done to the reputation of an entire region—how many families had been devastated by the tragic loss of innocent loved ones in this country, of course, but also how a terrible shadow would be cast upon all immigrant children from the region, all people of Middle Eastern Arab background everywhere. This was something that was going to go on and on, that might never be resolved in our lifetimes. But my fury at the perpetrators of such crimes, their incredible selfishness—made me write that piece. I just had to

write it in that personal tone. To anyone who might be contemplating horrible acts—that's not how you get things done in the world. It's like taking a
thousand steps backward, reverting to Stone Age times. By the way, I do
have a bumper sticker here taped on my file cabinet that says, "War is ter-
rorism with a bigger budget."

Susan: How does that impact your own writing and how you decide what
you'll write?

Naomi: Well, I think we have to keep responding to what's going on out
there. I think it's important to send poems to the White House regularly or
to write e-mails to the White House regularly, even if young staffers are the
only ones reading them. It's important to write letters to the editor. I think
it's very important that, as citizens, we're constantly speaking out, saying,
"This is wrong! What our country is doing is absurd. It is wrong!"—if we
think it is, obviously. Some people seem to have a great deal of reluctance
and fear to speak out during these dark times. We're the writers, the speakers, the educators. I think every act of violence, whether sanctioned or
unsanctioned, is a betrayal of language. It boils down to that for me as a writer.
So I have to keep saying, "I feel betrayed as an American by the acts of my country." Without freedom of speech, who are we? People should be speaking out
more. Many of my cousins, out of economic necessity, have emigrated to the
United States. But there are still quite a few in the Middle East.

Susan: I remember when you said, "My heart will probably always belong to
the Middle East, travelwise."

Naomi: I long to be doing something useful over there. I wish that the
model of Neve Shalom–Wahat al-Salaam Peace Village in Israel—half Arab,
half Jewish; the wonderful, deliberate village of dialogue and positive col-
laborations—could spread like the "wildfire of peace" that Israeli poet
Yehuda Amichai yearned for. I love the work that [Palestinian Arab scholar]
Dr. Edward Said and [Israeli musician] Daniel Barenboim were doing—taking musicians into Ramallah, doing music education for kids. You know, if
we can't converse politically in language that ends up feeling satisfying to
our cause of living and working together, maybe we could do it through music, art, and culture. I have Arab-American writer friends who've gone and
done summer writing and art workshops with Palestinian kids in refugee
camps and community centers. I'd like to do that. Back in the 1990s I was
visiting a lot of universities over there—schools, orphanages, and so forth—
but I haven't lately. My great doubts about the 21st century have so far all
been confirmed. The 21st century has been very nasty so far. I don't look on
it fondly yet.

Susan: Have you seen any changes since you started writing poetry and books for children?

Naomi: I think there's more and more call for books that are humanity-based. I really believe in the innate wisdom of most people. Normally I think most human beings have big hearts. Most humans share similar basic desires, don't they? They want to be with family, to feel comfort and plea-sure, to come home and find that their tree is still their tree and their house still their house. None of us would be thrilled to find our property seized by anyone else or our neighborhood bombed for some abstract reason that an-other country had. One of my favorite quotes leading up to the Iraq War was when a Canadian said to the United States, "We'd like to come down and examine your weapons of mass destruction." I thought that was great!

There's more of a tendency these days for books that cross borders and represent us all us as human beings. I love the book by the Israeli writer Daniella Carmi (2000), *Samir and Yonatan*, in which she writes in the voice of a Palestinian boy. It won the Batchelder Prize a few years ago. The boys are hospital roommates and become friends, sort of reluctant friends, but very haunting, beautiful friends. It's a wonderful, unpredictable book, and I think it was quite risky that she writes in the voice of a Palestinian. She made a leap, and the voice is utterly believable. That's the kind of book we need. There's a memoir from Farrar, Straus & Giroux, I'm happy to say, written by a friend of mine, a beautiful young Palestinian writer named Ibtisam Barakat, called *Tasting the Sky: A Palestinian Childhood*. It's a deeply moving memoir about what happened to her family when she was growing up—their difficult attempt to maintain some semblance of regular life and joy in the midst of war and occupation. That it's being published by a mainstream publisher is wonderful news.

Susan: We haven't had that many books about Middle Eastern experiences.

Naomi: That's right. We could use more. However, if you check the offer-ings of Interlink Distribution, you will see how many there are that you haven't yet read. I think more and more publishers and editors are very open to books about the region, and they want them from various perspec-tives. My anthology of poems from the Middle East, *The Space Between Our Footsteps*, reprinted in a little paperback, *The Flag of Childhood* (2002), is being used by some schools now, and it makes me glad—this is a spectrum of voices that we should be listening to. These are ancient cultures and countries we keep hearing about in the news—how much do we know the voices of the real people there?

I try to read poems from Iraq in classes I visit. I started doing that dur-ing the Gulf War, and I've been doing it during this horrible Iraq War, which I think the teachers really appreciate. They want their students to know human voices writing about human subjects. I think of that as being quietly political. You're acknowledging that these people have voices and a right to live. I always say that when I read the poem "The Train of the Stars" by Iraqi poet Abdul-Raheem Saleh Al-Raheem, (Nye, 1998) that "The man who wrote this poem was a teacher in Baghdad; he had five children; let's hope he's still alive." We believe in human voices; we trust them; we want to know what they have seen and heard. I just met the children's book writer and illustrator Molly Bang a couple of weeks ago. We were at a children's literature festival sponsored by the fabulous Reading Reptile bookstore in Kansas City, and she was presenting from a book of hers, *Nobody Particular* (1980), that takes place in my state, Texas, along the coast, and it includes city and water issues within Texas, critical environmental issues. The book has a real hero, a woman activist named Diane Wilson. Here I am, living right next to the ongoing story, and I had never heard of this person before. It wakes you right up. How little we know about what is close to us.

Susan: And it's amazing how much you learn from a good children's book!

Naomi: I know! Molly Bang's book opened up a whole saga that's been going on for years right here in my backyard. Recently there was an op-ed piece in the Dallas newspaper written by a teenage girl, with the title: "I Really Don't Know Much About Iraq." I cut it out and took it to a high school where I was working that day and interestingly, a bunch of the kids had also cut it out and had it with them. The writer was admitting that when you're a teenager you wish your country wasn't in a war. You'd prefer to be having fun and thinking of frivolous things, but there's a nagging part of you that knows, as a responsible citizen, that you should be asking a lot of questions about what's going on and forming real opinions. If you're studying history in school, shouldn't you be studying the "history" you're living at that moment? We should *all* be asking a lot more questions and caring about the answers, it seems to me! I think *asking* has long been one of the central impulses of children's books. Becoming part of community, questioning what we know and don't know. I think that the world of children's books—politically, environmentally—is definitely more conscious than it was when many of us were growing up.

Susan: I so agree with that. There are such riches of books available on so many vital topics and in such a variety of genre and formats. What haven't I asked you, or what would you say to teachers who are sharing your books and poetry with children? Or what might you say to children themselves who are reading your works?

Naomi: Well, what would I say to teachers? I think that many teachers sometimes feel they have to be an expert on poetry before sharing it with their students. They don't. They just need to share poems they can be genuinely enthusiastic about. Some feel uncomfortable sharing poetry if it contains mystery or if there are variant possible interpretations. But that's how poetry wants to be! "What does this really mean?" is the question many of us were asked about poems we read in school, as if poems were subliminal coded messages. That's not quite as open-ended or inviting as "What does this make you think of?" or "Does anyone like this poem?" or "What do you like about it?" or "Where does it take you?" or "What questions do you ask after reading this poem?" or "What does it remind you of in your own life?" There are so many questions we can ask about poems that could engage *all* of us in different ways, rather than implying that there is only one right way to read a poem and that some people get it and some don't.

Susan: Those are the kinds of questions that rarely get asked. I don't remember ever being invited to give my personal interpretation of a poem until I got into my doctoral studies at Ohio State and took a poetry class with Charlotte Huck. I remember an undergraduate college class that was deadly. There was only one right answer. To this day poetry still makes me nervous!

Naomi: Absolutely. And it shouldn't. Teachers sometimes feel a little nervous about poetry because they were taught that it is tricky. They ask themselves, do I know what it really means? We can just say, "Does anyone like this poem?" Let the children guide you in their response to the poem and with a discussion of the poem. If we can do that, we will have more fun talking about the images, metaphors, ideas, connections, and leaps; it engages the students more. If three kids in a class can emphasize three different things in a poem after reading it, that's a good thing. That would make the poet happy.

A poem doesn't want everybody to come away with the same exact emphasis. A poem wants to engage us in dialogue, so if we talk about the poem, we talk with the poem. We talk about issues that are raised by the poem, as opposed to saying, "Okay, figure out what this really means. There's one right answer." That's not the way to teach poetry. So I try to encourage teachers to feel more comfortable with poetry, to have it read out loud more in their classes so students can hear it and find ways to model and shape their own writing. I think that's a critical part of it, that we encourage students to write in response to poems, to create their own parallel poems, or to be stimulated from a poem to another poem. That's much more meaningful than writing an analytical paper in another kind of language about a poem. I think that poems are happier and poets are happier if students are encouraged to model their own poems on existing poems. This is not plagiarism; this is inspiration.

When I went to visit the American Embassy School not long ago in Delhi, India, some of the kids had done this fantastic modeling exercise using my poems before I got there. They presented them to me—playing off of

"My Father and the Fig Tree." For example, they wrote poems like "My Grandfather and the Lemon Bush" or "My Uncle and the Mint Bed." Their poems were great, too. And their attitudes were, interested, compassionate, and loving, because they had been invited into their own experiences, not just into mine. It's an ongoing chain of images.

Susan: And do they all have to rhyme, Naomi?

Naomi (*laughing*): Never! Never, never, never! I strongly urge kids to write without rhyme, to open up, expand the possibilities of language, surprise themselves with noun-verb combinations, to know rhyme as one of the many devices of language but not the most crucial one, for goodness' sake, not the heart and soul. Unfortunately, if kids aren't exposed to open-form poems or free-verse poems—which are by far the way the majority of poems that have ever been written were composed—or if they are exposed to more interesting ways to use rhyme (like internal rhyme, occasional rhyme), then their worlds of language will open up. But unfortunately, if some teachers just share little cutesy rhyming poems, then you end up with kids who don't like writing, or who write all the wife-knife poems. Once when our son was little and I was getting ready to read him some poems, he said, "You don't have to read me any more poems that rhyme, Mom. Rhyming was okay till I was about 2. But I got over it." And I thought, "That's really good."

Susan: It's a generational thing in your family.

Naomi: After I had stopped reading to our son at bedtime (a beautiful, precious ritual), when he said, "Hey, by the way, I'm 13 or 14 now, I think I can read for myself!"—I started reading to him as his morning wake-up call. I read three poems every morning. I would march upstairs to his room, read him three poems, the first words out of my mouth every day—we wouldn't have a conversation about them or anything, but he would know, okay, now it's time to get up. I learned this from a farmer in Oklahoma. Selecting poems to read to someone else early in the morning was a peaceful and inspiring enterprise. I found myself reading American poets like W. S. Merwin, Robert Bly, Mary Oliver, and Denise Levertov; Shuntaro Tanikawa from Japan; Paul Durcan from Ireland; Norman McCaig from Scotland; Mahmoud Darwish and Yehuda Amichai from the Middle East.

I urge teachers to find poems they love, sneak them into that chaotic moment before they go home, read a poem to open or close the class, or invite students to read poems out loud regularly. Any way that we can share that kind of language and detail with one another is a good thing. I think that teachers should have fun with poetry; it should be a place of refuge for them. It should be a moment when they can take a deep breath, pause, and hear the words. Have confidence to put words out there and not always feel you have to explain them—just share them.

Susan: That's the big message, I think.

Naomi: Yes. Poetry is often so short we can sneak it in all the time. Well, a big hug to you, Susan. Thank you for letting me participate in this way. You've been very gracious. Good wishes to you and your mama.

Susan: Thank you, Naomi.

References

Bang, M. (1980). *Nobody particular.* New York: Holt.

Barakat, I. (2007). *Tasting the sky: A Palestinian childhood.* New York: Farrar, Straus & Giroux.

Carmi, D. (2000). *Samir and Yonatan.* New York: Scholastic.

Shihab, A. (2007). *Does the land remember Me?* Syracuse, NY: Syracuse University Press.

Nye, N. (1994). *Sitti's secrets.* New York: Simon & Schuster.

Nye, N. (2006). *You and yours.* Rochester, New York: BOA.

Nye, N. (1998). *The space between our footsteps.* New York: Simon & Schuster.

Nye, N. (2002). *The flag of childhood.* New York: Simon & Schuster.

Part IV

*Voices From the Field:
Issues of Literature
in the Classroom*

Bold New Perspectives: Issues in Selecting and Using Nonfiction

Janice V. Kristo, Penny Colman,
and Sandip Wilson

"Nonfiction was to me a smelly old textbook that described the habitats of pelicans in Florida." This was the first line of a poem by Shannon Viaggiano, a teacher, describing her insights about nonfiction. The poem continues:

> Is an author authentic?
> Is she writing the truth?
> If so, can you show me
> Well-researched proof?
>
> Nonfiction is everywhere
> Sharks, deserts, dinosaurs
> Native Americans
> Crocodiles, a praying mantis
>
> September is looming
> Can I be as passionate
> And teach what is real?

What is it about nonfiction that changed this teacher's opinion of it—from being bored by it to being passionate about it? How are words and phrases like *authentic*, *writing the truth*, *well-researched*, and *passionate* all linked with nonfiction? Why does learning about it matter? In this chapter we explore bold new terrain about nonfiction. We build the case that "non-fiction is everywhere. It is the stuff of everyday life—the infinite list of activities and duties and decisions and desires and feelings and fears and happiness. . . Nonfiction is there and here and everywhere" (Colman, 2004, p. 4).

We start by questioning and defining terminology—the use of *nonfiction* versus *informational* and how this gives rise to confusion in the field. Next, we describe misconceptions that prevail about nonfiction. We describe some of the concerns and challenges that nonfiction authors face in their research and writing. We also examine the process of how a national committee chooses award-winning nonfiction and look briefly at trends in writing non-fiction. Finally, we share ideas for teaching nonfiction and why it matters that we do teach it and do it well at all grade levels. We end the chapter with action steps for using nonfiction to its fullest and best capacity.

Defining Nonfiction: What's in a Name?

Inconsistencies abound in the field about what to label this genre. A survey of eight children's literature textbooks published between 2002 and 2007 re-vealed inconsistencies in the chapter titles that deal with nonfiction litera-ture. Three of the textbooks discuss nonfiction books under the chapter title "Nonfiction." The other five textbooks used the chapter title "Informational Books." This is also found in professional trade books and journal articles (see Duke & Bennett-Armistead, 2003; Hunt, 2005; Kristo & Bamford, 2004; Stead, 2006). As for awards, there is the Robert F. Sibert Informational Book Award and the Orbis Pictus Award for Outstanding Nonfiction for Children.

Colman (1999a) tracked the emergence of the term *informational* to 1972; At that time, Zena Sutherland coined the term *informational books* (that same year, Margery Fisher proposed *information book*) as another term for nonfiction books for children and young adults. Sutherland and Fisher never intended that the term would limit people's understanding of the complexity, richness, and literary nature of nonfiction. However, in time that is exactly what happened—the term got carried forth without the con-text and content of Sutherland's and Fisher's understanding of it. This is problematic, because the semantic association that most adults and young-sters make when they hear the term *information books* is encyclopedias or textbooks. The term does not readily trigger associations with the variety of nonfiction books—biographies, history, true adventure, science, sports, photographic essays, memoirs—that are available and accessible for chil-dren and young adults and that can be just as compelling, engaging, and beautifully written as good fiction.

The terms *information* and *informational* miseducate children and young adults about what to expect from fiction as well as nonfiction. Students are often not taught to look for information in fiction, despite the fact that many fiction books for children convey information that the author researched and, in some cases, included notes about. For example, in *Al Capone Does My Shirts,* Gennifer Choldenko (2004) conveys information about autism, about families dealing with an autistic child, and about what life was like for both prisoners and nonprisoners on Alcatraz Island in 1935. At the end of the book, there is an author's note about the information. Other examples are Mary Hoffman's (2003) *Encore Grace*, which deals with jealousy and death and a parent's remarriage, and Jean Craighead George's (1972) *Julie of the Wolves*, which conveys information about nature and ecosystems, a wolf pack, falcons, owls, weasels, foxes, prairie dogs, alpine tundra, and tropical rain forests (Colman, 2005a).

We believe that it is time for the field to reach consensus on a uniform definition. Given the above discussion of the limitations of the term *informational books*, we propose the exclusive use of the term *nonfiction*. Rybcyznski (2001) suggests thinking of nonfiction as "a positive thing unto itself" instead of as "a non-something" (p. 8). Gerard (1996) writes, "We lie a lot. . . . We don't mean to—not always. . . . So when we label a piece of writing nonfiction, we are announcing our determination to rein in our impulse to lie" (p. 5). Rosenthal (2006) asserts: "I've been drawn to nonfiction. . . . The word *nonfiction* beckoned me, with its self-assured first three letters. NON fiction. NON made-up. NON not true" (p. 15).

Here are some of the definitions currently in print:

- "Although it is difficult to pin down precisely what nonfiction is, its major purpose is to inform." (Mitchell, 2003, p. 326)
- "A genre created mainly to inform readers about a particular subject, issue, or idea." (Temple, Martinez, Yokota, & Naylor, 2002, p. 394)
- "Informational books are nonfiction and present current and accurate knowledge about something found in our universe." (Jacobs & Tunnell, 2004, p. 146)
- "Nonfiction—informational texts about the way things are." (Nodelman & Reimer, 2003, p. 128)
- "Nonfiction is the literature of fact—or the product of an author's inquiry, research, and writing." (Kristo & Bamford, 2004, p. 12)
- "The term *nonfiction* describes books of information and fact." (Galda & Cullinan, 2006, p. 261)
- "Books about subjects such as history, space, animals, plants, geography, and how things work." (Norton, 2007, p. 500)
- "For us, the real world is rich, fascinating, and compelling. Young kids know this, which is why furry caterpillars, sparkling rocks, and medieval knights sweep them away. Kids can't resist the real world." (Harvey & Goudvis, 2000, p. 118)

- "Nonfiction. Why don't we just call it Life?" (Tomie dePaola, in Stead, 2006, p. viii).

Colman (2005c) has discussed the issue of a definition from her own perspective as a writer of both fiction and nonfiction:

> In thinking about definitions, I kept asking myself what is the essence of the difference between fiction and nonfiction. Both can have facts and information. Both can have expository and narrative and descriptive writing. Both can express universal truths. Both can have literary devices. As a writer, I asked myself, what is the difference in terms of what I can or cannot do? The answer is: make up material. With fiction, I can. With nonfiction, I cannot. That insight led me to these definitions: Nonfiction is writing about reality (real people, events, ideas, feeling, things) in which nothing is made up. Fiction is writing in which anything can be made up. *Hybrid* is my term for books that are labeled nonfiction (or "juvenile literature" in the Library of Congress schema) *but* contain made-up material (e.g. *The Magic School Bus* series). (p. 9)

We put Colman's definition forth as one for the field to consider.

Next, we consider myths and misconceptions about nonfiction that have found their way into classrooms (Bamford & Kristo, 2000; Colman, 1999a, 2005c). Table 22-1 lists some of the more common misconceptions and a brief look at the realities and classroom implications for each.

Table 22-1. Myths About Nonfiction

Myth	Reality
Nonfiction is boring.	Some nonfiction can be boring, but so can some fiction.
	Children are interested in learning about life and everything in it! They're curious and want to learn. Many children cut "their literary teeth" on concept books about shapes, colors, numbers, reptiles, and trucks. Children love to have these books read and shared over and over.
	Caswell and Duke (1998) indicate that young children can read and write nonfiction. Research also supports that early experiences set a firm foundation for nonfiction reading in the later grades (Newkirk, 1989; Pappas, 1991).

Table 22-1. Myths About Nonfiction *(Continued)*

Myth	Reality
Boys prefer nonfiction more than girls do.	Pappas (1991) indicated that kindergartners of both genders like both genres—fiction and nonfiction—equally. Genuard (2005) found that fourth, fifth, and sixth grade boys and girls in her study liked nonfiction equally. She also found that fourth graders preferred nonfiction to fiction. Teachers we know report that gender differences disappear when their students have access to nonfiction that covers a wide range of topics. For example, sharing nonfiction books about the life cycles and habitats of animals appeals to most everyone.
Nonfiction is for skimming or dipping in and out of, not for reading from beginning to end.	Some nonfiction books can be skimmed, especially if the book is structured with subtopics or has an enumerative structure, or if the reader is knowledgeable about the topic and is looking for specific information. However, if the book is organized chronologically, or if the author is illustrating a theme or supporting a thesis, then the reader needs to start at the beginning and read to the end (Wilson, 2001). To read a nonfiction book, one must know the structure the author used as well as one's purpose for reading (Bamford & Kristo, 2000; Robb, 2004).
Nonfiction books are not "real" books or considered literature.	There are plenty of examples of *fiction* books that are boring, irrelevant, difficult, and guaranteed to turn off readers. Think of nonfiction books that have had a lasting impact on readers, such as *Anne Frank: The Diary of a Young Girl* (1995). Change the perception that nonfiction isn't literature by sharing and reading high-quality nonfiction books—ones that captivate listeners, provide interesting role models, and contain fascinating stories about life.
Nonfiction books only provide information.	High-quality nonfiction has the power to offer life lessons and to stimulate readers to think in different ways. There is also a great deal of nonfiction that has narrative, such as biographies and narrative nonfiction. Plan nonfiction displays as a way to advertise and introduce students to a variety of nonfiction.

Table 22-1. Myths About Nonfiction *(Continued)*

Myth	Reality
Nonfiction is not relevant.	Nonfiction offers role models and life lessons for students. Nonfiction engages young readers in topics they want to know about and in topics that relate to the world they experience. They are drawn to nonfiction when they might resist reading fiction (Caswell & Duke, 1998). Be selective in choosing good nonfiction. Weed out inaccurate and outdated books. This selection and weeding procedure also applies to fiction. Talk to students about criteria for selecting high-quality books for the classroom—strive for quality!
Nonfiction is too hard for kids to read and understand.	Some nonfiction contains complex concepts and topics, as some fiction also does. Teach students to successfully read challenging text by using read-alouds, shared reading, and guided reading to scaffold and support reading. (See Kristo & Bamford, 2004)
Nonfiction is devoid of an author's voice.	High-quality nonfiction writers have a distinctive, identifiable way of writing, just as high-quality fiction writers do. Some nonfiction writers include themselves and their experiences in their books. Colman (1997) does this in *Corpses, Coffins, and Crypts* and in *Adventurous Women: Eight True Stories About Women Who Made a Difference* (2006b), and so does Virginia Wright-Frierson in her books. Nonfiction books aren't limited to those that only list facts. Find many types of nonfiction books to share with your students so that they can listen to and read a variety of nonfiction writing. See Bamford and Kristo (2000) for a description of types of nonfiction. The variety of authors' voices from a range of nonfiction provides opportunities to hear rich language that authors use in expressing their ideas, arguments, and experiences in their writing.
Nonfiction is not aesthetic or creative.	Many book covers, such as for James M. Deem's (2005), *Bodies from the Ash: Life and Death in Ancient Pompeii*, show dramatic content and include chilling photographs that touch on topics in the book. Also, the design of the book, with photographs displayed prominently or as strategic sidebars, will engage readers and keep them turning pages. The aesthetic features of a book, such as design elements, contribute to engaging the audience for whom it is intended, such as Burleigh's (1991) *Flight: The Journey of Charles Lindbergh* and Colman's (1997) *Corpses, Coffins, and Crypts: A History of Burial*.

Table 22-1. Myths About Nonfiction *(Continued)*

Myth	Reality
Nonfiction is hard to find.	Nonfiction appears in many formats, from newspapers to magazines to all sorts of books—atlases, biographies, reference books, life-cycle books, identification books, and other specialized books. Become aware of the various types of nonfiction and see how many varieties and forms are available for today's readers of all ages. Access book lists from national organizations that offer good nonfiction suggestions, such as the National Council of Teachers of English. Go to the library yourself and browse through the nonfiction books and other material. Solicit recommendations from nonfiction-loving teachers and librarians.
Nonfiction reading does not help students learn how to write.	Nonfiction offers models for learning how to write nonfiction, which, after all, encompasses much of what students (and adults) have to write. Dissect a nonfiction writer's work and ask: How does this writer establish a point of view, use voice, create a sense of time, or use metaphor? Read a wide range of nonfiction and study how each piece is structured—how it begins and ends. Share lots of good nonfiction with students of all ages and invite them to look carefully at these books to talk about the craft of the writing, the visual information used, and the design and layout of the book. This careful study and talk influences how children will design and write their own nonfiction.
Kids won't read nonfiction. They'll only read fiction.	Just as many adults enjoy reading nonfiction, so do students of all ages. Teachers we know report that students happily read nonfiction when it is available. Make nonfiction books visible and accessible to kids in your classroom.

What Authors Say About Writing Nonfiction

Another area of misinformation is about what nonfiction authors do. For example, in various books and articles about nonfiction, the typical motive or purpose ascribed to nonfiction writers is that they write to provide information. But is that what nonfiction writers themselves say? Not according to our sampling. For example, in her book, *The Forbidden Schoolhouse: The True and Dramatic Story of Prudence Crandall and Her Students*, Jurmain (2005) says that her purpose was to tell an "extraordinary story" (jacket copy). For Colman (2004), it was a sense of responsibility and community that motivated her to write *Corpses, Coffins and Crypts: A History of Burial*

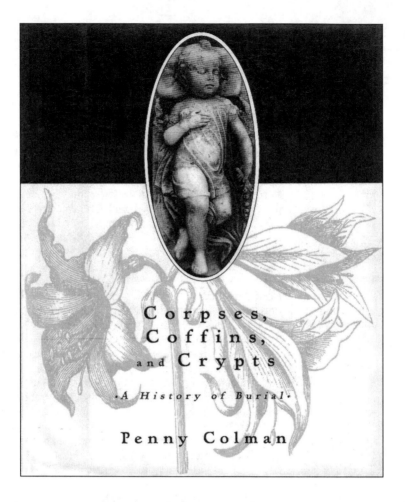

(1997) and weave in her own personal experiences. Jim Murphy (Vandergrift, retrieved July 7, 2006) "wanted readers to experience what it was like to see the fire approaching, hear its terrible roar, and feel the intense heat" in his book *The Great Fire* (1995). He specifically did not want his book to be "loaded with dry statistics and information." Montgomery (2004) takes astonishing risks in her field research to understand wildlife and is a zealous supporter and advocate of protecting endangered species.

Colman (1999a), who has written both fiction and nonfiction, concludes the following:

> Creating a high-quality nonfiction book is not for the faint-hearted because it is a challenging, complex, time-consuming, and intense experience. Many of us do extensive research, including finding illustrative material that has to be carefully coordinated with the text. We spend countless hours thinking about structure and discovering

> the narrative. We glue ourselves to our chairs for endless days as we craft our writing in a way that will keep readers turning the page. (p. 223)

Sid Fleischman (2006), biographer of Harry Houdini, states the following:

> I have been a fiction writer by choice and instinct for a long professional life. It has been a leap for me to tell the truth. In a delightful way, nonfiction is easier to write. The plot and characters are already served up, as joyful as breakfast in bed. But nonfiction has a harrowing downside. I could not invent new scenes or punch up old ones. As I was six years old when Houdini died, I couldn't ring him up to pin down some elusive detail. I was boxed in by the recorded past. I was unable to pluck Houdini's conversations out of thin air. (p. xi)

A challenge that authors face is the number of pages to allocate to material such as notes and sources. Colman wrestles with that issue in some of her books. She has had to make hard decisions because of a publisher's page limitations. In her book *Where the Action Was: Women War Correspondents in World War II* (2002), she had to decide whether to include follow-up material on the subject or use the space for endnotes. She chose to include the follow-up material because she decided that that would be more interesting and engaging for readers and motivate them to read more about the women.

The Business of Publishing Nonfiction

The business of publishing nonfiction is not for the faint-hearted. According to an executive editor at a major publishing company:

> Nonfiction is more expensive and time-consuming on all fronts. Straight fiction does not usually require photo placement and heavy design, extensive fact-checking, indexing, and often substantive changes in first proofs. Also, [nonfiction] books are more costly to produce because the paper stock needs to be better for photo reproduction, and this drives up the cost and price of the book, often to $20. We are very selective in whom we publish and what content we publish, given the stakes. (Personal communication, November 18, 2005)

The realities of a publisher's bottom line can affect everything, from the number of pages in a book, to the quality of paper stock, to the hiring of fact checkers, to the type of cover and the amount of promotion and marketing.

Colman (2005a) had an experience that affected the actual publication of a book. The incident happened in 1994, shortly after the midterm congressional elections, when Newt Gingrich and his Contract with America enabled the Republican Party to regain the majority in the House of Representatives for the first time in 40 years. A book by Colman entitled *Mary McLeod Bethune and the Power of Education* was in production when the editor—with whom she had already published several books—called to report the following: "In light of the recent election, the sales staff has reevaluated our forthcoming books and decided to pull seven books out of production, including *Mary McLeod Bethune*." The editor explained that the sales staff was convinced that "women's history was not going to sell in this climate" (p. 2).

That is why you can see *Mary McLeod Bethune and the Power of Education* by Penny Colman listed in Books in Print and on various Web sites, but you can never find the actual book. Fortunately, Colman was finally able to publish an essay, "Mary McLeod Bethune: Passionate Educator" in her 2006 book *Adventurous Women: Eight True Stories About Women Who Made a Difference* (2006b).

The Orbis Pictus Award Committee:
A Look Behind the Scenes

The Orbis Pictus Award, established in 1989 by the National Council of Teachers of English, promotes and honors outstanding nonfiction published in the United States for kindergarten through middle school readers. The committee members serve for 3 years and come from professions related to children's literature. Anyone can nominate books for consideration. The committee also writes letters to publishers inviting submissions or requesting copies of books that have been nominated.

Deciding what is high-quality nonfiction requires careful assessment of multiple aspects of a book. The criteria for selection by the Orbis Pictus Committee include the quality of the book design, accuracy, organization, writing style, and how all these aspects blend together to make appealing, engaging nonfiction literature. One criterion does not have priority over another; they function together and members consider them all.

Assessing the degree of accuracy is not easy. The extent to which authors include sources, notes, and a discussion of how information was gathered and selected is a step in assessing accuracy, although even those are not absolute guarantees that books are accurate.

Orbis Pictus Committee members may have expertise in some fields and not others; they judge books from an array of fields. This makes assessing accuracy all the more challenging. Members who have expertise in particular topics and periods of history, for instance, serve as fact-checkers, and other members might consult historians. If the committee is reading a book on a science topic and no member has scientific expertise, then scientists are consulted.

Committee members engage in a careful reading of each book to examine content, style, and sources, and then they reread it several times to focus on different aspects. For example, in one reading they might look at whether quotations are cited in source notes. In another reading, members look at how well primary sources are integrated into the text. For example, in her book *Clara Schumann: Piano Virtuoso*, Reich (1999) illustrates the challenges that Schumann faced in pursuing a celebrated performing career while accommodating the needs of her husband. The author explains how Robert was not a good traveler, although he yearned to travel with his wife, and Reich includes letters in which Robert wrote how much he bemoaned Clara's absence.

One factor that the committee considers is whether authors present information about the research process. For example, in her book, *The Tarantula Scientist*, Montgomery (2004) explains how scientists do their work as she describes their investigation, observation, and data collection. She not only shares information about the tarantula but also describes the scientists' methods in finding out about the tarantula in its habitat. In *The Great Fire* Murphy (1995) reflects on conflicting sources about the Chicago fire of 1871 and explains what was known and what was conjecture—where the fire started, how it spread, and who was responsible. In *Secrets of a Civil War Submarine: Solving the Mysteries of the H. L. Hunley*, Sally Walker (2005) explains how historians have learned about a Civil War submarine and includes archival illustrations. She explains how scientists have investigated the mysteries of the vessel and includes photographs that show steps in the process of their investigation.

The Orbis Pictus Committee also considers a book's appeal as a source of pleasure and literary experience. The members think about whether the book would be of interest to children, whether it would be good for sharing aloud, and if it has connections to the curriculum. Throughout the year, before the final award selections, the members share nominated books with groups of children in informal classroom settings during read-aloud sessions and book talks. They observe how students interact with the books and what they find engaging about them.

Trends in Nonfiction

Over the decades, nonfiction literature has grown and expanded in the range of topics covered, attention to style and quality of writing, accuracy of information, and artistic design and layout. In the 1930s, biographies included dialogue and scenes for which there might be no documented evidence and "in which known facts are often presented in dramatic episodes complete with conversation" (Sutherland, 1997, p. 426). The *Childhood of Famous Americans* series, an example of such an approach, enjoyed popularity for decades (Giblin, 2000). Biographies excluded certain historical events deemed difficult for young readers, such as Lincoln's assassination, which was not mentioned in the picture book *Abraham Lincoln* (D'Aulaire & D'Aulaire, 1957).

One of the trends is that a growing number of authors include source material both within the text and at the end. The rigors of documented evidence are as applicable to nonfiction literature for younger readers as they are to any scholarly work. For example, in her book *Adventurous Women: Eight True Stories About Women Who Made a Difference,* Penny Colman (2006b) describes Mary Gibson Henry, who, as a child, fell in love with a particular flower, *Linnaea borealis*, during her family's summer trips—a love that launched her life's work. The description is not Colman's interpretation, nor is it an image she describes in the narrative to engage readers; it is an actual quotation from Henry herself. At the end of the book is a footnote to reference the quotation.

Some current biographies focus on the lives of ordinary people and reflect the emergence in the 1960s of the field of social history, with its emphasis on daily life and the lives of people beyond presidents and politicians, wars and business. In her book, *Pioneer Girl: Growing Up on the Prairie,* Warren (1998) writes a detailed chronicle of a young pioneer girl whose life mirrors the changes in family and work throughout the 20th century. Myers (1991), Tillage (1997), and Govenar (2000) all write social history from the perspective of ordinary lives of African Americans.

Today's nonfiction deals with a variety of topics in the sciences, social sciences, art, and religion. In the biological sciences, for instance, no longer are "books confined to those about familiar plants and animals—today they cover almost every topic from a hen's egg to cryogenics and space medicine" (Sutherland, 1997, p. 481). *Tasting the Sky: A Palestinian Childhood* (Barakat, 2007) is a memoir. *Quest of the Tree Kangaroo: An Expedition to the Cloud Forest of New Guinea* (Montgomery, 2006) chronicles scientific research as does *ER Vets: Life in an Animal Emergency Room* (Jackson, 2005). *Jane Addams: Champion of Democracy* (Fradin & Fradin, 2006) is a biography full of archival photographs. Sensational topics and titles immediately pique the attention of student readers and shock adults, such as *Hands-On Grossology* (Branzei, 2003), *Oh Rats! The Story of Rats and People* (Marrin, 2006), and *Oh Yuck! The Encyclopedia of Everything Nasty* (Masoff, 2000). These books demonstrate the range of topics and treatments in contemporary nonfiction. Social and political issues are also subjects of nonfiction literature in today's world. For example, Blumenthal (2005) points out the ongoing challenge to achieve gender equity in athletics and the workplace. Current nonfiction uses advances in photographic technology to not only present information but to stimulate aesthetic experiences not available until the end of the 20th century; for example, the digestive system (Simon, 2005) and the brain (Newquist, 2004).

Sy Montgomery has an engaging writing style that draws young readers into the book. Yet the style does more than engage readers with lively language, it also serves a critical purpose in books about topics in science. She shows how scientists do their work and how they think. She has the scientist explain his observations. In her book *The Tarantula Scientist* (2004), Montgomery follows Sam Marshall, an arachnologist who studies spiders in the rain forest of French Guiana. At the beginning of the chapter about the spider's burrow, she watches Sam investigating one and encouraging the spider to come out. She writes, "'Strike, Strike. Backing up...strike!' Sam is lying in the dirt again looking down into a tarantula burrow. Like a sportscaster, he's narrating what he sees: ...'It doesn't look like she wants to come out.' But he can't blame her. A few minutes earlier Sam had enticed her out with his 'twizzle' stick. Once she figured out that that was a hoax, she wisely decided to stay in her burrow."

Of the spider's burrow, Montgomery writes, "It's a nice place to stay after all," and explains how the spider keeps her burrow clean. Then she writes what Sam observes, "'Tarantulas are tidy little homemakers...It's not a messy, smelly, hole. It's a nice hole, clean and dry inside, and lined with silk.'"

Montgomery delivers more than information and a close-up view of how scientists do their work. She shows how scientists pursue their passion to do something about problems they see in the world. For Example, in the book *Quest for the Tree Kangaroo: An Expedition to the Cloud Forest of New Guinea* (2006) she introduces the life and work of scientist Lisa Dabek. Montgomery chronicles the research of one of the rarest creatures on the Earth, which is becoming rarer as forests are cut down and kangaroos are killed. She tells readers the purposes of the study undertaken by a crew of international and local explorers: "What do they eat? How many are left? What do they need to survive? We hope to find out answers—before it's too late" (p. 8). Montgomery shows how science can be a result of people living and working together with a common purpose, employing the skills and experiences of all

the members of the crew. Each member has a crucial role in the work of the study, local villagers work along side scientists.

Sy Montgomery puts a human face on science and conservation as she portrays science in a cultural context. The people of Papua New Guinea speak a language common among villages and other languages unique to local areas, which means more than one thousand different languages are spoken. She shows how the local people, who donated land to protect the lives and habitat of the tree kangaroo, share common goals with the scientists. Montgomery writes, "Lisa's friends in the village will be our partners and guides at the field site. Without them, we could never find the tree kangaroos" (p. 28).

Children's Books Cited

Montgomery, S. (2006). *Quest for the Tree Kangaroo: An Expedition to the Cloud Forest of New Guinea.* Boston: Houghton Mifflin Co.

_____. (2004). *The Tarantula Scientist.* Boston: Houghton Mifflin Co.

Nonfiction in the Classroom

Curiosity! Inquisitiveness! A sense of wonder about the world! These are all key ingredients for effectively teaching nonfiction in the classroom. Be interested yourself and model how you select and read a variety of nonfiction texts—books, newspaper articles, magazines, letters, journals, and diaries. Invite your students to be inquisitive, nosy, and full of wonder when approaching nonfiction text. Wonder about how a writer presents information, question the author's knowledge base, and be curious together about how the author helps a reader to enter a book. There are several ways to make that happen.

As teachers read *Corpses, Coffins, and Crypts: A History of Burial* (Colman, 1997), they write about their reading process. This is an exercise that Colman uses with her students of nonfiction children's literature at Queens College. An eighth-grade teacher, Teresa Donoghue, wrote:

The important thing I realized was that the way in which I teach my students how to read nonfiction is not at all what I do myself when I read! For example, when teaching my children how to read captions in school, I often teach them to read the entire page first and then go back and read the caption. However, I often found myself turning ahead and skipping ahead to read the caption if the picture caught my attention. Once I had read the caption, then I went back and read the page; however, it got me thinking about what I do and had me questioning the techniques that I teach my students . . . maybe I need to change them a little bit!

Mary Evans, a fourth-grade teacher in Bangor, Maine, immersed her students in a complex inquiry about nonfiction with her question "How does the author help me read the book?" Evans played a central role in this inquiry. She read aloud portions of nonfiction books, did think-alouds, and planned for practice through shared and guided reading experiences that provided multiple opportunities to explore and make discoveries about the text together. Along with her question, she looked for acknowledgments and author credentials to find out who helped the author and whether the author was credible. For Evans, this preliminary exploration was important in the sequence of inquiry.

Evans's question about how an author helps a reader was an invitation to students to ask their own questions. Students wondered about how headings and titles might help readers. They questioned and studied how captions elaborated on the information and how they had to read back and forth between the text and the captions. They investigated features of nonfiction such as the table of contents, maps, glossaries, sources, notes, author bios, and captions. Students even considered the effect on their reading when maps were provided at the beginning of a book. They questioned whether glossaries at the back were as helpful as definitions in the text.

The inquiry led to a second question: "How does the author know that?" Evans's students asked questions during instructional read-aloud sessions and in small-group reading. The students began to examine the front matter and back matter for sources and information that elaborated on the text. Evans and her students flipped back and forth between the text and the sources, charting quotations and notes about them. They also checked Web sites listed in the source material and charted information relevant to the book. This led to questions about the information the author had selected: what was new information, what information would add to the book they were reading, and was there conflicting information?

Older students, in the fifth and sixth grades, can pursue the question of what the author knows by looking for descriptions of people in nonfiction books, highlighting the adjectives that are used, and then asking, "How does the author know that?" Together, the students and the teacher can assess whether there is enough information in the text and in the sources and source notes to support the description. Students can work together in small groups to look for descriptions; they can chart the words and phrases in one column and the information and sources that provide the evidence in the other column. Then they can explain how they arrived at their decisions about what the author knows with other members of the class.

Van Sledright and Kelly (1998) found that teacher modeling and guidance help students to become competent in assessing sources and examining the extent to which an author shows supporting evidence for ideas and information. Their study suggests that what the teacher values in reading nonfiction will be reflected in what is taught and what students learn.

The following is a list of action steps that teachers can use to make learning about nonfiction a critical component of their classrooms:

- Examine your attitudes toward nonfiction. If you are quick to say that you don't like nonfiction, familiarize yourself with the amazing array of nonfiction books available today. It is a given that your enthusiasm and genuine interest in nonfiction and a desire to learn more about it will rub off on your students.

- Have your students see you reading nonfiction—for pleasure! Share the parts that make you wonder, that raise your spirits, and that make you think twice.

- Show students the benefits of reading nonfiction; in other words, what's in it for them—a great read, learning new and wonderful things about the world around them, and learning how writers investigate and research subjects they are passionate about. Most important, share your excitement and sense of wonder about the world.

- Take an inventory of what nonfiction is available in your classroom or library. Make sure that you have a wide range of current and high-quality nonfiction material available—from survey books to identification books to specialized titles. Look for old and outdated titles that might have inaccurate information. Children tend to remember misconceptions or inaccurate information.

- Use nonfiction from the newspaper or other sources to explore provocative issues. Show students how to use the Internet productively to find information. Provide guidelines and practice, and help kids to see that the Internet and nonfiction books work together and complement one another. Point out that nonfiction books have advantages that the Internet doesn't—they're tactile, readers will get to know nonfiction authors and grow to have favorites, and readers can take these books anywhere! Nonfiction books (once you have a copy) are permanent, whereas Web sites disappear. Knowing these things will help kids to see that nonfiction books are truly a great resource for learning even in our technological age.

- Create nonfiction displays on a topic or on titles by the same author. Make it a centerpiece of your classroom—give nonfiction the visibility it deserves.

- Take an inventory of your students' interests and have nonfiction books available that pertain to those topics. Invite browsing; make it easy for kids to access nonfiction.

- Invite students to create summer reading lists of must-read nonfiction, and include nonfiction as free-choice reading.

- Let your librarian know about units and themes that you develop; encourage purchasing and creating text sets—a variety of nonfiction books on a topic that can be used for theme and unit work.

- Make learning about nonfiction fun and informative. Design nonfiction literary telegrams. Gather a selection of nonfiction books—as many as you have students in the class or enough for pairs of students. The collection could be on the same theme or on a variety of topics. Look through each book carefully and then design a question about the book and type it on a slip of paper—that's the "literary telegram." For example, you might say the following: "In this book, you'll find out about Broca's area." (The answer can be found in *The Great Brain Book* [Newquist, 2004].) You can also design literary telegrams around features of nonfiction, such as the table of contents, maps, timelines, or diagrams. Put all the telegrams in an envelope and have the students select one. Have all the books displayed. The students' task is to find the right book by using the telegram as a clue. For the finale, everyone shares his or her telegram, and you have a chance to add a few words about particular books. This activity is fun and informative for everyone.

- Plan a nonfiction book pass. Give each student two to four nonfiction titles to look at for a brief time—maybe 3 minutes or so, just enough time to whet the appetite and then say "book pass." Each student's books are then passed to the next student. This is an effective and enjoyable way to see a lot of nonfiction titles in a short amount of time. You can also design a simple rating or comment sheet for students to keep track of the books during the book pass.

- Take advantage of "nonfiction moments" (Colman, 2006a). Turn everyday nonfiction events into an opportunity to savor nonfiction and use them as possible springboards for lessons across the curriculum: find out about the hottest day of the year in your town, the first snow day, the interesting bird that you saw out your kitchen window that morning, the bat someone found in the school, how pencils are made, who the school is named after, the monument in the town square. Create a list with your kids of interesting and ordinary things to investigate. You and your students will come up with some extraordinarily intriguing information.

- Teach what you know about nonfiction by modeling what you do as a reader. Read aloud and do think-alouds that demonstrate how you read nonfiction. Plan shared and guided reading and writing experiences (Kristo & Bamford, 2004).

- Talk about the kinds of books you share with your students and select some nonfiction to read aloud. What and how much you share depends on your purposes and goals for the read-aloud. Hearing nonfiction read aloud will help your students to develop an ear for how good nonfiction sounds. Enjoy the experience!

- Deepen and strengthen the conversation from read-alouds by comparing how information is presented and what is the same or different by selecting several nonfiction books on a topic, written by different authors. Find books with different formats, such as picture books, longer books, and books that were published at different times.

- Provide students with lots of time to talk about nonfiction. The more that students discuss content, the more control and comfort they'll feel for the topic. This makes writing about a topic much easier. When kids don't understand content, they tend to copy it word for word, and the writing sounds stilted and contrived.

- Use quality nonfiction—essays, books, articles—to teach writing (Colman, 2004). Some teachers report to us that fiction is more often the model for teaching writing. Mark Twain (Bainton, 1890) observed the following in a letter he wrote in 1888: "Whenever we read a sentence and like it, we unconsciously store it away in our model-chamber; and it goes with a myriad of its fellows to the building, brick by brick, of the eventual edifice which we call our style." Good nonfiction is a great tool to use for writing mini-lessons to show how authors craft leads, organize topics, integrate visual information, use illustrations and captions, and include access features, such as a table of contents or glossary. Share good examples of these and talk about them as mentor examples for their own writing—examples they can go back to as they craft their own nonfiction writing. Remember that most writing (fiction and nonfiction) is a combination of expository and narrative writing. Fiction writers often have to research their topics.

- Host an after-school nonfiction book–sharing club to talk about new books with kids.

- Undertake a teacher study group to talk about new books and discuss ways to share nonfiction with kids.

- Enjoy your own immersion in nonfiction and make discoveries right along with your students. Share what you learn!

Implications

Speculate, question, imagine, and wonder about the world! See the possibilities that nonfiction literature offers you and the students you teach. Nonfiction, after all, is a major source of content and learning about life and the world we live in for all of us—students and teachers alike. Content is, of course, essential for comprehension. Learning as much as we can about the world we live in is critical to becoming informed citizens in our global community. Colman (2004) says:

> Nonfiction is the language of everyday things—news, instructions, reports, presentations, letters, email, records, documents, court decisions and extraordinary things such as Abraham Lincoln's Gettysburg Address and Elizabeth Cady Stanton's Declaration of Sentiments. Nonfiction is the language of all debates of policies and issues—social, economic, political and environmental—that affect everyone's life throughout the world. Nonfiction is the currency with which public policies and legislation are enacted, societal needs are discussed, cultural aesthetics are defined, life lessons are conveyed, historical narratives are transmitted. *The currency with which matters of war and peace are decided.*
>
> Nonfiction is everywhere. It is the stuff of everyday life—the infinite list of activities and duties and decisions and desires and feelings and fears and happiness. It is birthdays and festivals and funerals. It is winning and losing and bouncing back. It is the WOW experiences of life—reveling in nature, witnessing an athletic achievement, marveling at an artistic creation or [a] theatrical or musical [one], fulfilling a dream, falling in love. Nonfiction is there and here and everywhere. That is why I'm hooked on nonfiction. How about you? (p. 4)

References

Bainton, G. (Ed.). (1890). *The art of authorship: Literary reminiscences, methods of word, and advice to young beginners, personally contributed by leading authors of the day.* New York: Appleton.

Bamford, R., & Kristo, J. V. (2000). *Checking out nonfiction, K–8: Good choices for best learning.* Norwood, MA: Christopher-Gordon.

Caswell, L. J., & Duke, N. K. (1998). Non-narrative as a catalyst for literacy development. *Language Arts, 75* (2), 108–117.

Colman, P. (1999a, Summer). Nonfiction is literature, too. *The New Advocate, 12* (3), 215–223.

Colman, P. (1999b, November). *With a passion: Turning kids on to nonfiction.* Paper presented at the National Council of the Teachers of English, Denver, CO.

Colman, P. (2004, January). *Hooked on nonfiction: How about you?* Paper presented at the Children's Literature Conference, Ohio State University, Columbus.

Colman, P. (2005a, June). *Bathrooms, burials, and women: Writing women's history for children and young adults.* Paper presented at the Berkshire Conference on the History of Women, Claremont, CA.

Colman, P. (2005b, April). *Birth of a book.* Paper presented at the University of Maine, Orono.

Colman, P. (2005c, November). *Writing, selecting, and teaching children's literature: A dynamic model.* Paper presented at Presidential Roundtable, Queens College, City University of New York, Flushing.

Colman, P. (2006a, February). *History and children's literature.* Paper presented at the Symposium in Honor of Janet Hickham, Ohio State University, Columbus.

Duke, N. K., & Bennett-Armistead, S. V. (2003). *Reading & writing informational text in the primary grades: Research-based practices.* New York: Scholastic.

Galda, L., & Cullinan, B. E. (2006). *Literature and the child* (6th ed.). Belmont, CA: Thomson Wadsworth.

Genuard, M. (2005). *Focus on nonfiction literature: Students' reading preferences and teachers' beliefs and practices.* Unpublished master's thesis, Queens College, City University of New York, Flushing.

Gerard, P. (1996). *Creative nonfiction.* Cincinnati, OH: Story Press.

Giblin, J. C. (2000). More than the facts: A hundred years of children's nonfiction. *The Horn Book Magazine, 76* (4), 413–424.

Harvey, S., & Goudvis, A. (2000). *Strategies that work: Teaching comprehension to enhance understanding.* York, ME: Stenhouse.

Hunt, J. (2005). Where *do* all the prizes go?: Thoughts on the state of informational books. *The Horn Book Magazine, 81* (4), 439–445.

Jacobs, J., & Tunnell, M. (2004). *Children's literature briefly* (3rd ed.). Upper Saddle River, NJ: Pearson/Merrill Prentice Hall.

Kristo, J. V., & Bamford, R. A. (2004). *Nonfiction in focus: A comprehensive framework for helping students become independent readers and writers of nonfiction, K–6.* New York: Scholastic.

Mitchell, D. (2003). *Children's literature: An invitation to the world.* Boston: Pearson.

Newkirk, T. (1989). *More than stories: The range of children's writing.* Portsmouth, NH: Heinemann.

Nodelman, P., & Reimer, M. (2003). *The pleasures of children's literature* (3rd ed.) Boston: Allyn & Bacon.

Norton, D. (2007). *Through the eyes of a child* (7th ed.). Columbus, OH: Pearson/Merrill Prentice Hall.

Pappas, C. C. (1991). Fostering full access to literacy by including informational books. *Language Arts, 68,* 449–462.

Robb, L. (2004). *Nonfiction writing from the inside out: Writing lessons inspired by conversations with leading authors.* New York: Scholastic.

Rosenthal, A. K. (2006, March 6). An agent, a publisher, and a polygraph test? *Newsweek*, p. 15.

Rybcyznski, W. (2001). The writing life. *The Washington Post Book World*, p. 8.

Sutherland, Z. (1997). *Children and books* (9th ed.). New York: Longman.

Temple, C., Martinez, M., Yokota, J., & Naylor, A. (2002). *Children's books in children's hands: An introduction to their literature* (2nd ed.). Boston: Allyn & Bacon.

Van Sledright, B. A., & Kelly, C. (1998). Reading American history: The influence of multiple sources on six fifth graders. *Elementary School Journal, 98* (3), 239–265.

Wilson, S. L. (2001). Coherence and historical understanding in children's biography and historical nonfiction literature: A content analysis of selected Orbis Pictus books. *Dissertation Abstracts International, 63* (01), 121A. (University Microfilms No. AAT30-39414)

Children's Books

Barakat, Ibtasin. (2007). *Tasting the sky: A Palestinian childhood.* New York: Farrar, Straus & Giroux.

Blumenthal, K. (2005). *Let me play: The story of Title 1X—the law that changed the future of girls in America.* New York: Atheneum Books.

Branzei, S. (2003). Hands-on grossology. New York: Price Stern Sloan.

Burleigh, R. (1991). *Flight: The journey of Charles Lindbergh.* New York: Philomel Books.

Choldenko, G. (2004). *Al Capone does my shirts.* New York: Putnam.

Colman, P. (1997). *Corpses, coffins, and crypts: A history of burial.* New York: Holt.

Colman, P. (2002). *Where the action was: Women war correspondents in World War II.* New York: Crown.

Colman, P. (2006b). *Adventurous women: Eight true stories about women who made a difference.* New York: Holt.

D'Aulaire, I., & D'Aulaire, E. P. (1957). *Abraham Lincoln.* New York: Doubleday.

Deems, J. M. (2005). *Bodies from the ash: Life and death in ancient Pompeii.* Boston: Houghton Mifflin.

Fleischman, S. (2006). *Escape!: The story of the great Houdini.* New York: Greenwillow Books.

Fradin, J. B., & Fradin, D. B. (2006). *Jane Addams: Champion of Democracy.* New York: Clarion Books.

Frank, A. (1995). *Anne Frank: The diary of a young girl.* New York: Doubleday.

George, J. C. (1972). *Julie of the wolves.* New York: Harper & Row.

Govenar, A. (2000). *Osceola: Memories of a sharecropper's daughter.* New York: Hyperion Books.

Hoffman, M. (2003). *Encore Grace.* New York: Dial.

Jackson, D. (2005). *ER vets: Life in an animal emergency room.* Boston: Houghton Mifflin.

Jurmain, S. T. (2005). *The forbidden schoolhouse: The true and dramatic story of Prudence Crandall and her students.* Boston: Houghton Mifflin.

Marrin. A. (2006). *Oh, rats!: The story of rats and people.* New York: Dutton.

Masoff, J. (2000). *Oh yuck! The encyclopedia of everything nasty.* New York: Workman.

Montgomery, S. (2004). *The tarantula scientist.* Boston: Houghton Mifflin.

Montgomery, S. (2006). *Quest for the tree kangaroo: An expedition to the cloud forest of New Guinea.* Boston: Houghton Mifflin.

Murphy, J. (1995). *The great fire.* New York: Scholastic.

Myers, W. D. (1991). *Now is your time!: The African-American struggle for freedom.* New York: HarperCollins.

Newquist, H. P. (2004). *The great brain book: An inside look at the inside of your head.* New York: Scholastic.

Reich, S. (1999). *Clara Schumann: Piano virtuoso.* New York: Clarion Books.

Simon, S. (2005). *Guts: Our digestive system.* New York: HarperCollins.

Tillage, L. W. (1997). *Leon's story.* New York: Farrar, Straus & Giroux.

Walker, S. M. (2005). *Secrets of a Civil War submarine: Solving the mysteries of the H. L. Hunley.* Minneapolis, MN: Carolrhoda.

Warren, A. (1998). *Pioneer girl: Growing up on the prairie.* New York: Morrow.

Chapter 23

Pitfalls of Using Social Studies Texts Exclusively: Analyzing Diversity and Filling the Gaps

Deborah L. Thompson

Eight fifth-grade students attending a Washington, D.C., public elementary school were discussing elements of Jerry Spinelli's *Maniac Magee* (1990) and Mildred D. Taylor's *The Friendship* (1986). (See Lehr & Thompson, 2000, for details of the comparative study of the two books.) The first exchange occurred as students were making text-to-world connections and discussing what makes a person a legend. They began naming people who they thought were legends:

Tony: Martin Luther King.

DLT: Why would he be a legend?

Tony: Because he helped Black people and because he helped the people during slavery.

Donna: Yeah, he helped free the slaves.

Teacher: Are you sure Martin Luther King freed the slaves?

Tony: Yeah.

DLT: But Martin Luther King didn't live during the time of slavery; how could he have helped free the slaves?

Sheila: He didn't?

This response and the students' certainty that Martin Luther King helped free the slaves perplexed me for some time. The answer to why the students thought this is addressed later in the chapter.

The next exchange came during a discussion of *The Friendship*. The students were shocked that violence would result if Mr. Tom Bee (a Black man) called John Wallace (a White man) by his first name (John Wallace shoots Tom Bee). The episode elicited a discussion of discriminatory practices in the Jim Crow South:

> *Alyssa*: I have a question [about racism]. Back then, did they really not let (Black) people go to the restaurants or drink cold water?
>
> *DLT*: Yes, laws had to be changed.
>
> *Alyssa*: They don't do this now, do they?

Alyssa (from mainland China) could not grasp the concept of not allowing people to enter a restaurant to get a drink of cold water because of their skin color. Alyssa's incredulity comes despite her earlier sharing of how the British and Japanese discriminated against the Chinese (in China) when they posted signs that said "No dogs, no Chinese." Further along in the discussion, when Carlos (from El Salvador) and Jimmy (an African American) discussed what the consequences of John Wallace's actions would be, Carlos thought he would go to jail, to which Jimmy replied, "Oh no, if a White man shot a Black man, they wouldn't do anything to him. He would not go to jail" (Lehr & Thompson, 2000, p. 490). Jimmy's response suggested that he had made a temporal shift from the book's events to something more immediate and personal.

Despite being well-read, above-average fifth graders, the student participants in this study showed a remarkable lack of historical understanding, especially related to slavery and race relations. Although Jimmy's response was rooted in history, more than likely his understanding came from his wider community, family members, and other acquaintances—what is called *vernacular history*. Vernacular histories are rooted in family and or community stories and are often used by people in marginalized groups to counteract the history of the privileged classes that is taught in school (Barton & Levstik, 2000). Alyssa's historical anecdote about the treatment of Chinese in the early 20th century more than likely was a combination of standard history and vernacular history. Few if any of the social studies texts published in the United States would have exposed elementary students to an account of history in which the privileged classes are shown in a constant negative light.

Additionally, when the response study was conducted at the end of the 1990s, high-stakes testing had already taken root in the Washington, D.C., public schools. Teachers were being held accountable for their students' literacy and math achievement (i.e., reading and math test scores). Even students as bright as the participants in this study, who had and could pass the reading and math tests with ease, were overwhelmed with the test-score frenzy. Their teachers probably spent little time exposing them to American or world history or disabusing them of faulty historical assumptions acquired from a steady diet of history as presented in their social studies textbooks.

The State of Elementary Social Studies Instruction

Except for literacy, perhaps, few school subjects stir the ire of education critics, education "experts," political leaders, conservative talk show hosts, and even some well-known and well-respected educators and historians—as social studies does. Florida has gone so far as to legislate what can be taught in history (Allen, 2006). "Just the facts" legislation states that Florida teachers cannot teach any social studies topic that is open to interpretation and will cause controversy; this means that Florida's students could be reduced to memorizing dates, major battles, and state capitals. Presidential elections could even be off-limits if they are controversial—and George W. Bush's ascendancy to the presidency in 2000 is just one of several disputed presidential elections in our nation's history (others were John Quincy Adams and Andrew Jackson in 1824 and Samuel Tilden and Rutherford B. Hayes in 1876). The ultimate goal of the legislation, says one educator, is to prepare students to take a new state social studies test.

By learning endless dates and battles, children will possibly be better prepared to answer questions on the next pop history quiz. Often when the results of the occasional "pop history survey" have been reported, there have been great proclamations about student ignorance and poor instruction. Paxton (2003) reveals that these proclamations of student ignorance have been a staple of public discourse for decades. He notes that in 1917, two researchers surveyed 1,500 Texas students (elementary through university) on basic historical facts—for example, the significance of the year 1492. The results of the survey showed that the percentage of students who knew the appropriate answers ranged from 16% for elementary students to 49% for university students.

A broader history facts survey was administered in 1943 to 7,000 college freshmen. The results of the survey were so abysmal that a *New York Times* headline trumpeted, "Ignorance of U.S. History Shown by College Freshman" (Paxton, 2003, p. 267). In successive decades, the results of history surveys have raised the same types of public responses: American students have a broad historical ignorance, and teachers are doing a poor job of teaching in general but particularly in social studies.

It is true that elementary social studies often receives short shrift in the daily instructional schedule. In a survey of teachers in a large West Coast urban school district, researchers (Berstein, Hutton, & Curtis, 2006) found that 50% of the teachers spent less than an hour a week teaching social studies. According to these teachers, the demands of No Child Left Behind (NCLB) prevented them from spending much time teaching subjects that were not going to be assessed. Some teachers did say they alternated between teaching science one marking period and social studies the next. If teachers were going to teach social studies, most of them (67%) reported that they used work sheets and the textbooks, no primary sources or core literature.

Zhao and Hoge (2005) found that the teachers in their study had negative attitudes toward social studies. They considered it a "second tier" subject on which not much instructional time should be spent. The teachers maintained that there were far more important subjects to teach (i.e., those that would be assessed), such as reading and math. Students in this same study described social studies as "boring and useless, reading the textbook, or not applicable to them" (p. 218). As in the previous study, the main source of instruction for the teachers in this study was the social studies text. Many other studies reveal similar results—social studies need only be taught if it fits in the daily instructional schedule (Jones, Pang, & Rodriguez, 2001).

Elementary social studies instruction suffers from more than teacher and student indifference. It also is a battleground across the political spectrum. The battle is not so much over how the subject is taught, although that is important, but more about what topics are taught and how those topics are presented in social studies texts. Waters (2005) states that K–12 social studies is taught from a "grand-sweep" perspective that focuses on names, dates, places, and the glories of the past (e.g., the Pilgrims, the Declaration of Independence and the Revolutionary War, the crafting of the Constitution, and the development of the American way of life).

Chester Finn of the Thomas Fordham Institute, a consistent critic of most things related to public schools, believes that the field of social studies has been taken over by lunatics. He says that these lunatics

> possess no respect for Western civilization; are inclined to view America's evolution as a problem for humanity rather than mankind's [sic] last, best hope; and they have pooh-poohed history's chronological and factual skeleton as privileging elites and White males over the poor and oppressed. (2003, p. i)

In other words, too much emphasis on American slavery, the treatment of American Indians, or women takes away from those (i.e., White men) who have made America the country that it is today. The real focus of social studies classes should be on the last best hope for the world—the United States of America.

Despite what Chester Finn believes about lunatics and the present state of social studies, the subject remains a cataloguing of famous people, events, and dates to be memorized that are often meaningless to students (Fertig, 2005). The privileged classes still control the formal history of the nation, and this formal history is transmitted through textbooks. As Waters (2005) notes, "Millions of glossy paged copies are produced to teach K–12 students the dominant explanation of why the nation is the way it is" (p. 17).

Not to be ignored, liberal pundits present arguments about why what is taught as social studies favors the oppressors over the oppressed. They contend that there is not enough page space devoted to diverse perspectives, but given the organized opposition of many conservatives, any view not adhering to the grand-sweep perspective is categorized as "liberal." Basically, both groups want to control the stories being told as American history and control how students think and respond to those stories.

The Social Studies Text

Social studies is the most textbook-driven subject in school (Loewen, 1995). More than likely, the social studies texts adopted for any school in the United States are published by one of four major publishing companies: McGraw-Hill, Houghton Mifflin, Harcourt, and—the nation's and perhaps the world's largest—Pearson Education. These four companies control 70% of the textbook market (Robinson, 2006).

The four major publishers tailor the social studies texts to suit the school boards and textbook adoption committees of two major states: California and Texas. Therefore, the texts published for use throughout the United States will carry topics and be written in a style that suits the political tastes and pedagogical sensibilities of the California and Texas Boards of Education. The textbooks that emerge from these companies are often a patchwork of facts and dates, with little conflict or real suspense. Anything in history that might contradict the stories (or myths) created to explain our national character and our role in the world (Hughes, 2003; Loewen, 1995) is subsumed and almost lost in broad historical themes.

For example, under the broad theme "The New Nation," the Founding Fathers solve the representation problem by agreeing to the Three-Fifths Compromise, wherein one male slave counts as three-fifths of an enfranchised White male (Boyd, Gay, Geiger, Kracht, Pang, Risenger, & Sanchez, 2005). Under the broad theme "A Changing Nation," the difficulties and discrimination the Chinese immigrants experienced as they completed the dangerous work on the Transcontinental Railroad is cited in one paragraph (Viola, Bednarz, Cortés, Jennings, Schug, & White, 2005).

Despite all that has been done to improve the social studies texts our students use, it appears that little has changed from when the alleged righteousness of the privileged classes dominated the pages in most texts. Attempting to present a broader view of American history, the authors of both of the above series included text-set titles for each chapter. *Text sets* are collections of related books grouped by a common theme or element that are used by a small group of students for discussion and comparison (Opitz, 1998).

The Social Studies Texts Analyzed for This Study

Two fifth-grade social studies texts, Scott-Foresman's *The United States* (Vols. 1 & 2) (Boyd et al., 2005) and Houghton Mifflin's *United States History: The Early Years* (Vol. 1.) and *United States History: Civil War to Today* (Vol. 2) (Viola et al., 2005) were selected and analyzed for this chapter. These texts were chosen because in the United States, fifth grade is the students' initial exposure to American history. These two series were chosen because they included the attacks of September 11, 2001, and the nation's subsequent responses (wars in Afghanistan and Iraq) to those attacks. Both series have been approved by the California Department of Education (2005) for use in California public schools—the largest consumers of textbooks in the country.

No recent editions (2005 copyright or later) of the Holt, Rinehart & Winston social studies series, one of five adopted by the Texas Board of Education (personal communication), could be obtained for the content analysis. A visit to the publisher's Web site reveals that there are various editions from which to choose. There is the full survey or a two-volume set, divided into U.S. history to 1877 (or alternately, to 1914) and from the Civil War to the present. There is no explanation of why there are two first volumes or why they are divided as they are—to 1877 or to 1914—or why the second volume overlaps by beginning with the Civil War.

The series selected for analysis were analyzed for how U.S. history is parsed, the types of events emphasized, the page coverage for different historical events (including 9/11 and the Iraq War), and the suggested literature selections.

The Literature Connection

Children's literature, traditional and multicultural, adds a dimension to social studies that textbooks do not have. Topics on which many chapters are spent, such as the American Revolution or the Civil War, can still appear commonplace and uninspiring as presented in the typical social studies text. Nonfiction, historical fiction, and even poetry can create contexts for students to actually acquire an understanding of social studies concepts. Good children's literature presents endless possibilities for children to read and think critically (Wolk, 2003).

Both series that I analyzed included leveled text sets to accompany each unit chapter. Leveled books are titles organized by topic, sentence complexity, vocabulary load, and genre. Single copies of titles from a variety of genres can be mixed and matched to support each chapter as needed. The text sets in the two series included awarding-winning authors and titles along with many biographies from a publisher noted for titles written especially for school libraries. Some of the books were notable, even award-winning, such as Fradin (2002) and Freedman (2004). In my analysis, however, I have included additional titles.

As I began analyzing the texts, one of the most perplexing responses from the students in the literature response study was finally answered. How could very intelligent students think that Martin Luther King had freed the slaves? How could they even think that he had lived during that era? The answer came from a fifth-grade social studies text (not analyzed in this study, for reasons noted above) published by Harcourt (Boehm, Hoone, McGowan, McKinney-Browning, Miramontes, & Porter, 2000). In the chapter "The Fight for Freedom Goes On," which focuses on the aftermath of the Civil War and Reconstruction, there is a two-page spread (pp. 192–193) on Martin Luther King. Moreover, on pages 194 and 195 is a pictorial timeline of slavery and Reconstruction. It appears that the intent of the text's authors was to make the period after the Civil War relevant to the students by having them make comparisons between the Reconstruction era and the Civil Rights Movement in the mid-20th century.

Such a comparison might have worked in the late 1970s or the 1980s, but these students were born in the late 1980s. To these students, the Civil Rights Movement was probably as far away and foreign as the Civil War. Furthermore, immigrant students have little or no prior knowledge of any American history. The students' responses in the study suggested that when (or if) Reconstruction was taught, the attempt to connect the two periods was unsuccessful. What they took away from the lesson was that Martin Luther King was an important person during some period, so if he was in the chapter with the newly freed slaves, then he obviously must have had something to do with their being freed.

Comparing the Series

American history is such a broad topic that it would be impossible to analyze every war, patriot, political movement, or explorer. Many possible themes emerged from analysis of the Scott Foresman and Houghton Mifflin series, including American Indians, the growth and spread of slavery, the contributions of minorities and women to the war efforts, women's fight for the right to vote, and the Civil Rights Movement. Instead of trying to choose the most important themes, and in order to avoid misrepresenting the series authors' purpose, I decided to analyze the series based on their nine units and how many alternate voices or views were presented in each—specifically, American Indians, African Americans, Asian Americans, Hispanics, and women.

Analysis of Volume 1: Units 1–4

The First Americans

For reasons not made clear in either series, information about American Indians was condensed and placed in the earliest sections of both series. The only differences were in the presentation of the many Indian nations and the ethnic terms that each series used. Unit 1, chapter 2 of the Scott Foresman text (Boyd et al., 2005) began with an east-to-west sweep of American Indian (the term used by this series) nations, starting first with the Eastern Woodland nations and ending with the Pacific Northwest. Each section began with a famous warrior (if possible), how the tribes lived in the past, and what members of the nations do today. The chapter was a hodgepodge of old and new, with incongruent sections, such as the Navajo Code Talkers intermingled with information on other American Indian tribes.

The section on the Navajo Code Talkers was very instructive. First of all, after chapter 1 there was no further discussion of these famous warriors, and no mention of them was made in the section on World War II. Given the time that elapses between the teaching of World War II (in the spring) and the early introduction (in the fall) of the Code Talkers, it would probably be safe to say that not all students will connect what they read in unit 1 (in September) to what they read in unit 9 (in April, May or June).

The second instructive piece is a photograph of George W. Bush presenting a former Code Talker with a medal. The Code Talker is being deferential by looking down and away from the president and not making eye contact. It is a sign of respect among many Navajos, especially the older and/or more traditional members, to look away from the subject or down and not make eye contact. The president is bending over, attempting to look the warrior in the eye. To make matters worse, he has his hand on the warrior's back. Such familiarity is common among Southerners, but not among many Navajos. These cultural taboos are ones that neither the president's advisors nor the book's editors appeared to have known. One can imagine the embarrassment that some Navajo students, and other American Indian tribes that have the same cultural mores about physical and eye contact, would feel seeing such a photograph.

In unit 1, chapter 3, on life in the Eastern Hemisphere, there are three pages dedicated to Asia's Silk Road and four pages dedicated to the African trading empires of Mali, Songhay and Ghana. Six pages are dedicated to European explorers, such as Vasco de Gama, who sailed around the Cape of Good Hope to India. The unit ends with a Lakota folktale, "The First Flute," retold by Joseph Bruchac. Aztecs, Mayas, and Incas are addressed in chapter 1 and are revisited in the chapter on Spanish settlements. Titles for reading aloud and for independent reading are listed at the beginning of each chapter in the teacher's edition.

In the Houghton Mifflin series (Viola, et al., 2005), chapter 2 is dedicated to Native Americans (the term used by this series). The chapter begins with ancient Amerindians—the Mound Builders. There is some mention of the Aztecs (who are addressed more fully in the chapter on explorers), and then the chapter moves in a west-to-east sweep of American Indian tribes, beginning with the Pacific Northwest and ending with the Eastern Woodland tribes.

Again there is a section on contemporary American Indians, such as the Mohawk ironworkers—known the world over for their work in skyscraper construction. There is also a folktale, this time from the Chinook of the Pacific Northwest. No editorial attributions are given, but there are a few David Diaz illustrations. A bibliography of titles for independent reading is included at the beginning of each chapter of the teacher's edition. The editors of this series chose to use primary sources as the read-aloud selection for each chapter. Inexplicably, the read-aloud selection for the chapter on Native Americans was "The Song of Hiawatha" by Henry Wadsworth Longfellow. Longfellow notwithstanding, this chapter had a better flow than did the chapter of the other series.

The next chapter covers the Asian and African trading empires. The basic information is the same as that found in the other series—for instance, Mansa Musa of the Kingdom of Mali. The section on the Asian Silk Road is paired with a picture of cellist Yo-Yo Ma. The books' authors are trying to connect Ma's Silk Road music project with the ancient Asian Silk Road, just as the Harcourt series (Boehm et al., 2000) noted above attempted to connect Martin Luther King with Reconstruction. In any lesson, execution is vitally important. If teachers do not make clear why Yo-Yo Ma is in a chapter with the ancient Asian Silk Road, some students might believe that he was a contemporary of Genghis Khan.

In the remaining two volumes, American Indians are highlighted in fewer than 20 pages. There is a page in each series on the Indian Removal Act and the Cherokee Trail of Tears. There are occasional sidebars or captions about chiefs who tried to resist the westward movement of the settlers. There is coverage of Little Big Horn in Scott Foresman (Boyd et al., 2005) and Little Big Horn and Wounded Knee in Houghton Mifflin (Viola et al., 2005). After that, American Indians make no appearances in the 20th century and beyond. It is little wonder that many children think that all American Indians are dead.

The Introduction of Slavery;
Pilgrims and the First Thanksgiving

The topics of slavery and the Pilgrims are introduced in unit 2 of both series. Because much has been written about Pocahontas—some good, some bad, some totally erroneous—I will not focus on her treatment in the two series. Instead, the focus of this section will be the arrival of enslaved Africans at Jamestown, Virginia, in 1619 and the Pilgrims at Plymouth, Massachusetts, in 1620. Africans arrived on this continent long before the Pilgrims or the 20 Africans on the Dutch trading ship to Jamestown (Palmer, 1994), but the two texts focus only on the arrival of Africans in English Jamestown. In 1619, a Dutch ship docked in Jamestown, where a trader sold 20 captured Africans for food. Both texts state that these 20 Africans were probably treated as indentured servants (people who were bonded to serve for a given length of time, such as 10 years). The texts note that eventually, Africans were no longer allowed to have indentures (the contracts stating the terms) and were enslaved. This made slavery, as practiced in the colonies and then the United States, the only slave system in the world based solely on the color of a person's skin.

One irritating piece of politically correct, but historically incorrect, terminology was used in both series—*African American*. Both series called the enslaved Africans *African Americans* from the time they disembarked in Jamestown all the way through the end of the Civil War and the ratification of the 13th, 14th, and 15th Amendments. At no time should the enslaved Africans be called *Americans*; that implies that these enslaved Africans were considered people and not property or real estate. A plantation owner would no more consider enslaved Africans as Americans anymore than he would have considered his house, his plow, or his horse as an American. Furthermore, in 1619, the plantation owners would not have called themselves Americans. It is probable that the colonists did not call themselves Americans until after they crafted the Preamble to the Constitution in 1787 (Berkin, 2006). Both texts call the settlers *colonists*. To call enslaved Africans *American* supports what Loewen (1995) calls the "optimistic approach" to American history, which allows students and teachers to avoid unpleasant historical truths, such as people being considered things instead of humans.

In 1620 the Pilgrims arrived in the New World. Authors of both series point out that the first year was very hard on the citizens of Plymouth. The next year, with the invaluable help of Squanto, the Pilgrims had a good harvest and decided to celebrate, or give thanks. Both series state that the Pilgrims invited the Wampanoags to feast with them. The books do say that the guests brought more food. Fact-checking (www.oyate.org) shows that when the Wampanoags heard much commotion coming from the Pilgrims' encampment, they were afraid that the settlers were planning war. Suspecting that there was trouble afoot, Masssoit and his people went to investigate. Upon discovering the settlers celebrating, the Wampanoags left and then returned, bringing deer and turkeys, and joined in the celebratory feast. There are no pictures of the Thanksgiving celebration in the Houghton Mifflin series (Viola et al., 2005), but in the Scott Foresman series (Boyd et al., 2005), the first thing the reader notices at the introduction to the Early Settlers unit is a very large portrait of a traditional view of Thanksgiving by J. L. G. Ferris. There is a female Pilgrim serving food to several American Indian guests. The picture is not quite an N. C. Wyeth rendition, but it is close enough to show that some stories in history cannot be discarded no matter how much they have been disproved.

The Spread of Slavery

Several things are noticeable in how the two series cover the spread of slavery in the colonies, apart from the use of the term *African American*. In neither book were there explanations of who captured the Africans to enslave them. There was no mention of kidnapping children from their homes, the separation in families from their loved ones, or the wholesale slaughter in some African villages. It is understandable, perhaps, not to want to expose children to the pillaging and plundering that the slave traders and their occasional African accomplices meted out, but to have the African captives show up miraculously at the slave ships ready to board without any sign of resistance or with no explanations of how they got there is a serious misrepresentation of the facts.

Hughes (2003) states that we pride ourselves as a good nation with only a few unsavory periods in our past. Since we would never do anything such as enslave Africans (or oppress American Indians or women) now, that untidy historical period need not be overemphasized. Hughes would say that this historical skimming feeds into the myth (or story) of an "innocent nation." The myth is that we are a good country and a good people. Kidnapping, pillaging, and raping are things that evil people and evil countries do, so we could not possibly have participated in such heinous acts involving enslaved Africans. To free the country (at that time, the colonies) of the burden of slavery's evils, the social studies series make the slave catchers faceless and without nationalities. In doing so, there is no one to blame for enslaving Africans, except maybe the Africans themselves for allowing others to enslave them in the first place.

A second historical taradiddle was that slavery was really a Southern phenomenon. It is true that there were more slaves in the South than in the North, but every colony had slaves. It is also true that being a slave in the South was more difficult than being a slave in the North. Both series noted that enslaved people in the North could work and save enough to buy their freedom. That is also true of enslaved people in the South. However, whether the enslaved person lived in the North or the South, until those freedom papers could be purchased, he or she was still considered property.

Women in the Colonies

There are very few women highlighted in the chapters on the early colonies. Aside from a brief statement about the first English women arriving in Jamestown and Anne Hutchinson and religious freedom, one would think that women were not present in the colonies until the Revolutionary War (and that there were very few of them). Eliza Lucas Pinckney was noted in both series as one who, after experimenting with indigo plants on her father's plantation, developed a plant that was easier to grow.

The American Revolution

In lockstep, the two series use their fourth units to focus on the American Revolution. Women were instrumental in making the boycott of British goods successful. The Daughters of Liberty were among the boycott leaders. Deborah Sampson, the young woman who disguised herself as a boy to fight with the Patriots; Mary Ludwig Hays (Molly Pitcher), who took over her husband's cannon when he was injured; Martha Washington, the General's wife; and Phillis Wheatley, the Black poet, were featured in both series. Mary Catherine Goodard, a printer, was given a caption revealing that she printed an official copy of the Declaration of Independence. Abigail Adams wrote to her husband, John, asking him to make sure that he and his fellow statesmen "remember the ladies" when they write the Declaration of Independence.

There are sidebars featuring the sailor Crispus Attucks, a former slave, who was killed at the Boston Massacre. Whether he was one of four, as the Scott Foresman text claimed (Boyd et al., 2005), or one of five, as the Houghton Mifflin text claimed (Viola et al., 2005), he was among the first to die in the Revolution. Scott Foresman highlighted Peter Salem, who mortally wounded British leader John Pitcairn at the Battle of Bunker Hill and who was instrumental at the Battle of Saratoga. Also cited was Prince Hall, a Black man who fought in the Revolution and who later successfully petitioned the Massachusetts Legislature to abolish slavery in the state. Houghton Mifflin highlighted Peter Salem and James Amistad, who served as a spy for the colonists. The only mention of American Indians was in the Houghton Mifflin series, which states that the Mohawks were allied with the British, hoping that the colonists' defeat would mean that the settlers would stop invading American Indian lands.

The last chapter of unit 1 in the Houghton Mifflin series (Viola et al., 2005) features the historic struggle to write the Constitution. Many issues drew heated discussions, but among the most contentious was slavery. These men, who so boldly declared that it was every man's inalienable right to life, liberty, and the pursuit of happiness, had great difficulty extending those same rights to the enslaved, women, and American Indians. The biggest problem centered on taxation and a state's representation in the House of Representatives. The Three-Fifths Compromise solved the problem, so that a state like Virginia, with tens of thousands of slaves, would receive a larger number of representatives than would states like New Hampshire, which had few slaves. The solution was to count each male slave as three-fifths of a White male. Or, as the Houghton Mifflin authors stated it, three male slaves equaled five propertied White males. Women of all races and American Indians received even less notice than did the male slaves, because neither group was of financial value.

Analysis of Volume 2: Units 5–9

The first chapter in the second volume of the Scott Foresman series focuses on writing the Constitution. Boyd, Gay, Geiger, Kracht, Pang, Risenger, and Sanchez (2005) do not discuss what the Constitution meant for women and American Indians, but they do highlight the issue of representation and the states with the largest slave populations. They cleverly avoided describing the Three-Fifths Compromise as meaning a male slave was equal to three-fifths of a propertied White male. Instead, they made the compromise more palatable, converting the fractions to whole numbers, saying that only three of five slaves could be counted for representation purposes. Three out of five might sound less offensive, but three-fifths it still is, meaning that one male slave counted as three-fifths of his master.

The Move Toward the Civil War

As the country grew, the settlers displaced American Indians from their lands. The Indian Removal Act and the Trail of Tears are explained in two pages (in both series). Several American Indian nations—the Choctaw, Seminole, and Creek—were removed from their lands just as the Cherokee were. The series do mention the other nations, but the major focus is on the Cherokee.

As the nation grew, and more states were added to the Union, slavery became a thornier issue for all and was considered an immoral institution by a growing number of antislavery leaders. By the time the importation of slaves into the United States was outlawed (1808), it had become a home-bred enterprise (Conniff & Davis, 1994; Kolchin, 1993; Segal, 1995). The dishonorable methods by which masters increased their holdings of enslaved people (e.g., the rape of female slaves) are not mentioned in either series, and perhaps the authors should not be expected to do so. What the two series do highlight are the growth of the abolitionist movement, the Underground Railroad, and the various compromises, such as the Missouri Compromise, which were enacted to stave off a looming civil war. Both series also had a few sentences on Dred Scott and the legal and human ramifications of the Dred Scott Supreme Court decision. There was special emphasis on Frederick Douglass; Harriet Tubman, the Underground Railroad's most famous conductor; and Sojourner Truth, who was known for her strength and her powers of oratory. Lucretia Mott and Susan B. Anthony were noted for their abolitionist work and their fight for women's rights. The Seneca Falls Women's Rights Convention received a brief mention. Elizabeth Cady Stanton's role in the fight for women's rights was also highlighted. Reformers Dorothea Dix, Frances Elizabeth Willard, and Lucy Larcorn were highlighted in sidebars.

The Civil War and Its Aftermath

The Civil War constituted a whole unit in both series. The usual battles, generals, heroics, victories, and defeats were given about the same coverage in both series. The one glaring piece of information missing from both was the role of slaves and ex-slaves in the Confederate Army. Toward the end of the war, the Confederates needed all the able-bodied men they could get, and that included slaves and some ex-slaves. Blacks had already been performing manual labor for the Confederate troops and the most dangerous and/or onerous tasks, such as retrieving fallen soldiers from an active battlefield. Robert E. Lee wanted to recruit slaves into the enlisted ranks by promising them freedom, but Jefferson Davis and his advisors did not want to use freedom as an incentive for slaves to enlist (Haskins, 1998). Reconstruction is covered in fewer pages than the Civil War, with the major focus being on how many ex-slaves were at the mercy of vengeful Whites when the Federal troops were withdrawn from the former Confederate States. Hiram Revels was noted as the first person of African descent to serve in the United States Senate.

The Transcontinental Railroad and the Push Westward

The nation's rapid growth westward kept pushing American Indians from their hunting grounds and homelands. In both series, the authors focused on the last great stands made by such American Indian warriors as Sitting Bull, Crazy Horse, and Chief Joseph. Among the famous warrior-leaders omitted from both series was the great Apache warrior Geronimo. The Black soldiers known as the Buffalo Soldiers, who gained fame in the Indian

Wars, were not mentioned until the turn of the century, when they charged up San Juan Hill with Teddy Roosevelt and his Rough Riders.

Although historians have shown that without Chinese immigrants, the Transcontinental Railroad would not have been built so efficiently and as quickly, the two series skimmed over the contributions of these Chinese immigrants, the unspeakable bigotry they suffered, and the horrid conditions in which they lived. They were paid much less than all the other workers, including ex-slaves. The most the two series could muster was a paragraph in the Houghton Mifflin series (Viola, et al., 2005) and two sentences in the Scott Foresman series (Boyd, et al., 2005). Another gap in this piece of history is the omission of any reference to the Chinese Exclusion Act of 1882, legislation that prevented Chinese immigrants from becoming citizens. Citing the Act would show that despite the prejudices of previous generations, the country has been strong enough to repeal bad legislation for the benefit of its citizens.

Reconstruction and the Late 19th Century Text Set

The recommended titles in this extended text set for the late 19th century (Table 23-1) highlight the following: (a) the struggles of ex-slaves attempting to live honorably and peacefully after being freed, (b) the difficult conditions and bigotry that Chinese immigrants experienced seeking a new life in the "Land of Gold Mountain," especially during their work on the building of the Transcontinental Railroad, (c) the consequences of the railroad crossing American Indian homelands, (d) a rarely told piece of American history about Jewish settlers in the West, and (e) how women and people of color went west to partake of this country's many opportunities and to live freely.

The 20th Century

As critical as the 20th century was to this country's standing in the world, the two social studies series crammed all the monumental events in two to three chapters. World War II, on both fronts, took all of seven pages in one series and eight pages in the other.

Cramming too much history in a few short pages and shortchanging the 20th century is not unusual for a social studies series. Beck, McKeown, & Gromoll (1989) analyzed four social studies series and found that 62% to 75% of them were to devoted to events from the age of discovery to the Civil War. They note that in one series, westward expansion, the Industrial Revolution, immigration, the two World Wars, the Korean War, the Cold War, the Civil Rights Movement, the Vietnam War, and the women's liberation movement were covered in 44 pages (p. 108). The two series in my study were not quite that stingy, but proportionally, the number of pages

Table 23-1. Text Set for Reconstruction & the Late 19th Century

Reconstruction

- *Cause: Reconstruction America, 1863–1877* (Bolden, 2005)
- *Into the Land of Freedom: African Americans in Reconstruction* (Greene, 2004)
- *Bury Me Not in the Land of Slaves: African-Americans in the Time of Reconstruction* (Hansen, 2000)
- *Children of the Emancipation* (King, 2000)
- *Black Voices From Reconstruction, 1865–1877* (Smith, 1996)

Native Americans

- *Geronimo* (Bruchac, 2006)
- *Navajo Long Walk: The Tragic Story of a Proud People's Forced March From Their Homeland* (Bruchac, 2002)
- *Death of the Iron Horse* (Goble, 1987)
- *Into the West: From Reconstruction to the Final Days of the American Frontier* (McPherson, 2006)
- *Buffalo Soldiers: African-American Soldiers* (Reef, 1993)
- *It Is a Good Day to Die: Indian Eyewitnesses Tell the Story of the Battle of Little Big Horn* (Viola, 1998)

Chinese Immigrants

- *Iron Dragon Never Sleeps* (Krensky, 1994)
- *Tales From Gold Mountain: Stories of the Chinese in the New World* (Yee, 1990)
- *Dragon's Gate* (Yep, 1993)
- *The Journal of Wong Ming-Chung: A Chinese Miner* (Yep, 2000)
- *Coolies* (Yin, 2001)

Western Expansion

- *Wagon Wheels* (Brenner, 1993)
- *Geography of Hope: Black Exodus From the South After Reconstruction* (Haskins, 1999)
- *Black Women of the Old West* (Katz, 1995)
- *Black Cowboy, Wild Horses* (Lester, 1998)
- *Journal of Joshua Loper: A Black Cowboy* (Myers, 1999)
- *Nothing Here But Stones: A Jewish Pioneer Story* (Oswald, 2004)
- *Women of the American West* (Sonneborn, 2005)
- *I Could Do That!: Ester Morris Gets Women the Vote* (White, 2005)

and chapters devoted to significant milestones in the 20th century were far fewer than the number dedicated to the Civil War and earlier.

Another problem with the two social studies series is how historically dependent events are presented as stand-alone occurrences, thus making it difficult for students to make connections among significant events. The authors cherry-picked events that happened concurrently and presented them as if they had occurred chronologically. For example, the final push for the 19th Amendment really took off during the first term of Woodrow Wilson. Women supported his election because he said that he supported women's suffrage. If students did not know that piece of history beforehand, they would never learn it from these two series. It was as if the authors were trying to protect Wilson from hoards of willful women who were angered because he reneged on his campaign promise (Bausum, 2004).

Wilson and his work for the League of Nations and other issues surrounding World War I were featured before women's suffrage was discussed; this was true of both series. Once elected, he was unsympathetic to women who were being abused in protest marches, jailed unnecessarily, and threatened with being committed to asylums by husbands and fathers. Wilson was definitely not thrilled to see women marching in the streets of Washington, D.C. However, the way Wilson's first term and the women's suffrage movement are presented, a student would never know that one had any relation to the other. Wilson was presented as if he had no notion that there was an active women's movement in the streets right outside the White House.

World War II

World War II was given little page space compared to the chapters dedicated to the Revolutionary and Civil Wars. Within seven or eight pages, students are expected to learn about Hitler, his Final Solution, Mussolini's alliance with Hitler, the U.S. ambivalence about entering the war in Europe, and finally, Pearl Harbor and the war in the Pacific. The country's internment of Japanese Americans was covered in four paragraphs (about half a page) in the Scott Foresman text (Boyd et al., 2005). In the Houghton Mifflin series (Viola et al., 2005) the information on Japanese internment was covered in about two paragraphs. The Holocaust received similar coverage, one short column (a long paragraph) in Houghton Mifflin, and two paragraphs in Scott Foresman. Women, represented by Rosie the Riveter, received caption and picture space and several sentences within a paragraph on the need for more tanks and uniforms. Finally, in the last sentences of the last paragraph on World War II on the Asian front, the bombing of Hiroshima and Nagasaki are mentioned. In one text Hiroshima is highlighted on the page, but Nagasaki is not. In the other series, the names of the two cities are almost lost in within the paragraph's verbiage.

Another thing about the way that World War II is presented in these texts is that the contributions African Americans made to the war effort seem to be very few (in one series) or not at all (in the other). Buried in a sentence about the overall number of people who enlisted was a showing that about 1 million Blacks joined the armed services. There was not a single sentence on the Tuskegee Airmen. The picture presented in the two series of the United States in World War II inferred that it was the White man's burden to save the country (and the world) from the Nazis, the Fascists, and the Japanese with just a little help from Navajo Code Talkers (that is, if students remembered that information from September).

The United States and the World at War Text Set

The two defining wars of the 20th century did not warrant individual chapters from either series. The Korean and Vietnam Wars were mere blips in the chapters. The titles in this extended text set (Table 23-2) support what little information was included about the world at war and our country's role in each, particularly titles that show the contributions of women and people of color during times of war. Unfortunately, there are also titles that show the depths to which humans can sink when they fear or hate those who do not look, speak, or believe as they do.

The Civil Rights Movement

The Civil Rights Movement has all the usual players—Martin Luther King (the March on Washington and his "I Have a Dream" speech), Thurgood Marshall, Linda Brown, and Rosa Parks. The counter sit-ins are given some page space, and the Little Rock Nine get one sentence in one series, but the Freedom Riders, the bombing of the church in Birmingham in which four little girls were killed, George Wallace's famous stand in the school doorway, and various peaceful protest marches are omitted. The authors' single-minded focus on Martin Luther King makes it appear that his was the only significant contribution to the Civil Rights Movement. This one-sided focus minimizes the significant contributions of other important, but often less recognized, civil rights leaders, such as Fannie Lou Hamer and Daisy Bates.

The Terrorist Attacks of September 11, 2001

The last aspect of the series that I examined was the 9/11 terrorists attacks. If ever there was an event that touched all colors and classes of people, the terrorist attacks on the Pentagon and the World Trade Center would be it. It is difficult to say if the weak coverage of the event was due to publishing deadlines, the fear that the events would be too frightening for fifth graders to digest, or both. Both series had the Iwo Jima–like photographs of the firemen in the rubble of one of the towers hoisting an American flag. There are pictures of many people and animals that helped in the rescue efforts. The short sections do nothing to help students reflect on the reasons that someone would ever consider flying passenger planes into buildings full of

Table 23-2. Text Set for the United States and the World at War

African Americans, Native Americans, and Women in War

- *American Patriots: The Story of Blacks in the Military From the Revolutionary War to Desert Storm* (Buckley, 2003)
- *Hell Fighters: African-American Soldiers in World War I* (Cooper, 1997)
- *Flying Free: America's First Black Aviators* (Hart, 1992)
- *Tuskegee Airmen: American Heroes* (Homan & Reilly, 2002)
- *Harlem Hellfighters: When Pride Met Courage* (Myers & Miles, 2005)
- *Those Extraordinary Women of World War I* (Zeinert, 2001)
- *The Unbreakable Code* (Hunter, 1996)
- *Warriors: Navajo Code Talkers* (Kawano, 1990)
- *Quiet Hero: The Ira Hayes Story* (Nelson, 2006)

The Holocaust

- *A Hero of the Holocaust* (Adler, 2002)
- *Hilde and Eli: Children of the Holocaust* (Adler, 1994)
- *Auschwitz: The Story of a Nazi Death Camp* (Lawton, 2002)
- *Luba: The Angel of Bergen-Belsen* (McCann, 2003)
- *Passage to Freedom: The Sugihara Story* (Mochizuk, 1997)
- *Smoke and Ashes: The Story of the Holocaust* (Rogasky, 2002)
- *The Cat With the Yellow Star* (Rubin & Weissberger, 2006)
- *My Secret Camera: Life in the Lodz Ghetto* (Smith, 2000)

The Atom Bomb and Japanese-American Internment

- *Weedflower* (Kadohata, 2006)
- *Hiroshima: The Story of the First Atom Bomb* (Lawton, 2004)
- *A Place Where Sunflowers Grow* (Lee-Tai, 2006)
- *Hiroshima No Pika* (Maruki, 1980)
- *Baseball Saved Us* (Mochizuki, 1993)
- *Dear Miss Breed: True Stories of the Japanese Incarceration During World War II and the Librarian Who Made a Difference* (Oppenheim, 2006)
- *I Am an American: A True Story of the Japanese Internment* (Stanley, 1994)
- *The Children of Topaz: The Story of a Japanese-American Internment Camp* (Tunnell & Chilcoat, 1996)

The Korean and Vietnam Wars

- *Sweet Dried Apples* (Breckler, 1996)
- *10,000 Days of Thunder: A History of the Vietnam War* (Caputo, 2005)
- *The Korean War* (Feldman, 2004)
- *I Remember Korea: Veterans Tell Their Stories of the Korean War, 1950–53* (Granfield, 2003)
- *The Land I Lost: Adventures of a Boy in Vietnam* (Nhuong, 1982)
- *Escape From Saigon: How a Vietnam Orphan Became an American Boy* (Warren, 2004)

people. This means that students should be asked to engage in serious reflection about the dangers in the world. They should be asked to think critically about how the United States affects the world, for good and for bad. Despite how the issues are presented by our leaders, this is not an issue of good versus evil. It is a major clash of worldviews. Students must consider these worldviews as they grow older, and fifth grade is a proper time to start these conversations about differences. They will need informed, not emotional, guidance from adults to help them understand people who live in countries far different from the United States. They will also need texts that will make them want to explore and think about living in a rapidly changing world. Unfortunately, the end of the chapter mentions the United States in Afghanistan and Iraq, with little background to help students understand the countries to which the United States has deployed troops.

Since the attacks of September 11, 2001, it has been very clear that Americans have very little understanding of the Arab and Muslim world, whether the countries are friendly or antagonistic. This lack of knowledge prevents many citizens from being able to separate the rhetoric of friend from that of foe. Because of the fear of vulnerable borders that the attacks of 9/11 sparked in many Americans, titles about immigration from Mexico and other countries have been included in the list (Table 23-3). Being more informed

Table 23-3. Text Set for Linking to the World

- *Ask Me No Questions* (Budhos, 2006)
- *Neve Shalom/Wahat Al-Salaam: Oasis of Peace* (Dolphin, 1993)
- *The Breadwinner* (Ellis, 2000)
- *Mud City* (Ellis, 2003)
- *Parvana's Journey* (Ellis, 2002)
- *Three Wishes: Palestinian and Israeli Children Speak* (Ellis, 2004)
- *Ramadan* (Ghazi, 1996)
- *Crossing the Wire* (Hobbs, 2006)
- *La Linea* (Jaramillo, 2006)
- *Children Just Like Me: A Unique Celebration of Children Around the World* (Kindersley & Kindersley, 1995)
- *Who Belongs Here?: An American Story* (Knight, 1993)
- *How My Family Lives in America* (Kuklin, 1992)
- *My Name Is Jorge on Both Sides of the River* (Medina, 1999)
- *Grandma Hekmat Remembers: An Egyptian-American Family Story* (Morris, 2003)
- *Being Muslim* (Siddiqui, 2006)
- *If the World Were a Village: A Book About the World's People* (Smith, 2002)
- *Alia's Mission: Saving the Books of Iraq* (Stamatay, 2004)
- *The Librarian of Basra: A True Story of Iraq* (Winter, 2005)

about the immigration issue empowers those who can see beyond the hyperbolic rhetoric. The more students read about societies different from theirs, the better able they will be able to live in a 21st century in which being a world superpower (at this writing, the only world superpower) no longer holds the value that it once did.

Conclusion

The history taught to children in American schools has many masters to satisfy—conservatives, college professors, school boards, professional organizations, standards writers, teachers, parents, and the students. As presented in these two series, the history content reflects what has been said about the American math curriculum during the late 1990s. The lead author of the Third International Mathematics and Science Study (TIMSS) described the American math curriculum as being "an inch deep and a mile wide" (Schmidt, McKnight, & Raizen, 1997). This shallow and wide history coverage is why Loewen (1995) states that history is the only school subject in which the more courses students take, the "stupider they become." History, as taught in grades K–12, has become so problematic that many college professors feel the need to reteach much of what has been learned in school (Waters, 2005). The history in these two series lacks so much depth that students who have had a steady diet of it might have to take remedial history when they enroll in college.

References

Allen, G. (Producer). (2006, August 19). Florida law stirs debate over teaching history. *All Things Considered* Washington, DC: National Public Radio.

Barton, K. C., & Levstik, L. S. (2000). "It wasn't a good part of history": National identity and student explanations of historical significance. *Teachers College Record, 99* (3), 478–513.

Bausum. A. (2004). *With courage and cloth: Winning the fight for a woman's right to vote.* Washington, DC: National Geographic.

Beck, I., McKeown, M. G., & Gromoll, E. W. (1989). Learning from social studies texts. *Cognition and Instruction, 6* (2), 99–158.

Berkin, C. (2006). "We, the People of the United States": The birth of the American identity, September, 1787. *OAH Magazine of History, 20* (4), 53–54.

Berstein, J. H., Hutton, L. A., & Curtis, R. (2006). The state of social studies teaching in one urban district. *Journal of Social Studies Research, 30* (1), 15–20.

Boehm, R. G., Hoone, C., McGowan, L. M., McKinney-Browning, M. C., Miramontes, O. B. & Porter, P. H. (2000). *United States in modern times.* Orlando, FL: Harcourt.

Boyd, C. D., Gay, G. Geiger, R., Kracht, J. B., Pang, V. O., Risenger, C. F. & Sanchez, S. M. (2005). *Scott Foresman Social Studies: The United States* (Vols. 1 & 2). Glenview, IL: Pearson Education.

California Department of Education. (2005). *California 2005 History–Social Science*. Available online at www.cde.ca.gov/ci/hs/im/sbehssadop.asp

Carr, K. S., Buchanan, D. L., Wentz, J. B., Weiss, M. L., & Brant, K. J. (2001). Not just for primary grades: A bibliography of picture books for secondary teachers. *Journal of Adolescent and Adult Literacy, 45* (2), 146–153.

Conniff, M. L., & Davis, T. J. (1994). *Africans in the Americas: A history of the Black diaspora*. New York: St. Martin's Press.

Fertig, G. (2005). Teaching elementary students how to interpret the past. *Social Studies, 96* (1), 2–8.

Finn, C. E. (2003). Foreword. In J. Lemming, L. Ellington, & K. Porter-Magee, *Passion without progress: What's wrong with social studies education?* Washington, DC: Fordham Institute.

Haskins, J. (1998). *Black, blue & gray: African Americans in the Civil War*. New York: Simon & Schuster.

Hughes, R. T. (2003). *Myths America lives by*. Urbana, IL: University of Illinois Press.

Jones, E. B., Pang, V. O., & Rodriguez, J. L. (2001). Social studies in the elementary classroom: Culture matters. *Theory Into Practice, 40* (1), 35–41.

Kolchin, P. (1993). *American slavery, 1619–1877*. New York: Hill and Wang.

Lehr, S. S., & Thompson, D. L. (2000). The dynamic nature of response: Children reading and responding to *Maniac Magee* and *The friendship*. *The Reading Teacher, 53*, 480–493.

Loewen, J. W. (1995). *Lies my teacher told me: Everything your American history textbook got wrong*. New York: New Press.

Opitz, M. (1998). Text sets: One way to flex your grouping—in first grade, too! *The Reading Teacher, 51* (7), 622–624.

Palmer, C. A. (1994). *The first passage: Blacks in the Americas, 1502–1617*. New York: Oxford University Press.

Paxton, R. J. (2003). Don't know much about history—never did. *Phi Delta Kappan, 85* (4), 265–273.

Robinson, W. C. (2006). *IS: 561—Textbook publishing*. Available online at http://web.utk.edu/~wrobinso/561_lec_textbk.html.

Schmidt, W., McKnight, C. C., & Raizen, S. A. (1997). *A splintered vision: An investigation of U.S. science and mathematics education—Executive summary*. East Lansing, MI: U.S. National Research Center for the Third International Mathematics and Science Study (TIMSS).

Segal, R. (1995). *The Black diaspora*. New York: Farrar, Straus & Giroux.

Viola, H. J., Bednarz, S. W., Cortés, C. E., Jennings, C., Schug, M. C. & White, C. S. (2005). *Houghton Mifflin Social Studies: United States History* (Vols. 1 & 2). Boston: Houghton Mifflin.

Waters, T. (2005). Why students think there are two kinds of American history. *The History Teacher, 39* (1), 11–21.

Wolk, S. (2003). Teaching for critical literacy in social studies. *Social Studies, 94* (3), 101–106.

Zhao, Y., & Hoge, J. D. (2005). What elementary students and teachers say about social studies. *Social Studies, 96* (5), 216–221.

Children's Books

Adler, D. A. (1994). *Hilde and Eli: Children of the Holocaust.* New York: Holiday House.

Adler, D. A. (2002). *A hero of the Holocaust.* New York: Holiday House.

Bolden, T. (2005). *Cause: Reconstruction America, 1863–1877.* New York: Crown.

Breckler, R. (1996). *Sweet dried apples.* Boston: Houghton Mifflin.

Brenner, B. (1993). *Wagon wheels.* New York: HarperCollins.

Bruchac, J. (2002). *Navajo Long Walk: The tragic story of a proud people's forced march from their homeland.* Washington, DC: National Geographic.

Bruchac, J. (2006). *Geronimo.* New York: Scholastic.

Buckley, G. (2003). *American patriots: The story of blacks in the military from the Revolutionary War to Desert Storm.* New York: Crown.

Budhos, M. (2006). *Ask me no questions.* New York: Atheneum.

Caputo, P. (2005). *10,000 days of thunder: A history of the Vietnam War.* New York: Simon & Schuster.

Cooper, M. (1997). *Hell fighters: African-American soldiers in World War I.* New York: Penguin.

Dolphin, L. (1993). *Neve Shalom/Wahat Al-Salaam: Oasis of peace.* New York: Scholastic.

Ellis, D. (2000). *The breadwinner.* Toronto, Ontario, Canada: Groundwood.

Ellis, D. (2002). *Parvana's journey.* Toronto, Ontario, Canada: Groundwood.

Ellis, D. (2003). *Mud city.* Toronto, Ontario, Canada: Groundwood.

Ellis, D. (2004). *Three wishes: Palestinian and Israeli children speak.* Toronto, Ontario, Canada: Groundwood.

Feldman, R. T. (2004). *The Korean War.* Minneapolis, MN: Lerner.

Fradin, D. B. (2002). *The signers: The 56 stories behind the Declaration of Independence.* New York: Walker.

Freedman, R. (2004). *The voice that challenged a nation: Marian Anderson and the struggle for equal rights.* New York: Clarion Books.

Ghazi, H. (1996). *Ramadan.* New York: Holiday House

Goble, P. (1987). *Death of the iron horse.* New York: Bradbury.

Granfield, L. (2003). *I remember Korea: Veterans tell their stories of the Korean War, 1950–53.* New York: Clarion Books.

Greene, M. (2004). *Into the land of freedom: African Americans in Reconstruction.* Minneapolis, MN: Lerner.

Hansen, J. (2000). *Bury me not in the land of slaves: African Americans in the time of Reconstruction.* New York: Scholastic.

Hart, P. S. (1992). *Flying free: America's first Black aviators.* Minneapolis, MN: Lerner.

Haskins, J. (1999). *Geography of hope: Black exodus from the South after Reconstruction.* Minneapolis, MN: Lerner.

Hobbs, W. (2006). *Crossing the wire.* New York: HarperCollins.

Homan, L. M., & Reilly, T. (2002). *Tuskegee airmen: American heroes.* Gretna, LA: Pelican.

Hunter, S. H. (1996). *The unbreakable code.* Flagstaff, AZ: Rising Moon.

Jaramillo, A. (2006). *La linea.* New Milford, CT: Roaring Brook Press.

Kadohata, C. (2006). *Weedflower.* New York: Atheneum.

Katz, W. L. (1995). *Black women of the old west.* New York: Atheneum.

Kawano, K. (1990). *Warriors: Navajo code talkers.* Flagstaff, AZ Northland.

Kindersley B., & Kindersley, A. (1995). *Children just like me: A unique celebration of children around the world.* New York: Dorling Kindersley.

King, W. (2000). *Children of the emancipation.* Minneapolis, MN: Lerner.

Knight, M. B. (1993). *Who belongs here?: An American story.* Gardiner, ME: Tilbury House.

Krensky, S. (1994). *Iron dragon never sleeps.* New York: Bantam Doubleday.

Kuklin, S. (1992). *How my family lives in America.* New York: Bradbury.

Lawton, C. A. (2002). *Auschwitz: The story of a Nazi death camp.* Cambridge, MA: Candlewick Press.

Lawton, C. A. (2004). *Hiroshima: The story of the first atom bomb.* Cambridge, MA: Candlewick Press,

Lee-Tai, A. (2006). *A place where sunflowers grow.* San Francisco: Children's Book Press.

Lester, J. (1998). *Black cowboy, wild horses.* New York: Dial.

Maruki, T. (1980). *Hiroshima no pika.* New York: Lothrop.

McCann, M. R. (2003). *Luba: The angel of Bergen-Belsen.* Berkeley, CA: Tricycle Press.

McPherson, J. (2006). *Into the west: From Reconstruction to the final days of the American frontier.* New York: Simon & Schuster.

Medina, J. (1999). *My name is Jorge on both sides of the river.* Honesdale, PA: Wordsong.

Mochizuki, K. (1993). *Baseball saved us.* New York: Lee & Low.

Mochizuki, K. (1997). *Passage to freedom: The Sugihara story.* New York: Lee & Low.

Morris, A. (2003). *Grandma Hekmat remembers: An Egyptian-American family story.* Minneapolis, MN: Lerner.

Myers, W. D. (1999). *Journal of Joshua Loper: A Black cowboy.* New York: Scholastic.

Myers, W. D., & Miles, B. (2005). *Harlem Hellfighters: When pride met courage.* New York: HarperCollins.

Nelson, G. (2006). *Quiet hero: The Ira Hayes story.* New York: Lee & Low.

Nhuong, H. Q. (1982). *The land I lost: Adventures of a boy in Vietnam.* New York: Harper & Row.

Oppenheim, J. (2006). *Dear Miss Breed: True stories of the Japanese incarceration during World War II and the librarian who made a difference.* New York: Scholastic.

Oswald, N. (2004). *Nothing here but stones: A Jewish pioneer story.* New York: Holt.

Reef, C. (1993). *Buffalo soldiers: African-American Soldiers.* Minneapolis, MN: Twenty-First Century.

Rogasky, B. (2002). *Smoke and ashes: The story of the Holocaust.* New York: Holiday House.

Rubin, S. G., & Weissberger, E. (2006). *The cat with the yellow star.* New York: Holiday House.

Siddiqui, H. (2006). *Being Muslim.* Toronto, Ontario, Canada: Groundwood.

Smith, D. (2002). *If the world were a village: A book about the world's people.* Toronto, Ontario, Canada: Kids Can Press.

Smith, F. D. (2000). *My secret camera: Life in the Lodz Ghetto.* San Diego, CA: Gulliver/Harcourt.

Smith, J. D. (1996). *Black voices from Reconstruction, 1865–1877.* Minneapolis, MN: Millbrook.

Sonneborn, L. (2005). *Women of the American west.* New York: Scholastic.

Spinelli, J. (1990). *Maniac Magee.* Boston: Little, Brown.

Stamatay, M. A. (2004). *Alia's mission: Saving the books of Iraq.* New York: Knopf.

Stanley, J. (1994). *I am an American: A true story of the Japanese internment.* New York: Crown.

Taylor, M. D. (1986). *The friendship.* New York: Dial.

Tunnell, M., & Chilcoat, G. W. (1996). *The children of Topaz: The story of a Japanese-American internment camp.* New York: Holiday House.

Viola, H. (1998). *It is a good day to die: Indian eyewitnesses tell the story of the Battle of Little Big Horn.* New York: Crown.

Warren, A. (2004). *Escape from Saigon: How a Vietnam orphan became an American boy.* New York: Farrar, Straus & Giroux,

White, L. A. (2005). *I could do that!: Ester Morris gets women the vote.* New York: Farrar, Straus & Giroux.

Winter, J. (2005). *The librarian of Basra: A true story of Iraq.* New York: Harcourt.

Yee, P. (1990). *Tales from Gold Mountain: Stories of the Chinese in the New World.* New York: Simon & Schuster.

Yep, L. (1993). *Dragon's gate.* New York: HarperCollins.

Yep, L. (2000). *The journal of Wong Ming-Chung: A Chinese miner.* New York: Scholastic.

Yin. (2001). *Coolies.* New York: Philomel.

Zeinert, K. (2001). *Those extraordinary women of World War I.* Minneapolis, MN: Millbrook.

Chapter 24

Books Matter: Literature Strategies That Work in Middle School

Laura Robb

When I support a school district in improving reading and in motivating middle school students to read, I always interview dozens of students from each grade during my first two visits. I find that middle school students are candid, and these interviews often spotlight students' needs and provide me with the data I need to work with administrators and teachers.

David (pseudonym) was the first seventh-grader I interviewed on my first day at his school. When I asked him how I could help to improve his reading, he blurted, "Give me words. Oh, yeah," added, "and stuff I can read." Indeed, when I reviewed David's standardized testing and the Independent Reading Inventories that teachers had administered in the past, I saw that David and too many other students at this school had weak vocabularies and were so far behind their grade level that they weren't able to read the grade-level anthology in language arts classes and the textbooks in science and social studies. Outside school David read "some comics," but not books or magazines. "Man, I don't touch those," he told me.

The language arts classrooms in David's school had no libraries. Moreover, the school's library was inadequate and staffed by parent volunteers who were not there all the time and who lacked the training and authority to order books and magazines. Readers like David, who needed access to books to practice reading to enlarge their vocabularies and background knowledge, lost reading ground each year. The first initiative that teachers, parents, and administrators rallied around was to raise money for rich and varied classrooms libraries. I helped them to understand that access to books, magazines, and graphic novels at a wide range of reading levels in a classroom library would enable the students to choose books that interested them and that they could connect to and enjoy (Cunningham & Allington, 2003). Immediate access to materials they could read and wanted to read would provide the practice reading that students needed to become better readers.

It's wrong to assume that books and other reading materials are available to all children in the United States. Moreover, differences in access to books cause gaps in reading achievement (Cunningham and Allington, 2003; Krashen, 1996). In this chapter I explore ways to make the classroom library not an "add on" to curriculum or a luxury item for independent reading but an embedded literacy strategy that promotes independent reading, unfettered by curriculum links.

Inspire Students to Read With Your Classroom Library

With schools using government-approved basal anthologies—one grade-level text for all—those learners who need the most reading practice to improve don't have easy access to books. Like Richard Allington (2006), I believe that readers who struggle need to read as much as, if not more than, proficient readers do. That's why I believe that if more schools put classroom libraries at the top of their wish lists, they could make it happen and meet the needs of all students.

A library should be one of the first resources schools buy. I want books to be central, and reading them the heart and soul of every middle school classroom. Books should be the first thing that catches students' attention when they enter a classroom, and books best serve students when they are arranged to "sell" themselves—not unlike how you find them displayed in a good bookstore. I organize and label my books and bookshelves by genre because I find that middle school students look first for a favorite genre—and then for a beloved author or a book recommended by someone. I then separate fiction and nonfiction genres into categories, such as realistic fiction, suspense, biography, and nature books. Come up with your own way of organizing your books to reflect your students' reading interests. Following are the genres I suggest you collect:

> *Poetry*, including fiction written in free verse, such as *Dark Sons* by Nikki Grimes (2005), *The Taking of Room 114* by Mel Glenn (1997), *Witness* by Karen Hesse (2001), and *Carver* by Marilyn Nelson (2001).

> *Short texts*: short stories, fairy tales and folktales, and myths and legends, such as *Lives of Extraordinary Women* (2000) and *Lives of the Athletes* (1997) by Kathleen Krull, *Her Stories* by Virginia Hamilton (1995), *Heroes and Monsters of Greek Myths* by Bernard Evslin and Dorothy Evslin, and *Bronx Masquerade* by Nikki Grimes (2002).

Fiction: realistic fiction, historical fiction, letters, diaries, suspense, fantasy, science fiction, graphic novels, and comics. Here are a few books my students rate as top-notch: *California Blue* by David Klass (1999), *Crash* by Jerry Spinelli (1996), *Miracle's Boys* by Jacqueline Woodson (2000), and *Somewhere in Darkness* by Walter Dean Myers (1992). A few all-time favorite authors are Richard Peck, Diana Wynn Jones, Avi, Barbara Cooney, Walter Dean Myers, Gordon Korman, and Jacqueline Woodson.

Nonfiction: informational chapter books and picture books, biography and autobiography, diaries, letters, journals. *Black Whiteness: Admiral Byrd Alone in the Antarctic* by Robert Burleigh (1998), *Harvesting Hope: The Story of Cesar Chavez* by Kathleen Krull (2003), and *Confucius: The Golden Rule* (2002) and *Lincoln: A Photobiography* (1987) by Russell Freedman are titles that students repeatedly check out. Beloved nonfiction authors are James Cross Giblin, Russell Freedman, Frederick McKissack and Patricia McKissack, and Milton Meltzer.

Suspense, mystery, horror, romance, series, graphic novels, and magazines: In addition to the above categories, I also include a section on horror and suspense, romance and "girlie" books (that's my students' name for these), comics, graphic novels, and magazines. Each year students bring comics and magazines for their peers to check out. I always permit students to choose what they enjoy and find interesting. Through book talks by me and their peers, most students branch out from comics to books. That's why my library contains books by R. L. Stine, Stephen King, Carolyn Cooney, John Bellairs, and Joan Lowry Nixon. Authors of series that are frequently passed from student to student are Gordon Korman and Aiden Chambers.

It takes time to build a large and varied classroom library. You can ask your parent-teacher association (PTA) to raise dollars for books, you can apply for grants, and you can order titles from book clubs and use your bonus points to enlarge your library. Make sure that you create appealing displays that shout to students, "Read! Read! Read!"

Keep Book Displays Dynamic

Books in a neat row with spines showing save space, but it's not an ideal display for browsing. Here are some strategies for enticing young readers to pick up a book:

- Create clear, colorful labels above each section (mysteries, biographies, etc.).
- On each shelf, place two or three books with covers facing outward.
- Use your entire classroom. Set up displays on windowsills, line some books up on the chalk tray of your chalkboard (after cleaning it, of

course!), on an extra table, on your desk, or on the top of book-shelves.

- Change the displays every 5–6 weeks and take a few minutes of class time to point out each new group of books that arrives. Pique students' interest by sharing the genre, author, and cover photo; if you have time, read the text on the back or inside cover. Advertise books so they invite students to browse and explore genres and authors that are new for them.

- When you think of ideas for the featured displays, be creative. For example, you can feature an author or a a genre; a period in history; a theme; or common issues such as justice and injustice, the struggle between good and evil, or the power of hope. Encourage students to create displays of an author or a genre and share their selections with the class.

> **Tips for Keeping Track of Library Books**
>
> - Put your name in each book.
> - Record each book title in a database on your computer.
> - Create a checkout system so students can take books home. I use a note-book in which students write their name, the book's title, the date checked out, and the date returned. Students can keep books up to a month.
> - If a student fails to return a book, I work with that student. Most of the time students return books. However, it's wise to accept that there will be some books lost each year that you have to replace.
> - Have students shelve the returned books.

When my students write about their personal reading lives, they give high marks to classroom libraries. Christa Doerwaldt notes, "I love having a library in our class-room! It has books at our reading levels, and it is easier to see what books are there than in a big library." Avery McIntosh agrees when she explains, "A library in class really helps me because I have so many books at the tip of my fingers."

Knowing students' interests early in the year can empower you to help them select books that will motivate them to continue to read.

Discover Your Students' Interests

At the start of the school year I find out my students' interests and perhaps discover a topic they're passionate about. This information helps me to suggest books to students that they might want to read. Note that I say *might* want to read, because I've found that students might not choose to read or finish reading a book I've suggested. This is especially true of reluctant readers, those who rarely engage with a book and enjoy reading. Try to get beyond your first natural reaction of *I'll never take time to help you again.*

Instead, try inviting a student with similar interests to recommend a book to his or her peer; it's often a more persuasive recommendation.

You can also buddy up reluctant readers or students who are reading below grade level with primary-level students and have the older students read aloud to their buddies. One day I brought in two crates of picture books for a group of seventh and eighth graders who were to choose a book and practice reading it aloud before sharing the book with a buddy. One seventh grader slowly turned the pages of Steven Kellogg's (2002) *The Mysterious Tadpole*, savoring each illustration. He brought the book to me, holding it open in the palms of his hands. "So *this* is a picture book," he said. Sad to say, this literacy-deprived young adult only had memories of completing work sheets and reading "boring" books. Having a younger buddy changed these students' attitudes toward reading because the younger children admired and adored their older buddies and saw them as expert readers. One eighth grader summed up every student's feelings this way: "I feel better about myself when I read to my buddy. He [the buddy] loves when I read to him."

Use the interest inventory (Table 24-1) to discover what books your students might want to read independently or read aloud to a young buddy. Remember to always offer students choice. Suggest two or three books that might interest a student, and empower the students to select what they want to read.

Table 24-1. Interest Inventory

> **Directions:** Write your name and the date at the top of a [separate] sheet of paper and answer the following questions.
>
> 1. What do you enjoy doing most in your free time?
> 2. What sports do you love to watch?
> 3. What sports do you enjoy playing?
> 4. Do you have a favorite school subject? Can you explain why you enjoy it?
> 5. If you could travel back in time, where would you go? Explain why.
> 6. If you could visit any place on Earth, where would you go?
> 7. Do you have a favorite author? Name the author and try to explain why you enjoy his or her books.
> 8. Do you read comic books? Name some that you enjoy.
> 9. Do you read magazines? Name the ones you read often.
> 10. What kinds of books do you enjoy most when reading on your own? This list can help you name some: mystery, suspense, funny books, folktales, series books, realistic fiction, fantasy, science fiction, biography, historical fiction, or informational books.

Providing Choice and Time to Read During Class

When I invite my students to write about their experiences with class libraries and what they value about them, two issues always surface: the opportunity to choose their own books and the time to read at school.

Choice

The word *choice* always reminds me of the Arthurian legend "Gawain and the Loathley Lady" in *The Sword and the Circle* (Sutcliffe, 1981). Gawain, a knight, loves and wishes to marry Lady Ragnell, who has been put under a spell that makes her hideously ugly half of each day and beautiful the other half of each day. Once Gawain tells his love to choose whether she wishes to be beautiful by day and hideously ugly at night, or vice versa, he breaks the spell on her. By giving the Lady Ragnell choice, Sir Gawain shows a deep understanding of a basic need that all of us have— to choose and exercise control over our lives. The right to choose was such a powerful force that it broke the enchantment and freed Ragnell to be her beautiful self all the time. Our students, too, crave opportunities to choose, for choice gives us control over our lives and supports growth in reading.

In addition to choice being a desire among all age groups, offering middle schoolers the right to choose books has extra advantages, because choice does the following:

- Develops students' literary tastes, enabling them to discover what they do and don't enjoy reading
- Cultivates students' personal reading lives, making it more likely that students will read at home, because they know the kinds of books that engage and interest them
- Shows students that you trust them to select books that meet their needs
- Builds students' self-confidence as they repeatedly choose books they want to finish
- Builds reading fluency and reading stamina, making it more likely that students will reread favorite books and deepen their understanding of them
- Helps students to learn to concentrate, because they are more likely to complete books they *want* to read

Amylee's writing about choice indicates students' need for autonomy in aspects of their school lives and also points out students' desire to decide what to read on their own:

> One thing that really made me read more is that Mrs. Laura Robb let me read the books I was interested in. All my teachers didn't encourage me to read what I want, we just read boring books. Another thing is that she encouraged me to step out of the box by slowly showing me other books she thinks would interest me. If I didn't like them, that was okay and I could go on reading my books.

In addition to offering students a choice of reading materials they can read, you can develop the habit of reading and concentrating on a book by reserving time to read at school.

Time

Equally as important as providing choice is providing time to read during class. Without exception, my own research and the research of others have shown that middle school students value class time to read because once they leave school, homework and after-school activities take up most of the day and evening. Eleanor, an eighth grader, noted an added benefit of time to read at school: "People who don't enjoy reading don't read out of school. But if you have to read in school, you might learn to enjoy it." Making the time for independent reading can be a challenge.

Consider the following suggestions, which have worked at my school and at schools where I coach teachers:

- Language arts teachers with daily, 90-minute class blocks can reserve 15–20 minutes a week for independent, silent reading. Teachers with 45-minute classes can set aside 15–20 minutes twice a week.
- Teachers with self-contained classes can schedule silent reading at least 4 times a week, preferably 5.

Independent, silent reading of books that students choose and can read with ease will improve their inferential thinking and their ability to make connections. In 2002, the National Assessment of Educational Progress (NAEP) conducted a survey among fourth graders, who are now considered "adolescent" readers (Biancarosa & Snow, 2004). Here's what the report (NAEP, 2002) said:

> Practice is important to reading development. Higher numbers of pages read daily in school and for homework were associated with higher average reading scale scores. Fourth-graders who reported reading 11 or more pages daily had the highest average score, outperforming their peers who reported reading fewer pages.

Silent reading at home and at school provides middle school students with the practice in reading that they need to enlarge their vocabulary and background knowledge; improve their reading rate and fluency; and develop their imaginations, mental imaging abilities, and inferential thinking (Allington, 2006).

Encourage Reflection With Book Logs

To help my students think about and share their independent reading, I have them keep a book log. Students can create a simple book log form: student's name at the top; title, author, and date completed for each book read. Book logs can encourage students to reflect on their independent reading lives, make book-to-book connections, and reveal their reading tastes and habits. However, they're effective only if they are used wisely.

First, students have to be given 3–5 minutes twice a week to update their book logs. Without this time set aside, the logs suffer the same fate as home exercise machines! Students come to see them as busywork. Second, students must interact with the data in the logs. Without this social component, the log will be of little value to students. For example, about halfway through the school year, book log writing will require an infusion of prompts. I set aside about 5–7 minutes for students to review their book logs. Next, I invite pairs or groups to brainstorm for a few minutes to create a list of discussion points and questions they would be eager to answer in future book log entries. I compile all the ideas on the chalkboard or chart paper. Here's the list one class of eighth graders composed:

- Books we loved and reread
- The number of books read early in the year compared to the number of books read at this point
- Comparing the amount of independent reading completed in past years to this year
- Thinking about the kinds of genres we're reading. Is it the same genre or is there variety?
- Are the books very long, short, or a mixture of both?
- Is there a certain author we really enjoy and seek out?
- Is there a book we have reread many times or one we plan to reread? What makes this book so special that we repeatedly reread it?
- Is there a book we'd recommend to a classmate? Explain why.

Next, I invite students to use the rereading of their logs—and the class list we just generated—to jump–start their thinking about what they learned about themselves as readers. To provide the entire class with a mental model of what such an entry might express, I compose one on chart paper. This is an important step, for students need to know what the teacher expects and recognize that the task is doable. Without modeling, students tend to jot down words and phrases instead of complete thoughts. Here's what I share with students:

> At the start of the year, I contracted to read the minimum amount of books—one in September and two in October. After that, I began to read more and more. For January I read four books, and the same for February. I found that I love fantasy, science fiction, and suspense, so I keep looking for those kinds of books. The fantasy books are pretty long, but that doesn't matter if I get into one. I read on the bus and at home if the book grabs me. I'm finding that the more I read, the faster I can finish a book. A book that I have reread three times already is *The Giver* by Lois Lowry [1993]. I'll probably reread it again, before the end of the year. That's the book I'd tell everyone in my class to read. The ending is cool, because you're not sure what really happens. I guess I should try some other genres. Connor says I should read *Houdini* [Cox, 2001]— that's a biography. Maybe I'll try it.

Before you invite students to write their own reflections in their own logs, it's helpful to invite pairs or groups to take a few minutes to discuss what you wrote. I ask students two questions to help them with this task: (a) What did you notice about my response? and (b) What did you learn from the response? Here are some comments and observations the eighth graders made:

- You didn't answer every idea on the list.
- You showed how you read more now.
- You read three genres. Maybe you should try another.
- You say that more reading helps you read faster.
- You recommended a book. We can ask more questions about it and see if we want to check it out.
- I never believed a book log could show all that.

Once students observe that reviewing their book logs can help them to gather insights into their personal reading lives, they tend to take more time to reflect on their lists of books. When you model your expectations for students, you not only remove the unknown from the task, you also show them how much they can learn about themselves as readers. Julian entered my eighth-grade class in January and caught the reading bug from his classmates. After 2 months, Julian's write-up about his book log reflects the change in his reading habits. Julian's goal of 10 books over the next 2½ months shows me that he is cultivating and loving his personal reading life.

Book logs help students to discover books that others have enjoyed. My students value book recommendations from classmates that come from their book logs, such as short 2- to 4-minute monthly oral book talks, and by reading one another's short but strong opinions about books on the graffiti board. Christa summed up the benefits of sharing books this way: "I love the book talks 'cause they give me ideas for reading I would never have chosen."

Book Talks for Students

Book talks are one of the surest ways to interest your students in reading. The four that follow take no more than 3–4 minutes, because each one has a narrow focus. Give students 3 or 4 days to prepare their book talks. Have them jot down notes on a 3 x 5 index card and practice at home so they only occasionally look at the note card. The students and I have established the following guidelines for book talks:

- Follow the criteria in the book talk you've chosen. In fact, keep the guidelines with you when you prepare your talk.
- Speak slowly and clearly.
- Practice and know your talk; avoid reading from the index card.
- Make eye contact with your classmates.
- Bring your book, if possible.

Some students who checked books out of a school or public library might not be able to show their book during book talks.

Book Talk 1: What's the Genre?

- Tell your audience the title and author.
- Identify the genre of your book. Is it mystery, fantasy, science fiction, historical or realistic fiction, short stories, myths, legends, biography, autobiography, or informational text?
- Offer two specific examples from the book that helped you to decide on the genre.
- Think of and share one big idea or theme the author was trying to convey. Explain what in the book helped you to figure out this idea or theme.

Book Talk 2: Thoughts on the Main Character

- Tell your audience the title and author.
- Identify the protagonist and a key problem he or she faced.
- Show how the protagonist deals with the problem.
- How does the problem affect the protagonist? What does he or she learn from coping with this problem?

Book Talk 3: Biography or Autobiography

- Tell your audience the title and author.
- Identify two problems the protagonist faced and the antagonistic forces that helped to create these problems.
- Were both problems resolved? If so, explain how. If not, explain why.

Book Talk 4: Think and Connect Information

- Tell your audience the title and author.
- Explain two fascinating and/or new facts that you learned.
- Explain the significance or importance of this topic and these facts by connecting them to a community or world issue.
- Show how the book changed your thinking about this topic or why this topic interests you.

Capture Strong Opinions With a Graffiti Board

After students complete a book that they adore or intensely dislike, they want to share their feelings immediately. Setting up a graffiti board satisfies students' desire to advertise strong feelings—without disrupting your class. Tape a large piece of construction paper to a wall or use thumbtacks to attach it to a bulletin board. Invite students to jot down their reactions to a book after completing it. The students and I have agreed on the following guidelines:

- Write the title and author.
- Write a one-sentence comment; avoid using inappropriate language.
- Sign your name.

During independent reading I encourage students to read the graffiti board, then chat quietly for a few minutes with a classmate about a book they might want to read. Some students become avid contributors to and readers of the graffiti board. Others find book talks and book log sharing more helpful. Students also benefit from conferring with one another about a completed book. The point is to offer students a variety of opportunities to communicate about their reading with others.

Pair Up for Peer Book Conferences

Peer book conferences are a good way to tap into students' social natures and love of chatting with one another. With large classes and limited teaching time, student-to-student conferences free you to support those who struggle while pairs document and turn in their conversations about books (Robb, 2006). Use a read-aloud text to model for students how you complete a peer book conference; record your notes on chart paper so students have an example to refer to while they confer.

Have partners take turns conferring, using different books. First, the speaker discusses the genre and the listener jots down notes. Next, the speaker chooses two to three topics from the list on the form (Figure 24-1) and discusses them. The listener asks clarifying questions, then jots down the key points discussed. Finally, the pair switches roles.

My Name _____   Date _____

Partner's Name _____

Title and Author of Partner's Book _____

Preparation Checklist: Came with: book _____ pencil _____ form _____

Directions:

1. Jot down some notes that reflect what you and your partner discussed.
2. Turn the completed form in to your teacher.

Discussion Points:

- What genre was your book? Can you give two or three examples that support your decision? Choose one or two of these topics, discuss it, and jot down the high points of your conversation.
- Discuss the information you learned and explain why it's important.
- Explain how the book changed your thinking about a topic, a theme, or an idea.
- Describe two settings and show how each was important to the text.
- Explain one key conflict and the outcome.
- Discuss the character or event you connected to and explain why.
- Discuss how and why you think the protagonist changed from beginning to end.
- Explain how the information you read about can change the way we live, save lives, help the environment, and/or protect our food supply.
- Select a favorite illustration, photograph, or passage from the text and explain why you chose it.
- State a problem a character faced and explain how it was resolved. If it wasn't resolved, explain why.

Figure 24-1. Peer Book Conference Form

Classroom Libraries Across the Curriculum

By the time students reach middle school, their enthusiasm for reading has diminished (Ruddell & Unrau, 1997), and the differences among students as readers widen. Add to this the ever increasing numbers of English-language learners who are trying to cope with middle school reading demands, and the need for students to practice reading—using real books, both in and out of school—becomes even more necessary. That's why I lobby for classroom libraries in social studies and science classes. Building rich collections of trade books in those subjects gives students access to fascinating, well-written accounts that might happen to catch their fancy more than fiction.

Content area–related trade books also allow students to get beyond the limited information in textbooks and gain multiple perspectives on a topic. For example, in addition to reading two pages about the Holocaust in a social studies textbook, students can choose from dozens of historical novels and informational books, such as the photographic essay *My Secret Camera: Life in the Lodz Ghetto* (Smith, 2000); an autobiography, *No Pretty Pictures: A Child of War* by Anina Lobel (1988); an informational text, *Surviving Hitler: A Boy in the Nazi Death Camps* by Andrea Warren (2001); historical fiction, *The Endless Steppe* by Esther Hautzig (1968); and poetry, *I Never Saw Another Butterfly: Children's Drawings and Poems From Terezin Concentration Camp, 1942–1944* (Weil, 1978).

Five Resources That Help You Choose Books for Science and Social Studies

There are five resources I repeatedly turn to when I want to find quality books for class libraries in all subjects.

Zarnowski et al. (2001) includes a history of the Orbis Pictus Ward, chapters where award-winning authors discuss their work, and an annotated bibliography of winners, honor books, and other recommended titles.

The Horn Book guide is a biannual publication that organizes books by genre, age, and subject. Reviewers rate books from 1 to 6, with ratings of 1 and 2 being the best.

With chapters written by respected, well-know educators, Bamford & Kristo (1998) contains teaching ideas and a wealth of excellent nonfiction titles for math, science, English, and social studies.

Beers & Samuels (2003) annotates over 1000 titles of interest to middle schoolers. Arranged by genre and topic, this booklist will help teachers find books for class libraries and multi-text units of study. NCTE updates *Your Reading* periodically. These resources have repeatedly helped me purchase books for themed and issues-based units of study.

Zarnowski (2006) does a remarkable job of linking the pursuit of literature with the quest for historical understanding. Includes lots of book recommendations.

Human Rights: An Issues-Based Unit of Study

When I speak of classroom libraries and make the claim that books matter, perhaps nowhere does the power of books become more evident than during class discussions of books read for a theme unit. The following example shows the power of a single trade book to expand one's thinking on the important topics of our society.

"Are my human rights being violated if someone pushes me when I'm in line to check out a book?" asked Francesca, during a class discussion of human rights.

Emily responded, "Violation of human rights are bigger things, like genocide, or arresting people without giving them a right to a lawyer and trial." This started a heated debate among the eighth graders.

"Pushing might seem small," noted Danny, "but it could grow into subtle bullying, like Archie and Brother Leon in *The Chocolate War* [Cormier, 1974]."

"I still think it's the big stuff, like Chu Ju [Whelan, 2004] having to run away so her family doesn't send her baby sister away because the family now has two girls and Chinese families should have a boy as one of the two children," said Francesca.

Discussions like these occur when my eighth graders start exploring the issue of human rights. I initiate this conversation by jotting this excerpt from the Declaration of Independence on the chalkboard: "We hold these truths to be self-evident, that all men are created equal, that they are endowed by their Creator with certain unalienable Rights, that among these are Life, Liberty, and the pursuit of Happiness." Next I invite students to write, in their journals, an explanation of human rights prior to reading and discussing books.

Here are some of the students' ideas about human rights at the beginning and near the end of this unit of study. Reading, discussing, and dramatizing events in the books they read enabled the eighth graders to construct new understandings of human rights. Excerpts from the journals of Christa, Emily, and Danny illustrate their ability to synthesize what they learned from their books and enlarge their understanding of human rights.

Christa, beginning: I think that all humans have a right to eat to survive, at least, whether it is fulfilled or not. If you cannot eat, it is inhumane.

Christa, end: Human rights means so much more than the right to eat. It's a right to travel, to earn a living and do well, to have medical care, a fair trial, to not be forced to abandon your family, as in *Red Scarf Girl* [Jiang, 1997].

Emily, beginning: I think human rights means no discrimination and free speech.

Emily, end: After I read *So Far From the Bamboo Grove* [Watkins, 1986], human rights took on a new meaning for me. Discrimination because of your cultural background violates a basic human right—like the family leaving their home in Korea 'cause they were Japanese. [It means] Creating horrible fear in people so it takes away their ability to do everyday stuff like buy food, sleep, be safe, go to school, ask for help—that shows no human rights.

Danny, beginning: I think human rights means that the color of your skin and where you come from make no difference in going to school and getting a job—like Marion Anderson [Ryan, 2002]. I think the right to not starve and not live like the family in *Childtimes* [Greenfield & Little, 1997] is a human right all human beings should have.

Danny, end: After listening to the group who read *Nothing but the Truth* [Avi, 1991], I got a whole new view on human rights. There are human rights violated every day, like Miss Narwin losing her job because of lies and parents acting on their kids' lies. It made me think of all the lies kids and grown-ups [tell] and how these can destroy.

Through a variety of experiences and by reading two or three of the suggested books to deepen their understanding of human rights, the eighth graders enlarged their knowledge of human rights and started to develop an awareness of their responsibility to their family, friends, community, and the world. One group ended its panel presentation on *Red Scarf Girl* (Jiang, 1997) by noting this point on the chalkboard: "Turning family members against one another and [putting] loyalty to Mao and his power-hungry officials above love for honest family members is the ugliest form of denial of human rights."

The following works are good for human rights study. For read-alouds, use Greenfield & Little (1997), Krull (2003), Newth (1989), Ryan (2002), and Whelan (2004). For students to read, use Avi (1991), Cormier (1974), Elliott (2001), Jiang (1997), Jiminez (1997), Klass (1999), Paterson (1996), and Watkins (1986).

Learning Experiences That Can Drive
A Study of Human Rights

View the list of learning experiences below as suggestions to choose from, and adapt them to the needs of your students. I ask students what they would like to do to explore human rights or any other theme, and many ideas on this list have come from my students. Questions and discussions should follow each student presentation.

Teacher read-alouds. This becomes a common text through which you can expose students to a range of human rights violations and show them how you respond to them. During a read-aloud, sometimes I stop in the middle of the text and ask students to jot down their connections to human rights in their journals. At other times I wait until I finish reading, then I invite partners to discuss, write in their journals, and share. It's the sharing that stimulates meaningful and often charged discussions. After whole-class discussions, I ask students to reread their journal notes and add ideas that the discussion raised.

Journal responses. These can include revisiting and redefining the concept of human rights as well as writing about how the denial of human rights evolved in a text, and how this denial affected the lives of the characters and affects real people.

Panel presentations. Individual presentations can include a discussion of the situations that violated human rights and the characters' or people's responses to these denials. Students can also include big ideas and themes the author conveyed as well as how the book changed their way of thinking.

Interviews of characters. This works best with partners. One partner steps into the shoes of a character in the book; the other takes the role of interviewer and develops a set of questions based on that character's experiences. The student answers the questions in character, using the details and information in the book.

Stick puppet plays. Small groups create a play that shows how the book highlighted violations of human rights. Members create stick puppets of the characters in their drama and use these to present their play. Plays can be written down or practiced informally and then presented to the class.

Re-creation of an event. This experience invites pairs or small groups to choose a powerful event from their book, then re-create that event as if they were there, reliving it. This type of drama benefits from a narrator, who comments on the action and moves the plot forward.

Original newspaper articles and editorials. These journalism tasks require that students have the background knowledge necessary to write a news article or an editorial. Individuals can use their journalistic talents to write about an event (from their books) that violates human rights.

Comments on present news articles. You can have students collect articles from newspapers and magazines that illustrate violation of human rights and what countries do to bring about change. Students can post these on an oversize piece of construction paper, summarize each, and discuss what they learned about human rights from these articles.

Synthesizing Information Based on Human Rights

Understanding human rights and the importance of protecting them are topics that middle school students should explore if they are to maintain the democratic traditions of this country and become socially responsible citizens. After students have completed their presentations, invite them to discuss ways countries can respond to violations of human rights. This moves them from gathering information to problem solving. Here's a list one class offered:

- Holding peaceful demonstrations
- Organizing peaceful marches
- Writing letters to the editor or to state congressmen
- Asking television, movie, and music celebrities to speak out
- Creating pamphlets with information and distributing them
- Raising money to help through walkathons and raffles
- Meeting with community leaders and asking them to get involved
- Writing letters to the president and to U.S. senators and representatives
- Joining the school newspaper and writing articles about these events

Summary

When I think of class libraries and giving students choice, I always remember Amylee and others like her who resented being forced to read books that were too difficult or books they could not connect to because they lacked background knowledge. Developing classroom libraries with diverse topics, genres, and reading levels can lead your students to cultivate a personal reading life as long as you honor choice and reserve time for them to read in class.

When you believe in the power of books and make reading central to your curriculum, students can mirror your positive outlook. In addition, books can raise your students' awareness of community and world issues such as injustice, power and control, and human rights. By understanding the plight of others in their community and the world, middle school students can develop social responsibility and move beyond themselves to considering the plight of others.

References

Allington, R. (2006). Fluency: Still waiting after all these years. In S. J. Samuels & A. E. Farstrup (Eds.), *What research has to say about fluency instruction*. Newark: DE: International Reading Association.

Bamford, R. A., & Kristo, J. V. (Eds.). (1998). *Making facts come alive: Choosing quality nonfiction literature, K–8*. Norwood, MA: Christopher-Gordon.

Beers, K., & & Samuels, B. (Eds.) (2003). *Your reading: An annotated booklist for junior high/middle school*. Urbana, IL: National Council of Teachers of English.

Biancarosa, G., & Snow, D. (2004). *Reading next: A visions for action and research in middle and high school literacy*. New York: Carnegie.

Braunger, J., & Lewis, J. P. (2005). *Building a knowledge base in reading* (2nd ed.). Newark, DE & Urbana, IL: International Reading Association and National Council of Teachers of English.

Cunningham, P. M., & Allington, R. L. (2003). *Classrooms that work: They can ALL read and write* (3rd ed.). Boston: Allyn & Bacon.

Guice, S., Allington, R. L., Johnston, P., Baker, K., & Michelson, N. (1996). Access?: Books, children, and literature-based curriculum in schools. *The New Advocate, 9* (3), 197–207.

Horn Book. (n.d.). *The Horn book guide*. Boston: Author.

Krashen, S. D. (1996). *Every person a reader: An alternative to the California Task Force report on reading*. Culver City, CA: Language Education Associates.

National Assessment of Educational Progress (NAEP). (2002). *Reading performance of students in grade 4*. Available online at http://nces.ed.gov/programs/coe/2002/section2/indicator07.asp

Neuman, S. B., & Celano, D. (2001). Access to print in low-income and middle-income communities: An ecological study of four neighborhoods. *Reading Research Quarterly, 36* (1), 8–26.

Robb, L. (1991). Building bridges: Eighth and third grades read together. *The New Advocate, 4* (4), 151–161.

Robb L. (1993). A cause for celebration: Reading and writing with at-risk students. *The New Advocate, 6* (1), 25-40.

Robb L. (2000). *Teaching reading in middle school*. New York: Scholastic.

Robb, L. (2002). Multiple texts: Multiple opportunities for teaching and learning. *Voices From the Middle, 9* (4): 28–32.

Robb, L. (2006). *Teaching reading: A complete resource for grades four and up*. New York: Scholastic.

Ruddell, R. B., & Unrau, N. J. (1997). The role of responsive teaching in focusing reader intention and developing read motivation. In J. T. Guthrie & A. Wigfield (Eds.), *Reading engagement: Motivating readers through integrated instruction*. Newark, DE: International Reading Association.

Zarnowski. M. (2006). *Making sense of history: Using high-quality literature and hands-on experiences to build content knowledge* New York: Scholastic.

Zarnowski, M., Kerper, R. H., & Jenson, J. M. (Eds.). (2001). *The best in children's non-fiction: Reading, writing, and teaching Orbis Pictus Award books.* Urbana, IL: National Council of Teachers of English.

Children's Books

Avi. (1991). *Nothing but the truth.* New York: Orchard Books.

Avi. (1997). *What do fish have to do with anything?* Cambridge, MA: Candlewick Press.

Burleigh, R. (1998). *Black whiteness: Admiral Byrd alone in the Antarctic.* New York: Atheneum.

Cormier, R. (1974). *The chocolate war.* New York: Pantheon Books.

Cox, C. (2001). *Houdini: Master of illusion .* New York: Scholastic.

Elliott, L. M. (2001). *Under a war-torn sky.* New York: Hyperion Books.

Evslin, B., & Evslin, D. (1975). *Heroes and monsters of Greek myths.* New York: Bantam.

Freedman, R. (1987). *Lincoln: A photobiography.* New York: Clarion Books.

Freedman, R. (2002). *Confucius: The golden rule.* New York: Scholastic.

Glenn, M. (1997). *The taking of room 114: A hostage drama in poems.* New York: Lodestar.

Greenfield, E., & Little, L. J. (1997). *Childtimes: A three-generation memoir.* New York: HarperCollins.

Grimes, N. (2002). *Bronx masquerade.* New York: Dial.

Grimes, N. (2005). *Dark sons.* New York: Hyperion Books.

Hamilton, V. (1995). *Her stories: African American folktales, fairy tales, and true tales* (L. Dillon & D. Dillon, Illus.). New York: Scholastic.

Hautzig, E. (1968). *The endless steppe.* New York: HarperTrophy.

Hesse, K. (2001). *Witness.* New York: Scholastic.

Jiang, J. L. (1997). *Red scarf girl: A memoir of the cultural revolution.* New York: HarperTrophy.

Jimenez, F. (1997). *The circuit: Stories from the life of a migrant child.* New York: Scholastic.

Kellogg, S. (2002). *The mysterious tadpole.* New York: Dial.

Klass, D. (1999). *California blue.* New York: Scholastic.

Korman, G. (2000). *No more dead dogs.* New York: Hyperion Books.

Krull, K. (1997). *Lives of the athletes: Thrills, spills (and what the neighbors thought).* San Diego, CA: Harcourt.

Krull, K. (2000). *Lives of extraordinary women: Rulers and rebels (and what the neighbors thought).* San Diego: Harcourt.

Krull, K. (2003). *Harvesting hope: The story of Cesar Chavez.* San Diego: Harcourt.

Lobel, A. (1998). *No pretty pictures: A child of war.* New York: Greenwillow.

Lowry, Lois. (1993). *The giver.* Boston: Houghton Mifflin.

Myers, W. D. (1992). *Somewhere in darkness.* New York: Scholastic.

Nelson, M. (2001). *Carver: A life in poems.* Ashville, NC: Front Street Books.

Newth, M. (1989). *The abduction.* New York: Farrar, Straus & Giroux.

Paterson, K. (1996). *Jip: His story.* New York: Lodestar.

Ryan, P. M. (2002). *When Marion sang.* New York: Scholastic.

Smith, F. D. (2000). *My secret camera: Life in the Lodz ghetto* (M. Grossman, Illus.). San Diego: Harcourt.

Spinelli, J. (1996). *Crash.* New York: Random House.

Sutcliffe, R. (1981). *The sword and the circle.* London: Hodder and Stoughton.

Warren, A. (2001). *Surviving Hitler: A boy in the Nazi death camps.* New York: HarperCollins.

Watkins, Y. K. (1986). *So far from the bamboo grove.* New York: Morrow.

Weil, J. (Ed.). (1978). *I never saw another butterfly: Children's drawings and poems from Terezin concentration camp.* New York: Schocken Books.

Whelan, G. (2004). *Chu Ju's house.* New York: HarperCollins.

Woodson, J. (2000). *Miracle's boys.* New York: Putnam.

Evolution of a Reader and a Writer: An Interview With Janet S. Wong

Barbara Chatton

I had the pleasure of reviewing Janet Wong's first book of poetry for young people, *Good Luck Gold*, in 1994. This first success was followed by a continual stream of poetry and picture books, each a delightful exploration of Janet's curiosity about childhood, family, and topics as diverse as dreams, driving, and superstition. When I first met Janet in person at a conference dinner, she took one look at my name tag and commented on my positive review of her first book. I remember that first dinner with Janet as one filled with talk about poetry, politics, personal stories, and a great deal of laughter. This is perhaps not surprising in a person whose magazine essay (Wong, 2006a) had been described as filled with "humor and bristling opinions" (Sutton, 2006, p. 647).

Since that time, Janet and I have participated in various poetry events sponsored by the National Council of Teachers of English (NCTE) and have held wonderful conversations in hallways, near publishers' displays, and at meals. Because of our acquaintance and Janet's easy way with words and ideas, we were able to conduct this interview by e-mail.

Barbara: Could you tell me a bit about your childhood? I know that you, like many of us, lived within American popular culture ("fast food, shopping, and TV," as you said in an article). Where did you grow up? Do you think the geography of your childhood influenced you as a writer?

Janet: I grew up in California, but in so many different Californias, in seven different places from birth through high school: smack in the middle of Los Angeles, where Koreatown is today; then in San Anselmo, a semirural suburb of

San Francisco where kids used to catch lizards after school for fun; back again in Los Angeles for middle school and high school, in a rather tough section of Hollywood; and also in Walnut, a suburban community of developments that were brand-new when we moved there.

My favorite home was in San Anselmo, from third through sixth grade. Those years were especially important for me because of memories of things like lizard-catching—the basis of my book *Minn and Jake* (2003b) and the inspiration for the cover of my Richard C. Owen "Meet the Author" book, *Before It Wriggles Away* (2006b). It also was important in a somewhat negative way: This was the first time that I felt truly different because of my Asianness. Living in Los Angeles until second grade, I grew up among children of many ethnicities, and—despite the fact that I occasionally suffered taunts of "ching chong Chinaman" from kids—I did not feel particularly strange because of my race. It was only when we moved to San Anselmo, where there were only two Asian families at my school, that I began to feel truly "other." Reflecting on that time in my life now, I'm pretty sure that being "other" in a rather "white-bread" environment contributed to the way I grew up, insisting on being seen as culturally American rather than Asian.

Barbara: Did you hear family stories as a child? Have these stories influenced you as a writer?

Janet: Absolutely. I'm sure that a large part of my ability to tell stories (or parts of stories, to describe moments in time, as poems do) is that I grew up hearing my Chinese grandfather, my GongGong, talk about his youth and early days in America. He had a habit of telling the same stories over and over, which used to annoy me, but his annoying habit is what helps me to remember the stories now.

Barbara: Do you think that you and/or your family were what I call "language-focused"? For example, in my family, my father, the son of Armenian immigrants, and a second-language English speaker, loved to think about the roots and meanings of words, about connections between words across languages, about rhyme, and about other language sounds. Did that occur in your family, or did it happen to you at some point?

Janet: My family was definitely not language-focused. First of all, there was the problem that my mother did not speak English when she came to this country, in her 20s, married to my father (who met her while he was in the U.S. Army in Korea). My father did not speak Korean. At home we spoke in English, which meant mainly that my father and I talked and played, and my mother spoke to me only about necessities—eating, cleaning up, and homework. Several years ago, though, when my mother stopped working and suddenly had a lot of time (and the need) to talk, I learned that she does have a strangely natural poetic sense. For instance, she was complaining a few years ago about my father's entrepreneurial failures, and she said (with hands grabbing at the air), "He is trying to catch the wind."

Some of this might be just a Korean thing; last year during a thunderstorm she said, "The tigers are marrying," explaining that this (or something like it) was a common Korean expression. Well, "common Korean" for common Korean country folk, at least—which she is, having had just 5 years of schooling because her parents needed her to work on their farm. (I don't know if people in the sophisticated big city of Seoul use the "tigers marrying" phrase; in my mother's rural hometown, though, there actually were tigers living in the mountains.)

Barbara: Were you a reader as a child? What books did you like? Did they influence you as a writer?

Janet: If you had asked me this 2 years ago, I would have answered that no, I was not a reader. This is because I didn't read a lot, bookwise, just for fun. I'd go to the library at school or with my father, check out a book, and feel really guilty the day it was due because I hadn't finished it. I still have this problem, to this day: I'm really bad at finishing things—books, scrapbook projects, closet-cleaning, everything!

Two years ago I changed my answer. When I visit schools, kids always ask, "Were you a reader?" and all of a sudden I felt comfortable answering yes. This is why: I realized that even though I didn't read a lot of books, I would read the cereal box and milk carton in the morning. If I sat on a toilet and there was graffiti on the stall wall, I would always read that, too. I couldn't *not* read it. I loved leafing through magazines, reading headlines and bits of blurbs. To this day, I still am compelled to constantly read "bits and pieces" of things around me. And yet I can finish only two or three novels a year. Perhaps this is why poetry is my favorite genre.

Barbara: Did you have any teachers in your K–12 schooling who influenced you? How?

Janet: I had many good teachers, but I was a pretty oblivious student. I worked hard in order to get good grades, but I really had very little passion for learning; I was just one of those students who "goes through the motions" and does the required work and gets lucky. I'm still pretty much that way today, which is why I think some kids like me; they sense that I'm as much a slacker as they are! In high school, though, I had a crush on one of my teachers, so I took his word as gospel. One day he told me not to refer to myself as "Oriental," explaining that his Chinese-American friends referred to themselves as "Asian." I remember thinking, "My, that is odd. What's wrong with 'Oriental'?!" But he told me that was an old-fashioned term, and so I ditched it that very moment. This likely was an important moment of awareness, even if I didn't realize it at the time: learning to evaluate labels, exploring the issue of self-identification versus identification by others.

Barbara: Did you read or listen to poetry as a child? What poets influenced you?

Janet: I read very little poetry as a child, listened to even less of it, and did no poetry at all on my own. My exposure to poetry was limited to what happened in the classroom. Unfortunately, one of my early experiences with poetry required memorizing a poem and performing it in front of the class. This is a wonderful experience for kids who are good at memorizing and performing poems; a memorized poem becomes part of you for the rest of your life. But for kids who are not good at memorizing and performing, this exercise is exactly the kind of thing that can make a person hate poetry. And so, in fourth grade, I decided that I hated poetry. It was only because of an encounter with Myra Cohn Livingston later in life that I changed my mind about poetry.

Barbara: I know that you developed your "inner poet" through your work with Myra Cohn Livingston. How did these experiences shape the types of writing you do? The topics? The forms of poetry?

Janet: Before I met Myra, I didn't think of poetry very often at all. If pressed, I would've confessed to thinking of poetry as difficult boring stuff that sounded mostly like what the warlock father in *Bewitched* used to recite when he popped into the living room. I didn't know poetry. I had no idea, especially, of the depth and variety of children's poems. As for serious children's poems about all kinds of contemporary subjects—the works of Arnold Adoff, Valerie Worth, Myra herself—I never had any idea that this existed. The first poems of mine that Myra liked were serious poems drawn from childhood memories, and because Myra's approval was such a hard thing to get, her bit of encouragement prompted me to continue writing that sort of thing. If she had praised me for nonsense poems, instead, my body of work might look quite different! Myra required me (and her other students) to write in a variety of forms. And while I did my homework like a good student, I quickly decided that I liked free verse and simple rhyming forms best. I think this was a bit of a disappointment to Myra, actually. She often used to say, "Can't you give it a little more form—a little more music?" To appease her, I started using more repetition and doing drafts of poems in a variety of forms, even if what I chose for the final draft happened to be free verse or simple rhyme.

Barbara: Your first two books of poetry were powerful portrayals of the experiences of Asian-American children. Did you consciously choose to write about your ethnic background when you first began writing for children?

Janet: My very first book—the first book I wrote after quitting my law job—had no ethnic reference at all. It was a middle-grade novel featuring talking insects. I put this book through five or six complete drafts, 100 pages or so, but I never sent it out. You can imagine my disappointment when, 2 years later, the movies *A Bug's Life* and *AntZ* came out! Most of my early rejected manuscripts also had nothing to do with being Asian. Several friends urged me to write Asian-theme books, insisting that "multicultural is in." The idea of profiting from my ethnicity bothered me, but soon I realized that my best stories and poems were about my family, and since my family is multicultural—my Chinese immigrant father, my Korean immigrant mother, and American-born me—writing a multicultural book was genuine, and not a sellout.

Barbara: Since you began publishing, your topics and themes have broadened to include driving, dreams, superstitions, and friendship. These books appeal to audiences from very young children through young adults. How do you decide what to focus on as a subject or whom to focus on as an audience? Does one thing come before another?

Janet: Many of my topics come from my daily life or childhood memories, and other ideas just pop into my head (or fingers) from nowhere. I have many topics that I know I want to write about, and I just haven't been able to focus and produce results. I'm always struck with ideas from my surroundings, from what I see and hear and experience. Several years ago I saw a chair that had been crafted out of old wooden skis. I asked the artist what inspired it, and he said, "Oh, I'm just a Dumpster diver!" I had never heard the term before, and it got my imagination going. The result was *The Dumpster Diver* (2007a), a picture book about Steve the Electrician who enlists the help of kids to build fanciful treasure from useful junk.

I'm hoping that the teacher's guide that Candlewick [the publisher] created will prompt teachers to use the book in their classrooms as a call to action to all of us to stop wasting so much stuff, to reduce, reuse, and recycle in the most creative ways. A prominent independent bookstore, All for Kids Books, is sponsoring a "Junk Is Good" contest (open to individuals, teams, and classrooms worldwide). Students are *not* to go foraging in the trash; in my book, Steve gets cut in the Dumpster and the kids decide that it's better to collect useful junk by asking neighbors for donations. Wouldn't it be great if kids who were inspired by this book started maniacally cleaning out their basements and garages? Contest details can be found at www.allforkidsbooks.com.

Barbara: Do you want to talk a bit about your notion of "postmulticultural" authorship?

Janet: There are certain subjects that, while not being explicitly tied to any ethnicity, might be more readily understood by one cultural group than another. For instance, if I were to talk about eating tripe, most American kids would shriek in disgust and utter disbelief. But many Asian kids and even some Latino kids would know exactly what I was talking about. Fried pork skin, coagulated blood, stewed chicken feet, grilled intestines, beef tendon— even if we don't like these things ourselves, we have seen our parents and grandparents eat them. We might express disgust, but there would be no disbelief. It's part of our awareness. Therefore, a book that has no mention of race or ethnicity but that features a grandmother who eats tripe might not be "multicultural," but it could be called "postmulticultural" because the audience most likely to accept and understand the book would be "culturally different" from the American mainstream.

Barbara: After having produced a significant body of work, are you allowed to have some say in who illustrates your work? Do you see the illustrations at any point? Are there some illustrations that you think have captured your ideas most clearly?

Janet: Many people believe that authors are allowed to choose the illustrators of their books. An author comes up with the story, after all, and often has very strong opinions about how the book should look. Unfortunately (for us authors), most editors and art directors would rather do the choosing. The way I explain it to aspiring writers is this: Think of a book as a child. The author is the father, who gets things started. The illustrator is the mother, who suffers for nine months to give shape to the creation. They both think of the book as their own. But the publisher owns the book; the publisher is God.

That being said, there is one illustrator that I have chosen: Julie Paschkis. We have done three books together, and each one was submitted as a package—my poems with Julie's art. *Night Garden: Poems From the World of Dreams* (2000) won the *New York Times* Best Illustrated Book award, which thrilled me because it validated my taste in art! *Knock on Wood: Poems About Superstitions* (2003) followed; one of my favorite illustrations ever is in that book, the one with a butterfly ear and a bee ear (corresponding to a right ear itching with *praise* and a left ear itching with *stinging*, (slanderous words). I wrote our third book, *Twist: Yoga Poems* (2007b), as a gift for Julie; she does yoga every day, and I wanted to give her a subject that she would be passionate about. She took inspiration from Indian miniatures for that book, which ties yoga to its Indian roots. When I work with Julie, I seek her advice on which poems to use or omit, but once we have the poems set, I leave her to work on her own.

Barbara: What is the best part about your life as an author? What is the worst part?

Janet: The worst part is that people usually assume that everything I write is autobiographical. A lot of what I've written has an element of truth, some basis in memories, but at least half of it is just plain made up. This can be somewhat limiting to me because I have to be careful while I'm writing; I'm afraid to write some things for fear that friends (or people who are less than friends) will think I'm writing about them.

The best part of my life as an author is the flexibility of my job. When my son was in elementary school, I spent a lot of time volunteering at his school, and that was time that I treasured. Now that he's in middle school and his life is tied to sports, I'm glad that I can be there for his games and meets. I can work at midnight or while I'm waiting at the dentist's office (if I need to do so). The very best part of my life is that I get paid to remember, to daydream, and to lie.

Some of my writer friends criticize me because I encourage people to write books of their own, but I think everyone has at least one book in them. Getting published is a complicated business (or game), and many great manuscripts are never published, so I don't want people to think that publication is a must. What is a must is getting our family stories down: We all have something inside that needs to be written, to be preserved, before it is lost forever.

References

Sutton, R. (2006, November/December). One by one. *The Horn Book Magazine, 82* (6), 647.

Wong, J. (2006a, November/December). Alien bunny bots—or not? *The Horn Book Magazine, 82* (6), 667–672.

Children's Books

Wong, J. (1994). *Good luck gold.* New York: Simon & Schuster.

Wong, J. (2000). *Night garden: Poems from the world of dreams* (Julie Paschkis, Illus.) New York: Simon & Schuster.

Wong, J. (2003a) *Knock on wood: Poems about superstitions* (Julie Paschkis, Illus.) New York: Simon & Schuster.

Wong, J. (2003b). *Minn and Jake* (Genevieve Cote, Illus.). New York: Farrar, Straus & Giroux.

Wong, J. (2006b) *Before it wriggles away.* (Anne Lindsay, Illus.) Katonah, NY: Owen.

Wong, J. (2007a). *The dumpster diver* (David Roberts, Illus.) Cambridge, MA: Candlewick Press.

Wong, J. (2007b). *Twist: Yoga poems.* (Julie Paschkis, Illus.). New York: Simon & Schuster.

Chapter
26

Working in the School Library: Delights, Dilemmas, and Disasters

Linda N. McDowell

As a school library media specialist, I believe that one of my roles is to teach students to love reading and to choose to read. I often ask myself how I can accomplish this. I try thinking about what has made me want to read. I recall my memories of the books I read or that were read to me. I think I came to love reading rather late in life—during graduate school. It was my children's literature professor who really sparked my interest in books. He himself loved to read, and he had a contagious passion that he passed on to his students. Frank Hodge would bring authors into our class or share his favorite stories about them. David Ross was one of them. I still treasure my copy of *Book of Hugs* (Ross, 1999a); I dreamed of reading it to my own child one day. I remember purchasing *Book of Kisses* (Ross, 1999b) when my son was born.

My strongest memory from Frank's children's literature class is of Paula Danziger's visit. She shared her stories of being a junior high English teacher. She had recently left the classroom to be a writer full time, so she told us what it was like to be a newly published author. Her books took on a new life as I read them. Having been an overweight youngster, I related to *The Cat Ate My Gymsuit* (1974). It was her voice I heard as I read her books. Many years later I met her at a conference, and I was immediately reminded of that memory.

With these experiences, Frank created a connection between the author and us. He made us want to read the books he introduced. It was during his class that he asked us to think about our early reading memories. I remember one book in particular that my mother read to my sister and me over and over: *The Pokey Little Puppy* (Lowrey, 1942). To this day, I see the cover with the adorable brown-and-white puppy's face. It reminded me of the beagle that we had as little girls. My mother loved to read; she always had a book. Later, my father built her a bookshelf wall that housed her book collection, some of which I now have in my bookcase wall with my collection. I also remember loving to read the Nancy Drew books. Her adventures became my adventures.

Author Visits

So how do I pass this love of reading on to my students? I try to make a connection to authors whenever I can. Author visits are the best. The first author who visited my school was Olivier Dunrea. I had met him at a whole-language conference in the Vermont mountains one summer. He has a charismatic personality and infectious sense of humor. I was a classroom teacher at the time, and I knew I just had to have him visit my classroom.

Upon returning to school that fall, I applied for and received a Teacher Center grant for $1,500. I set out on my own crusade to bring authors to our school as often as possible. Fortunately, the Parent-Teacher-Student Organization (PTSO) president at the time also believed in this endeavor and convinced the board to fund my projects. That year, Ben Mikaelsen visited our school.

An author visit is now a line item in the PTSO yearly budget. Since that time we have been fortunate to bring such authors as Daniel Kirk, John Reynolds Gardiner, J. Patrick Lewis, and Gordon Korman. They have left lasting impressions on our students. At a recent book fair, we couldn't keep enough of Gordon Korman's books stocked. They flew off the shelves as quickly as we put them out. The students know that I have a passion for reading and that they can, too.

I try to help the students see authors as real people. I think it's important to meet as many authors and illustrators as I can. Therefore, I attend at least one professional conference each year. While there, I seek out the sessions at which the authors talk about their lives and experiences. I look for sessions that introduce authors and illustrators who share stories that I can relate to my students. One of my favorites is the time I met Patricia Polacco and actually held in my hands the family heirloom quilt that was her inspiration for *The Keeping Quilt* (1998). I also tell my students about the time that I had brunch with Martin Waddell, and he read us his latest book.

I talk with my students about my favorite books. I encourage books to be read and reread. Phoebe Gilman's (1992) *Something From Nothing* was a favorite reread in one of my kindergarten classes. It had all the necessary elements: rhyme, rhythm, and repetition. To this day, whenever I see Brittany, one of my students who is now sixteen, she will mention how many times she borrowed that book from the classroom library.

Creating a Safe, Inviting Library

If you have a passion for children's books (and you probably do since you are reading this book), being surrounded by books day in and day out is like a dream come true. A component of my job as school library media specialist is to manage the library media center. This includes the physical space. We wanted students to feel safe when they entered what can be for some an intimidating environment. Students of any age can feel overwhelmed if they are unfamiliar with the library's organization. I worked at achieving their comfort in several ways.

One way was the use of signage. There are signs throughout the library, and we have enlisted students to help create them. A big sign on the circulation desk welcomes patrons to the library. It was important that it be written in a student's handwriting. This helps to set the tone that this is their space. Another sign tells them to ask if they want help. Students are greeted with a smile and, whenever possible, by name. We make this clear to all who work and volunteer in our library; we have made it a priority.

I am fortunate to work with a part-time library aide who has a similar vision for the library media center as an inviting, welcoming, comfortable space for both students and teachers. We use plants, displays that change with the seasons, and topics of study related to the curriculum to help make the space visibly welcoming. The local dollar stores have made this possible since the budget does not include such items. I am always on the lookout for bargains that I can use. We also have classical or light jazz music playing in the background. Many teachers have commented that they like the music.

Parent Volunteers

One of our biggest influences is the large number of parent volunteers who work with us in the library on a regular basis. This year we have 10 parents who volunteer two hours each week. They take care of most of the circulation responsibilities: checking in, checking out, and reshelving. Most books are reshelved the day they are returned, which helps to make the books accessible to students—our original goal.

The number of parent volunteers has grown from the original one or two. Each year we advertise in the monthly school newsletter. Classroom teachers mention the opportunity for parents to be involved at their "Let's Get Acquainted Night" and at kindergarten roundup. Our principal also promotes this at his principal coffees, as well as every chance he gets.

New parents are trained when they start. We see them taking on more responsibility as they become more comfortable with the system. Some want to work on displays, whereas others like to work on ordering the books on the shelves. We build on their individual strengths.

The Library Collection

Maintaining the library's collection is another aspect of my position. This includes staying current on new titles and weeding out titles that are no longer suitable, appropriate, or in good shape. No one wants to pick up a book that is falling apart or looks as if it had been dropped in the trash. It's easy to understand that books in a library should be current, with up-to-date information. This is particularly obvious for such topics as science and technology, but it might not be as obvious—although it is equally important—for fiction books that describe interpersonal relationships and reflect the cultural values of the time.

For instance, the roles of men and women are not the same now as they were 50 years ago. This needs to be reflected in the literature our students are reading. That is why many schools have policies that relate to collection age and acquisition procedures and policies. A former student approached me one day about a biography he had read and reread when he attended our school more than 20 years ago. When it came time to weed that section, I was able to pass the book on to him for a keepsake. A few weeks ago, I saw him again, and he commented, "Boy, is that book ever politically incorrect!" He understood why it had no place in our collection anymore.

Blending Instruction and Teacher Collaboration

My job as a school library media specialist is multifaceted. There is also a very important instructional component: information literacy, or teaching children to access information. Because we are a small school, I have an opportunity to get to know many of the students and their reading interests. I work on a flexible schedule and see all the students in our K–6 building. We like being able to refer a newly delivered book to a student who has read others by that author or on that particular topic. Jackson, an avid reader, had just finished his latest book and was browsing the shelves for what to read next. We suggested Kathryn Lasky's (2003) *Guardians of Ga'hoole* series. It was a good match, and he was back for the second in the series within days.

Working on a flexible schedule allows me to work with students and teachers and teach the information literacy skills within the existing curriculum. I am able to team-teach; I work with a small group of children in the library while the classroom teacher works with another group in the classroom. This integration helps the students to make the necessary connections to ensure that learning takes place. Integration is the key to accomplishing all that we need to teach students nowadays. Given the short amount of time that teachers have with students, it is the only way that the teachers can accomplish everything. As the library media specialist, I am in the perfect position to help them implement children's literature.

Another aspect of my job as library media specialist, therefore, is collaboration. I collaborate with the teachers to plan ways that we can teach together. I recently attended a regional library workshop with Ross Todd from Rutgers University. He is head of the library science program at Rutgers, which is recognized nationally as being one of the top programs to prepare school librarians. His advice to the audience was "Start small," so I did.

One of the teachers in my building, Mary Anne, introduces a different genre each month. She assigns her students a minimum of two books to read and then write a response. I asked her if she would like me to read an example of a personal narrative poem and have each student select one to begin the project. She wrote out the times she met with her groups and indicated what days would be best for her. I constructed a schedule wherein I would meet with a group of her students in the library while she met with the others in her classroom. Since she had four reading groups, we worked this out over two days— two groups each day. I talked with the students about the organization of the library and how to use the Online Patron Access Catalog (OPAC), which replaced the card catalog, to find the stories in rhyme, and then I gave students an opportunity to find a book they wanted to use for the assignment. I read one of my favorite poems: *Gilbert de la Frogponde: A Swamp Story* (Rae, 1997). This is a delightful story of a lazy frog named Gilbert that doesn't want to end up as a gourmet delicacy. So Gilbert convinces his would-be captors that insects are the delicacy of the moment.

My objectives for teaching students to search the OPAC were met. Mary Anne's objectives for introducing a different genre were met. Because I met with students when she was with the other groups, it didn't take away from her instructional time.

Another time I worked with a teacher named Kelly and her students on a research project for social studies. Kelly and I met one afternoon after school for about an hour to create a plan and a schedule. She had 21 students for reading instruction. Our plan involved my working with half of her students while she worked with the other half. She introduced the project and helped the students choose a topic. The theme was animals of the Arctic. Kelly explained to the students the kind of information she wanted them to gather—description, habitat, food, predators— and then I worked with them on the steps to follow when researching. We talked about sources, where to find them, and how to proceed. Each student chose one book about an animal.

Be sure to check the availability of books on a topic *before* you assign them to students. That first year was more than a little frustrating because several students chose an animal for which we did not have a book or had only a book that mentioned the animal briefly. I had assumed that the library would have whatever book I needed on whatever topic I wanted, but this was not so. Now I ask the teacher to either check the catalog or give me a list of topics so that I can check it.

I met with the groups two other times, once to teach them how to use an electronic encyclopedia and to discuss plagiarism, and the other time to teach them how to cite the sources they had used. Children as young as 7 years old were learning the Modern Language Association (MLA) format for citing book and electronic sources.

Mary Anne and Kelly became my biggest advocates. They helped to spread the word by telling other teachers. I started out by asking teachers, but now teachers are coming to me with ideas on how they would like me to collaborate with them and their students. This year I worked with all our primary (first- and second-grade) and intermediate (third- and fourth-grade) students on research projects. My focus is teaching students to access, evaluate, and use information. These objectives appear in the national and state language arts standards, science standards, and social studies standards. By taking a look at the curriculum maps that teachers complete each year, I can see when topics are being taught and approach teachers about working together at that time. By teaming up, we can accomplish twice as much.

I recently approached one of the math teachers about working with his students on a practical reason for understanding decimals. In order to find a book with a call number of 645.78, students need to be able to understand how decimals work. So much for the comment "Why do I need to know this?"

Making Connections

Another hat I wear is that of information specialist. I love this part! This can include helping teachers to find books for an author study, resources for a unit of instruction, or maybe a read-aloud. This is where I really get to utilize my 30 or more years of experience as a classroom teacher and combine it with my acquired knowledge of library science. I am still a teacher: I teach students and teachers, but I have a much bigger classroom—the library media center.

I recently came across a video clip of an interview with Kate DiCamillo. I approached one teacher, Judy, about sending her reading groups to me one at a time to view the interview. Students took notes and talked about what surprised them. We were all surprised that DiCamillo didn't start writing until she was 29. The students liked that she had worked at Epcot (an amusement park) on a ride that many of them had ridden. This was a perfect springboard for Judy to use *The Miraculous Journey of Edward Tulane* (DiCamillo, 2006) as her next read-aloud.

Reflections on the Delights and Dilemmas

For many years, I was a kindergarten teacher in the same school where I am currently the library media specialist. I loved that level. Five-year-olds love to please—themselves and the people around them. What a delight it was to read a book to my group during a language arts instruction. I had favorites that seemed to capture the students' interest each year.

One class was particularly interested in Joanna Cole's (1986) *The Magic School Bus at the Waterworks*. We read it and learned about the water cycle. One of the student's fathers worked at a local hydroelectric plant. He arranged for us to take a tour— complete with hard hats. Later the students picked up this book during their playtime. Sometimes they matched the words; sometimes they retold the story line. Either way, there was a certain magic about the activity. As educators, we need to build on this magic and make it grow. The experience I had as a classroom teacher has significantly impacted how I am able to work with students as the librarian.

As for all educators, time is my biggest dilemma—time to accomplish all that we want, time to meet with each other to plan, time to collaborate, time to practice what we have taught. It's up to us to make this happen. Our school has designated Tuesdays to be meeting days. We use this time to meet within our teaching teams. People know not to make appointments after school on Tuesdays. Our kindergarten team also decided that we would eat lunch together one day a week so that we could plan collaboratively then. Planning time has to become part of the schedule. It must be nonnegotiable and a priority.

Trust is another issue. We need to trust in ourselves and what we hold as important and valuable. I was fortunate to be a teacher during the whole-language heyday. I think I have to attribute my passion for children's literature, in part, to this phenomenon. We immersed ourselves in reading and writing. We surrounded ourselves with authors and illustrators, musicians, and poets. We learned from the artists themselves. We attended conference after conference, seeking others of like mind.

There were no basal readers or teacher's manuals to follow. We studied theory. We wanted to know how kids learn to read, to write, to talk, and listen. We discovered how children learn to communicate, how children learn language by being immersed in that language. We were professionals. One wouldn't presume to tell a surgeon how to operate on a patient. Why, then, would a teacher need to be told how to teach his or her students? As professionals, we are the ones who know our students. Knowing the theory, we could use our knowledge and expertise to teach. We trusted ourselves to know our craft, and therefore the parents and administrators—the other stakeholders—trusted us.

What happened to that trust? That's a big dilemma for me these days. I hear teachers talking about teaching to the test. There has always been assessment. Schools have been using standardized tests for many years. In New York, the state standards for what we teach have not changed—only the assessment tool has. I hear some teachers say they want a basal to follow. I hear other teachers saying they wish they had time to read to their students. How can one be a teacher of reading and *not* read to students? The purpose of the tests is to drive instruction. We need to look at the test results and see how we can improve our instruction, but we also have to look at our own practices and make changes wherever we can.

Having a Voice and Taking a Stand

We need to have a voice, and we can accomplish that by belonging to professional organizations—not only at the local level, but at the state and national levels as well. We need to support our professional organizations. National organizations, like the International Reading Association and the National Council of Teachers of English, have a political action component. Part of the dues from these organizations is spent for lobbying in Washington. By joining the state affiliates of these organizations—the New York State Reading Association and the New York State English Council—I put my voice together with thousands of teachers. Together we are strong, and our voice is louder.

We don't have control over state and national mandates, but we do have a choice of how to look at them. It's time for us to change our attitudes. The mandates are not going away. We will always have noneducators making decisions about education, but what we do with those decisions is within our control. I believe it's much like the case of whether the glass is half empty or half full. Personally, I think we can accomplish more by taking a positive approach.

Recent studies have shown that a strong library program has a positive impact on student achievement. These studies support library programs run by certified school library media specialists who function in the capacity of teacher-librarian. As a library media specialist, I have to be proactive. I need to seek out teachers and not wait for them to approach me. I have to find curriculum connections and opportunities for collaboration. I need to attend curriculum meetings and stay on top of what teachers in my building are teaching and when they are teaching it. As the saying goes, "It takes a village to raise a child." In our case, it takes a school to teach our students. Here's to working together!

Children's Books

Cole, J. (1986). *The magic school bus at the waterworks.* New York: Scholastic.

Danziger, P. (1974). *The cat ate my gymsuit.* New York: Dell.

DiCamillo, K. (2006). *The miraculous journey of Edward Tulane.* Cambridge, MA: Candlewick Press.

Gilman, P. (1992). *Something from nothing.* New York: Scholastic.

Lasky, K. (2003). *Guardians of Ga'hoole.* New York: Scholastic.

Lowrey, J. S. (1942). *The pokey little puppy.* New York: Golden Books.

Polacco, P. (1998). *The keeping quilt.* New York: Simon & Schuster.

Rae, J. (1997). *Gilbert de la Frog Ponde: A swamp story.* Atlanta, GA: Peachtree.

Ross, D. (1999a). *Book of hugs.* New York: HarperCollins.

Ross, D. (1999b). *Book of kisses.* New York: HarperCollins.

Chapter 27

New Teacher Voices: Snapshots From the Trenches

Amy Dunbar, Elyssa Brand, Kara Pirillo,
Peter Stiepleman, Miquelina Vasquez,
Beverly Rawson, Suzy Burke, and Rebecca Brand

Introduction

~Susan S. Lehr~

The following essays explore simple yet effective ways to connect children and books. The teachers writing these essays have been teaching for about 5 years, and are all former students of mine at Skidmore College. The students they teach range from grade 1 to grade 5. From a first-grade author-illustrator study of Kevin Henkes's books to a fifth-grade study of racism in *The Night Crossing* (Ackerman, 1995), these eight teachers talk about their core beliefs about literacy and how they enact them every day in the classroom. Their enthusiasm and freshness are apparent in the way they describe their classrooms and their students. They love great books and are passing that love on to their students.

I am struck by how literature directly impacts children's thinking. When they experience the lives of book characters, they can make connections and explore meaning in their own lives. "Cheap talk" can be replaced with meaningful dialogue. Through a study of Kevin Henkes's books, Amy Dunbar's first-grade children link the problems of literary characters to their own worlds, which include real problems like being mean to a sibling or being jealous of a new baby in the family or missing a father in the military who is stationed far from home. Elyssa Brand talks about her trepidation of teaching literature authentically alongside traditional veterans who teach strict phonics programs. New teachers are vulnerable and can be anxious about being vocal about their literacy beliefs. After talking to her principal, Elyssa was able to find a balance by making the phonics component a limited but intense focus on word study. I applaud Elyssa as an empowered new teacher who immerses her first-grade children in literature.

Similarly, Kara Parillo immerses her third graders in life's moral dilemmas through a study of Aesop's fables. Kara encourages her children to interpret the fables and applauds diverse interpretations, thereby including all children at the literary table. Through comparison charts and links to Arnold Lobel's book of fables, the children make leaps from the texts to support their own ideas and to make connections between literature and their own lives.

Peter Stiepleman worked with bilingual children in Oakland and taught from the mandated Open Court series. He discusses how one size can never fit all children by describing his children's encounter with *Make Way for Ducklings* (McCloskey, 1941). Peter brought in books like *Chato's Kitchen* (Soto, 1995) to balance the cultural bias in the Open Court series, and to provide his students with characters, settings, and themes that related to their lives. Peter's experiences underscore the necessity of bringing in multiple perspectives and multiple texts for all children.

Miguelina Vasquez's urban students explore what it means to show courage and consider their own behavior in the classroom after studying Bernard Waber's (2002) *Courage*. Many of her fourth grade students understand that their success in the classroom depends on the personal choices they make.

Beverly Rawson shows her early evolution with book clubs. In the beginning she used a tight model for scaffolding student talk about books, but as her confidence grew Beverly began to trust her students and found that they took on roles and explored diverse perspectives naturally. Sometimes it's like putting a child on a bicycle and slowly letting go.

Suzy Burke's older readers explore powerful themes of the American Revolution in social studies while reading *My Brother Sam is Dead* (Collier & Collier, 1974), thus making rich and natural interdisciplinary connections.

In Rebecca Brand's fifth-grade class you'll find classics by Katherine Paterson and poems by Maya Angelou alongside picture books by Dr. Seuss and Eve Bunting. In a sophisticated study of Eve Bunting's work, students examined complex themes in illustrated books including illiteracy, homelessness, flight from oppression, and building relationships with stepparents. One fifth-grade student describes her own personal response to Eve Bunting's work: "I just love it. It's so intense and vibrant."

These emerging teachers are equally intense and vibrant. Their enthusiasm and passion for literature are contagious.

Building Connections Through
Author Kevin Henkes

~Amy Dunbar~

"Chrysanthemum, Chrysanthemum, Chrysanthemum" (Henkes, 1996) reso-nates through my memories when I reflect back on the 3 years that I have taught first grade at Schuylerville Elementary School in Schuylerville, New York. I am reminded that I have been able to stir a love of literature in my students through the works of Kevin Henkes. Each year I change my lesson plans to fit the needs of the students, but one unit that remains constant is the Kevin Henkes author study. Since I co-teach in an inclusive classroom, I am always striving to find a common forum for my students, both socially and academically. When I implement a whole-class unit, it must cater to the large range of abilities and needs of the students. The Kevin Henkes author study provides the students with a congenial environment in which they can enthusiastically learn and grow through literature.

Kevin Henkes allows young children to take a peek into their own lives. First graders are often egocentric, but through characters like Lilly, Chry-santhemum, Owen, Chester, and Wilson they are able to contemplate them-selves, their lives, and their relationships. A comprehension skill that students are expected to learn is the ability to make connections with books, including text-to-self, text-to-text, and text-to-world connections (Keene & Zimmerman, 1997). It is a skill that I teach directly to the students, and Kevin Henkes's books allow the children to make those sincere and natural connections.

By sharing their text-to-self connections with the class, the children are able to connect with each other, breaking through their egocentric tenden-cies. Henkes's lovable characters provide an avenue through which children can share common experiences. Two students might discover that they each have a baby sibling after reading *Julius, Baby of the World* (Henkes, 1995a). In this story, Lilly's parents bring home a new baby brother, Julius. Lilly torments Julius repeatedly, until her cousin mistreats Julius; she then stands up for her brother. The students can recognize the complex feelings they might have about their own younger siblings by relating to Lilly's initial jealousy of Julius and eventual embracement of him. The students who have older siblings relate to Julius.

After we have read *Julius, Baby of the World*, I ask the students to em-body either Julius or Lilly and to write a letter to the character's sibling to explain his or her feelings toward that sibling. A student who truly em-braces his or her own text-to-self connection will rely on personal experi-ence to compose the letter. Many of the students are able to recognize that Julius would be angry or upset about the way Lilly treated him, but one student recognized from his own experience that Julius might have unchari-table feelings. He wrote, "I wish you weren't so mean. I loved it when you had a nightmare. It would be funny to see you having a nightmare." The student identified that Julius could have felt satisfied that Lilly had a night-mare of a giant version of Julius, with menacing claws, trying to capture her.

Another student might be reminded of how to play cooperatively with a friend after reading *A Weekend With Wendell* (Henkes, 1995b). The story helps students to better understand the Golden Rule that we often ask them to follow. When Wendell continually bosses Sophie around, she finally gives him "a piece of his own medicine," as one of my students described it. Wendell realizes what it feels like to be bossed around, and he learns to play cooperatively with Sophie.

After reading *Wemberly Worried* (Henkes, 2000) and *Owen* (Henkes, 1993), each student brings in a security object to share with the class. Shar-ing the security objects allows the students to explain and understand how the characters were feeling in the two stories. It helps students to sympathize with Owen's determination to keep his baby blanket, because they have affec-tion for their own security objects. They might even have struggled with their parents, who wanted to take it away. One student had a parallel con-nection with Owen; "My mom cut my blankie in half so I could keep one half at my grandma's and one half at my house. Then I have a blankie piece wherever I go, just like Owen brought his blanket pieces wherever he went."

Another connection is not as direct, but it still helps students to under-stand the character's feelings. Students can relate to how Wemberly used her doll, Petal, to calm her down when she worried. One student brought in a picture of his dad, who was in the military. He was able to explain that he looks at the picture when he misses his dad or when he is upset. The emo-tions relate to Wemberly rubbing Petal's ears when she was upset. Not only are the students able to make text-to-self connections with these two books, they are also able make a text-to-text connection between the two books. Students are able to identify that both Wemberly and Owen had security objects that supported them during difficult situations.

It is a treat to share these stories with the students. They enjoy hearing stories to which they can relate. The characters that Kevin Henkes intro-duces to us are engaging and lovable. As I read the stories aloud to the class, I look around and can see the children's eyes twinkle as they make a connection to the characters. As the children catch on to the repetitive text that is often characteristic of Kevin Henkes's books, they join me with flu-ency and enthusiasm in chanting, "Chrysanthemum, Chrysanthemum, Chrysanthemum." The story ends, and the children look around at each other; then you hear a round of applause. Each time I hear that round of applause, I feel the excitement and passion ignite deep within my soul. I've accomplished a teacher's dream: I am teaching my students to be compre-hending and fluent readers—and they are enjoying it!

Finding the Balance: The Road to Literacy

~Elyssa Brand~

As I gazed around my first-grade classroom in early May, I saw children sprawled around the room, busy reading individually and with partners. One conversation between two students caught my attention. They were perusing a book about a child who was learning to read. One child commented that he had been reading since he was born. The other child enthusiastically agreed, commenting, "I get better and better at it every day." This is how all children, regardless of ability, should view their journey toward literacy. It is my job, as the teacher, to facilitate this natural process, both for learners who pick up reading quickly and for those most in need of support.

Teaching first-grade literacy is a delicate balancing act. When I began teaching 4 years ago, first-grade reading instruction at my school was largely phonics based. As a kindergarten teacher at the time, I reveled in the freedom of being able to teach literacy in authentic ways. I taught phonemic awareness through poems and songs; we wrote shared letters to the class next door, acted out read-alouds, and made the alphabet with our bodies on the playground. When I was given the opportunity to continue with my students to first grade, I accepted, but not without trepidation. How would I incorporate my ideas about literacy with the more traditional views that many of the teachers in my school held? How would I find the time to teach the strict phonics program that was required and still have time for more authentic reading and writing experiences?

As fall approached, I began to set up my classroom. New crayons and markers filled their respective containers, and storage pockets hung on chairs. Colorful book baskets lined the shelves, each with a label that clearly denoted its contents. Some were labeled by genre, some by author, some by topic; and, of course, there was an empty basket for the books that the class would deem First-Grade Favorites. With blank walls awaiting the first graders' work, I mulled over my 2½-hour literacy block and carefully made a schedule. With my principal's blessing, I determined that the required phonics curriculum would be a small but intense part of the literacy block, which the students and I would call Word Study. During the remainder of the allotted time, I endeavored to engage the students in reading and writing activities that were authentic and meaningful in nature.

During the ensuing 10 months, the children participated in reading and writing workshop, read and wrote for various purposes, conferenced with myself and with each other, spent time at literacy centers and in guided-reading groups, and listened to hundreds of read-alouds. From the beginning, I treated the students as readers and writers. We talked about how there are many ways that beginning first graders read. They can "picture read," read the words, or tell the story of a book with which they are familiar. We collaboratively wrote class books that we added to our classroom library. We chorally read short stories and poems. The children read ABC books and simple rhyming books, but they knew that when they entered the room they would be reading "real" books for real reasons.

I also had the children write for various purposes. We wrote letters, lists, small moment stories, how-to books, nonfiction reports, journal entries, and poems. We talked about why we use each genre and the components of each. I expected the students to write every day, and they rose to the challenge.

They also engaged in rich responses to literature. We read *Click, Clack, Moo: Cows That Type* by Doreen Cronin (2000), and the children wrote letters to the farmer from the perspective of the ducks. We made comparison charts and Venn diagrams for books such as *The Carrot Seed* by Ruth Krauss (1973) and *Leo the Late Bloomer* by Robert Kraus (1971), and for *Amazing Grace* by Mary Hoffman (1991) and *Oliver Button Is a Sissy* by Tomie de Paola (1979). The children wrote their own "Three Little Pig" stories after reading *The True Story of the Three Little Pigs* by John Scieszca (1989), and acted out a poem entitled "The Aquarium" by Valerie Worth (1996).

As the year progressed, we had engaging literary conversations that displayed the children's insights. For example, one of my struggling readers had written a poem about his best friend, Alex. During a writing conference, I commented that I thought it was interesting that he never actually mentioned Alex's name. The student replied, "I meant to do that. I want my friends to have to infer who[m] my poem is about."

On another occasion, we studied the strategy of asking questions before, during, and after our reading. We talked about "our wonderings" and how we might go about answering them. Sometimes the children would find them in the text, sometimes they would have to infer the answer, and sometimes they would have to look elsewhere. As Laura, an extremely high-level learner told us one day, "It is crazy, because sometimes I think so hard, but I never find an answer to my wonderings."

As I observed my classroom at the end of the year, I remembered my students as emergent readers, slowly learning to decode words one sound at a time on their way to increased levels of automaticity, fluency, and understanding. I noticed every child engaged in a "just right" book and listened as the students shared their reading with each other. Ultimately, I was glad I had invested the bulk of our literacy time on more authentic experiences. Not only did my students understand the mechanics of reading and writing, but they functioned as a learned and literate community who at a first-grade level understood that the purpose of these activities transcended work sheets and isolated sounds and letters.

In sum, I feel privileged to work under administrators who value their teachers' instincts and realize the importance of allowing teachers the freedom to teach in the way that best serves their unique students. In fact, the tides, schoolwide, are changing. In the 3 years since I began teaching first grade, my school has begun a balanced literacy initiative; training was provided, study groups were established, and a more balanced approach to literacy was initiated schoolwide. What a relief! Now instead of closing my door to teach, I find myself peeking into adjacent classrooms.

The Richness of Fable Study

~Kara Pirillo~

> What is most truly valuable is often underrated.
>
> —Aesop, *The Stag at the Pool*

It was the middle of March, and I was sitting on the rug surrounded by my third graders. We had just finished reading the Aesop's fable "The Lion and The Mouse" (1999). I shared the moral "Little friends may prove great friends" with my students and asked them to explain what Aesop meant. After multiple responses along the lines of "Just because you're little doesn't mean you can't do something an adult could do" and "You shouldn't think someone can't do something just because they're smaller than you," I asked the class to create an alternative moral for the fable. After giving them some time to think, I called on Chris, a small, thoughtful boy who shared, "I think another could be [to] always keep your promise, because if the mouse didn't keep his promise to the lion, he would have stayed caught and hunters would have gotten him." Chris's simple yet reflective remark helped me to introduce the main focus of fables—a short story that teaches the reader a lesson, and there isn't always one moral that can be derived from the tales. As I watched more hands rise into the air, I was excited by their enthusiasm, and we were ready to begin our journey.

One of the first activities I used to introduce the study was to complete a comparison chart of Aesop's fables. This helped to familiarize my students with the characteristics of a fable as well as the story elements. Together we read a story aloud and then filled in a giant chart, which included sections on characters, setting, problem, solution, and moral. Throughout this activity we found time to discuss the meaning of the story elements and their importance to the fable. We began to use the terms *setting* and *conflict* during our conversations, not only during our reading but in our writing as well. After we'd read multiple stories, we stepped back and looked at our chart. Using the completed document, we were able to discuss the overall themes, patterns, and characteristics that fables share. At that point I felt confident that the students had the necessary tools to identify the key elements without my direct instruction.

Next, students worked in pairs and read a chosen story out of the book *Fables* by Arnold Lobel (1980). The students completed a miniature comparison chart with a new section that required them to create an additional moral for the story they chose. As I moved from pair to pair, I found my students discussing and debating which moral to choose and why. They supported their thinking with quotes from the text, and I often overheard students making connections between fables. I loved circulating the room while this process was happening; it provided real insight into my students' thinking and informed my instruction for future lessons. It was amazing to stop and listen to the deep discussions that occurred between students; these are the times for which, I think, most teachers live.

In culmination, the students had the opportunity to create their own fables. Together we created a rubric of the required components and discussed story ideas. After many weeks of writing and rewriting, we were ready to share our creations. Sharing and modeling writing is a big part of our classroom; it's a time for students to gain ideas from their peers as well as gain confidence as writers. Furthermore, it's a time we're all able to sit back and realize what we've accomplished as a community of readers and writers.

In reflecting on this fable study, I often think about things I might change or update for the future. I would love to be able to find fables from other cultures and incorporate them into my study. Perhaps I could learn more about the life and times of Aesop and put that into context with his stories. I could even find a way to use music or theater to heighten the comprehension of morals or lessons. I'm constantly searching for ways to provide rich, powerful experiences for my students.

I have seen such growth in my students as a result of this fable study. Our discussions have become more involved, and students are using the text to support their ideas and make connections between literature and their lives. Furthermore, students question and form discussions on what they've read. Through completing this project, I found that my students were challenged in their thinking, which pushed them as readers and writers. I realize how fortunate I am to be part of a school community that not only supports innovative teaching but actually encourages it. I truly believe that without this freedom, my students would not gain the knowledge or have the opportunities to become independent, expressive, and fluent individuals.

It is now the end of April, and I'm again sitting with my students around me. This time I ask, "Why do you think fables are used to teach people lessons?" Again, I give the students some time to think, and I am not surprised when I see Chris's little hand shoot high into the air. I call on him, and he says the following:

> Well, I think that fables are good for a lot of reasons. Everyone likes to read about animals, because they're fun. The stories aren't too long, and that's good, too, because then the reader doesn't forget too much of what they've read. But I think the main reason is that fables help people figure out stuff they already know, but they just don't want to admit it. Fables make it safer for people to make choices that might be hard.

It had been a long journey, but sitting there listening to Chris's response, I knew that we were almost at our destination.

Treasured Texts and English Language Learners
~Peter Stiepleman~

When I began a career in education in 1998, California was in a time of dramatic teacher shortages. Governor Pete Wilson had just signed a class-size reduction law, and smaller class sizes meant that many more teachers were needed, especially in large urban districts. I was hired as a Spanish bilingual third-grade teacher, and all of my students spoke Spanish as their first language. Untrained in working with English language learners (ELLs), I found myself particularly confused and anxious when teaching English reading.

I wasn't alone. Many teachers worked at cross-purposes because the district lacked a coherent vision for teaching English to ELLs. In an attempt to solve this, the district adopted Open Court, a phonics- and skills-based basal reading program, because it provided a standardized approach to teaching reading. New teachers in low-performing schools, many of whom had been hired to fill the positions of teachers who had sought less demanding employment at high-performing schools, would have their reading curriculum made explicit through the Open Court scripts.

School communities, however, soon became aware of the negative aspects of any scripted program. The entire class read the same story, regardless of a child's literacy level. Open Court's rigid design made it impossible for a teacher to create units of study based on the students' needs. Despite this, the district continued to be inflexible and used frequent assessments that championed fluency over comprehension as a way to monitor students, teachers, and principals. The program's adoption, undertaken without teacher input, created a toxic culture—a culture of distrust and low morale.

One especially criticized part of Open Court is the teacher's obligation to use basal readers that are often too difficult for children to understand, either because cognitively the writing is too demanding or because they simply do not comprehend the context. *Make Way for Ducklings* (McCloskey, 1941), an Open Court selection, is a beloved classic for its illustrations and use of narrative. The setting (Boston in the 1940s), however, presents a particular challenge for a class of ELLs. These students lack the background knowledge necessary to create meaning from the book.

I'll never forget when I first read this book during our daily read-aloud. My students kept interrupting me with questions about the text. Marco Gomez, a slender 8-year-old boy with brown hair and brown eyes, asked, "What is Boston?" I stopped reading, stood up, and pulled down the map of the United States. I pointed to Boston. "Boston," I said, "is the capital of Massachusetts." Perla Garcia, an 8-year-old girl with long braids, looked confused. She raised her hand and asked, "What's a capital?" Before I could reply, Marco broke in again, "And what's a Massachusetts?" I tried to answer their questions, but I found it difficult to explain that the states form a nation and that each state has its own capital. "I don't get it," said Marco. "Yeah, me neither," concurred Perla. Agreeing to talk about it after we finished the book, I continued reading.

I hadn't gotten very far before I was answering questions about the illustrations. The children noticed that the cars and the clothing were different from what they observed in Oakland. Perla raised her hand again. "Mr. Stiepleman, is that what Boston looks like?" I tried to explain the concepts of past, present, and future. Perla, Marco, and the rest of my students stared at me blankly before joining in chorus, "I don't get it!" It was I who didn't get it. They were unprepared for the story, and I was to blame for creating so much confusion.

What took me time to discover, and what I hope to convey, is that when choosing books for students, a teacher must be given the freedom to consider the students' needs. In the case of ELL students, it's about building background knowledge. I found myself opting for stories like *A Chair for My Mother* (Williams, 1982), *Chato's Kitchen* (Soto, 1995), *Pablo Remembers* (Ancona, 1993), *Two Mrs. Gibsons* (Igus, 1996), and *Yo Yes?* (Raschka, 1993) because their narratives reflected the kinds of lives my students could comprehend. With these stories, they made connections between the books and their own lives.

Many of my students had hardworking, exhausted, single mothers like Rosa's mother in *A Chair for My Mother* (Williams, 1982). I remember when Edwin Dominguez, a fair-skinned boy with tight curly hair, connected his life to that of the narrator's. Like Rosa, Edwin gave his mother a foot rub when she came home from work each night. He understood the sacrifices she made for his two siblings and him.

Iris Sanchez, a new student from Los Angeles, identified with the mouse family's fear and trepidation upon moving into Chato's neighborhood in *Chato's Kitchen* (Soto, 1995). Her new home, a ground-floor apartment with one, barred window, was jammed between two equally bleak structures. The noise, garbage, and poor light caused her to declare, "I got to get me a dog like that!" when she saw the mice's "low-rider" friend.

Fernando Nemecio, a recent immigrant from rural Mexico, connected with Pablo's experiences in *Pablo Remembers* (Ancona, 1993). Like Pablo, Fernando and his family honored their ancestors in a three-day celebration of the Day of the Dead. His greatest worry when he was in my class was who was going to sweep his ancestors' graves now that he and his family were living in California.

Daisi Aquino, a Latina and Filipina, enjoyed reading *Two Mrs. Gibsons* (Igus, 1996) because, like the narrator in the story, she came from a multiracial family that shared different customs. *Yo Yes?* (Raschka, 1993) was a big hit in my classroom because my students related to the encounter and budding friendship formed by the two boys, especially my ELL students at the onset of speaking English.

When my students read these types of stories, the discussions were rich and the comprehension skills became easier to model. In fact, some of these titles have now been translated into Spanish, providing the scaffolding for a smoother transition into the English versions.

Although I think it is essential for a teacher to choose contextually embedded texts—books for which children possess the background knowledge so they can understand them immediately—when teaching new concepts, a teacher will be stifled if he or she limits the literature selections only to those books that are contextually embedded. It is equally important to challenge your students' cognitive development with contextually reduced books—books for which the students possess no background knowledge—because otherwise you have stifled their opportunities to learn new concepts.

Students need individualized opportunities to read books based on their independent level (i.e., books the students can handle on their own) and their instructional level (i.e., books that might require teacher intervention). However, this is not possible unless teachers are properly supported. That support does not come from what Oakland teachers referred to as the "Open Court police" (i.e., teachers assigned to monitor their peers), but rather from ongoing opportunities that emphasize comprehension over fluency and that encourage student-facilitated literature groups over teacher-led, whole-class lectures. During the 7 years I worked in California, I observed how a dearth of meaningful professional development opportunities contributed to a collective struggle for authentic instruction. Teachers need to understand how to teach the academic English present in literature and how to build on what students already know (i.e., schema). When teachers learn how to relate new material to the content that students already know, the acquisition of new vocabulary and new concepts happens faster. Good books are not enough. Good instruction is paramount.

Courage in the Fourth Grade

~Miqueline Vasquez~

The Community Elementary School where I teach is located in the Bronx, New York. Approximately 600 students, grades K–6, attend this school. This year we have a new principal who is dedicated to using good literature in the school. Each month she selects "books of the month" for the entire school. All K–6 teachers are given a list of response activities, from which we select those that are most appropriate for our students. We also have the opportunity to share and display the work.

Courage by Bernard Waber (2002) was the book-of-the-month selection for November 2006. In this book Waber describes the many ways that children have courage in their daily lives. For instance, "courage is nobody better pick on your little brother" and "courage is two candy bars and saving one for tomorrow." Although there are situations included in the book that some of my students have not yet experienced, they are still able to understand the emotions that Waber describes—for instance, "courage is riding your bicycle for the first time without training wheels." Some students, like myself when I was younger, might not have had a bike to ride; however, they understand the idea that is expressed. Another example is "courage is a spelling bee and your word is *superciliousness.*" Despite the fact that most of my students have not participated in a spelling bee, they are aware of the emotions one goes through in it.

In this book there is friendly vocabulary with which my students are familiar, such as the following: "Courage is being the new kid on the block and saying, flat out, 'Hi, my name is Wayne. What's yours?'" By adding the words *flat out,* the author is using slang that some students use or have heard outside school. It's vocabulary they can relate to, which seems to make the book easier for them to understand.

The first thing I asked my students to do after hearing the book read aloud was to have them define courage in their own words. When we revisited this book in June, the students reflected on their experiences in fourth grade and defined the kinds of courage they had throughout the year. First, we gathered in our meeting area and I reread parts of the book. Although this book remained in our classroom library and was available for them to read, I decided to reacquaint them with the book by rereading parts of the book aloud. Second, I presented a task on chart paper. I asked the students to describe a type of courage that they had experienced in the fourth grade.

Then I shared a personal answer about my own courage. I wrote, "Courage is not quitting fourth grade. I need to survive and hope that things will get better." I talked about my response and let them know that it was a very difficult year for me, because being a fourth-grade teacher and going to school at the same time was very stressful. I explained that I needed to have courage in order to continue working and going to school simultaneously. Some students still had difficulty understanding the assignment; therefore, I asked others to explain and give personal examples. Asking other students to explain courage in their own words made it easier for all the students to understand the assignment and think about times that they showed courage. Below are some examples of how my students described courage in the fourth grade:

"Courage is not quitting reading. I needed to read more and I did not like reading."

"Courage is coming in at the middle of the school year and trying to do your best to catch up."

"Courage is not being shy to go on stage for a show. Courage is not being scared to do something."

"Courage is to ask people to be my new friend in fourth grade."

"Courage is to try hard to understand my math homework."

One student wrote, "Courage is not stopping to work hard in the 4th grade. I want to go to 5th grade and be smart," and another wrote, "Courage is not to give up being good in fourth grade. I will never stop behaving good [sic] in fourth grade." Both were among my brightest students. Their parents attended parent-teacher conferences and often called me on evenings or weekends to find out how their children were doing. These children came from supportive homes and were aware of their responsibilities as students and knew that they must work hard and behave in class.

In contrast, some students focused on troubled classmates. They wrote the following: "Courage is ignoring some students in the fourth grade. I needed to ignore some students [who] were getting me mad." "Courage is ignoring kids who behave badly and not getting mad at the teacher." In our classroom we had students who were off-task, disruptive, and angry. These behavioral problems often interfered with my teaching and their learning. Therefore, when these two students stated that they needed to ignore certain students, they were referring to that small group of students who at times made it difficult for all of us to focus.

The students wrote their responses and paired up with each other to share their definitions of courage, a technique called *think, pair, share*. As I circulated the meeting area, students were having meaningful discussions about their responses. Reading, writing, and talking about Waber's (2002) book was a meaningful experience for my students, because it gave them the opportunity to think about their own actions and to share their emotions. As a result, they understood each other just a bit better.

Book Clubs as a Way to Invest in Rich Conversation

~Beverly Rawson~

"Talk is cheap."

Whoever first said this must not have been a teacher. In my experience, talk is invaluable. As a fifth-year teacher, I look back at my naïveté now and can laugh; I was shocked to discover, in my first year of teaching, that my fifth-grade students simply did not know how to talk to one and other. The shock quickly wore off as I began to pursue a solution. How could I foster the rich, meaningful talk I envisioned in my ideal classroom?

The answer came in what I naturally knew and saw in popular culture around me: My students needed something to talk about that interested them, that they had access to and power over. These are all aspects of book clubs, also called literature circles, in which students read a common book in small groups. Maggie Moon, of the Teachers College Reading and Writing Project, explains that "book clubs are a social structure meant to encourage semi-independent conversation" (personal communication, March 20, 2006).

My first attempt at using book clubs was incredibly structured. Each student was given a specific task or role for the day, such as finding a text-to-world connection or a great quotation. I picked five books that were on the fifth-grade level, despite having a class that ranged from second-grade to sixth-grade reading levels. Each group chose the book its members wanted to read. I sat back and watched what I thought must surely work. I was bombarded with the fact that I had one smoothly working group and four rebellious ones—the teacher's nightmare of a flat, undeveloped 5-minute conversation followed by anything but being focused on the literature.

The following year, I organized the students into homogeneous groups according to reading level and scaled down the clubs so that there were no more than four students per club. I eliminated the segregation of daily roles. It is more natural that all students learn all the roles, or strategies of reading and talking about reading, because readers naturally employ all these roles simultaneously. The result was that my students were talking!

Not only were they talking, they were also referencing the text, citing outside sources (whether from the real world or from other texts), politely debating, searching together to find answers and create questions, problem-solving as a group, and working with each other to understand the text. They read daily and talked regularly during our reading period. These readers used self-stick notes to record ideas, questions, connections, or simply a passage they really liked. A few minutes of conversation preparation time were included in our daily reading routine.

Recently, a group of four students discussed the social issue of bigotry, based on the account of antisemitism in *The Night Crossing*, Karen Ackerman's (1995) story of Clara, a Jewish girl living in Austria during World War II. These students, all minorities and almost all from families receiving public assistance, were deep in discussion over Clara's plight. I sat just outside their circle and noted their conversation:

> *Mike*: It's not fair.
>
> *Doneisha*: Yeah, it's not fair. Just because she's Jewish she be hated. You can't even look at her skin and know that.
>
> *Emily*: It is like when people say, "Oh, I don't like you because you're Puerto Rican or you're Black or you're in a wheelchair."
>
> *Mike*: These people were whack.
>
> *Emily*: I have a, a, a part here about it: turn to this page.

Emily then directed her three group members to an excerpt from the text, which they read aloud and continued to discuss. It is important to note that these students had no direction from me besides this: "Take 2 minutes to look over your notes" and "When you are ready, you may begin your conversations."

These students have been preparing for this moment since the first day. They practice accountable talk during read-alouds and in reading partnerships (and, really, in all subjects throughout the day, every day). They read daily and know that they are expected to talk about that reading. They have been handed rich, well-written books.

The group cited above is reading at below grade level, yet their conversation is far from remedial. After they finished *The Night Crossing* (Ackerman, 1995), they chose to move on to Mildred D. Taylor's (1998) *The Well*, which also deals with prejudice, but this time the racism of the American South in the 1930s.

It is so simple that it is easy to overlook: Students talk about what interests them. If they cannot read and draw meaning from the book, they will not talk about it; if the book is boring, they will not push themselves to become enchanted. I am fortunate enough to be in a school where quality literature is recognized, and all efforts are made to get the best there is into the hands of our readers.

It takes daily preparation and work, but by the time we begin our first book club, I, as the teacher, have stepped back. I compare it to pushing a child on a bicycle and then letting go. I'm there watching in case of any bumps and to shout out encouragement, but the child is the one who is biking. I touch base with each group each day. On some days, the meeting is brief, and on others it is necessary to have a longer conference. My role is to facilitate while the students converse about books they feel strongly about and cite.

Just as in any other classroom activity, there are groups that sail along smoothly and those that need more help. Daniels (2002) writes about his work with book clubs:

> They shared responses with peers, listened respectfully to each other, sometimes disagreed vehemently, but dug back into the text to settle arguments or validate different interpretations. In short, our kids were acting like real readers, lifelong readers. Oh, sure, there were problems, too: kids who didn't do the reading, off-task discussions, and really noisy rooms. But mostly, it was working. (p. 1)

I have to agree that that has been my experience, too. By shifting the power to the students, giving them interesting, engaging books that they are able to read, I find that we are far from "cheap talk." As the clichéd credit card advertisement might go: Cost of books? $3.50. Cost of plastic chairs arranged in circle? $25.95. Cost of meaningful, lively conversation centered around a good book? Priceless.

The Most Well-Planned Lesson

~Suzanne Burke~

It's 11:00 A.M., and as we wander back to the classroom from art class, the children grab their snacks, come to their seats, and assemble themselves, as we do every day, for our read-aloud. I begin to read the last chapter from *My Brother Sam Is Dead* by James Collier and Chris Collier (1974). As I scan the room, I see that a few children have their heads resting on their hands and that others are curled up in beanbag chairs. Many stop chewing their snack when they hear that Sam—the hero they have come to know, love, and appreciate—has been shot after being wrongly accused of stealing his own family's cattle. As I read with passion and enthusiasm, I spot, out of the corner of my eye, two girls, hands clasped together, cringing as I read the last pages of the book.

That was February, and we had all come to work by the same routines. My class and I worked together throughout the year to get into a rhythm and learn each other's personalities and learning and teaching styles. Each year I strive to find that delicate balance between setting and following a routine and still allowing room for flexibility. Flexibility in my teaching allows me to grasp the teachable moments. I feel very fortunate to work in a school that encourages and supports teachers to use their own experiences and knowledge to enhance the children's learning.

Upon reflecting on that experience, I had to ask, "Why are these children so enthralled?" We had been reading and writing about the Revolutionary War for weeks, using primary-source documents and other nonfiction texts. Much of our class time was spent exploring the growing tension between the colonists and the English as the colonists' desire for independence grew. Primary-source documents, such as the original newspaper article on the Boston Massacre trial and the engravings of Paul Revere, exposed children to actual historical artifacts. Those texts, along with class discussions, helped the social studies curriculum become both exciting and accessible. This enabled students to make connections among what they were reading, their own lives, the world, and other literature.

My school follows a balanced literacy model and encourages a variety of experiences to immerse children in the world of reading and writing. Read-alouds are a vital part of my classroom, and *My Brother Sam Is Dead* (Collier & Collier, 1974) complemented the social studies curriculum perfectly. At first the boys and girls were mainly interested in the blood, guts, and gore of war; however, as we continued to delve deeper into the novel, they became invested in the characters.

Many of my students, both boys and girls, identified with Tim, a 12-year-old boy who struggled to develop a sense of independence. Throughout the book, Tim's feelings about the war were inconsistent; his father supported the war and was loyal to the king, whereas his brother Sam ran off to fight with the rebels. When students were posed with a hypothetical situation similar to Tim's, they found it hard to choose between their siblings, whom they idolize, and their parents, to whom they've always listened.

We also created inside-outside charts, which are life-size outlines, to further analyze the internal thoughts and outward movements of some major characters. Students wrote on a character's hands, feet, heart, stomach, brain, mouth, and ears what that character thought, felt, smelled, tasted, touched, and so on. This gave the students a concrete way to discuss with their peers some of their thoughts and knowledge about each character. They used the book as a reference and discussed story elements as they analyzed the thoughts, actions, and perceptions of each character.

This enhanced their comprehension of the complex book events and helped them to understand what motivated each individual character. This was a great way to differentiate instruction, because as some students were solidifying their understanding and sequencing of events, others were able to make informed predictions about what could have happened at the end of the book. Now, in May, our charts are still displayed, and I still catch students reflecting on their work and thinking about the book experience.

However, what struck me the most during this novel study was an authentic, unintentional, motivating writing piece that blossomed unexpectedly from the students' own enthusiasm.

As I read the last sentence of the book, you could hear a pin drop. The students were so invested in the story that their faces reflected their emotions. Some were outraged, some were upset, and some couldn't wrap their minds around what just happened to their beloved Sam. "Could we write another ending?" To be honest, this didn't mesh with my plans, but I couldn't resist their need to rebuild a palatable ending. They had very little to say but had a strong need to write.

We abandoned other plans and brainstormed alternative endings together. The students mapped out what would happen to the main character. We tried to capture Tim's voice. Together we went down to the computer lab with 10 copies of the book as a reference point. Over the next week and a half, I set my students loose to craft their own endings.

One student, Julie, took this opportunity to make the story her own. She was totally focused, but I assisted when she asked, and I patiently awaited to see what was to be her masterpiece. I was literally moved to tears when I read the "perfect ending" from Julie's perspective:

I sat there with the note in my hand and cried. I didn't care if Betsy saw me. It was too painful.

Then I heard the clanking of horses' hooves. It was the British. They were barging into some of the other Patriots' houses. Then I saw a Patriot who was in the war. I looked closer and it was Sam. I checked the note he sent, and it was dated 3 weeks ago. He must've been let out.

I heard myself scream, "Sam!"

But it was too late. A bullet was shot from the British army and Sam fell off of his horse. He didn't move. And I just watched the sun go down.

This is my fourth year of teaching, and this was one of my most memorable teachable moments. The work that my students produced was absolutely incredible, because the content of their pieces was substantial. This new writing opportunity also gave me a chance to address skills such as paragraph structure, perspective, and sequencing of events.

Before this impromptu project, I rarely gave my students the opportunity to write in the historical fiction genre. I always kept them safely housed in the world of personal narratives, persuasive essays, and other pieces that were directly linked to their own lives. They collectively proved that they were ready for much more complexity in their writing. Reflecting on my own teaching practices is something that has had an invaluable effect on my teaching. I value the experiences that this group of students brought to me. They taught me that being flexible in my teaching often leads to the richest reading and writing experiences. In this instance, clearly, the most "well-planned" lesson was the one that was unplanned.

Riding the Tiger: Real Conversations by Real Readers
~Rebecca Brand~

It is early March and the fifth graders gather eagerly around the circle. With books in hand and self-stick notes haphazardly arranged, the students become quiet as Andrew begins to speak:

Today I was reading *Life Doesn't Frighten Me* by Maya Angelou [1993]. It's a picture book that illustrates her poem by the same name. At first, I didn't understand the meaning of the poem. I also don't have much schema for Maya Angelou's writing. I know she is a famous poet and author, but not much else. I think her poem is kind of creepy, and I had a lot of questions while I was reading. Why does she keep repeating, "Life doesn't frighten me at all"? What is causing her to be afraid? Is she talking about herself or someone else? I was confused. Then I looked at the afterword. I marked this part with a [self-stick note] because it helped me make sense of this poem. In the afterword, it says that Maya Angelou had some bad things happen to her in her life. I am inferring that she wrote this poem to help her deal with how she got through some of those bad things.

As I thank Andrew for sharing and we hear some responses to his thoughts, I marvel at the way these fifth graders have evolved into a learning community of real readers and writers. Each day, they read and write for authentic purposes, think metacognitively, investigate new strategies and concepts, and share what they find with each other and with their teachers. They discuss what they read in pairs and in book clubs, make book recommendations, and choose books, genres, and topics that will help them to grow. As a community, we integrate these strategies into our content area classes and make them an integral part of our day. I feel privileged to lead, as well as to participate in, such a productive learning group.

That I can cultivate and be part of such a community is due to the insistence of my school district, specifically of my curriculum coordinator, that our school implement a workshop model that incorporates a balanced literacy approach. Despite the overwhelming pressures of state testing, budget cuts that impact funds for reading support, and a few school committee members who lean toward a "back to basics" approach, teachers at my school are encouraged to provide authentic reading and writing experiences for our students—experiences that are differentiated, provide choice, and incorporate modeling, guided practice, and independent work.

One morning at the beginning of May, the students examined the picture books of Eve Bunting, an author of numerous award-winning picture books for intermediate readers. The students browsed through several of Bunting's books in pairs and small groups, including *Fly Away Home* (1991), *Train to Somewhere* (1996), *Dandelions* (2001a), *The Wall* (1990), and *The Memory String* (2000). Bunting's picture books are especially powerful for upper elementary readers because they encompass mature themes such as homelessness, oppression, illiteracy, and other contemporary issues.

Over several days, the students shared excerpts representing "really effective writing" with the rest of the group. We met as a class to discuss characteristics that are indicative of Eve Bunting's style and voice as a writer. The students came to the conclusion that Eve Bunting writes in the genres of historical fiction and realistic fiction, that she likes to write about children, and that her texts expose issues that are both realistic and poignant. First they commented that Bunting's writing is very descriptive, but a small group later clarified that her writing is not descriptive in a wordy manner; she creates sensory images in a more simple way, carefully placing similes and other description so as to enhance the mood of her story. They were also astounded by the various mediums and styles of the illustrations in Bunting's books. They concluded that she meticulously chooses illustrators whose styles help her to convey the moods and themes of her works to the reader.

In the next few days, the students wrestled with the sophisticated themes addressed in Bunting's writing by applying what they learned this year about being active readers. They demonstrated their knowledge of voice, perspective, and theme by delving deeply into one of Eve Bunting's books and by responding to it through writing and art. In the process, they engaged in partner and individual reading, did some freestyle writing and freestyle drawing, and brought a piece of writing to final draft. In addition, they discussed in depth one theme of their picture book and what kinds of symbols they could use to portray that theme as a visual piece of art.

Despite the open-ended nature of this project, the students were not participating without significant teacher input and guidance. This class had worked all year to get to where they were now. They knew that each day in reading workshop, they would participate in a directed mini-lesson (5–15 minutes of teacher-led instruction on a focus skill), and that after the instruction they would practice the skill in small groups, on their own, or with a teacher or volunteer. Furthermore, they knew they would be expected to share what they had learned at the end of our workshop each day.

They were exposed this year to reading strategies such as visualizing, asking questions, making connections, inferring, and synthesizing a text. They had extensive guided practice through book clubs and through whole-class discussions about what it should look like and sound like to have an authentic conversation about literature. As a class, they developed awareness of genre, voice, and the author's craft. Additionally, they tackled the literary concepts of plot, setting, theme, and, to a certain degree, symbolism. Therefore, the demands of this particular project required that the students build upon and select from the skills they had been practicing since September.

On one particular day, the focus of our mini-lesson is inferring the theme of a book. We review that the theme is the big idea, or the message of a text. I pull out three books we've read as a class this year: *Bridge to Terabithia* by Katherine Paterson (1987), *The Lorax* by Dr. Seuss (1971), and *The Bee Tree* by Patricia Polacco (1998). The students know these books well because we've examined them in depth and have used them as examples in many of our mini-lessons. As a class, we make a quick anchor chart about the big ideas or themes we've inferred from each of the books. We discuss why we've chosen each theme and give verbal examples.

During the last 5 minutes of the mini-lesson, I remind the students about freestyle writing, a mechanism that we use to express our ideas about a piece of text or a content-area concept. During freestyle writing, each student writes whatever comes to mind related to a topic or a prompt for a prescribed amount of time. Today the assignment is for each group to discuss its book briefly, and then to spend 10 minutes doing some independent freestyle writing to the following prompt: "What are one or more themes that you have inferred from your book? Give examples that support why you chose the theme." Finally, the students will discuss their responses with each other before coming back to share those findings with the class.

As I send the students off to work, I watch them settle around the room. Three students sprawl on the rug with *Fly Away Home* (Bunting, 1991), a book about a homeless boy and his dad who find refuge in an airport. Two of my struggling readers sit down with a parent volunteer to discuss *The Memory String* (Bunting, 2000), a book about a young girl's changing relationship with her stepmother. Another group is already busy writing about *Riding the Tiger* (2001b), a provocative text about the difficulty of making wise choices. One group appears as if it didn't hear the directions—the students are sliding across the linoleum on a rolling chair—and so I hurry over to help them settle into their reading of *Smoky Night* (Bunting, 1994).

"What are you thinking about the theme of this book?" I ask as I sit down on the rug and motion for the two boys to sit beside me. We take a minute to page through *Smoky Night* as they point out the vivid, abstract illustrations. During my conference with this group yesterday, I had helped them to make the connection that the book is actually a fictional account of two families who lived through the 1992 Los Angeles riots. The students had very little schema on this event (it happened before they were born), but they did have quite a bit of background knowledge about the themes of prejudice, race, and divisions between individuals and groups. I had sent them to print up some basic information on the riots, and they refer to their findings today as they discuss the main characters: an African-American boy, his mother, and their Asian neighbor, who become friends in the aftermath of the fires. The boys earnestly profess their amazement that previous to this catastrophic event the two parties had never spoken. As the boys finish their conversation, I encourage them to begin writing.

"What message do you take away from the book? Why did you choose this message?" I ask as they take out their pencils. Then, as I move away, I say, "I'll be back, and I can't wait to hear you share what you've written!"

Before I return to check on the parent volunteer, I confer briefly with Rebecca, who is working on her freestyle writing in response to *Riding the Tiger* (Bunting, 2001b). Her response reads as follows:

> In the beginning I felt a little scared for the boy. In the middle, I felt like the tiger was sucking power from the boy. Toward the end, I was happy because the boy finally found the courage to get off the tiger's back...by looking at the pictures you can tell that the tiger is kind of sneaky and makes the boy think he's something he's not....I keep thinking about how much strength it takes to not get sucked into a trap, especially when you are the new kid. I think that the major message of this book is that sometimes choosing something just to fit in is not all it is cracked up to be.

As we chat about Eve Bunting's perspective and connect the book to Rebecca's schema on what it is like to crave a sense of belonging, I think about how fortunate I am that I have the liberty to use authentic texts with my students. They are reading real books, with real topics, for real reasons.

Several weeks later, my students invite their parents to a culminating exhibit entitled "Responding Through Words and Art: An Author Study of Eve Bunting." On each of the glass windows outside our auditorium is a 28-inch masterpiece, a visual symbol that represents a theme of each of the 14 Bunting books chosen by the students. The visual symbols are stunning and well executed; some are painted, and others were completed with colored pencils or markers. A few are decorated with tissue paper, cotton balls, and other materials, and one is decidedly three-dimensional. Under each work of art is a written piece describing the theme of the book and how the group chose to represent that theme as a visual symbol. The students are visibly engaged and excited. They drag their parents over to the windows and explain the project and their learning. Equally encouraging are their written reflections on what they learned about both the process and the ultimate product.

Chris commented, "I learned that I can visualize more while reading. I also learned that art isn't just a picture. Sometimes colors and shapes can mean things, too!"

Josh observed, "I learned that reading, writing, and art are related, and that reading can teach you valuable lessons."

Some students revealed insights they had about themselves. "I learned that I can really look at books as a person and that I'm a great reader," Taylor commented.

Finally, the students were asked whether they thought the project was worth the time and effort that they expended over a 3-week period. The students' responses were almost unanimously positive; they wrote comments along the lines of how this endeavor made them think, how it forced them to work together, and how they enjoyed responding to literature through art. Regarding student engagement, perhaps Bekka's comment was the most telling, "I loved our project. It was so intense and vibrant. That's what we were going for. It was worth it because when I was done, I kept thinking 'Wow! That's mine—that's mine!'"

References

Daniels, H. (2002). *Literature circles: Voice and choice in book clubs and reading groups.* New York: Stenhouse.

Keene, E., & Zimmerman, S. (1997). *Mosiac of thought.* Portsmouth, NH: Heinemann.

Children's Books

Ackerman, K. (1995). *The night crossing.* New York: Yearling.

Aesop, (1999). *The classic treasury of Aesop's fables* (D. Daily, Ed.). Philadelphia: Running Press.

Ancona, G. (1993). *Pablo remembers: The fiesta of Day of the Dead.* New York: Lothrop, Lee & Shepard Books.

Angelou, M. (1993). *Life doesn't frighten me.* New York: Stewart, Tabori, and Chang.

Bunting, E. (1990). *The wall.* New York: Clarion Books.

Bunting, E. (1991). *Fly away home.* New York: Clarion Books.

Bunting, E. (1994). *Smoky night.* New York: Voyager Books.

Bunting, E. (1996). *Train to somewhere*. New York: Clarion Books.

Bunting, E. (2000). *The memory string*. New York: Clarion Books.

Bunting, E. (2001a). *Dandelions*. New York: First Voyager Books.

Bunting, E. (2001b). *Riding the tiger*. New York: Clarion Books.

Collier, J., & Collier, C. (1974). *My brother Sam is dead*. New York: Scholastic.

Cronin, D. (2000). *Click clack moo: Cows that type*. New York: Simon & Schuster.

de Paola , T. (1979). *Oliver Button is a sissy*. Orlando, FL: Harcourt Brace.

Henkes, K. (1993). *Owen*. New York: HarperCollins.

Henkes, K. (1995a). *Julius, baby of the world*. New York: HarperCollins.

Henkes, K. (1995b). *A weekend with Wendell*. New York: HarperCollins.

Henkes, K. (1996). *Chrysanthemum*. New York: HarperCollins.

Henkes, K. (2000). *Wemberly worried*. New York: HarperCollins.

Hoffman, M. (1991). *Amazing Grace*. New York: Dial.

Igus, T. (1996). *Two Mrs. Gibsons*. San Francisco: Children's Book Press.

Kraus, R. (1971). *Leo the late bloomer*. New York: HarperCollins.

Krauss, R. (1973). *The carrot seed*. New York: HarperCollins.

Lobel, A. (1980). *Fables*. New York: HarperTrophy.

McCloskey, R. (1941). *Make way for ducklings*. New York: Viking Press.

Paterson, K. (1987). *Bridge to Terabithia*. New York: HarperTrophy.

Polacco, P. (1998). *The bee tree*. New York: Putnam and Grosset.

Raschka, C. (1993). *Yo yes?* New York: Orchard Books.

Scieszca, J. (1989). *The true story of the three little pigs*. New York: Penguin Putnam Books.

Seuss, Dr. (1971). *The lorax*. New York: Random House.

Soto, G. (1995). *Chato's kitchen*. New York: Putnam Books.

Taylor, M. D. (1998). *The well*. New York: Puffin Books.

Waber, B. (2002). *Courage*. Boston: Houghton Mifflin.

Williams, V. B. (1982). *A chair for my mother*. New York: Greenwillow Books.

Worth, V. (1996). Aquarium. In *All the poems and fourteen more* (p. 11). New York: Farrar, Straus & Giroux.

About the Authors

Susan S. Lehr, Editor

Susan S. Lehr, Ph. D. served two terms as the chair of the education department at Skidmore College and is a full professor who teaches language, literature, and literacy courses. Lehr has a strong commitment to constructivist models of teaching and learning and is passionate about preparing pre-service teachers to teach literacy and literature in relevant and innovative ways. Her first reader response study explored the child's developing sense of theme and has evolved into an exploration of how children actively read and respond to literature focused on themes of social justice. Lehr analyzes how children construct meaning in interactive contexts.

Lehr earned her Masters in Education at St. Louis University in 1975 and her Ph.D. at The Ohio State University in 1985, studying with Charlotte Huck and Janet Hickman. She spent six years teaching in early childhood programs and in the elementary classroom and has been in the college classroom for 25 years.

Her first book, *The Child's Developing Sense Of Theme*, published by Teachers College Press in 1991, examines the young child's developing sense of theme in individual and interactive classroom contexts. Recent books by Lehr include edited volumes of teacher, author and educator voices examining controversial issues, the construction of gender, and the politics of children's literature: *Battling Dragons: Issues And Controversy In Children's Literature* (1995), and *Beauty, Brains And Brawn: The Construction Of Gender In Children's Literature* (2001).

Her reader response research has been published in journals, e.g. *Reading Research Quarterly, The Journal of Research in Childhood Education,* and *The Reading Teacher.* Lehr has also published chapters about themes and genre in children's literature in edited textbooks including: *Extending Charlotte's Web,* edited by Cullinan, Hickman, and Hepler, *Booktalk: Books That Invite Talk, Wonder And Play With Language,* edited by McClure and Kristo, *Parents And Teachers: Helping Children Learn To Read And Write,* edited by Rasinski, *Journeying: Children Responding to Literature,* edited by Holland and Hungerford. She has conducted dozens of interviews with children's authors for her edited books and for journals like *The New Advocate* and *The Journal of Children's Literature.*

Lehr's current research focuses on the feminist children's writers of the eighteenth century, women who wrote radical texts for children but were eventually dismissed as didactic authors. Lehr's research has led her to the primary documents of these writers in the Rare Books Room at the British Library.

Lehr served as the president of the Children's Literature Assembly for the National Council of Teachers of English, has chaired committees for state and national book awards, including NCTE's Notable Books in the Language Arts, and on the editorial boards of professional journals like *The Reading Teacher* and the *Language Arts.* In 1990 she developed and chaired the first Charlotte Award, a children's choice book award for the New York State Reading Association.

She and a colleague, Karen Brackett, developed and co-directed Journeys And Reflections: An Educational Study Program in South Africa, leading groups of college students on three remarkable journeys that focused on the educational system of this multi-lingual society and included reader response studies and interviews with teachers.

Elyssa Brand

Elyssa Brand has taught kindergarten and first grade for the past four years. She is extremely interested in literacy instruction and enjoys creating a classroom community where her students believe in themselves as readers and writers.

Rebecca Brand

Rebecca Brand has been teaching 5th and 6th grade for the past four years. She is committed to providing authentic, challenging and rich literacy experiences for her students.

Joseph Bruchac

Joseph Bruchac is a writer and traditional storyteller whose work often draws upon the American Indian (Abenaki) part of his ancestry. The author of over 100 books for both young and adult readers, ranging from critical essays and collections of his own poetry to historical fiction and picture books, he is also (with his wife Carol) the founder and editor of The Greenfield Review Press. His most recent books include *At The End Of Ridge Road* (Milkweed Editions), described as a "colorful memoir (that) explores the links between Bruchac's native Abenaki culture and his long-held views on human dignity and social justice," and the novel *Jim Thorpe, Original All-American* (Dial).

Suzanne Burke

Suzanne Burke taught first grade for one year and is now in her fourth year of teaching fifth grade. Teaching first grade gave her valuable perspectives in teaching her fifth graders the reading and writing process. She loves developing a tight knit classroom community that encourages her class to comfortably take risks.

Barbara Chatton

Barbara Chatton is a Professor in the Department of Elementary and Early Childhood Education at The University of Wyoming. She teaches courses in children's and young adult literature. She writes and speaks on children's poetry, historical fiction, books for beginning readers, and literature across the curriculum. Her books include *Using Poetry Across the Curriculum* and *Blurring the Edges: Children's Literature and Writing Across the Curriculum* (with Lynne Collins).

Penny Colman

Penny Colman is a widely published author of books, essays, stories, and articles. The awards for her books include the American Library Association Best of the Best for the Twenty-first Century and the National Council of English Teachers Orbis Pictus Honor Award for Outstanding Nonfiction. In addition to her research and writing, she does the picture research and takes photographs for her books. She is a Distinguished Lecturer at Queens College, The City University of New York. Her web site is www. pennycolman.com

Christopher Paul Curtis

Born in Flint, Michigan, Christopher Paul Curtis spent his first 13 years after high school on the assembly line of Flint's historic Fisher Body Plant #1. His job entailed hanging car doors, and it left him with an aversion to getting into and out of large automobiles—particularly big Buicks.

Curtis's writing—and his dedication to it—has been greatly influenced by his family members, particularly his wife, Kaysandra. With grandfathers like Earl "Lefty" Lewis, a Negro Baseball League pitcher, and 1930s bandleader Herman E. Curtis, Sr., of Herman Curtis and the Dusky Devastators of the Depression, it is easy to see why Christopher Paul Curtis was destined to become an entertainer. Christopher Paul Curtis made an outstanding debut in children's literature with *The Watsons Go to Birmingham—1963*. His second novel, *Bud, Not Buddy*, is the first book ever to receive both the Newbery Medal and the Coretta Scott King Author Award.

Amy Dunbar

Amy Dunbar has taught in a range of situations, including third grade in Charlotte, North Carolina, an in-patient psychiatric hospital and a private laboratory school. Amy has settled outside Saratoga where her teaching career first began as an undergraduate student at Skidmore College, and now uses her varied teaching experiences to team-teach first grade in an inclusion classroom.

Deborah Ellis

Deborah Ellis lives in Simcoe, Ontario. She has published nine books for young readers and one for adults. Her work has been translated into 18 languages, and has won awards in several countries.

Dr. Evelyn B. Freeman

Dr. Evelyn B. Freeman is Dean and Director of The Ohio State University-Mansfield. A professor of Education, she teaches courses in children's literature and language arts. She has served as co-editor of the *Journal of Children's Literature* and *Bookbird: A Journal of International Children's Literature*. She helped found and chaired the first committee of the Orbis Pictus Award for Outstanding Nonfiction for Children of the National Council of Teachers of English. She has co-authored three books, numerous book chapters and journal articles, and has presented at professional conferences nationally and internationally. She currently serves as President of the Children's Literature Assembly of NCTE.

Marjorie R. Hancock

Marjorie R. Hancock is a Professor of Language Arts at Kansas State University. She is the author of two literature-based textbooks—*A Celebration of Literature and Response* (2nd ed.) and *Language Arts: Extending the Possibilities*. Both texts have links to the theoretical foundations of Louise Rosenblatt. Marjorie's extensive research in reader response has resulted in publications in *The Reading Teacher*, *Language Arts*, and the *Journal of Children's Literature*, several book chapters, and national and international presentations at IRA and NCTE. She is the past-president of the Children's Literature Assembly of NCTE.

Shelley Harwayne

Shelley Harwayne has been affiliated with the New York City Public Schools for more than 35 years, serving as a teacher, staff developer, co-director of the Teachers College Writing Project, founding principal of the Manhattan New School and Superintendent of Community School District # 2. Although she is currently providing daycare for her four grandchildren, she continues to carve out time to consult with school districts throughout the country and publish professional books on literacy and school leadership. Her most recent publication is *Novel Perspectives: Writing Minilessons Inspired by the Children in Adult Fiction*. She is the recipient of the 2006 NCTE Outstanding English Language Arts Educator Award.

Frank Hodge

Frank Hodge has spent 25 years bookselling at his children's bookstore, HODGE-PODGE BOOKS, INC in Albany, NY. His interest in the field started in 1962 when he took his first course in Children's Literature at Cornell University with poet-author Katherine Reeves. In 1965 Frank started teaching a course called Literature For Reading Programs which covered both children's literature as well as young adult literature. This course has been taught in the graduate programs at The University at Albany, Russell Sage College and Saint Rose College. Frank was named a Fellow of the NYS English Council for his work with teachers of English and named Friend to Reading by the NYS Reading Association. Currently he organizes conferences, GOT

BOOKS/ LET'S READ!! bringing authors/illustrators together with teachers/librarians and principals to help bring the magic back to reading classes through the use of literature.

Barbara Kiefer

Barbara Kiefer is the Charlotte S. Huck Professor of Children's Literature at The Ohio State University. She was formerly Robinson Professor of Children's Literature at Teachers College, Columbia University. Originally trained in art education, she taught grades one, two, four, and five in several regions of the U.S and in overseas schools. She served as the elected chair of the year 2000 Caldecott Award Committee of the American Library Association and was a member of the 1988 Caldecott Award Committee. She has published numerous articles and book chapters about reading and children's literature and is author of *The Potential of Picturebooks: From Visual Literacy to Aesthetic Understanding*, and the co-author of the books *An Integrated Language Perspective in the Elementary School: Theory Into Action*, with Christine Pappas and Linda Levstik, and the Sixth, Seventh, Eighth, and Ninth Editions of *Children's Literature in the Elementary School*, with Charlotte Huck, Susan Hepler, and Janet Hickman.

Dr. Janice V. Kristo

Dr. Janice V. Kristo is a Professor of Literacy at the University of Maine. She is co-author and editor of several texts, including *Nonfiction in Focus: A Comprehensive Framework for Helping Students Become Independent Readers and Writers of Nonfiction, K–6* and *Living Literature: Using Children's Literature to Support Reading and Language Arts*. She serves on the Editorial Review Board of the Journal of Children's Literature and Language Arts. Jan is a co-recipient of the University of Maine's Presidential Research and Creative Achievement Award and is a recipient of the New England Reading Association's Special Recognition Award.

Linda Leonard Lamme

Linda Leonard Lamme is a professor of education at the University of Florida, where she teaches courses in children's literature, international children's literature, the picture book, and multicultural literature. Linda requires that her future teachers read books outside their own culture.

Linda has two children, Laurel and Ary, and lives with her partner, Elaine, in Gainesville, Florida. Linda and Laurel have written articles and conduct workshops on welcoming children with LGBT parents into our schools.

Barbara A. Lehman

Barbara A. Lehman is Professor of Teaching and Learning at the Ohio State University, where she teaches graduate courses in children's literature and literacy at the Mansfield Campus. She co-edited with Marilou Sorensen *Teaching with Children's Books: Paths to Literature-Based Instruction* (National Council of Teachers of English, 1995) and co-authored with Evelyn Freeman *Global Perspectives in Children's Literature* (Allyn & Bacon, 2001). She has co-edited the *Journal of Children's Literature* (Children's Literature Assembly of NCTE) and *Bookbird: A Journal of International Children's Literature* for the International Board on Books for Young People. Her scholarly interests focus on international children's literature and child-centered literary criticism.

Belinda Louie

Belinda Louie is a professor of Education at the University of Washington, Tacoma. She has written articles for the *Reading Teacher,* the *Journal of Adolescent and Adult Literacy, Language Arts, English Journal, Children's Literature in Education, Journal of Children's Literature, Social Studies and the Young Learners, Journal of Higher Education,* and the *Bookbird.* Belinda is active at the local and nationals level in children's and young adult literature.

Dr. Amy McClure

Dr. Amy McClure is Rodefer Professor of Education and Chair of the Education Department at Ohio Wesleyan University, where she teaches courses in children's literature and early literacy and supervises student teachers. She also coordinates the University's Honors Program and the Early Childhood Education program. Dr. McClure is the author and editor of several books including *Sunrises and Songs: Reading and Writing Poetry in an Elementary Classroom, Booktalk: Books That Invite Talk, Wonder and Play with Literature, Inviting Children's Response to Literature, Adventuring with Books,* and *Living Literature: Using Children's Literature to Support Reading and Language Arts.* She is also the author of numerous book chapters and articles and has presented at conferences throughout the United States and the world. She is the Past-President of the Children's Literature Assembly of NCTE, IRA's Children's Literature SIG and the Ohio International Reading Association. Dr. McClure was selected NCTE's Promising Young Researcher and her dissertation won Kappa Delta Pi's Outstanding Dissertation of the Year Award. She also received Ohio Wesleyan's Herbert Welch Meritorious Teaching Award.

Linda N. McDowell

Linda N. McDowell is the School Library Media Specialist at Lake George Elementary School in Lake George, New York. This position follows more than twenty-five years as a classroom teacher. Linda has experience with readers at all levels from early childhood, to developing readers, and independent readers, having taught students in all grades from kindergarten through fifth grade. Linda is past president of the local reading council as well as the New York State English Council. Other experiences include serving on NCTE's *Notable Children's Books in the Language Arts Committee* and IRA's *Notables Books for a Global Society Committee.*

Caroline E. McGuire

Caroline E. McGuire is a PhD Candidate in the Reading/Writing/Literacy Program at the Graduate School of Education at the University of Pennsylvania. She graduated from Princeton University with a bachelor's degree in French and Italian and worked with a hospital-based early literacy program in

New York City. She has been part of a multi-year curriculum research project in Head Start classrooms, and teaches undergraduate and graduate level courses in children's literature at the University of Pennsylvania. She is currently working on her dissertation, which involves classroom-based research on the development of young children's understandings of literary genre across reading and writing experiences. Her research interests include children's responses to wordless picturebooks and picturebooks with sparse verbal text, the concept of children's "identification" with literary characters, and children's use of picturebooks as models for their own writing.

Naomi Shihab Nye

Photo by Michael Nye

Naomi Shihab Nye lives in San Antonio, Texas. Her recent books include *You & Yours, Going Going, A Maze Me, 19 Varieties of Gazelle; Poems of the Middle East, Come with Me: Poems for a Journey, Fuel, Red Suitcase* and *Habibi ,*a novel for teens. She has edited seven anthologies of poetry for young readers, including *This Same Sky, The Tree is Older than You Are, The Space Between our Footsteps: Poems & Paintings from the Middle East, What Have You Lost?* and *Salting the Ocean.* A visiting writer for many years all over the world, she has been a Lannan Fellow, a Guggenheim Fellow and a Library of Congress Witter Bynner Fellow.

Kara Pirillo

Kara Pirillo currently works as a 3rd grade teacher in a small suburban town just north of Boston, Massachusetts. In the past she's taught special needs students, and as a part of an enrichment based after school program. Kara holds a BS in Elementary Education from Skidmore College and an MA from Cambridge College.

Beverly Rawson

Beverly Rawson attended Skidmore College, where she majored in Education with a concentration in English. Upon graduation she embarked on an educational tour of South Africa. That adventure was followed by a second: Teaching in rural China. After returning to the States, she settled in New York City. She has spent the past few years teaching in a public school on the Lower Eastside. She continues to teach today while also working towards her Master's degree at Teachers College, Columbia University.

Laura Robb

Teacher, author, and coach, Laura Robb has just completed her 43rd year in the classroom. This year she will be coaching and running professional study at Powhatan School in Boyce, Virginia. Robb also trains teachers in other Virginia districts and speaks at conferences. She has published more then 15 books. Her most recent titles are a three ring binder for Scholastic: Teaching Reading: A Complete Resource for Grades four and up, and also for Scholastic, Nonfiction Writing From the Inside Out, a book about teaching expository writing.

Pam Munoz Ryan

Pam Munoz Ryan, has written many books for young people that include books for the very young, picture books for older readers, to middle grade and young adult novels. Awards include the Pura Belpre Medal, the Jane Addams Peace Award, the Americas Award Honor, ALA Schneider Family Award, the Tomas Rivera Award, and other accolades. She received her bachelor's and master's degrees at San Diego State University and now lives in north San Diego County.

Patricia L. Scharer

Patricia L. Scharer is a Professor of Education at The Ohio State University. Her research interests include early literacy development, phonics and word study, and the role of children's literature to foster both literary development and literacy achievement. Her research has been published in *Reading Research Quarterly, Research in the Teaching of English, Educational Leadership, Language Arts, The Reading Teacher, Reading Research and Instruction* and the yearbooks of the National Reading Conference and the College Reading Association. She has served as co-editor of the *Journal of Children's Literature, Bookbird: A Journal of International Children's Literature,* and the Children's Books column of *The Reading Teacher.* Professor Scharer is also co-editor of *Extending Our Reach: Teaching for Comprehension in Reading, Grades K–2* and co-author of *Rethinking Phonics: Making the Best Teaching Decisions.* Currently, she is conducting federally-funded research in partnership with University of Chicago, Lesley University, and Stanford University.

Lawrence R. Sipe

Lawrence R. Sipe is an Associate Professor in the Reading/Writing/Literacy Program at the University of Pennsylvania's Graduate School of Education, where he teaches courses in children's literature. His PhD is in children's literature and emergent literacy from The Ohio State University. He taught in a one-room school in an isolated fishing village in Newfoundland, Canada and in an independent school (K–2) in Princeton, New Jersey. He has also served as a coordinator of language arts and early childhood education for a school district in Newfoundland. His research centers on young children's literary understanding and the aesthetics of picturebook design. His awards include the Outstanding Dissertation Award (College Reading Association and the International Reading Association); the Student Outstanding Research Award and the Early Career Achievement Award from the National Reading Conference; the Promising Researcher Award from NCTE; and the Teaching Excellence Award from Penn's Graduate School of Education.

Peter Stiepleman

Peter Stiepleman began his career in Oakland, California where he worked as a Spanish bilingual teacher, an instructional facilitator for English language development, and an administrator. Now living in Columbia, Missouri, Peter is the assistant principal at West Boulevard Elementary School.

Alfred Tatum

Alfred Tatum is an assistant professor in the Department of Literacy at Northern Illinois University. His research interests are teacher professional development in urban middle schools and high schools, adolescent literacy, and the literacy development of African American males. He has published in the three major journals of the International Reading Association. Among his works are "Breaking down barriers that disenfranchise African American adolescents in low-level reading tracks" and "A road map for reading specialists entering school without exemplary reading programs." His book, *Teaching Reading to Black Adolescent Males: Closing the Achievement Gap* was published in May 2005. Dr. Tatum earned his Ph.D. from the University of Illinois-Chicago He began his career as an eighth-grade teacher on the south side of Chicago.

Deborah L. Thompson, Ph.D.

Deborah L. Thompson, Ph.D. is an associate professor of education at The College of New Jersey in Ewing, NJ. She teaches courses in emergent and early literacy, elementary and middle school reading instruction, and children's literature. She holds a Bachelor of Science in Elementary Education from Tennessee State University and a Masters and Doctorate in Language Arts/Literacy/Literature from The Ohio State University. She has conducted numerous professional development workshops on effective reading and writing instruction, using children's literature (traditional and multicultural) in the reading program, and whole school reform. Her writing and research areas include children's responses to literature, children's early vocabulary development, and the uses of multicultural children's literature in the literacy curriculum.

Roberta Seelinger Trites

Roberta Seelinger Trites is a professor of English at Illinois State University, where she teaches children's and adolescent literature. She is the author of *Waking Sleeping Beauty: Feminist Voices in Children's Novels* (1997) and *Disturbing the Universe: Power and Repression in Adolescent Literature* (2000). She has served as the editor of the *Children's Literature Association Quarterly* (2000–2004) and as President of the Children's Literature Association (2006–2007).

Miguelina Vasquez

Miguelina Vasquez was born in the Dominican Republic and raised in New York City. She completed her undergraduate degree at Skidmore College and graduate degree at City College. She spent three and a half years teaching Spanish to high school students in Vermont and Manhattan. For the past two years she has been teaching fourth grade in the Bronx. Her goal is to be the best teacher for her students, one who knows them as students and as individuals so that she can fulfill their needs.

Linda Wedwick

Linda Wedwick is an assistant professor in the Center for Reading and Literacy at Illinois State University and a former middle school teacher of Language Arts. Her current projects involve research into students' self-selection of texts for independent reading and middle school students' attitudes about reading. Her publications have appeared in *The Reading Teacher*, *Voices from the Middle*, and *Illinois Reading Council Journal*.

Sandip Wilson

Sandip Wilson is an Assistant Professor in the School of Education at Husson College, in Bangor, Maine, where she teaches courses in children's literature, language arts, and reading. She conducts workshops in literacy and children's literature with elementary and middle schools teachers and served as Curriculum Coordinator and Literacy Specialist in Washington County, Maine. A member of the Orbis Pictus Award selection committee of NCTE from 2001 to 2004, she served as chair from 2004–2007, and is a member the Advisory Board of the New England Reading Association. Her recent article, "Getting Down to Facts in Children's Nonfiction Literature: A Case for the Importance of Sources" appeared in the *Journal of Children's Literature.*

Janet Wong

Janet S. Wong (www.janetwong.com) is the author of eighteen books for children and teens, mainly poetry collections and picture books. Her latest books are: Before It Wriggles Away, an autobiography that describes her transition from lawyer to poet; The Dumpster Diver, an ode to creative reuse and recycling; and Twist: Yoga Poems. She lives in Hopewell, NJ.

Junko Yokota

Junko Yokota is Professor of Reading and Language and Director of the Center for Teaching through Children's Books at National-Louis University in Chicago, Illinois. For ten years, she was a classroom teacher and school librarian. Her publications include articles and review columns as well as the editing of *Kaleidoscope: A Multicultural Booklist for Grades K–8 (3rd ed.).* She coauthored the textbook *Children's Books in Children's Hands (3rd ed.)* and served on the Caldecott and Newbery Award Committees, chaired the Batchelder Award Committee, and was president of USBBY. She received the Virginia Hamilton Award for Contribution to Multicultural Literature, and served on the 2006 IBBY Hans Christian Andersen Award Jury.

Index